The Institute of Chartered Accountants in England and Wales

BUSINESS STRATEGY AND TECHNOLOGY

For exams in 2019

www.icaew.com

Business Strategy and Technology
The Institute of Chartered Accountants in England and Wales

ISBN: 978-1-50972-083-5
Previous ISBN: 978-1-78363-771-3

First edition 2008
Twelfth edition 2018

The content of this publication is intended to prepare students for the ICAEW examinations, and should not be used as professional advice.

British Library Cataloguing-in-Publication Data
A catalogue record for this book is available from the British Library

Originally printed in the United Kingdom on paper obtained from traceable, sustainable sources.

Contents

The Study Manual reference column highlights where the questions in this Question Bank have been explicitly referred to in the Study Manual. The references in the Study Manual highlight how key business strategy and technology concepts and theories have been examined in past exam questions. This should be used as a guide to help you with your studies and is not intended to provide any insight into those syllabus areas which may be examined in future sittings.

Title	Study manual reference	Marks	Time allocation Mins	Page Question	Page Answer
March 2015					
19 Rocket Co (amended)	Ch12,15,16	46	69	40	262
20 The Scottish Woodlands Commission (amended)	Ch2	34	51	43	270
21 WeDive Ltd (amended)	Ch7	20	30	44	275
June 2015					
22 Reyel plc (amended)		42	63	46	278
23 Home of Leather plc		34	51	48	286
24 Zuccini plc (amended)		24	36	50	292
September 2015					
25 Kentish Fruit Farms	Ch4	43	64	52	297
26 Premier Paper Products plc (amended)	Ch10	30	45	54	305
27 Taxi Tracker		27	41	56	311
March 2016					
28 Outil plc	Ch8	43	64	58	315
29 Dreamy Potato Products Ltd (amended)	Ch5	33	50	60	324
30 The Zed Museum		24	36	62	329
June 2016					
31 The Healthy Vegetarian plc		44	66	64	334
32 Elver Bloom Recruiting plc		35	52	67	342
33 TechScan Ltd		21	32	69	346
September 2016					
34 Guayaporto Ltd	Ch16	44	66	71	349
35 MHD (amended)		31	47	73	356
36 Thistle Engineering Services Ltd	Ch9,13	25	37	75	363
December 2016					
37 Pinter Shipping Panels plc		40	60	77	368
38 Zeter Domestic Chemicals plc	Ch16	30	45	80	375
39 Hartley's Traditional Footwear Ltd		30	45	82	382
March 2017					
40 Ignite plc	Ch4,12	44	66	84	388
41 Eclo Ltd	Ch9	36	54	88	395
42 Gighay Ltd (amended)	Ch6,14	20	30	89	401

Question Bank topic finder

Set out below is a guide showing the Business Strategy and Technology topic areas, with the relevant syllabus learning outcomes and related questions in the Question Bank for each topic area. If you need to concentrate on certain topic areas, or if you want to attempt all available questions that refer to a particular topic, you will find this guide useful.

Topic area	Syllabus learning outcome(s)	Question number(s)	Key Study Manual chapter(s)
Alternative strategies (including methods of development)	2a,2g,3e	3,6,12,13,14,30,35,40,44,46,48,52,55,56	6,7,11
Ansoff's matrix	2a,2i,3e	1,16,21,26	7,8
Automation and intelligent systems	1b,1d, 3b	31,44, 47,49,55	6
Balanced scorecard	1g,2b,3h	19,30,35	12
BCG matrix (product portfolio)	1c,1d,2h	24,39,58	6
Benchmarking	1d,2b,3h	18,50	6
Break-even and sensitivity	2j,3h	4,20,23,27,36,53,59	10
Budgeting and forecast analysis	1g,2j,3h	31,36,49	12
Business plans	3f,3g	7,36,56	13
Change management	3j	6,12,19,23,28,44,50,54,60	15
Competitive strategies (including Porter's generic strategies)	1a,1c,2i,3i	44,46,53	2,7
Core competences and critical success factors	1a,1d	1,5,26,50	6,12
Corporate governance	1e,3d	10,20,35	9,10
Corporate responsibility and sustainability	1b,2e	10,13,29,35	16
Cyber risk and security	1f,2d,3e	1,2,47,53	9,10,14
Data analysis (including performance evaluation)	1g,2b,3h,3i	5,7,9,12,16,22,25,28,31,32,38,43,46,49,52,55,58	12
Data analytics and big data	1d,2b,3i	3,5,42,43,49,57,58	6,14

Topic area	Syllabus learning outcome(s)	Question number(s)	Key Study Manual chapter(s)
Decision making (including relevant costing and decision trees)	2j,3h	3,4,21,28,31,32,33,37,38,39,44,45,46,49,52,53,55	10,12
Developing technologies (including digital assets and cryptocurrencies)	1d, 3b	3,9,26	6
Environmental analysis (including PESTEL and Porter's Five Forces)	1b	1,5,17,25,29,32,40,52,60	4,5
Ethical issues	1h, 2f,3k	6,7,10,16,19,22,25,29,31,35,38,41,43,46,49,52,57,58	16
Evaluating strategic options	2a,2e,2g,2j	3,4,17,23,24,26,28,29,33,39,45,49,53	12
Human capital and human resources	1d,3a,3b	3,6,12, 19, 26, 47	6,13
Information technology strategy	1f,2d,3h,3i	2,5,15,42,43	14
International trade and expansion (including international structures)	1b,2a,2g, 3e	6,14,21,23,28,36,50,54,55,56	4,11
Knowledge management	1d,3i	12	6,14
KPIs and performance measures	1a,1g, 2b,3h	9,18,25,30,31,35,38,39,42,50,52	6,12
Lynch expansion matrix	2a,3e	1,16,26	11
Marketing strategy	2b,2f,2i,3a	1,13,15,17,28,39,54	8,13,16
Methods of expansion (including joint ventures, strategic alliances, and franchising)	2a	3,8,9,16,52,55,56,59	11
Mission statements, vision and objectives	1a	10,47,51	3
Natural capital	1b,2e	10,13,26	4, 16
Operations management (including capacity management)	3a	3,9,22,43,45,53	13
Organisational structure	3c	12,14,36,41,43,54	9

Topic area	Syllabus learning outcome(s)	Question number(s)	Key Study Manual chapter(s)
Outsourcing	1d,2e,3e	2,41,42	6
Pricing	2i	11,22,27,32,39	8
Procurement (purchasing)	1d,3a	8,31,37,56	13
Product/industry lifecycle	1d,2h	8,24	5,6
Quality control	3a	25,39,41,53	13
Research and development strategy	3a,3b	33,47	13
Risk management	1f,2d,2g,3e	2,4,7,9,20,26,34,36,43,47,48,53,56	10
Scenario planning	1b,2j	34	4,10
Shared service centres	3b	12, 19	6
Stakeholders and their objectives	1a,1b,2c, 3d	4,23,28,30,47,51,59	3,9,16
Strategic fit	1a,2g	20,48	2
Supply chain management and distribution	1b,1d,2e, 3a	8,39,41,56	6,8,13
Transfer pricing and divisionalisation	3c	12,16,28,38,43,46,50,54	9
Value chain (including value drivers)	1d	9,27,44,53	6
Workforce flexibility	1d,3a,3b	22, 57	6,13

ICAEW 2019

Exam

Your exam will consist of:

3 questions	100 marks
Pass mark	55
Exam length	2.5 hours

The ACA student area of our website includes the latest information, guidance and exclusive resources to help you progress through the ACA. Find everything you need, from exam webinars, past exams, marks plans, errata sheets and the syllabus to advice from the examiners at icaew.com/exams.

Question Bank

Questions

1   DA plc (amended)

DA plc (DA) is an information solutions company, listed on the London Stock Exchange.

Company background

DA began trading a number of years ago, providing credit reference services for business customers. Although this remains its primary activity, it has grown organically and now provides financial and statistical information to a variety of UK businesses to help them manage the risk of commercial and financial decisions.

The company is split into three divisions:

- Credit reference services – provides factual information to clients, via credit searches of an individual's financial history, to assist them to lend profitably or offer trade credit.

- Decision software – assists clients in improving the consistency and quality of business decisions in areas such as credit risk, fraud prevention and customer account management.

- Vehicle history – provides financial and statistical information to the automotive industry to help clients understand the risks associated with the purchase or sale of a particular second-hand vehicle.

A breakdown of key data, by division, for 20X7 is as follows:

	Credit reference services	Decision software	Vehicle history	Total
Sales (£m)	166	115	64	345
Operating profit (£m)	41	34	13	88
Growth in sales from 20X6	3%	15%	0%	6%
Number of employees	686	490	300	1,476

Credit reference services

Clients for credit reference services can be split into two groups:

(1)   Banks, credit card companies and other financial services organisations which need help assessing the risk associated with lending decisions; and

(2)   Commercial companies seeking credit references before supplying goods on credit to other businesses and private customers.

When an individual or business makes an application for credit, the lender or supplier usually asks a credit reference agency (CRA) for a credit search to check the applicant's identity and credit worthiness. The database system operated by a CRA enables different lenders, such as banks, to share information about their customers' credit accounts and repayment histories. Applicants have to give permission for their credit report information to be shared when they apply for credit.

Although a number of companies are currently licensed as CRAs in the UK, DA is the largest, with a 58% market share. DA has built its market position by compiling and managing the most comprehensive credit database in the UK. Communication and information technology are a core part of DA's business. Online systems allow lenders to update data directly, resulting in more accurate information and efficiency gains for DA.

DA's main competitor, CC Inc (CC) is an American-based business with an acknowledged expertise in credit scoring (a statistical technique that combines several financial characteristics to form a single score to represent a customer's creditworthiness). CC has recently announced that, as part of its global expansion strategy, it plans to increase its share of the UK credit market, which is currently 32%. CC intends to use low cost web-based systems to deliver online consumer credit scores directly to lenders and companies extending trade credit. In this way, it hopes to reduce DA's market dominance in the UK.

DA's strategic development

Decision software

Having created a reputation for holding the most comprehensive credit database in the UK, DA has embraced the increasing use of data analytics software and has developed its own in-house analytical software to enable clients to process credit applications and manage customer credit accounts more efficiently.

The software takes data from DA's own credit management database and a range of other sources, such as the client's own customer account information, and uses analytical tools and scoring systems to provide decision support. Typical users of this product are banks, credit card companies, mortgage providers and other organisations that grant personal or trade credit. DA's software has helped to revolutionise the service offered to clients by enabling them to quickly and accurately assess in 'real time' whether to accept a new customer or extend credit arrangements for existing customers. The software can also define the processes the businesses should adopt in managing an account that has fallen into arrears. In recent months a number of large financial institutions have contacted DA with a view to making a use of the service.

Vehicle history

Recognising that it had a core skill in the management of large databases for the financial services industry, DA also decided to provide similar services to the automotive industry. It compiles and manages data on the histories of 30 million vehicles and 25 million car insurance policies in the UK.

This data is used to provide vehicle history information to car dealers, finance providers and insurers. Fraudulent representation of used vehicles is a significant risk for private consumers and a potential financial liability for the businesses involved in the sale or purchase. The vehicle history can assist in establishing the market value of a vehicle; and whether a vehicle is registered as stolen or has outstanding finance.

Proposed diversification

Recently, DA has decided to target a new market, the individual consumer market, with a new online service: 'Checksta'.

Under current UK legislation, individuals have a legal right to see the information about them held by a CRA. In return for a statutory fee of £2, the CRA is legally obliged to provide a written copy of the information held on the individual's credit report. Instead of making a written application for a statutory credit report, individual consumers will be able to pay to subscribe to Checksta.

The Checksta service will allow individuals to check online that their credit report is accurate and up-to-date, as many times as they want. Checksta will send a text or email alert every time there is a significant change to the information held on an individual's credit report. This alert service assists in identifying identity fraud (where somebody applies for credit in another person's name). Individuals will also be able to order a credit score, based on their DA credit report, which will give them an idea of how a lender would view the information, if they were to apply for credit.

The introduction of Checksta is partly in response to the aggressive marketing stance currently being adopted by CC and also as a reaction to the following changes in the external environment:

- **Changing attitudes to money and credit**

  An increase in spending has led to an increase in demand for credit and it is very easy to apply now, both by telephone and online. This means that individuals are more likely to shop around for credit and lenders have to carry out more credit checks.

- **Changes in legislation**

  DA has to conform to the UK laws that govern the way it does business. Government concerns that debt levels are too high have caused a tightening of the legislation to give consumers better access to information held on them, more rights regarding disputes with lenders and more protection from rogue lenders. As a result, CRAs have had to implement a consumer education programme, working closely with consumer organisations to help consumers understand how credit referencing works.

- **The growth of e-commerce (products bought online)**

  This has necessitated more frequent and rapid credit checks and a subsequent upgrading of DA's information technology systems.

- **An increase in identity fraud**

  Identity criminals steal people's personal information and use these details to commit crimes, usually obtaining credit illegally.

Marketing

To date, DA has worked mainly with business clients, attracting business customers through personal selling and retaining them by developing strong client relationships. The sales director is aware that to succeed in the consumer market, DA will need to use a different marketing strategy for Checksta.

Preliminary market research suggests that those most likely to be interested in using the Checksta service are people who are internet users, credit users and those keen to manage their financial affairs effectively. Such people are likely to read the financial pages in newspapers or visit personal finance websites.

Requirements

1.1 Explain the factors that are likely to have contributed to DA's competitive advantage.

(6 marks)

1.2 Using relevant strategic models, analyse the ways in which DA has chosen to expand its business since it began trading, including its plans for Checksta. **(10 marks)**

1.3 Prepare a PESTEL analysis on the credit reference industry, clearly explaining the implications for DA's plans to implement the Checksta product. **(8 marks)**

1.4 Advise DA on an appropriate marketing strategy for Checksta. **(8 marks)**

1.5 Identify the strategic and cyber security risks arising from DA's use of Information Technology and Information Systems and outline the measures that can be implemented to deal with such risks. **(8 marks)**

Total: 40 marks

2   e-Parts Ltd (amended)

e-Parts Ltd (EP) is an online retailer which sells spare parts and accessories for a variety of domestic appliances. EP was established two years ago by Kamal Sheikh, who identified a gap in the market after he struggled to find a reasonably priced replacement part for his oven. EP has two types of customer:

- Small specialists who repair and service domestic appliances for individuals and need to access parts quickly at low cost; and

- Individuals who need either parts such as door hinges and seals to carry out their own simple, non-electrical repairs, or accessories such as fridge shelves or dishwasher cutlery baskets.

EP has grown as people try to save money and seek to extend the life of their existing domestic appliances by servicing them rather than replacing them. It now has a database of over two million customers that have opted to receive marketing and promotional information from EP. 90% of orders are placed and paid for online, with the remaining 10% handled by a call centre, which also offers after-sales service and support for online customers. In its warehouse, EP stocks 100,000 different products covering the appliances of 250 different manufacturers. EP's inventory control system allows it to despatch most items on the day that the order is placed.

Competition

Domestic appliance manufacturers charge premium prices for spare parts and accessories, primarily to encourage customers to buy new appliances, but also because they do not find it cost-effective to supply parts and accessories directly to customers. Domestic appliance retailers only stock items for the most popular appliances. EP prices are significantly lower than those charged by the appliance manufacturers. As a result, its only real competition is from other similar online businesses.

Brand and marketing

Kamal has positioned EP as "a service business which helps customers to repair and enhance appliances". Via the EP website's advice page, customers can access articles and videos to guide them through the most common repair processes. EP also takes advertising revenue from repair businesses in exchange for listing their services on the website. EP relies heavily on customer feedback. As well as a 'product and service review' facility on the website, Kamal has recently created a social networking page where customers can take advantage of special promotions, exchange information and access free advice from experts.

Risk management and business continuity

At a recent management meeting, Kamal made the following comments:

"Keeping our website operational is key for our business. If the site is down we don't make any money. If new customers visit our site and the online shop is not functioning effectively, they don't come back again. The other key issue for us is our inventory control system which allows us to identify quickly whether an item is in stock and where it is located. So far we have handled everything ourselves, but as a result of our rapid growth I am thinking of outsourcing all our operational systems to a specialist information technology (IT) provider. I have also been told that we should have a formal risk management policy, including a business continuity plan, for the business as a whole, so that if a major incident occurs we can continue to function."

Requirements

2.1 Explain the relevance of risk management to the business as a whole and identify the main factors that would be covered in EP's business continuity plan. **(6 marks)**

2.2 Identify the key IT risks including cyber risks arising for EP as a result of its reliance on IT (other than those relating to business continuity) and recommend how they can be managed. **(8 marks)**

2.3 Explain the factors to be considered by EP in deciding whether to use outsourcing as a method of implementing its IT strategy. **(7 marks)**

Total: 21 marks

3 Marcham plc (amended)

Marcham plc (Marcham) is a major supermarket chain with a loyal customer base and a 30% share of the UK supermarket sector.

MarchamBank

Marcham is proposing to take advantage of recent turmoil in the banking sector and public mistrust of some retail banks by launching its own banking services, under the name of MarchamBank. This will reduce the pressure felt by Marcham's traditional, mature retail business as a result of lower consumer spending, and will take advantage of rising margins for financial products. MarchamBank will operate from 30 branches within the largest existing Marcham stores and will also provide online banking facilities. The strategy is to offer Marcham customers simplified financial products and the marketing literature will emphasise "face-to-face, relationship-driven banking from a name that our customers can trust". Initially MarchamBank will offer simple savings products, short term loans, and a credit card. Once these have all been launched successfully, it will offer current accounts and a mortgage broker service to source mortgages for customers. It does not intend to offer mortgages itself. In the longer term, Marcham's operations director is keen for MarchamBank, once established, to explore the possibilities of offering web-based accounts capable of holding cryptocurrencies on behalf of account holders.

Unlike other competitors which have moved into selected personal finance products via joint ventures with major UK banks, Marcham is planning to control its own banking operations. It will hire its own financial services specialists to run its branches and staff its customer service call centre. In view of the collapse of several banks during the financial crisis a number of years ago, the UK government is keen to increase competition in the banking sector and Marcham has already been granted a banking licence. Establishment of the customer service call centre in Scotland (rather than Asia where most competitors base their support services) will allow Marcham to receive a £5 million grant from the UK government.

Customer loyalty card scheme and integrated information system

Marcham has over 20 million customers in the UK and manages its relationship with them via a customer loyalty card. The loyalty card allows customers to earn points in return for cash spent in Marcham stores. Points can be converted into vouchers that can be used to reduce the cost of future purchases. When customers sign up to take out a loyalty card they give their consent for Marcham to use their personal data in exchange for receiving money-off vouchers. The money-off vouchers are customised to appeal to individual customers based on their previous purchases. The need to obtain customer consent to issue such promotions is a requirement of data protection regulations. The loyalty card forms part of an integrated data analytics and knowledge management information system which allows Marcham to track the shopping habits of its customers.

The other key element of the integrated system is a sophisticated electronic point of sale (EPOS) and inventory control system. As soon as a sales transaction is recorded, this system updates inventory records, provides valuable sales information regarding product demand and profitability, and facilitates automated purchasing from suppliers. This has enabled Marcham to reduce costs by increasing the frequency and accuracy of ordering, leading to lower levels of inventory and wastage.

The data collected from the various elements of the integrated system are logged in a centralised database with an advanced search engine. The data analytics feature of the system allows Marcham to build a profile of each customer with a loyalty card. This profile can then be used for a variety of purposes including pricing, decisions as to which product ranges to stock, research, marketing and customer service. One of the key benefits is improved customer segmentation, enabling Marcham to promote low price or high quality items as appropriate. Marcham's own internal information about its best-selling products is sold to a number of its suppliers, which in turn use it to refine and develop their products. Customer personal data is not sold to third parties.

Whilst most other supermarkets operate similar customer loyalty schemes, none is as far-reaching as Marcham's, which was the first of its kind. Marcham's research suggests that one in four UK adults belongs to its customer loyalty scheme. A key advantage for Marcham is that the scheme enables it to extend its share of customer spend by identifying other products that the customer is likely to be interested in, based on their profile and spending patterns.

Marcham plans for the loyalty card scheme to be a key driver of competitive advantage for its expansion into banking services, especially as none of the existing retail banks operates a loyalty card scheme. Marcham intends to contact its loyalty card customers to request their permission to send them marketing and promotional materials in respect of MarchamBank's services.

Marcham criticised

The following is an extract from an article that appeared recently in a national newspaper:

"Supermarket giant Marcham has been criticised recently. Its customer loyalty card scheme has been labelled as a sophisticated spy system by some critics, allowing it to exploit customers by using it to sell them things they don't need. As well, there is a risk that this private shopping information could fall into the wrong hands and might one day be used against people.

"Marcham has also been accused of further tightening supplier payment terms to improve its own cash flow, despite continuing to make huge profits – indeed this may be where the money for its proposed expansion into banking services is coming from. Suppliers are, of course, prevented from complaining about low margins and onerous terms and conditions because of fears that they will lose Marcham's business."

Requirements

3.1 In preparation for a meeting of Marcham's senior executives, the operations director has asked you to prepare a report which:

  (a) Explains the potential benefits of an effective data analytics and information system for a supermarket and discuss how Marcham has used its information systems to create competitive advantage in the supermarket industry. **(8 marks)**

  (b) Assesses the suitability, feasibility and acceptability of Marcham's proposed expansion into the banking sector. **(12 marks)**

  (c) Discusses the relative merits of Marcham's intention to expand into banking via organic growth rather than having an established bank as a joint venture partner. **(8 marks)**

3.2 Discuss the ethical issues raised by the newspaper article in respect of Marcham's customer loyalty card and its treatment of suppliers. **(8 marks)**

Total: 36 marks

4 Bigville Council

Bigville Council (the Council) is the local government body responsible for providing community services to residents of Bigville, a large city in the UK. The Council is financed by central government, together with local taxes paid by residents and businesses in the area. Bigville is relatively strong economically. It has a respected university and is well-known as both a business and tourist destination. Around 500,000 people live and/or work in Bigville.

Demand for a community stadium

Bigville's professional rugby club leases its current sports stadium from the Council. As a result of recent success, the club is attracting large crowds to matches played at its stadium (home matches) and this stadium is at full capacity. Aware that Bigville's professional football club is also in need of a new stadium, the rugby club has asked the Council to consider the creation of a council-owned community stadium on a new site, with a shared pitch suitable for both rugby and football. It would also incorporate additional sports facilities which would be available for use by schools, colleges, clubs and other community groups throughout the year. On days when there are no home matches for either rugby or football teams the stadium could be used for a range of other commercial and social events (concerts, weddings, etc).

In the UK, football clubs compete in a series of hierarchical leagues, with the top clubs being promoted to the league above at the end of the playing season and the bottom clubs being relegated to the league below. The same system applies to rugby.

The attendance (number of people attending home matches at the club's stadium) and financial performance of any club is heavily dependent on its team's performance in the league. Bigville's two clubs currently play home matches on different days (football on Saturdays and rugby on Sundays) and their seasons overlap. The football season runs from August through to April, and the rugby season runs from February to September. Both clubs have a strong support base but have lower attendance than their respective league competitors due to restricted capacity. Neither stadium has the scope to be extended.

A new stadium would benefit the two clubs by allowing for increased attendance, which generates revenue from ticket sales, refreshments and merchandising. The improvement in facilities would increase the scope to raise some ticket prices by offering premium seating. For this reason, if the shared stadium goes ahead, the rugby and football clubs have pledged to make initial contributions of £1 million and £2 million respectively towards the capital cost.

Council's strategic priorities

The Council has recently stated publicly that its strategic priorities are as follows:

- To maintain and develop Bigville's successful economy and provide suitable employment opportunities for residents

- To ensure accessible opportunities for all to engage in culture, leisure and recreational activity

- To promote and provide support for local people to make healthy lifestyle choices

- To create, enhance and maintain cleaner, safer and more sustainable environments

The Council believes that a new community stadium would potentially assist in meeting some of these aims. It is therefore making a preliminary assessment of the business case for the community stadium. If this indicates viability, a more detailed feasibility study and financial analysis will be undertaken. The vision is to create a stadium with 6,000 seats, which both the football and rugby clubs will use for home matches and training.

The new stadium will incorporate a community sports centre with an athletics track and all-weather sports pitches. There is an option to enhance the stadium by adding a second level, which could be used commercially as a conference and events centre.

The Council has identified three criteria which it will use to assess the business case:

(1) Ability to raise finance for the initial capital investment
(2) Whether it is a commercially sustainable venture
(3) Alignment with the Council's overall strategic priorities

Council-owned land has already been identified as a suitable site for the stadium. This land is expected to meet the necessary planning criteria. The stadium would be partly sunk into the ground to limit noise problems, reduce the impact on the landscape and maximise environmental efficiency.

Capital costs and financial projections

The new stadium would be partly funded by the sale of the council-owned land on which the rugby club's current stadium stands. If sold to a developer for the construction of a retail site, this land would be expected to realise in the region of £6 million. Initial research suggests that some additional public sector funding would be available in the form of central government grants, provided certain criteria are fulfilled by the new stadium. These criteria include whether it can be demonstrated that the stadium actively increases community participation in sports, creates additional employment or contributes to the sustainability of the local environment. A sponsorship deal would be sought with a large credit card company, Finanex plc, whose headquarters are in Bigville and which is Bigville's largest private sector employer. The company has indicated that it would be prepared to pay an initial £1 million for the stadium to be named 'The Finanex Stadium', and then it would also contribute an amount annually for the right to display its company logos on the exterior and interior of the stadium.

The stadium is likely to cost a total of £10 million to construct. This comprises £6.75 million for the basic stadium and £3.25 million for the community sports facilities. An enhanced stadium, with an additional second level for conference and events facilities, would cost a further £1.1 million. Any shortfall in funding would need to come from the Council's cash reserves and/or debt finance. The Council's strategy department has researched similar community stadia funded by other councils and has produced some initial forecasts for the potential costs and revenue streams associated with the new stadium. These are set out in **Exhibits 1 and 2**.

Management and operation

If the new stadium goes ahead as planned, it will be owned by the Council and operated by a stadium management company (SMC) created as a joint venture between the Council and the two sports clubs. The Council will lease the stadium to SMC, which will then retain any profits or losses made from its operation. The Council, the football club and the rugby club will each have two directors on the board of SMC, although the Council will have a casting vote on certain specified issues. The Council is keen to ensure that it minimises its level of risk and, in particular, the financial liability to which it is exposed. It also wants to retain the ability to control the governance of SMC and the pricing, events scheduling and promotion of the stadium.

Exhibit 1: Forecast annual match revenues and costs for new stadium

	Number of home matches	Expected attendance per match	Total annual attendance	Total annual revenue	Total annual contribution	Traceable annual fixed operating costs	Forecast annual profit/ (loss)
	Note 1	Notes 2 and 3		Note 4			
Football	25	3,200	80,000	£800,000	£640,000	(£644,000)	(£4,000)
Rugby	15	3,000	45,000	£450,000	£270,000	(£214,000)	£56,000

Notes

1. Based on the average number of home matches played last season in each club's existing stadium. This can increase if a club is successful in various additional competitions which are run during the season.

2. Initial estimate of expected future attendance provided to the Council by each club, on the basis that it increases its capacity by moving to the new stadium and remains playing within its existing competitive league.

3. The average home match attendance at each club's current stadium is: football: 2,863; rugby: 2,234. Comparable data for similar clubs are as follows:

	Average attendance per match for typical club in:		
	League below	Existing league	League above
Football	1,800	3,050	5,000
Rugby	1,900	2,840	4,000

4. Based on expected average total spend per visitor on tickets, refreshments and merchandising.

Exhibit 2: Forecast annual non-match revenues and costs for new stadium

	Basic stadium £	Enhanced stadium with conference facilities £
Revenues		
Net income from community use of facilities	50,000	50,000
Stadium advertising/sponsorship from Finanex plc	200,000	250,000
Revenue from non-match day activities	187,000	537,000
Costs		
Stadium running costs, not directly traceable to rugby or football matches	(375,000)	(525,000)

Requirements

4.1 Discuss how the objectives of the key stakeholders (the Council, the rugby club and the football club) may conflict in relation to the shared stadium. You should ignore SMC as a separate entity for the purposes of this requirement. **(7 marks)**

4.2 (a) Using the quantitative data in Exhibit 1 relating to the new stadium, estimate the breakeven attendance figures for each rugby and football match. **(4 marks)**

(b) Explain the implications of your calculations in (a) for the forecast match profits and discuss the potential variability in the annual attendance for each club, including the impact this is likely to have on the forecast in Exhibit 1. Show any supporting calculations. **(9 marks)**

4.3 Using the quantitative data in Exhibits 1 and 2 and the other qualitative information provided, prepare a report for the Council which evaluates the business case for the new stadium against the Council's three stated criteria, clearly identifying any further information required. **(14 marks)**

4.4 Assess the key risks for the Council in relation to the construction of the stadium and its operation by SMC. **(8 marks)**

Total: 42 marks

5 Mayhews Ltd (amended)

The date is March 20X3.

Mayhews Ltd (Mayhews) is a family-owned business which runs three garages from freehold sites in prime locations in central England. Each garage operates a filling station, which sells fuel (petrol and diesel), and has a facility offering maintenance and repairs for motor vehicles.

Fuel retailing in the UK

Fuel retailing in the UK is a high volume, low margin business, characterised by strong competition. In the industry there are three types of filling station:

- Branded filling stations are either owned and managed by one of the major fuel wholesalers or operated on their behalf by licensees.

- Independent retailers, like Mayhews, are free to obtain fuel supplies from any wholesaler. Over 50% of all filling stations in the UK are independently owned.

- The big supermarket chains operate filling stations alongside their major stores. In recent years, whilst the number of branded filling stations and independent retailers has declined, the number of supermarket-owned sites has increased. This has coincided with the expansion of large out-of-town supermarkets with more people driving to do their shopping and buying fuel at the same time. As a result of their supply chain efficiencies and the large volumes of fuel that they sell, the supermarkets incur lower overheads per litre of fuel sold and are able to charge lower prices. In addition, many offer discounts on fuel based on the amount customers spend on goods in the main store. The average retail price charged by supermarkets in 20X2 was 130.9 pence per litre compared to an overall UK average of 133.8 pence per litre.

Supply of fuel and pricing in the UK industry

The wholesale supply of fuel to retailers is dominated by a few large companies which produce and refine crude oil into a range of products including fuel. These wholesalers supply fuel to their own branded filling stations and to the supermarkets and independent retailers. 60% of the UK retail fuel price per litre consists of fuel tax and sales tax. On average 35% is paid to the wholesaler and the retailer earns 5% towards overheads and profit. Wholesale fuel prices in the last three years have been very volatile as the price of crude oil has varied significantly. Price volatility is a major problem for independent retailers. When market prices fall, independent retailers are often left with fuel supplies previously bought from the wholesaler at a high price. If they reduce the retail price then they may make a loss. If they keep retail prices high this is likely to have a negative effect on sales volumes. Conversely, when wholesale prices rise, the independent retailer may struggle to afford the increased cost of replenishing fuel supplies.

Demand for fuel in the UK market

Despite increased numbers of cars on the road, sales volumes of fuel are under pressure because of the improved efficiency of vehicle engines, increased fuel prices and the difficult economic climate. Government figures suggest congestion on motorways and major roads has been falling, indicating that people are undertaking fewer journeys by car.

Fierce competition between fuel retailers has led to a significant decline in the number of filling stations. There are now fewer than half the 18,000 filling stations that existed 20 years ago (**Exhibit 1**).

A fuel station's viability depends on two key factors: the gross margin per litre and the volume of fuel sold. Independent filling stations and those in less well-populated rural areas are at the greatest risk of losses due to declining sales volumes and below average margins. They also struggle to justify the additional capital expenditure required to comply with increasingly strict environmental and safety regulations. Many have tried to reduce their reliance on fuel revenue by creating alternative revenue streams such as on-site shops selling snacks, groceries and vehicle accessories. Mayhews does not currently operate a shop at any of its garages.

420 filling stations closed in the UK in 20X2, of which two-thirds were independent. Some of these filling stations have been bought by property developers, although because of environmental regulations, sites have to be closed and the fuel tanks filled with concrete before being capable of alternative use.

Mayhews' business

The first Mayhews garage was set up a number of years ago by John Mayhew. The boom at this time in vehicle ownership and the later development of the UK motorway network led to a significant increase in demand for fuel and maintenance/repairs and Mayhews soon opened a further two garages. The business is now owned and managed by John's son Barry (aged 60), who is a well-known businessman in the region. After many successful years, Mayhews has been finding the filling stations market increasingly difficult and this is reflected in the company's recent results (**Exhibit 2**).

Although Mayhews has been experiencing a decline in fuel sales, the revenue and profit from maintenance and repairs have been increasing. This part of the business undertakes MOT testing (a compulsory annual test of safety for vehicles over three years old); replacement of parts due to wear and tear (brakes, tyres, wiper blades, lights etc); annual maintenance; and repairs.

Due to the economic climate, people have been slow to replace their old vehicles with new ones. Time pressure, lack of skills and the complexity of vehicles mean people no longer maintain their own vehicles, but they are reluctant to pay the high prices charged by the vehicle retailers for maintenance. Because of its longstanding presence in the region, and also as a result of Barry's contacts, each Mayhews garage has a loyal base of local customers. Mayhews also has contracts with a number of local companies for the maintenance of their corporate vehicles.

There are 32 million vehicles on the UK's roads and the maintenance and repairs market is fragmented. There are around 24,000 garage outlets in the UK offering motor vehicle repairs and maintenance. They are operated by retailers of vehicles, national and regional repairs and maintenance chains, fast-fit centres (specialising in tyres, exhausts and brakes) and many independents.

Strategic dilemma

Your firm acts as business advisers to Mayhews. At a recent meeting, Barry commented:

"We seem to be selling so little fuel these days I can't believe we are making much money from this side of the business. What do you think about us closing one or more of the filling stations and focusing on maintenance and repairs? This is a service-based market with many different providers where trust is really important to the customer. We already have a reputation for being honest and reliable and our brand is well-known locally.

"We also have much lower overheads and labour costs than the main vehicle retailers. We can use this to differentiate ourselves by offering vehicle retailer quality service at affordable local garage prices.

"Unfortunately, we simply don't have the appropriate technology to deal with the engine management systems in the more modern vehicles so currently we have to refer them to the vehicle retailer. We would need to invest in information technology by purchasing the relevant engine diagnostic equipment and a new computer system.

"The new IT system would improve parts management and have marketing benefits. By maintaining their vehicles in good working condition our customers can improve fuel efficiency and drive safely. A key way we can help customers is to anticipate their needs for MOTs and maintenance and contact them in advance, provided they give their consent to receive reminders from us. The new system would provide us with an advanced data management system incorporating data analytics functionality. This should enable us to offer customers online booking for repairs and maintenance."

Requirements

5.1 Prepare a Porter's Five Forces analysis of the UK fuel retailing industry which might be used to inform further discussions regarding the viability of Mayhews' filling station operations.

(9 marks)

5.2 Using the quantitative data in the Exhibits, your answer to requirement (5.1), and the other information provided, evaluate the performance of Mayhews' overall business and compare the performance of the individual garages. Make and justify a preliminary conclusion as to whether Mayhews should consider closing one or more of its filling stations to focus on maintenance and repairs. **(16 marks)**

5.3 Discuss the advantages and disadvantages of making the investment in information technology referred to by Barry. You should refer to the use of data analytics in your answer. **(7 marks)**

5.4 Explain how the use of critical success factors (CSFs) may assist Mayhews in establishing a strategic control system. Justify three CSFs for Mayhews' maintenance and repairs business and suggest one appropriate key performance indicator for each CSF identified. **(9 marks)**

Total: 41 marks

Exhibit 1: UK filling stations - market data 20X2

	Branded filling stations	Independents	Supermarkets	Total
Number of sites	2,605	4,425	1,470	8,500
Millions of litres sold	10,520	7,425	14,950	32,895

Exhibit 2: Mayhews Ltd recent financial performance					
	Breakdown of 20X2			Total company	
	Garage A 20X2 £'000	Garage B 20X2 £'000	Garage C 20X2 £'000	Mayhews Ltd 20X2 £'000	Mayhews Ltd 20X1 £'000
Sales:					
Fuel (Note 1)	878	738	776	2,392	2,686
Maintenance and repairs	688	454	755	1,897	1,604
Total sales	1,566	1,192	1,531	4,289	4,290
Gross profit:					
Fuel	103	76	91	270	304
Maintenance and repairs (Note 2)	355	218	415	988	836
Total gross profit	458	294	506	1,258	1,140
Operating costs (Note 3)	269	184	219	672	679
Profit	189	110	287	586	461
Litres of fuel sold (millions)	1.63	1.34	1.43	4.40	5.21

Notes

1 Fuel revenue is stated net of tax, ie, at 40% of the retail fuel price.

2 The gross profit on maintenance and repairs is based on the sales value of work done less the cost of parts and materials.

3 Operating costs include the wages and salaries of all garage staff. The operating costs for garage A also include £45,000 for Barry's salary.

6 Chiba

Chiba is a Japanese company which manufactures a range of liquid foods including rice vinegar and soy sauce.

Different countries make vinegars from their indigenous crops, for example rice vinegar in Japan, oat vinegar in Korea, cider vinegar in the US, wine vinegar in Europe and malt vinegar in the UK. Rice vinegar has no fat or cholesterol and is very low in calories. It is also known for its anti-bacterial properties.

UK expansion strategy

Malegar, a division of a large UK listed food business, makes the UK's leading brand of malt vinegar. The division is currently for sale because Malegar's parent company (VM plc) has incurred significant borrowings and is now moving to a strategy of focusing on a few key profitable food brands.

Chiba wants to increase its market share in the UK and is considering setting up a subsidiary company, Chiba UK, to acquire Malegar, because of Malegar's strong UK heritage and identity. As well as targeting Malegar's traditional food market, Chiba is also keen to promote vinegar as a health product and as a cleaning product. However, Chiba's marketing director is concerned that VM plc would not be selling Malegar if it were a profitable business.

Contamination issue

The directors of Malegar are aware of a recent complaint from a major wholesaler concerning a contaminated batch of malt vinegar. The cause has not yet been confirmed and they are unsure whether the contamination arose in the glass bottles, which are purchased from an external supplier, or within the Malegar factory. Malegar takes health and safety and quality control very seriously, so the directors believe the fault is most likely to lie with the supplier. As Malegar was probably not responsible for the incident, the directors are planning to keep this issue confidential from all parties, including Chiba.

Human resource management

If Chiba's acquisition of Malegar goes ahead, all Malegar employees will transfer their contracts to Chiba UK following an appropriate consultation process. This may take up to 12 months.

Chiba's approach to human resource management is very different from Malegar's. Malegar has a hierarchical structure with a focus on short-term results, and with individual functional managers held accountable for the performance of their function. Employees within Malegar's factory have little involvement in the decision-making process and there is high staff turnover. In contrast, Chiba's approach emphasises job security for core employees, cooperation and mutual trust between employees and managers, collective responsibility and shared decision making. Chiba's directors are concerned about the change management issues that will arise from the integration of the Malegar employees into the Chiba culture.

Requirements

6.1 Explain the ethical issues that arise for Malegar's directors in relation to concealing the possible contamination. **(5 marks)**

6.2 In light of the comments by Chiba's marketing director, discuss the possible reasons for the divestment of Malegar by VM plc and the benefits to Chiba of growing by acquisition in the UK. **(8 marks)**

6.3 (a) Contrast Chiba's and Malegar's differing approaches to human resource management. **(5 marks)**

(b) Explain the change management issues that Chiba is likely to face when integrating the Malegar employees. Refer to relevant models where appropriate. **(9 marks)**

Total: 27 marks

7 Hire Value Ltd

The date is June 20X3.

Hire Value Ltd (HV) operates in the car hire industry throughout the UK.

The UK car hire industry has two sectors: renting cars to users for the short term, typically between one day and two weeks (the car rental sector); and leasing cars to users for the longer term (the leasing sector). These sectors are of approximately equal size in terms of revenue.

The UK car rental sector

There are about 100 companies operating in the car rental sector in the UK. In 20X2, these companies generated total revenue of £5,000 million. A few large companies dominate the sector. These larger companies tend to be international, with some companies being subsidiaries of car manufacturers. The car rental sector is also characterised by many medium-sized companies. Some of these have a regional focus, but most operate throughout the UK from airports, where there are clusters of car rental companies providing wide consumer choice.

The larger companies tend to maintain a modern fleet of cars, usually owning each vehicle for an average of only 13 months.

The car rental sector can be segmented in two main ways: by customer (business or leisure) or by location of outlets (airport or non-airport). A high proportion of rentals are dependent on the airline industry. Business customers tend to be companies which negotiate flexible contracts for renting many vehicles for short periods so that, for instance, visiting overseas executives can drive to meetings straight from the airport. An account is set up for each business customer and preferential prices are offered, compared with those for individual customers hiring cars for leisure purposes.

The car rental business tends to be seasonal, with spring and summer (the peak periods for leisure customers) each generating about 30% of annual revenues.

Strategic partnerships are common in the sector. The main examples are partnerships between car rental companies and airlines, which allow the customer to book car rentals online with a partner company at the same time as booking flights.

UK car rental market leader

Kerr Karrs plc (KK) is the UK market leader in the car rental sector, which is the only sector in which it operates. KK offers a high level of standard service by renting out modern, relatively good quality cars, charging a price premium compared with the industry average. In addition to its standard range of vehicles, it has a premium range of luxury cars for affluent individuals and senior business executives.

KK operates throughout the UK. It has many large, listed companies as its business customers and has partnerships with many airlines including special arrangements for their first class and business class customers. It tends not to have partnerships with budget airlines.

Hire Value Ltd – company history

HV was established a number of years ago by the current members of its board. HV's business model is to operate in the car rental sector throughout the UK. Its particular focus is to locate its outlets at airports in order to attract business and leisure travellers. The airport outlets also serve customers living or working in the cities closest to these airports. Each outlet consists of a customer service desk in the airport terminal, plus a vehicle collection site in the parking area. Both are distinctively branded to attract travellers and promote brand image. Staff are well trained in customer service.

HV's accounting information system provides an analysis of revenues from business customers and leisure customers separately. However, there is no separate analysis of costs or profit for each of these customer groups, as individual cars are used interchangeably between them.

HV aims to operate mid-market in terms of the service it provides. However, in order to control costs, HV buys cars which are about two years old and then operates them for a further three years. HV has adopted this policy as it believes that customers are more sensitive to price and the type of car they hire than its age.

All customer bookings are made online. Car rental charges are payable by credit card or debit card at the time of booking by leisure customers. Business accounts are on credit terms.

Expansion and the business plan

In March 20X2, the HV directors obtained new equity finance from a venture capital company, TopFin, to expand the business. The business plan included the acquisition of more vehicles and the development of more locations to provide greater economies of scale and more efficient operations. A forecast of rapid growth was therefore a key element in obtaining the new finance from TopFin. The original board members continue to hold 60% of the ordinary share capital of HV; the remaining 40% is owned by TopFin.

A formal agreement was made between the director-shareholders and TopFin that there would be an independent review after a year to monitor the success of HV's growth strategy. In April 20X3 accountants and business advisers, Gatter LLP, therefore reviewed how the business plan was being implemented and monitored. They reported that, for the year ended 31 March 20X3, revenues had grown, but the projections in the business plan had not been achieved (see **Exhibit**). TopFin has now asked for a detailed analysis of the data to explain why actual performance has varied from the business plan.

Ethical issues

The review by Gatter LLP also reported that executive directors used some HV assets for personal use, raising a number of ethical issues:

(1) HV cars are sometimes loaned overnight to various executive directors when not rented out to customers. This is done on a casual basis without records. It appears to be accepted by employees as part of HV's corporate culture but, as no records are kept, TopFin has, to date, been unaware of this practice.

(2) One director, Mike Knight, provided an HV car to his friend for a few hours without charge. He told one of the other directors about this, prior to lending the car.

(3) Another director, Sandra Bevan, rented out an HV car for cash under a private arrangement. Initially, she held the cash received in her personal bank account but, after a month, paid it over to HV. This was just prior to the start of the Gatter investigation.

Requirements

7.1 For the year ended 31 March 20X3 compare the actual performance and competitive position of HV with that of the market leader, KK. Use the data in the Exhibit and the other information provided. **(10 marks)**

7.2 Using the quantitative data in the Exhibit and the other information provided, analyse and explain the shortfall between HV's actual performance for the year ended 31 March 20X3 and its forecast performance in the business plan for the same period. In addition, you should indicate **three** significant matters which require further investigation in order to provide a more complete analysis. **(16 marks)**

7.3 Prepare a risk register for what you consider to be the **four** most significant risks of HV. Use a table with three columns which, for each risk, explains:

   (a) The nature of the risk
   (b) The possible impact of the risk and likelihood of it occurring
   (c) Possible risk management procedures **(9 marks)**

7.4 Prepare notes for a presentation to the HV board which explain the ethical issues, and the implications that arise from these, for the HV directors (both individually and collectively) as a result of the review by Gatter LLP of HV asset use. **(10 marks)**

Total: 45 marks

Exhibit: Financial and operating data for HV and KK			
Year ended 31 March 20X3	HV forecast in Business Plan	HV actual	KK actual
Revenue:			
Business customers (£'m)	13.00	7.00	620.00
Leisure customers (£'m)	17.00	20.00	580.00
Operating profit (£'m)	1.20	1.00	56.00
Number of cars owned (average in year)	3,000	2,800	68,000
Total days of hiring ('000 days)	870	820	21,100
Market values of assets:			
Cars (£'m)	20.25	16.80	816.00
Other assets (£'m)	10.00	10.00	664.00

8   The Foto Phrame Company

The date is December 20X3.

The Foto Phrame Company (FPC) is a listed company manufacturing mid-market cameras from a single factory in Germany.

The camera industry

The first camera was produced over 100 years ago and, since that time, new technology has enabled improved products to be launched with increasing frequency. Nearly all cameras now produced are digital cameras, which first appeared 30 years ago. However, technology advances quickly in the camera industry and each model of digital camera has a limited life cycle of five to eight years, before being replaced with an updated model. Within this life cycle, minor changes in technology mean that small variations in design, to improve a given model, are implemented each year.

Currently, there are broadly three types of camera: the compact camera (at the lower end of the market); the mirrorless camera (mid-market); the digital SLR (single lens reflex) camera (at the upper end of the market). Smartphones are a major competitor for compact cameras, but are less of a threat to mirrorless and digital SLR cameras.

Research and development (R&D) is a key feature of product improvement and replacement. The industry is very competitive and owning intellectual property for the latest technology can be important in gaining competitive advantage. However, as technology changes rapidly, any such competitive advantage can be quickly eroded. Industry employees tend to be highly skilled.

The Foto Phrame Company

FPC products

FPC manufactures only mirrorless cameras. It has a highly skilled workforce and it spends a significant amount on R&D. FPC's markets are global. 40% of sales revenues are from European countries and 30% from the United States.

The lens is one of the highest cost components in a camera. FPC currently purchases all of its camera lenses from a German company, Zeegle, which has a factory located 40 kilometres from FPC's factory. Zeegle is in daily communication with FPC procurement staff regarding delivery quantities. However, there have been occasional delays in supply, so FPC holds the equivalent of 15 days of average usage of lenses in inventory. FPC believes that Zeegle's prices are higher than they should be. The Zeegle board has refused to lower the prices, but it has constantly sought to improve product quality and service delivery for FPC.

In June 20X4, FPC intends to launch a replacement model for its best selling MirrorMinus3 (MM3) camera. This is the MirrorMinus4 (MM4), which has been redesigned to be smaller and lighter, with industry-leading technology. FPC undertakes a strategic review at the end of each model's life cycle. It is currently reviewing its procurement strategy and supply chain management policy as part of the strategic implementation of the new MM4.

Procurement and supply chain management

Two issues have arisen in terms of procurement and supply chain management:

Issue 1:   FPC is unsure whether to procure its lenses for the MM4 from: (1) one supplier, Zeegle; or (2) a range of five suppliers, producing a single type of lens, but competing on price, product quality and service. One of the suppliers would be Zeegle, two other suppliers would be French, and two would be Japanese.

Issue 2:   The MM4 has over 60 other separate components and FPC wishes to reduce costs. It wants to assess the benefits of undertaking a procurement review of all its direct suppliers ('tier 1' suppliers) in order to identify efficiencies. It is also considering managing further up the supply chain to ensure its suppliers' suppliers (ie, 'tier 2' suppliers) are reliable and cost efficient. FPC is unsure whether to conduct its own review of operating procedures in tier 2 suppliers or to ask its tier 1 suppliers to carry out this task on its behalf.

Distribution

A further concern for the FPC board relates to distribution, particularly in the US which is a major and growing market for FPC. US sales have increased from 15% to 30% of FPC's total sales revenue in the last 10 years. Up to now, distribution for this market has occurred from Germany either to US wholesalers or directly to large US retail clients (eg, large chains of specialist camera shops). No inventory is currently held by FPC in the US. However, demand in the US is variable and there have been an increasing number of complaints from US customers that lead times are too long and too uncertain.

The problems have been magnified by the fact that the version of the MM3 sold in the US differs in design from the MM3 sold to other global customers, due to the particular demands of US consumers. As a consequence, production runs for US design cameras at the factory in Germany only take place in the first week of each month. The company expects that variations in design for the US product will also be required for the new MM4.

FPC is considering developing its distribution facilities in the US by one of the following:

Distribution strategy 1: Open a distribution centre in central US to hold significant inventory for distribution throughout the US using a third party courier.

Distribution strategy 2: Set up a joint venture with a Japanese camera manufacturer to operate a distribution function in the US. The joint venture would acquire a distribution centre and vans to deliver the cameras of both companies to clients throughout the US.

Under both strategies, distribution would be both to wholesalers and directly to large retailers. However, a greater proportion of deliveries could be made directly to retailers, rather than through wholesalers, compared with existing distribution from Germany. Neither distribution strategy would involve FPC carrying out any further modification of cameras in the US.

Requirements

8.1 Explain the concept of the product life cycle and describe the factors which may affect the length of the product life cycle for FPC's cameras such as the MM3 and the MM4. **(8 marks)**

8.2 Prepare a report for the board which explains the factors that FPC should consider in evaluating:

(a) The two procurement and supply chain management issues identified by FPC, providing reasoned advice; and **(13 marks)**

(b) Each of the two US distribution strategies identified by FPC, providing reasoned advice. **(14 marks)**

Total: 35 marks

9 Emelius Ltd (amended)

The date is March 20X4.

Emelius Ltd (Emelius) offers document storage and management services in England. Its clients are organisations which typically process large volumes of paper and need to retain documents for a certain amount of time, for commercial or regulatory purposes. Clients include banks, professional services firms, local government organisations, utility companies and medical practices which find that managing their own documents requires significant amounts of time and storage space.

Document management companies benefit from economies of scale and can provide fast, cost-effective access to business-critical information. They use sophisticated systems to index information, protect documents from loss and alteration, and allow authorised access. Companies in the industry range from large global businesses, which offer comprehensive document storage and electronic data management, to smaller local or regional providers of paper-based storage facilities.

Company information

Emelius' current focus is the physical storage of paper documents. Documents requiring storage are collected from the client and taken to the nearest Emelius facility where they are bar-coded. This allows the documents to be catalogued and computer-indexed. Where relevant, a document is assigned an end-of-life destruction date, selected by the client, before being placed in long-term storage. When the agreed destruction date arrives, the document is shredded and the waste is recycled wherever possible.

Emelius' long-term storage system is suited to paper documents which clients are unlikely to need to access regularly. If access is required, the relevant documents can be retrieved from the storage facility and delivered to the client. Each Emelius storage facility is fitted with advanced fire detection systems and has comprehensive security with 24-hour off-site monitoring of the premises via surveillance cameras.

The document storage and management industry is quite capital intensive. In addition to premises and equipment, significant investment in IT systems is required. To reduce the amount of capital required, Emelius operates its business on a franchise model, with each franchisee granted an exclusive right to run the Emelius business in an agreed region of England. Strict franchise agreements allow Emelius to have tight control over the operations and quality of service provided, and to ensure Emelius' business model is applied consistently. Confidentiality of information and customer satisfaction are important and Emelius takes a strict approach to breaches of security and customer complaints.

Emelius has recently developed a new digital data capture service, which franchisees will have the option to offer as an alternative to their customers. The new service converts paper documents into digital files known as digital assets. The paper documents turned into digital assets are often those that clients need to access on a regular basis. Paper documents are taken to the company's single central scanning house, where they are converted and saved in digital form. The original paper document is destroyed and the digital version is made available for clients to access using Emelius's web-based digital asset management system. A value chain analysis for Emelius' new digital data capture service is included in **Exhibit 1**.

Emelius Northern franchise

The Emelius Northern franchise (EN) was set up in 20X2 by Lee Gryphon. The maximum storage capacity of its existing paper-based facility is 100 million sheets of paper. The business has been experiencing rapid growth (see **Exhibit 2**) and capacity could be increased to 150 million sheets by incurring additional fixed costs of £750,000 pa. EN does not currently offer the new digital data capture service.

Lee is in discussions with a large firm of solicitors, Swinburne LLP (Swinburne), about a potential new contract. Swinburne has five offices in the north of England and its paper document archive consists of 12 million sheets of paper. It wishes to outsource paper-based storage of all these documents to EN.

Swinburne has expressed an interest in using Emelius' new digital data capture service but Lee is unsure whether EN should start offering this service. Swinburne estimates that, once stored, 40% of its archive will need to be accessed regularly. The remainder needs storing for regulatory purposes but is unlikely to be accessed before end-of-life.

Requirements

9.1 Prepare a risk register setting out one significant risk facing Emelius' current paper-based document storage business, in each of the following four risk categories: strategic, operational, hazard and financial.

Use a table with four rows and three columns which explains, for each risk category:

- The nature of the one significant risk you have identified;
- The possible impact of the risk and the likelihood of it occurring; and
- Appropriate risk management procedures. **(12 marks)**

9.2 Explain four key drivers in the value chain for Emelius' new digital data capture service (Exhibit 1). **(12 marks)**

9.3 Using the quantitative data in Exhibit 2 and the other information provided in relation to the Emelius Northern (EN) franchise:

- Calculate the expected operating profit for 20X4, without the Swinburne contract. Analyse the reasons for the improvement in performance of the EN franchise over the period 1 January 20X2 to 31 December 20X4.

- Quantify the impact on EN's 20X4 expected operating profit of accepting the contract to manage Swinburne's document archive in paper format only.

- Explain your results and their implications for EN's decision about whether to introduce the digital data capture service. State any assumptions you have made. **(14 marks)**

9.4 Draft a letter on behalf of Lee Gryphon, the EN franchisee, to Swinburne, which covers the following:

- The benefits that digital data capture might offer Swinburne

- A justification of three performance measures that should be incorporated in the service level agreement for the contract between EN and Swinburne **(10 marks)**

Total: 48 marks

Exhibit 1: Value chain analysis for Emelius' new digital data capture service

FI	10 regional franchises in England; head office provides support services (accounting, marketing, training) and centralised purchasing of all equipment and IT requirements; single centralised scanning house				
TD	Automatic checks on quality/legibility of scanning and exception reporting of scanning errors	Documents stored in standard image and text format to ensure maximum system compatibility	Powerful indexing system with multiple search function allows rapid document retrieval of main and any linked supporting documents		Multiple secure access controls to prevent and detect unauthorised creation, access, alteration or deletion of records
HRM	Relatively unskilled employees at scanning house, minimum wage, strict document processing targets			Existing franchisee responsible for deciding whether to offer new service in their region	Existing head office customer service team responsible for all customer support in relation to digital data service
P	Use of 24-hour national couriers to deliver paper documents from clients to central scanning house	Sole supplier agreement for all IT needs	Maintenance of online platform for document access is outsourced to specialist provider		
PA	High-speed scanners at single central facility, able to cope with multiple document formats and batch-process large volumes Once scanned, paper documents are destroyed	Key data captured and used to index documents Validation of accuracy of indexes Copies of digital documents stored across multiple servers	Web-enabled system allows multiple users to access the same files at the same time Paper copies of documents can be requested by authorised individuals	Distinctive Emelius branding on vans, staff uniforms, correspondence, website and social media	Certificate of destruction issued to client at end-of-life in accordance with regulatory requirements
	Inbound Logistics = Converting paper documents to digital files by scanning	**Operations =** Indexing and storage of digital documents	**Outbound Logistics =** Providing clients with access to digital documents 'digital assets'	**Marketing and Sales =** Informing customers and persuading them to buy	**Service =** Ongoing service support

Margin (shown at right of chart)

KEY: FI = firm infrastructure; **TD** = technology development; **HRM** = human resource management; **P** = procurement; **PA** = primary activities

Exhibit 2: Emelius Northern (EN) franchise – operating performance summary

Year ended 31 December	Volume (sheets of paper)	Revenue £'000	Variable costs £'000	Fixed costs £'000	Operating (loss)/profit £'000
20X2 actual	50 million	1,800	675.0	1,500	(375.0)
20X3 actual	75 million	2,700	937.5	1,650	112.5

20X4 working assumptions (without Swinburne contract):

Maximum storage capacity = 100 million sheets of paper.
Anticipated volume = 90 million sheets of paper.
There will be no change in 20X3 prices to customers.
Variable cost will be 1.15 pence per sheet.
Expected fixed cost = £1,755,000.

10 Boom plc (amended)

Boom plc (Boom) is a large, profitable mining company. It is engaged in extracting natural shale gas from underground rock formations at various sites around the world.

The hydraulic fracturing industry

Shale gas represents an important type of natural capital for many mining companies around the world, and is projected to be one of the fastest-growing components of world energy consumption, with production expected to more than double between 2000 and 2020. A plentiful supply of shale gas is contained worldwide in underground rocks. It is much more abundant than conventional gas but cannot be reached by traditional vertical drilling. Instead a mixture of water, sand and chemicals is injected at high pressure, deep underground, to break up rocks and release the gas they hold. This process is known as hydraulic fracturing (fracking). The benefits claimed for shale gas include: reduced reliance on traditional forms of natural capital such as fossil fuels, increased security of energy supply, reduced carbon emissions, and socio-economic development through jobs and tax revenues.

Project SA

Boom has recently discovered a new site in a remote but populated area of South America (Project SA). The local government is willing to grant Boom a lease to proceed with the fracking and the central government anticipates that there will be significant economic benefits from the production of shale gas, in terms of job creation, gross domestic product and tax revenues. Also, an abundant domestic supply of natural shale gas could be used to produce cleaner, cheaper electricity and fuel for the region.

However, there is opposition from environmental groups which claim that the local population has not been sufficiently informed about the long-term environmental issues associated with fracking. They claim that the development would place large demands on already restricted water resources and that Boom would compete with local farmers and residents for water. They also claim that fracking risks contaminating drinking water supplies. Industry experts disagree, pointing out that it is possible to make some use of saline (non-drinking) water and recycle the waste water from the fracking process.

Boom's mission

Boom's mission statement is 'to maximise the return on investment for our shareholders whilst striving to recognise our corporate responsibility to wider society.'

At a recent board meeting to discuss Project SA, Boom's finance director commented: "Our responsibility as directors is to look after our shareholders. If we have to spend money keeping these environmentalists happy, at best we will reduce profits and at worst some of our projects will not be viable. I think the two parts of our mission statement contradict each other."

One non-executive director (NED) took a different view. "I recently attended a conference looking at the NED's role. They said that, as directors, we have a legal duty to promote the success of the company for the benefit of its members as a whole. This means having regard to the long-term consequences of any decision and the impact of the company's operations on the community and the environment as well as its employees, suppliers and customers. This leads to a sustainable business. Surely therefore we need to consider these environmentalists, if only from a risk management point of view."

Requirements

10.1 Discuss the views of the two directors in relation to Boom's mission statement. In doing so, you should explain the directors' duties in respect of corporate governance and corporate responsibility. **(12 marks)**

10.2 Discuss the commercial and ethical issues for Boom which are involved in the decision to extract shale gas in South America. **(10 marks)**

Total: 22 marks

11 ElectroInfo Ltd

ElectroInfo Ltd (EIL) operates in the electrical and IT services industry. The EIL board is currently reconsidering the company's pricing policy to customers.

Operations

EIL offers electrical and IT services to customers for their homes. These two types of service are offered independently and are provided by different EIL employees. The electrical services provided by EIL include traditional home electrical services, such as wiring and fuse box installation, and also broadband installation and maintenance. The IT services offer solutions to basic software problems experienced by customers on their home PCs, laptops and tablets.

EIL operates from 30 depots located on business parks in towns throughout the UK. The depots are located about 50 kilometres away from each other in places where there is less competition than in large cities and where local reputation can be established more easily. EIL employs qualified electricians and IT specialists. Typically there are three electricians and three IT specialists operating from each depot. Customers all live within 25 kilometres of a depot. The company aims to offer good quality customer service.

EIL has a centralised structure so prices and wages, plus most other aspects of operations, are determined centrally. Each depot head reports directly to EIL's board of directors.

Competition

EIL aims to have a market position between large service companies and small sole proprietor businesses which operate from proprietors' homes. The large service companies tend to carry out both commercial and consumer work, but charge higher prices at £38 per labour hour upwards. Sole proprietor businesses offer lower prices, charging £28 per labour hour or less, but they often lack the most up-to-date training.

Pricing

EIL charges all its services, to all its customers, at a single rate of £32 per chargeable hour. The average variable cost to the company for both IT and electrical services is £20 per chargeable hour.

To increase profits, some directors suggested raising EIL's price to all customers for both types of service, but the **finance director**, Denise Jones, was concerned about this. "Some customers are willing to pay more, but many are on low incomes. They are resistant to price increases and many would move to lower priced competitors if we raised our price. Instead, I believe we should consider charging a different price for each of our two different services, IT and electrical, to all customers, even though it costs us the same to provide these services in terms of both wages and other costs."

The **marketing director**, Amy Ashad, disagreed: "We should be charging different prices to different customers, but pricing each of the two types of service the same."

Market research

The board agreed to obtain more information about customers' attitudes to price through market research based on questionnaires and examination of actual behaviour in response to previous price changes. This research revealed the following information about the sensitivity of demand (chargeable hours per year) to selling price (£ per chargeable hour):

Selling price per chargeable hour	£30	£32	£34	£36
Demand (chargeable hours per year)	250,000	230,000	200,000	160,000

Further market analysis was completed, using two different approaches to segmenting the customer market for electrical and IT services, firstly by customer income, and secondly by service type.

Segmented by customer income

Selling price per chargeable hour	£30	£32	£34	£36
Demand (chargeable hours per year)				
Low income customers (Note)	85,000	70,000	45,000	20,000
Other customers	165,000	160,000	155,000	140,000

Note: Classified using the estimated value of the customer's house as a rough measure to indicate the level of the customer's income.

Segmented by service type

Selling price per chargeable hour	£30	£32	£34	£36
Demand (chargeable hours per year)				
IT services	125,000	120,000	110,000	100,000
Electrical services	125,000	110,000	90,000	60,000

The **chief executive** has now made a further suggestion: prices should be set locally by each depot head, rather than centrally for all the depots by the directors.

Requirements

11.1 Assume that the same price is charged for both electrical and IT services and that prices are set centrally:

(a) From the four choices of price identified in the tables above, calculate the price per chargeable hour that EIL should charge in order to maximise total contribution under each of the following alternative assumptions:

- A single uniform price is charged to all customers (as per the current policy).

- One uniform price is charged to low income customers and a different uniform price is charged to all other customers.

(b) Discuss the feasibility and benefits of Amy Ashad's suggestion of charging different prices to different customers based on income. Refer to your calculations in (a) above.

(12 marks)

11.2 Evaluate Denise Jones' suggestion that a different price should be charged for the two different service types, IT and electrical. Provide supporting calculations. Assume the same single uniform price continues to be charged to both low income and all other customers, and that prices are set centrally. **(9 marks)**

11.3 Evaluate the chief executive's suggestion of depot heads setting prices locally and explain the issues which are likely to arise in implementing this policy. **(11 marks)**

Total: 32 marks

12 Forsi Ltd (amended)

The date is September 20X4.

Forsi Ltd (Forsi) provides forensic science services to private clients and UK public sector organisations, such as the police and HMRC.

Industry information

Forensic scientists examine materials and provide scientific evidence to assist in an investigation or court proceedings. As well as criminal cases, forensic science is used in private disputes concerning accidents, medical negligence, insurance claims and product liability.

For a number of years, the government-owned Forensic Science Service (FSS) accounted for 60% of the total forensic science market in the UK and handled the majority of the public sector work. However, in 20X0 a decision was taken to reduce the activities of FSS, leading to its complete closure in 20X3. As a result there have been several new entrants to the market, which is now very competitive.

Forsi was founded in 20X0 by four scientists who previously worked for FSS. Forsi and one other key competitor now dominate the UK market. Both offer a wide range of forensic science services to all types of client. A number of smaller providers have also emerged which typically specialise in one particular scientific field eg, fire investigation, toxicology or genetics. Various UK police forces also have their own in-house forensic science laboratories but there is no national police policy, so many police forces outsource work to businesses such as Forsi.

Company information

From the outset, Forsi has operated with an informal structure, to minimise bureaucracy and focus on technical expertise and scientific analysis. The original founders spend little time on administration and management tasks, and instead concentrate on attracting clients and undertaking analytical work. Many support functions (including payroll, accounting and human resources) are outsourced.

As a result of the founders' reputations and technical expertise, and the range of forensic science services provided, Forsi has experienced steady growth. It now employs 40 scientists and five administrators. Work is organised on a project basis, with an appropriate project team created for each specific client request. On smaller projects, scientists may work alone. When they are not working on projects, Forsi's scientists are expected to undertake research to develop new scientific techniques or more efficient processes.

Although Forsi does undertake one-off projects for clients, most of its business is on a repeat basis, eg, a succession of accident investigations for an insurance company. Obtaining such clients is key to revenue growth. Once Forsi has been confirmed as a client's approved supplier, client retention becomes important. Depending on the client and the nature of the work, some projects are negotiated at a fixed price and some are priced on a cost-plus basis. Increasingly clients prefer fixed-price projects so that they can avoid unexpected increases in costs. All dealings and discussions with clients are handled by the four founders.

As a result of the increased competition, Forsi's informal structure has started to present some difficulties and threatens to inhibit its growth. There has been a lack of collaboration between staff, with scientists preferring to work independently on each project, and Forsi has not maximised opportunities for shared learning.

Often, requirements change during the course of a project and delays have arisen whilst one of the founders renegotiates with the client, leading to client complaints. There are few in-house financial controls and although a budgeted cost is established for each project before work starts, this is often exceeded. As a result of these issues, Forsi's profits have fallen (**Exhibits 1 and 2**). It has started to lose some potential projects to competitors and has also had to accept lower margins on repeat business in order to retain clients.

A possible new owner

Recently, Forsi has been approached by an Australian multi-national, Aussi Ltd (Aussi), which undertakes work for global private and public sector clients. Aussi consists of several divisions, each offering a different scientific service (eg, pharmaceutical research, forensic science, aerospace). All support services are provided by a centralised shared service centre which operates from Aussi's head office.

Aussi's forensic science division is the market leader in Australia and Asia. In 20X3 it spent £4.4 million on research and development and £9 million on marketing, and it generated sales revenue of £220.3 million (all figures translated from Australian dollars into £ sterling).

Aussi wants to acquire Forsi to further its expansion in Europe. However, it does not want to destroy Forsi's research-centred culture as it acknowledges that Forsi's success to date has been driven by the founders' knowledge and contacts, and by the skill of the scientists it employs. If the founders agree to sell their shares, Aussi will either allow Forsi to operate autonomously as a separate subsidiary company or integrate it within Aussi's forensic science division.

Whichever structure is chosen, Forsi will be required by Aussi to achieve a target return on capital employed (ROCE) of 15%. It will also have to comply with Aussi's formal project screening process whereby:

- All new projects are required to meet an expected minimum 20% gross margin
- The final agreed project price has to be signed off by Aussi's central finance department

In 20X3, Aussi's forensic science division generated a gross margin of 25% and ROCE of 18% on net assets of £183.5 million. **Exhibit 2** sets out additional operating data for Aussi.

Requirements

12.1 Using the quantitative data in the Exhibits and the other information provided, analyse the performance of Forsi, contrasting it with Aussi's where appropriate. Suggest other non-financial information that may be useful in ascertaining the causes of the deterioration in Forsi's performance. **(16 marks)**

12.2 Discuss the appropriateness of Forsi's existing structure, referring to relevant models. **(7 marks)**

12.3 Assuming Forsi's founders do **not** agree to be taken over by Aussi, explain why knowledge management is important to Forsi and recommend the steps that Forsi could take to implement a knowledge management strategy. You should refer to the concept of human capital in your answer. **(8 marks)**

12.4 Assuming Forsi's founders **do** agree to be taken over by Aussi:

(a) Discuss whether Forsi should be operated as a subsidiary of Aussi or as part of Aussi's forensic science division; and

(b) Recommend how Aussi should manage the change when the takeover is announced. **(14 marks)**

Total: 45 marks

Exhibit 1: Financial data for Forsi for the years ended 31 December

	20X2 £'000	20X3 £'000
Sales revenue	5,400	5,088
Direct costs	(4,175)	(4,165)
Gross profit	1,225	923
Research & development	(254)	(260)
Marketing	(108)	(90)
Other operating expenses	(268)	(270)
Operating profit	595	303
Net asset value	4,020	3,910

Exhibit 2: Operating data for Forsi and Aussi

	Forsi 20X2	Forsi 20X3	Aussi forensic science division 20X3
Number of employees	45	45	2,000
Number of projects undertaken in year	108	106	2,448
% of projects completed on time	83%	76%	89%
% of projects completed within budgeted cost	72%	65%	92%
Sales value of projects awarded, but not yet undertaken, at year end	£1,350,000	£855,000	£65,080,000

13 Water On Tap (amended)

The date is September 20X4.

'Water On Tap' (Ontap) is a small social enterprise operating in central London. A social enterprise is a business which meets social and environmental aims by trading in a profitable and sustainable way.

Ontap's specific aim is 'to provide a cheaper and more sustainable alternative to bottled water.' Its founder, Nala Delmar, a keen athlete, founded Ontap because she was frustrated by the large amount of money she was spending on bottled drinking water. Nala's concerns were heightened after she read a news article which reported the increasing problems being caused by the number of one-time use, plastic water bottles in circulation. The article also highlighted the negative impact that the global consumption of mineral water is having on the planet's natural capital.

Ontap's operations need to be financially viable because it relies on its business activities, not donations, for funding. 70% of Ontap's profits are donated to fund clean water projects in India. Remaining funds are reinvested in the business or used to raise awareness of the damaging effects of bottled water on the environment.

Bottled water industry in the UK

The retail market for bottled water in the UK is worth approximately £1.6 billion, by annual sales revenue. Industry statistics show that the average consumer drinks 33 litres of purchased bottled water per annum.

Despite legislation that requires any establishment serving alcohol to have free tap water available, it has become the social norm to purchase bottled water in such establishments. This has reduced the acceptability of asking for free tap water in restaurants, cafes and bars. It has also created a huge increase in plastic bottle waste. An estimated 18 billion plastic bottles are consumed annually in the UK, of which 75% are not recycled and therefore end up in landfill. The packaging and transportation involved means that bottled water also has a much higher carbon footprint per litre than tap water.

In 20X2 several UK supermarkets were criticised for selling a product that should have been free, when it became apparent that some of their own-brand bottled water was simply filtered, purified tap water. Some multi-national bottled water companies have also attracted adverse publicity for spending huge sums on advertising in an attempt to make their brand fashionable and appear to offer variety for what is essentially a homogenous product.

About Ontap

The Ontap concept involves a re-fillable water bottle made from recycled aluminium foil, which carries the Ontap logo. Once purchased from Ontap, at a cost of £8, the bottle can be taken to a range of participating cafes and shops (currently only in central London) and re-filled with tap water. These businesses provide their re-filling services for Ontap's customers free of charge, in the hope they will purchase additional products. The Ontap website and free mobile app provide a list of refill sites, all of which prominently display the Ontap logo.

Plans for expansion

In London, Ontap has been a success and proved popular with athletes, commuters and students plus the participating cafes and shops. Ontap has received lots of social media coverage and the brand is currently very fashionable. Nala is keen to expand her original concept.

She is considering two possible options for expansion:

(1) A corporate sales scheme. Nala would like to persuade companies to buy water bottles to replace the plastic cups typically found beside water coolers in most offices. She has read a recent survey reporting that, on average in such offices, each employee throws away four plastic cups a day. Instead, the company would bulk purchase Ontap bottles for their employees, which would then be co-branded with the company's own name.

(2) Geographical expansion. This would necessitate finding cafes and shops outside the central London area which would be willing to be Ontap partners.

Requirements

13.1 Discuss the extent to which Ontap is a sustainable enterprise. **(7 marks)**

13.2 Compare and contrast the ethics of the marketing activities of Ontap with its competitors in the bottled water industry. **(8 marks)**

13.3 Discuss the problems Ontap will face in any expansion of the business and evaluate the two proposed options. **(10 marks)**

Total: 25 marks

14 Drummond & Drew LLP

The date is December 20X5.

Drummond & Drew LLP (DD) is a large firm of commercial architects, based in a single office in London.

The industry

Architects plan, design and oversee the construction of buildings for clients. Architects belong to professional bodies and usually operate in professional partnerships or companies.

The scale of architectural projects varies from large commercial buildings (such as offices, shops and factories) to residential housing. Some architect firms specialise in one type of project, others operate across a spectrum of different project types. A project may involve constructing a new building or altering an existing building.

A client's project usually requires two phases of work: the planning and design phase, and the construction phase. Both phases are normally managed by the same architect firm.

The planning and design phase involves the architect ascertaining the client's requirements in detail. The architect then prepares design drawings and graphics which comply with local building and other regulations.

The construction phase requires the administration, monitoring and coordination of the construction process by the architect. This can include, for a large project: site inspections, surveys, procurement of contractors, cost appraisal, certification, valuations and project management. Most aspects of this phase require architects regularly working on site with construction company staff.

Company background

DD's structure and staffing

DD has grown gradually over many years, increasing its revenue and staff, and has built a reputation within the UK as a good quality architect firm specialising in commercial, rather than residential, projects. In recent years, however, DD's UK growth has slowed due to increasing competition from existing firms and new market entrants.

DD has 12 partners (all qualified architects) plus 93 other qualified architects, and a further 77 support staff including managers, IT specialists, chartered surveyors, semi-skilled staff and administrative staff.

The 12 partners together take all the key decisions. Jeff Drummond is the senior partner. The other qualified architects have various levels of seniority and differing specialist skills.

All DD architects are fee-earning other than the technical and regulatory team, comprising three architects, which deals with adherence to technical standards and compliance with regulations.

Additional qualified architect time is sometimes acquired on a short-term contract basis, for both complex projects and more routine work. Using short-term contract architects has helped DD manage capacity where there are variations over time in the number and size of client projects.

Individual DD architects have significant autonomy in the design process and professional decision making, but they report to the partners regarding progress compared to plan, time spent and profitability of each project.

In the design and planning phase, most architects work at the London office, with occasional visits to clients. In the construction phase, most of the architects' time is spent at the construction site, with occasional visits to the London office.

Clients and projects

DD's client portfolio includes large companies requiring the design and construction of offices, factories and other large commercial buildings.

Whilst historically most of DD's projects have been in the UK, over the past five years there has been an increasing number of overseas projects. Almost all of the growth in project numbers has been in Dubai and the other Gulf States, where there is significant commercial construction activity as the region recovers from a recent economic downturn.

The scale of projects won in the Gulf States has grown as DD's reputation has spread in the region. To date, projects in the Gulf States have been serviced by London-based DD staff, but this has proved increasingly difficult as the number and scale of projects in the region have increased. In 20X4, the equivalent of 10 architects spent all their chargeable hours on Gulf State projects. A majority of DD partners believe that many more projects could be obtained in the Gulf States if the firm had an office in the region.

A potential new project in Dubai

To be eligible to bid in January 20X6 to provide planning, design and construction services for a major building in Dubai, called the Sunrise, DD must make a commitment to establishing an office in the region from 1 January 20X7. It therefore needs now to make an urgent decision about operating an office in Dubai. If the bid is successful, design work on the Sunrise project will start in January 20X7.

DD would aim to obtain commissions for additional commercial projects in the Gulf State region during 20X6. However, to make the investment in an office in Dubai viable in the longer term, DD would also need to work on smaller projects, especially residential buildings.

The number of architects and support staff required to be located in an office in Dubai is estimated to be:

| | **Number of Dubai staff** | | |
Projects	20X7	20X8	20X9 and each year thereafter
Sunrise	12	18	0
Other commercial	10	14	16
Residential	5	7	10

If this international expansion does take place, there are two alternative methods: acquire an existing architect firm in Dubai; or set up a new DD office there.

Requirements

14.1 Using appropriate models, explain the nature and suitability of the existing organisational structure of DD as a professional service organisation. Ignore any new development in the Gulf States. **(10 marks)**

14.2 Explain the factors that DD should consider in deciding whether or not to expand internationally by establishing an office in Dubai. Ignore the issue of whether this is by acquisition or by an office being set up by DD. **(12 marks)**

14.3 Assuming DD does decide it needs an office in Dubai, explain the factors that should be considered in determining whether it should acquire an existing architect firm in Dubai or open a new office there itself. **(8 marks)**

Total: 30 marks

15 Mississippi Muzic Ltd

Mississippi Muzic Ltd (MM) operates four London nightclubs, each with a restaurant. The four clubs are the same size but are located in different areas of London. They all aim to attract a similar clientele and are open every night of the week.

There is a small fee for life-time membership when a person first visits a MM club, but the entrance charge for each subsequent visit by a member is high, and drinks and meals are expensive. The target market is young, high-income professionals who wish to socialise, dine, drink and network with people from a similar background. The high entrance charge is viewed favourably by many club members as it keeps the environment exclusive to professional groups.

MM has attracted a loyal core of members and the clubs are, on average, 95% full on Friday and Saturday nights. The capacity of each club at any one time is 250 people. The clubs are significantly less busy for the remainder of the week as members tend to work long hours.

MM has a database of all its 7,800 current members. All of MM's members have consented to MM using their personal data for marketing purposes. The membership grows each week as new members join. However the chief executive of MM, Jane Flinkstein, believes that the company is not making best use of this database for marketing. The core database includes the member's: name; contact details; gender; age; job; and interests. Each member has a membership card with a bar code to be shown at each visit to the club. Data is then recorded so the timing and frequency of each member's visits are held on the database.

MM wishes to increase revenue by marketing its clubs more effectively and has identified two possible strategies, which are not mutually exclusive.

Strategy 1 – MM would encourage existing members to visit the clubs more frequently, and dine in the restaurants more often, by using its database more effectively for relationship marketing purposes.

Strategy 2 – MM would appeal to new types of customer, other than young professionals, in order to fill its spare capacity from Sunday to Thursday.

Requirements

You are a business adviser who has been asked by Jane Flinkstein to prepare a report outlining elements of a marketing strategy for MM:

15.1 Explain how MM can use its database more effectively to market to existing customers (Strategy 1). **(8 marks)**

15.2 Outline and explain the market research that MM should undertake for Strategy 2.

(8 marks)

15.3 For Strategy 2, identify and explain:

- a segmentation strategy; and
- a pricing strategy. **(8 marks)**

Total: 24 marks

16 Confo plc

The date is December 20X4.

Confo plc (Confo) is a listed company, operating in the packaged confectionery products (boxes of sweets) industry.

Confo was established a number of years ago, manufacturing boxes of sweets in its factory and selling them in its own shops throughout the UK. Since this time, some of the 240 shops have been operated under exclusive franchise arrangements, while the remainder are still owned by Confo. All products sold at Confo shops (both owned and franchised) are produced in Confo's factory. The company was structured as two separate divisions, Manufacturing and Retail, until 30 September 20X3 (**Exhibit 1**).

Recovery plan

After a difficult period of trading, a new board was appointed in December 20X2 and, following a detailed review, it implemented a radical three-year recovery plan from 1 October 20X3. The recovery plan included: the closure of 70 owned shops; the opening of 30 franchised shops; and the creation of two new sales channels, commercial sales (to UK supermarkets) and export sales (to overseas retailers). As a result, Confo now has two additional divisions, Commercial and Export, and a revised system for pricing transfers (**Exhibit 2**).

Following preparation of the management accounts and operating data for the year ended 30 September 20X4 (**Exhibit 3**), a board meeting was called to review progress in implementing the three-year recovery plan, and to consider whether any changes to the plan are needed.

Board meeting

The chief executive complained: "This year's results are disastrous. This was supposed to be a recovery plan, but performance seems to have got worse, not better. Profit has fallen compared with last year."

The marketing director disagreed: "I believe that we have great potential for future growth from the commercial and export sales that we started this year. However, we need to give them time to get established and show their potential. You cannot judge performance on one year's figures."

An ethical issue

From 1 October 20X3, the sales manager of Confo's Commercial Division, Kirsty Keller, met regularly with John Drake, the procurement manager of a large customer, Lenton Supermarket (Lenton). In November 20X3, John asked if he could have two small boxes of sweets for his family for Christmas. This type of small gift to customers' staff is common in the sweets industry. In December 20X3, Kirsty delivered some Confo sweets, with a total value of £10, to John's home as a gift to promote good relations between Confo and Lenton. She informed Confo's commercial director about what she had done and he was happy with this action.

From January 20X4, John made further requests for gifts of sweets, gradually increasing in both value and frequency. In order to keep a good business relationship with John, Kirsty continued to provide these gifts, but she stopped disclosing them to the commercial director in March 20X4 when the value of the gifts reached £30 per week. In July 20X4, when John started asking for gifts valued at £100 per week, Kirsty refused.

In September 20X4, Lenton stopped purchasing from Confo. Kirsty never made any personal gain from the gifts and there is no documentary evidence relating to them.

Requirements

16.1 Compare and evaluate Confo's pricing of transfers before and after the changes made by implementing the recovery plan on 1 October 20X3. Suggest and justify alternative methods of pricing transfers that Confo could have adopted on 1 October 20X3. **(9 marks)**

16.2 Analyse and evaluate the performance of the Manufacturing Division and the Retail Division in the year ended 30 September 20X4 compared with the year ended 30 September 20X3. Highlight any problems in comparing the data and set out any additional information that would assist your analysis. **(15 marks)**

16.3 As part of the appraisal of the first year of the recovery plan, prepare a report which:

    (a)   Reviews the strategies adopted by the Export Division and the Commercial Division, and evaluates their performance. Include any relevant strategic models in your appraisal.

    (b)   Evaluates the success of the recovery plan for Confo to date. **(15 marks)**

16.4 Explain the ethical issues for Kirsty, and for Confo, arising from the matters occurring with Lenton and John Drake. Set out, and justify, the actions that Kirsty and Confo should now take. **(7 marks)**

Total: 46 marks

Exhibit 1: Company structure and pricing of transfers – pre 30 September 20X3

Up to 30 September 20X3, both Confo divisions, Manufacturing and Retail, were profit centres. The factory's output was transferred by the Manufacturing Division to all Confo shops (owned and franchised) at the same price, full cost plus 20%. In addition to the Retail Division's profits from the owned shops, Confo also earned a total of £1.2 million annually from the fixed fees it charged to franchisees for use of the Confo brand name and for operational and management support.

Consumers are charged the same list prices at all Confo shops. Franchisees are also required to charge these list prices in order not to undercut the prices charged by owned shops, and to avoid cheapening the Confo brand.

The setting of the same prices for transfers from the factory to both owned and franchised shops caused some internal debate. The Retail Division management claimed that prices for transfers to owned shops were too high and should be lower than the prices charged to franchisees. They also believed that the annual fixed fees paid to Confo by franchisees were too low. Confo products are unique and valid comparison with the prices charged by rival manufacturers and retailers cannot be made easily.

Exhibit 2: Company structure and pricing of transfers – post 1 October 20X3

Since the commencement of the recovery plan on 1 October 20X3, Confo has operated with four divisions: Manufacturing, Retail, Commercial and Export.

Changes in the Manufacturing Division

From 1 October 20X3, the Manufacturing Division became a cost centre. It transfers all its output at full cost to the Retail Division, to franchisees, and to the new Commercial and Export Divisions. The reduction in the price of transfers was, in part, intended to increase the volume of sweets purchased by existing franchisees and to encourage more franchises to be taken up. To offset the lost revenue, Confo increased the fixed fee charged to each franchisee. These fixed fees now total £2.5 million.

Changes in the Retail Division

Confo continues to make UK retail sales via owned and franchised shops. The Retail Division still comprises owned shops and remains a profit centre. The review by the new board identified that many owned shops in the retail network were under-performing. On 1 October 20X3, as part of the recovery plan, 70 poorly performing owned shops were closed. Of these closed shops, 30 were immediately reopened under the management of new franchisees.

The new Commercial and Export Divisions

The Commercial and Export Divisions were opened on 1 October 20X3 as separate profit centres.

The Commercial Division makes sales to UK supermarkets. The products are all made in Confo's factory, but are packaged by Confo in the client's brand and wrapping (ie, 'own labelled') in order to minimise the loss of sales at Confo shops, and to make price comparisons by consumers more difficult. Prices charged by the Commercial Division are negotiated separately with each client. The supermarkets sell the products at retail prices that are lower than the list prices in Confo's owned and franchised shops.

The Export Division sells only Confo branded products, in bulk, to overseas retailers. It has taken some time to establish relationships with new clients and develop brand awareness, but sales have started to grow.

Exhibit 3: Management accounts and operating data

Confo: Management accounts for the year ended 30 September 20X3

	Manufacturing £'000	Retail £'000	Total £'000
Transfers to franchised shops by Manufacturing Division	8,100	–	8,100
External sales	–	24,000	24,000
Divisional transfers	18,000	(18,000)	–
Variable costs	(13,050)	(2,400)	(15,450)
Fixed costs	(8,700)	(4,000)	(12,700)
Divisional profit	4,350	(400)	3,950
Fixed franchise fees			1,200
Operating profit			5,150

Confo: Management accounts for the year ended 30 September 20X4

	Manufacturing £'000	Retail £'000	Commercial £'000	Export £'000	Total £'000
Transfers to franchised shops by Manufacturing Division	7,500	–	–	–	7,500
External sales	–	14,400	4,320	1,760	20,480
Divisional transfers	13,000	(9,000)	(3,000)	(1,000)	–
Variable costs	(12,300)	(1,080)	(720)	(320)	(14,420)
Fixed costs	(8,200)	(3,000)	(300)	(240)	(11,740)
Divisional profit	0	1,320	300	200	1,820
Fixed franchise fees					2,500
Operating profit					4,320

Confo: Operating data for the years ended 30 September		
	20X3	**20X4**
Number of boxes of sweets sold externally:		
Retail Division (owned shops) ('000s)	12,000	7,200
Franchised shops ('000s)	5,400	6,000
Commercial Division ('000s)	–	2,400
Export Division ('000s)	–	800
Total products sold externally	17,400	16,400
Number of Confo shops:		
Owned shops	150	80
Franchised shops	90	120

17 Radar Traditional Radios Ltd (amended)

The date is December 20X8.

Radar Traditional Radios Ltd (RTR) is a family-owned company which manufactures high quality portable radios at a factory in the UK. The particular styling of the radios, which appeals to UK market tastes, means sales are made in the UK only.

Radio broadcasting

In the UK, radio stations broadcast radio programmes via two main platforms:

- Analogue, using traditional analogue frequencies (AM/FM)
- Digital, using newer digital audio broadcasting (DAB)

Digital broadcasting was publicly launched in the UK 20 years ago. The broadcasting industry is encouraging digital radio broadcasting as it offers a wider choice of radio stations than analogue, is easier to use, and is resistant to localised signal interference.

However, on the negative side, the overall audio quality on digital is poorer than analogue, and digital reception is restricted in certain areas of the UK, so a lower percentage of the population can receive digital, compared with analogue. Digital reception was available to 80% of the UK population 10 years ago and is today available to 90% of the population. Analogue reception is available to 99% of the UK population.

Radio listening

In 20X7, 35% of radio listening hours in the UK were on digital, 60% on analogue and 5% on other platforms.

Radio programmes that are broadcast on the analogue platform can be listened to only on analogue radios. Digital radio broadcasts can however be listened to on a variety of devices. The devices used to listen to digital audio broadcasts in the UK in 20X7 compared to 20X2 were as follows:

Radio listening to digital broadcasts by device

	20X2	20X7
	%	%
Digital television	25	27
Digital radios	23	25
Internet	15	22
Smartphones	10	20
Other devices	27	6

In the years before 20X7, there was significant optimism about the future of digital radio broadcasting. The UK government predicted that it would switch off the analogue platform in the UK by 20X9. As a result, in 20X5 a major UK electrical retailer announced that it would shortly stop selling analogue radios. In spite of this early optimism, however, growth in sales of digital radios has been much lower than anticipated. Digital radios are currently owned by a little less than half of UK households.

The government is now expected to require the switch-off of analogue radio frequencies in the UK in the next 5 years. Some industry analysts believe that digital may take many years to overtake analogue due to the modest levels of ownership of digital radios.

Radio manufacture

The manufacture of radios is a global industry with some multinational companies producing radios as part of a wide range of consumer electrical products. There are however many small national companies, like RTR, specialising in radio manufacture only for their home markets. Some companies have stopped making analogue radios. Most companies in the industry, however, currently manufacture both analogue and digital radios, though some have plans to greatly reduce, and then cease, the production of analogue radios, as analogue is being switched off in an increasing number of countries.

The price of radios to consumers in the UK varies widely. Analogue radios are significantly cheaper than digital radios, retailing from around £25. The cheaper digital radios retail at £35, and mid-market digital radios are typically £50 to £100, while top-of-the-range models are considerably more expensive.

With advances in technology, some radio manufacturers are adding additional features to digital radios including, for example, internet access. They have also added 'Bluetooth' technology, which allows the user to stream music wirelessly through a digital radio from other devices such as MP3 players and smartphones.

Company information – RTR

RTR manufactures both digital and analogue radios. Its radios contain up-to-date technology and are known for their quality, but they deliberately feature old-fashioned styling. This gives RTR a niche market, but there is continued pressure in the industry to keep the technology up-to-date to compete, not just with other radios, but also with the other devices, such as smartphones, which can receive digital broadcasts.

RTR radios are only distributed through upmarket stores in the UK, and are at the top end of the market. RTR's analogue radios sell for an average of £150 and their digital radios average £200. Over the past few years, RTR's annual sales volumes have remained constant at 100,000 radios, as follows:

RTR sales (units)	20X2	20X7
Analogue radios	65,000	60,000
Digital radios	35,000	40,000

RTR has always had a policy of investing in research and development (R&D) to ensure its radios are innovative in function, as well as being distinctive in style. Recently it has added Bluetooth to one model in its digital range, but further investment is needed to introduce Bluetooth across the digital range and develop additional technology features.

It has become difficult for RTR to compete with larger manufacturers given rapidly advancing technology, both in radio broadcasting and in listening devices. RTR needs to decide whether to cease R&D and marketing expenditure on analogue radios, effectively phasing out their production over the next two to three years, so that all the R&D and marketing budgets can be focused on digital radios. A board meeting was arranged to discuss these issues.

Board meeting

The R&D director was pessimistic: "We are a small company in a big industry. We need to focus our R&D expenditure on digital products or the budget will just be spread too thin."

The marketing director disagreed: "We cannot abandon analogue, which is still our largest market. I agree we need to focus our resources. However, I would try to focus marketing expenditure at our target consumer groups for both analogue and digital radios, not just concentrate on one type of product. I agree the digital radio market is more challenging, so I have provided some data (**Exhibit**) to help us decide on a marketing strategy for digital radios."

Requirements

17.1 Using Porter's Five Forces Model, explain the impact on competitiveness in the radio manufacturing industry, for the UK market, of the following **two** forces only:

- Substitutes
- Competitive rivalry amongst existing firms **(10 marks)**

17.2 Explain how market segmentation can be used by RTR to identify target groups of consumers for its digital radios, and discuss how each of the components in the marketing mix (4Ps) can be used by RTR to promote its digital radio product range to these groups. **(12 marks)**

17.3 Discuss and evaluate the factors to be considered by the RTR board in determining whether, and if so when, it should decide to abandon the manufacture of analogue radios to focus resources on developing and selling only digital radios. **(9 marks)**

Total: 31 marks

Exhibit: Analysis of UK consumers for digital radios

	UK industry average	RTR radios
Age of consumer	45	55
Average annual income	£23,000	£37,000
Gender	60% male	45% male

---

18 The Norgate Bank plc

The date is December 20X4.

The Norgate Bank plc (NB) is a bank whose customers are small businesses and individuals living in either the UK or France. It has no physical branches for customers to visit. Internet banking is therefore important to NB, but also its telephone call centres are key to communication and to building customer relationships.

Until last year, NB had only one telephone call centre, which was near London and served all its existing customers. Call operators included fluent French speakers to serve French customers. In December 20X3, a major new investment was made in a new call centre in Vietnam, where some of the local population speak French. At that time, Ron Terry was appointed as the director in charge of all call centre operations.

Under the new arrangement, the UK call centre serves only UK customers. French customers are served by the call centre in Vietnam, where call operators are from the local, French-speaking population. Property costs and staff costs are much lower in Vietnam than in London. At both call centres there are two groups of call operators: one for business customers and one for individual customers.

Ron wants to conduct a post-implementation review of both call centres to ensure that physical and human resources are being used efficiently. Over the past year, Ron has used three Key Performance Indictors (KPIs) to measure call centre performance (**Exhibit**). These are:

- average time taken to answer a customer call
- average length of a customer call
- scores from customer satisfaction surveys for handling calls (where: 1 = poor; 5 = excellent)

Ron is concerned about the validity of these KPIs, and he is unsure whether they are the most appropriate means of measuring performance. He is also unsure how they might be utilised to improve the efficiency of the call centres.

Wendy West, a senior manager reporting to Ron, used to work at a call centre in a large insurance company. She believes that NB's KPIs are poor by comparison to those of her previous employer.

Requirements

18.1 Evaluate the validity of the three KPIs used for measuring the performance of NB's call centres and suggest alternative measures.   **(12 marks)**

18.2 Explain the benefits and problems of NB using benchmarking to evaluate performance, and to improve efficiency, in its call centres. Refer to different types of benchmark and use the data in the Exhibit where relevant.   **(11 marks)**

Total: 23 marks

Exhibit: Data for the year ended 30 November 20X4				
	UK call centre (UK customers)		Vietnam call centre (French customers)	
	Business	Individuals	Business	Individuals
Number of calls in the year ('000s)	120	1,200	90	600
Number of call operators	20	100	12	30
Time to answer a call (minutes)	2	2	1	1.2
Length of call (minutes)	10	4	8	3
Average customer satisfaction score	3.9	4.1	3.1	3.3

19 Rocket Co (amended)

The date is late March 20X5.

Rocket Co (Rocket) is an accountancy practice with four partners. It operates from a single office in a European country that is not part of the EU and whose currency is the franc.

Information about Rocket

Rocket employs 17 professional staff, both qualified and part-qualified accountants, and five support staff. It specialises in accounting and tax advisory work in the sports and leisure sector. Rocket's clients are typically wealthy self-employed sportsmen and sportswomen. It competes with a number of big regional and national accountancy practices which service sports and leisure clients as part of a more general client portfolio.

Rocket has experienced impressive growth rates but the partners are concerned that growth appears to be slowing. An extract from Rocket's balanced scorecard for the years ended 31 December 20X3 and 20X4 is provided in the **Exhibit**, showing both financial and non-financial information. The partners' financial returns in 20X4 were affected by a number of factors, including a fall in billable hours, a rent review and increased professional indemnity insurance (PII) premiums. Most significantly, Rocket had to pay higher salaries to its employees. Professional staff working on sports and leisure clients normally command a premium of around 10% on market salaries. During a recent economic downturn in Rocket's home country, Rocket had been paying its 17 professional staff just below the market rates for general accountancy staff. This was accepted by staff while they had few other employment options available, however the market is now improving and external job opportunities are growing. As a result, during 20X4, Rocket was forced to give professional staff a substantial pay rise.

Change in strategy: creation of a multi-disciplinary practice

A new regulatory framework for the legal services market was recently introduced in Rocket's country, to increase competition and encourage efficiency. This removed the previous restrictions on lawyers forming partnerships with other professions and created a new type of professional services firm, known as a multi-disciplinary practice (MDP). An MDP is a professional firm consisting of professionally qualified lawyers and accountants working together in client-facing roles. To operate as an MDP, a licence is required from the newly-created regulatory authority which is responsible for monitoring quality and compliance.

In February 20X5, Rocket's four partners decided to take steps to become an MDP. Clients in the sports and leisure sector often need more than one professional service to deal with matters such as contract negotiations, sponsorship deals and personal injury claims. Rocket's intention is to capitalise on this by offering legal, tax and accounting advice to its existing clients. This should also allow it to attract new clients. Typically both legal and accounting firms face high fixed costs for salaries, premises and PII. The synergies involved in becoming an MDP will allow Rocket to provide a greater volume of client services more efficiently and cost-effectively, thereby increasing both revenue and margins.

Rocket estimates it initially needs six fully-qualified lawyers, with a view to increasing this to a team of 10 once demand is established. Two possible ways of resourcing the change to an MDP are being considered:

(1) Recruit qualified lawyers on an individual basis

(2) Acquire a specialist team of qualified lawyers from a law firm to which Rocket has previously referred work

Announcement of the change in strategy

On 1 March 20X5, Rocket issued the following email to its professional staff and support staff, in order to announce the firm's change of strategy and to set out the partners' expectations. There had been no prior consultation with the recipients of the email and it has caused considerable anxiety among all staff.

CONFIDENTIAL EMAIL

To: allstaff@Rocket.com
From: Rocket partners
Date: 1 March 20X5

Re: New business structure and strategy

The partners have decided to take advantage of recent changes in legislation so, with effect from 1 June 20X5, Rocket will become a multi-disciplinary practice (MDP) offering both legal and accounting/tax services. As you are aware, our high-profile sporting clients frequently also need legal services and this change in strategy will allow us to attract a greater share of their expenditure on professional advice, and to improve our competitive position. We are in the process of recruiting the necessary qualified lawyers.

We will be spending heavily on marketing the new services and to fund this over the next month we will be examining the potential for cost savings and efficiencies across the firm. This may have some impact on our staffing and management structure.

We estimate that 75% of a fully-qualified staff member's total workload is dependent on having completed their professional qualification. The remaining workload could be carried out by a combination of part-qualified professional staff and support staff. Therefore, we require all fully-qualified staff to identify immediately which parts of their work they can begin to pass on to other staff. This will result in financial benefits to clients as we can reduce certain fees, and it will allow our fully-qualified staff to focus on more value-added advisory work, which will enhance revenues.

From 1 June 20X5, each client will be serviced by a multi-disciplinary account management team headed up by a partner, with at least one qualified lawyer and one fully-qualified accountant. There will be a new shared service centre providing administrative assistance to both legal and accounting/tax professional staff, so that clients receive a coordinated service. To improve productivity we will staff the shared service centre on the basis of one member of support staff for every six professional staff (including partners). We expect all staff to be as cooperative as possible and ask you to do everything you can to make our new legal colleagues welcome. Please give them open access to your clients and all relevant client information.

Ethical issue

Alina Jay, an ICAEW Chartered Accountant with Rocket, has recently been involved in preparing a statement of personal assets and liabilities for a long-standing client of the firm, who is currently seeking loan finance. The final statement which was submitted to the client's bank was very different from the initial draft which Alina prepared and submitted to her manager at Rocket. She suspects that the Rocket manager, who is a personal friend of the client, may have agreed to a misstatement of the client's personal affairs. Alina is unsure whether she should report the client and/or the manager to her superiors, and is concerned about the impact on her job and career if she were to do so.

Requirements

19.1 Using the balanced scorecard in the Exhibit and the other information available, analyse and evaluate the performance of Rocket between 20X3 and 20X4.　　　　　　**(18 marks)**

19.2 Analyse the impact of the following factors that may influence Rocket's ability to create a multi-disciplinary practice:

- Human resource capabilities
- Legal and regulatory issues
- Competitors and market structure **(10 marks)**

19.3 In relation to the email announcing Rocket's proposed change in strategy, discuss the extent to which Rocket's approach meets best practice in change management. Refer to an appropriate change model such as Gemini 4Rs. **(10 marks)**

19.4 Discuss the ethical issues associated with Alina's concerns and advise her on appropriate actions to take. **(8 marks)**

Total: 46 marks

Exhibit: Extract from Balanced Scorecard for Rocket

	Year ended 31 December	
	20X4	20X3
Financial		
Note: All monetary amounts are expressed in francs (F)		
Total fee income (F'000)	7,091	6,653
Growth in fee income	+6.6%	+9.2%
Mix of fee income – Accounting Tax	47:53	45:55
Average fee charged per billable hour (F):		
Accounting services	335	300
Taxation services	415	360
Fee income per partner (F'000)	1,773	1,663
Net profit as a % of fee income	20.8%	23.1%
Clients		
Market share (sports and leisure sector)	12%	14%
% of satisfied clients (based on annual survey)	75%	85%
Innovation and learning		
Average training hours per qualified employee	14	14
Total staff turnover	23.5%	17.6%
Internal business processes		
Error rates (% of client assignments undertaken where mistakes by rocket employees are detected)	10%	8%
Utilisation rate (% of total professional staff hours spent on chargeable client work)	70.5%	66.5%
Staff ratio:		
Number of support staff: number of professional staff and partners	5:21	5:21

20 The Scottish Woodlands Commission (amended)

The Scottish Woodlands Commission (SWC) is a government department. It is responsible for all state-owned forests in Scotland.

SWC's mission and activities

SWC's mission is to 'manage, protect and expand the public woodlands in Scotland and to increase their value to society and the environment'. It is authorised to carry out woodland management, nature conservation and the provision of facilities for public recreation.

Woodland management requires a long-term planning process, typically involving a timescale of more than 20 years. Activities include:

- maintenance of existing trees and removal of deadwood

- felling of trees and extraction of timber

- planting of new trees

- identification and management of threats to woodland (eg, fire, pests, disease, impact of wildlife, soil erosion)

In addition to woodland management, SWC's secondary aims are:

- to protect and maintain habitats for wildlife and to manage wildlife populations

- to provide the general public with widespread access to the natural woodland environment and to promote the woodlands as a location for sports and leisure activities

SWC is governed by a board of trustees whose role is to make strategic decisions, monitor performance and liaise with stakeholders including the general public and other government departments. SWC is allocated a share of central government funds annually, but it is prohibited from borrowing money in its own right. Money is spent on replanting, making grants to private organisations and individuals engaged in woodland creation and improvement, providing education, and research. SWC is able to generate some revenue from the harvesting and sale of timber for use in house-building, paper, fencing and bio-fuels.

Holiday village

SWC has been approached by CabinCo Ltd (CabinCo), a private company, which operates a number of up-market, self-catering holiday villages in England and Wales. CabinCo has a database of around 400,000 customers. All of the customers in the database have given their consent to receive marketing and promotional details from CabinCo. Its mission is 'to be one of the UK's leading providers of luxury short-breaks in natural surroundings'. CabinCo has been highly successful because of the high occupancy rates it achieves in its holiday villages. It wants to take advantage of the rapid growth in the short-break market (holidays of 3–5 days) and the increased demand for 'sustainable tourism' to create a new, high-quality holiday village in Campbell Forest, one of SWC's woodlands in Scotland. Customers will be able to rent a luxury self-catering log cabin and participate in a variety of activities in woodland surroundings. Due to Campbell Forest's location, on the edge of a lake surrounded by mountains, it is envisaged that there will be demand all year round and cabins will be available 365 days a year.

Structure of venture

A limited liability public/private partnership (LLP) will be set up specifically for the new venture. The LLP will have two members: CabinCo and SWC. CabinCo will provide capital in the form of £2 million cash for building the cabins and developing the site, and will provide holiday management experience.

SWC will make its capital contribution by making available Campbell Forest (current market value £2 million) for use in the venture. It will also provide expertise in woodland management and woodland activities. The LLP will be operated as a commercial venture, with the members sharing profits and losses equally. The new venture will be known as Woodsaway LLP

(Woodsaway). CabinCo and SWC will each be entitled to appoint three representatives on Woodsaway's senior management committee.

Campbell Forest will continue to be owned by SWC, which will grant a long lease to Woodsaway in exchange for an annual rent of £30,000. Woodsaway will have day-to-day management responsibility for operating the holiday village and the surrounding woodland. The village will consist of 100 high-quality two bedroom log cabins, built to a unique, eco-friendly design. Construction of the village will take approximately 12 months at an expected cost of £2 million, to be funded by CabinCo's contribution to the LLP.

The government has granted preliminary approval for creation of the public/private partnership, as it believes this is the most appropriate format for the management of risk and the exploitation of benefits from the village. The financial projections for Woodsaway make it clear that cabin occupancy levels will be critical to the venture breaking even:

	%	%	%
Cabin occupancy	40	65	90
	£'000	£'000	£'000
Cabin revenue	1,752	2,847	3,942
Variable costs	(526)	(854)	(1,183)
Contribution	1,226	1,993	2,759
Fixed costs	(1,502)	(1,727)	(1,985)
Rent to SWC	(30)	(30)	(30)
Operating (loss)/profit	(306)	236	744

If the initial venture proves successful then the concept may be expanded to other SWC woodland locations and Woodsaway will be given first right of access for the development of any new holiday villages in these locations.

Governance

At a meeting of SWC's trustees, one trustee expressed concern: "Given SWC is a public sector body and we have a responsibility as trustees to deliver public benefit, by demonstrating selflessness and objectivity among other things, won't our involvement in Woodsaway give rise to possible corporate governance issues?"

Another trustee disagreed: "Surely corporate governance isn't relevant. As the term **corporate** suggests, it is a matter for companies and their directors only, not a public sector body like SWC".

Requirements

You are a strategic business adviser engaged by the government. Prepare a report for SWC's trustees, evaluating the proposed venture using the following headings:

20.1 Strategic fit	**(9 marks)**
20.2 Financial benefits	**(10 marks)**
20.3 Risks	**(7 marks)**
20.4 Governance issues	**(8 marks)**

Total: 34 marks

21 WeDive Ltd (amended)

WeDive Ltd (WeDive) is a company which produces and sells high-performance drysuits for divers. It was set up some years ago, by a group of friends, after they experienced severe discomfort whilst scuba diving in cold waters because of leaks in their hired drysuits, which are supposed to work by keeping water out. The friends sourced a single supplier that was able to provide a special thermal fabric and designed a very tight-fitting durable suit with a unique neck seal, to offer maximum protection.

WeDive's drysuits are very expensive (up to £2,000 each) and are typically bought by professional divers (police, armed forces, oil companies, rescue organisations and salvage businesses). To achieve optimum fit the company produces a wide range of different sizes for both men and women. Each drysuit has a three year warranty and any repairs are undertaken at WeDive's production facility, located in the UK.

WeDive has grown successfully. It now has a number of major contracts with professional divers, but also distributes its drysuits to diving retailers for recreational users who want a high quality product. Total sales last year were approximately £13 million, comprising 65% professional divers and 35% recreational users. All sales were in the UK.

Drysuit production is very labour intensive. The market for recreational drysuits is dominated by several large manufacturers in China and South East Asia which benefit from economies of scale, although there are a significant number of smaller producers, like WeDive, which sell in niche markets.

WeDive's directors are keen to expand the business and are considering the following two mutually exclusive strategies:

Option 1: Expand the range of products for the UK market

WeDive would source supplies of lifestyle clothing (t-shirts, jackets and accessories) and sell them under its own brand. The products would be aimed at consumers in the UK market and distributed and sold through existing channels (diving retailers). This option would require marketing but, because of limited funds, WeDive primarily intends to use social media.

Option 2: Produce drysuits for export markets

Entering export markets would involve finding and partnering with new distributors, which WeDive hopes would promote the product on its behalf. A key aspect of WeDive's high-performance drysuit is the fit, so the product may need some redesigning or additional tailoring depending on the height and weight of the local population in each export market.

If Option 2 is pursued, a possible key market is New Zealand. If WeDive enters this market, there is a 90% chance that New Zealand market conditions will be favourable and it will generate a profit of £300,000. However, if market conditions are unfavourable, a loss of £100,000 is expected. Alternatively WeDive could delay its decision until it has undertaken market research, at a cost of £15,000, which would accurately predict the expected market conditions in New Zealand.

Requirements

21.1 So far as the information permits, evaluate the two strategic options being considered by WeDive's directors. Refer to models where appropriate. Ignore the specific information about the New Zealand market for this requirement. **(14 marks)**

21.2 Using a decision tree, calculate whether it would be worth WeDive paying for market research on the New Zealand market. Discuss your findings. **(6 marks)**

Total: 20 marks

Tutorial note

Please note that when this question was set candidates were asked to draw a decision tree diagram. In your computer-based exam if you are asked to prepare a decision tree diagram then it is perfectly acceptable to present your work in a tabular or columnar format.

22   Reyel plc (amended)

The date is June 20X5.

Reyel plc (Reyel) is an international company which owns and operates mid-market hotels.

On 31 March 20X4 a new division, 'The Extended Stay Hotel Division' (the ESH Division), was set up so Reyel could enter the extended stay hotel market.

The extended stay hotel market

Hotels in this market target customers who wish to stay in a hotel for at least eight consecutive nights. Whilst customers can stay for as little as one night, the high prices charged for short stays discourage this.

The extended stay hotel market has two segments, business and private:

*   Customers in the business segment include: project managers; professionals working on assignments; staff on short-term secondments; and contract workers.

*   Customers in the private segment include individuals who are in the process of relocation, while looking for more permanent accommodation, or who have had to evacuate their houses due, for example, to floods or fire.

The business segment typically represents a higher proportion of total revenue than is the case for traditional hotels.

In order to meet the needs of the extended stay market, the guestrooms are larger than in traditional hotels and include living space with a kitchen as well as a bedroom. When averaged across the duration of the stay, the price per night is typically cheaper than traditional hotels, but the costs incurred are lower as the number of room change-overs (ie, when one guest leaves and another arrives) is greatly reduced, and guestrooms are cleaned weekly on average, rather than daily. Occupancy is also typically higher than for traditional hotels.

The extended stay hotel market is well developed in the US, but it does not represent a significant proportion of the European hotel market, although it is growing.

The ESH Division

The ESH Division's business model is designed to: appeal to a different type of customer than Reyel's traditional hotels; exploit cost advantages; and strengthen the wider company brand in the business market segment.

The Clarre

In order to test the business model, the ESH Division commenced trading on 1 April 20X4 with one hotel, called The Clarre, which is located in London. It has large guestrooms, each including a living area and a kitchen, but it does not have a restaurant or bar as there are many in the local area which guests can use. The hotel offers good quality rooms, but provides a limited range of services to guests. Each guestroom is identical.

The performance of The Clarre has been closely monitored and assessed each quarter. Sales appear to have been seasonal, with the quarters ending 30 September and 31 December being the periods of highest demand. Within each quarter, there is variation in demand where occupancy in some weeks is 100% (ie, all guestrooms are full) and customers have to be turned away. There are fewer fluctuations in demand between days of the week than is the case with traditional hotels due to the longer duration of each guest's stay.

Kevin Kloster, the manager of The Clarre, has expressed concern over managing capacity and pricing:

- Managing capacity is a short-term concern involving coping with weekly and monthly fluctuations in demand. It is also a long-term concern in terms of being able to meet trends in demand over time.

- Pricing is complex with different standard prices at different times of the year. There is also a range of discounts available on the standard prices according to type of customer (business or private), length of stay and frequency of visits. Kevin also has discretion to offer a discount to achieve a booking when negotiating with customers.

The Zoy – a comparison

Performance measures monitored by the Reyel board include internal benchmarking in comparing The Clarre with a traditional hotel, called The Zoy, which is also owned by Reyel and is located nearby in the same area of London. The Zoy is a long-established traditional hotel, in a building the same size as The Clarre, but it has a restaurant and a bar which generate additional revenue. The Zoy's guestrooms are much smaller than The Clarre's, but there are more of them. Guestrooms are cleaned daily at The Zoy, but usually only weekly at The Clarre.

Quarterly financial and operating data is provided for The Clarre. Annual data is provided for The Zoy (**Exhibit**).

Concerns of The Zoy's manager

At a Reyel internal meeting, the manager of The Zoy expressed some concerns: "Reyel should not be entering the extended stay hotel market. Our business is in traditional hotels and there will be customer confusion. Also, the cheaper prices for extended stays will damage the Reyel brand name. In the year ended 31 March 20X5, revenues from The Zoy were 10% lower than the previous year and I think this is due to the opening of The Clarre in the same area of London, less than two kilometres away. I also believe Kevin Kloster is undercutting us on price and we just cannot compete as we need to offer a much wider range of services, which increases our costs.

"When we look at the performance of The Clarre we should look from a company-wide perspective and consider lost sales for other group hotels, not just the sales The Clarre is recording."

An ethical problem

Most business customers in the extended stay hotel market are individuals who choose which hotel to stay in, then recharge the cost to their employers. To induce some of The Clarre's regular business customers to agree to pay a premium over the standard price for a guestroom, at their employer's expense, Kevin has been giving these individuals Reyel discount vouchers for private holidays with their families at Reyel hotels.

Requirements

22.1 Using the quantitative data in the Exhibit and the other information provided:

(a) Analyse the performance of The Clarre for each of the four quarters to 31 March 20X5. Briefly identify additional information that would help provide a more comprehensive assessment of performance.

(b) Compare the performance of The Clarre and The Zoy for the year ended 31 March 20X5. **(18 marks)**

22.2 Explain, for the year ending 31 March 20X6, the factors that the manager of The Clarre should consider in respect of:

- capacity management; and
- pricing. **(10 marks)**

22.3 Explain how the Reyel management could estimate the loss in revenue of The Zoy for the year ended 31 March 20X5 arising from the opening of The Clarre. **(7 marks)**

22.4 Discuss the ethical issues arising from the inducements given to individual business customers and advise on the actions that Reyel should take. **(7 marks)**

Total: 42 marks

Exhibit: Financial and operating data

Management accounts for the year ended 31 March 20X5

	The Clarre					The Zoy
	Q1 £'000	Q2 £'000	Q3 £'000	Q4 £'000	Year ending 31 March 20X5 £'000	Year ending 31 March 20X5 £'000
Guestroom revenues	1,058	1,279	1,280	1,028	4,645	6,264
Other revenues	–	–	–	–	–	1,200
Operating costs	(864)	(920)	(920)	(857)	(3,561)	(6,106)
Operating profit	194	359	360	171	1,084	1,358

Operating data for the year ended 31 March 20X5

	The Clarre					The Zoy
	Q1	Q2	Q3	Q4	Year ending 31 March 20X5	Year ending 31 March 20X5
Occupancy	72%	80%	78%	70%	75%	58%
Average guestroom price per night	£68.0	£74.0	£76.0	£68.0	£71.7	£100
Average length of stay (nights)	14	15	18	13	15	3

Notes

1 Both The Clarre and The Zoy are open for 90 days each quarter.

2 The Clarre has 240 guestrooms and The Zoy has 300 guestrooms.

3 Occupancy refers to the average number of nights that guestrooms are occupied as a percentage of the total available guestrooms.

4 'Other revenues' comprise restaurant and bar sales.

5 Quarterly accounting periods are as follows:

- **Q1** is the quarter ended 30 June 20X4
- **Q2** is the quarter ended 30 September 20X4
- **Q3** is the quarter ended 31 December 20X4
- **Q4** is the quarter ended 31 March 20X5

---

23 Home of Leather plc

The date is June 20X5.

Home of Leather plc (HoL) is a company which manufactures good quality leather furniture. The company is located in the small town of Puddington in the South of England, where its site is comprised of a factory, distribution centre and office.

Company background

HoL was established many years ago and has been important to the Puddington economy throughout its existence. Most of the employees, who are mainly skilled workers, live in or around Puddington. Many of the suppliers, including suppliers of leather, are also from the local area. HoL is Puddington's largest employer.

Over the past 15 years, the reputation of HoL's products has grown. Its furniture is now sold throughout Europe, although 70% of sales are still in the UK market.

However, revenue growth has slowed in recent years. There has been increasing competition in the UK and European markets from overseas suppliers producing good quality leather furniture. These suppliers incur lower property and labour costs than HoL, and can therefore charge lower prices. The HoL board fears that sales could start to decline unless costs can be reduced to enable more competitive pricing.

A particular concern is that half of the UK sales come from a single customer, Grint plc (Grint), under a long-term contract. The contract is due for renewal on 31 December 20X6 and the Grint board has already stated that the contract will be put out to tender. Grint's expectation is that prices will need to be reduced from their current average of £400 per unit to, at most, £360 per unit.

Strategic choices

The HoL board has decided that a fundamental change needs to be made in the next six months in order for HoL to continue to compete in the market. It has not yet made any announcement to the employees (including managers), but three alternative strategies have been proposed to reduce costs.

The board has set a target annual profit of £7.2 million, to be achieved irrespective of which strategy is selected.

Strategy 1 - relocate within the UK

Close the whole Puddington site and relocate all operations to a larger site in the UK about 150 kilometres away. Most, but not all, employees would be offered continuing employment at the new site, but only about 40% of existing employees are expected to agree to relocate and carry on working for HoL at the new site. The new factory would have more automated production processes than the old factory and many of the working practices of skilled employees would need to change, along with the managerial reporting structure. The employees who do not relocate would be made redundant. HoL would continue to use most, but not all, of its existing suppliers.

Strategy 2 - relocate manufacturing overseas

Close the factory in Puddington and relocate manufacturing to a larger factory in a lower cost, developing nation in South America. This would involve making 96% of existing employees redundant. The remaining 4% would continue to be employed in the existing distribution centre in Puddington, with senior managers operating from the Puddington office.

Strategy 3 - cease manufacturing and import

Close the factory in Puddington and import furniture from overseas suppliers, thereby making HoL a wholesaler. Most employees would be made redundant. Only 4% of existing employees would be retained, operating from the Puddington distribution centre and Puddington office, as in Strategy 2.

Pricing

The quality of the output under Strategy 1 will be higher than under the other two strategies. As a result, the selling price for Strategy 2 and Strategy 3 will be about 90% of the selling price for Strategy 1. However, the sales volumes will be the same under all three strategies.

Estimated data is provided for costs and revenues for each of the three strategies (**Exhibit**).

Requirements

The board of HoL has asked you, as a business advisor, to prepare a report for it as follows:

23.1 Calculate each of the following, using the information in the Exhibit, for **each** of the three proposed strategies:

    (a)   The breakeven selling price

    (b)   The volume of sales which would achieve an annual profit of £7.2 million   **(9 marks)**

23.2 Evaluate **each** of the three proposed strategies. Refer to your calculations in (a) above and make any further appropriate calculations. Ignore change management issues.   **(10 marks)**

23.3 For Strategy 1 **only**, explain power-interest using Mendelow's matrix for each of the following stakeholders:

- Existing employees
- Grint   **(7 marks)**

23.4 Identify and compare the change management issues for Strategy 1 and Strategy 2.

    (8 marks)

    Total: 34 marks

Exhibit: Estimated data on costs and revenues

	Strategy 1	Strategy 2	Strategy 3
Expected sales volume	120,000 units	120,000 units	120,000 units
Average price per unit	£360	£324	£324
Average variable cost per unit	£200	£160	£280
Annual fixed costs	£14.4 million	£10.8 million	£1.8 million

24 Zuccini plc (amended)

The date is June 20X5.

Zuccini plc (Zuccini) is a listed company manufacturing motorbikes, which it sells mainly in European countries.

The motorbike industry

Motorbike technology is constantly changing. As a result, research and development (R&D) is a key feature of product improvement and replacement. The industry is very competitive and implementing the latest technology can be important in gaining competitive advantage. However, as technology changes rapidly, any such advantage is difficult to sustain.

There were 1.2 million new motorbikes sold in the Europe last year. Many of the most popular motorbikes sold in Europe are manufactured in Japan by multinational companies, which also make cars and other automotive products. There are also several smaller niche motorbike manufacturers located throughout Europe, such as Zuccini.

Company background

Zuccini is a relatively small company in the global motorbike industry. Currently it has an annual sales volume of 4,800 motorbikes. It has an R&D centre in Italy and two factories, one in Italy and one in the UK. The head office is in the UK.

The existing models

Zuccini currently manufactures two models of motorbike: the Typhoon4, a mid-market to upmarket motorbike; and the StormRaider, an upmarket motorbike.

The StormRaider is manufactured at the UK factory and was launched in 20X3. Its launch was successful and monthly sales are continuing to increase. It is estimated to have a product life cycle of six years before it needs replacing in 20X9.

The Typhoon4 is made at the factory in Italy. It is reaching the end of its product life cycle and sales have been gradually falling in recent months. The Zuccini board has not yet decided whether to:

(1) Replace the Typhoon4 with a completely new model, the Typhoon5; or

(2) Modify the Typhoon4 to produce a slightly updated version, the Typhoon4A, then replace the Typhoon4A with the Typhoon 5 two years later (ie, in 20X7 if the Typhoon4 were to be modified as the Typhoon4A immediately).

New capital investment will be needed for either alternative. The Typhoon5 would be a much more significant change than the Typhoon4A, although either of these alternatives could be implemented without much delay, once a decision is made. The board has not yet decided how long to carry on manufacturing the Typhoon4, but the timing of any change is under active consideration.

A new model under development

Another model of motorbike, 'the Hurricane', is currently in its R&D phase, but technical difficulties have caused delays and some uncertainties. It could be brought to market in June 20X6 as a basic product selling at £6,000 or, with a further two years' development, it could be brought to market in June 20X8 as a mid-market product selling at £9,000. The life cycle would be seven years from launch for the basic version of the product, as it is less susceptible to new technology developments and would sell on the basis of price rather than features. The life cycle would be six years from launch for the mid-market version. No estimate of production costs or volumes for either of these alternatives can yet be made.

Liquidity issues

Liquidity has started to become a concern for Zuccini. There is no immediate crisis, but cash flow projections indicate that further financing will be needed by 20X7, unless sales improve.

Requirements

24.1 Referring to appropriate models, provide reasoned advice to the Zuccini board to help it decide:

- When production of the Typhoon4 should be ended; and

- Whether to replace the Typhoon4 with the new Typhoon5, or to modify it, initially, as the Typhoon4A. **(12 marks)**

24.2 Explain the strategic, operational and financial factors which would determine whether the Hurricane should be launched:

- In June 20X6 as a basic product; or
- In June 20X8 as a mid-market product. **(12 marks)**

Total: 24 marks

September 2015 exam questions

25 Kentish Fruit Farms

The date is September 20X5.

Kentish Fruit Farms (KFF) is a UK organic fruit farm that is owned and run by the Fielding family. KFF grows apples and produces apple juice, both of which it sells at local markets and to retailers.

UK organic farming and food industry

Organic food must be produced using environmentally-friendly farming methods, so no genetically modified (GM) crops, growth enhancers, or artificial pesticides and fertilisers may be used. Any farmer claiming to be organic must be certified by a government-approved body, such as the UK Soil Association. Food producers must also comply with Food Standards Agency regulations regarding the production, packaging and labelling of food.

Regulatory bodies can impose sanctions for breaching regulations. They can:

- forbid the use of misleading labels and product descriptions
- issue fines for inappropriate production
- close down operations
- seek punishment of those responsible for wrongful operations

Consumers increasingly want food that is healthy and is sourced both ethically and locally. Consequently, although initially perceived as a luxury niche product, organic food is now seen as a lifestyle choice by those consumers who regard non-organic products as more harmful to health and the environment. Major supermarkets have started to stock more organic and locally grown food.

A key issue for all farmers is the weather, which significantly affects the volume (yield) and quality of a crop and hence the market price. Organic farmers are unable to use artificial fertilisers or pesticides, so have developed alternative high-tech farming methods to improve profitability and cash flow. Weather information systems help plan planting, harvesting and irrigation. Climate-controlled growing tunnels and stores provide a pest-free environment with temperature, light and humidity control. These methods increase yields, extend the possible growing season and allow crops to be stored for longer before usage or sale, with no loss of flavour or quality.

KFF operations

KFF's profitability depends on crop yields and fruit quality, and its ability to use or sell all of the apple harvest. It is also affected by the overall level of supply in the market in any given year. KFF has a weather information system and uses climate-controlled technology.

The best of KFF's apples, which conform to retailers' specifications in relation to size, shape and quality, are sold to retailers as fresh fruit. Apples that do not meet retailers' specifications are either sold at local markets or used to produce KFF own-brand organic pressed apple juice in one-litre bottles. The juice is sold at local markets and has proved very popular so it is now also being stocked by retailers.

KFF's harvest normally begins in early summer and ends in late autumn. The production of juice follows on from the harvest cycle and, because of KFF's ability to store fruit, continues after the harvest has ended. KFF has a permanent labour force for its growing, production and bottling operations and additional seasonal workers are employed for harvesting and packing the fruit.

KFF uses its own vans to transport goods to the local markets. Distribution of products to the retailers, most of which are within 80 kilometres of the farm, is outsourced.

New strategies affecting the 20X4 results

Demand for KFF's apples and juices in year ended 31 December 20X3 exceeded KFF's production capacity. In 20X4, capacity increased as a result of implementing the following strategies:

Strategy 1: KFF had acquired 15 hectares of land from a neighbouring farmer in 20X0. The land was then intensively planted with apple trees of a modern variety which were expected to produce yields 30% higher than existing varieties. The first apple crop from these new trees was harvested in 20X4. KFF's existing trees continued to give the same yield as in 20X3, at the same cost per hectare.

Strategy 2: In 20X4 KFF started to buy apples from other local farmers to use in its organic juices.

KFF's board set medium-term business objectives at the start of 20X4. These were to:

- Achieve average annual revenue growth of 15%
- Increase gross profit margin to 45%

Financial and operating data for 20X3 and 20X4 is available **(Exhibits 1 and 2)**. The current management information system does not separately analyse cost of sales between the fresh fruit and juice operations.

Supply chain problem

In August 20X5, a batch of KFF's organic apple juice was tested by the Food Standards Agency and found to contain artificial pesticides. The juice was made in a large production run using fruit from one of KFF's new suppliers. 20% of this production run has already been distributed to a major retailer which has just started to sell KFF organic juice. KFF is considering whether to issue a public recall of these bottles.

KFF's marketing manager, Joe Fielding, thinks this could be disastrous for KFF's reputation locally and has suggested that they do nothing in relation to the bottles that have already been distributed, but re-label and sell the remainder as non-organic. "The thing that most concerns me," said Joe, "is why we didn't identify this as a problem earlier?"

Requirements

25.1 Identify and analyse the **three** key factors from the PESTEL model which are most relevant to the UK organic fruit industry. **(9 marks)**

25.2 Using the quantitative data in the Exhibits and the other information provided, evaluate the impact that KFF's two new strategies had on its performance in 20X4. Identify any specific information that you require to explain more fully the effect of each strategy. **(18 marks)**

25.3 Discuss the ethical issues for KFF arising from the supply chain problem, and advise KFF on appropriate actions. **(8 marks)**

25.4 Explain how control procedures could be used by KFF to identify and prevent quality problems with suppliers. You should give specific examples of information that could be used to measure and monitor supplier performance. **(8 marks)**

Total: 43 marks

26 Premier Paper Products plc (amended)

The date is September 20X5.

Premier Paper Products plc (PPP) prints banknotes and identity documents for a variety of central banks and governments. It operates three divisions: Banknotes, Cash Processing and Identity Systems.

Company background

PPP started over 100 years ago with a contract to produce paper banknotes for its own country. Its reputation for high quality, elegant designs and innovative security features has made it a market leader – PPP now prints paper banknotes for over 100 countries, mainly in Europe and Asia.

To capitalise on its customer base, 60 years ago PPP started to produce banknote counting and sorting machines and banknote inspection equipment to assist banks in processing cash and detecting forgeries. It then applied its expertise in designing and printing security paper for government identity schemes. 15 years ago PPP won its first contract to print passports and driving licences, for its own government. PPP has continued to invest in the development of sophisticated security solutions. It produces passports and identity cards for 65 countries, including machine-readable e-passports with biometric data incorporated on an electronic chip.

Banknote production

A country's currency is issued by its central bank. The world's largest central banks produce all of their country's banknotes using their own state-owned printing works. However many smaller central banks outsource production to large paper and printing companies which benefit from economies of scale. As a result, PPP and its competitors print 20% of all banknotes worldwide.

Since security is a major issue, banknote-printing companies must be certified and the ordering and distribution process is tightly controlled. Normally central banks outsource banknote printing to a single supplier, under a long-term contract, renewable every 10 years.

Smaller countries outsource banknote printing for economic and technical reasons. Machines required to print modern currency are expensive and are designed to produce large volumes of notes which may significantly exceed a smaller country's requirement.

Some state-owned printing works attempt to achieve critical mass by producing notes for other countries. Rapid changes in technology make it difficult for a small state-owned printing works to keep up with constantly evolving anti-counterfeiting features.

New technology means that several central banks recently decided to change from using paper banknotes to plastic (polymer) notes. Polymer notes are lighter, cleaner and have more embedded security features to protect against counterfeiting. They are also more environmentally sustainable as on average each polymer note has a life of seven years compared to three years for a paper note.

Future strategic direction: Banknote division

Although PPP remains committed to the production of paper notes, its board is unsure whether the demand for polymer notes merits investing in the new technology.

The private banknote printing sector is dominated by PPP and two other companies, one of which, Uniquel, produces polymer notes. Uniquel's share of the banknote market has increased as 25 countries have recently moved from paper to polymer notes, because costs to the central bank are reduced over the life of the banknote despite high initial costs.

Several of PPP's central bank contracts for paper notes are due to come to an end in 20X6 and some of the banks concerned are likely to adopt polymer notes. Producing and printing polymer notes would require a more highly skilled workforce and different machinery. To achieve critical mass for both existing and new machinery, PPP would need to find new customers for paper notes whilst persuading some existing customers to switch to polymer.

Extract from Banking trade journal article:

Is there a future for cash?

Society is increasingly moving away from cash to card-based and smartphone/contactless payments systems. Last year only 4.5% of the UK's money existed in the form of physical cash and the average value of a cash transaction was £9.50. Furthermore, a handful of online retailers have started to explore the opportunities offered by accepting customer payments made using digital currencies, known as cryptocurrencies.

Will polymer bank notes help stop this move to a cashless society?

Polymer notes are waterproof, cleaner, more durable and more environmentally friendly than paper money and this will help them compete with plastic payment cards. Unlike credit cards, contactless payment systems and cryptocurrencies, notes are not subject to identity theft.

In the UK cash is still important for person-to-person transactions and elsewhere around the world, cash prevails. In many emerging economies over 70% of all consumer transactions still take place in cash. Between 20X5 and 20X7 banknote volumes are expected to grow in some parts of Africa by up to 50%.

Requirements

26.1 Using relevant strategic models analyse the ways that PPP has expanded its business and identify the critical success factors (CSFs) which have facilitated this growth. **(10 marks)**

26.2 Prepare a risk register, setting out what you consider to be **three** significant business risks facing PPP's Banknote division.

You should present your answer in a three-column format, explaining, for each risk:

- The nature of the risk
- The possible impact of the risk and the likelihood of it occurring
- Risk management strategies **(9 marks)**

26.3 You are the manager of the PPP Banknote division. Prepare a memorandum for the board which explains the issues that should be considered in deciding whether to invest in polymer banknotes technology. **(11 marks)**

Total: 30 marks

27 Taxi Tracker

The date is September 20X5.

Taxi Tracker (TT) is a company which is trying to change the taxi market in a major capital city. The market currently consists of council-regulated city taxis (Citicabs) and private-hire vehicles (PHV).

Citicabs operate from taxi ranks and are also able to pick up passengers in the street. The city council controls the number of Citicab licences available and regulates fares. Critics argue that this increases waiting times and imposes high fares on customers. The council also issues licences to drivers of individual private-hire vehicles. PHVs cannot use the taxi ranks or pick up passengers in the street. They must be pre-booked but can charge whatever they like in fares. Some PHV drivers work for themselves, others register with private-hire companies which operate a centralised booking service and take a percentage of each fare charged in exchange for putting the driver in contact with passengers.

TT's business model

TT began operations in 20X2 when it launched a 'driver for hire' application (app) for smartphones. The customer downloads the TT app for free and registers their personal details and payment card information. They can then see which PHVs are near their location, receive estimates of price and journey time, tap on the desired PHV to book, and track its arrival on their phone. TT fares are calculated according to distance and time, with the customer's phone acting as a meter. At the end of the journey the customer's registered payment card is automatically debited. TT promises to 'have a car with you within five minutes'. It seeks customer feedback on every journey and drivers are required to achieve a minimum average score of 4 out of 5.

TT does not own vehicles or employ drivers. Instead it acts as an intermediary between PHV drivers and customers. Drivers with an existing PHV licence can apply to TT, which carries out a criminal record check, and verifies licence and insurance details. Drivers who pass TT's screening process are then issued with a TT smartphone which allows them to be registered and tracked on the TT system. TT passes 80% of the fare it charges to the driver, retaining 20% as commission to cover costs and margin. TT's main operating costs are technology and marketing.

Since its launch, TT has faced intense opposition from Citicab drivers, who have argued to the city's transport regulators that TT essentially operates an unlicensed city taxi service. To the consumer, TT's service was initially cheaper than a Citicab, but more expensive than a conventional PHV. Due to the ease of booking, cashless payment, and improved customer service compared to both Citicabs and existing PHV, the number of journeys booked through TT grew rapidly.

Dynamic demand-based pricing

As a result of its initial success, in 20X4 TT switched to a dynamic demand-based pricing model. When demand is high in relation to the number of cars available, the fare goes up in an attempt to balance supply and demand. The higher price encourages more PHV drivers to make themselves available, helping to avoid unfulfilled customer requests. For example, when it is raining, and during peak hours, the average fare typically increases by 50%. There have been some angry responses on social media suggesting this is unfair to TT's customers.

Proposed short-term fare reduction

Recently TT has been made aware of rumours that a rival firm is planning to launch its own taxi booking app in the city. TT is keen to protect its 'first to market' position. In order to generate brand loyalty from existing customers and attract new ones before the rival's launch, TT is considering cutting its fares by 25% for a limited period of four weeks. However it needs to retain the loyalty of its PHV drivers so wants to make sure it minimises the impact on them.

Requirements

27.1 Explain the concept of cost drivers and value drivers and briefly explain **three** key drivers in TT's value chain. **(8 marks)**

27.2 Discuss the benefits of TT's dynamic demand-based pricing model and comment on whether it is unfair to TT's customers. **(8 marks)**

27.3 You have been asked to evaluate for TT the impact of its proposed short-term 25% fare reduction. Assume that currently 130,000 journeys a week are booked through the TT app, at an average fare of £10 per journey.

(a) Calculate the impact on TT's profit for a four-week period if:

- demand is unaffected by the fare cut, and TT retains 20% commission

- demand increases by 15% and TT commits to maintaining PHV driver revenue at its current level

(b) Assuming that TT retains 20% commission, calculate the increase in demand that would maintain revenue for both TT and the PHV drivers at the same level as before the fare reduction.

(c) Evaluate the proposed fare reduction strategy in light of your results in both (a) and (b). **(11 marks)**

Total: 27 marks

March 2016 exam questions

28 Outil plc

The date is March 20X6.

Outil plc (Outil) is a large home improvement retailer, listed on the London Stock Exchange.

It operates three divisions:

- Homestyle Division (UK only)
- Fixings Division (UK only)
- Targi Division (Eastern Europe only)

UK home improvement industry

The home improvement industry derives its income from homeowners undertaking repairs, maintenance and improvements to houses. Industry revenue has been in decline for several years. Approximately 60% of industry revenue derives from homeowners themselves (domestic customers) and the remainder from tradespeople such as builders, electricians and plumbers (trade customers). The market is influenced by the state of the economy and the volume of transactions in the housing market, with homeowners typically repairing and improving their houses either before a house sale or after a purchase.

Despite recent recovery in the UK housing market, homeowners have been slow to increase spending on home improvements. Industry experts believe this is partly due to younger homeowners lacking the necessary skills to do the work themselves, and preferring to spend their time and money on leisure activities. As a result, there is a move away from a 'Do-it-yourself' (DIY) approach to home improvements to a 'Do-it-for-me' approach, with homeowners hiring tradespeople. Retailers who service trade customers as well as domestic customers have therefore generally performed better.

Some home improvement retailers have responded by launching services to link their trade and domestic customers, and recommending local tradespeople to homeowners. Some retailers have switched to UK suppliers to reduce the need to hold inventory. Many bigger retailers are also increasing online sales or reducing the size of stores.

Company history: UK

Outil was established a number of years ago with 10 home improvement stores in the UK. It grew organically and the original chain now operates as the Homestyle Division with 252 stores.

Homestyle stores sell to both domestic and trade customers. The stores stock a vast range of home improvement products (30,000 to 50,000 different products). Approximately 30% of the store space is accessible to customers and 70% is used for storage. Stores have extended opening hours and specialist staff are available to provide advice. Homestyle stores vary considerably in size from 5,000 to 15,000 square metres. Newer large stores have demonstration areas for DIY classes plus display kitchens, bathrooms and bedrooms so that customers can plan a major home improvement project with the help of design consultants. However the availability of suitable large sites for new stores is limited by transportation and traffic problems, and by planning restrictions. New stores also require large capital investment.

The Fixings Division was created in 20X0 when Outil purchased a UK business that sold screws and fixings. The Fixings Division sells a wide range of small items (tools, nuts, bolts, piping etc) via a catalogue, website and its 395 stores. The division has grown rapidly, opening 50 new stores in 20X5. Fixings stores are specifically designed to satisfy the needs of trade customers, although they do sell to domestic customers as well. There is a simple layout with emphasis on convenience, and the majority of store space is visible to customers as it is used to display inventory. Stores carry a limited range (up to 15,000 different products) and are, typically, smaller than the Homestyle stores (up to 5,000 square metres). Their smaller size makes it easier for Outil to find sites to establish new Fixings stores, obtain planning permission and finance the necessary capital investment.

Company history: Eastern Europe

In January 20X5, Outil acquired a chain of 115 stores branded 'Targi' in Eastern Europe, which it operates as the new Targi Division. Targi only sells to trade customers. It provides equipment and materials for professional building companies and tradespeople. Stores carry a limited range of products which are sold in large quantities at low prices. This division currently operates only in Eastern Europe.

Board meeting

Outil's most recent management accounts (**Exhibit**) show a decrease in profit in 20X5. This is despite the acquisition of Targi. Outil's board has been concerned for some time about the performance of the Homestyle Division, which is a mature business.

The managing director commented at a recent board meeting:

"Given the excellent performance of our other divisions, we should refocus as a business that sells to trade customers only, so we should close the Homestyle Division. Smaller Homestyle stores could be re-branded and operated as Fixings stores, or used to establish Targi as a brand in the UK. Larger Homestyle stores are too big so would need to be closed outright. Employees, where possible, would be transferred to remaining divisions. There would be a cost in terms of lease penalties and redundancies but overall I believe that results would improve."

The director of the Homestyle Division advocated continuing the current strategy:

"20X5 was a very tough year and one of the Division's major competitors closed, but we still managed to keep sales revenue constant. Margins were affected by customers choosing lower margin products, increased delivery costs and more pricing promotions but I am confident that the market will improve eventually in line with activity in the housing market."

A different approach was proposed by the Fixings Division director:

"An alternative is to sell the Homestyle Division outright. This would generate funds for Outil to expand the Targi and Fixings brands. Our website has recently attracted lots of attention from international customers. I would like to test the market for our international expansion by initially opening four Fixings stores in Germany, on a trial basis, with a dedicated German website."

Requirements

Prepare a report for the board on the future strategic direction of Outil.

Your report should:

28.1 Use the quantitative data in the Exhibit and the other information provided to:

- evaluate the company's overall performance between 20X4 and 20X5, and
- compare the performance of the three divisions in 20X5. **(17 marks)**

28.2 Discuss the proposals for the future of the Homestyle Division. Refer to your calculations in 28.1 and the directors' comments where appropriate. Ignore the proposed German expansion for the purpose of this requirement. **(10 marks)**

28.3 Identify **two** stakeholder groups that are likely to be affected by a decision to close the Homestyle Division, and advise on the strategies that Outil could adopt to reduce any barriers to change. Refer to relevant models where appropriate. **(8 marks)**

28.4 In relation to the Fixings division, discuss:

- the merits of undertaking test marketing before a full international expansion, and
- the strategy of opening four stores in Germany, on a trial basis. **(8 marks)**

Total: 43 marks

Financial information: Year ended 31 December (£ million)

| | 20X5 | | | | | 20X4 |
	Home style	Fixings	UK Total	Targi	Outil Total	Outil Total
Revenue	2,635	1,955	4,590	835	5,425	4,343
Gross profit	771	821	1,592	251	1,843	1,560
Traceable divisional costs	(620)	(672)	(1,292)	(178)	(1,470)	(1,167)
Divisional contribution	151	149	300	73	373	393
Apportioned central costs	(20)	(14)	(34)	(6)	(40)	(35)
Operating profit	131	135	266	67	333	358
Net assets (at carrying amount)	728	495	1,223	266	1,489	1,160

Operating information: Year ended 31 December 20X5

	Homestyle	Fixings	Targi
Number of employees	14,595	7,200	3,430
Number of stores	252	395	115
Average store size (square metres)	10,000	3,500	5,600
Average number of product lines per store	43,500	13,750	10,750

29 Dreamy Potato Products Ltd (amended)

The date is March 20X6.

Dreamy Potato Products Ltd (DPP) is a food processing company based in the west of England.

Company operations

DPP purchases potatoes from local farmers then peels, washes and processes them into two uncooked forms: whole or cut. It sells these products to food manufacturers which choose to buy from companies, like DPP, that benefit from economies of scale in procurement and processing.

DPP has grown steadily. Approximately 80% of its revenue comes from four food manufacturing clients that produce ready-meals for UK supermarkets. DPP's contracts are, typically, renegotiated every three years, although terms change frequently. This is often as a result of specific demands by supermarkets in relation, for instance, to quality or type of potato.

The food processing industry is highly regulated for health and safety. DPP's clients, prompted by the major supermarkets, also have their own strict quality control requirements. DPP's workforce consists mainly of weekly-paid workers, on the UK minimum wage. DPP is subject to legal restrictions on working hours.

DPP's raw material costs and selling prices are driven by the market price of potatoes, which fluctuates considerably, depending on the availability and quality of the annual crop. DPP acquires its potatoes from local farms, with which it has exclusive purchase agreements. The company owns a fleet of trucks for distributing products to its clients.

Competition

The market-leader, Estima plc (Estima), has a 30% share of the UK market for processed uncooked potatoes. It is a vertically-integrated, national business which grows its own potatoes and supplies both uncooked and cooked potato products to the catering industry and food manufacturers.

A further 35% of the UK market consists of DPP and two other competitors – one in the south and one in the east of England. The rest of the market is fragmented. Many farms supply unprocessed potatoes direct to the catering industry. Some potato farmers operate their own processing plants, but these are regional businesses, often specialising in particular market niches eg, supplying processed uncooked potatoes to local schools or hospitals.

Proposals

In the year ended 31 December 20X5, DPP generated an operating profit of £352,000 on sales of £10.8 million. It is considering two opportunities for future growth:

Proposal 1: fast-food contract

DPP has been approached by a national fast-food chain that wants to buy uncooked cut potatoes. The initial contract would be for three years, at a fixed price of £210 per tonne. To implement this strategy, DPP would need to acquire a new machine to grade and cut the potatoes and rent a further 9,000 square metres of premises. Working assumptions for this contract are provided in the **Exhibit**.

Proposal 2: use of waste

Starch residue from washing the potatoes could be sold to local farmers as cattle food. DPP is also considering investing in a digester machine, which can convert potato waste into gas to power DPP's processing plant. As well as potentially improving profits, better use of waste would be positive for sustainability and help differentiate DPP from Estima.

Client request

Potters Pies (Potters), a major client, buys processed uncooked potatoes from DPP to produce pies for two supermarkets: Giant (a low-cost retailer) and Quality (a high-quality retailer). Potters' contract with Giant is due for renewal shortly and Giant has told Potters to reduce its prices if it wants to retain the business. Andrew Baxter, a director at Potters, wants DPP to drop the price that it charges Potters for potatoes for the Giant contract by 5%.

Andrew explained to DPP's sales director: "If you drop the price on the Giant contract, I am prepared to increase the price per tonne we pay DPP for potatoes for the Quality contract by the same percentage.

"I am confident that I can go to Quality and persuade them to pay more for our pies. I will convince them by pretending that we have had to pay our supplier more because they have started to supply higher quality potatoes.

"This will help ensure that we don't lose the Giant contract, which would be bad news for both Potters and DPP. If you agree, I will make sure that DPP is our preferred supplier when we renegotiate contracts later this year. If not, then I may have to move our business to Estima."

Requirements

29.1 In relation to the potato processing industry, prepare an analysis of the following elements of the Porter's Five Forces model:

- Barriers to entry
- Power of suppliers
- Power of customers

You should explain the relevance of each force for DPP. **(9 marks)**

29.2 Evaluate the fast-food contract in Proposal 1 and discuss whether it should be undertaken. Show supporting calculations. **(10 marks)**

29.3 Assess Proposal 2 for the use of waste and suggest further actions that DPP could take to enhance its sustainability. **(7 marks)**

29.4 Discuss the ethical issues for DPP and Potters that arise from Andrew Baxter's request.

(7 marks)

Total: 33 marks

Exhibit: Working assumptions for Proposal 1: fast-food contract

1. Expected sales volume: 9,000 tonnes pa at £210 per tonne, for three years.

2. Direct labour and variable costs of processing are expected to be £65 per tonne pa.

3. In 20X5 DPP's fixed overhead absorption rate was 12% of revenue pa. Fixed operating expenses will increase by £25,000 pa as a result of this contract.

4. For the first year of the contract DPP has agreed, with its existing suppliers, a purchase price of £125 per tonne of potatoes. Industry price forecasts assume that Year 3 potato prices are conditional on market prices in Year 2. The predicted average purchase prices are as follows:

	Year 2 Probability	Year 2 Price/tonne (£)			Year 3 Probability	Year 3 Price/tonne (£)
Low price	0.40	125	{	Low price	0.45	115
				High price	0.55	135
High price	0.60	160	{	Low price	0.65	150
				High price	0.35	170

---

30 The Zed Museum

The Zed Museum (Zed) opened in Venice, Italy, a number of years ago. It hosts one of the finest collections of sculptures and modern art in the world and is a popular destination for locals and tourists.

The museum is a not-for-profit organisation, managed by trustees and largely staffed by volunteers. It charges nominal admission fees and relies on private donations. For the last three years, Zed's income has just covered the costs of operating the museum, insuring the exhibits and running educational programmes. After the recent death of Zed's wealthy founder, Emilio Zissi, the museum is experiencing a financial crisis and some of the staff and donors feel that it lacks direction. Without a significant injection of cash, the museum may have to close and, if it is found to be insolvent, the trustees may be liable for any losses.

Zed has a sizeable collection, only a small proportion of which is on display at any given time. Most of the items in the collection are not owned by Zed but were given in trust to Zed to hold, conserve and use in exhibitions or programmes for future generations. Despite their value, the items are not liquid assets and Zed is prohibited from selling them to pay for operating expenses.

The trustees have appointed a new chief executive to address Zed's financial situation and to attract a wider audience and additional revenue streams. She is keen to operate the museum on a more commercial basis and exploit its collection, as she explained at a recent meeting of the museum's trustees:

"Zed's ability to remain open rests purely on how fast we can raise sufficient additional funds – a task that I believe may be accomplished, in part, by licensing our brand and collection. I have been approached by a well-known billionaire, Kazuo Tada, who owns a Japanese island. Mr Tada is developing the island into an exclusive cultural destination. A 20-year licence to operate a Zed-branded museum on the island will attract wealthy international tourists and other world-class visitor attractions. In addition to paying the annual licensing fee for the Zed brand, Mr Tada has promised us a substantial one-off donation. The Japanese museum will be stocked by us with exhibits from our collection, in return for the annual licensing fee. Other international museums have successfully licensed their brand and collection, and I believe that we should do the same."

Some of the trustees disagree with the chief executive's proposal. They do not believe that the licence deal is appropriate for a world-class museum, which is seen as an educationally-driven entity and a steward of Italian culture. They also argue that the proposal may be contrary to the founding principles established by Emilio Zissi:

Founding principles of the Zed Museum

- Hold the collection in trust for society and safeguard the long-term public interest in the collection
- Recognise the interests of the people who made, owned, collected or donated items in the collection
- Encourage visitors to explore the collection for inspiration, learning and enjoyment
- Consult and involve the local community, users and supporters
- Review performance to innovate and improve

The chief executive is aware that some stakeholders have expressed concerns about the museum's future. She also believes that some of Zed's problems have arisen because of a failure to monitor performance adequately, and is evaluating how best to measure the museum's success. Historically, Emilio Zissi simply counted the number of visitors each year.

Requirements

30.1 Analyse the interests and influence that the following stakeholders are likely to have in their relationship with the museum:

- Trustees
- Donors
- Staff **(9 marks)**

30.2 Explain the advantages and disadvantages for Zed of pursuing a licensing strategy with a third party and any specific considerations relating to the proposed Japanese museum.

(8 marks)

30.3 Recommend an approach to performance measurement that is suitable for Zed and some specific performance measures to assist the chief executive in measuring Zed's performance. **(7 marks)**

Total: 24 marks

June 2016 exam questions

31 The Healthy Vegetarian plc

The date is June 20X6.

The Healthy Vegetarian plc (THV) is a listed company which operates 200 shops throughout the UK. THV shops sell ready-to-eat food, plus hot and cold drinks. All products are suitable for people who eat no meat or fish products (vegetarians). THV does not prepare food on the premises, although some snacks can be heated in the shop, on request, at the time of purchase.

Company background

Company history and development

THV has expanded organically by reinvesting operating cash flows to finance the opening of new shops. The board is not willing to borrow or raise new equity capital at this time.

Food products and operations

THV carries a range of 40 types of food and drink products. All products are purchased centrally by head office from four suppliers. Products are delivered by suppliers directly to each shop. All shops are charged the same price for each product, which is agreed by head office with suppliers.

One week in advance, the shop manager informs head office of the quantities of food and drink required for each day. Drinks can be displayed on shelves for a long time from the delivery date, but most foods can be displayed for only one or two days before being discarded, in line with hygiene regulations. Excessive delivery quantities therefore reduce the operating profit of the shop.

Each shop has one manager who decides on the number of staff to employ, but wage rates are set centrally at head office.

Head office determines capital expenditure. Depreciation on each shop's non-current assets is charged in arriving at the shop's operating profit, but no central head office costs are allocated to shops.

Markets

The target market for THV is customers who are healthy eaters. The company markets itself as selling healthy, vegetarian products, as reflected in the company's name.

Selling prices are determined by head office so, for each product, all shops charge the same price to customers.

Budgeting, performance assessment and closure review procedures

An annual budget is set for each shop at the start of each year, and the performance of each shop is assessed annually using key performance indicators (KPIs) and internal benchmarks (**Exhibit 1**). The worst performing shops are placed under 'closure review procedures' following assessment, and are then given three months to demonstrate substantial improvement, or be closed.

June board meeting

Closure review procedures

At the June 20X6 board meeting, the performance director, Tina Thomson, expressed concern about the company's closure review procedures. "There is increasing stress amongst staff about these procedures. Staff do not understand how they operate and fear the possible loss of their jobs at short notice.

"We need to develop and communicate more objective criteria for placing shops under closure review procedures. To help determine which criteria are appropriate, I have provided illustrative data for two poorly performing shops, in Leeds and Hull, which have recently been placed under closure review procedures. I have also provided relevant internal benchmarks from THV shops across the performance range (**Exhibit 2**)."

Procurement processes

The head of management information systems, Paul Potter, suggested a change in procurement processes. "Currently each shop manager has responsibility for determining the quantities of food and drinks ordered each day. I believe that we could use information technology to have automated reordering centrally. The IT system would use data on the amount and timing of historic sales for each shop to predict future sales as the basis for ordering from suppliers. Shop managers would therefore no longer be responsible for ordering.

"I have consulted one group of managers about this, who suggested an alternative approach. Their suggestion was to allow shop managers to use their discretion to purchase up to (say) 20% of their shop's products, by value, directly from local suppliers, rather than ordering through head office. These managers argued that this would better enable them to satisfy local tastes using their local knowledge. The remaining 80% of products would continue to be ordered by shop managers through head office."

Ethical concerns

In a private conversation, Andrew Aimes, a non-executive director of THV, raised a concern with the marketing director, Diana Dunn.

Andrew said: "A major element of THV's marketing is that our products are not only vegetarian, but also are healthy because they are vegetarian. However, there is high sugar content in many of our products, and it is well-established that eating too much sugar can badly affect people's health."

Diana responded: "Look, Andrew, the sugar content in grams is marked on all our products in a small, detailed table of the ingredients. If people don't want to read it, or don't understand what number of grams is high or low for sugar content, then that is their problem."

Requirements

31.1 In respect of assessing shop performance:

    (a)   Evaluate and explain the performance of the shops in Leeds and Hull (Exhibit 2). So far as the information permits, give a reasoned opinion as to whether each shop should be closed. State key additional information that you would require to make a more complete assessment of the performance of the two shops; and   **(10 marks)**

    (b)   Critically appraise the effectiveness of THV's KPIs (Exhibit 1) in identifying under-performing shops. Suggest and justify further relevant KPIs that would improve the process for implementing closure review procedures.   **(8 marks)**

31.2 Explain how THV can make better use of budgeting (Exhibit 1).   **(7 marks)**

31.3 In respect of procurement processes, explain the merits and problems of:

    •   permitting shop managers to purchase some of their products from local suppliers, rather than ordering only through head office; and

    •   using IT systems to automate ordering for all products centrally for each shop.

    Assume these two proposals are mutually exclusive.   **(11 marks)**

31.4 Explain the ethical issues for Andrew and THV arising from the matters discussed by Andrew and Diana. Set out any actions that Andrew should now take.   **(8 marks)**

Total: 44 marks

Exhibit 1: Performance assessment and budgeting

Performance assessment and closure review procedures

THV's accounting year end is 31 May. The annual performance of every shop is assessed in June each year. The performance of each shop is measured and the shops are ranked in order (from best to worst) for each of the following three KPIs:

- Revenue

- Operating profit

- Return on capital employed (ROCE) – calculated using the depreciated historic cost of the shop's non-current assets.

Staff in the best performing 50 shops are paid a bonus.

At the discretion of the board, shops which are placed bottom in the ranking for at least one KPI may be placed under closure review procedures. During these procedures, the shop manager must implement a three-month recovery plan, and the shop's monthly performance is measured against this plan. Unless the shop shows substantial improvement over the period of the recovery plan it is likely to be closed.

The closure review procedures were introduced to give an incentive to shop managers and other staff to perform well, as all the staff working in shops that are closed are normally made redundant.

The final decision to close a shop is made at the discretion of the board after considering all relevant factors.

Budgeting

Annual budgets are set for each shop, and the actual performance of each shop is compared to its budget annually. This is an additional, and separate, process to the annual closure review process.

Budgets are used for planning purposes, and also to motivate all shop managers, whether they are performing well or badly. The budgets are set by negotiation with each shop manager. However, head office does not accept shop budgets which have a lower revenue or operating profit than was actually achieved for the previous year. If a shop budget is consistently not achieved, the shop manager may be dismissed, although the shop would not be closed on this basis alone.

Exhibit 2: Performance data and related internal benchmarks

Year ended 31 May 20X6

	Shops under closure review procedures		Benchmarks		
	Leeds shop	Hull shop	Average for all shops	Average for 50 worst performing shops	Average for 50 best performing shops
Revenue	£425,000	£325,000	£480,000	£390,000	£580,000
Operating profit	£17,000	£11,000	£30,000	£20,000	£45,000
ROCE	3.1%	3.7%	9.7%	6.8%	10.0%
Number of years since opening	11 years	2 years	5 years	3 years	13 years
Floor space (square metres)	130	80	80	80	120
Non-current assets *	£550,000	£300,000	£310,000	£295,000	£450,000
Number of employees	11	7	7	7	10

* Non-current assets are property, plant and equipment valued at depreciated historic cost. At 31 May 20X6 there were no leasehold properties.

32 Elver Bloom Recruiting plc

The date is June 20X6.

Elver Bloom Recruiting plc (EBR) is a medium-sized employment recruitment agency. It recruits staff, on behalf of its clients, to work on permanent employment contracts in the finance industry.

The employment recruitment industry

Recruitment agencies attract, identify and select suitable candidates as employees for their clients. Staff recruited may be for permanent or temporary contracts.

Recruitment agencies may also offer other services, such as training, project management (eg, redundancy schemes and large-scale recruitment initiatives), advice (eg, on employment law) and staff appraisal. Frequently, these services are provided to existing regular clients.

Advertising available jobs in the most efficient manner, and identifying potential employees, are key processes for any recruitment agency. Increased use of the internet and social media in recent years has facilitated these processes for all companies in the industry.

Key constraints on recruitment agencies are legal issues regarding both who can be recruited and the process by which employees can be recruited.

Smaller agencies tend to specialise in: a particular industry (eg, finance, IT, hospitality, education, construction); a category of employee (eg, new graduates, seasonal workers); or a geographical region (eg, major cities or a single country). Larger recruitment agencies operate across a broad spectrum of services and sectors.

The majority of the revenue of recruitment agencies comes from charging fees to clients for achieving successful recruitment. The fee for recruiting a permanent employee is normally based on a percentage of the employee's first year salary. This can range from 10% (for large-volume, regular clients) to 30% (for a one-off assignment).

If the recruited employee does not stay in employment for more than three months, the agency pays a rebate to the employer, which is typically between 50% and 100% of the fee.

The market for recruitment agency services was weak during the recession 4 to 8 years ago. However, more recently, revenue in the industry increased by 10% in 20X4 and by 9% in 20X5. Profitability growth has been highest in the recruitment of permanent employees, with average increases in profit in the sector of 18% in 20X4 and 16% in 20X5. Many new entrants to the recruitment agency industry are being attracted by increasing profits.

EBR – company background

EBR was formed 10 years ago by Amy Cheng and Mark Prost, who had worked together in the human resources department of an investment bank. Shortly afterwards they set up an office in the financial district of London and now have 35 staff. EBR has established a base of regular clients, but it also carries out one-off assignments. The industry is competitive and new clients and assignments are gained through tenders. Each year, existing regular clients put pressure on EBR to reduce fees.

EBR specialises in permanent appointments in the finance industry (eg, banking, investment management, financial services and accounting). It seeks to attract candidates with a minimum of five years' relevant work experience. The average first-year salary of EBR's recruits is £80,000.

A further specialism is that EBR attempts to recruit candidates both in the UK and internationally, mainly for clients based in London.

Mark summarised this policy: "We use social media, the internet and industry electronic journals to recruit the best financial candidates in the world and bring them to London, which is one of the largest global financial centres. These international candidates bring language skills and knowledge of international financial markets. We recruit in three regions: Europe, North America and East Asia."

Fees – a new approach

During the recession, market conditions for EBR were difficult, as they were for all companies in the industry. Then, as the UK economy began to emerge from the recession, EBR continued to find it difficult to win new tenders, retain existing clients and increase revenue.

The EBR board therefore decided to reduce all its fees by 10% for each employee recruited from 1 April 20X5. This reduction was aimed at winning tenders and retaining clients, and thereby gaining a greater volume of business.

A board meeting in May 20X6 reviewed the success of the fee reduction policy.

Mark Prost opened: "The policy to reduce fees has been a disaster. I have produced some financial information and operating data (**Exhibit**) which shows that, while revenue has increased, operating profit has fallen. I think we should revert to our previous fee levels."

The marketing director, Nick Drapp, disagreed: "I think the policy has been a success. We have won more tenders in the year ended 31 March 20X6 than in the previous few years, and we have retained nearly all our regular clients. This gives the agency a better basis to market itself to existing and new clients and therefore to build for the future."

Amy Cheng had a different view: "I think we need to move upmarket and increase fees by 20% from their current, reduced, level. Clearly, we must offer something in return to clients, so I think we should go beyond the industry norm for offering rebates. I suggest we offer a 100% rebate to clients if our recruits leave their employment within six months of joining, and a 75% rebate if recruits leave between six months and 12 months of joining. We will then be giving a really clear signal that we have confidence in the quality and suitability of the candidates we have recruited."

Requirements

32.1 Using the PESTEL framework, explain how the following factors affect the employment recruitment agency industry:

- Economic
- Technological
- Legal

You are **not** required to discuss the other PESTEL factors. **(10 marks)**

32.2 Use the available quantitative data (Exhibit) and other information to evaluate the decision to reduce fees by 10% from 1 April 20X5. In a report to the board advise, with reasons, whether this price reduction should now be retained or reversed. Ignore Amy's proposal. **(16 marks)**

32.3 Explain the factors that should be considered in deciding whether to implement Amy's proposal. Provide a reasoned recommendation. **(9 marks)**

Total: 35 marks

Exhibit: Financial information and operating data

Financial information – years ended 31 March

	20X6 £'000	20X5 £'000
Recruitment		
Revenue: fees	12,480	11,900
Less:		
Rebates	(1,498)	(1,200)
Variable costs (eg, advertising)	(2,496)	(2,142)
Fixed costs	(3,300)	(3,300)
Operating profit from recruitment	5,186	5,258
Operating profit from other services	610	560
Total operating profit	5,796	5,818

Operating data – years ended 31 March

	20X6	20X5
Number of permanent appointments	780	700
Number of active clients	168	142

Working assumption: if the change in pricing policy on 1 April 20X5 had not taken place, the financial information and operating data for the year ended 31 March 20X6 would have been the same as that for the year ended 31 March 20X5.

---

33 TechScan Ltd

The date is June 20X6.

TechScan Ltd (TechScan) develops and manufactures complex electronic scanners, which are used by hospitals in the UK. The company has a large research and development (R&D) department.

The basic TechScan technology is common to all its products and is protected by patents. However, the patent protection ends in 20X7 and, unless new technology can be found, there will be a significant fall in profitability.

The TechScan board has identified two options:

- **Option 1** – TechScan's R&D department develops and patents new advanced scanner technology.

- **Option 2** – TechScan obtains a licence for the right to use new scanning technology which has already been successfully developed in the US by Ursa Inc, a rival company.

While the technologies under each option would be different, if TechScan's R&D is successful, the two different technologies are expected to be equally effective. It is therefore estimated that, using either technology, sales of scanners would be the same in quality, volume and price terms. The useful life of either technology would be five years, before being replaced by newer developments. Both technologies could be available to TechScan in 20X7 and 1,000 scanners could be manufactured and sold over the following five-year period, under either option.

Option 1 – R&D project

TechScan's R&D department has been working on an R&D project to develop new advanced scanner technology for six years. It has incurred substantial expenditure over that period and, while some progress has been made, there remain significant uncertainties with the project. An immediate additional investment of £45 million is required to finance the final phase of the R&D project but, even with this investment, there is only a 60% probability of its success. If the project fails, no benefit would arise. However, the licence from Ursa Inc could still then be purchased (as per Option 2).

If the R&D project succeeds, the present value of all future costs to manufacture 1,000 scanners would be £20 million (in addition to the £45 million R&D investment). All costs would be incurred in £ sterling.

Option 2 – purchase a licence

TechScan could abandon the R&D project immediately and purchase a licence from Ursa Inc. This would give TechScan the sole rights to include Ursa technology in all its scanners sold in the UK over the next five years. The present value of all future costs to develop and manufacture 1,000 scanners using Ursa technology would be £100 million, including the licence fees. All costs would be incurred in £ sterling.

Sales

The total sales volume over the five years of manufacture would be 1,000 scanners under either option. Over this period, the selling price would be subject to the same uncertainties for either option. There is a 70% probability of high prices, in which case the present value of revenues would be £160 million for either option. There is a 30% probability of low prices, in which case the present value of revenues would be £110 million for either option.

Requirements

33.1 If the board were to choose Option 2, discuss the likely impact of this decision on the R&D department and on TechScan's future R&D strategy. **(6 marks)**

33.2 (a) Calculate the expected net present values of the two options.

(b) Using the calculations in 33.2(a), and taking account of other relevant factors, advise and explain which of the two options should be selected. **(15 marks)**

Total: 21 marks

34 Guayaporto Ltd

The date is September 20X6.

Guayaporto Ltd (GPT) is a company based in Fantasia in South America. It manufactures discs (CDs and DVDs) that store digital data in audio, video or text format. It supplies these to order to Fantasian businesses in the publishing, music, education and home entertainment sectors.

Disc production process

To produce each set of discs, a template is required. GPT outsources the creation of this to a specialist supplier in Asia. For every order placed, the customer provides GPT with a confidential data file. This is sent, electronically, to the Asian supplier, which uses the data to create a glass master-disc as a template. This master-disc is transported from the supplier to GPT by secure courier.

GPT manufactures discs in-house, from polycarbonate, which it sources locally. Using the master-disc, the digital data are transferred onto each disc. A metallic reflective layer is then applied which allows the disc to be played. Once these stages are complete, colour and graphics are added to one side of each disc, according to the customer's specifications. Finally, the discs are packaged into individual plastic wallets or cases.

Quality control is very important for customer satisfaction and because high error rates and wastage result in low margins for GPT. Testing for quality consistency is undertaken at various points in the production process and any defective discs are rejected. The intellectual property contained in the confidential data files and the master-disc belongs to GPT's customer and must be kept secure at all times. The terms of GPT's standard contract with the customer requires GPT to destroy the master-disc on completion of each order.

Industry demand

CDs were introduced 30 years ago, and DVDs followed 10 years later, when use of the internet was becoming popular. For 20 years, disc-based technology dominated the market for film, music and gaming. However, use of the internet for downloading data, and the rise of on-demand services for streaming film, music and games, has meant that discs are increasingly obsolete.

As businesses move away from releasing their products in disc form, retailers are devoting less shelf space to CDs and DVDs. Traditionally discs were used for storage of digital data, but they are being replaced by other devices and cloud-based storage. Computer manufacturers are increasingly producing computers and tablets without disc drives. As a result, worldwide demand for CDs and DVDs has fallen to 30% of its peak of 20 billion discs at the beginning of the 21st century.

Weakening demand has led to some manufacturers stopping disc production entirely or diversifying into other products. However, not all markets are declining at the same rate and there is still a core demand for discs for certain purposes. For example, some film producers refuse to make their films available for streaming, preferring to release them as DVDs in an attempt to maintain their revenues. 3D movies, which are increasingly popular, are often released on disc due to the large file sizes involved. DVDs, rather than downloads, are still preferred by many video-game players.

GPT's results and future direction

GPT's machines are capable of producing up to 45,000 discs per week but are not currently being used at full capacity. Most of GPT's production line is highly mechanised, but all the final packaging is carried out manually. The directors understand that manual packaging is less efficient, but they have been prepared to sacrifice some margin because they believe it is important to provide employment for the local labour force.

GPT's results have declined considerably in the last 12 months (Exhibit). GPT has not lost many customers, but typically customers are placing orders for smaller volumes. In addition, Fantasia's currency (the franc) has weakened against most other currencies. This has increased the cost to GPT of buying master-discs from the Asian supplier, despite the purchase price in Asian $ remaining constant.

Production director's suggestion

To reduce costs, the production director has suggested that GPT acquires a new machine to undertake all its packaging requirements. This would increase capacity and avoid delays currently caused by the manual packaging process. If the proposed machine purchase takes place, 60% of GPT's packaging workforce would be made redundant. The remaining 40% would be trained to operate and maintain the packaging machine.

Sales director's suggestion

The sales director has suggested that, because falling demand for its products is the problem, GPT should establish alternative revenue streams. He has made one specific suggestion already: one of GPT's regular customers, Alegre Education (Alegre), produces a range of disc-based revision guides for college students. A college has approached GPT and asked to buy some of the revision guides directly from GPT at a price that is lower than Alegre's. Since the master-disc already exists, GPT could produce own-brand versions of the Alegre revision guides, on disc, at relatively low cost.

Requirements

34.1 Explain how GPT might benefit from scenario planning to help it develop strategic responses to the uncertainty facing its industry's future. **(7 marks)**

34.2 Using the quantitative data and the other information provided, identify and explain the key causes of the decline in GPT's performance, and analyse the impact that each cause has had on its financial results. You should, where feasible, provide calculations to quantify the financial impact and set out any further information that is required to make a fuller assessment. **(18 marks)**

34.3 Discuss the issues that GPT should consider when sharing confidential data files through the supply chain and explain how these might be addressed. **(7 marks)**

34.4 Discuss the advantages and disadvantages of the proposals made by the production director and the sales director. **(12 marks)**

Total: 44 marks

Operating data		
	20X5	**20X4**
Total number of discs sold	1,050,000	1,476,000
Average number of discs per order	1,000	1,200
Number of orders	1,050	1,230
Purchase price per master-disc (Asian $)	$25	$25
Average exchange rate: Fantasian francs (f) per Asian $	f20=$1	f13=$1

35 MHD (amended)

MHD is a large mental health charity based in the UK. It provides services for people with mental health problems. The charity owns and operates a number of residential and day-care centres which are subject to inspection by government regulators. It also funds research into mental health conditions.

MHD is governed by a board of trustees (the board) chaired by John Adams. The board oversees the charity's activities and is accountable for the charity's performance. It ensures that MHD is run in the public interest and for the benefit of sufferers of mental health problems. The board has delegated responsibility for the day-to-day operations of the charity to a small management team, led by chief executive Vishal Garcia. The charity has over 200 employees plus many volunteers.

MHD receives some government funding, but it relies heavily on donations and sponsorship. It has experienced financial difficulties recently and its cash balances are now very low. The chief finance officer resigned from the management team three months ago and Jennifer Studley has been recruited to take over the role. Jennifer previously managed the finances for a much smaller organisation in the charity sector.

Jennifer wants to make some changes to the way MHD functions but she has encountered some resistance from the board. John and Vishal have both been involved with MHD for over 15 years. The majority of the trustees are volunteers who have been recruited by John and Vishal from among their close friends and former colleagues in the mental health sector.

Jennifer met recently with Vishal and John to discuss how to improve MHD's financial position and raised a number of agenda items:

Agenda item A: Governance and the role of trustees

Jennifer started the meeting: "I think that we should recruit some new trustees with a wider range of commercial experience. They would be able to challenge the way MHD is managed, and identify opportunities for innovation and development. This would allow the board to take a more strategic view in future."

Vishal was not convinced: "One of the big advantages of working with the current board of trustees is the fact that we all know each other and the charity well, having spent many years working together. As a result, there is little conflict in our meetings and we are usually able to reach quick, unanimous decisions. Also, some of our trustees are very wealthy and their companies have given us large donations in the past. I would not want to upset them by suggesting they have not been doing their jobs properly."

John commented: "Since MHD is a charity, I believe our role as trustees is to make sure that the management team avoids risk, wherever possible, and chooses safe strategies. This approach has served us well in the past."

Agenda item B: Sustainability and performance measurement

Jennifer suggested that MHD should consider seeking more funds to prevent any solvency issues: "There is a critical need for MHD to provide more mental health services but, as we have minimal cash, we would need to raise new funds. We will be more able to access funding, and therefore become a more sustainable organisation, if we can clearly demonstrate good performance.

"As far as I can tell the charity has done little in the past to measure its performance. If we are to attract more funding we need to be able to demonstrate to our fund-providers the impact that MHD is having in the mental health sector."

Agenda item C: Adverse publicity about MHD's ethics

Finally Jennifer said: "I feel awkward raising this, but it has come to my attention that MHD has attracted some adverse publicity recently, in a negative article about the charitable sector in a national newspaper. The journalist expressed concerns about the ethics of high salary packages paid by charitable organisations, and in particular the recent pay rises awarded by MHD to its senior management.

"The article also queried the ethics of MHD's aggressive fund-raising. As you know we are under pressure to raise more funds so we outsourced this process to a professional fund-raising organisation FundsForYou Ltd (FFY). We agreed to pay them commission based on the amount of funds raised. FFY initially sent a mailshot and an email to all the previous donors listed on our database that had consented to receiving such messages from MHD. It then used its call centre staff to follow this up with repeated texts and phone calls."

Requirements

Agenda item A:

35.1 With reference to the views expressed at the meeting, critically appraise the governance procedures of MHD and assess their impact on the charity's ability to achieve its objectives.

(8 marks)

Agenda item B:

35.2 Explain what sustainability means for MHD and discuss the extent to which MHD is a sustainable organisation.

(6 marks)

35.3 Explain an approach to performance measurement that MHD could use to assess the impact of its activities. You should give examples of specific performance measures relevant to MHD.

(9 marks)

Agenda item C:

35.4 Discuss the ethical implications arising for MHD from the issues raised in the newspaper article.

(8 marks)

Total: 31 marks

36 Thistle Engineering Services Ltd

The date is September 20X6.

Thistle Engineering Services Ltd (Thistle) was formed 20 years ago by engineer Joshua Woodburn. The company is based in Scotland and provides engineering and construction services. Thistle specialises in the design, construction and installation of storage tanks and high-pressure steel pipelines for the oil and gas industry.

Management team

Joshua Woodburn (aged 60) – Managing director and Sales director (shareholding 50%)
Tom Tabinor (aged 53) – Operations director (shareholding 35%)
Anya Clough (aged 45) – Finance director (shareholding 15%)

Joshua and Tom have run the business for many years. Joshua has 30 years' experience in the engineering sector and has overall responsibility for the company. Tom joined Thistle soon after it was formed, having previously worked in the oil and gas industry. Anya originally joined Thistle as financial controller many years ago. She manages its administration and finances. Thistle also employs 100 staff, the majority of whom are skilled engineers. They are all based in Scotland.

Operations

All structural steelwork is manufactured at the company's factory in Scotland, by experienced, fully-qualified welders. Pipelines and tanks are then transported to the customer's site for installation. Unlike many competitors, which rely on contract labour, all Thistle's site installation teams are directly employed by the company. Thistle also provides pipeline testing and off-site fabrication and welding services.

Thistle uses a range of Scottish suppliers for tools and other materials. It also has contracts with preferred suppliers for metals, pumps and specialist equipment. The majority of these suppliers are located in the UK.

Thistle has an established customer base in the UK and the majority of its business is on a repeat basis. 60% of sales are made to four large global companies that distribute oil and gas around the UK. Other customers include utility companies and businesses specialising in the removal of liquid waste.

Thistle has built a reputation for quality and innovation. It has developed a unique, patented 'pipe-wrapping' system which allows customers to maintain the flow of product through their pipelines whilst Thistle undertakes repairs.

The company is committed to maintaining the highest standards of health and safety. It is certified as compliant with global oil and gas regulatory standards and is acknowledged as an industry leader in environmental awareness and compliance.

International expansion

One of Thistle's major customers, Romiou Inc (Romiou), is a global company. It has asked Thistle to provide it with services for a major infrastructure project outside the UK. Exploratory drilling has identified large gas reserves at a new offshore site in the Mediterranean, and an undersea pipeline is required to transfer the gas to an onshore plant in Malta. Initial industry research has indicated that there is enormous potential for extracting natural gas in the region. Thistle believes there is a strong likelihood that Romiou will be the first of many customers seeking contracts for Mediterranean operations. As a result, Thistle is considering setting up a new base in Malta.

Setting up a Maltese base on 1 July 20X7 will require an initial investment of £425,000 and Thistle has approached its UK bank for loan finance. The bank has asked Thistle to produce a business plan in support of its loan application, specifying certain sections that are required. You work in Thistle's strategy team and have been asked to help draft information that should be included in the business plan. Anya has supplied you with the following financial information:

Three year forecast – new Maltese base

	Year 1 £'000	Year 2 £'000	Year 3 £'000	Total £'000
Sales	633	1,266	1,582	3,481
Gross profit	190	443	634	1,267
Fixed costs	(310)	(335)	(365)	(1,010)
Operating (loss)/profit	(120)	108	269	257

Thistle Ltd – summary of UK results, year ended 30 June 20X6

	£'000	Notes
Sales	6,574	
Cost of sales	(4,565)	
Gross profit	2,009	Gross margin 30.6%
Overheads	(1,593)	
Operating profit	416	Operating margin 6.3%
Interest	(49)	Interest cover = 8.5 times
Profit before tax	367	
Net assets	1,850	ROCE = 22.5%

Requirements

You are required to assist in preparing three specific sections of the business plan for a loan for the new Maltese base that would be of use to Thistle's bank.

For each of the sections set out in 36.1 to 36.3 below you should:

- prepare the section;
- explain why the section is important for the loan application; and
- identify any further information that would be useful to complete the section.

36.1 Risks of the new Maltese base, and any mitigating factors **(8 marks)**

36.2 Analysis of the three year forecast for the new Maltese base, including sensitivity **(10 marks)**

36.3 Appropriate organisational structure for international expansion **(7 marks)**

Total: 25 marks

37 Pinter Shipping Panels plc

The date is December 20X6.

Pinter Shipping Panels plc (PSP) is a listed company which manufactures steel panels for the shipbuilding industry. Shipbuilding is a global industry which is extremely competitive.

You have recently joined PSP, reporting to the chief executive, Ashley Adams. Ashley has asked you to report to him on a few important issues that have arisen recently:

"I know you are new to PSP so I have provided you with some background information (**Exhibit 1**).

"The board is concerned about performance. Although profits have improved this year the directors are not convinced that this improvement is sustainable. The finance director has provided some financial and operating data for 20X5 and 20X6 (**Exhibit 2**).

"There are also two issues for you to evaluate. Firstly, our sole supplier of steel has recently informed PSP that it will cease production on 31 December 20X6. We need to address this problem urgently, using either a sole new supplier or multiple new suppliers (**Exhibit 3**). Secondly, one of our two customers, Tinner, is challenging our pricing policy (**Exhibit 4**)."

Requirements

37.1 Using the quantitative data and other information provided in Exhibits 1 and 2, analyse the performance of PSP in 20X5 and 20X6, identifying and explaining the key drivers of profit.

(18 marks)

37.2 Explain the factors to be considered in deciding how to source supplies of steel (Exhibit 3). Provide reasoned advice regarding which supplier should be selected or whether both suppliers should be used in a multiple supplier agreement. **(13 marks)**

37.3 Prepare a formal response to the email from Tinner's procurement director, Kelly Jones (Exhibit 4). **(9 marks)**

Total: 40 marks

Exhibit 1: PSP – background information

Operations

PSP uses steel as a raw material to manufacture its panels. The panels are used by PSP's customers to build ships. The size and shape of the panels are standardised. The cost of manufacturing each panel is similar for all customers, although delivery costs vary according to the customer's requirements and location.

After taking account of wastage rates, one tonne of steel makes four steel panels.

Raw material – steel

Due to overcapacity in the steel industry, the global price of steel has fallen significantly from a high of £350 per tonne in 20X4 to a price of £130 per tonne in December 20X6. This has caused many steel producers to cease production.

Supply chain – upstream

For many years PSP has used a sole supplier of steel, Coastal Inc (Coastal), which is based in Brazil. Until recently Coastal supplied steel to PSP under annual fixed price contracts in which the price of steel per tonne for the next year was fixed in £ sterling on 1 January each year.

In October 20X6, Coastal Inc informed PSP it would cease production from 31 December 20X6 because it had become insolvent. Since October, the PSP board has been looking for new sources of steel and has found two possible suppliers, Lipp plc and Kerr Inc (Exhibit 3).

Supply chain – downstream

PSP has only two customers: Tinner plc (Tinner) and Falchetti Marine Construction (FMC).

Tinner

Tinner builds cargo ships at its dockyard which is five kilometres from the PSP factory in the UK. PSP is the sole supplier of steel panels to Tinner.

PSP agrees an annual contract with Tinner on 1 January each year, which fixes the price of steel panels in £ sterling for that year. PSP delivers to Tinner every two weeks, with similar quantities of panels each time. Deliveries are agreed a few months in advance. Tinner holds large inventories of steel panels in order to deal with any variations in its manufacturing requirements. PSP could deliver panels more frequently, but it has not been required to do so by Tinner.

Tinner has recently appointed a new procurement director, Kelly Jones. She wishes to negotiate the supply contract with PSP for 20X7 on revised terms and has sent an email to PSP about this (Exhibit 4).

FMC

FMC builds cargo ships at a dockyard in Italy. It uses several suppliers of steel panels. PSP supplies 35% of FMC's total requirements for steel panels.

PSP supplies FMC under quarterly contracts. These are agreed on 1 January and at three-month intervals thereafter. Each contract fixes the price of steel panels in euro for the following three months.

Exhibit 2: PSP financial and operating data – prepared by the finance director

Extracts from the financial statements for the years to 31 December:

	20X5			20X6 (Estimated)		
	Tinner £'000	FMC £'000	Total £'000	Tinner £'000	FMC £'000	Total £'000
Revenue	24,000	16,400	40,400	18,720	16,720	35,440
Cost of steel	(9,000)	(6,000)	(15,000)	(3,900)	(3,300)	(7,200)
Other variable Operating costs	(7,200)	(5,200)	(12,400)	(6,760)	(6,160)	(12,920)
Fixed operating			(9,000)			(9,000)
Operating profit			4,000			6,320

Operating data for the years to 31 December:

	20X5	20X6 (Estimated)
Steel used (tonnes)	50,000	48,000
Number of steel panels sold:		
Tinner	120,000	104,000
FMC	80,000	88,000
	200,000	192,000

Note: The figures for 20X6 comprise actual data for the year to November 20X6, with estimates for December 20X6.

Exhibit 3: Potential supply arrangements for steel

Only two potential new suppliers of steel for PSP have been identified for 20X7: Lipp plc (Lipp) and Kerr Inc (Kerr). PSP can select one of these companies to be its sole supplier, or it can use both companies in a multiple supplier arrangement.

Lipp

Lipp is a UK steel producer. It has been struggling financially recently, so it wants to win the contract to supply steel to PSP. It has offered an annual contract from 1 January 20X7 at a fixed price of £180 per tonne of steel under a sole supplier arrangement. If there is to be a multiple supplier arrangement it has offered a fixed price of £190 per tonne of steel under a similar annual contract. Deliveries can be made weekly.

Kerr

Kerr is a US steel producer. It is willing to supply steel to PSP from 1 January 20X7. Each delivery would be under a separate contract. Each contract's price would vary according to a pre-agreed formula based on the spot price of steel on global commodity markets on the day of ordering. Prices would be charged to PSP in US dollars. For a delivery on 1 January 20X7, the contract price is expected to be equivalent to £185 per tonne of steel.

Multiple supplier arrangement

PSP has agreed with Lipp and Kerr that, in any multiple supplier arrangement, each supplier would supply at least 40% of PSP's total annual steel requirements. The Lipp contract would be renegotiated after one year.

Exhibit 4: Extract from email to PSP from Tinner's procurement director, Kelly Jones

In the last two years, PSP has benefitted from large reductions in the global price of steel. However, because of the current fixed price contract, PSP has not shared this benefit with Tinner in the form of lower prices for its steel panels. It is not acceptable for this to continue.

I have also reviewed the level of service that PSP has been offering Tinner.

I require the following amendments to the terms in the new contract for 20X7:

- The current system of a delivery every two weeks will cease. We will require several deliveries per week. These will be of varying quantities, notified to you one day in advance of delivery.

- There will be a separate contract each week. The price for each week's deliveries will be determined separately according to an agreed formula in the contract that takes into account the spot price of steel.

If we cannot agree on these revised terms Tinner will terminate PSP's status as its sole supplier and, in future, source its steel panels from other suppliers in addition to PSP. This would result in a significant reduction in the volume of steel panels that Tinner purchases from PSP

38 Zeter Domestic Chemicals plc

The date is December 20X6.

Zeter Domestic Chemicals plc (ZDC) manufactures domestic cleaning products that are used by individual consumers.

Company background

ZDC processes raw chemicals to make domestic cleaning products, which it packages and sells to retailers.

The cleaning products are collected and distributed by lorry from ZDC's factory in the south of England. They are delivered directly to retailers which are located in the UK and France.

The acquisition of Trann Ltd

ZDC acquired Trann Ltd (Trann) on 1 October 20X4.

Prior to the acquisition, Trann had been one of three distribution companies used by ZDC.

The decision to acquire Trann was the result of a vote at a ZDC board meeting. The Chief executive, David Xuan, and the Marketing Director, Kevin Hilton, voted in favour. The Finance Director, Lisa Long, and the Chairman voted against. David Xuan had the casting vote and so the acquisition was approved.

First year post-acquisition review: October 20X5

On 1 October 20X5, ZDC's board held a meeting to review the first year of ZDC's ownership of Trann.

The board heard that, for this year, Trann's management had been allowed the autonomy to take all decisions which it believed to be appropriate for Trann. As a result, little had changed since ZDC's acquisition: Trann was still providing similar distribution services for ZDC and its other customers, and was charging similar prices as it did before the acquisition. ZDC's distribution managers also continued to use the two other distribution companies in addition to Trann.

David Xuan was unhappy: "I am wondering why we acquired Trann. In effect, it is being run as a separate entity from ZDC. Why are we still using the other two external distribution companies as well as Trann, and incurring unnecessary costs? We now have our own distribution company which we can use for all our distribution needs."

The ZDC board agreed that ZDC should use Trann for all its distribution with immediate effect. To give ZDC's distribution managers an incentive to use Trann, the Trann board was instructed to reduce its transfer prices to ZDC by 10%. Trann was also instructed to terminate its contracts with all its other customers immediately in order to create sufficient capacity to satisfy all of ZDC's transport requirements.

Second year post-acquisition review: October 20X6

In October 20X6, the ZDC board met for a further review of Trann. Financial extracts for Trann were provided to the ZDC board (**Exhibit 1**).

Lisa Long commented on these results: "It is clear that the performance of Trann was poor in the first year after acquisition and it has continued to decline in this second year. I disagreed with the decision to acquire Trann and these figures have proved me right."

Kevin Hilton disagreed: "The acquisition of Trann has been a success. I have produced key performance indicators (KPIs) (**Exhibit 2**) to show how much ZDC's distribution has improved in terms of efficiency and customer satisfaction in the year ended 30 September 20X6."

An ethical issue

David Xuan and Kevin Hilton had a conversation after the October 20X6 review.

During the conversation Kevin said: "In talking to Trann staff, I discovered that your niece has worked for Trann as a manager for several years. There is a rumour that, in supporting ZDC's acquisition of Trann, you were helping your niece. I note that she has been promoted twice within Trann since the acquisition. At the time the ZDC board voted on the acquisition, I felt that you applied pressure on me to vote with you. I hope that this was because you thought the acquisition was in the best interests of ZDC, not because of concern for your niece's career."

David responded: "At the time of the vote I said nothing about my niece's position at Trann because I did not want to influence the board, favourably or unfavourably, in the acquisition decision. ZDC's distribution function is part of your role and you are responsible for Trann. If the acquisition is not successful for ZDC, I will be asking for your resignation. The matter of my niece's employment is confidential. If you break that confidence I will dismiss you."

Requirements

38.1 Analyse the decisions made on 1 October 20X5, at the first year post-acquisition review, to:

- use Trann for all of ZDC's distribution needs, and require Trann to terminate the contracts with all its other customers; and

- reduce the transfer prices charged by Trann to ZDC by 10%.

Note: Ignore the data in Exhibit 1 and Exhibit 2. **(11 marks)**

38.2 Evaluate the views and information put forward by Lisa Long and Kevin Hilton, in October 20X6, at the second year post-acquisition review. Use the information in Exhibits 1 and 2 to provide supporting calculations. These should include, but not be restricted to, return on investment and residual income for Trann. **(11 marks)**

38.3 Explain the ethical issues for David Xuan and Kevin Hilton arising from their conversation. Set out the actions that they should each now take. **(8 marks)**

Total: 30 marks

Exhibit 1: Financial extracts for Trann – prepared by the Finance Director

Extracts from the management accounts of Trann for years ended 30 September:

	20X5	20X6
	£'000	£'000
Revenue	16,610	15,120
Operating profit/(loss)	983	(640)
Fair value of net assets	7,000	7,000

The annual cost of capital for both ZDC and Trann is 10%.

Using the fair value of its net assets, excluding Trann, ZDC has a return on investment of 18% per annum.

It is estimated that variable costs for Trann were £1.40 per kilometre in both the years ended 30 September 20X5 and 30 September 20X6.

KPIs – years ended 30 September	20X5	20X6
Percentage of on-time deliveries	91%	96%
Number of customer complaints related to delivery journeys	184	163
Percentage of full loads operated (ie, % of all deliveries when the lorry is full to capacity on the outward journey)	44	56
Number of delivery journeys made:		
• For ZDC	4,250	8,000
• For other customers	3,300	–
Average distance per delivery journey (kilometres)		
• For ZDC	1,100	1,050
• For other customers	1,100	–

Each delivery journey may involve deliveries to several retailers.

39 Hartley's Traditional Footwear Ltd

The date is December 20X6.

Hartley's Traditional Footwear Ltd (HTF) is a retailer of high quality shoes and boots (footwear) from 20 shops located throughout the UK.

Company background

HTF was established a number of years ago as a retailer of traditional leather footwear. Customers were typically from high-income groups and over 40 years old. HTF's shops are located in premium locations in shopping centres of major cities.

The HTF brand is well-known amongst high-income individuals in the UK as having high quality footwear, supported by good customer service.

A new product – Ayres boots

From January 20X5, HTF entered into a two-year contract with an Australian manufacturer of boots, The Ayres Boot Company Ltd (ABC), for the exclusive right to sell its Ayres brand boots in the UK. At that time, the Ayres brand was not well known in the UK. The contract specified that HTF could buy each pair of boots for £40 a pair from ABC until December 20X6. Sales globally were typically to consumers in the 20 to 30 years age group. Ayres boots are made mostly from synthetic fur.

For the first year, sales of Ayres boots were low. Some HTF board members started to argue that they were not suitable for HTF's customer base and had damaged the HTF brand.

In December 20X5, several celebrities were photographed wearing Ayres boots. Via social media, the boots quickly became a global fashion phenomenon. They became in huge demand as a premium product from the start of 20X6.

Global sales of Ayres boots increased rapidly and, despite retailers raising the selling price to consumers substantially, ABC could not manufacture enough boots to satisfy global demand. From January 20X6, ABC therefore limited supplies to HTF to 10,000 pairs of boots per month in the UK for the remaining term of the contract.

The following data are provided:

	20X5	20X6
Sales volumes (pairs):		
Ayres boots	8,000	120,000
Traditional footwear	40,000	36,000
Average sales prices:		
Ayres boots	£60	£200
Traditional footwear	£150	£150
Average cost:		
Ayres boots	£40	£40
Traditional footwear	£100	£100

Contract extension – December 20X6

HTF continues to sell traditional leather footwear through its shops, but HTF's reputation and brand are now closely identified with the Ayres brand.

The end of the two-year contract period with ABC is now imminent. ABC has stated that it is still willing to continue to sell its boots to HTF. However, it is considering increasing its price to HTF and ending the exclusivity agreement by making sales to other UK retailers from 1 January 20X7.

ABC's board has said that it will consider extending the existing contract with HTF, as the exclusive UK retailer, for one more year. This would be in return for a one-off payment by HTF. The extended contract would continue to run until 31 December 20X7 on the same terms of 10,000 pairs per month, at £40 per pair. To open negotiations, ABC has asked the HTF board to suggest an appropriate amount for the one-off payment.

Importing boots from Russia

As a possible alternative to buying any boots from ABC from January 20X7, HTF has found a Russian company that can supply boots of a similar design as the Ayres boots, but without a brand name. The cost to HTF would be £40 a pair. HTF estimates that these boots will sell in similar quantities to the Ayres boots if it charges customers £60 a pair.

Some HTF board members are concerned that the Russian boots may have a risk of poor quality and have suggested that sourcing from this supplier may necessitate new quality control procedures.

Requirements

39.1 In respect of HTF's branding strategy:

   (a) Compare the HTF brand and the Ayres brand; and

   (b) Explain the benefits and problems for the HTF brand arising from the association with the Ayres brand. **(8 marks)**

39.2 Explain why the same Ayres boots sold for £60 in 20X5 and for £200 in 20X6. Use appropriate pricing models and concepts. **(7 marks)**

39.3 Identify and explain the quantitative and qualitative factors that HTF should consider in determining the amount of the one-off payment to offer ABC for the one-year extension of the exclusive supply contract for the UK. **(7 marks)**

39.4 Explain how quality control procedures could be used to identify and mitigate problems with the supply of the Russian boots. You should give specific examples of information that could be used to measure and monitor supplier performance. **(8 marks)**

Total: 30 marks

March 2017 exam questions

40 Ignite plc

Assume the date is March 2017.

Ignite plc (Ignite) is a listed company which makes a range of products that are capable of world-wide use. These include: cigarette lighters; multi-purpose lighters; lighter fuel; and a limited range of accessories (including torches, sunglasses and pens).

You have recently joined Ignite as a corporate strategy advisor, reporting to the strategy director, Hannah Smith. Hannah has asked for your help with a report that Ignite's board has requested on the company's product portfolio.

"As you are new to the team and the business, I am hoping you will bring some innovative ideas. Our most important product has always been the Ignite cigarette lighter. Our most important market has historically been the UK, though the anti-smoking movement has caused us a number of issues here. The board has recently been discussing the sales forecasts and it is very concerned about the declining sales of Ignite cigarette lighters in the UK. I have provided some background information for you about the company's history and product range (**Exhibit 1**) and the UK cigarette industry (**Exhibit 2**). More widely, the board has asked us to evaluate Ignite's global product sales and current product portfolio, because of concern about their implications for the company's future profitability (**Exhibit 3**).

"Ignite has a strong brand image but traditionally it has struggled to attract female consumers, other than those purchasing Ignite products as gifts. One of our directors believes that this is a failure on the part of the advertising department; another director believes that the problem is the design of our product range, which appeals primarily to males in the age group 18–34.

"The board wants us to consider opportunities for growth. I believe that we should extend the current portfolio to other related products in different markets and with different customers. I have suggested some ideas (**Exhibit 4**). The board is keen to report better results for 2017. It has set targets of 15% sales growth (compared with 2016), and a 38% gross profit margin."

Requirements

Draft sections for the report on the company's product portfolio that Ignite's board has requested:

40.1 Analyse the external factors that have influenced the changing demand for Ignite's cigarette lighters in the UK between 1950 and 2016. Use the data provided in Exhibits 1 and 2 to support your analysis. **(9 marks)**

40.2 Using the data in Exhibits 1, 2 and 3 and the other information provided, evaluate Ignite's existing product portfolio:

(a) Make appropriate calculations to:

- analyse the global historic and forecast financial information for 2015-2017 (for this purpose ignore the new products in Exhibit 4)

- analyse Ignite's existing product portfolio using the Boston Consulting Group (BCG) matrix.

(b) Discuss the implications of your analysis in (a) for Ignite's future corporate strategy. Use the following headings:

- Sales growth
- Profitability
- Risk **(22 marks)**

40.3 In relation to the board's requirements for future growth:

    (a)   Calculate the forecast sales and gross profit margin that the new products (Exhibit 4) must achieve to meet the board's targets for 2017.

    (b)   Discuss the growth strategies proposed by Hannah Smith (Exhibit 4). Refer to relevant models.

(13 marks)

Total: 44 marks

Exhibit 1: Company history and product range

Ignite was established in the late 1940s as a UK manufacturer of high quality cigarette lighters. The health risks of smoking are now widely known but, at that time, smoking was marketed as a fashionable and elegant activity.

Cigarette lighters

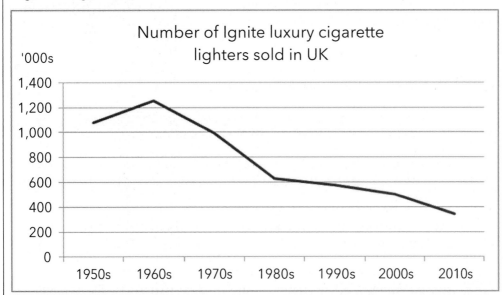

Ignite's first product was a luxury cigarette lighter with a fuel cylinder that could be refilled. The fuel could be purchased only from Ignite. As a result of their innovative design, Ignite lighters quickly became collectors' items, even being purchased by non-smokers.

In 1961, a competitor launched the first disposable cigarette lighter. Ignite reacted by introducing a lifetime guarantee for its products, promising that: "It works or we will fix it for free". This was attractive to loyal customers who valued Ignite's quality standards. However, by 1980, the use of very cheap, disposable lighters was widespread and several makers of refillable lighters went out of business.

During the 1980s, Ignite developed and patented new technology to produce lighters with a wind-resistant flame which would remain lit in all weather conditions. Ignite also expanded its marketing internationally, making use of product placement in films, television and sponsored events, to raise brand awareness.

Since 2007, as in many countries, smoking has been banned in the UK in enclosed public places. The fact that smokers are forced to go outside has increased demand for Ignite's wind-resistant lighters. However, the ban has also led to some of Ignite's customers switching to electronic cigarettes (e-cigarettes) which do not need a lighter.

To stimulate demand, every year Ignite brings out a limited-edition cigarette lighter which is widely publicised on social media. Each lighter carries unique artwork and is engraved with a date code and the initials of the worker who assembled it.

The UK market is declining so the international market is becoming increasingly important for Ignite. Today, Ignite lighters are sold in over 160 countries, and Ignite is a popular brand in Asia.

Multi-purpose lighters

In the 1990s, as UK social habits changed and outdoor entertaining became more popular, Ignite used its wind-resistant flame technology to develop multi-purpose lighters for candles, barbecues and cooking stoves. These are proving increasingly popular.

Lifestyle accessories

To capitalise on its brand name, in 2010 Ignite launched a range of lifestyle accessories for men: sunglasses, torches and pens. However whilst the technology behind the wind-resistant flame is difficult to copy, this is less true of fashion accessories. A number of cheap 'Ignite' counterfeits have been produced which has provided publicity for the Ignite brand, but reduced Ignite's sales and detracted from its quality image. The accessory range also included a range of male fragrances in cigarette lighter-shaped bottles. However, demand for Ignite fragrance has been lower than for other accessories.

Exhibit 2: Key dates influencing the UK cigarette industry

1920s-1950s	Cigarette smoking was extremely popular and increased rapidly. By 1959, in the UK, 60% of men and 40% of women smoked.
1960s	Various research papers were published about the addictive nature of cigarettes, showing a statistical link between smoking and reduced life expectancy.
1971	UK government health warnings were placed on cigarette packs for the first time.
1990s (and ongoing)	Research suggested that a 10% increase in price leads to approximately a 5% reduction in demand for cigarettes. Successive UK governments adopted a strategy of raising the price of cigarettes, through taxes, to reduce smoking.
2002	UK legislation banned cigarette advertising, promotion and sponsorship.
2004	The first electronic 'e-cigarette' was developed.
2007	UK legislation banned smoking in enclosed public places (bars, restaurants, workplaces).
2016	UK users of e-cigarettes increased from 700,000 in 2012 to 2.6 million in 2016.

Exhibit 3: Extracts of management information for Ignite's global product portfolio

Global product sales and profitability (based on 31 December year end):

	Luxury cigarette lighters £ million	Multi-purpose lighters £ million	Lighter fuel £ million	Lifestyle accessories £ million	Total £ million
Actual 2015					
Sales	127.0	34.0	32.0	20.0	213.0
Gross profit	52.1	8.2	6.1	12.0	78.4
Actual 2016					
Sales	108.0	38.0	30.0	24.0	200.0
Gross profit	43.2	9.1	5.4	14.4	72.1
Forecast 2017					
Sales	92.0	40.0	30.0	28.0	190.0
Gross profit	35.0	9.6	5.1	16.8	66.5

Global market data for the year ended 31 December 2016:

Product	Ignite's market share	Market leader's market share	Estimated market growth rate pa
Luxury cigarette lighters	26%	38%	(5%)
Multi-purpose lighters	18%	22%	14%
Lighter fuel	11%	45%	2%
Lifestyle accessories	Negligible	Note	12%

Note: No single company has more than 5% of the market.

Exhibit 4: Growth strategies, suggested by Hannah Smith (strategy director)

- **New lighter**

  In response to health concerns about smoking and the success of fitness apps, Ignite has developed a new product, the Trackr. The Trackr is a cigarette lighter which includes a digital screen to monitor the number of cigarettes that have been lit that day. This enables a person to keep track of their smoking habit. This will be marketed as a device to help customers cut down on their smoking. The Trackr can be used on its own or integrated with a fitness app which monitors a range of other health-related issues (diet, exercise, alcohol etc) on a daily basis.

- **Outdoor range**

  Ignite's multi-purpose lighters are already used by many camping enthusiasts. Ignite is currently developing a range of high-quality gas barbecues to capitalise on its wind-resistant technological expertise. The negative association with smoking has been bad for Ignite's brand image. Developing more of an outdoor focus will appeal to health and fitness fans and counteract this. Once it has been established as a barbecue brand, Ignite will then develop a range of camping equipment.

- **Female market**

  To attract more customers, Ignite is also considering a new range of products for the female market: candle lighters, sunglasses, pens, fragrances. Unlike existing products, these will be designed specifically to appeal visually to women.

41 Eclo Ltd

Eclo Ltd (Eclo) sells environmentally-friendly uniforms to corporate clients. The garments are customised with the client's business logo. Eclo's target market is organisations that have created brands based on sustainability.

Company background

Eclo is a social enterprise which aims to trade in a profitable and sustainable manner. It was set up five years ago by Eve Carter, a textile engineering expert.

Eve is passionate about the environment. She wanted Eclo to avoid the traditional linear supply chain model: "take resources, make a product, use it, discard it". Instead, Eclo adopts a circular model where product materials and packaging are re-used multiple times as they are recycled into the supply chain to aim for zero waste.

Eve designs all Eclo garments with the aim that they can be repaired, re-used or re-manufactured. Customers are offered discounts off future orders as an incentive to return old products if they do not need them any longer.

Eclo has a small workforce. It operates with a very flat organisational structure, with all employees encouraged to contribute ideas and participate in decisions. It has strategic partnerships with three different Indian suppliers which currently produce all of Eclo's garments in India to standard specifications. Eclo pays an agent in India which arranges for the garments to be transported from the suppliers' factories to an Indian printing company for customisation according to the client's requirements. The agent then arranges shipping to the UK.

Sustainable production

Eclo uses environmentally sustainable processes which conform to a global certification standard. This requires Eclo to comply with high-level environmental and social criteria along its entire supply chain. A key marketing message of Eclo is that every Eclo garment can be traced back to its origins. Eclo has developed a simple eco-labelling system to evidence this.

All suppliers are required to have a fair and consistent wage policy and there are strict regulations on workers' age and working conditions. Eclo prohibits the use of poisonous chemicals and toxic additives that might damage workers' health and the environment.

Eclo's garments are made in factories that are powered by wind and solar energy. The garments incorporate wool, organic cotton and recycled polyester (RPET) fabrics. RPET is created from recycled plastic bottles which are turned into fabric so it has a much lower carbon footprint than other synthetic fabrics. The customised printing process uses environmentally-friendly dyes and low-waste, bio-degradable ink.

Supply chain management

Eclo's reliance on Indian suppliers has caused delays between client order and delivery. There have been an increasing number of client complaints about product quality and errors in printing. Eve is now considering whether to change to an entirely UK-based supply chain for garment production, and whether to establish an in-house printing operation in the UK. Eve has identified a suitable factory unit at a low rent. Eclo would need an additional equity investor to provide £100,000 for the installation of environmentally-friendly printing machines. Eve wants to acquire technology to allow clients to connect directly to Eclo's printing operation using an app so that they can upload their logos and designs and place orders without the need for Eclo's intervention.

Ethical issue: wastewater contamination

One of the Indian suppliers (AMG) makes garments for several companies, not all of which conform to the certification standard used by Eclo. Toxic wastewater from AMG's factory has been discharged, untreated, into the nearby river causing a severe impact on aquatic life and plants.

AMG has emailed Eclo to inform it about the incident, which arose during a production run for a high-fashion retailer. The contamination has not yet been made public, however AMG intends to publish an honest and open apology next week and to make appropriate compensation payments. AMG has asked Eclo to keep this information confidential until it has had a chance to publish all the facts.

Eclo's marketing manager wants to avoid any bad publicity. "Our products do not use any toxic chemical dyes so this issue cannot be anything to do with us. I think we should cancel our contract with AMG immediately. We should also make a public statement now, before the news comes out, explaining the contamination was not our responsibility. We can name the high-fashion retailer as the culprit. That way our reputation should remain intact."

Requirements

41.1 Discuss whether Eclo operates with a flexible organisational structure. Refer to relevant models. **(7 marks)**

41.2 Assume that Eclo continues with its existing supply chain arrangements in India.

Discuss the control procedures that can be used to ensure suppliers are compliant with Eclo's sustainability processes and to monitor the quality of their output. **(9 marks)**

41.3 Explain the strategic and financial considerations that will determine whether Eclo should bring its supply chain to the UK and whether to invest in an in-house printing operation. **(12 marks)**

41.4 Discuss any ethical issues arising for Eclo as a result of the wastewater contamination and the proposals made by Eclo's marketing manager. Advise Eve on appropriate actions. **(8 marks)**

Total: 36 marks

42 Gighay Ltd (amended)

Gighay Ltd (Gighay) is a technology company which provides managed services to small and medium-sized enterprises (SMEs) in respect of information technology (IT). It specialises in creating flexible, cost-effective managed IT service solutions for its clients. Gighay's promise is "to enable you to make the best use of IT in your business, whatever your size, whatever your budget".

Gighay employs a team of technical experts with industry-accredited IT qualifications. It has strategic alliances with leading hardware and software providers. As a result, Gighay has access to the latest technological developments, and knowledge and experience in a range of IT specialisms. It has particular expertise in data capture and data analytics.

Gighay's managed IT services are provided by a 24-hour team which is based at its operations centre. Gighay monitors the configuration, availability and performance of client systems and applications from the same centre. It holds regular service review meetings and all clients receive a monthly reporting pack with tailored key performance indicators (KPIs).

Gighay has been approached by two potential clients, Oxna Ltd (Oxna) and Feltar Ltd (Feltar).

Oxna

Oxna is a publishing business. Many of Oxna's employees work remotely in different countries and time zones. They depend on being able to connect to Oxna's network, 24 hours a day. Oxna's business is growing rapidly and the demands on its systems are increasing. On two occasions recently, Oxna's server has crashed. This caused periods of costly downtime and required Oxna to pay for expensive emergency support. It appears that one of these incidents was the result of a targeted attack by a hacker who used malicious software to disrupt the company's systems. Oxna is therefore increasingly worried about cyber-security. It has limited in-house IT expertise and is considering whether to use Gighay's managed IT services. Oxna's operations director has asked for a document which sets out the benefits of outsourcing management of all its IT needs to Gighay and explains how Gighay will manage the service contract between itself and Oxna.

Feltar

Feltar sells speciality coffee in two forms, whole-bean and ground coffee, to individual consumers and independent cafes. It currently makes online sales via a basic website. When placing an order, customers are required to provide limited details, including their name, address, contact and payment details. Feltar's managing director has approached Gighay for advice: "One of our employees tells me that we should be making more use of social media. He also says we could use big data and data analytics to direct our marketing efforts better and to determine inventory and pricing strategies. I am not sure I even understand what big data is, let alone how we could use it to our competitive advantage. And as a small business, I am concerned about the practical implications for us of capturing and using more data about customers".

Requirements

In response to the requests by Gighay's potential clients:

42.1 Explain the benefits and problems for Oxna of outsourcing all of its IT needs to Gighay and suggest some KPIs that could be included in the service contract between the companies.

(11 marks)

42.2 Explain how Feltar can use data analytics to achieve competitive advantage. Address the managing director's concerns about the practical implications of implementing a big data strategy.

(9 marks)

Total: 20 marks

June 2017 exam questions

43 Holidays Direct plc

The date is June 20X7.

Holidays Direct plc (HD) is a UK-based, online holiday company which sells package holidays to locations outside the UK, directly to UK consumers.

The package holiday industry

Package holiday companies arrange both accommodation (ie, hotel stays) and flights, then sell these together as holiday packages. Sales are made either directly to consumers or through travel agents acting as intermediaries.

Most package holiday companies do not own aircraft or hotels. Instead, they enter into block contracts to purchase flights and hotel stays in advance from airlines and hotel operators.

In relation to flights, the package holiday company charters entire aircraft for return flights to and from a pre-agreed destination airport at a pre-agreed time. The package holiday company then sells individual seats as return flights to consumers as part of the holiday package.

The increasing use of the internet has made holiday package companies' marketing more effective, including the use of mobile devices and social media.

Company background

Company history and development

HD was established a number of years ago in the UK as an online holiday company selling holiday packages to mainland Europe, direct to UK consumers.

In 20X2, HD acquired another UK online holiday company, Helio Ltd, which sold holiday packages to worldwide destinations. Helio's European activities were quickly integrated into HD's operations, forming the European Division. Helio's operations outside Europe formed a separate Worldwide Division within HD.

In the year ended 31 May 20X6, demand was low and HD's financial performance was poor. The CEO was removed in November 20X6 and a new CEO, Oliver Orrs, was appointed in April 20X7.

The year ended 31 May 20X7 was an unexpectedly good year for HD with high demand, which exceeded forecasts.

Sales and bookings

All HD bookings are made online directly by consumers. Each booking combines return flight seats plus hotel stays (averaging one week) under a single contract for a group of two or more people. HD does not sell flight seats and hotel stays separately. Bookings can be made many months in advance, but can also be made just a few days before departure.

Flights

HD charters flights from three different airlines. Two of these airlines serve only European destination airports and one operates worldwide. Each destination airport may serve a number of different holiday sites. The fee paid by HD for each chartered flight is the same no matter how many seats are occupied on the flight.

HD agrees the number, dates and destination airports of chartered flights for the year with each airline under one large annual contract (block contract). Block contracts, which are binding, are entered into for an entire calendar year in September of the previous year. The capacity of the flights, timings and destination airports are based on HD's estimates of demand from consumers for each destination airport.

HD offers late discounts on its website to attract last-minute bookings from consumers where there are unsold seats. If HD overestimates demand for a destination airport, then some seats on some flights may remain unoccupied despite such discounts.

If HD underestimates demand for a destination airport, then it may charter some additional flights from airlines, but at a much higher price than the original block contract price.

Harriet Hubber is the manager for HD's flight chartering. She reports to the head of HD's European Division regarding European flights, and to the head of HD's Worldwide Division regarding non-European flights.

Hotels

HD purchases hotel stays from 84 different hotel operators at holiday sites throughout the world. Most of the hotel operators own hotels both in Europe and the rest of the world.

Typically, HD signs block contracts with each hotel up to three years ahead, to secure an appropriate number and type of bedroom accommodation (hotel stays). These are based on HD's estimates of demand from consumers for each holiday site.

The block contracts are binding and the full price must be paid by HD, whether or not it eventually sells the hotel stays in the block contracts to consumers.

HD offers late discounts to attract consumers if it has overestimated demand for a particular hotel. If it has underestimated demand, HD tries to purchase additional hotel stays, often at a higher cost.

Penny Price is the manager for hotels. She reports to the head of HD's European Division regarding European hotels, and to the head of HD's Worldwide Division regarding non-European hotels.

Challenges identified by the new CEO

Following his initial assessment of the company, Oliver Orrs required data to be collected and analysed to support his strategic and operational decisions. Some limited initial information has been prepared (**Exhibit**).

Oliver believes that HD's current organisational structure of two divisions, European and Worldwide, is not promoting operational efficiency. Therefore, he is considering making changes to the organisational structure.

A critical success factor for HD is matching actual consumer bookings with the block contracts made in advance to purchase flights and hotel stays. Oliver is concerned about the scale of the variances between HD's estimates and actual demand. He wants to understand the possible consequences in financial terms and wishes to mitigate this operating risk.

Ethical issue

Penny Price made the following comments, in confidence, to Harriet Hubber:

Penny said: "HD has a contract with a global car rental business to promote their car hire as an additional service to consumers. HD receives a commission on each car rental contract that our consumers book. However, I am concerned that consumers are being overcharged.

"I have a friend who operates a small car rental firm in Spain and I have told just a few consumers that it would be cheaper for them to hire through his company, rather than the car rental company that HD promotes. I have not taken any money for doing this."

Requirements

43.1 Use the quantitative data in the Exhibit and the other information provided to:

(a) Evaluate HD's operating and financial performance in the year ended 31 May 20X7, comparing it with the year ended 31 May 20X6, identifying any key further information required; and

(b) Explain the operating and financial risks which arise for HD from the potential differences in quantities between:

- The number of flights and hotel stays that have been acquired through the block contracts; and

- Demand from consumers. **(19 marks)**

43.2 Explain how monitoring the use of its website by consumers may help HD estimate future demand. **(8 marks)**

43.3 Critically appraise HD's current organisational structure. Explain and justify a revised structure. **(9 marks)**

43.4 Explain the ethical issues that arise for HD and Penny from the matters in Penny Price's comments. Set out the actions that should be taken by Harriet Hubber. **(8 marks)**

Total: 44 marks

Exhibit: Financial and operating data for years ended 31 May		
Revenue	**20X6**	**20X7**
European destinations (£'000s)	348,000	360,000
Worldwide destinations (£'000s)	148,000	184,000
Total (£'000s)	496,000	544,000
Other financial data		
Value of discounts given to consumers (£'000s)	14,880	5,440
Cost of additional flights and hotel stays purchased by HD outside block contracts (£'000s)	4,960	27,200
Number of bookings by consumers		
European destinations ('000s)	290	300
Worldwide destinations ('000s)	74	92
Total ('000s)	364	392
Operating data		
Average time of booking by consumer before departure (days)	87	76
Number of hotel stays booked by consumers ('000s)	473	470
Number of return flight seats booked by consumers ('000s)	1,092	1,176
Number of block contract hotel stays left unoccupied ('000s)	14.2	4.7
Number of block contract flight seats left unoccupied ('000s)	32.8	11.8
Website data		
Number of website visits (000s)	6,916	8,624

Definition of terms

Bookings by consumers – a booking is when a person (representing a group of two or more people) enters into a single contract for a holiday package which includes flight seats and hotel stays for everyone in the group.

Cost of additional bookings – this is the price paid by HD to make late purchases of whole flights and hotel stays in addition to block contracts.

Hotel stay – this is one bedroom, irrespective of the number of occupants. Hotel stays average one week.

Return flight seat – this is one return flight per person.

Value of discounts given to consumers – these are the discounts given to consumers in order to make late sales of unsold flight seats and hotel stays.

Website visits – a visit to the website is counted each time a consumer accesses any part of the HD website.

44 Jason Smyth Textiles Ltd (amended)

The date is June 20X7.

Jason Smyth Textiles Ltd (JST) is a manufacturer of soft furnishings including bedding, cushions and curtains.

Company background

The entire ordinary share capital of JST is owned by Jason Smyth.

A number of years ago Jason established JST and immediately acquired a factory, located in the UK, and good quality machinery at low cost from the liquidator of another company.

JST's business model has been one of cost leadership. Jason personally maintains strict operational and financial control over all the company's activities in order to minimise costs.

Price competition throughout the supply chain is intense. Whilst design and quality are important, contracts are frequently won and lost on the basis of price. JST makes sales to low-price soft furnishings retailers throughout the UK.

The main raw material used by JST is polyester, which is a cheap synthetic fabric. Polyester is imported by JST from a small number of suppliers located in developing nations. JST uses only a few suppliers to obtain larger quantity discounts and to increase the efficiency of its procurement system. It is the responsibility of suppliers to arrange delivery directly to JST's factory. The fabric purchased by JST is of basic quality, but it is fit for the purpose of manufacturing soft furnishings for JST's customers.

The labour-intensive manufacturing process involves colouring, processing and cutting the raw material polyester fabric, before making it into soft furnishings designed by JST. The colouring and design are particular features of JST products that have enabled the company to distinguish its products from those of competitors.

JST uses its own lorries for distribution to customers. It is a low-cost service which operates efficiently using an information technology (IT) system to schedule and control deliveries.

Ordering of raw materials and the scheduling of deliveries are controlled centrally by skilled employees using the company's IT systems. This permits strict inventory control. The large overall quantity of raw materials ordered by JST from each supplier enables it to impose a just-in-time inventory system.

JST managers take a strict approach to staff discipline, especially regarding customer complaints. Some training is provided for skilled staff, but little for unskilled staff.

Financing and marketing support is provided by skilled JST staff, again using the company's IT systems. This includes providing and administering credit facilities for customers. A strict 30-day credit policy is applied. Marketing is mainly through customer relationship management using captured data on each retailer customer.

Competition and pressures on costs

There has been a long-term trend for soft furnishings to be manufactured in developing nations using low cost production and locally produced fabrics. These goods are imported into the UK, and other developed countries, and sold at prices which undercut JST's prices.

The machinery that Jason originally acquired from the liquidator has given JST a cost advantage. However, it is now nearing the end of its useful life so it is becoming unreliable. As a result, an increasing number of defects have been found in batches of production. JST always replaces such items for its customers.

In the year ended 31 May 20X7, JST made an operating loss. Two factors have been identified which suggest that costs will rise in future and, as a result, financial performance is expected to worsen:

(1) The legal minimum wage in the UK has recently increased and will further increase in the next few years. 75% of JST's staff are unskilled and paid the current legal minimum wage. Skilled staff are paid a little above the legal minimum wage. Staff turnover is high, but there is high local unemployment, so finding replacement employees is not difficult.

(2) A fall in the value of sterling, compared with many currencies, has meant that the cost of fabric imported by JST has increased in sterling terms.

A proposed new business model

The JST board believes that the company's cost leadership position is no longer sustainable. It has proposed changing the company's strategic direction with a new business model. This involves a move upmarket by producing better quality soft furnishings in a new range of fabrics. The company will mainly use natural fabrics including cotton, wool, linen and silk. It will still use some polyester fabric, but this will be better quality than the type currently used.

The new business model will require transformational change. It will include replacing most of the old machinery and increasing automation through the use of advanced robotic machinery operated by an intelligent control system. The JST board believe that the introduction of the new machinery will lead to significant efficiencies in the manufacturing process. The change in business model will require new management roles and reporting structures to be created. The model is planned to be introduced on 1 January 20X8.

Fewer unskilled staff will be needed and so many of these employees will be made redundant. Skilled staff will be retrained to upgrade and adapt their skills. There will also be recruitment of new staff with specialist skills more relevant to automated production.

Requirements

44.1 Prepare a report to the JST board in which you:

    (a) Prepare a value chain diagram for JST's existing business model and include brief descriptions of each of JST's relevant activities in the diagram. Present your value chain diagram in a tabular format.

    (b) Explain how the elements of JST's value chain support its current low cost strategy.

    Ignore the proposed new business model. **(19 marks)**

44.2 With respect to JST's proposed new business model:

    (a) Describe its benefits and problems, and make a reasoned recommendation as to whether JST should implement the new business model; and

    (b) Explain the change management issues for JST. **(14 marks)**

Total: 33 marks

45 Portland Prawns Ltd

The date is June 20X7.

Portland Prawns Ltd (PP) processes high-quality fresh prawns and sells them to upmarket restaurants.

Company background

PP owns a processing and packaging factory in Scotland, about 750 kilometres north of London. It purchases high-quality, freshly caught prawns from a small number of suppliers located at fishing ports in Scotland.

The prawns are processed, packaged and delivered fresh to customers throughout the UK within 24 hours of being caught.

In recent years, PP's annual sales have been constant at 400,000 kilos, priced at £10 per kilo. This level of production is 80% of the factory's operating capacity.

The budgeted performance of PP for the year ending 30 June 20X8 is as follows:

	£'000	£'000
Revenue		4,000
Production costs:		
Variable	1,800	
Fixed	1,000	
		(2,800)
Variable distribution costs		(400)
Fixed administration expenses		(200)
Operating profit		600

Proposed new contract

Finlay's Finest Fish Ltd (FFF) is a chain of large, upmarket fish shops based in and around London.

FFF has offered PP a one-year contract, from 1 July 20X7, to supply FFF with frozen prawns. The following terms are not negotiable:

- Selling price per kilo will be £8.

- A minimum of 150,000 kilos will be supplied in the year, but up to 200,000 kilos in total must be supplied by PP if FFF requests this amount.

- The quality must be at least equal to that now being supplied to PP's existing customers, but prawns must be frozen rather than fresh.

- FFF will collect the frozen prawns from the PP factory, so there will be no incremental distribution costs incurred by PP.

- Large financial penalties will apply if the contract conditions are not satisfied.

- FFF has the option, but not the obligation, to renew the contract for a further year from 1 July 20X8 on the same terms. The contract may be renewed yet again on 1 July 20X9 on terms to be agreed between the two parties at the appropriate time.

- PP will be FFF's sole supplier of frozen prawns.

Variable production costs per kilo will not change in the next three years, with or without the new FFF contract. All annual fixed costs will remain the same in future if the new FFF contract is rejected, but will increase by £420,000 from 1 July 20X7 as a result of accepting the FFF contract in order to acquire and operate freezing facilities.

Market research

New market research has determined the following demand schedule from PP's existing customers (ie, excluding FFF) for the year ending 30 June 20X8:

Selling price	£10.00	£10.50	£11.00
Sales volume (kilos)	400,000	350,000	300,000

New capacity – a possible rental agreement

PP has the opportunity to sign a three-year rental agreement for an additional local factory, including machinery. The rental agreement would commence on 1 July 20X7 and would give PP annual processing capacity for an extra 150,000 kilos of prawns. The annual rental cost is £65,000.

Requirements

45.1 Determine the maximum operating profit achievable by PP for the year ending 30 June 20X8 under each of the following alternative assumptions:

    (a)   The FFF contract is rejected.

    (b)   The FFF contract is accepted and FFF demand in the year ending 30 June 20X8 is 150,000 kilos.

    (c)   The FFF contract is accepted and FFF demand in the year ending 30 June 20X8 is 200,000 kilos.

Advise PP's board on whether the new FFF contract should be accepted, considering all relevant factors. Ignore the rental agreement. **(15 marks)**

45.2 Explain, with supporting calculations, whether PP should sign the rental agreement. Assume that the FFF contract has been accepted. **(8 marks)**

Total: 23 marks

46 Blakes Blinds Ltd

The date is September 20X7.

Blakes Blinds Ltd (BB) manufactures and installs high-quality door and window blinds for the corporate market.

Customers

BB's customers are UK-based. They include restaurant chains, hospitals, educational establishments and owners of commercial buildings. BB undertakes one-off contracts but also has repeat business with existing customers who refurbish their premises or re-locate. BB acts as sub-contractor to several large building firms for the installation of blinds in new-build developments.

Competitive strategy

The blinds market is divided into domestic and commercial segments. It is dominated by a small number of key companies, with large marketing budgets, who compete aggressively on price. The rest of the market is fragmented. Smaller operators, like BB, often focus on one market segment or one geographical area.

Most companies that sell blinds buy low-cost, finished products from Asia and sell them to UK customers. However BB manufactures all its own products in its UK factory, based in Lemchester, which allows it to control quality. BB purchases over 60% of its components from China, mostly from one supplier, Ren Xiao Ltd (RX), with whom it has a good trading relationship.

BB offers a wide range of blinds for the control of light, heat and privacy, with a complete service from design to installation. When a customer makes an enquiry, BB carries out a site survey to advise on the best option for the customer's individual requirements. BB's blinds are then made to measure. The service is tailored to take into account customer needs in relation to delivery dates, installation times and specific budgets. Once the blinds have been manufactured, they are installed by a team of specialist fitters, who are all employed by BB.

Blinds are often subject to high usage and can therefore be damaged easily. After installation, BB offers customers the option to pay for a service contract with a three-year warranty on all components. The price of the service contract depends on the quantity and type of blinds installed. Under the service contract, BB checks all operating mechanisms on each anniversary of the initial installation. Damaged components are replaced free of charge within the three-year warranty period, but are chargeable to the customer thereafter. Service contracts help to tie customers into BB and most customers extend their contracts beyond the initial warranty period. As a result, where repairs and upgrades are necessary, BB is likely to be asked to undertake them.

In January 20X5 BB launched its innovative 'Auto-Close' system. This allows blinds to be operated by remote control or by using an app on a smartphone or tablet. The system's motorised technology can be fitted as part of an initial installation of new blinds or fitted to a customer's existing blinds, even if they were originally installed by another company. Auto-Close has proved very popular with corporate customers who need to respond quickly to changes in light and weather conditions, to maintain constant internal temperatures and to reduce energy consumption. Since BB introduced Auto-Close, several competitors have launched similar products. The only intellectual property right that BB has protected is the use of the Auto-Close brand name.

Financial performance

As a result of introducing Auto-Close, BB achieved high revenue growth in 20X6. However, the board was disappointed that, although selling prices were relatively constant, the operating profit was lower than in 20X5. Extracts from the most recent management accounts, including key performance indicators and the 20X7 budget, are provided (**Exhibit**). The board would like to understand how profitability to date has been affected by the performance of each of BB's three main revenue streams:

(1) Blinds
(2) Auto-Close systems
(3) Service contracts

Possible acquisition of supplier

BB is considering the acquisition of its major Chinese supplier, RX. The board believes that eliminating the margins currently paid to RX may help improve profitability. If the acquisition goes ahead, RX's business would be operated as the component division of BB and would supply all the required components to BB's manufacturing division. In addition BB's board hopes that the acquisition will give it an opportunity to start selling blinds in Asia, by using the local knowledge and contacts of RX.

Grant application

Lemchester City Council has recently made grants available to help revive the area's manufacturing industries. Grants will be awarded to businesses which provide local employment and also have an entirely local supply chain. BB's Managing Director (MD) has told the Financial Controller to apply for a grant and to certify on the form that BB fulfils all the application criteria. The MD's justification is that all BB's blinds are manufactured locally. The Financial Controller, a qualified ICAEW Chartered Accountant, is concerned that BB does not meet the grant conditions because it buys components from China.

Requirements

46.1 Identify the factors that have contributed to BB's competitive advantage and assess the extent to which this is likely to be sustainable. **(7 marks)**

46.2 Using the data in the Exhibit and the other information provided, analyse BB's financial performance to:

- explain the key reasons for the differences in performance between 20X5 and 20X6
- assess the likelihood of achieving the 20X7 budget, highlighting any areas of concern.

Identify specific further information that would assist your analysis. **(20 marks)**

46.3 In relation to the proposal to acquire RX:

- Discuss the advantages and disadvantages of the acquisition.

- Assuming the acquisition takes place, briefly explain the factors that should be considered in determining transfer prices between BB's new component division and its manufacturing division. **(11 marks)**

46.4 Discuss the ethical issues arising for BB and the Financial Controller as a result of the grant application, and recommend appropriate actions. **(7 marks)**

Total: 45 marks

Exhibit: Extracts from BB's management accounts

Summary of financial performance (£'000)

	Actual results Year ended 31 December		6 months to 30 June	Budget Year ending 31 December
	20X5	20X6	20X7	20X7
Revenue	10,530	16,460	10,370	24,165
Cost of sales	5,980	9,790	6,225	14,260
Gross profit	4,550	6,670	4,145	9,905
Fixed costs	4,133	6,260	3,694	6,970
Operating profit	417	410	451	2,935

Note: Cost of sales consists of labour and components. It includes the cost of components bought from China and invoiced in Chinese yuan renminbi (CNY). Actual costs have been translated into sterling (£) at the appropriate exchange rate:

Components bought from China	Year ended 31 December		6 months to 30 June
	20X5	20X6	20X7
Actual cost (CNY'000)	19,616	26,456	16,123
Actual cost (£'000)	2,060	3,043	1,935

Analysis of sales and gross profit by revenue stream

Year ended 31 December 20X5	Blinds £'000	Auto-Close systems £'000	Service contracts £'000
Revenue	7,660	560	2,310
Gross profit	2,756	252	1,542
20X6			
Revenue	10,299	2,869	3,292
Gross profit	3,055	1,411	2,204

Key performance indicators	Year ended 31 December	
	20X5	20X6
Gross profit margin	43.2%	40.5%
Operating profit margin	4.0%	2.5%
Revenue growth	6.7%	56.3%
Warranty costs as % of cost of sales	5.0%	8.0%
Research and development costs as % of revenue	9.8%	5.1%

47 Air Services UK Ltd (amended)

Air Services UK Ltd (ASU) is responsible for providing airspace management services to all airports and aircraft using UK airspace.

Company ownership

The company was originally a non-profit making government body. However, a number of years ago it was established as a limited company. ASU is 49% owned by the UK government and 51% privately owned. Private shareholders include several UK-based airlines and ASU staff. In the interests of national security, the government intends to retain its shareholding for the foreseeable future.

Operations

ASU's airspace management services comprise:

- **Air traffic control**

  ASU staff manage take-offs, landings and traffic in and around each UK airport. This is done from a control tower located at each airport.

- **In-flight navigation services**

  ASU is responsible for authorising access to all UK airspace and providing in-flight navigational guidance for aircraft over the UK. This is handled at ASU's two operational centres in the UK.

ASU's activities in the UK are licensed and regulated by the Civil Aviation Authority (CAA). The CAA ensures that the UK aviation industry treats consumers fairly, meets the highest safety and security standards and complies with environmental targets. The CAA, with the UK government, has committed to reducing aviation emissions.

ASU operates as a commercial company. It charges fees to the airports for managing their air traffic and to the airlines for its in-flight navigation services. Since ASU is in a monopoly situation, the CAA sets limits on the fees that ASU can charge.

Human resources

ASU operates 24 hours a day, 365 days of the year. The company employs 6,000 people comprising air traffic controllers, analysts, researchers and support staff. The majority were appointed when ASU was still a government body and have long-standing employment contracts. Up to 2,000 senior employees are expected to retire over the next 10 years (half of ASU's analysts and a third of its air traffic controllers).

Information technology

Timely and accurate management of data and information is vital for airports, airlines and air traffic control. Air traffic control systems are complex, integrating many diverse technologies, components and data. Technological developments play a key role in allowing the airline industry to meet operational efficiency and environmental targets.

Airports want to increase their capacity to handle flights, whilst maintaining safety and reducing operating costs and emissions. Airlines face high costs which are increased if there are flight delays and flight inefficiency. Effective air traffic control systems help airlines and airports to reduce costs by improving runway usage, reducing delays for inbound and outbound aircraft and designing more efficient flight routes. This also reduces the levels of emissions.

ASU has invested heavily in technology to allow better sharing of information. ASU's IT systems are connected across a wide range of organisations in different countries, with many users having real-time access. This enables controllers to manage high volumes of aircraft safely in crowded airspace, but presents increased cyber-security risks.

Through investment in research and development, ASU has developed expertise in managing unmanned aircraft systems (drones). Drones can pose a threat to air traffic management. ASU's innovative cloud-based system features cutting edge intelligent system design, as it is capable of capturing, analysing and responding to all available data about a drone's flight plans. The system monitors the drone in-flight and sends out electronic commands, where necessary, to redirect the drone or make it land immediately.

Suspected cyber-security incident

Recently there was a suspected hacking incident at one of ASU's operational centres. This occurred during a technical upgrade of the system responsible for airspace monitoring and aircraft control. ASU immediately shut down the system and implemented its business continuity plan. However, 300 flights were cancelled and 1,500 were delayed. After the incident, the CAA made ASU pay £7 million compensation to the airports and airlines affected.

A new global vision

Since the suspected cyber-security incident, ASU has appointed a new Chief Executive, Joan Louli. Joan previously led Germany's state-owned traffic control operation. She is keen to develop international revenue streams for ASU. Her stated vision is for ASU to become "the global leader in innovative airspace management."

Joan has set out the following three-year goals for the company:

- Achieve business growth by diversification
- Reduce the risk of accidents linked to airspace management
- Reduce emissions arising from inefficient airspace management
- Increase the efficiency of ASU's internal operations.

Joan has identified two specific international growth opportunities:

European airspace reorganisation

An agreement has been signed to reorganise Europe's airspace into nine blocks. ASU has been invited to tender to manage airspace within one or more of the blocks. Airspace management in most European countries is currently provided by state-owned operations. Joan believes that ASU's public-private ownership gives it a competitive advantage. Contracts will be awarded via a competitive tender process, based on four key criteria: safety, cost-efficiency, capacity management and environmental impact.

Drone traffic management

ASU has been asked to tender for a contract with the government of a Middle Eastern country to implement a drone traffic management service. ASU was approached after an incident involving a drone which closed the country's main airport for an hour.

Joan believes that ASU's ability to grow will depend on its information systems, its people and its ability to innovate. She wants to ensure that ASU has the right functional strategies in place to win the tenders and deliver these new contracts.

Requirements

47.1 Analyse the extent to which the three-year goals set out by Joan Louli are consistent with both her stated vision for ASU and the objectives of ASU's key stakeholders. **(10 marks)**

47.2 Explain the following two functional strategies that ASU could implement to achieve Joan Louli's stated vision:

- Human Resources (HR); and
- Research and Development (R&D). **(10 marks)**

47.3 Explain the cyber-security risks that ASU faces and how these risks can be managed.

(9 marks)

Total: 29 marks

48 Purechoc Ltd

Purechoc Ltd (Purechoc) is a family-owned business that makes premium chocolates and chocolate bars, on a small scale for a niche market. It was established three years ago by Marine Bernard and her brother Thomas. Purechoc has four UK shops, each managed by a member of the Bernard family, who are all directors (see **Exhibit**). Purechoc's share capital is owned as follows:

Marine	35%
Thomas	35%
Jonathan (Thomas's son)	15%
Anne (Marine's daughter)	15%

Over 80% of chocolate products sold in the UK are made by three dominant confectionery producers. Some of these businesses have attracted adverse publicity recently due to the way they source their cocoa and their treatment of cocoa producers in the supply chain. This has created an opportunity for businesses like Purechoc to exploit growing niche markets.

All Purechoc products are hand-made at each shop and are available in a wide range of exotic flavours. Instead of making products from pre-processed cocoa, Purechoc starts with high-quality, fair-trade cocoa beans from a single country of origin.

Purechoc sells only to individuals and not to supermarkets or other retailers. Its products are priced at about three times the price of standard chocolate confectionery. Purechoc shops have a loyal following of local customers, although Purechoc has done no marketing. It relies instead on word-of-mouth to generate business.

A large, American confectionery manufacturer, Koreto Inc (Koreto), has recently offered to acquire the entire share capital of Purechoc. Koreto's products are very popular in the USA but relatively unknown in the UK, and Koreto wants to enter the UK confectionery market. Marine Bernard is unwell and wishes to reduce her role in the business. As a result she wants to accept Koreto's offer for her shares.

If its offer is accepted, Koreto has promised that Purechoc will keep its brand identity and that the current board can run it as a semi-autonomous subsidiary. Koreto will provide funds to allow Purechoc to expand the number of shops. However, one of the terms of the offer is that Koreto would appoint a new Chief Executive to run Purechoc.

Jonathan and Anne do not want to sell their shares. However they recognise that opening four shops in three years has created a cashflow constraint. They have put forward an alternative proposal to resolve the constraint whilst retaining control of the growth of the business. This would involve expanding the number of shops by offering exclusive franchise agreements. Each franchisee would have the right to operate a Purechoc shop, and would be provided with the recipes to make and sell Purechoc products. Purechoc would receive an upfront franchise fee and commission based on sales revenue generated. Thomas however is concerned that franchising will destroy the unique and personal image of the Purechoc brand.

Requirements

Prepare a report for the directors that will help them to evaluate the two alternative proposals for the future of the Purechoc business: the sale of shares to Koreto Inc and the expansion by franchising.

Use the following headings:

48.1 Control
48.2 Risks
48.3 Strategic fit
48.4 Preliminary advice

Total: 26 marks

Exhibit: Directors and shareholders

- Marine (aged 58)

  Marine was the driving force behind setting up Purechoc. The business is currently her sole source of income and the proceeds from the sale of her shares in Purechoc will be her main source of funds in future.

- Thomas (aged 50)

  Thomas is married to a wealthy landowner and was happy to help provide initial capital for Marine to set up Purechoc. Thomas does not need income. He works in the business because of his family loyalty and his passion for Purechoc's products.

- Jonathan (aged 27)

  Jonathan joined Purechoc after completing a degree in business. He is entrepreneurial and has ambitious plans to create a larger, more successful business.

- Anne (aged 30)

  Before joining Purechoc, Anne worked for a large catering business but left because she wanted to be her own boss. She relies on the business as her main source of income.

49   Fullerton Office Furniture Ltd

The date is December 20X7.

Fullerton Office Furniture Ltd (FOF) manufactures office furniture which it sells to UK businesses and schools. It has a single factory, with administrative offices, in Birmingham.

Industry and market background

The office furniture industry manufactures a range of products including desks, chairs and shelving.

The UK market for office furniture in 20X7 is expected to be £560 million at wholesale prices (20X6: £544 million).The market has grown at 3% per annum for several years and this rate of growth is expected to continue.

There is significant competition, with 900 manufacturers in the UK, but only 300 of these have more than £1 million of annual sales revenue each. In addition to furniture sales, some larger manufacturers offer related services, such as office planning, interior design, project management, finance and storage.

Company background

FOF has two segments – Business and Schools – which operate as separate divisions, serving different markets. All furniture is made from wood and carries the FOF brand. FOF does not deal with retailers because it makes all its sales direct. FOF's existing Birmingham site is a central location for distribution to customers.

Forecast financial and operating data (**Exhibit**) are provided for the year ending
31 December 20X7.

The Business Segment

The Business Segment has customers of varying sizes located throughout the UK. Most customers make regular purchases every few years or, in some cases, every year. New Business Segment customers are a major source of long-term growth. However, sales to existing customers make up the majority of sales revenue, so relationship marketing is important. Sales are made either through the FOF website or via a direct sales team. The FOF website currently needs upgrading.

Prior to 20X7, sales prices were determined using fixed list prices, and direct sales staff were only paid fixed salaries. However, to increase revenue, from 1 January 20X7 FOF started to pay commission to sales staff of 3.5% of the revenue they generate, in addition to salary. Since 1 January 20X7, sales staff have also been permitted to offer discounts to all Business Segment customers of up to 5% off the fixed list price.

The Schools Segment

A local education authority (LEA) is the local government department responsible for schools in a given geographical area. An LEA has responsibility for purchases of furniture for schools under its control. Suppliers submit tenders for all school furniture purchases. The chief procurement officer in each LEA evaluates tenders and has significant discretion in deciding which furniture manufacturer is successful. In any one year, a single school has furniture provided by only one supplier.

Due to reductions in government expenditure, the total budget for school furniture purchases made by LEAs was lower in 20X7 compared with 20X6.

FOF's Schools Segment is headed by Trevor Williams. It has a small number of sales staff, but they are not paid commission. The Schools Segment sells only to the Birmingham LEA, which controlled 475 schools in both 20X6 and 20X7. In 20X7, FOF'sSchools Segment won tenders for 125 of the Birmingham LEA's schools (150 schools in 20X6).

The Schools Segment's main competitor is Educational Eco-fittings Ltd (EE) which, in 20X7, won tenders for 263 of the Birmingham LEA's schools (254 schools in 20X6). EE only sells furniture to schools. Ten smaller companies also supply furniture to the Birmingham LEA.

An increasing number of furniture items have been returned to FOF from schools in 20X7, compared with 20X6. A frequent cause of faults is the wood splitting. FOF's directors fear that the company's reputation is being damaged.

The directors are also concerned that the decline in performance of the Schools Segment is due to increasingly competitive conditions for tenders.

Operations and procurement

Schools Segment furniture differs from Business Segment furniture in style and quality, so they are made on separate production lines. The Business Segment production line uses good quality wood and modern, automated equipment. The Schools Segment production line uses lower quality wood and older production technology.

Wood from all FOF's suppliers is imported into the port of Liverpool, which is 150 kilometres north of the FOF factory, and is then transported by road to the FOF factory. Wood is delivered to FOF monthly. FOF's transport costs from Liverpool are £1,000 per month and are allocated equally between the two segments. FOF's suppliers pay the transport costs by sea to the port of Liverpool.

From 1 January 20X7, the Schools Segment started to buy wood from a new Estonian supplier at lower cost.

New premises

FOF has been negotiating to renew the lease for the Birmingham premises, which expires on 31 December 20X8. The current annual lease rental is £240,000. However, from 1 January 20X9, the owner is demanding a minimum 10-year term for a new lease agreement and a 50% increase in annual lease rentals.

FOF has found suitable alternative premises, but they are in Liverpool. The rentals would be £260,000 per annum for a five-year lease agreement.

The Liverpool premises are larger than the existing Birmingham premises. This would enable FOF to have additional office space and to introduce new design and production technology.

New technology

The new design technology would comprise an upgrade of the existing website plus an additional feature which would allow Business Segment customers to design their office layout and plan their furniture installations online. It would not be possible to charge customers more for this service, but it would enhance sales volumes for the Business Segment. It would also be possible for FOF to analyse and monitor customer activity using the design technology's data analytics package. This would provide data on customer usage regarding the timing and nature of website visits, which could then be used to forecast customers' furniture replacement decisions.

The new production technology would decrease variable costs on the Business Segment production line by £1.50 per furniture item, by reducing wastage and improving operating efficiency.

The additional costs for the new design and production technology together would be £180,000 per annum, excluding any allocation of the lease rental for the new premises.

Potential ethical issues

While visiting the Birmingham LEA on 10 November 20X7, Trevor Williams overheard a conversation between two LEA employees. The employees said that they believed the chief executive of EE had been providing free tickets for major sports events to Jayne Oliver, the LEA's chief procurement officer. The employees thought that, as a result, Jayne might have been favouring EE when awarding school tenders.

On 26 November 20X7, Trevor questioned Jayne about this issue during a business lunch. Jayne refused to answer his questions and said she would report Trevor to her line manager for attempting to intimidate her. Trevor has not received any further communication on this matter since the business lunch. Jayne is continuing to deal with FOF tenders, but her communications with Trevor are now limited to very formal emails. Previously Trevor and Jayne had been on good terms.

Requirements

49.1 Using the data and other information provided, analyse FOF's forecast performance in 20X7 compared with actual performance in 20X6 for:

(a) the Business Segment: and
(b) the Schools Segment.

Determine and explain, with supporting calculations, the key drivers of the change in operating profit for each segment. **(22 marks)**

49.2 Explain the factors to be considered by FOF in deciding between using the Birmingham premises or the Liverpool premises from 1 January 20X9. **(10 marks)**

49.3 Evaluate whether FOF should invest in the new design and production technology, assuming the company relocates to Liverpool. Provide supporting calculations. **(7 marks)**

49.4 Explain the potential ethical issues for Trevor and Jayne arising from the events described. Set out the actions that Trevor should now take. **(8 marks)**

Total: 47 marks

Exhibit: Financial and operating data for FOF

Financial data – years to 31 December

	Business Segment		Schools Segment	
	Forecast 20X7 £	Actual 20X6 £	Forecast 20X7 £	Actual 20X6 £
Sales	7,761,600	7,200,000	800,000	960,000
Fixed production costs	3,000,000	2,800,000	240,000	240,000
Variable production costs	3,484,800	2,880,000	240,000	307,200
Sales staff commissions	194,040	–	–	–
Returns inwards – costs	2,000	2,000	10,000	1,000
Administration expenses – fixed	250,000	250,000	100,000	100,000
Distribution costs				
Fixed (inward – wood from Liverpool)	6,000	6,000	6,000	6,000
Variable (outward – furniture to customers)	633,600	576,000	16,000	19,200
Operating profit	**191,160**	**686,000**	**188,000**	**286,600**

Operating data

	Business Segment		Schools Segment	
	Forecast 20X7	Actual 20X6	Forecast 20X7	Actual 20X6
Total number of items sold	79,200	72,000	16,000	19,200
Number of business customers	300	320	-	-
Number of new business customers	12	18	-	-
Total sales to new business customers	£480,000	£756,000	-	-
Number of school tenders won	-	-	125	150
Distribution costs outward per item	£8	£8	£1	£1

Working assumption

Sales revenue and sales volumes in the Business Segment would have been the same in 20X7 as in 20X6 if the new policy of offering discounts to customers and paying commissions to sales staff had not been introduced.

50 Berlina Kitchen Appliances

The date is December 20X7.

Berlina Kitchen Appliances (BKA) manufactures electrical appliances for use in domestic kitchens.

Company history

BKA was established over 50 years ago as a government-owned business in Ruritania, Eastern Europe.

For many years, most Ruritanian industries were owned by the government and there was limited international trade. As a result, almost all of BKA's revenue was generated from sales within Ruritania to government-owned retail organisations. These sales were under long-term contracts, which gave financial stability to BKA.

Internally, BKA operated a hierarchical and centralised organisational structure with a rigid control system.

Current operations

BKA has one site in Ruritania where it makes washing machines, tumble dryers, refrigerators and cookers. Each of the four products is made on a separate production line. In total, 1.2 million units are produced annually, in equal proportions for each type of product.

BKA's major competitor, Muskov, sells similar products to BKA. Until the end of 20X6 all the sales of both companies were within Ruritania.

Acquisition of BKA

From 20X6, following a change of government, there has been a movement towards free market liberalisation of the Ruritanian economy and a desire to open up to international trade by encouraging foreign direct investment into Ruritania.

In May 20X7 the Ruritanian government sold BKA's assets to Stigel GmbH (Stigel), an international electrical appliances manufacturer which sells high quality products and is headquartered in Germany. Due to rising production costs in Germany, Stigel's board wanted to acquire a factory in a low-cost environment, but with the ultimate aim of achieving the same high production quality in the acquired factory as in its German factories.

Stigel appointed a new chief executive of BKA, Jurgen Muller. He immediately reviewed BKA's business and operations, and found the following:

- Production technology is old and inefficient.

- All components are purchased from other Ruritanian companies or are made by BKA.

- BKA's sales have fallen significantly since the end of 20X6, as many expiring long-term government contracts have not been renewed.

- BKA's existing products are difficult to sell internationally as they are of poor quality and design compared with international standards in the industry.

- Employee wages are about 40% of the amounts typically paid in the industry outside Ruritania.

- BKA's management and factory employees have a continuing culture of resistance to change.

Change management plan

Jurgen drew up a change management plan which includes the following:

- Each of the four products will be operated as a separate division, with more autonomy given to new divisional heads. Divisions' performance will be measured as profit centres.

- To help set achievable goals for the change management plan, a benchmarking exercise will be carried out to compare BKA's processes, products and performance with best practice.

- Following the benchmarking exercise, critical success factors (CSFs) and key performance indicators (KPIs) will be set for a new performance measurement system for BKA. The target for each KPI will change each year to reflect expected improvements (**Exhibit**).

- There will be continuing investment over time to modernise production, but this will be conditional on achieving the KPI targets. Any division not achieving them may be closed.

- The number of units produced per employee will increase significantly.

- The short-term aim will be to use the low-cost Ruritanian environment to make products which are capable of being sold internationally under the BKA brand.

- From 1 January 20X8, Stigel's German factories will supply BKA with some major components (eg, washing machine motors) to achieve an immediate improvement in quality.

The long-term aim, at the end of the change management plan's implementation, will be to have high quality standards so that products manufactured in Ruritania will be of the same quality as those manufactured in Germany. These high-quality products will then be branded with Stigel's trademark and sold internationally.

Jurgen has proposed that the plan should be implemented in stages over a five-year period from 1 January 20X8. However, one of his fellow directors has counter-proposed that the whole plan should be implemented rapidly, and should be completed within two years.

Requirements

50.1 Identify appropriate types of benchmarks for BKA, providing examples. Explain how BKA may benefit from the use of each type of benchmark. **(9 marks)**

50.2 Critically appraise the proposed performance measurement system for BKA (Exhibit), and suggest alternative KPIs, where appropriate, for each CSF. Assume that the CSFs have been agreed. **(11 marks)**

50.3 In respect of the change management plan, explain:

(a) the factors that the board should consider when choosing between staged implementation (over five years) and rapid implementation (over two years); and

(b) the cultural and personnel barriers to change that are likely to arise, describing how their effects might be mitigated. **(11 marks)**

Total: 31 marks

Exhibit:
Performance measurement system for the three years ending 31 December 20X9

Agreed CSFs	KPI	Expected achievement for 20X7	Target for 20X8	Target for 20X9
Customer satisfaction	Proportion of customers responding to questionnaires as overall being 'satisfied' or 'very satisfied'.	72%	90%	95%
Production quality	Proportion of products reported as faulty in the first year after sale.	18%	10%	5%
Penetration of international markets	Proportion of sales outside Ruritania.	2%	10%	30%

Note: The targets for 20X8 and 20X9 assume a staged implementation of the change management plan over five years.

---

51 Cancer Concern Ltd

The date is December 20X7.

Cancer Concern Ltd (CC) is a not-for-profit, UK-based charity.

Background information

CC was established over 20 years ago as a charitable trust. Its board of trustees has ultimate responsibility for governing and managing CC. CC uses available funds to support its two main charitable activities:

(1) **Cancer research**

CC supports specific research projects in universities and hospitals in the UK which are aimed at the prevention, diagnosis and treatment of cancer. CC awards funds only to established cancer research groups for projects with specific objectives and timescales. Amounts awarded range from £30,000 to £1 million per project. Awarded funds are normally released in stages over the period of the project, and the release of later payments is subject to annual progress reviews. There have been some project successes, but also many failed projects.

(2) **Hospices**

CC operates 10 hospices which provide expert care for terminally ill cancer patients and support for their families. Hospices are staffed by volunteers and by medical professionals employed by CC.

Restrictions on CC raising funds

CC's income comes from gifts from individuals, events, grants and other types of fundraising. Total income for the year ended 30 September 20X7 was £164.2 million (£188.3 million in the year ended 30 September 20X6). New government regulations restricting some types of charitable marketing mean this lower level of income is expected to continue in future.

Restrictions on CC's use of funds

When giving to CC, some individuals specify that the funds must be used for a particular activity (eg, a specific hospice). These funds are 'restricted' and can be used only for the specific charitable activity specified by the individuals.

Other funds received by CC are 'unrestricted' and therefore trustees have discretion to use these for any projects or causes within the broad activities of cancer research and hospices. CC's policy has been to split the unrestricted funds equally between these two main charitable activities.

A charity's trustees must choose between allocating available funds to current charitable activities or retaining some funds as reserves, to maintain financial stability and to use for future charitable activities.

CC has limited reserves and therefore, given the reduction in income in the year ended 30 September 20X7, its trustees must choose how much it allocates to each of its two main charitable activities. It must also choose which specific projects within each of these activities should suffer cuts.

Review of CC's strategy and mission

As a result of the funding reduction and restrictions, the trustees are reviewing CC's strategy and mission, but this has caused conflict amongst trustees and between stakeholders.

CC's current mission statement is: "To find cures for cancer and to care for those suffering from cancer".

All CC trustees agree that this mission statement is too short to be useful and does not help in determining priorities for future fund allocations to be made by CC. In addition, it does not recognise the impact of the financial constraints being faced by CC.

The CC trustees agree that a new and more detailed mission statement must be produced. This will be used to help determine a new strategy and new fund allocation priorities.

Requirements

51.1 Prepare a report for the CC trustees which:

    (a)   describes the potential impact on relevant stakeholder groups arising from CC reducing its allocation of funds to its main charitable activities; and

    (b)   explains the factors that the CC trustees should consider in deciding how much to allocate to each of its main charitable activities. **(14 marks)**

51.2 Prepare a revised mission statement for CC. This should identify CC's key purposes and values. It should also recognise the impact of financial constraints.

    Justify your revisions of the existing mission statement. **(8 marks)**

Total: 22 marks

March 2018 exam questions

52 Just Houses Ltd

The date is March 20X8.

Just Houses Ltd (JH) is a residential estate agency in North West England.

UK estate agency industry

A residential estate agency (the agency) acts on behalf of a person (the seller) who wishes to sell a property such as a house or apartment. The agency estimates the market value of the property, agrees with the seller the price at which it should be marketed (the asking price), advertises the property for sale and sends an agency employee to accompany potential buyers to view it. Once a buyer is found, the agency assists with price negotiations between the seller and buyer. The agency receives payment for these services from the seller, in the form of commission based on the final selling price of the property.

Agencies are regulated in the UK by the Estate Agents Act, which aims to ensure that agents act in the best interests of sellers, and that both buyers and sellers are treated honestly and fairly. Agencies must also comply with money laundering legislation. Agency employees are not currently required by UK law to be either licensed or formally qualified. However many employees belong to a professional body and must comply with that body's code of professional ethics.

Traditional estate agency model

The traditional model for an estate agency is to operate from several retail outlets (branches). As well as administrative staff, each branch has several employees who provide services to sellers in a relatively small geographical area. These employees receive an element of performance-related pay. The estate agency industry is highly fragmented. There are some well-known national agencies with branches across the UK. There are also many local, independent agencies and the average agency has only two branches.

In the last ten years technology has led to rapid changes in the estate agency industry in the form of online agencies and online advertising.

Online agencies

There are 35 online agencies in the UK. It is estimated that they will represent sellers in 15% of UK property sales during 20X8. Online agencies charge sellers a fixed fee, regardless of the value of the property, and are significantly cheaper than traditional agencies. An online agency values the property and lists it for sale on its own website. Sellers can monitor the progress of their sale online and buyers can undertake virtual tours of each property, reducing the need for accompanied visits. However online agencies do not provide face-to-face services and may lack the local knowledge of a traditional estate agency.

Online advertising on property portals

When looking for a property, buyers prefer to have all available properties listed in one place, rather than accessing multiple sources of information. 95% of buyers start their search by viewing properties advertised for sale on one of two online property portals: Pozla and Nextstep. These provide an advertising service to estate agencies by listing residential properties for sale on their portals. They use large databases to provide additional market intelligence but do not themselves offer estate agency services. The estate agency industry typically spends half of its advertising budget on listing properties with Pozla and Nextstep.

JH business model

JH was set up by Jaini Haldar and is owned and operated by the Haldar family. It is a traditional estate agency with seven branches, located in major towns, and a central office. The branches deal primarily with the sale of residential properties, for which JH charges the seller a commission of 1.5% of the final selling price. JH also offers services relating to rental properties. People who choose JH to sell their houses typically live within 25 kilometres of the relevant JH branch. JH's branch and office premises are leased.

JH markets each property for sale by displaying property details in the relevant branch and on its own website, distributing brochures and paying to advertise in local newspapers and on local radio. It does not advertise with Pozla or Nextstep.

JH's level of completed property sales has been declining, due in part to political and economic uncertainty which has affected both sellers and buyers. In 20X7 JH's commission revenue and profits reduced as a result, although this decline was not consistent across all its branches.

Branch closure criteria

The JH directors are considering whether to save costs by closing the two worst performing branches. They have decided to use commission revenue and operating profit margin as the closure criteria and branches A and B have been selected for possible closure on this basis. Performance data for the year ended 31 December 20X7 are included in the **Exhibit**.

Strategic alliance

Jaini's daughter, Rebecca, is one of JH's youngest directors. Rebecca believes that JH has failed to embrace the changes in technology which are challenging the traditional industry model. She has suggested a strategic alliance between JH and OurCasa Ltd (OurCasa), a small online agency that recently started trading.

OurCasa charges sellers a fixed fee of £650 to register, advertise and sell a property via its website. Once a seller has registered, an OurCasa employee values the property using available online data about the property's location. The employee also visits it to record details (eg, size, age, layout) and take photos and videos to produce a virtual tour. The details and tour are then posted on OurCasa's website. Potential buyers can ask to view a property or make offers to buy a property by emailing OurCasa. OurCasa passes these requests to the seller by email. OurCasa does not organise viewings or negotiate the final sale on the seller's behalf.

Rebecca said:

> "Our knowledge and expertise in our local property market is no longer enough to persuade sellers to use JH. We don't have the capital to launch an online agency ourselves, and our IT expertise is limited, so an alliance with OurCasa is the best way forward. We will be able to list all of our sellers' properties on the OurCasa website, which offers an online service 24 hours a day. In return we will provide traditional estate agency services to support OurCasa in introducing a new "premium sales package" for its properties in our local area. Sellers will pay OurCasa a fixed fee of £1,250 per property, which will include accompanied viewings and assistance in price negotiations. OurCasa will retain £750 of this fee and pay the rest to JH for the support we provide. OurCasa have given us first refusal but plan to talk to other agents if we reject these terms."

Ethical issue

You are the financial controller at JH. You overheard a JH employee, Sarah, who is a member of a professional body, talking to her brother Jim about a customer's property sale that she is handling. Jim is a local property developer. He wants to buy the property but is in competition with Vera, a private individual who wishes to buy it. JH's customer wants to achieve the highest price so Jim and Vera have been asked to submit confidential offers to JH, in writing, indicating the maximum price each is prepared to pay. Jim told Sarah that he will pay an additional 1%

commission to JH if Sarah tells him the price submitted by Vera. This will allow Jim to submit a higher price and ensure that his offer is accepted.

Requirements

52.1 Analyse the barriers to entry that exist in the estate agency industry and explain the impact that technology has had on these. **(8 marks)**

52.2 Using the data in the Exhibit and the other information provided, evaluate the comparative operating and financial performance of branches A and B in 20X7. Provide an initial assessment of whether JH should close either branch, identifying any further information or closure criteria that would assist the directors in making this decision. **(19 marks)**

52.3 Discuss the advantages and disadvantages for JH of the proposed strategic alliance with OurCasa. **(10 marks)**

52.4 Explain the potential ethical issues arising for you, Sarah and JH as a result of the conversation that you overheard, and recommend appropriate actions. **(8 marks)**

Total: 45 marks

Exhibit: JH performance data for year ended 31 December 20X7

Financial data	JH Total £'000	Average JH Branch £'000	Branch A (note 1) £'000	Branch B (note 2) £'000
Total value of completed property sales (based on final selling price)	240,000	34,286	24,500	28,100
Commission revenue (1.5% of completed property sales value)	3,600	514	368	422
Revenue from other services	1,200	171	170	140
Total revenue	4,800	685	538	562
Branch costs	(2,900)	(414)	(326)	(408)
Central office costs	(700)	(100)	(100)	(100)
Operating profit	**1,200**	**171**	**112**	**54**

Operating data	JH Total	Average JH Branch	Branch A (note 1)	Branch B (note 2)
Number of employees	47 (*)	6	5	7
Number of properties sold in year	660	94	70	84
Number of initial enquiries from potential sellers	1,200	171	225	153
Average time taken to sell a property (weeks)	15	15	12	18
Number of accompanied viewings	7,920	1,131	675	1,176
Final selling price as a % of original asking price	93%	93%	94%	89%

(*) includes five central office staff

Notes

1 Branch A is located in a town with a population of 180,000 people. The town has a university and is home to the regional headquarters of a major bank.

2 Branch B is located in a town by the sea with a population of 140,000 people. The town was popular as a holiday destination for many years, but its economy has suffered due to the rising popularity of foreign holidays. A significant number of people living in the town are retired.

53   Bagaj Lux Ltd

The date is March 20X8.

Bagaj Lux Ltd (BL) designs and manufactures luxury luggage (leather bags and suitcases) at its UK factory, located in South West England.

Company information

BL sells luggage through its website to customers around the world, who order and pay online using a debit or credit card.

BL luggage is instantly recognisable because all items are made from leather which is printed with the distinctive BL logo. Each item fastens with a buckle, strap and lock. Product designs are frequently updated but remain very distinctive.

BL sources the very best leather from a single supplier in Belgium, which dyes it by hand and then prints it. All additional components (buckles, straps, locks) are supplied by a Turkish company.

BL's luggage production process at its factory is very labour intensive. Highly skilled craftspeople cut, stitch and finish each item by hand. At full capacity the factory can produce 600 items per week. Inventory of finished luggage is kept to a minimum because most items are only made after the customer has placed an order. BL luggage sells for between £1,200 and £1,500 per item and BL makes an average 48% gross profit margin. Because BL luggage is in demand, customers are normally willing to wait up to three months for delivery. All BL luggage is guaranteed for life and BL offers an after-care service whereby customers can send their luggage back to the factory for any repairs.

BL places great emphasis on the fact that its luggage is "hand-made in England" and customers are willing to pay premium prices for this distinctive feature. BL offers a range of styles and colours but in limited quantities to maintain the image of exclusivity.

Marketing is a significant expense. In addition to TV, radio and print advertising, BL uses a range of product placement strategies and upmarket promotions. Demand for BL's luggage has increased following a recent rise in its popularity amongst celebrity internet bloggers, and also due to a direct competitor receiving adverse publicity after a hacking incident in which customer details were stolen.

BL outsources distribution to an international logistics company, Pello Ltd (Pello). Finished luggage is sent directly from BL's factory to Pello's UK warehouse, and from there to appropriate global distribution centres. In the UK, Pello employs a dedicated team responsible for the BL contract who provide value-added services, such as pre-wrapping and care-label tagging, before despatching the items. Pello's information systems are fully integrated with BL's, so Pello can view customers' orders and provide real-time reporting on deliveries. Pello's distribution operations are regularly inspected by BL to ensure that they comply with BL's strict quality and security standards.

Competition

Competition in the luxury luggage market consists of:

- two global companies that produce luggage for a range of market segments

- several well-known manufacturers of luxury goods that make luxury luggage as one of their many product ranges

- many smaller independent businesses, such as BL, that focus on the luxury luggage segment only.

New contract

BL has recently been asked to tender for a contract to design and supply two flight bags for each member of the cabin crew of Taraf Air Ltd (Taraf). Taraf is a global airline specialising in luxury travel. The contract would run for two years from 1 May 20X8 and would require BL to supply 4,500 bags during the contract period. The bags would use lower quality leather and fastenings from new suppliers but would still be printed with the BL logo.

To help BL's sales director decide what price to quote for the new contract, the production director has prepared the following cost estimate:

- Each flight bag requires one metre of leather in total, of two different types: 60% of the leather would be purchased at a price of £95 per metre, and the remainder would be purchased at a price of £105 per metre.

- Labour and other variable costs would be £185 per bag and the additional components would cost £26 per bag.

- BL normally recovers fixed production overheads at a rate of 50% of the total variable cost for each item of luggage. The production director estimates that fixed production costs would increase by £405,000 per annum as a result of the new contract.

Requirements

53.1 Explain how the key elements of BL's value chain support its competitive strategy. You are not required to draw a value chain diagram. **(10 marks)**

53.2 Identify and explain the key cyber-security risks that BL faces and suggest how these risks can be managed. **(8 marks)**

53.3 Explain the financial and non-financial factors that BL should consider in deciding whether to tender for the new contract with Taraf. Show relevant supporting calculations.

(12 marks)

Total: 30 marks

54 Jacmel Products plc

Jacmel Products plc (Jacmel) produces disposable pens and razors. It operates in the USA and Europe. Jacmel sells to retail outlets such as supermarkets, pharmacies, convenience stores and shops that sell stationery and office supplies. Jacmel's products aim both to meet a specific consumer need and to perform a specific function, and are offered at highly competitive prices for the quality provided.

Products are carefully designed to include only essential features. They are mass-produced in huge volumes by two factories, one in Europe and one in the USA. Packaging is minimal and products are sold in multipacks, with pens packaged in boxes of 10 units and razors in bags of five units. The pens and razors are not refillable so the products have a limited life.

Jacmel's products have typically appealed to average-income consumers in Europe and the USA. However these markets are maturing and Jacmel has attracted criticism for producing disposable products that are not sustainable. At Jacmel's latest board meeting this criticism was rejected by Tom Sykes, the chief executive, who stated:

> "Our products are sustainable. They offer long-lasting performance with more than two kilometres of writing for a pen, and at least 10 shaves for a razor. Since they are designed with no superfluous parts or features, they require a minimum of raw materials and packaging.

> "The problem we have though is that consumers in our existing markets are becoming increasingly demanding. We need to look elsewhere for markets that are at a different point in their lifecycle."

Jacmel has two product divisions, Pens and Razors. Each division has a management team, led by a general manager who is responsible for manufacturing and marketing the product on a global basis. Tom wants to target new markets in developing economies, starting with East Africa. To allow Jacmel to respond to the needs of both its existing and new markets, Tom wants to change the organisational structure to a matrix. This would be organised by geography (Europe, USA, East Africa) and by product (pens and razors).

In the new markets, Jacmel pens and razors will typically be purchased by lower income consumers from small local kiosks and stalls, so Jacmel will need to adapt its products to make them even more basic and affordable. Products may have to be packaged in single or double unit packs rather than multipacks.

Tom commented to the board:

> "We have performed data analytics on consumer preferences in our existing markets but I am not sure that this sort of desk research is going to help much with our new markets. We need to think about how we can get better information to target our marketing efforts successfully."

Requirements

Prepare a report for the directors of Jacmel to include the following:

54.1 In relation to the proposed change in organisational structure:

- Discuss the benefits and problems of the proposed matrix structure.

- Explain the challenges that Jacmel may face from its managers in implementing the change to the new organisational structure. **(12 marks)**

54.2 To assist Jacmel in developing a marketing strategy for the new markets:

- Explain the factors Jacmel should take into account when deciding on appropriate market research.

- Discuss how Jacmel's marketing mix can be developed to take account of the ways in which the new markets differ from the existing ones. **(13 marks)**

Total: 25 marks

June 2018 exam questions

55 Ten Ten Burgers Inc

The date is June 20X8.

Ten Ten Burgers Inc (TTB) is a US-based restaurant chain specialising in high-quality burgers.

Company background

TTB was established by two friends who opened a restaurant in New York over 30 years ago selling burgers made with high-quality, fresh beef, cooked to order and eaten in comfortable, good quality surroundings.

The TTB business model proved popular and the company expanded throughout the US, with over 750 restaurants by 20X4 in prime, city centre locations.

Expansion into the UK: TTB board meeting – September 20X5

TTB's board held a meeting in September 20X5 to discuss expansion outside the US.

The marketing director said: "We have agreed that we do not want to open more restaurants in the US for now. If we are to continue to grow, we need to develop the brand internationally, but the TTB brand is not known outside the US, which adds to the risks. It will not be easy, as other countries have different cultures and tastes, but I suggest we start by expanding in the UK."

The operations director offered some ideas: "We should manage risks by expanding using a mixture of owned and franchised restaurants. Operating in the UK lets us experiment with a new business model in this way."

The IT director added: "We can also experiment in the UK with our new app, called the 'Lima'. I believe this will show us how to improve marketing and the efficiency of operations in all markets."

The board agreed that expansion outside the US would start in the UK, by opening a separate division, TTB UK, and that a 10% return on investment would be required.

Progress: TTB UK board meeting – June 20X8

A meeting of the TTB UK board in June 20X8 reviewed the first two years of UK operations, during which time:

- four restaurants opened on 1 April 20X6, all owned by TTB UK

- a further six restaurants opened on 1 April 20X7, four of which were franchised and two owned

- the Lima app operated from 1 April 20X7.

The IT director presented some quarterly data for the year ended 31 March 20X8 which was extracted from the Lima app, along with some notes on its use (**Exhibit 1**).

The finance director presented financial data for the two years ended 31 March 20X8 (**Exhibit 2**) and information on the franchise agreements (**Exhibit 3**).

At the meeting, the directors started to evaluate whether to expand in the UK in future using franchised restaurants only.

Requirements

55.1 Explain, using Exhibit 1, how the information captured by the Lima app can be used by TTB UK to:

- increase revenues; and
- improve operating efficiency   **(8 marks)**

55.2 Using all the Exhibits:

- compare and evaluate the performance of owned restaurants and franchised restaurants for the year ended 31 March 20X8;

- evaluate and explain the performance of TTB UK in the year ended 31 March 20X8 compared with the year ended 31 March 20X7; and

- evaluate the effect of the Lima app on revenue, so far as the information permits.
  (27 marks)

55.3 Explain the factors to be considered by TTB UK in deciding whether to expand further within the UK by opening:

- new franchised restaurants; or
- owned restaurants.   **(9 marks)**

Total: 44 marks

Exhibit 1: The Lima app

TTB developed an application (the Lima app) that can be used by customers on smartphones and tablets. From 1 April 20X7, the Lima app was made available to TTB customers in the UK. Customers consent to provide their basic details (name, gender, age, job, address, email address) before they can download the app.

TTB customers access the Lima app to place an order for a meal and book a table at a specified restaurant (subject to availability) up to 20 minutes before the specified time of arrival. Payment must be made, using the app, at the time of booking. This means that the meal and a table are ready for the customer on arrival, thereby reducing waiting times.

Tables are allocated by an algorithm to ensure maximum usage. As payment is made in advance, nearly all customers take up their bookings.

The marketing slogan associated with the app is: "Quality burgers, faster than fast food".

After every meal, the Lima app awards the customer electronic credits which give a discount off the full (ie, gross) menu price of the next booking. This encourages customers to return in future. Credits can be time-limited or restricted to use at non-peak times. They can also be tailored to individual customers' basic details (age, gender, job, location) or to their historic spending characteristics (total spend, number of people in their group, time taken to eat a meal).

Customers can give feedback on their TTB experience on social media accessed through the Lima app. In return, they are awarded extra credits.

TTB UK plans to increase, over time, both full menu prices and the value of credits awarded by the app. This will allow TTB UK to implement a flexible pricing policy, based on knowledge of individual customers or attributes of types of customer groups.

Reminders and special offers can also be sent to customers using the app once their spending patterns are established.

Customers who visit TTB restaurants without accessing the Lima app must pay the full menu prices. They must also wait to obtain a table and for meals to be cooked to order.

Lima app – quarterly data for the year ended 31 March 20X8

	Three months ending			
	30 June 20X7	30 Sept 20X7	31 Dec 20X7	31 March 20X8
Number of times downloaded app accessed	68,000	166,667	196,154	194,286
Number of meals ordered via the app	27,200	66,667	78,462	77,714
Value of sales made via the app (before credits)	£272,000	£680,000	£816,000	£816,000
Total value of credits awarded to app users	£13,600	£40,800	£57,120	£65,280
Average full price of a meal	£10.00	£10.20	£10.40	£10.50

Lima app data relates to all UK restaurants, owned and franchised.

Exhibit 2: Financial data

Franchisees retain net profits, after paying fees to TTB UK.

Performance of TTB UK restaurants – for years ended 31 March

	20X7	20X8	
	Owned	Owned	Franchised
Number of restaurants	4	6	4
	£	£	£
Revenue	4,000,000	6,480,000	4,400,000
Operating profit	360,000	960,000	660,000
Fees paid to TTB UK:			
- Fixed			(120,000)
- Variable			(440,000)
Net profit retained by franchisees			100,000

TTB UK: total income – for years ended 31 March

	20X7	20X8
	£	£
Fees from franchised restaurants:		
- Fixed (as above)		120,000
- Variable (as above)		440,000
Costs incurred by TTB UK in respect of franchises (see Exhibit 3)		(200,000)
Net operating profit from franchised restaurants		360,000
Operating profit from owned restaurants (as above)	360,000	960,000
Total operating profit	**360,000**	**1,320,000**

Impact of the Lima app

TTB's marketing team has estimated that revenue per restaurant for the year ended 31 March 20X8 would have been 5% lower if the Lima app had not been available.

> **Exhibit 3: TTB UK franchise agreements**
>
> Four 10-year franchises were set up in the UK on 1 April 20X7.
>
> The average total cost of setting up a TTB UK restaurant (whether owned or franchised) is £400,000 for property, fixtures and fittings. For franchised restaurants, this is paid for by the franchisee.
>
> TTB UK charges each franchisee, per restaurant, a fixed annual fee and a variable fee which is a percentage of annual revenue. The same terms regarding fees apply to every franchisee.
>
> In return, the franchisee is permitted to operate using the TTB brand name and to benefit from the Lima app, national advertising and operational support.
>
> The annual franchising costs incurred by TTB UK of £200,000, are for running the franchise, providing management support, running systems including the Lima app and marketing on behalf of franchisees.
>
> Franchisees must comply with the terms of the franchise arrangement so TTB can protect its reputation.
>
> Franchisees must purchase all ingredients for meals from TTB and can offer only TTB's standard menu. Franchisees must charge at least the full menu price, unless credits awarded by the Lima app apply.

56 Maya plc

Maya plc (Maya) is a chemical company with global operations, which is listed on the London Stock Exchange.

Company background

Maya currently has three operating divisions: Pharmaceutical, Industrial and Personal. Each operating division has multiple locations throughout the world.

All the operating divisions are supported by a centralised research and development (R&D) division in the UK, which develops innovative new products and processes. The R&D division is a profit centre and makes an internal charge to operating divisions based on the sales of the products it has developed.

New Agrochemicals division

A recent research project by the R&D division had an unexpected outcome in developing an innovative new chemical, Vardex, which is suitable for use in agriculture. Robust scientific testing in the Maya laboratories has shown that Vardex significantly increases agricultural productivity for a range of food crops. It also enhances crop protection from a wide variety of diseases and pests.

Initial laboratory testing suggests that Vardex is an important agrochemical which is superior to products being offered by other agrochemical companies.

The Maya board held a strategy meeting and agreed, in principle, to set up a new operating division, Agrochemicals, in South America.

Despite great enthusiasm for Vardex, however, the meeting identified two problems:

(1)   Agrochemicals, including Vardex, do not fit into the business models of any of Maya's existing three divisions.

(2)   Although Vardex has been shown to be effective in laboratory tests, it has not yet been demonstrated as effective on large commercial farms. This means there are likely to be initial credibility problems with potential customers.

Developing a business plan for Agrochemicals

The purpose of the Agrochemicals division will be to produce, market and distribute agrochemical products for the protection of crops and the enhancement of agricultural productivity.

Initially, Vardex will be the Agrochemicals division's only product, but other new agrochemical products will be developed by R&D.

The Maya board appointed a planning team to set up the new Agrochemicals division and develop a business plan for the production, marketing and distribution of Vardex.

The board provided the planning team with background information to assist in preparing the business plan (**Exhibit**). It emphasised that, before Maya would provide investment funds to the Agrochemicals division to finance the Vardex venture, the business plan should:

- evaluate whether the new division will be successful
- present a balanced, objective appraisal.

You work in the planning team for the new Agrochemicals division.

Requirements

Prepare the following sections of the business plan required by the Maya board.

56.1 **Risks**

Explain the risks of operating the new Agrochemicals division and describe appropriate actions for mitigation of each risk.

Note: Ignore the possibility of a strategic alliance. **(11 marks)**

56.2 **Supply chain management**

Explain the factors to consider in choosing either Veng or Gomex as sole suppliers, or using both in a dual supplier arrangement. **(11 marks)**

56.3 **Strategy**

Analyse whether Maya should set up the Agrochemicals division in South America:

- as an independent operation; or
- through a strategic alliance with AMB.

Provide a reasoned recommendation. **(11 marks)**

Total: 33 marks

Exhibit: Background information for preparation of the business plan

The Vardex agrochemical

Evidence indicates that Vardex is most effective in protecting crops in warmer climates.

Food production can be enhanced by Vardex, thereby improving the quality and quantity of food supplies in both poor and rich countries.

Location

The board wants to investigate the desirability of establishing the Agrochemicals division in South America, possibly in Brazil.

The board believes that labour costs and other production costs will be lower in South America than in the UK. R&D activity will remain centralised in the UK.

Customers

Markets for Vardex will be in warmer climates globally. Because it is a bulky agrochemical, distribution costs for Vardex will increase in proportion to the distance between the sites where it is used and where it is produced.

The major customers for Vardex will be large commercial farms and wholesale distributors of agrochemicals.

Suppliers

A rare chemical, HaDx, is required to make Vardex. This can be obtained from only a few suppliers. One possible supplier is Veng, which is a current supplier of other products to Maya's Industrial division, and is based in Europe. Veng's products and lead times are known to be reliable, but its prices are high.

An alternative supplier of HaDx is Gomez, which is based in South America. Maya has not dealt directly with Gomez before. The board believes Gomez has reasonable prices but long, variable lead times and product quality that is, very occasionally, very poor. HaDx cannot be stored for more than six weeks. It cannot be transported by air economically.

A potential strategic alliance

Initial discussions have taken place with a South American company, AMB, regarding a potential strategic alliance with Maya's new Agrochemicals division.

AMB is a well-established company, based in Brazil, which makes agricultural machinery. It makes sales throughout South America to large commercial farms.

Whilst no agreement has been finalised, the following have been identified as possible elements of any strategic alliance between Maya and AMB:

- Maya will locate next to AMB's existing production site in Brazil, using surplus land owned by AMB. Maya will construct a new factory on this land and buy the plant and equipment for Vardex production in Brazil.

- AMB will provide introductions to its existing customers (ie, large commercial farms) to help Maya market Vardex.

- Profits will be shared between Maya and AMB in respect of sales of Vardex within South America. The profit share ratio is still to be negotiated. Maya will keep all the profits from sales of Vardex outside South America.

The initial agreement will be for a four-year period, which may be extended if both parties agree.

57 Muple plc

The date is June 20X8.

Muple plc (Muple) is a retailer which owns a chain of large consumer technology stores. Each store has three separate departments, selling:

- mobile phones, tablets and communications equipment
- entertainment equipment
- software and computers.

Scheduling staff time

A major proportion of Muple's costs are labour costs. Department managers are responsible for scheduling staff time. The schedule varies daily so there are sufficient staff on duty in the stores to deal with customers who require advice and to complete sales transactions.

When scheduling staff time, there have been problems matching the number of staff on duty with the number of customers in the store, leading regularly to both over-staffing and under-staffing.

A technology solution

Pergola Ltd (Pergola) has approached Muple with a technology solution, Sensorex, for staff scheduling. Sensorex provides predictive data analytics to measure, and help retailers forecast, in-store customer traffic using video, audio and mobile 'fingerprinting' to capture customer movements.

Sensors are installed throughout a store to capture data. The following data was captured in a pilot test for one Muple store for one week in May 20X8:

- **Footfall**: the number of customers entering the store. This varied between 975 people per hour at 13:00 on Saturday afternoon, to 128 people per hour at 09:00 on Monday morning.

- **Dwell time**: the time a customer spends in the store. This varied between 90 minutes at 12:30 on Sunday lunchtime, to 24 minutes at 16:00 on Tuesday afternoon.

- **Conversion rate**: the volume of sales transactions as a percentage of the footfall (calculated by the data analytics package). This varied from 31% on Saturday to 44% on Wednesday.

The above data can be reported to management minute by minute in real time using a data dashboard of key information. Footfall and dwell time can also be measured separately for each department within a store.

The data can be used to forecast customer volumes and hence staffing needs in each department on an hour by hour basis.

Sensorex can also be used to improve Muple's response to forecasts of real-time staffing needs. Using smartphones, staff can link to a scheduling system within Sensorex then, in real time, indicate their short-term availability to work or change their indicated availability to work.

If there is an unexpected surge in customers in a department, then staff who are shown as indicating availability can be quickly called in to work, or can be transferred from less busy departments to meet customer demand.

Discussions are continuing between Muple and Pergola, but no agreement has yet been reached. A three-year agreement for Pergola to supply Sensorex to Muple is one possible outcome.

Ethical issue

The IT director of Muple, Tony Torry, has been offered a senior job at Pergola by the CEO of Pergola, Harriett Hobb.

Harriett opened a meeting with Tony: "I want to delay your start date with us for six months. As you know, Pergola is still in negotiations over a contract to supply Sensorex to Muple. I want to make sure that the contract is finalised before you join us, as I want you to work on delivering Sensorex to Muple if the contract goes ahead. Please don't mention to anybody at Muple that you have been offered a job with Pergola as, for the moment, this is confidential."

Requirements

57.1 Explain how using Sensorex could improve Muple's efficiency and profitability. **(16 marks)**

57.2 Explain the ethical issues for Tony and Harriett arising from their meeting. Set out the actions that Tony should now take. **(7 marks)**

Total: 23 marks

58 Innotoy Ltd

The date is September 20X8.

Innotoy Ltd (Innotoy), a small UK-based company, designs and sells novelty toys for children. It began trading in January 20X6 with the launch of four products. Innotoy outsources its manufacturing, then sells its products to a variety of retailers.

Innotoy's products are developed in-house by its research and development (R&D) team. Innotoy protected its intellectual property (IP) by obtaining trademarks for the product brand names. Due to the time and expense involved, however, Innotoy decided not to patent its product designs. Innotoy has a preferred supplier agreement with a Chinese manufacturer which requires Innotoy to pre-order in December each year for the following 12 months. All Innotoy toys are sold to retailers at a mark-up of 55% on cost.

Digiwhirl toy

Digiwhirl, a hand-held spinner toy, is Innotoy's most successful product. Digiwhirl was unique in the market in 20X6 and it quickly became the 'must-have' children's toy in the UK.

During 20X7 Innotoy's board decided to keep the price to retailers constant but to limit supply, to maintain the perception that Digiwhirl was an exclusive product. Also, as demand was hard to predict, the board did not want to have a large number of unsold toys. However, consumer demand far exceeded supply in 20X7, especially after Digiwhirl was featured on social media in April and suddenly became popular with young adults. Having failed to meet demand fully during 20X7, in December 20X7 Innotoy pre-ordered 25% more Digiwhirls for 20X8.

In October 20X7 several competitors launched cheaper hand-held spinner toys that were copies of Digiwhirl. Innotoy's competitors range from large entertainment corporations to young entrepreneurs making products with 3D printers and advertising on social media. On average, these copies retailed at 20% less than Digiwhirl's selling price.

Despite the increasing competition, Innotoy decided to maintain its constant price in 20X8, but attempted to retain market share by promoting its product as 'Innotoy's original Digiwhirl spinner'. Forecasts for 20X9 suggest that the UK hand-held spinner toy market is now saturated and sales volumes are expected to be 60% lower than in 20X8.

Comments at a recent Board meeting

Poor sales

The finance director stated: "We need to evaluate Digiwhirl's sales performance since its launch. I want to understand whether the decline we have seen during 20X8 is because of poor management decisions or is an inevitable result of short product life cycles in the toy industry. I have prepared some sales information (**Exhibit 1**) to help with this evaluation."

Data capture and analysis

The IT director responded: "Part of the problem is that our management information system is too focused on internal performance and does not produce all the information required to make the right decisions. We were taken by surprise when Digiwhirl became popular on social media. There are always so many photos, videos and conversations online. We need to do more to capture this external information, then combine it with existing information, so we can monitor market trends and make better predictions of consumer demand. I have supplied some illustrations of the type of data that I believe is relevant (**Exhibit 2**)."

Future sales growth

The marketing director commented: "What matters is the future. I propose that, to improve profitability, we should look for other markets for Digiwhirl. It could be marketed as a desk toy for stressed executives and as a concentration aid for children with attention problems. This would help address the fact that 40% of sales volume in the children's toy market is concentrated in the last quarter of the calendar year."

The sales director added: "I agree that this idea would help to reduce seasonality, but I believe there is still scope for growth in sales of Digiwhirl as a children's toy. I suggest that we offer a wider range of Digiwhirl models with added features such as LED lights, Bluetooth speakers and personalisation so that brand-loyal consumers will buy more than one version. We should continue to sell all versions of the Digiwhirl product at our premium price so we do not destroy its brand image.

"If we really want to be successful though, R&D needs to develop Innotoy's next new product. More than half the toys sold each year in our market are newly-developed products, but R&D seems to have been struggling for ideas recently."

A new product opportunity

The R&D director responded: "Recently I was approached with a good idea for a new toy by an inventor who did not have sufficient funds to develop it or to patent the design. The inventor offered to give Innotoy her design for free, in exchange for half the profits on all future sales of the toy.

"I suggest that, instead of taking up the inventor's offer, we launch a copy of the toy ourselves so that Innotoy can retain all the profits. Competitors copy our Digiwhirl product design and we can do nothing about it. Our lawyer has suggested that if we make small variations to the product design, the inventor will not be able to sue us for breach of IP, and she is unlikely to have the money to start legal proceedings."

Requirements

58.1 Using the data in the Exhibits and the other information provided, identify and analyse, for Innotoy's finance director, the reasons for Digiwhirl's sales performance since its launch in January 20X6. **(17 marks)**

58.2 Discuss the IT director's comments about Innotoy's management information system. Explain how Innotoy could improve its capture and analysis of information to gain competitive advantage. **(8 marks)**

58.3 Assess the merits of the marketing and sales directors' strategies for future sales growth. Refer to relevant models. **(10 marks)**

58.4 Discuss the ethical implications for Innotoy of the R&D director's proposal for a new product and recommend appropriate actions. **(8 marks)**

Total: 43 marks

ICAEW 2019

Exhibit 1: Sales information

Innotoy sales revenue
Year ended 31 December 20X7

Digiwhirl: Quarterly sales revenue analysis

	Q1 £'000	Q2 £'000	Q3 £'000	Q4 £'000	Total £'000
20X6	750	1,950	3,300	4,500	10,500
20X7	2,750	5,550	3,700	3,000	15,000
20X8	1,200	2,400	3,600*	4,800*	12,000

* based on latest estimates

Hand-held spinners – volumes ('000)

	20X6	20X7	20X8
Digiwhirl			
Purchased from supplier	700	1,000	1,250
Sales volume	700	1,000	800*
Unfulfilled orders from retailers	100	250	0
Total UK toy market			
Hand-held spinners sales volume	700	1,450	1,600*

* based on latest estimates

	20X6	20X7	6 months to 30 June 20X8
Number of visits to Innotoy website ('000)	3,200	5,000	2,000
Average rating of Digiwhirl on product review websites	5/5	4.5/5	3/5
Number of #Digiwhirl references on social media ('000)	1,400	3,000	1,000
Number of brands of hand-held spinners on a leading online retailer site	1	20	150
Number of results from internet search for 'hand-held spinner' ('000)	6,507	17,430	23,512

59 Balad Ltd

The date is September 20X8.

Ambrosia is a small country with a strong economy and a thriving financial services sector. Its currency is the Ambrosian dollar ($). Ambrosia attracts many foreign nationals (expatriates) who are employed in technology roles and are temporarily resident in Ambrosia on 5–10 year working visas.

Education in Ambrosia

The Ambrosian Government offers state-funded education for children born and resident in Ambrosia. Children must be in full-time education until they are at least 16. The state funds education leading to two qualifications:

- Certificate of Ambrosian Education (CAE) - taken by all state-funded children at age 16

- Final Award of Ambrosian Education (FAE) – taken at age 18 by state-funded children who choose to continue in post-16 education

80% of children up to age 16 who are eligible for state funding attend state-run schools. 60% of eligible children continue in education to age 18.

In addition to state-run schools, there are several privately-run schools in Ambrosia. These offer two internationally-recognised qualifications:

- International GCSE (IGCSE) – taken at age 16
- International Baccalaureate (IBAC) – taken at age 18

Privately-run schools are commercial organisations which charge fees to parents. They are primarily attended by the children of expatriates and the remainder are children of Ambrosian residents whose parents opt to pay for education.

Balad School – background information

Balad Ltd (Balad) is a company owned by the Balad family which operates Balad School, a privately-run school in Ambrosia. Balad School has a reputation for providing high-quality education for children aged 11–18. All children take IGCSE at age 16 then at age 18 they can take the IBAC. 30% of children attending Balad School were born in Ambrosia.

Children must pass an exam to gain entry to Balad School. Demand for places on Balad School's IGCSE programme (aged 11-16) is very high and there is always a waiting list. However, Balad School has spare capacity on its IBAC programme post-16, as many expatriate children return to their country of origin to continue post-16 education.

Balad's board consists of members of the extended Balad family, all of whom were born in Ambrosia. The board's primary objective is profit maximisation.

Government plans for education

The Ambrosian Government wants to maintain its strong economy and achieve year-on-year growth. An extract from the Government's latest strategic plan for education states that its priorities are to:

- increase the number of Ambrosian-born children who continue in post-16 education; and

- develop technological expertise to provide Ambrosia with resident IT specialists in the future.

The Government has approached Balad with a proposal to create a new College of Technology (College) for children post-16.

All children passing the exam to attend the College would study for both the IBAC and an International Diploma in Technology (IDT). The course would last for two years.

The Government would pay fees to the College for children born in Ambrosia. This would cost the Government an extra $1,500 per year per child than if the child attended a state-run FAE programme. Children of expatriate families would be encouraged to attend the College, but their parents would be required to pay the fees in full.

Joint venture

If the College goes ahead, it will be operated as a joint venture company (JV), with the Government and Balad each owning 50% of the shares and sharing profits and losses equally. The JV will run for five years initially. The Government and Balad will each be able to appoint two members of the College's senior management team.

The Government will close an existing state-run school, for children post-16, that has considerable spare capacity and the College will operate from these buildings. The Government will pay a one-off sum of $250,000 to refurbish the buildings to an appropriate standard. The Government will retain ownership of the buildings and make them available to the JV in return for rental payments of $225,000 each year.

To equip the College, Balad will provide the JV with $250,000 initial capital for learning resources, including IT equipment. Balad will manage the College's day-to-day educational operations and will be paid $375,000 each year by the JV for doing this.

If the JV goes ahead, Balad will continue to operate Balad School as a separate independent company, but will offer only the IGCSE programme for children aged 11–16. Balad School will close its IBAC programme and encourage children completing IGCSE at 16 to move to the College. Balad School's specialist IBAC teachers will move to the College.

Closing the IBAC programme will increase Balad School's capacity so it can offer more places on its IGCSE programme for children aged 11–16. Closing the IBAC programme will result in an estimated net reduction in profits for Balad School of $400,000 each year.

The following estimates have been made for the College:

- Variable costs such as tuition materials will be 15% of tuition fees.

- Fixed costs of operating the College, including teacher salaries, will be $794,000 each year. This excludes any payments to the JV parties.

- Course fees will be $8,000 each year per child. These will be paid by the Government for children born in Ambrosia.

- The first intake will be 120 children and the intake is expected to grow by 20% each year.

Requirements

59.1 Discuss the extent to which the government's objectives for the College of Technology may conflict with Balad's objectives. **(9 marks)**

59.2 Calculate the number of children that need to attend the College each year for it to break even, stating any assumptions. Comment briefly on the implication of your result for the financial success of the College. **(10 marks)**

59.3 Evaluate the benefits and risks of the joint venture for both Balad and the Government. **(16 marks)**

Total: 35 marks

60 Vision Bank

BanksUnite.com – the banking sector blog

1 September 20X8

Open banking – a threat or an opportunity?

Thanks to Europe's new open banking regulations, which came into force in early 20X8, the banks' monopoly on their customers' account and payment information may soon disappear. Individual personal customers could soon look to technology firms, internet giants and online retailers ('digital challengers') to meet their needs for financial services.

All banks are now required to create an open data platform, which – provided the customer consents – will give authorised third parties access to all the financial information a bank holds on a customer.

A recent industry report estimates that traditional European banks may lose up to 31% of profits to these digital challengers. There are three key reasons why the threat to traditional banks is now more real than ever:

(a) By having instant access to banks' databases, digital challengers can immediately enter the financial services market.

(b) Digital challengers can meet customer requirements in a more innovative way than many traditional banks as they do not need the same large, complex infrastructure. For example, a single digital challenger could focus on providing just credit cards, and then it could connect customers wanting additional services to other banking providers through cloud-based solutions or open banking platforms.

(c) In a world of contactless payments and mobile apps, consumers are increasingly demanding a digital approach. They want financial services that are faster, more personalised and more easily accessible.

Motan Inc (Motan), a new digital challenger bank, has already acquired a banking licence in Europe. Yesterday Motan's CEO announced its intention to use open banking to become the digital bank of choice: "Our open platform will allow software developers to build apps that can improve our service. For instance, someone could develop an app that connects to Motan's open platform and customers could authorise the app to access their account and extract information on their business expenses."

Not everyone agrees that open banking will be an immediate success. A spokesman for the body that represents the banking sector in Europe said:

"Open banking has the potential to transform banking, but this depends on people's willingness to embrace it. A survey of customers in 20X7 found that:

- Only 5-10% identified themselves as early adopters who are keen to embrace new technology

- 53% said that they would not share their bank account information with third-party providers and would be reluctant to change their existing banking habits

"The banking sector believes there are still questions around data security and privacy that need to be answered. Third parties will need appropriate security in place to protect against fraudsters – and do not forget that any digital challenger which wants to offer banking services will still need to apply for a banking licence from the relevant regulator."

Vision Bank

Vision Bank (VB) is a small European bank which currently operates a traditional banking model. It has a modern, high-specification computer system. VB recognises the significant change occurring in the banking industry because of the new open banking regulations. It wants to capitalise on this by launching a banking app (the VB app) and implementing a new, digital-only banking strategy.

VB's CEO outlined her plans at a recent board meeting:

"We want to provide individual customers with a digital platform that offers them a more efficient way to manage their money. Because of open banking, our new VB app will be able to give our customers a complete view of all aspects of their financial life, whatever products they have and whichever bank provides them. As part of this strategy, we will shut down our large processing centre which is currently responsible for paper services (printing bank statements, cheque books and correspondence). Customers will be informed of the change on 1 October 20X8 and all paper services will cease on 31 December 20X8.

"From 1 January 20X9 all customers will need to switch to electronic payment methods. Customers will use the VB app to access statements for all the financial products they hold with VB and other banks. No paper copies will be available.

"This change will require significant education and support for some of our existing customers. Although they all currently have the facility to use online banking, a surprising number prefer to receive paper statements and correspondence. Some of our customers are still writing and banking cheques as their only means of accessing banking services.

"Inevitably, we will have to make some employees redundant. Other employees can choose to retrain and transfer to the Digital Help Centre that we will set up to answer customer queries. We will also need to recruit new employees with appropriate technological skills."

Requirements

In relation to VB's proposal for a digital-only banking strategy, prepare a report for VB's board which:

60.1 Identifies and analyses **three** key external factors that are creating change in the European banking industry. Refer to relevant models. **(10 marks)**

60.2 Explains the change management issues that arise for employees and customers and advises VB on how to manage these issues. **(12 marks)**

Total: 22 marks

Answer Bank

Business strategy and technology answers

Guidance on mark plans

Introduction

This guidance has been put together by the examining team. It is possible, over time, as a result of candidates' performance in the real exams, that there may be further developments in the way in which mark plans are constructed. A document such as this can only ever provide broad guidance. The examining team set mark plans for each question on an individual basis, taking account of the overall structure of the question, the scenario, and the complexity of the analysis and argument required.

Marking documents

Business Strategy and Technology has one of the highest skills content of all the Professional Stage examinations as it leads on to the Technical Integration and Case Study exams. This is reflected in the marking process where the available marks for each requirement are divided into two pools: Knowledge marks (K) and Skills marks (S), with more marks awarded for skills than knowledge.

For any particular exam there are three separate marking documents:

- A detailed mark plan for the exam (a full answer, containing all the likely points that candidates may make, as published for students)

- A marking grid which breaks the exam down into the K and S mark pools available for each requirement

- A separate marking guidance document issued to markers, giving an overview of the typical K and S points for each requirement, to be used in conjunction with the detailed mark plan

The marking grid and marking guidance for the September 2017 exam are included in Chapter 1 of the Study Manual.

Knowledge and skills marks

Broadly speaking, the K marks are for demonstration of appropriate and accurate knowledge and understanding from the learning materials, explicit or implied (eg, where the answer is developed using recognised models, tools and frameworks, not just common sense).

The S marks are for:

- Assimilating and using information
- Structuring problems and solutions
- Applying judgement
- Conclusions and recommendations
- Communication

For example, if the requirement was to 'analyse the competitive forces within an industry' then K marks would be available for selecting the right model and knowing the meaning of the key headings, in this case that 'competitive forces' suggests Porter's Five Forces model should be applied.

S marks would be gained for example by:

- Applying a model to the context in the question, eg, identifying relevant information from the scenario

- Analysing the information, eg, identifying causal factors that explain changes in data

- Reasoning and judgement, eg, providing reasoned advice relating to the specific terms of the scenario

The marking information set out below is used to mark the questions.

Allocation of marks

Typically it is not possible to allocate a half/one mark per point as it is in the more numerical exams. This type of approach would encourage a scatter-gun approach and reward answers making a long list of minor points, even where they fail to identify and explain the key issues.

Marks are therefore awarded in small pools which attempt to give an assessment of a candidate's performance for each sub-set of a requirement. Markers are encouraged to use discretion and to award partial marks where a point was either not explained fully or made by implication.

It is often the case that the more succinct answers are better, since it is the quality rather than the number of points which attracts marks in Business Strategy and Technology.

As a general rule, the mark plan is constructed according to the following principles:

- **Numerical elements**

  Where the requirement includes a specific calculation, the total marks available will be broken down into a series of computations for the components of the calculation. Marks will be awarded for workings and not just for the correct final figure. Additional marks will be available for stating assumptions.

- **Data interpretation/analysis**

  Specific marks for any necessary calculations/numerical analysis will be awarded as for numerical elements above. Also, however, appropriate calculations will need to be identified by the candidate and marks will be awarded for addressing the key issues.

  A greater proportion of the total marks available will be awarded for the following skills:

  - Interpretation of data (both qualitative and quantitative)
  - Considering cause and effect relationships
  - Identifying implications of the analysis
  - And for linking the data analysis to the wider strategy or issue in the scenario

  In these respects 'making the numbers talk' will be a key feature.

  Additional marks will be awarded for highlighting additional information required and/or the limitations of the analysis undertaken, even if not specifically asked for (although this may form part of the requirement).

- **Use of specific theories/models**

  Requirements will generally be open ended and candidates may be expected to identify the appropriate model to use in a particular situation. For example, a requirement to analyse the ways in which the business has grown might be answered by considering Ansoff and Lynch.

  Where a requirement calls for the application of a particular theory or model, there will be a limited number of knowledge marks for identifying the correct model and explaining its use. A greater proportion of the total marks will be awarded for the skills shown in applying the model to the scenario and discussing its limitations in the particular context.

- **Narrative elements**

  Each component of the requirement will be assigned a 'pool' of marks. An element of the marks in the pool will be available for demonstrating the correct knowledge but the majority will then be awarded to a candidate based on the degree of application, analysis and judgement demonstrated by the answer. Thus it is possible to identify the characteristics of various possible answers, together with their mark scoring potential:

  (a) Generic comments from the learning materials, which are not expressed in the context of the scenario. Answer includes lists of unprioritised, undeveloped and/or irrelevant points. Points listed but not explained.

  This constitutes a poor answer, scoring less than half the marks available in the pool and hence a 'fail' on the particular section of the requirement.

  (b) A number of generic comments but with some attempt to apply knowledge to the scenario in the question and to link points together in the form of key issues.

  An adequate attempt, scoring a little over half the marks available in the pool normally generating sufficient marks to attain a marginal pass.

  (c) Succinct points, made in the context of the question with little irrelevant comment. Some insights demonstrated. Logical argument backed up by analysis of the data/scenario. Demonstrates judgement by providing clear recommendations or advice where required by the question.

  A high scoring answer which would be awarded the majority of marks available in the pool (in some cases the maximum) and achieve a clear pass.

Presentation marks and workings

Generally, where specifically requested in the requirement, one knowledge mark would be awarded for presentation of a report/memo/briefing notes in an appropriate format. It is important to note that when using the exam software candidates need to be mindful that the examiner can only see answers as they appear on the screen. The examiners cannot see the formulae used by candidates in their answers nor can they make the window larger to view narrative answers which extend beyond the view of the screen. As such candidates need to ensure that there is an audit trail for numerate answers, and ensure that all text is clearly visible so that the examiners can fully review the answers provided.

Headroom

All questions contain a degree of 'headroom' (ie, potentially there are more marks available than the maximum for the requirement), as a range of different answers are possible. For example, the requirement totals, say, 20 marks, but the mark plan contains a total of, say, 23 marks. This means that a candidate could, in fact, score 100% without producing an ideal answer.

The published answers are detailed mark **plans** and are designed to encompass many possible valid comments that a marker may see. As a result they are often more detailed than even a strong candidate would give in their answer.

Mark plans in the learning materials

The summary mark plans in the learning materials have been reviewed by the examining team.

However, tutors should bear in mind that the mark plans in the learning materials have not undergone the full development process as those for the real exams where mark plans are tested over a large sample of candidates' answers.

Nonetheless, the above guidance can be illustrated by looking at the past real exams included in the question bank.

The mark scheme provided with each solution indicates relative emphasis of the sub-areas of the question.

> **Tutorial note**
>
> The marks awarded in the real exam may exceed these where the candidate's answers merit this.

1 DA plc (March 2008, amended)

Marking guide

	Knowledge	Skill	Marks
1.1 Factors creating competitive advantage	2	5	6
1.2 Analysis of strategic development	4	8	10
1.3 PESTEL analysis	2	7	8
1.4 Marketing strategy	2	7	8
1.5 Strategic and cyber security risks	2	7	8
	12	34	40

1.1 Factors creating competitive advantage

Competitive advantage is anything that gives one organisation an edge over its rivals. Critical success factors (CSFs) are the areas where an organisation must excel if it is to achieve sustainable competitive advantage. DA's critical success factors concern not only the resources of the business but how these can be used to advantage in the competitive environment in which it operates.

Here a key strategic resource is the possession of a licence to operate as a CRA. Complying with the terms of this licence is fundamental to DA's ability to continue in operation. Possession of the licence acts as a barrier to entry and while it does not give DA an advantage over CC Inc, it does protect its market share from new entrants.

DA may gain competitive advantage over CC Inc by virtue of being the only UK-based CRA.

According to the resource-based view of strategy, firms develop competencies and then exploit them. Sustainable competitive advantage is obtained by the exploitation of unique resources. Thus a firm should focus only on products where it has a sustainable competitive advantage and focus on core competences which competitors do not possess or would find it difficult to copy.

A threshold competence for CRAs is compliance with the relevant UK legislation, eg, consumers have specific rights in relation to the information CRAs hold about them. Complying with this and other relevant legislation is crucial to DA's business, as it is to the business of competitors. Going beyond mere compliance, eg, by extending its free advisory and education services may give DA a competitive advantage over CC Inc.

The key factors that appear to have given rise to DA's competitive advantage would include:

(1) First to market – DA began business a number of years ago and as one of the first to market, and a primary player, it has created a strong reputation and market dominance as a result of this.

(2) Scale – with 58% of the market there are scale economies in search costs and IT costs which would give DA an advantage over its main competitor and any potential entrants.

(3) Information and knowledge systems – DA's core competences are its ability to compile and manage vast quantities of data, and extract meaning from it. This has been achieved partly by the data analytics software that it developed in-house. This has helped to give DA 'the most comprehensive credit database in the UK'. It also maintains a large database for the automotive industry.

For competitive advantage DA must have superior skills in database management and data analytics:

- Continuous access to a wide range of data sources to ensure that the consumer profile or vehicle history is complete and accurate

- The ability to integrate vast quantities of information and organise it in a user friendly form

- Maintenance of up-to-date information that can be used by large credit providers to make enhanced decisions in 'real time'

(4) Product development skills/Innovation – DA have a core competence in helping businesses reduce risk. This is best illustrated by the development of data analytics software which has enabled DA to expand the products and services it offers and the markets it serves, eg, the development of the analytical decision business. The demand for this service is evident given the fact that a large number of financial institutions have expressed an interest in using this in recent months. By making this proprietary software, DA is able to protect their competitive position and prevent copying.

(5) Relationship management skills – DA's experience in personal selling has attracted business customers in the first instance. These customers have been retained through relationship management and by developing additional products to meet their risk management needs. As a result there is significant brand loyalty.

(6) Technical resources – DA's IT systems will be important in delivering an efficient service to customers, where customers will particularly value:

- Speed of processing
- Flexibility of delivery (online, phone etc)
- Confidentiality

(7) Organisation structure – DA has divisionalised by product or brand. This should facilitate communication and decision-making, at the level of the brand and allow a fast response to a rapidly changing market.

As a listed company DA will also have good access to finance.

1.2 Analysis of strategic development

The Ansoff model is a two-by-two matrix of Products (new and existing) and Markets (new and existing).

By relating product opportunities to markets, this mix identifies four broad alternative strategies open to DA.

Market penetration

This involves selling more of existing products to existing markets. This increases the organisation's market share. DA is the largest credit reference agency in the UK market and in this field the company has only one major competitor, CC Inc. As a result each company can only increase market share at the expense of the other, unless they can each persuade businesses to carry out searches with both organisations. To some extent DA's position is protected by the fact that organisations wishing to compile credit information need a licence. As DA is clearly the market leader it could be argued that they have been very successful in achieving market penetration. This has been based on their ability to create and retain successful client relationships and their core skills of database compilation and management.

Product development

This means developing new products for existing markets. As a credit reference business, DA initially focused on financial services businesses as its potential customers. It was then able to expand by developing the technology around its existing product. Knowledge of the specific needs of this market in terms of speed of decision making, reduction of risk etc enabled DA to build and develop a wider range of products relevant to its customers, eg, the decision analysis software that DA introduced was based on the premise that businesses would value analytical rather than just factual information.

Market development

This strategy takes existing products and finds new markets for them. Having recognised a core competence in database management, DA used this strategy to offer information products to the automotive industry. This market is similar to the financial services market, in that customers value information that assists in reducing the risk associated with decisions.

Diversification

This involves moving away from core activities and developing new products for new markets. Diversification stands apart from the other strategies. It involves the greatest risk of all strategies. It requires new skills, new techniques and different ways of operating.

Having focused on the business-to-business market, DA plans to diversify into the business-to-consumer market with its new product Checksta. While the broad product area is still credit information there are overtones of diversification because it is for individual consumers. This decision recognises that many consumers want to be more in control of their credit status, to be able to monitor their credit report at any time and to protect themselves against identity fraud.

Tutorial note

Although the company perception is that Checksta represents a new market, it could be argued that this is product development rather than diversification, since DA already offers the statutory credit report to the consumer market.

Lynch Expansion method matrix

The Lynch model is another two-by-two matrix of company growth (organic growth and external development) and geographical location (home (domestic) and international). Under this model, all of DA's growth appears to have been carried out organically and products/markets have been developed domestically rather than internationally.

DA has been able to grow organically as a result of having been an initial player in the market, allowing it to develop critical mass.

Overseas expansion

It is likely that a large number of existing customers, who value the DA brand, are global businesses. In the same way that CC Inc has expanded into the UK, DA could exploit this brand loyalty and apply its information management skills to Europe or the USA. If it wishes to target overseas markets in the future, then growth by acquisition might be considered as a faster way of getting access to the necessary licences and databases.

1.3 PESTEL analysis

Political

- Only companies that are licensed CRAs can provide credit reference services and access to consumer credit files. DA and CC Inc are the two largest CRAs. Lending organisations and retailers offering trade credit have a choice of organisation with which to do a credit search, and consumers may not know which business their prospective lender will use, thus consumers are likely to want to access their file with each organisation.

- Changes in regulation may restrict DA's freedom of operations, eg, regarding pricing or ability to advertise.

- Government may choose to discourage credit, reducing the need for credit checks and hence DA's product.

Economic

- A consumer's willingness to take on credit depends on his or her confidence in their ability to repay the money. This confidence comes in part from job stability and faith in the economy. The relatively low and stable interest rates and stable employment have made consumers more willing to take on credit. While currently favourable, future changes, eg, in interest rates, may reverse this trend.

- Consumer spending is often used as an indicator of how well the economy is doing. Credit is a key factor in fuelling an economic boom. Any boom in consumer spending will mean that there is an increase in the number of credit checks lenders make through DA.

- The rejection of credit applications, especially if it is unexpected, may be an opportunity for DA as it is likely to cause individuals to want to access their credit report.

Social

- Changing attitudes to money and credit have meant it is no longer traditional to save up for things. More and more people use credit as a way of buying things they do not have the money for.

- People can apply for credit from almost anywhere: over the internet, by telephone, in a shop or supermarket, or in response to marketing campaigns.

- Consumers are much less loyal to one bank or finance provider and are more likely to shop around and approach several lenders to find the best deal. The above factors mean that individuals are more likely to shop around for credit and lenders have to carry out more credit checks. A desire to obtain credit on the best terms is likely to increase consumers' awareness of their credit history and increase demand for the credit scoring service provided in conjunction with Checksta.

Technological

- The credit industry has made huge technological advances. Financial products and services can now be bought online and e-commerce is now an important part of the global economy.

- The boom in e-commerce will continue to necessitate more frequent and rapid credit checks by businesses and increase the number of consumers who are likely to want real time online access to their credit history.

- DA has already upgraded its IT and knowledge management systems in response to changing technology but will need to ensure that these are kept up to date and that the necessary security systems are in place.

- The increase in identity crime represents a major opportunity for Checksta as individuals become increasingly aware of the possibilities of fraudulent access to their information and identities and will be keen to protect themselves against this.

Environmental

- Not really of major significance, though there could be a reduction in credit if society moves towards consuming less and conserving energy and resources.

- Environmental concerns, such as the desire to go 'paperless' may boost demand for an online product.

Legal

- UK legislation exists which governs how organisations can collect, use and share personal information and giving consumers specific rights in relation to the information CRAs hold about them. Continuing to comply with this and other relevant legislation is crucial to DA's business. DA needs to ensure that its plans for Checksta do not contravene this legislation or the terms of its licence.

- The consumer education programme that DA had to implement as a result of the tightening legislation has given it an opportunity to increase the awareness of its brand name among consumers and also consumer organisations.

In conclusion the environmental analysis would suggest that there is considerable scope for a product such as Checksta and that its planned introduction is well timed.

1.4 Marketing strategy

In the first instance DA should ensure that it has undertaken the appropriate market research. Market research is the systematic gathering, recording and analysing of information about problems relating to marketing of goods and services. Market research will therefore involve gathering information about the 7Ps of marketing (see below).

Target market

To the extent that it has identified customer needs and developed a product accordingly, DA would appear to have undertaken some preliminary market research and used this to identify the segments containing those potential customers that it wants to target.

In DA's case it wants to target a specific type of customer: personal rather than business, with certain behaviour preferences: users of credit and also of the internet. As a result it will need to take account of people's ages, their gender and socioeconomic grouping in deciding on an appropriate marketing mix.

Checksta is a new UK brand. It is important to develop an image that would be appropriate for the product that is being offered. Having a profile of the most likely customer will help DA to develop a promotional campaign that positions the product in the minds of its potential customers.

Marketing mix

Next, DA needs to develop its marketing strategy using the marketing mix, which is traditionally done using the 4Ps.

Product

Checksta is based on a product that existed already – the consumer credit report. The product has been developed by allowing real time online access and augmented via support for ID fraud.

In this case, the service needs to be considered in terms of the attributes that are likely to generate demand (eg, 24-hour availability; convenience of online access; security of information; ability to predict lender's scoring).

Checksta's unique selling points (USPs) are that it allows consumers to see their credit reports online and automatically alerts them to important changes to the information held about them. This helps consumers understand what makes them creditworthy and can help them to manage their credit commitments. If there is a problem, consumers get free phone advice from credit reference specialists.

Price

The price that potential customers are willing to pay could clearly be a specific objective of any market research exercise.

DA needs to consider whether there are any regulations governing the pricing of their service. Presumably the starting point for price is the price of the statutory report = £2.

It then needs to assess the value of real time access to the customer and the value of the other services on offer.

One possibility is to price elements of the package separately eg, a basic price for online access, and then extra charges for the additional service elements such as the alert service, credit score and so on.

Some form of monthly membership scheme, with an initial free trial period would encourage new users to consider take up of the service. If they do not think the service is for them, members would then have to remember to cancel their membership, say at the end of the 30-day free trial.

DA could consider price skimming for early adopters or alternatively discounts for those who are quick to sign up, so as to build market share quickly.

Place

Checksta was developed because of the growth in e-commerce communications technology. Its 'place' or channel by which it reaches its users is the electronic medium of the internet – Checksta is an e-commerce product, available online for consumers.

Some of the support services are offered online but also via different channels – the alert service is offered via email or text (mobile phone) and the free phone help-line can presumably be accessed via landline or mobile. Thus in addition to internet users, DA is also targeting those with mobile phones.

Promotion

As a new venture, the initial impact of advertising and other promotion on price and demand should be considered.

Until recently, DA has worked mainly in the business-to-business (b2b) market. Its expertise is based on personal selling and relationship building. To succeed in the business to consumer (b2c) market, DA will have to use a different promotional mix and needs to develop a range of different promotional strategies.

As a result of the tightening of credit legislation DA has already implemented a consumer education programme and been working with consumer groups. When DA launches its Checksta product in the UK, it should build on this existing awareness of its brand by ensuring that all free advice guides, consumer education programmes and conferences it attends also promote Checksta.

It could produce literature both online and as a paper product informing people of the dangers of identity fraud and explain how a monitoring service like Checksta could help protect them from the effects of this crime.

DA should consider using a public relations agency to help advertise the new online credit report with press releases and a television advertising campaign.

Advertising could be placed in the money/financial review sections of the press and appropriate financial/credit/consumer advice magazines.

DA could sponsor exhibitions such as the Ideal Home Show and events such as Credit Awareness Week 20X7, which its target customers may attend.

As the product is an online one and DA are targeting internet users, web-based advertising would also be appropriate. DA need to ensure there are links to its website from the various money supermarket and personal finance websites. Research should be done to ensure that DA and the Checksta brand appear when a potential customer uses a search engine.

DA could exploit links with other areas of its business, eg, advertise the Checksta service to those customers seeking finance for vehicle purchases. This could be achieved by direct mailing those individuals that consent to receive marketing materials promoting DA's other products and services.

Tutorial note

As DA is a service company, the marketing mix could be extended to consideration of 7 Ps.

People

This refers to anyone that is to have regular interaction with the customer. In this case a lot of the service will be provided automatically and a substantial amount of any interaction will be electronic by text or email. Customers may make personal contact if they use the free advice phone line.

DA needs to ensure that the nature of any communication gives a good impression of the company, that staff have appropriate training on the new product and the flexibility to provide a good service and that staff manning the helpline are informative and suitably concerned and reassuring.

Processes

Accuracy of information, secure access and confidentiality will be key to determining how effective the service is. DA needs to implement standard operational procedures and ensure that staff apply these consistently.

The ease of application for membership and navigation through the website will be important.

There will need to be security systems in place to verify the identity of members both online and by phone.

DA needs to ensure that the IT systems operate efficiently and that there are no significant delays in the provision of the real time information or periods when the website is down.

Physical evidence

This is the evidence that the service has been performed. It may include electronic confirmation of membership, the online report, any alerts. DA could issue a credit card sized Checksta membership card, with membership number and key contact numbers/website addresses.

1.5 IT/IS risks

Strategic risks	Risk management
DA will lose competitive advantage if it fails to utilise IT/IS as effectively as CC Inc, particularly given its renewed focus on the UK market. If the use of analytical software among DA's competitors increases and DA fails to innovate its own processes then this may result in falling behind its rivals.	DA needs to keep up to date with new technology, continuously upgrade systems and ensure continuous advancements in the products/services offered. It should undertake regular benchmarking against competitors such as CC Inc.

Strategic risks	Risk management
Since all of DA's information management and in particular the Checksta product depends on IT/IS, a breakdown in its operations threatens the business. This could arise from systems failure or natural threats such as fire, flood, and electrical storms.	DA should ensure that if major failures or disasters occur, the business will not be completely unable to function. It should implement protection measures to ensure continuity of operations and to minimise the risk of systems failures, eg, back-up servers in alternative locations and regular back-ups of data.
The cost of updating and maintaining IT/IS and implementing the necessary security controls and risk management systems may reduce the operating margins that DA has enjoyed to date (currently around 25% on average). This is particularly true if, as a result of CC Inc offering a low cost web-based solution, DA has to reduce the price of its services.	The costs of the necessary systems controls and security measures need to be considered in the light of the benefits that these will bring.
Market dominance may result in DA being criticised for anti-competitive practices or investigated by the Competition and Markets Authority.	Care should be taken to ensure DA does not abuse its position and actively lay itself open to criticism.

Cyber security risks	Risk management
Loss of information as a result of corruption of the system by viruses or human error.	Particularly important is protection from viruses and the need for regular back-ups. DA needs to protect data and systems from unauthorised modification, eg, via passwords and levels of access/modification authority.
Theft of sensitive financial information or deliberate misuse of data by hackers/employees.	DA must recruit trustworthy employees, and ensure detection and reporting of security-related incidents, eg, unauthorised activity. Training is particularly important, with the aim that users are aware of information security threats and concerns and are equipped to comply with the security policy.
Penalties or intervention as a result of non-compliance with regulations such as the *Data Protection Act (2018)* which could be imposed by courts if data is wrongly used or control procedures are not in place.	DA must put controls in place to ensure it monitors compliance with any relevant legal requirements such as the *Data Protection Act (2018)*.

2   e-Parts Ltd (September 2010, amended)

	Knowledge	Skill	Marks
2.1 Relevance of risk management/contents of BCP	3	4	6
2.2 Key IT risks and management	4	5	8
2.3 Outsourcing to implement IT strategy	3	5	7
	10	14	21

2.1 Risk management and business continuity planning

Risk management is the process of identifying and assessing the risks facing EP's business and the development, implementation and monitoring of a strategy to respond to those risks, in order to reduce threats to acceptable levels.

When running a business, risk is unavoidable and will include financial, strategic, operational and hazard risks arising from both internal and external sources. Risk management is a corporate governance issue as there is the danger that directors of companies might take decisions intended to increase profits without giving due regard to the risks. They may also continue to operate without regard to the changing risk profile of their organisation.

The point of risk management is that risks can be mitigated if management have plans to deal with problems if they occur. Risk management should be carried out by all businesses and involve all levels of staff and management. The aim is to prioritise the risks according to the ones that threaten the business most and then to take action to reduce or otherwise address the risk.

In addition to the general risks faced by all businesses, as a retailer EP faces additional IT and cyber risks because it carries large volumes of inventory and also because business is largely done online (see below). Cyber risk is any risk of financial loss, disruption or damage to the reputation of an organisation from some sort of failure of its IT systems. A key issue for an online business is that technical failure has a significant and immediate impact. Problems with the ecommerce site are immediately visible and it is easy for customers to switch to a competitor if the website is unavailable. Thus cyber security is an important issue for EP. EP needs to take action to prevent/reduce losses due to excessive risk exposure that may include theft, fraud and data insecurity.

Kamal must ensure that all staff are trained and fully aware of ecommerce security issues and fraud risk.

Whether EP thrives or fails will partly be dependent on how as a business it manages risk and exploits opportunities. The aim is to reduce the probability and/or consequence of failure but retain as far as possible the benefits of success. Thus effective risk management is integral to EP's competitive advantage and will help ensure EP's survival in the longer term.

Business continuity planning is the process through which a business details how and when it will recover and restore operations interrupted by the occurrence of a massive (but rare) risk event eg, natural disaster such as a warehouse flood or fire or a major breach of security causing the website to be down for an extended period.

Where risk management is largely pre-emptive, BCP is designed to deal with the consequences of a major realised risk. The difference is also linked to the extent of the impact – for instance the difference between website disruption due to a temporary loss of internet connection and a denial of service attack that places the business's existence in jeopardy.

A BCP is concerned with crisis management and disaster recovery. It must specify the actions to be taken in order to recover from any unexpected disruptive event. Factors that should be considered by a BCP include the following:

- Securing interim management and staff
- Inventory replacement
- Restoration of data and other IT systems
- Securing interim premises
- Management of the PR issues

Methods of recovery might include the following:

- Carrying out activities manually until IT services are resumed (eg, via the call centre)

- Moving staff at an affected building to another location

- Agreeing with another business to use each other's premises in the event of a disaster

- Arranging to use IT services and accommodation provided by a specialist third-party standby site

All members of EP staff should be aware of the importance of business continuity planning, training should be given and the plan tested regularly.

Examiner's comments

The first requirement asked candidates to explain the relevance of risk management to the business as a whole and to identify the main factors that would be covered in a business continuity plan. Overall answers were of a poor standard with many candidates failing this requirement because they were uncertain about the nature and content of a business continuity plan, despite the clear hint given in the scenario about ensuring the business could continue to function in the event of a major incident. Explanations of risk management tended to be extremely generic and only the best candidates pointed out that risk management was critical given the risks faced by EP as a result of its inventory levels and the e-commerce nature of the business. Weaker candidates often mentioned Turnbull, which demonstrated a lack of understanding of its application.

2.2 IT risks including cyber risks and how to manage them

EP must take steps to minimise the risk of systems failure, protect the integrity of its systems, safeguard information and ensure the continuity of its operations.

Risks may be transferred, avoided, reduced or accepted.

Specific IT and cyber risks arising for EP and recommendations for risk management:

- Inaccessible website/website too slow/payment system for ecommerce website goes down. This is critical given that 90% sales are online and is likely to result in frustrated customers and lost sales as they can easily switch to another online competitor.

  Risk can be reduced by ensuring appropriate systems development and maintenance takes place and by having back-up servers. EP could also reduce the risk by providing other channels to market and ensuring that customers are directed to alternatives such as the call centre in the event of system delays or failures.

  EP could transfer the risk by outsourcing the provision of the website to a specialist provider (see below).

- Identity theft/credit card fraud arising due to online payments – this would damage EP's reputation and may result in lost customers.

EP should ensure it reduces the risk by having access controls, appropriate payment verification software, firewalls and secure communication.

- Loss of critical data, particularly given there are 2 million customers on the database and 100,000 different products to control. Failure of the inventory control system may cause inaccurate information to be provided regarding inventory levels or wrong products to be despatched. Failure to comply with the *Data Protection Act (2018)* could also result in penalties/litigation.

    EP should reduce the risk of inadequate or inaccurate information by performing regular physical inventory counts and reconciling these to computerised records.

    EP must ensure the inventory system and customer database are kept up-to date, backed up regularly and hard copies kept off site. It must have systems in place to monitor compliance with data protection regulations and ensure all data held is secure (eg, via encryption). Furthermore, customer data should not be held for longer than is needed.

    Reduce the risk by ensuring all feedback is screened regularly and ensuring appropriate security features are in place to control access and content. A process for identifying and removing customer data held on the database needs to be determined.

- IT system becomes out-of-date or is less capable than that of online competitors.

    Systems need to be upgraded regularly to ensure they are capable of providing the necessary capacity, particularly given the growth EP has experienced.

Where risks cannot be reduced or eliminated it may be possible for EP to transfer them via the following:

- Insurance (however this may be costly and it may be problematic to quantify the extent of business loss from a security incident)

- Contracting out the management of ecommerce to a third party who can host the system. The loss may still occur and impact on the business, but the service level agreement can stipulate penalties

Other more generic IT risks include the following:

- Virus attacks and/or hackers exploiting vulnerabilities in the system (steal data, damage system or corrupt information)

- Website defacement (impact on reputation/brand image)

- Denial of service

- Infrastructure failure eg, loss of internet connection

- Software/hardware systems malfunction

- Loss of key IT personnel eg, website designer/IT manager

- Risk to corporate information/intellectual property

- Human error

- Deliberate sabotage

- Fraud

- Natural threats (fire, flood, electrical storm)

More generally EP can reduce vulnerability and increase its level of confidence in its technical environment by:

- Installing firewalls, using strong authentication processes and secure communication

- Implementing policies to manage activities eg, internet and email usage

- Setting standards for firewalls, servers and procurement of PCs

- Establishing a high level of Information security and access controls, and measuring to detect unauthorised access
- Ensuring there are regular back-ups
- Undertaking appropriate systems development and maintenance
- Ensuring physical and environment security
- Complying with relevant legislation

Examiner's comments

The second requirement asked candidates to identify the key IT risks including cyber risks arising for EP as a result of its reliance on IT and to recommend how they could be managed. Answers were quite variable. Good answers concentrated on relevant IT and cyber risks for EP, including the possible failure of the website, loss of customer database information, identity theft and the possibility of damaging reviews on social networking sites. A significant number of answers discussed IT risks and the TARA model for risk management in very generic terms. The weakest candidates failed to concentrate on IT and cyber risks, mentioning any types of risk they could think of.

2.3 **Considerations in outsourcing the provision of the website and inventory control system**

EP is considering outsourcing all its systems relating to the website and inventory control.

Factors to consider include the following:

- EP has experienced substantial growth and its current systems may no longer be able to cope with the increasing volume of transactions. Outsourcing may reduce the chance of system breakdown and give EP access to back-up servers and systems.
- Outsourcing would provide access to specialist IT knowledge and allow Kamal to concentrate on the strategy of the company.
- As specialists, with the potential for economies of scale, an outsourcer may be able to provide better, more efficient systems for EP at a lower cost. They are also more likely to be able to keep the systems up-to-date and develop new applications which may help EP maintain its competitive advantage.
- By outsourcing, EP can transfer the risk of systems failure to the IT provider and may have recourse to compensation in the event of financial loss.

However:

- EP has a database of 2 million customers. Outsourcing would require it to share confidential information with the IT provider, who may also work with competitors. Care needs to be taken to ensure compliance with the *Data Protection Act 2018*.
- Any problems experienced when transferring the systems over may disrupt EP's business and cause it to lose sales/customers.
- Once EP has decided to outsource it may find it difficult to switch suppliers and is unlikely to be able to revert to in-house provision as it will no longer have its own web designers/IT experts.

Other factors to consider:

- Fees charged by contractor
- Costs currently incurred in own service provision
- Potential redundancies of staff no longer required
- Time and cost involved in agreeing and monitoring service level agreement
- Attitude of influential stakeholders
- Previous incidence and consequence of system breakdown

Conclusion: if EP does decide to outsource it will need to choose a partner carefully, and assess their financial stability and track record of delivering suitable services elsewhere.

It must then agree a series of performance targets and penalties in the event of the contractor's failure to deliver.

Examiner's comments

In the third requirement candidates were asked to explain the factors that should be considered by EP in deciding whether to use outsourcing as a method of implementing its IT strategy. Candidates were clearly well rehearsed for this requirement in terms of knowledge but many weaker candidates failed to obtain the available skills marks. This was due to the fact that they produced largely generic lists of pros and cons, with minimal application of EP and its IT strategy, which could have been applied to almost any outsourcing scenario. Better answers focused specifically on the factors that would influence the choice between in-house and outsourced IT provision and the impact on risks for EP.

3 Marcham plc (September 2010, amended)

Marking guide

	Knowledge	Skill	Marks
3.1 Report format			
(a) Info system benefits/competitive advantage	3	6	8
(b) SFA of expansion into the banking sector	3	10	12
(c) Organic growth v joint development	3	6	8
3.2 Ethical issues	3	6	8
	12	28	36

3.1 Report

To:	Operations Director
From:	AN Other
Date:	XX/XX/XX
Re:	Data analytics and information systems and proposed expansion into banking

(a) **Benefits of a data analytics and information system for competitive advantage**

- Increased revenue (from customers by analysing customer shopping data and also from the sale to suppliers of data related to best-selling products)

- Reduced costs (better inventory control)

- Increased customer service and hence improved customer retention – effectively the loyalty card acts as a barrier to exit for the customer

- Improved decision making (forecasting, scenario planning, market analysis)

- Existing database for direct marketing to those customers that have opted-in

- Targeted discount coupons as a form of price discrimination based on analysed customer purchase data

- EPOS system facilitates better inventory control, allowing for a Just-in-Time approach which reduces costs and wastage

Marcham's competitive advantage (CA)

In the supermarket industry, most players have EPOS systems and loyalty card schemes. In order for CA to arise, Marcham not only needs to be better at capturing data than competitors but also better at using it.

The loyalty scheme is a form of relationship marketing whereby Marcham is trying to build a long-term relationship with the customer. Marcham's CA arises because in terms of capturing the data:

- It was the first of its kind to introduce the scheme and therefore captured (and retained) an initial loyal customer base, obtaining first-mover advantage

- Its dominance within the market (30% market share and one in four adults in the UK belong to its customer loyalty scheme) means it has a more extensive database than any other competitor (data about more customers and also collected for longer). Crucially, Marcham has the data analytics software to be able to extract meaning from the data it holds.

In terms of its ability to use the data:

- It has reduced costs by increasing the frequency and accuracy of ordering, leading to lower levels of inventory and wastage

- It has more effective marketing which facilitates market segmentation and targeting, so low price goods can be promoted to certain customers and high quality ones to others

- It has better price discrimination and hence increased margins

- It can trade up sales by targeting promotions

- The percentage of customer spend can be extended by identifying products customers are likely to buy but may currently be buying elsewhere

- It has higher margins – it is cheaper to keep existing customers and to sell more to them than it is to attract new ones

- It is likely to result in a higher success rate for new product lines as it has already identified what customers want

- It provides internal sales data to suppliers, thereby generating additional revenue, promoting better captive relationships with the supplier and improving the matching of products with demand

Within the financial services sector none of the competitors has loyalty cards so Marcham will have first mover advantage if it is able to obtain consent from its loyalty card customers to send them promotional details about MarchamBank's services.

(b) **Suitability, feasibility, acceptability**

Suitability (strategic logic and fit)

There is a precedent as Marcham would not be the first major retailer to get involved in financial services (Tesco, Sainsbury, M&S) although it would be the first to set up a full banking service.

Strong brand name – timing is good given some people's loss of faith in the banking sector and perceived lack of transparency surrounding banks' behaviour. The issue is whether Marcham will be seen by consumers as a credible provider of banking services, although the fact that they have been granted a licence suggests the financial services regulator, the Financial Conduct Authority (FCA) believe they are.

Both banks and supermarkets are about serving personal customers and Marcham already possesses core competence in customer service and responsiveness.

There is also a strong link between retail spending and the need for credit.

Both banks and supermarkets require a presence on the high street and Marcham can use existing infrastructure.

However:

- Are financial services a core competence for retailers?

- It is a very competitive market

- Relatively, Marcham will be a very small player faced with large competition from existing banks

- Core competences in procurement and logistics would be less relevant in banking than if it expanded into other retail areas

- There are onerous compliance requirements related to data protection, identity confirmation, regulatory compliance and money laundering of which Marcham has limited experience

- Many customers now use online banking so MarchamBank's presence in stores may not be that attractive to them. Although, a longer term intention, plans for MarchamBank to become involved in offering banking services related to cryptocurrencies may lead to reputational damage. This is likely given the criminal associations and volatility in the value of such currencies.

Feasibility (can the strategy be implemented?)

This looks at whether Marcham have the necessary resources.

Marcham has already been granted a licence which demonstrates government support.

Branches will be located in existing stores which reduces the overhead costs associated with the operation.

Cash appears to be available although there is an opportunity cost if it is not invested in other new stores.

The loyalty card may provide a starting point for obtaining customer consent to send out marketing material promoting MarchamBank.

Marcham already has systems in place to collate data about customers and process applications, so credit assessment would simply be a bolt-on.

Marcham would need to invest in its human capital by hiring new staff and management with appropriate financial services knowledge – there is likely to be a big training requirement.

The pricing of financial services and processes are much more complex than individual retail transactions eg, selling a loaf of bread.

The banking sector will entail onerous compliance requirements related to data protection, identity confirmation and money laundering.

Financial services are long-term in nature so Marcham will need to commit resources for a significant period. It will take time to recoup initial set-up costs and for the venture to become profitable.

Acceptability (to stakeholders)

This considers the likely benefits to stakeholders (returns) and the likelihood of failure and its associated consequences (risk).

Returns

More information is required to assess the proposed financial impact of the strategy. Here we are told that it will offer access to higher margins at a time when the retail business is under pressure, so it may result in increased profitability for shareholders. The core retail business is mature and growing slowly so this offers an opportunity for continued growth.

The government grant reduces the cost of setting up the call centre.

Customers may perceive the strategy as enhancing the service on offer which may help retain/attract new customers for the retail business.

Given the government's stated aim to increase competition they may well look favourably on the venture by Marcham.

It may provide additional career opportunities for some employees.

Risk

The biggest risk is that management have no experience/expertise in financial services products, which are complex.

From a risk point of view, adding financial services spreads the risk profile of Marcham's business. However according to Ansoff this strategy would be classed as unrelated diversification and as a result is a high risk approach to increasing profits. Banking is no longer the safe and secure business that it was once deemed to be. Institutional shareholders will already have well diversified portfolios and it could be argued that if shareholders wanted ownership of a bank then they could just buy shares in one themselves.

Shareholders may be concerned that management will be distracted from the core business.

There is a big reputational risk for the existing business if Marcham gets it wrong and it would need to ring fence this area of the business as a separate company.

Marcham may lose customers from the retail business if it rejects applications for loans or credit cards.

Conclusion:

The fact that a number of other supermarkets have launched financial services products suggests that the strategy is viable, although further consideration needs to be given to the best method of implementing the strategy.

(c) **Organic growth versus joint venture**

Arguments against organic growth (in favour of joint venture)

Gaining competences via organic growth takes time. Marcham does not have any expertise in financial services so will need to buy it in. A partnership with an existing bank would ensure rapid access to the relevant expertise.

There are significant regulation and compliance issues in the banking sector, including barriers to entry such as the licence. Although Marcham has already been granted a licence it will lack expertise and systems to ensure compliance in areas such as money laundering legislation.

The financial services regulator, the Financial Conduct Authority (FCA), may be more favourable in the long term towards a venture that has already demonstrated financial expertise and compliance.

Most other retailers have chosen to move into financial services through partnership with banks, thus combining banking expertise with the retailer's brand strength and reputation.

Risk is shared.

Arguments in favour of organic growth (against joint venture)

Organic growth gives Marcham full control over the venture and avoids the need to share profits.

Having to buy-in operational expertise from a bank may restrict the scope for Marcham to do banking in a different way, which is a key driver for its strategy.

An alliance with a bank would not address the issue of the public's mistrust of the banking sector. Marcham's loyalty card may provide access to existing customer base.

The government grant may not be available if Marcham expands with a partner.

The available choice of partner would be limited as there would be relatively few options available to choose from in terms of a bank with a reputation still intact.

It avoids placing reliance on the future reputation of the chosen partner.

Organic growth avoids any potential clash of strategy or disagreement – banking partners may be reluctant to sanction new financial services products that are critical of their own service provision or that overtly compete.

It saves the time and cost of negotiating terms of a JV agreement, profit share, exit options etc.

Conclusion:

Other supermarkets have chosen to enter financial services with banking partners for a reason and Marcham needs to consider carefully the risks involved in pursuing this strategy alone.

3.2 Ethics

Tutorial note

This answer includes more points than is necessary for the marks available but a full range of points has been provided for marking purposes.

Loyalty card:

The issue concerning the loyalty card is really one of ethical marketing and relates to the collection, use and sale of the data gathered in this way. Is Marcham behaving in a fair and transparent manner and what is the likely effect on its customers?

It is partly a question of boundaries – how much data is legal to collect, what is acceptable use?

Collection of data

The ethical argument is that collection of the data is an invasion of privacy and that it could be abused if it falls into the wrong hands.

Consumers who join the loyalty scheme consent to provide their personal information in exchange for receiving product savings. Some consumers may join the scheme as they believe that this will help Marcham to better understand their needs, thereby improving the range of products offered. Customers have a choice as to whether to shop at Marcham and whether to join the loyalty card scheme. The fact that one in four adults belong implies they do not have a problem, or perceive that the benefits are sufficient to compensate for the lack of privacy.

The *Data Protection Act (2018)* strictly regulates the confidentiality, storage and use of personal information and Marcham is likely to have sophisticated security and access systems to ensure it does not fall into the wrong hands. Furthermore, personal data can only be processed in accordance with the consent provided by the customer, which in this case is to receive customised promotions, thereby allowing Marcham to track the shopping habits of its customers and to improve its product offering.

Marcham will also have a stated policy explaining what data is collected and how it is used plus consumers do not have to take out a loyalty card if they are unhappy with sharing their personal data.

The key ethical issue here is therefore transparency and whether informed and willing consent has been given by consumers to Marcham to utilise data in an agreed manner in return for the benefits of the scheme.

Use of data

Issues concern motives and transparency.

The debate about marketing centres on whether it is about meeting people's needs and expectations or selling people things they don't need.

It could be argued that Marcham uses the loyalty card to better identify the specific needs of different groups of customers and so wastes fewer resources because marketing is targeted. As a result it becomes more efficient at stocking shelves with products consumers want, and can therefore pass the savings on in lower prices, although some argue that this is at the expense of higher prices paid by non-loyalty card holders (lack of fairness/negative effect on some).

Profiling could however also be used negatively to exclude undesirable customers or to concentrate on a wealthier class of customers, and this would be regarded as unethical.

Conclusion

Ultimately Marcham is no different than a whole host of other retailers also operating loyalty card schemes and consumers have the choice of whether to belong to the scheme or not. They can also shop elsewhere if they don't like it.

Treatment of suppliers

Business ethics covers the way a firm as a whole behaves and thus any victimisation of suppliers by Marcham would contravene this. Corporate responsibility would also suggest that Marcham owes a responsibility to society and its wider stakeholders and that a balance needs to be struck between making profits for the shareholders and treating suppliers fairly.

Marcham is being blamed, like a number of other supermarkets and large retailers in the press, for exacerbating the poverty of farmers and other weak suppliers.

The issue centres on whether Marcham is merely implementing good supply chain management or is guilty of unethical treatment due to exploitation.

Marcham's ability to dictate terms and conditions to suppliers is evidence of its bargaining power as a customer (Porter) – the bigger the company the greater its likely power to push prices down and demand better payment terms. Lower prices achieved from suppliers may benefit consumers if they are passed on. Thus terms and prices may differ between suppliers depending on their relative bargaining power in relation to Marcham.

The policy of extending payment terms is good cash flow management and could be argued to be in the interests of shareholders.

Even if it adopted standard payment terms, Marcham would be a relatively cash rich business – cash sales mean it has few receivables and JIT policies keep inventories relatively low, leading to an effective cash operating cycle.

The argument against extending payment terms is that Marcham's monopoly position in the market allows them to exploit suppliers by driving prices down, which can force smaller suppliers out of business. Marcham's terms could be compared to the industry average and to other organisations of its size to assess whether they are reasonable. Marcham might be said to be being unfair if it significantly differentiates terms between large and small suppliers, thus abusing its position of power, or if it is not adhering to Industry codes of practice.

However it is unlikely to be in Marcham's interest to drive suppliers out of business as it would then be faced with disruptions in supply or emergency supplies at premium prices. As a major player in the market and a successful plc, Marcham will not want to risk damaging its reputation. Outwardly at least Marcham it is likely to argue that that it supports local businesses and works in partnership with suppliers, adopts ethical procurement policies with transparent payment terms and conditions agreed in advance, and has grievance procedures available to unhappy suppliers.

A lack of personal ethics might lead individual managers to abuse their position or make threats to suppliers and Marcham must ensure it creates an ethical culture and has procedures in place to deal with such inappropriate behaviour.

Note that the Competition and Markets Authority has the power to act if it believes that a firm in a dominant position within an industry is abusing its monopoly power.

Finally it is worth pointing out that the newspaper article may be guilty of sensationalism and some of the criticisms may be unfounded.

4 Bigville Council (September 2012)

Marking guide

	Knowledge	Skill	Marks
4.1 Key stakeholders	2	6	7
4.2 (a) Breakeven	–	4	4
(b) Implications	–	10	9
4.3 Business case (raise finance, sustainable value and alignment)	3	13	14
4.4 Key risks	2	7	8
	7	40	42

4.1 Stakeholder conflict

The clubs and the Council will have different objectives, which will themselves be linked to their different stakeholders. Key stakeholders for the clubs will include the players, the fans and the governing body. Key stakeholders for the Council will be residents, local businesses, the wider community and central government.

The Council as a Not For Profit (NFP) organisation has a wider range of stakeholders and is likely to have to balance the use of limited resources to ensure it provides the best possible services and maximises benefits for the wider community. The clubs are likely to have two main aims:

- To achieve the best sporting success possible in order to retain/attract new fans
- To generate as much profit as possible in order to be able to acquire better players

In certain cases these aims may coincide with the Council's eg, if the clubs achieve sporting success, this will generate additional attendance and income which will increase the wealth of the stadium and facilitate the Council's objectives. However there is also scope for conflict between the individual clubs and between the clubs and the Council:

Construction of the stadium:

The clubs are likely to be predominantly interested in the main stadium and pitch. There may be conflict between them as to the best layout and surface of the pitch for their particular requirements. Each club will be interested in any stipulations or health and safety regulations set out by its ruling league body. Since the football club is contributing more capital, it may expect priority over decisions.

The Council will also be interested in the additional community facilities and there may be conflict between the Council and the clubs if the siting or construction of these is seen to negatively affect anything in relation to the main stadium eg, a running track around the pitch may cause the fans to feel separated from the game. Similarly the environmental sustainability of the stadium is of key importance to the Council whereas this may be a low priority for the clubs, particularly if it affects the visibility of fans or anything to do with the playing surface or training/changing facilities. The clubs may also be reluctant to pay additional capital costs for community facilities.

The two clubs may also conflict on the seating capacity if for instance there is little prospect of the rugby club ever being promoted and filling a larger stadium but there are realistic prospects of the football club achieving the new capacity. The clubs may also disagree over the size and nature of the playing surface.

Operation of the stadium:

Again the clubs are likely to have their own interests at heart. Although the clubs typically play matches on different days there may be conflict between them over scheduling of training and cup match scheduling.

Similarly if the rugby club has a big championship match on a Sunday they may not take too kindly to the football club having churned up the pitch on the previous day.

The clubs are likely to want priority over the use of the stadium on match days and for weekday training sessions (unless, like some professional clubs, they have access to separate training pitches). Weekday use may conflict with the Council's desire to make the stadium available for the community. Also the Council may want to use profits generated by the stadium to cross-subsidise the use of the community pitches for example, which may conflict with the clubs' profit motives.

Similarly the Council may want to hire out the stadium for events such as concerts. These may benefit the clubs by attracting a wider audience however the clubs may be concerned about the impact that such events might have in terms of damage to the stadium or the playing surface.

Sharing of joint costs between the Council and the clubs is also likely to be an issue.

Operational Issues for the Council will include: crowd safety and security; noise, lighting, energy, waste management, traffic and transport. In respect of these issues the clubs will be focused on the needs of the clubs and their fans, whereas the Council will also need to take into account the needs of the wider community which may conflict with those of the fans/clubs.

Clearly the arrangements for the SMC will need to be carefully established and agreements drawn up to minimise the potential for conflict between the parties and to protect the interests of the Council.

Examiner's comments

The first requirement asked candidates to assess the potential for conflict between the three key stakeholders (Council, rugby club and football club). On the whole this was very well done. The majority of candidates recognised that the Council was a not-for-profit organisation and were able to discuss the potential for conflict between the clubs – who were likely to be focused on commercial and league success – and the Council's need to satisfy the wider community (and possibly the stadium sponsor). Better candidates also pointed out that in addition to this conflict, there was also likely to be conflict between the two clubs over the type of pitch, match scheduling etc, and that the football club might expect to have priority given that it was contributing a larger share of the capital. In their desire to apply models, candidates must be selective - a number of weaker candidates had learnt and churned out Mendelow's matrix which tended to result in too much focus on power and interest rather than on conflict between stakeholders. Some weaker candidates also dwelt exclusively on the stakeholders' objectives and did not get round to conflicts at all.

4.2 Breakeven

(a) **The breakeven attendance is as follows:**

Contribution per visitor

Football   £640,000/(25 × 3,200) = £8

Rugby   £270,000/(15 × 3,000) = £6

Breakeven

Football £644,000/£8 = 80,500 visitors p.a which with 25 matches = 3,220 per match

Rugby £214,000/£6 = 35,667 visitors p.a which with 15 matches = 2,378 per match

(b) **Discussion**

Implications of calculations

The BE attendance for the football club is marginally higher (by 20 visitors per match) than the attendance figure used in the forecast, which explains the predicted loss (20 × £8 × 25 = £4,000).

The BE figure is 12.5% higher than the current attendance enjoyed by the football club and 5.6% higher than the average for the league. Thus the projections may be quite optimistic and if the initial attendance is below this figure then the football club will make a bigger loss than predicted. (It can be seen from the appendix that there is a loss of £71,400 based on current attendance and a loss of £34,000 based on the average for the current league.) It would be useful to know what the capacity of the existing football ground is and whether, like the rugby club, it is already at full capacity.

In respect of the rugby club the BE figure is 6.4% higher than the current attendance (which would result in a loss of just under £13k) but 16.3% lower than the average for the league. As the club's existing ground appears to be at capacity there is likely to be an implied waiting list of fans wishing to attend and so the estimated attendance level of 3,000 seems reasonable and provides a margin of safety of 20.7% (3,000 - 2,378/3,000).

Variability of attendance levels

The attendance and financial performance of any sports club is heavily dependent on its team's performance. Thus the financial success of both the football and rugby club will depend on their ability to retain their current league position or the chances of being relegated/promoted, which can be seen from Exhibit 1 to significantly affect attendance levels.

(On average, attendance levels for football clubs are 64% higher in the league above and 41% lower in the league below.)

As the breakeven levels of attendance for both clubs are above the average attendance for either club in the lower league, then relegation of a club would lead to significant losses or the need to curtail costs. The financial impact of promotion/relegation is set out in the Appendix, based on the figures for a typical club in the league. These calculations make it clear that the profitability of the football club is much more at risk than the rugby club because of the high level of traceable fixed costs (discussed further below). As a result the potential results for football range from a loss of £284k if relegated to a profit of £356k if promoted, which compares to a loss of £43k and a profit of £146k for the rugby club.

In addition to variations in attendance, success in non-league tournaments during the year would lead to more matches, further increasing profits. Each additional football match would contribute an additional £25,600 on projected attendance levels, with an extra rugby match generating £18,000. Using the expected attendance levels provided, it can be seen from the appendix that 26 football matches and 12 rugby matches would be more than sufficient to break even.

To better assess the accuracy of the forecasts and the likelihood of profitability, it would be useful to know each club's position in the current league to assess the likelihood of promotion/relegation. Also the attendance levels and number of matches for the previous two or three seasons would indicate any trend – in reality the attendance is likely to vary between matches depending on the recent success of the team and who the opposition is.

Revenues and costs

The calculations of breakeven attendance depend on assumptions about the average spend per visitor, contribution and traceable fixed costs. If the forecasts have been based on existing ticket prices and spending on merchandise/catering, these may increase with the new stadium, in which case the contribution per visitor might increase and the required attendance would be lower. A breakdown of the average spend per visitor between ticket price and merchandising and details of the different ticket prices, which presumably include concessions for the young and elderly, would be useful.

One of the reasons the football club is predicting a loss is because its traceable fixed costs are significantly higher than those of the rugby club leading to a greater variability of profits if relegated/promoted. This may be because of the level of wages in the market place for footballers but more information is required here.

Appendix: Financial analysis

Estimated profits at various attendance levels: £'000

	Current attendance	If relegated	League average	If promoted	Per forecast
Football					
Attendance	2,863	1,800	3,050	5,000	3,200
	£	£	£	£	£
Contribution	572.6	360	610	1,000	640
Fixed costs	644	644	644	644	644
Profit	(71.4)	(284)	(34)	356	(4)
Rugby					
Attendance	2,234	1,900	2,840	4,000	3,000
	£	£	£	£	£
Contribution	201.06	171	255.6	360	270
Fixed costs	214	214	214	214	214
Profit	(12.94)	(43)	41.6	146	56

Sensitivity to number of matches

	Fixed costs	Forecast contribution per match	BE no of Matches (fixed cost/contribution)
Football	£644,000	640,000/25 = £25,600	25.16
Rugby	£214,000	270,000/15 = £18,000	11.89

Tutorial note

A variety of calculations were possible and other sensible approaches involving marginal increases/contribution would have attracted credit.

Examiner's comments

Part (a) of the second requirement asked candidates to calculate the breakeven attendance figure per match for both rugby and football and then in part (b) to discuss the implications of the variability of attendance on the forecasts, providing supporting calculations.

Answers to part (a) were good with a large number of attempts scoring full marks. The most common mistake was to provide the answer in the form of annual attendance rather than per match. Only a small minority seemed unfamiliar with the breakeven formula or divided fixed costs by revenue instead of contribution.

Answers to part (b) were slightly more disappointing ranging from a discussion with very little use of supporting data, to a set of calculations with no discussion. The key issue here is that the breakeven attendance for football is in excess of that currently forecast, whereas rugby has some margin of safety, although it is not clear how the traceable fixed costs (which are considerably higher for football than they are for rugby) have been arrived at. The calculation also makes assumptions about the number of matches and is based on average spend per visitor which will almost certainly vary. Using the data provided for the 'average' club to estimate attendance, it is evident that the forecast for match profits will not be realised if either club is relegated since they will be loss making, and conversely that league promotion would considerably increase the profits available. Also the risks arising from variability in attendance are higher for football than rugby. This was capably demonstrated numerically by the better candidates. Candidates would be well advised to note that when supporting calculations are asked for, it is very hard to produce a high-scoring discussion without reference to at least some numbers.

4.3 Report

To: Bigville Council
From: A N Consultant
Date: XX/XX/XX
Re: Community stadium

The council has identified three criteria which it will use to assess the high level business case:

(1) Ability to raise finance
(2) Commercially sustainable venture
(3) Alignment with council's overall strategic priorities

(1) **Ability to raise finance**

The costs of the proposed stadium are as follows:

	£m
Stadium construction	6.75
Community facilities	3.25
Basic stadium	10.0
Additional level	1.1
Expanded stadium	11.1

Currently the following funding appears to be available:

	£m
Sale of council land	6
Club contributions	3
Finanex payment for naming rights	1
	10

Thus the Council would appear to have sufficient funding in place for the basic stadium, with a shortfall of £1.1 million if the additional conference and events facilities are built. The forecasts suggest that an enhanced stadium would increase profits by £250,000 p.a. which means the additional investment would payback in less than 4.5 years (1.1m/250,000) and therefore appears on the face of it to be worthwhile.

It would be useful to know what information the build costs have been based on and whether these make any allowance for potential overruns which are often incurred on this type of project. The amount budgeted and actually spent on comparable stadiums would help assess whether the costs being put forward by the Council fall within the range of other stadiums.

If a 10% allowance was made for overruns and the Council wished to build the enhanced stadium then they would need to find around £2 million extra finance. It appears that some grant funding may be available and the Council needs to ascertain the amount that is likely to be forthcoming and the relevant conditions attached (which appear to be quite closely linked to the Council's own priorities in terms of employment, participation in sports and environmental sustainability).

A significant element of the finance is to come from the sale of the land so any uncertainty over the price or timing of this would need to be considered. For example work may need to start on the new stadium before the old one is demolished and the Council will need to ensure sufficient finance is available. In addition the Council is likely to have limited resources and therefore has a duty to consider the opportunity cost of using the money for the stadium in terms of the other projects that require funding.

Overall the initial findings suggest that there is a viable funding proposition provided the Council can find a suitable buyer for the land and receive some grant income. If this is not forthcoming then the Council would need to draw on any existing reserves or use debt finance. An alternative might be to consider the costs of building a smaller stadium since at 6,000 seats the capacity exceeds the maximum attendance for either club if promoted to the league above.

(2) **Commercially sustainable venture**

Basic stadium

	Football £	Rugby £	Non-match £	Total £
Club income				
Current profit/(loss) from clubs	(4,000)	56,000		52,000
Other income				
Community pitches/sports facilities			50,000	
Stadium advertising/sponsorship			200,000	
Revenue from non-match day activities			187,000	
			437,000	
Costs				
Stadium running costs			(375,000)	
				62,000
Overall surplus				114,000

Enhanced stadium

Incremental costs/revenues				
Non-match day activities (537 – 187)			350,000	
Advertising (250 – 200)			50,000	
Stadium running costs (525 – 375)			(150,000)	
Additional income generated				250,000
Total surplus (114,000 + 250,000)				364,000

The financial projections suggest that the basic stadium would generate £114,000 of annual surplus, increasing to £364,000 for the enhanced stadium (this is before the interest cost associated with any borrowing requirement, and assumes the forecasts of revenue and costs from the clubs are achieved).

This equates to a ROCE of 1.14% (114k/10m) for the basic stadium and 3.3% for the enhanced (364/11.1m). More importantly the additional tier generates a return of £250,000 on an investment of £1.1 million (22.7%) and would therefore seem to be a sensible option.

The commercial viability of the venture is quite heavily dependent on the ongoing sponsorship to be received from Finanex. Without this the basic stadium would generate a loss (ignoring match revenues/costs) of £138k, with the additional commercial activities from the enhanced stadium leading to only a small profit of £62k. If the venture fails however the Council will still be in the position of owning the land on which the stadium is built.

One of the considerations for the Council will be the extent to which it shares in the profits generated by the stadium. Were the clubs to keep their own profits/losses then the predicted income for the Council would be £62,000 from the basic stadium and £312,000 from the advanced. However it appears that the suggested agreement is for the SMC to pay rent to the Council for the stadium and for the members of the SMC (of which the Council is one) to then share the profits/losses from its operation. It is not clear whether the costs of the lease are included in the forecasts provided and what the nature of the profit sharing agreement between the three parties to the SMC will be. To better assess the commercial viability from the Council's perspective it would be useful to compare the Council's share of the incremental costs and revenues of the proposed stadium with the current situation where the Council receives lease payments from the rugby club for its existing ground.

(3) **Alignment with council's overall strategic priorities**

Bigville Council's recently stated strategic priorities are:

- To maintain and develop Bigville's successful economy and provide suitable employment opportunities for residents

- To ensure accessible opportunities for all to engage in culture, leisure and recreational activity

- To promote and provide support for local people to make healthy lifestyle choices

- To create, enhance and maintain cleaner, safer and more sustainable environments

Basic stadium

A shared community stadium should provide job opportunities and if the stadium is used for events on non-match days eg, concerts this may attract more visitors to the area, thus stimulating the economy. However the existing football and rugby grounds are likely to employ local people currently and amalgamation of two grounds into one may actually lead to a reduction of jobs in some cases.

Providing a new and improved stadium is consistent with the Council's aims of ensuring accessible leisure and recreational activities and promoting healthy lifestyle choices. The all-weather sports pitches and athletics track will be of benefit to Bigville's clubs, schools and colleges, thus increasing the opportunities available in the area for local people to have a healthy lifestyle. Concerts and other events on non-match days may also increase the cultural activities available.

Finally the design of the stadium appears to focus on environmental sustainability. However, it would be necessary to assess in more detail the impact on the environment of the construction activities and then the ongoing running of the stadium in terms of pollution, noise, use of resources etc.

Enhanced stadium

The extension of the stadium to provide a conference and exhibition centre is likely to significantly increase local employment opportunities, attract more visitors to Bigville, provide opportunities for its businesses and provide more economic benefit than the basic stadium.

In addition it will widen the scope of the activities available in the area. There may also be operating synergies which help the Council to minimise the costs involved in the provision of services or cross-subsidise the community activities from the profits generated by corporate hospitality etc.

Thus the plans for the community stadium do appear to be aligned in overall terms with the Council's four stated priorities and the enhanced stadium is likely to improve rather than worsen the strategic fit.

Conclusion

There does appear to be a positive high level business case for the shared stadium and the preliminary indications are that the enhanced stadium would be the most commercially viable and more likely to help achieve the Council's strategic priorities. The Council should arrange a meeting with the key stakeholders to discuss the project, their requirements and their potential involvement and then create a steering group to take the project forward and undertake a more detailed financial analysis and feasibility study.

Examiner's comments

In the third requirement, candidates were required to prepare a report for the Council assessing the high level business case for the stadium using the Council's three stated criteria from the scenario: ability to raise finance; commercial sustainability and alignment with strategic priorities. Generally candidates made a good attempt at assessing the ability to raise finance. The vast majority produced calculations showing the estimated costs of construction and the amount of finance already secured, recognising that cash was available to fund the basic stadium but that government grants would be required to build the enhanced version. The better answers pointed out the risk of over-runs and also the fact that there may be some uncertainty associated with the sale of the land to the developer. The evaluation of commercial sustainability was less well done, with the weaker candidates concentrating their discussion on the environmental aspects of the stadium (thereby overlooking the commercial element of sustainability) or merely reiterating their discussion of the variability of match profits, already addressed in part (b) of the second requirement. Using the projections in the scenario it is clear that the enhanced stadium increase profits significantly and that the additional £1.1 million investment would be worthwhile. The best candidates pointed this out, some producing ROCE or payback calculations which were encouraging, and a number recognising the reliance on income from the sponsor. Only a few candidates pointed out that the Council has a dual role – as lessor of the stadium (which will guarantee a fixed rental income) and as a partner in the SMC (which will entitle them to a share of the profits (losses). Candidates felt more comfortable evaluating whether the stadium met the Councils' strategic priorities, although surprisingly few discussed whether these were better met by the enhanced rather than the basic stadium. The weakest candidates simply made passing reference to the stated priorities and failed to analyse whether and how the stadium would achieve these. Disappointingly some candidates continue to ignore the presentation mark available for formatting their answer appropriately (in this case as a report) and the marks available for further information and a preliminary conclusion (both of which were specifically asked for). Better marks were scored by those candidates who attempted to tailor their request for further information to the scenario.

4.4 Risks

The risks for the Council in relation to the construction of the stadium and its operation by SMC include the following:

Construction

Funding requirement

Risk arises because of the uncertainty regarding the level of capital requirement and the funding available, especially in terms of grants. Should there be a shortfall then the Council may need to find more capital by diverting it from other needs or by borrowing.

The Council may not find a developer willing to buy the land on which the existing stadium is built or one who is prepared to pay the asking price for it. Even if the sale can be arranged there is a risk that it takes time and that construction of the new stadium needs to be started before the finance from the sale of the land is available. Local residents may also decide that the money would be better spent on services such as health and education.

There are uncertainties regarding stakeholder commitment to the project. It is unclear how the football club for example would react to a shared stadium and to the fact that they are contributing more capital than the rugby club. In the current economic climate Finanex may face budget constraints and decide that it has higher priorities to spend its money on.

A major capital cost overrun, which is not uncommon in such projects, would leave the Council with the residual funding risk.

Location and planning

It appears that a site has been earmarked but a potential risk is that it turns out not to be suitable. Planning permission for the new venture is critical. There is a risk that issues arise during the construction period in relation to the environment eg, protestors complaining about the impact on the landscape or local residents unhappy about the noise/traffic etc.

Timing

Any delays in construction, as well as increasing costs, could result in adverse publicity for the Council if the clubs do not have a stadium to play in at the start of the season.

Construction company

The council will need to ensure that the building contractor is carefully selected in accordance with policy to avoid the risks associated with the work not being done properly.

Operation by SMC

The current plans are for an SMC jointly controlled by the Council and the clubs. The joint venture potentially reduces risks for the Council (as does the receipt of an annual lease payment) but an agreement will need to be carefully drawn up to minimise the potential for conflict between the parties and to specify profit sharing arrangements, contributions to ongoing costs etc.

Financial

As discussed in relation to the second and third requirements, the financial models are dependent on a number of assumptions and estimates. The Council should undertake more detailed sensitivity analysis/scenario planning to get comfort regarding best and worst case scenarios. Should the venture be loss-making, or Finanex decide to cease their sponsorship, the Council is likely to have to provide further ongoing support/financial assistance.

It appears that the profits of the whole venture will be shared between the three parties but this needs to be clarified. If one or other club starts to perform poorly and/or gets relegated this would cause the stadium to become financially unsustainable and would affect the SMC's ability to make the lease payments.

Alternatively the clubs may be expecting to retain match-day profits in which case the SMC may only share the profits from the rest of the stadium and conferencing. This may reduce the amount of community activities that can be undertaken as the Council is likely to need a share of the profits from the clubs to subsidise such initiatives.

Legal

There is likely to be a range of regulations affecting the Council, its role and powers and, in particular, the Council's legal position if the revenue targets are not achieved.

Changes in regulations of the rugby and football governing bodies may also affect the stadium and/or the number of matches eg, there is a risk that increased pitch specifications or health and safety requirements increase the running costs.

Other stakeholders

As commercial entities, the clubs may have more in common with each other than they do with the Council and, if the objectives conflict, the Council may find itself in a minority over certain decisions, resulting in the venture not achieving its strategic priorities.

There is a risk that the clubs fall out or that one of them becomes insolvent and that, as a result, the Council loses one of the parties to the joint venture. Any change in ownership and/or management of the clubs may significantly affect the venture. For example if the football club is acquired by a wealthy investor it may decide that it wants a stadium for its own use.

The fourth requirement asked candidates to consider the risks for the Council associated with the construction of the stadium and its operation by the stadium management company (SMC). This was the least well done element of the question. Most, but not all, candidates split their discussion between construction and operation, although some candidates chose instead to structure their answers by using a model such as PESTEL and as a result sometimes lost focus on the specific requirement. A common weakness was to produce a list of risks that would be faced by all parties rather than specifically the council and to make only passing reference to the SMC. In this regard better answers were produced by those candidates who clearly appreciated the dual role of the council (referred to above) and their position as stakeholder within the SMC.

5 Mayhews Ltd (March 2013, amended)

Marking guide

		Knowledge	Skill	Marks
5.1	Porter's Five Forces analysis	3	7	9
5.2	(a) Performance evaluation	2	11	
	(b) Conclusion	–	6	16
5.3	Advantages/disadvantages	2	4	7
5.4	Critical success factors (CSFs)	3	7	9
		10	35	41

5.1 Five Forces analysis – filling stations

Threat of new entrants – low

Barriers to entry for fuel retailing are high. As well as needing sites in prime locations, there is the capital required to set up the filling station (underground storage tanks, fuel lines etc) and to comply with ongoing regulatory requirements. In addition the market is dominated by major brands (oil companies and supermarkets) and these larger players have significant cost advantages as a result of scale economies. Entry to the industry is also likely to be unattractive in the current environment given low margins and high levels of competition. As a result of these factors, the threat of new entrants is low although supermarkets may continue to open more filling stations at existing supermarket locations or new out-of-town sites.

Competitive rivalry – high

Because the industry is low margin, high volume, the level of competition is intense.

The supermarkets are keen to compete with each other on the price of fuel since if they can attract customers to the filling station they are also likely to buy other goods. The effect of competition is evidenced by the reduction in the number of filling stations and the failure of a significant number of the smaller independent filling stations.

Power of suppliers – high

Fuel supply is dominated by a few large petrol wholesalers who therefore wield significant power. This is increased by the fact that most are vertically integrated and also control some retail outlets. Suppliers are likely to exert more power in relation to the smaller independent filling stations than the supermarket-owned sites.

Power of customers – varied

Customers are fragmented so in that sense they have relatively low bargaining power in relation to the industry as a whole and the market price will largely be dictated by the petrol wholesaler and government taxes. However switching costs are low and petrol is a homogeneous commodity product so there is little brand loyalty. As a result customers are easily able to transfer business and in this respect they become more important to an individual operator within the industry as they are likely to choose the lowest price filling station in their area. Corporate buyers may have slightly more power because of the higher volume of business they represent.

Threat of substitutes – low

The threat of substitutes is limited although there is some scope for the manufacture and use of bio-fuels from vegetable oils and animal fats. The greater threat for the fuel retailing industry is that as the price of fuel increases people reduce their consumption by driving less, switching to electric cars and/or using alternative means of transport.

Conclusion

This is a highly competitive industry, which is particularly challenging for the smaller independent operators who struggle to compete with the economies of scale and brand loyalty of the supermarkets. With only three sites, Mayhews may lack sufficient throughput to sustain profitability in the fuel retailing industry in the longer term.

Examiner's comments

The first requirement asked candidates to prepare a Porter's Five Forces analysis of the UK fuel retailing industry which might help inform Mayhew's discussions regarding the viability of its filling station operations. This requirement was extremely well attempted by the majority of candidates. Whilst many were able to extract salient information from the question and use it to assess the strength of each force, only the better candidates concluded that the industry is extremely competitive, with high supplier power and that the future is relatively bleak for smaller independents such as Mayhews. A minority of candidates discussed only four of the five forces, omitting the need to consider competitive rivalry, which in the context of the scenario was one of the most important issues. A common error by weaker candidates was to discuss supermarket-owned filling stations under the heading substitutes instead of discussing substitutes for the purchase of fuel eg, the use of electric cars or public transport.

5.2 **Analysis of Mayhews' performance and closure plans**

> **Tutorial note**
>
> The data to support the following commentary can be found in the Appendix.

Mayhews' overall business performance

Between 20X1 and 20X2, despite the total revenue for the business remaining almost static at £4.29 million, there has been a 10.4% increase in gross profit and a 27.1% increase in net profit, resulting in an absolute increase in profit of £125,000. On the face of it therefore the business has done well in a difficult economic climate.

Although the revenue in overall terms has remained static, this masks the fact that the 11% reduction in fuel revenues has been almost exactly compensated for by an 18% increase in repairs revenue.

The movement in fuel revenue is explained by a 5.4% increase in price but a 15.5% reduction in volume. Within the industry fuel volumes are under pressure due to the economic climate and increased engine efficiency but the drop in volume of fuel sold by Mayhews may suggest that they are losing market share to competitors. This is not surprising since their average retail price is 136p/litre, over 2p/litre higher than the 20X2 UK average and 5p per litre higher than the average supermarket price.

On average Mayhews is selling 1.47 million litres per site which is not only considerably lower than the branded petrol stations but also less than the 1.68 million litres sold by the average independent. The lack of volume will probably result in Mayhews having to pay higher prices to the wholesaler and will also result in higher overhead costs per litre, which may explain the higher prices being charged. This is also reflected in Mayhews' gross margin, which is only 11.3% whereas on average retailers keep 5% of the retail price, equating to a gross margin of 5/40 = 12.5% of the net of tax price.

The repairs revenue has grown by 18%. Given the economic climate it is unlikely that Mayhews will have put its prices up significantly and this is probably due to volume increases as a result of people needing more repairs and servicing as they hold on to their cars longer. It is also likely to reflect a move away from the dealers to local garages as customers attempt to keep their costs down.

Repairs and servicing now accounts for 44% of the total sales (compared to 37% in 20X1). Since the gross margin on the repairs business is much higher at 52.1% than the margin on fuel (11.3%), this change in sales mix towards repairs has had a positive effect on the company's overall profit.

Operating costs have also remained relatively static at just under 16% of revenue. A breakdown of these would be helpful – since the premises are owned, in addition to the wages and salaries of the owner, filling station staff and garage mechanics, these costs are likely to consist of utilities, marketing and other administrative expenses. More information is required although on the face of it the business appears to have kept these under control.

Individual garages

If we consider the performance of the individual locations, it is clear that some garages are doing better than others. Garage C is performing best of all and contributing 40% of Mayhews' gross profit, which directly reflects its reduced reliance on fuel sales and a greater proportion of high margin servicing.

Garage B is the least successful. It is charging the highest price per litre (£1.38), selling the lowest volume of fuel (1.34 million litres) and has lower margins on both fuel and repairs than the other two garages. It is also the most reliant on fuel revenues (over 62% of total revenue).

More information is required about the location of garage B but this may be in one of the less well populated rural areas or alternatively it may face strong competition in the vicinity eg, it could be close to a filling station operated by a major supermarket.

Garage A appears to be performing reasonably and accounts for 36% of Mayhews' revenue and gross profit. Comparing the net margins is not particularly useful as the operating costs of garage A include the £45,000 salary cost of Barry which, once removed, shows garage A making a net margin of 14.9%.

If Mayhews is to focus more on repairs it should try and establish what garage C is doing to achieve margins of 55% and replicate that elsewhere (eg, considering the procurement policy it has adopted for parts).

Interdependence of revenues and costs

A key issue for Mayhews is the extent to which the fuel and repairs revenue are interdependent. Should Mayhews decide to close one or more of the filling stations then they may lose some customers for repairs and servicing also.

Depending on how closely located the three garages are to each other, the Mayhews brand may be strong enough to close one garage completely but transfer its repair customers to one of the other locations.

Another consideration is the extent to which operating costs at a particular location will be reduced by closing the filling station part of the business.

Preliminary Conclusions and Recommendations

Mayhews has several choices available:

- Continue as it is

- Close some/all of the filling stations but retain all three repairs and servicing businesses

- Close one or more garages in their entirety and sell off the sites to help fund investment in the new IT system and the repairs business at the remaining garage(s)

There is intense competition in fuel retailing, and the Porter's Five Forces analysis above suggests that this is a difficult industry for a business the size of Mayhews to make sustainable profits. Thus continuing as it is, is unlikely to guarantee long-term future success.

Currently the filling station at each garage is making a positive contribution towards fixed operating costs. However the evidence between 20X1 and 20X2 indicates that it would be possible to improve profitability by increasing the proportion of the servicing and repairs business. Barry's comments about reputation indicate that there may be an opportunity to capitalise on the Mayhews brand and their reputation for honesty and reliability.

A preliminary assessment suggests that garage B is underperforming compared to the others and might be considered for closure. However more information is needed about the detailed performance of the individual garages, the likely savings in operating costs and the exit/compliance costs before deciding whether to close individual sites. An important consideration is the extent to which revenue and costs for the filling stations and repairs business are interdependent.

In the event that Mayhews decided to retain some/all filling stations, it could follow competitors and attempt to service local community needs through product diversification (forecourt shops).

In deciding on the future strategic direction of the business, another issue is succession planning, since Barry is 60. It is important to establish his personal aims and objectives for the business, including any exit plans. He may be keen to realise some of the capital tied up within the business, which the sale of one or more sites to a developer would allow him to do.

Further information required

- Details of the locations, markets and customer profiles of each garage

- Previous year's accounts for each garage

- Repairs revenue/margins split between individual and corporate customers

- Breakdown of operating costs between fuel/repairs/other to ascertain the likely savings in operating costs if one or more filling station is closed

- Exit costs associated with closure of one/more filling stations

- Breakeven analysis of fuel sales
- Pricing policy for fuel sales
- Likely value of sites to developer
- Industry/sector information re gross margins/average labour costs/overheads

Appendix: Data analysis

Sales volumes and prices:

	Garage A	Garage B	Garage C	Mayhews 20X2	Mayhews 20X1
Litres sold (millions)	1.63	1.34	1.43	4.4	5.21
Ave price net of tax/litre	53.9pence	55.1pence	54.3pence	54.4pence	51.6pence
Ave retail price/litre (net of tax price/0.40)	£1.35	£1.38	£1.36	£1.36	£1.29

20X2	Branded	Independent	Supermarkets	Mayhews
Litres sold per site (millions)	4.04	1.68	10.2	1.47
Ave retail price/litre	UK ave (whole market) = 133.8p		130.9p	136p
Ave price net of tax/litre	53.5p		52.4p	54.4p

Analysis by product/market:

Sales mix (%)

	Garage A	Garage B	Garage C	20X2	20X1
Fuel	56	62	51	56	63
Repairs	44	38	49	44	37

Gross margin (%)

	Garage A	Garage B	Garage C	20X2	20X1
Fuel	11.7	10.3	11.7	11.3	11.3
Repairs	51.6	48.0	55.0	52.1	52.1
Total	29.2	24.7	33.1	29.3	26.6

Breakdown of 20X2 revenue by location (%):

	Fuel	Repairs	Total
Garage A	37	36	36
Garage B	31	24	28
Garage C	32	40	36

Breakdown of 20X2 gross profit by location (%):

	Fuel	Repairs	Total
Garage A	38	36	36
Garage B	28	22	23
Garage C	34	42	41

Gross profit mix (%)

	Garage A	Garage B	Garage C	20X2	20X1
Fuel	22	26	18	21	27
Repairs	78	74	82	79	73

Operating costs and net profit

	Garage A	Garage B	Garage C	20X2	20X1
Operating costs as % of revenue	17.2 14.3%*	15.4	14.3	15.7	15.8
Net profit margin (%)	12.1 14.9%*	9.2	18.7	13.7	10.7
	(*) = adjusted for Barry's salary				

Mayhews: Overall change in performance 20X1:20X2

Decrease in fuel revenue	-10.9%
Increase in repairs revenue	+18.3%
Decrease in total revenue	Negligible
Decrease in fuel gross profit	-11.2%
Increase in repairs gross profit	+18.2%
Increase in total gross profit	+10.4%
Reduction in operating costs	-1.0%
Increase in net profit	+27.1%
Decrease in litres sold	-15.5%
Increase in average retail price/litre	+5.4%

Examiner's comments

The second requirement asked candidates to evaluate the performance of Mayhew's overall business and the individual garages and to justify a preliminary conclusion as to whether the company should close one or more filling stations to focus on maintenance and repairs. There were some excellent attempts at this requirement with even the weaker candidates typically scoring over half the marks available.

Most candidates produced a range of calculations for Mayhews business as a whole and for each of its garages, typically including margins, sales mix and revenue/profit growth. Better candidates also used the data to assess Mayhews' fuel prices and volumes in relation to the competition/market. At the other end of the spectrum, some weaker candidates produced hardly any numerical analysis and simply copied out absolute figures from the question or only made a vague attempt at analysing increases/decreases.

Most candidates identified the fact that despite falling fuel volumes, Mayhews has performed well, generating a 27% increase in profit from relatively static sales revenue. The key reason for this is that the mix of sales has changed in favour of maintenance and repairs, which has a significantly higher gross margin than fuel.

In relation to the individual garages, most candidates commented that Garage C is performing best of all and that garage B is the least successful. Better answers explained that this reflects C's reduced reliance on fuel sales, whereas B - the most reliant on fuel sales - is charging the highest price per litre and selling the lowest volume of fuel. A pleasing number of candidates identified that comparing the net margins of the three garages is not particularly useful since the operating costs of garage A include the £45,000 salary cost of the owner, which needs to be removed for a more accurate assessment. Better candidates did this calculation and commented on its results.

The strongest candidates identified that more information is required about the location of the garages and that B may be in one of the less well populated rural areas or alternatively face strong local competition. The lowest scoring candidates merely made assertions describing the changes in ratios, with little, if any, attempt at an analysis of causality.

Candidates were requested to make a preliminary conclusion about the closure of one or more filling stations and most did this, recommending that the filling station at either B or C be closed. Only the better candidates went on to qualify their conclusion, pointing out that more information would be required before making a final decision. The very strongest candidates raised the issue of the possible interdependence of costs and revenues, identifying that the filling station business was making a positive contribution at all garage locations and that failure to supply fuel may lead to the loss of customers for repairs.

5.3 Benefits of new information system

There are two aspects to the investment in IT: a new engine diagnostic system which will allow Mayhews to service more modern vehicles and a new IT system which will improve parts management and have marketing benefits.

Advantages

- Mayhews will be able to handle all types of car and therefore attract greater volumes of business. It will also be able to undertake business that has previously had to be referred to the main dealer.

- A customer database coupled with data analytics functionality will increase marketing opportunities provided the customers provide consent to receive promotional material. Capturing data relating to previous garage services provided to Mayhews customers would enable the company to send out promotional offers. For example if 12 months earlier a customer had purchased a new set of a particular brand of tyre then the system could automatically generate an email offer promoting the same brand of tyre at a reduced price if purchased within a set time frame.

- There will be increased revenue opportunities eg, online booking of services and repairs, which might attract a different customer profile. When customers book a repair online the system could request some basic details of the identified fault. The data analytics software could combine the data captured from the customer with external data sources such as online databases of known vehicle manufacturer faults. This may enable Mayhews garage staff to pre-order parts in advance of the customer bringing their car into the garage.

- The database management system could be used to flag up, in advance, those customers needing an MOT or a vehicle service so that Mayhews staff can contact the customer to remind them and arrange a booking (again customer consent would be required to comply with data protection regulations). This should improve the quality of the customer experience and enhance service levels. This may increase customer retention and lead to a greater share of their spend.

- The system should provide Barry with better management information and improve decision making – forecasting, customer profitability analysis, assessment of performance by location/product stream. The data analytics software could provide details on the make of vehicles which generate the greatest level of work and profit. Mayhews could then specialise in those repairing those vehicles.

- A new system may help reduce costs through more efficient work scheduling, parts control etc.

- The system may help with knowledge management and reduce the business' reliance on Barry.

Disadvantages

- The costs of acquiring and installing the system may be prohibitive for a small business like Mayhews.

- Existing staff may lack the skills to use the system and/or to do work on modern cars. Mayhews will need to train staff to use the new IT system and may encounter resistance. The requirement to employ individuals with experience in operating data analytics software is likely to be inappropriate given the size of the business.

- If Mayhews is currently receiving commission on referrals to main dealers it will lose this income.

- Implementation issues with the new IT system and the risk of system failures/downtime may cause delays/affect customer service levels. Data protection and cyber security issues will need to be addressed.

- As the technology is likely to change in the future, particularly in relation to engine diagnostics, the system may need replacing or upgrading regularly.

- There is a risk that competitors will do this too – is it competitive advantage or catch up?

Conclusion

As Mayhews currently does not have the facility to carry out repairs to cars with more modern engine management systems, it appears that investing in a new system will be critical to the success of the strategy to increase the focus on the servicing and repairs business.

A detailed cost benefit analysis should be carried out to ensure the new IT system is commercially viable.

Examiner's comments

The third requirement asked candidates to discuss the advantages and disadvantages of the proposed investment in information technology. The key to a good answer here was to identify that there were two aspects to the investment in IT: an engine diagnostic system that would allow Mayhews to service modern cars that they currently had to refer to the main dealers, and a new computer system which would provide a customer database and assist with parts management. Candidates who identified the two aspects tended to score well. Weaker candidates often listed the generic pros and cons of information systems, without applying this to Mayhews. Only the best candidates came to any form of conclusion – pointing out that the investment would be critical to Mayhews proposal to focus on repairs and maintenance and identifying the need for some form of cost/benefit analysis before such investment was undertaken.

5.4 CSFs for repairs and servicing

CSFs

Johnson, Scholes and Whittington define critical success factors as "those product features that are particularly valued by a group of customers and therefore, where the organisation must excel to outperform the competition." Mayhews has both individual and corporate clients and they may value different things eg, corporate clients may be more concerned about speed of service whereas individual customers may focus on trust and reliability.

Alternatively a wider definition of CSFs is "a small number of key goals vital to the success of an organisation – things that must go right." Thus CSFs can consider not just the actual product/service but other factors vital to commercial success eg, availability, competitive knowledge, cost or performance control.

Using CSFs for strategic control

The process of identifying CSFs will help Mayhews' management focus attention on what is important and the things that need controlling/improving. It will also identify areas of little value-added where for example costs could be eliminated.

Mayhews can measure achievement of the CSFs by calculating KPIs for periodic reporting (see below). These KPIs will assist in benchmarking the garages against each other and also against rivals. They can also help to guide the development of the new information system to ensure that Barry and the garage managers receive information about the factors that are critical to the performance of each location.

Possible CSFs for Mayhews repairs and servicing business

Tutorial note

A number of CSFs have been identified below for marking purposes. Only three were required.

(1) Ability to attract and retain customers – Barry has identified that in this service-based market Mayhews has a reputation for being honest and reliable. Attracting and retaining customers will provide a stable source of income from annual MOTs and servicing and lead to word-of-mouth referrals which should generate growth. Maintaining and winning new corporate contracts will also be important.

(2) Providing top quality service levels – Mayhews wants to differentiate itself by providing dealer quality service. Customers will expect that repairs carried out are of the highest quality and comply with safety regulations and that they are undertaken as quickly as possible.

(3) Offering a competitively priced service – Mayhews has lower overheads and labour costs than the main dealers and its strategy is to capitalise on this by offering the same quality service but at affordable local garage prices. In the difficult economic climate, price may be a key factor for many customers.

(4) Ability to recruit and retain mechanics with appropriate expertise – Mayhews' ability to offer a fast and reliable service will depend on this, particularly if it starts to undertake more complicated engine diagnostics.

(5) Appropriate technology and information systems strategy to support business needs – without investing in the new engine diagnostic system, Mayhews will struggle to compete with the main dealers. The reliability of the new IT system will also affect online bookings and will enhance the customer experience by predicting service needs.

Performance measures (KPIs) linked to CSFs:

Tutorial note

A wide range of KPIs has been identified below for marking purposes. Only one relevant KPI was required for each of the three CSFs identified.

(1) **Attraction/Retention of customers:**

Number of cars referred to main dealer (measures Mayhews' ability to carry out work)
Number of contracts for corporate servicing
Average Customer satisfaction scores on post work feedback survey
Level of repeat business for MOTs and annual servicing
Geographical area of customer base
% of enquiries converted to booking for MOT/service

(2) **Quality service levels**

Quality of work undertaken:
% of defects rectified
Warranty costs as a % of revenue
Level of complaints
% of vehicles maintained/repaired which have to be subsequently rechecked

Speed of service

Lead time between customer call and date job scheduled
Availability of parts
Hours taken per repair/service
% of jobs finished on time

(3) **Competitively priced service**

Final price as a % of original quotation
Hourly labour charge compared to main dealers' labour charges
Price of various work (MOT/routine service etc) compared to competitors
Recovery rates: hours recharged to customers/hours worked

(4) **Staffing**

Qualifications undertaken/mechanic
Number of sick/absent days
Staff turnover compared to total number of staff

Number of vehicles that Mayhews is unable to diagnose/need referring to main dealer
Number of mechanics trained in the new engine diagnostic system
Number of computer system breakdowns

Examiner's comments

In the fourth requirement, candidates were asked to explain how the use of critical success factors might assist Mayhews in establishing a strategic control system. Candidates were required to justify three CSFs for the maintenance and repairs business and suggest one appropriate key performance indicator for each. This part was surprisingly quite poorly done. Many candidates restricted their marks by completely ignoring the element of the requirement relating to establishing a strategic control system and simply provided a list of CSFs and KPIs. The weakest candidates were clearly unsure about the distinction between KPIs and targets or goals. For some, the CSFs and KPIs described could have been those for any business and it was not obvious that the candidate was discussing Mayhews' repairs and maintenance business. Whilst customer satisfaction is relevant to all businesses and therefore customer feedback is vitally important, the information in the question could have been used to produce some higher quality answers. The better candidates produced a reasoned justification of their choice of each CSF and then demonstrated clearly how this could be measured. Some candidates provided a long list of KPIs, despite the specific request for only one for each CSF identified – these additional measures wasted time and did not attract marks.

6 Chiba (March 2013)

Marking guide

	Knowledge	Skill	Marks
6.1 Ethical issues	2	3	5
6.2 Divestment/growth by acquisition	3	6	8
6.3 (a) Human resource management	2	3	5
(b) Change management issues	3	7	9
	10	19	27

6.1 Ethical issues

The issue here is whether it is legal and ethical for the directors to keep the contamination confidential. As well as possibly damaging Malegar's reputation, the contamination will potentially have an effect on the wholesaler(s), the supplier of the bottles, the consumers of the vinegar and the potential purchaser, Chiba.

The directors need to investigate the cause of the problem and consider whether there has been any breach of the law or other regulations that may apply to the industry eg, health and safety or food standards. It could be argued that since Malegar takes health and safety and quality control very seriously, there should have been procedures in place to avoid/detect the contamination before the product reached the wholesaler, irrespective of whoever caused the problem.

In the context of the potential acquisition by Chiba, the directors of Malegar have a duty to act in the best interests of the company and to obtain the best value for shareholders. However, since Malegar's parent, VM plc, is a UK listed company it is likely to have certain obligations regarding the disclosure of any information that could materially affect the purchase price. To this effect there may be a conflict of interest between the directors' duty to obtain the best price for their shareholders and their duty to treat Chiba fairly. The directors should therefore seek legal advice as to how much information they are required to disclose to a prospective purchaser and to what extent it is a case of 'buyer beware'. Chiba is likely to undertake due diligence to help understand the risks before taking on ownership and this will almost certainly involve an investigation into potential liabilities and warranties.

Knowingly making statements that are misleading or inaccurate is likely to be considered dishonest and unethical. The omission of information, which is a matter of transparency, is perhaps less clear cut, particularly where it might be argued that this is an acceptable treatment eg, if the directors believe that the contamination issue has arisen with the supplier and is likely to be fully compensated.

Malegar's directors need to establish the facts and ascertain the cause of the contamination and then seek legal advice before deciding on the most appropriate course of action which fulfils their ethical obligations but minimises the risk of reputational damage for the company.

Examiner's comments

The first requirement asked candidates to explain the ethical issues that arise for Malegar's directors in relation to revealing the possible contamination.

The quality of answers to this requirement varied considerably. The question required candidates to assess the ethical issues arising from the directors' intention to keep the contamination confidential and the responsibility of Malegar to its customers and the potential acquirer, Chiba. Many candidates approached this requirement in terms of a transparency, fairness and effect framework. However only the better candidates went on to develop the next steps or draw any sort of conclusion. The weaker candidates only considered the issue in relation to Chiba, ignoring the other stakeholders in the scenario (namely the wholesaler, glass supplier and end consumers). They often failed to see any grey area and simply stated that Malegar's directors must reveal the potential contamination or risk being sued by Chiba after it had acquired the business. Stronger candidates discussed the fact that the cause of the contamination was uncertain, and that the directors needed first to establish the facts and then decide whether to disclose. The best candidates also discussed whether Malegar would have any legal duty to disclose the issue to its customers or Chiba, which might be expected to undertake its own due diligence, or whether in the context of the acquisition it would be a case of 'buyer beware'.

6.2 Strategy evaluation

As Chiba's marketing director notes, the UK parent may want to sell Malegar because the market is challenging and it is struggling to maintain margins etc. Even so, Malegar may still be worth buying as Chiba may be better placed to exploit benefits due to synergy with its existing brands and the ability to target other markets based on health benefits and alternative uses (eg, cleaning).

However it could also be that the Malegar business is viable and that other reasons can be put forward for the divestment by the UK parent:

Reason for sale by UK parent

- Rationalisation of the business as a result of portfolio analysis – here we are told that VM plc wants to focus on a few key food brands (a reversal of diversification strategy). VM plc may have decided that there is a lack of strategic fit between vinegar and its other more profitable brands.

- VM may wish to generate funds for investment in other markets that will generate better growth opportunities. Malegar may be generating insufficient returns for the amount of management time/investment required.

- We are also told that the parent company has incurred significant borrowings. These may be incurring high interest costs and putting a strain on liquidity. A sale would raise funds to reduce this debt burden.

- If exit barriers are high (eg, redundancy costs, termination penalties on leases etc) then it is better for VM to sell the business as a going concern rather than just withdraw the product.

- Finally the company may be trying to sell Malegar before the contamination becomes widely known and damages its brand/reputation.

Chiba's growth by acquisition

The Ansoff model is a two-by-two matrix of 'Products' and 'Markets'. In the context of this matrix the acquisition of Malegar would involve market development and, to the extent that malt vinegar is deemed to be different from rice vinegar, product development. The Lynch expansion model is another two-by-two matrix of company growth and geographical location. Under this model, Chiba's proposed acquisition is international external development.

Arguments for growth by acquisition

- Chiba's management has identified a desire to increase its presence in the UK. Chiba has no track record in the UK market and the strong market presence of brand names such as Malegar creates barriers to entry that would make organic growth hard to achieve. Acquisition is likely to be faster than organic growth and potentially less risky.

- Acquisition of the market leader creates instant market dominance for Chiba and at the same time removes a significant player from the market.

- It will provide access to a strong brand name/reputation in the UK market and facilitate a better understanding of the UK market for a Japanese company. This reduces cultural risk and having a 'local image' may also reduce xenophobic tendencies.

- Acquisition gives Chiba instant access to the existing factory location and resources, including employees.

- The acquisition of a business in the UK may give rise to other future opportunities, eg, expansion into Europe.

The price of the acquisition will be a major factor in assessing the overall merits of sale or purchase.

The second requirement asked candidates to discuss the possible reasons why the UK owner might be divesting Malegar (in light of the comments of Chiba's marketing director) and the benefits to Chiba of growing by acquisition in the UK.

Candidates are used to being asked to discuss growth by acquisition and were well-versed in the arguments here, with the majority able to apply their knowledge to the scenario. Some were less prepared for a discussion of reasons for divestment, although most were able to expand on the two reasons given in the question regarding the parent company's desire to reduce borrowings and focus on core brands. Better answers discussed other possible reasons such as product portfolio and life-cycles, liquidity and return. Stronger candidates queried whether the contamination may have had an impact on the decision to sell. Despite the comment in the requirement, relatively few candidates linked their discussion to the marketing director's concerns that Malegar might be loss-making. The best scripts did address this however, often in some form of conclusion, explaining that the fact that Malegar might be making insufficient return for its UK parent did not necessarily mean that it would be an unprofitable acquisition for Chiba, although only the top decile pointed out that the overall benefit of the acquisition might depend on the price to be paid.

6.3 HR strategy and change management

(a) HR management by Malegar

Malegar does not seem to have adopted a strategic approach to HRM. Its approach, which is very authoritarian, treats the staff merely as another resource, rather than as a valued asset. It may have resulted in a high degree of job-related tension, poor working relationships and some manipulation of data by functional managers accountable for their performance. There are likely to be limited prospects for career development.

The disadvantages of such an approach include the following:

- There is evidence that staff motivation may be a problem as there is a high staff turnover. The loss of staff loses experience and skills for the company with the costs of retraining and learning for new staff.

- There may be dysfunctional behaviour by staff in response to short-term targets instead of focusing on longer-term value-enhancing activities eg, this may mean that short-term sales are made at the cost of long-term customer relationships.

- The hierarchical nature of the business and centralised approach to decision making may also have impeded team-working and stifled innovation.

HR management by Chiba

Chiba on the other hand appears to take a more strategic approach with emphasis on the human element. This recognises that collectively the staff are a valued asset and can contribute to competitive advantage.

Chiba is likely to do more to focus on personal and career development, gaining employees' commitment to the organisation's values and goals and creating a more participative environment.

As a result tension and manipulation are reduced and relationships are likely to be better.

The shared approach to decision making is likely to increase goal congruence, although a potential downside of Chiba's approach to HRM is that decision-making may be slower than in Malegar.

(b) **Managing the change of culture**

It is clear that the two businesses are very different and that acquisition by Chiba will transform the existing structure, culture and values. As a result of the acquisition, Chiba's management will need to develop a strategy for creating and maintaining the necessary culture change, although the fact that the transition will take up to 12 months may help as the changes can be made gradually.

The changes may cause resistance from those wishing to preserve the existing state of affairs and the way that the changes are put forward and implemented will be crucial to Chiba's success. However given Chiba's approach to HRM, the change may be welcomed by many Malegar employees as better than they are used to.

Barrier to change

Barriers to change may be cultural or arise as a result of things which affect individuals and cause them to see the change as a threat (personnel barriers).

Cultural resistance arises as a result of structural inertia, group inertia and power structures.

- Structural inertia - Malegar has operated with a rigid hierarchy and short term targets which will take time to change. Its recruitment and promotion processes are likely to have resulted in certain types of employee who may not fit with Chiba's collective approach and participative decision making.

- Group inertia - this may be less relevant as Malegar's existing structure is unlikely to have led to cohesive teams. However the functional managers may act as a group in resisting change implementation and if employees are in one geographical location this may be a factor in increasing group resistance.

Power structures are threatened by the redistribution of authority or changing communication lines. This will in particular affect higher management in Malegar whose roles may change significantly after the new structure is implemented, as participation and collective responsibility is encouraged. Such management may be reluctant to implement changes which will be against their own interests. For example, managers may have viewed Malegar as having been very successful in the UK, therefore resenting the need to integrate and adopt the new values of a Japanese company.

Other Malegar employees who have been discontented under the existing system may however be supportive at the outset.

Personal barriers

There are also barriers which affect individuals and result in them seeing the change as a threat.

Malegar employees may feel threatened by the changes to their habitual way of working and the lack of familiarity (fear of the unknown). Junior employees may lack the confidence or skills to take on a new challenge and may take time to get used to the participative approach with its emphasis on shared responsibility. It is important that Chiba offers support and training to assist them.

Employees may have concerns over potential income levels and job security, although given the high staff turnover this does not seem to have been a feature of employment with Malegar. Chiba could provide statistics on staff turnover to help reassure employees about employment prospects and their earning capacity.

Selective information processing may cause employees to misinterpret or ignore the arguments for change put forward by Chiba's management.

Change management

Resistance to cultural change can be managed or reduced with genuine and visible support for the change by top management and good communication/participation systems associated with the change.

Chiba's management should identify the key stakeholders and influencers among the Malegar employees and provide communication and appropriate training.

Communication should focus on the benefits of the change to employees. Management needs to communicate Chiba's vision of the future and show how the Malegar employees can contribute to this. Given the gradual nature of the transfer of contracts, a negotiation strategy may be implemented where the process of bargaining leads to a situation of compromise and agreement. The advantage of a negotiation strategy is that Chiba can note possible conflict and deal with it in an orderly fashion, which prevents such problems as industrial action. Also ex-Malegar employees are more likely to support changes made and give positive commitment if they 'own' the change or have a stake in the future of the company.

Lewin suggests that managers should recognise the current state of equilibrium with forces pushing for change on the one hand and, equally, forces resisting change aiming to maintain the present situation. As a result Chiba's management would need to adopt the following process:

- **Unfreezing** – where management convince staff of the undesirability of the present situation, creating the initial motivation to change by emphasising the benefits of Chiba's longer term, participative approach.

- **The change process itself** – which will often involve new information, new attitudes and new concepts. This would involve the communication, negotiation and training outlined above.

- **Refreezing** – which reinforces the new pattern of work or behaviour by rewards, developing the belief that the changed situation satisfies organisational and personal values. Under Chiba's management employees are likely to have more opportunities for career development, staff turnover should reduce and Chiba can also implement non-financial motivators rather than focusing on the achievement of short term targets.

Tutorial note

This answer includes a wide variety of points for marking purposes and is far more comprehensive than would be expected for the marks available. As an alternative to Lewin, the Gemini's 4Rs framework for planned change could also be applied: Reframe, Restructure, Revitalise, Renew.

Examiner's comments

In the third requirement, candidates were required to (a) contrast Chiba and Malegar's differing approaches to human resource management and (b) explain the change management issues that Chiba is likely to face when integrating the Malegar employees.

Some candidates seemed less well prepared for part (a), with many weaker candidates restricting their answers to a comparison of structure and decision-making, which often was in fact little more than a repetition of points made in the scenario. Better candidates contrasted Malegar's 'hard' approach to HRM which treats employees as a short-term commodity, with Chiba's 'softer', more collective approach where employees are seen as a valued asset, and discussed the impact that this is likely to have on motivation, quality of decision-making and commitment to the organisation.

As usual candidates demonstrated good knowledge of change management in part (b), with most discussing barriers to change and Lewin/Schein's iceberg model (although the Gemini's 4Rs framework could also have been used). It was disappointing that more candidates did not focus on the change in the context of the very different HRM strategy and culture/values of the Japanese company – a point that part (a) had been intended to highlight; weaker candidates instead discussed at length the general change management issues associated with acquisitions. The best candidates recognised that the change will transform the existing culture but is to take place over a gradual period of 12 months and, given some explanation, may be welcomed by most employees as better than their current position. Candidates who went on at length about structural inertia, group norms and job security failed to recognise that these might not be particularly relevant given Malegar's existing high staff turnover.

7 Hire Value Ltd (June 2013)

Marking guide

		Knowledge	Skill	Marks
7.1	Performance and competitive position	2	9	10
7.2	Shortfall in performance and matters requiring further attention	–	18	16
7.3	Risk register	3	7	9
7.4	Ethical issues, and implications of them	3	8	10
		8	42	45

Data for 7.1 and 7.2

	HV plan	HV Actual	Variance	%	KK
Revenue					
Business £'000s	13,000	7,000	–6,000	–46.15	620,000
Leisure £'000s	17,000	20,000	+3,000	+17.65	580,000
TOTAL REV £'000s	30,000	27,000	–3,000	–10%	1,200,000
Profit £'000s	1,200	1,000	–200	–16.67%	56,000
Vehicles	3,000	2,800	–200	–6.67%	68,000
Days hiring ('000 days)	870	820	–50	–5.74%	21,100
Asset values					
Cars £'000s	20,250	16,800	–3,450	–17.04%	816,000
Other £'000s	10,000	10,000	0	0	664,000
Total assets £'000s	30,250	26,800	–3,450	–11.40%	1,480,000

	HV plan	HV Actual	Variance	%	KK
Analysis					
% REVENUE					
Business	43.3%	25.9%			51.7%
Leisure	56.7%	74.1%			48.3%
PROFIT/REV	4%	3.7%			4.7%
REV per car pa	£10,000	£9,642.85			£17,647
REV per day hiring	£34.48	£32.93			£56.87
Days hire per car	290	293			310
Profit/assets	3.97	3.73			3.78
Profit/value of cars	5.93	5.95			6.86
Value of cars/cars	£6,750	£6,000			£12,000
Rev/value of cars	1.48	1.61			1.47

7.1 Key differences between KK and HV which make performance comparisons more difficult are: the larger size of KK; and a different business sector, with KK being upmarket compared to HV's business model. However, both companies operate in a similar product and geographical market, being in the UK.

Competitive position

In assessing market share of KK and HV they are both operating in the short term rental sector which has revenues of £5,000 million. Any assessment of competitive position appears valid in relation to this market sub-sector.

With revenue of £1,200 million this gives KK a substantial 24% share of the short term car hire sector. In contrast, HV has a market share of about 0.5%. With a total industry revenue of about £5,000 million and 100 companies, the average company has a revenue of about £50 million giving it a 1% market share – almost twice that of HV.

As a consequence, HV is very much a niche player in the industry. It appears to adopt a slightly confused business model of a mid-market position in all respects except the key asset of the quality of the vehicles, which is downmarket. Perhaps, as a consequence, it is particularly weak in the business customer sector with only 26% of revenue from business customers.

In contrast, KK generates 52% of its revenue from the business customer sector. It also competes at the upper end of the market with a wide range of large company business customers and a series of partners offering exclusive access to some airlines making it impossible, in the short term at least, for smaller car hire companies, including HV, to compete.

KK's size enables it to have economies of scale and economies of scope for cost advantages and these also provide barriers to entry into this sector of the market making it hard for smaller companies, like HV, to compete.

Performance

In absolute terms, it is clear that KK earns a greater profit than HV. However this is to be expected from a larger company and it does not follow that it has performed better on this basis.

In terms of margins, the data table shows that KK has significantly better operating profit margins at 4.7% compared to 3.7% for HV. This may be due to: better cost control; economies of scale; or premium pricing.

Similarly, revenue per car is much greater for KK at £17,647 per year compared to only £9,643 for HV (83% higher). It would be misleading to conclude however that KK has better revenue generation from its assets on this basis. The table shows that the average value of a KK car is £12,000 while the average value of a HV car is only half that at £6,000. Thus, while

KK's car value is 100% greater than that of HV, the revenue per car is only 83% higher. As a consequence, the data table shows that HV's annual revenue per £1 of car value is £1.61, compared to only £1.41 for KK. This may give some support for the HV business model of sourcing two year old used cars.

A key piece of data that indicates market positioning is the price per day of hire. For HV it is only £32.93, whereas KK is able to charge an average of £56.87, although this average may reflect some very high quality vehicles.

In terms of operating efficiency, KK also appears to outperform HV. KK cars are hired out 310 days per year giving a utilisation of 85% (on a 365 day year) compared to that of 80% already noted for HV.

It is clear therefore that in financial and operating terms KK has overall outperformed HV, but nevertheless the strategy of HV may have some favourable aspects and HV may have more potential to grow if it is able to win some large business customer accounts.

Examiner's comments

The first requirement asked candidates to compare the performance and competitive position of HV with that of the market leader, KK. Attempts at this part were reasonable with most candidates producing some calculations including operating profit margin, average price per vehicle hired and average number of days hired. However, the interpretation of the data was, in many cases, limited. Candidates struggled with the comparison of a large business with a smaller business with many concluding little more than that KK had greater revenue and profit through its relatively greater size. Some of the reasons for the differences were very general, such as 'KK has economies of scale'. The comparison of competitive position was omitted altogether by a significant minority of candidates.

7.2 Revenue

The above data analysis shows that overall revenues are lower than the business plan by £3 million, which is a 10% shortfall on planned sales revenues.

The analysis by sector shows that there is a shortfall of £6 million in the business customer sector, but that sales revenue in the leisure sector has exceeded the business plan by £3 million. The reason for the shortfall in leisure needs to be investigated further in terms of the assumptions that were expected to lead to growth (eg, number of new business customers, new lines of business, pricing policy, one or a few larger business customers expected to be won). It may be that negotiations are continuing on some accounts that are expected to be won in 20X2/X3 and that will come to fruition in 20X3/X4.

The excess over plan of leisure customer revenues should also be investigated further to continue to exploit any successes in the next period.

The impact of the revenue variances has made the company much more dependent on the leisure sector compared to the business sector (74% v 26%) than was envisaged in the business plan where the relative shares were reasonably equal (57% v 43%).

There is limited additional data on each customer sector but, looking at revenue overall, it can be seen from the above data table that the number of days hiring has fallen short of the plan by 50,000 hire days. In terms of volumes this is a 5.7% shortfall. The fact that sales revenues have fallen by 10% and volumes by only 5.7% implies that the rental charge has been lower than expected. This notion is substantiated by the revenue per vehicle hire day which was £34.48 per hire day in the business plan, but only £32.93 was actually achieved.

This result could be explained by: additional discounting, proportionately more hires of cheaper vehicles or failure to implement intended price increases. The result is, however, inconsistent with the shift in the proportion of business customers to leisure customers as business customers have 'preferential rates' and so one would expect the revenue per hire day to increase with a greater proportion of leisure customers. This matter requires further investigation and analysis by sector.

Profitability

The above data table shows that overall profit before tax is lower than the business plan by £200,000, which is a 16.7% shortfall on profit in the business plan.

The fall of 16.7% in profit based on a 10% fall in revenue may, in part, be due to operating gearing whereby fixed costs still need to be covered and therefore profit falls by a greater amount than revenue.

Profit margins are also lower than planned at 3.7%, compared to the forecast 4%. This also may be due to high operating gearing and lower sales than expected.

Return on assets

Having considered profitability in absolute terms, it is necessary to consider profitability in relation to the asset base generating that profit.

The revenue earning asset base (cars) is smaller than planned, with an actual average count of 2,800 vehicles rather than the 3,000 planned. The reasons for this need to be established. It may have been that with lower demand it was decided to reduce the number of cars held in order not to have surplus underutilised assets. It is possible however that the direction of causation is the other way around ie, that it has proved difficult to source the right type of cars at the right price and the shortfall in vehicle capacity has meant that revenues have been affected. This latter explanation seems less likely, but further investigation is needed.

The return on total assets from the data table is 3.7% compared to the level in the business plan of 4%. This has occurred as, even though the asset base is £3.45 million (11.4%) lower than expected, the profit is down 16.7% on the planned level.

Further analysis of assets shows that general non-revenue earning assets are constant at £10m. As a result the entire £3.45 million fall in the asset base relates to hire cars. This is a 17% reduction. As a consequence, the return on the revenue generating asset base of cars is 5.95% which is slightly higher than the planned rate of 5.93%.

Further analysis shows that the reason for the lower hire car asset base is partly volume with 2,800 cars compared to the planned level of 3,000 (6.7% lower). However the value per car is also lower than planned at £6,000 compared to the planned value of £6,750. This may be due to: a higher proportion of purchases of smaller and cheaper cars than planned; the acquisition of older cars in the period; or a greater than expected fall in the value of the entire vehicle holding due to market conditions. Further investigations would be needed to ascertain the reasons.

Efficiency and utilisation

The number of days per year that cars are out on hire reflects utilisation and is a key factor in determining profitability. The data table shows that cars were out on hire 293 days per year compared to the planned level of 290 days (ie, on a 365 day year this is 80% utilisation). The most obvious reason for the higher level of utilisation is that despite lower sales volumes than expected (ie, hire days are 5.7% lower) the number of cars available is 6.7% lower.

The high utilisation rates are good in one respect as they reflect high usage of revenue earning assets. In another respect however the high utilisation could be seen as excessive. In particular as the business is seasonal then it may be significantly higher than 80% in peak season.

On the basis of the information provided, 30% of annual sales come in each of spring or summer. If there is on average 80% utilisation then in summer/spring there is 80% × 30/25 = 96%. At a peak time of the week in peak season there may be 100% utilisation for at least some types of vehicle. This may mean lost sales or lack of consumer choice in vehicle selection.

The utilisation and sales loss arguments need to be balanced. Further investigations are therefore needed regarding the number of lost sales from the inability to supply suitable vehicles to customers.

The business plan and professional scepticism

The shortfall from the business plan may have been due to over-optimistic forecasts in setting the plan rather than poor performance in delivering the plan. In particular, in order to raise finance from the venture capitalists, the HV board may have been incentivised to present the forecasts expected by the venture capitalists.

Examiner's comments

The second requirement asked candidates to analyse and explain the shortfall between actual performance and the business plan forecast, then to highlight three matters for further investigation. The weakest candidates produced few or no calculations for this part, thereby providing purely qualitative answers. These types of data analysis and interpretation questions require numerical analysis of data but also explanations of underlying cause and effect relationships indicating why variances may have occurred in order to 'make the numbers speak'.

Many better candidates produced calculations which normally considered days hired, operating profit margins, return on assets and efficiency/utilisation ratios. Better answers also considered the validity of the projections in the business plan itself, questioning whether they were too optimistic in an attempt to obtain venture capital finance. The correct observation was often made that the necessary investment in new vehicles had not taken place hence somewhat diluting the firm's ability to expand the business sector.

Most candidates provided reasonable suggestions for further investigation. For example, some candidates indicated that prior year performance data would be useful in order to assess the reasons for the shortfall.

7.3 (a), (b), (c)

Risk	Impact and likelihood	Risk management
Legal liability from the operation of cars by customers and employees.	• High significance if there is personal injury. • Lower impact as damage will be to only one car. • With many vehicles being operated a reasonably high probability that accidents will occur.	• Insure risk. • Put in place procedures to ensure terms of insurance agreement are complied with. • Implement procedures to minimise the probability of accidents (eg, restrict hires to 'clean' licence holders).

Risk	Impact and likelihood	Risk management
Regulation risk which may change the terms of business or the need for compliance costs to be incurred, including tax.	• Increased environment and tax legislation to reduce pollution seems likely. • With so many vehicles owned the impact could be significant.	• Consider acquiring more environmentally friendly vehicles. • Join industry pressure group to influence government.
Strong dependence on airline industry.	• Any problems with airline industry (recession, taxation, strike) are likely to affect the car rental industry.	• Form partnerships and work together with airline industry. • Diversify with partners in other industries (eg, insurance).
Competition risk. The internet has made capture of new bookings much easier for smaller companies to compete at the lower end of the market.	Competition may significantly affect price and have a major impact on profits of small companies such as HV. This is likely to occur and at the smaller end of the market there is already significant competition with over 100 UK operators.	• Develop reputation and identity. • Holding slots at airports is one way to restrict competition.
Seasonality means a risk of redundant assets in low season and insufficient capacity in peak season.	If seasonality is pronounced then the effects at the margin may be moderately significant. Highly likely as an established demand pattern.	• Price discrimination according to season. • Rent assets to acquire vehicles to meet short-term peak rather than owning 100% of car pool. • Model seasonality so timings are predictable.
Car prices could change If cars increase in cost then this is the major capital asset and will affect profitability and liquidity.	The car industry is competitive which makes major price changes unlikely. However should it occur it may have significant impact.	• Have portfolio of different types of car of different ages. • Hold cars for longer if car prices temporarily increase.
Second hand values weaken meaning lower residuals at end of car life and greater depreciation and costs of ownership.	Second hand market is competitive but new legislation could mean older cars which are less environmentally friendly may become more costly to run and this reduces their value. Effect possibly significant.	• Lease some cars. • Monitor second hand market and new legislation affecting cars. • Hold cars for longer.

ICAEW 2019

Risk	Impact and likelihood	Risk management
Operating cost increases – eg, repairs, petrol, insurance, road tax.	Very likely given past evidence. Cumulative effect likely to be significant, although customers pay for own petrol.	• Review maintenance operations. • Industry wide effect so would not materially impact upon competitive position in the industry which may enable industry wide price increase to offset cost increases.
Online communication or other computer failure would prevent all bookings for period of problem.	Likely to be short term and isolated but loss of customers to rivals and reputation risk.	IT back up facilities and contingency provisions for disaster recovery.

Tutorial note

Only **four** risks were required from candidates.

Examiner's comments

The third requirement asked candidates to prepare a risk register. There were some very general answers. For example some candidates merely cited operational or financial risk without being specific as to what these could be. That said, there were some really good answers at the other end of the spectrum which clearly identified very specific risks, their classification (eg, financial or strategic), their impact and likelihood and what could be done to mitigate them. The higher scoring answers included the risks of the airline industry and their implications, issues with the online systems, as well as increase in fuel prices, values of vehicles and the ageing and depreciation of cars. Weaker answers typically displayed some or all of the following: covering only three risks; little detail or explanation of each point: highlighting insignificant risks; or identifying unlikely circumstances which were not suggested by the scenario. Most, but far from all, candidates used the columnar format suggested in the question.

7.4 Introduction

In assessing the ethical issues and implications of the three matters raised it is important to assess both whether they are unethical, and the degree of ethical/unethical behaviour. This is particularly the case for the implications of the actions.

In the first instance, it is necessary to establish the full facts in each of the cases highlighted by Gatter LLP. At the moment they are merely accusations which need to be substantiated. An appropriate degree of professional scepticism must be applied to all concerned.

Issue 1 - private use of company vehicles by executive directors

The company is a separate legal entity from the directors and shareholders, and no-one has rights to use or take the company's assets without due authority. Potentially, the use of company assets by directors, even where there is no loss of revenue, is an illegal act in breach of their statutory duties. In addition, it appears there is a corporate governance problem in that the directors, who are the company's agents, are pursuing their own ends rather than those of the company. It may be necessary to take legal advice. Initially it will be necessary to speak to each director to gather evidence of actions. It will also be necessary to examine director employment contracts with the company to investigate whether they confer rights to use company assets under any conditions. Additionally, it should be established whether there was any direct benefit to the company in directors using the assets in this manner.

The key potential ethical issue is honesty/integrity.

In addition however there is the issue of transparency to shareholders, even if only retrospectively, of the nature and extent of any actions of this kind.

In terms of effect, it needs to be established whether there has been any direct loss to the company (eg, lost revenue) or additional cost (eg, petrol used) which needs to be made good by the directors concerned.

The fairness of the transaction is in question, in that it may be contrary to the interests of the shareholders. Even where the directors are shareholders it is contrary to the interests of the other shareholders, in particular TopFin.

If any of the directors belong to a professional body, then there may be a code of conduct and guidelines to ensure members behave in an ethical and professional manner, with disciplinary action if they do not. Any director who is a member of ICAEW for instance would face disciplinary proceedings unless the actions were legitimately within the terms of their employment contract.

There may also be an issue in directors not declaring a taxable benefit.

Issue 2 – the lending of a company vehicle by a director to a third party

The issues are similar to issue 1 except as follows:

- With issue 1, the practice appeared to be at least well known to the other directors. It is not clear whether there was any internal transparency over this incident, other than the one director who was informed.

- It seems implausible that this type of action is part of an employment contract with the director.

- There is potential for the director receiving some benefit from the friend in return for the loan of the car. This would be a key effect and would amount to a personal gain.

- Are there any further undisclosed transactions of this type?

In order to gain transparency internally amongst the directors, as well as externally to shareholders, these facts need to be established in addition to those in issue 1.

Issue 3 – the hiring of a private company vehicle by a director to a third party for personal gain

This is potentially the most serious ethical issue as there is an increased risk of fraud against the company. The distinguishing features from the first two issues are:

- there is a probability of a direct financial gain by a director from deliberate misuse of company property, in breach of her statutory duties as a director

- there is a potential direct effect on the company from loss of revenue on this contract

- assuming the other directors were unaware of the incident, then there is an issue of internal control and transparency

The facts to be established are:

- why and how this transaction occurred

- what happened to the proceeds gained? Why were they returned to the company after such a delay?

- are there any further undisclosed transactions of this type?

In the fourth requirement, candidates were asked to explain the ethical issues and implications arising from a series of transactions by directors.

Candidates' answers to this requirement were the weakest in the exam. Whilst most candidates were familiar with ethical language in terms of transparency, fairness and effect, only a small number of candidates considered honesty/integrity, legality and steps which should be taken to deal with each issue. Moreover, few candidates indicated that the full facts would need to be established prior to forming a firm conclusion. It was apparent in this question that candidates do not adopt a logical, methodical approach, which considers any additional information needed. Instead, many candidates merely concluded that the behaviour is illegal without questioning why or whether they have the legal knowledge or sufficient information to come to this firm conclusion. A significant number believed that Sandra Bevan's conduct amounted to money laundering. More balanced and questioning answers were required that do not assert conclusions without supporting reasoning and evidence. Few candidates questioned the powers and responsibilities of directors in the context of corporate governance or their legal duties.

8 The Foto Phrame Company (December 2013)

Marking guide

		Knowledge	Skill	Marks
8.1	Product life cycle	2	7	8
8.2 (a)	Procurement and supply chain	4	10	13
(b)	Two distribution strategies	3	12	14
		9	29	35

8.1 The product life cycle (PLC) describes the phases of development that a product goes through. The key stages of the life cycle are:

- **Introduction** – a newly invented product or service is made available for purchase and organisations attempt to develop buyer interest.

- **Growth** – a period of rapid expansion of demand or activity as the product finds a market and competitors are attracted by its potential.

- **Maturity** – a relatively stable period of time where there is little change in sales volumes year to year but competition between firms intensifies as growth slows down.

- **Decline** – a falling off in sales levels as the product becomes less competitive in the face of competition from newer products.

The way in which a product is defined is important in determining the life cycle. It could be defined in terms of the broad technology being used, such as digital cameras. Alternatively, it could be defined in terms of a particular model of camera, such as the MM4 for FPC. Typically, the wider definition of a digital camera would have a much longer life cycle which will only reach maturity when there has been a fundamental shift in industry technology.

From the perspective of FPC's new MM4 camera it is intended to introduce this in one year. It does not however follow from this the MM3 will be replaced immediately. FPC may carrying on producing the MM3 (or at least carry on selling it from existing inventories).

In this way, the PLC for successive products may overlap. As one product is declining, another is simultaneously being introduced. This may be because of continuing product loyalty by consumers for the old MM3. Alternatively, it is common to sell only the new product into key markets (eg, Europe and the US) but sell the older product at lower prices into other geographical markets such as developing nations where there is higher price elasticity. This will prevent internal competition between the two products, so long as there is no leakage between the two types of market.

If it is the intention for FPC to extend the PLC of the MM3 then this could be achieved through minor technological improvements and design modifications to the MM3.

Turning to the MM4, its PLC is likely to be uncertain as it is only about to enter its introductory phase and there are many uncertainties about the future. However factors that may affect the life cycle of the MM4 are:

- Success of R&D activities by FPC in developing replacement technology

- Success of R&D activities by FPC's rivals which may reduce MM4 sales and cause it to enter the decline phase sooner than expected

- Changes in customer tastes and preferences

- Pricing policies of FPC and its rivals

- New entrants to the industry

- Developments in competing technologies (eg, mobile phones)

- Willingness and ability of FPC to engage in product improvement for the MM4 to extend its product life

Examiner's comments

The first requirement was the best answered part of the exam. Most candidates exhibited good knowledge of the product life cycle model, often providing a diagram to explain it (although, of those who did provide a diagram, many did not label the axes correctly).

For weaker candidates, discussion of the factors affecting the length of the product life cycle tended to be generic, on the whole, with little, or no, application to the MM3 and MM4 products. Some omitted this element of the requirement altogether. The answers of the better candidates were more specific and discussed the influencing factors in terms of technology, social status, tastes and competition on the product life cycle of MM3 and MM4.

8.2 (a) **Issue 1**

There are two key issues:

(1) Whether to have one supplier or many suppliers

(2) Whether to continue solely with a current supplier or to engage with new suppliers as well

The current arrangement with Zeegle can be described as one of strategic procurement. This is the development of a partnership between a company and a supplier of strategic value. The arrangement is usually long-term, single-source in nature and addresses not only the buying of parts, products or services, but product design and supplier capacity.

ICAEW 2019

This type of relationship can be beneficial for some organisations which may need to establish close links with companies in the supply chain to meet their own production needs or strategic objectives.

Some of the advantages to FPC from single sourcing with Zeegle may include the following:

- Consistent lenses (shape, size, quality, clarity) from a single supplier.

- Easier to monitor quality.

- Zeegle may be dependent on FPC as a major customer, and therefore is more responsive to FPC's needs, if a large amount of its income is being earned from FPC.

- More scale economies can be earned by Zeegle to reduce costs which can then be passed on to FPC in reduced prices.

- Communication, integration and synchronisation are easier (eg, integrated IT systems).

- Collaboration is easier and more mutually beneficial in developing new products because all the benefits come to one supplier.

- Zeegle has an existing relationship with FPC and therefore there is less risk and greater awareness.

However, there may also be some problems with Zeegle as a single source supplier, some of which have already been experienced by FPC in producing the MM3:

- If there is disruption to output for Zeegle there is disruption to supply for FPC. This may be indicated by the fact that "there have been occasions when there have been delays in supply" which means FPC has needed to hold inventories.

- If there are variations in demand by FPC, a single supplier such as Zeegle may not be able to satisfy these in the short term (which may be another reason for FPC to hold inventory).

- Zeegle might exert upward pressure on prices if it knows FPC is tied into it for a number of years (over the product life cycle) and therefore has no alternative source of supply.

If FPC has multiple suppliers (ie, five) there are a number of benefits:

- FPC can drive down prices charged to it by encouraging competition between suppliers who know that FPC has a choice of alternative suppliers.

- Switching sources of supply is possible by dropping a supplier altogether if it is delivering a poor quality product or service.

- FPC can benefit from innovation in future product development from many companies rather than just one.

However, if FPC has multiple suppliers there may be a number of problems:

- Each supplier has a smaller income from FPC than a single source supplier and so may lack commitment.

- Multiple communications become more difficult and more expensive for FPC (eg, more difficult to integrate multiple IT systems).

- Reduced scale economies.

- Suppliers are less likely to invest in bespoke equipment and produce a bespoke product for FPC as production volumes may be insufficient.

- The lead times and uncertainty of delivery time are greater if the geographical distances are greater, such as with Japan.

- Cross-border supply chains may produce regulatory, language, cultural, exchange rate and tax problems. These are reduced because France and Germany are both in the EU, but this does not apply to Japan.

- Four of the five potential suppliers would be new and therefore this may create some initial uncertainty and front-end costs in establishing new relationships and communications systems.

Advice

The current supplier, Zeegle, has proved reliable and therefore reduces risk and gives assurance over quality. FPC may thus be best continuing with Zeegle as sole supplier but, in negotiations on price and service, the possibility of multiple suppliers could be raised in order to obtain the best possible contract terms.

Issue 2

The integrated supply chain model proposes that it is whole supply chains which compete and not just individual firms. Integration with, and information about, not only FPC's own suppliers (tier 1) but its suppliers' suppliers (tier 2) is consistent with this model.

If tier 2 suppliers can save costs, then this can be passed on to tier 1 suppliers in the form of reduced prices, which in turn can be passed on to FPC. While the integrated supply chain model is about more than cost reduction, this can be a key benefit, particularly where the components are fairly generic. Supply chain management is therefore needed to be able to obtain these benefits.

Supply chain management (SCM) is the management of all supply activities from the suppliers to a business through to delivery to customers. This may also be called demand chain management, reflecting the idea that the customers' requirements and downstream orders should drive activity or end-to-end business (e2e). In essence it refers to managing the value system.

In **Issue 2** the key theme is upstream supply chain management as it does not deal with customers.

The main themes in SCM are Responsiveness, Reliability and Relationships but the focus requested is solely on costs and the reliability aspects of SCM.

While **Issue 2** highlights reliability and cost reduction, responsiveness and building relationships can contribute to this.

While FPC, as the customer, has no legal right to investigate a supplier it can make transparency and openness conditions of FPC doing business with tier 1 suppliers. While such an investigation may appear to be an imposition on a tier 1 supplier (eg, a supplier of an electronic component) there may be mutual benefits of greater efficiency and establishing better relationships with a key customer.

The willingness of tier 1 suppliers to do this may depend on how large the supplier is and how important FPC is to it as a customer.

There is no direct contractual relationship between FPC and tier 2 suppliers. As a consequence, at first sight, there may be increased reluctance by tier 2 suppliers to grant access to FPC to investigate cost reduction and reliability of supply. However, a tier 2 supplier (eg, the manufacturer of a microchip that is used in an electronic component supplied by a tier 1 supplier to FPC) may be aware of the indirect relationship, and the fact that if FPC ceases to purchase from the tier 1 supplier then the tier 1 supplier may purchase less from the tier 2 supplier.

In terms of who would do the investigation, there may be more certainty if FPC does it itself, but FPC staff may be remote from the industry in which tier 2 suppliers operate and lack, not just the technical knowledge, but the detail of delivery schedules and processes as, unlike tier 1 suppliers, FPC is not a direct user of the output.

Advice

Managing costs down the supply chain seems entirely appropriate and in common with best practice. However, the cost-benefit trade-off from investigating tier 2 suppliers directly may not be favourable, as there is a lower proportion of FPC's costs at stake as we proceed further up the supply chain. Monitoring how tier 1 suppliers review tier 2 suppliers may therefore be the best compromise.

Examiner's comments

Part (a) of the second requirement produced some very general, and often brief, answers on the difference between a single supplier versus a multiple supplier strategy. Whilst there was some relevant discussion on how supplier management can be seen as a collaborative relationship, it was surprising that the information in the question was not always put to good use.

Quality and cost are issues in any type of supplier relationship and whilst these were mentioned, points were often not developed enough. What was expected was how the quality of the lenses could impact FPC, how lead times may be affected and what the resulting impact on customer goodwill may be if suppliers were not geographically proximate.

It was only a minority of candidates that discussed the Rs model (responsiveness, reliability and relationships) in a structured manner.

A number of candidates surprisingly considered the supplier tiers issue to be equivalent to vertical integration. Also some candidates confused the supply chain with the value chain, without attempting to link these concepts. A surprising number of candidates omitted discussion of the supplier review at all, thereby severely limiting the number of marks they could score on this requirement.

(b) Distribution is a key aspect of marketing. Distribution is also part of the supply chain. It has already been noted that supply chain management is the management of all supply activities through to delivery to customers. Distribution is therefore part of demand chain management, reflecting the idea that the customers' requirements and downstream orders should drive activity or end-to-end business (e2e).

The distribution channel comprises a number of stakeholders including: manufacturer (FPC); wholesalers; retailers; consumers. Either of the proposals shortens the channel between FPC, as manufacturer, and wholesalers/retailers. The local holding of inventory in the US also enables the distribution channel to be shortened in some cases, by cutting out the wholesaler and selling directly from FPC to retailers.

Distribution strategy 1 - acquire a US distribution centre

Benefits

- Inventory can be held 'locally' in the US to meet surges in demand more quickly and with less uncertainty for customers than by supplying directly from production output in Germany.

- As a consequence, this strategy is driven by customer need, which is central to the end-to-end business model. The US presence means that FPC is closer to the customers and could perhaps better understand their needs.

- If FPC owns the distribution facility then it has more control over this aspect of operations than with a JV.

- Presence in the US, rather than delivery directly from Germany, means we can use local employees with local knowledge.

- Reputation with customers may improve if they know they are being supplied locally (ie, the supply chain is within the US to a greater extent).

- FPC needs to respond to having 30% of its sales in the US and it appears FPC has not kept up with growth. Managing customer service for this extent of sales directly from Germany seems inappropriate, and a distribution facility seems to be a minimum response to satisfy the needs of the US market.

- A more substantial response to US sales growth would be to have a US production facility. However, having a distribution facility holding inventory is a much cheaper alternative than a second manufacturing site in the US which would increase fixed costs and would need an appropriate skills base without any history of production in the US.

Problems

- Mere location within the US still leaves a large geographical distance between the distribution facility and much of the US population. A single distribution facility may therefore only be a partial solution to the need to improve customer service. A network of multiple distribution facilities may be warranted for 30% of FPC's total sales.

- It would appear that little inventory of US-style cameras is currently held in Germany. An intermediate solution, to reduce lead time, would be to hold inventory in Germany rather than in the US.

- The fixed production facility increases fixed costs and therefore increases risk from operating gearing.

Strategy 2

Benefits

- Collaboration with the Japanese manufacturer takes advantage of common aims of both companies and sharing fixed costs from owning a distribution facility. This will give economies of scale.

- Given that both companies have common customers there are economies of scope from deliveries to the same location. Even if this were not the case, there are likely to be economies of scope from deliveries to the similar locations.

- Without a JV there may be insufficient volumes of sales for either company to sustain a feasible distribution network.

- The joint venture means that ownership of vans to make the distribution directly to customers is possible, so there is more control over all aspects of physical distribution without needing to trust third party couriers.

Problems

- There may be a conflict of interest in prioritising deliveries of each company where their needs, or the timing of needs, do not coincide.

- With a JV, one party may wish to terminate the agreement. This may require exit costs and create uncertainty over continuing viability.

- If there is common control between the two companies then issues of governance may arise if a key decision needs to be made that the two parties disagree about (eg, a decision to expand or develop).

- Governance could be contractual or through a JV entity. This would impact upon risk sharing, exit costs, control and cost sharing. This would need to be clearly agreed.

- If one party is larger than the other, and therefore gains more benefit from the JV, the issues of sharing costs, sharing benefits and sharing control arise. Unless there are transfer prices from the parent entities, the JV is not revenue generating which may create a range of problems over how the benefits and costs are shared.

Advice

The JV arrangement permits fixed costs to be shared and would facilitate operations in the US and support marketing there. The terms of the contract need to foresee the above potential problems and permit flexibility to enable alternative strategies to be pursued over time as conditions change or sales expand. Alternatively, if a JV partner decides to withdraw from the arrangement, there needs to be protection for FPC from excessive exit costs and options to facilitate alternative distribution strategies.

Examiner's comments

Answers to part (b) of the second requirement were sometimes very brief. Benefits of acquiring the US distribution centre focused on access to US customers and use of specialist employees. Risks included exchange rates, but often little else. There was inadequate consideration of the fact that acquisition of an additional distribution centre would increase fixed costs and could therefore impact profit and operating gearing.

The joint venture appeared to be the favoured option as this 'mitigated the risk'. It would have been encouraging to have an analysis of what the 'risks' were as this was not always clear.

Service level agreements were mentioned in this part of the question and marks were awarded for this.

A number of candidates merged their answers for the two distribution strategies. Many of these answers failed to identify the key issues for each of the options.

9 Emelius Ltd (March 2014, amended)

	Knowledge	Skill	Marks
9.1 Risk register	3	10	12
9.2 Value chain drivers	4	8	12
9.3 Emelius Northern franchise	5	12	14
9.4 Letter (benefits of digital data/performance measures)	3	8	10
	15	38	48

9.1 Key risks

Business risk is the variability of returns due to how a business operates, its markets, competitors etc.

It can be sub-divided into:

Strategic – risk relating to the company's strategic position with respect to competitors and environment

Operational – risk arising from how the business is managed and controlled on a day to day business, which also includes compliance issues

Hazard – risk arising from accidents or natural events

Financial – risk associated with how the business is financed

The key risk facing Emelius in each category is set out below:

Risk	Impact and likelihood	Risk management
Strategic – technological change renders the need for a paper-based document service obsolete	Technological developments clearly have a big impact on the nature of storage and the storage systems. This is evident given the increasing use of digital asset management systems. Changes in technology may reduce the volume of business but are unlikely to remove the need for paper entirely, which to some extent may be regulatory.	Avoid/reduce risk by developing the digital data capture side of the service so Emelius will retain customers even if they switch archive method. Emelius may actually use this trend in their favour when nearing capacity in a warehouse.

Risk	Impact and likelihood	Risk management
Operational – poor standards of service by a franchisee damage the company's reputation	Emelius works with large organisations, many of which (banks, professional services) are likely to be national businesses expecting consistent standards. The existence of a number of competitors increases the likelihood that customers will go elsewhere if they are dissatisfied, which will have a large impact on Emelius.	Reduce risk by screening franchisees carefully and drawing up strict franchise agreements. Emelius already takes a strict approach to breaches of security and customer complaints which will help.
Hazard – data loss through fire at storage warehouse	Document security is of paramount importance. Loss of a client's records would be very damaging to Emelius' reputation and may result in litigation. The impact would be severe, the likelihood is unknown.	Reduce likelihood by having preventative measures such as advanced smoke detection and sprinkler systems, plus 24-hour monitoring Transfer through insurance Digital back-ups would also reduce this risk
Financial – failure to attract franchisees prevents further expansion	Capital investment requirements to continually open new outlets are significant. Emelius relies on franchise model to fund expansion. High operating gearing means franchise may take time to become profitable so it is not necessarily an attractive proposition. Likelihood: To date Emelius has 10 regional franchises so this does not appear to have presented a problem, although we do not know how this compares to target numbers	Reduce risk of low take-up by ensuring good profit incentives for franchisees Emphasise support offered Need to continually be on look out for prospective partners Again the digital data capture service may also attract different franchisees

Tutorial note

Other relevant and important risks were awarded some credit.

The first requirement asked candidates to prepare a risk register for Emelius' paper-based document storage business, setting out one key risk in each of four categories: strategic, operational, hazard and financial. The standard of answers was generally very good, with almost all candidates following the tabular approach requested. Some candidates did not appear to be clear about the nature of the different types of risk, failing to distinguish the longer term nature of strategic risk from the more day-to-day operational risk, with the financial category being least well understood. That said, there were some really good answers at the other end of the spectrum which clearly identified very specific key risks, their impact and likelihood and what could be done to mitigate them. Weaker answers typically displayed some or all of the following: little detail or explanation of each point; highlighting insignificant risks (or more than one); or failing to discuss both impact and likelihood. A minority identified risks to the digital data capture service which were not relevant.

9.2 **Value chain**

The value chain is the sequence of business activities by which value is added to the products or services of an entity so that in the end it makes a profit. Value chain analysis can be used to help identify the cost and value drivers behind Emelius' digital data capture strategy and the strategically significant activities of this side of the business. Primary activities are those that create value and are directly concerned with providing the digital data capture service. The support activities do not create value of themselves, but they enable Emelius' primary activities to take place with maximum efficiency.

Porter's generic strategies suggest that a company should pursue a strategy of either cost leadership or differentiation. Some low cost features are present in the value chain and will help Emelius achieve profitability, although its competitive advantage is more likely to centre on the speed, security and reliability of access to digital information, once captured. As might be expected with digital data (digital assets), Emelius makes heavy use of technology throughout the chain to address these critical success factors.

Key drivers:

(1) **Centralisation of scanning process (inbound logistics)**

Inbound logistics involves converting paper documents into digital assets. A key cost driver is Emelius' use of a single centralised facility with large high-tech, high-speed scanners. The central facility can batch-process large volumes and multiple formats, reducing machine set-up costs. The use of relatively low skilled employees at the scanning house with strict targets will also help control costs although this may be counter-productive if it increases error rates, slows down the scanning process or leads to a high number of resubmissions. However Emelius's use of technology to check legibility and errors should prevent this affecting service levels.

(2) **Indexing of documents (operations)**

A key value driver is the way in which the documents are indexed (operations). The powerful indexing system supports a multiple search function which should make it easier for users to retrieve a range of documents without knowing the exact title (outbound logistics). This functionality is a key component of modern digital asset management systems. Emelius has also built in internal controls to validate the accuracy of indexing which will increase the chance of fast and accurate retrieval. The fact that the system can also generate any linked documents is likely to differentiate Emelius and be something that customers may be prepared to pay a premium for.

(3) **Security of documents (service)**

Another key value driver is the security associated with preserving the confidentiality of documents and access to them. Multiple levels of system security exist to prevent unauthorised access but also to ensure records are not created, altered or deleted inappropriately and Emelius is able to offer clients a clear document audit trail. The fact that Emelius keeps copies of digital documents across multiple servers reduces the risk that data will be lost and increases the reliability of the service offered to customers.

(4) **Use of outsourcing/extended chain (procurement)**

Linkages between activities in the chain or the wider value system of suppliers and customers also drive costs or value eg, the national courier chain has been chosen on the basis of the 24-hour secure service it offers. Centralised purchasing of all equipment and sole supplier agreement for all IT requirements are likely to lead to better prices/discounts. The maintenance of the online platform is outsourced to a specialist provider who is more likely to be an expert in this area than Emelius. Management of these wider linkages will allow Emelius to provide a better service and help to prevent Emelius' competitors from replicating its value chain.

> **Tutorial note**
>
> Other relevant and important drivers were awarded some credit.

Branding (marketing and sales)

Limited marketing beyond existing branding will help keep costs down. The existing franchise manager will be responsible for attracting new customers. Since Emelius uses a franchise model, brand image is likely to be important and will be strengthened by the distinctive branding on vans, staff uniforms, website, and social media.

Examiner's comments

The second requirement asked candidates to explain four key drivers in the value chain for Emelius' new digital data capture service. This was a slightly different take on the normal value chain requirement, as a detailed value chain diagram was already provided in the Exhibit. Weaker candidates had a tendency to merely repeat chunks of the diagram without explaining how the factor they had identified would help Emelius drive value or keep costs down. Better answers: discussed their answer in the context of Emelius' generic strategy using value chain terminology; identified and explained a range of both cost and value drivers; and brought out the importance of linkages in the value chain.

9.3 **Data analysis**

Expected profit 20X4 (without Swinburne contract)

	Working	£
Revenue	90m × 0.036	3,240,000
Variable costs	90m × 0.0115	(1,035,000)
Contribution	90m × 0.0245	2,205,000
Fixed costs		(1,755,000)
Expected profit		450,000

WORKING

Revenue per sheet 20X3 = 2.7m/75m = 0.036 ie, 3.6 pence

Comparison of results 20X2-20X4

Year	Volume (millions of sheets)	Revenue £'000	Variable costs £'000	Fixed costs £'000	Profit/ (Loss) £'000
20X2 actual	50	1,800	675	1,500	(375)
20X3 actual	75	2,700	937.5	1,650	112.5
20X4 forecast	90	3,240	1,035	1,755	450

	20X2	20X3	20X4
% of capacity	50%	75%	90%
Revenue/sheet	3.6p	3.6p	3.6p
VC/sheet	1.35p	1.25p	1.15p
FC/sheet	3p	2.2p	1.95p
Increase in volume (and revenue)	–	50%	20%
Increase in FC	–	10%	6.4%
Decrease in VC/sheet	–	7.4%	8%

The EN franchise started in 20X2 and has experienced strong growth in storage volumes (50% in 20X3 and a further 20% expected in 20X4), possibly due to a strong brand image and the increasing regulatory requirements requiring customers to store documents securely. Since the selling price charged per sheet has remained constant, all the revenue growth is due to this volume increase. Whilst the selling price has remained constant, the VC per sheet has fallen from 1.35 pence per sheet to 1.15 pence. This is likely to be due to economies of scale being achieved as volumes increase.

Given the high fixed costs of the business, the franchise needs to achieve high capacity in order to be profitable (the breakeven volume in 20X4 is 1,755/(0.036 – 0.0115) = 71.6 million sheets). As utilisation of capacity has increased, so has profitability but EN is now close to maximum and initially, because of the stepped fixed cost model, results are likely to deteriorate if it wants to increase the capacity beyond 100 million sheets.

20X4 forecast with Swinburne contract:

	Working	£
Revenue	102m × 0.036	3,672,000
Variable costs	102 × 0.0115	1,173,000
Fixed costs	1,755 + 750	2,505,000
Expected loss		(6,000)

This turns EN's profit into a small loss.

Assumptions:

Pricing and variable costs for Swinburne contract would be the same as for the existing business:

Revenue per sheet = 3.6p, VC per sheet = 1.15p (assumes no further economies of scale)

Swinburne contract of 12 million pages requires additional capacity and hence the step in fixed costs will be incurred.

Accept alternative calculations/justifications of impact of contract:

Store 12m additional sheets by increasing capacity

Contribution 12m × (0.0245) = £294,000
Incremental FC = £750,000
Net change in profit = £(456,000)

Store 12 million sheets by turning away 2 million existing business or destroying 2 million documents at end of life to stay within existing capacity.

Incremental profit = incremental contribution 10m × (0.0245) = £245,000

Explanation of results and implications

Comparison of Profitability 20X4:

Year	Volume (millions of sheets)	Revenue £'000	Variable costs £'000	Contribution £'000	Fixed costs £'000	Profit/ (Loss) £'000
Without contract	90	3,240	1,035	2,205	1,755	450
With contract	102	3,672	1,173	2,499	2,505	(6)

Assuming that Emelius Northern achieves its expected volume of 90 million sheets in 20X4, the Swinburne archive would take the storage volumes beyond the capacity of the existing facilities, necessitating a £750k increase in fixed costs. Emelius Northern has enjoyed rapid growth but 20X4-X5 represents the point at which it reaches a step in fixed costs if it is to expand further.

In this case it is perhaps unfair to treat the £750k as an incremental cost of the Swinburne contract. Assuming that demand generally for EN's services continue to grow, the opportunity for the Swinburne business is simply bringing forward the need to expand the business to 20X4 rather than 20X5. Even without the Swinburne contract, the expansion point may be reached in 20X5, since the business has been growing rapidly and it would only require growth of 100/90 = 11.1% before full capacity is reached without the Swinburne contract.

Emelius Northern might be able to avoid or delay expanding the existing warehouse facility and incurring the £750k if it:

(1) Identifies documents still being stored that have reached end-of-life and writes to the relevant clients suggesting destruction

(2) Starts to offer the digital data capture service and persuades existing clients to transfer some/all of their current paper storage to digital – particularly for those clients who need to retrieve documents regularly

Certainly in relation to the Swinburne contract it appears that offering the digital capture service for 40% of the archive (4.8 million documents) would delay the required expansion until 20X5. However before making a decision to implement the digital data service, EN needs to consider the costs involved and the expectations of revenue.

Examiner's comments

The third requirement started off by asking candidates to calculate EN's expected profit for 20X4, ignoring the Swinburne contract, and to analyse the reasons for the improvement in EN's performance since 20X2. Attempts at the initial profit calculation were normally very good, with most candidates producing the correct figure, although some made errors with variable cost. However the quality of the subsequent analysis was much more variable. The weakest candidates ignored this part of the requirement entirely, or simply used the absolute figures from the question, with no additional calculations, which limited the quality of any discussion. Better candidates spotted that as the selling price has remained constant, the increase in revenue is entirely down to volume growth and that, given the high operating gearing, capacity utilisation is the key to EN's profitability.

Candidates were then asked to quantify the impact on 20X4 profitability of accepting the Swinburne contract. The ability to tackle this part of the question was extremely varied. The key issue was that the new contract for storing 12 million pages would take EN over its existing capacity, necessitating a £750k step in fixed costs, which would not be covered by the additional £294k contribution. As a result the expected 20X4 profit would become a loss. Some insightful candidates identified that it might be possible to avoid the incremental costs and accept the Swinburne contract within the current capacity, either by destroying documents at end-of-life or by turning down business from smaller clients. This approach to the calculation, if explained, was awarded full credit.

Finally candidates were asked to consider their results and the implications for EN's decision about whether to introduce digital data capture service. The point here was that if EN could digitally store the 40% of documents that Swinburne need to access regularly it might be able to accept the contract without the increase in capacity.

Better candidates discussed other relevant factors: in light of the business' current growth, other clients would probably be found in 20X5 to help utilise the additional storage capacity created by the step and that the decision to expand should perhaps be separated from that of accepting the Swinburne contract.

9.4   Swinburne LLP
Albany Court
Leeds
L2 6FD

Emelius Northern
Unit 12,
Weyhill Industrial Park
Waverley
WY4 3XZ

19 March 20X4

Dear Sirs,

Data storage and management

Following our recent discussions, I am writing to you to explain the benefits of outsourcing your data management to Emelius Northern and to recommend the most appropriate data management service for your current needs.

Recommended service package

I recommend that you use a combination of our data management services: paper document management for the 60% of documents that you are unlikely to need to access from the archive, and digital data capture for the remaining 40%.

Why digital?

- Storing paper records reduces your ability to retrieve business critical information quickly, and convenient access to the documents by a wide range of users is limited. Digital data capture allows for rapid distribution of critical information and reduces the inefficiencies of having to handle, copy, distribute, file, store and retrieve paper documents, which slow the execution of tasks and negatively impact the productivity of your employees. Using our web-based digital asset management system, solicitors in your five offices will be able to access the same files at the same time, with minimal effort.

- Digital data (digital assets) prevents many of the human errors that occur with manual paper-based procedures, as well as minimising misplaced information, and allows for increased security measures in relation to identity theft and legal liabilities. We have multiple controls to prevent unauthorised access and tampering and this will be of great benefit to you given the confidential nature of your legal documents.

- The immediate availability of files and other data and our comprehensive indexing system will allow you to retrieve the main document quickly plus any linked supporting documents. This may be particularly useful to you in relation to prolonged legal cases or if information is suddenly required in a court case.

- There are many other benefits of capturing documents digitally:
  - It is more efficient and therefore will be cheaper for documents that are to be accessed regularly
  - Back-up files and records will be stored on multiple servers for disaster recovery
  - A certificate of destruction will be issued at end of life in accordance with regulatory requirements

Performance measures

The quality of our data management services can be assured and controlled through a service level agreement, with agreed performance measures. I would suggest the following three key performance indicators (KPIs):

Security of information – this is critical given the nature of your business and the data you hold about clients and cases. An appropriate KPI would be (any **one** of):

- Number of reported security breaches
- Number of unauthorised attempts at access
- Number or % of documents reported lost or unavailable

Speed of retrieval – this will assess the efficiency of the service we provide. An appropriate KPI would be (any **one** of):

- % of information retrieved within stated target time
- Average time taken to retrieve a document
- % electronic searches resulting in a document being retrieved and opened

Cost-effective service – a key benefit of our digital service is that it should help you reduce costs. An appropriate KPI would be:

- Monthly document storage and access costs

Tutorial note

Other relevant and important KPIs, with justifications, were awarded some credit, eg:

- Number of documents not removed/destroyed after end of life
- % of documents where end-of-life certificate not issued within an agreed time limit
- % of documents not accessed after more than one year (or other appropriate time period)

We very much look forward to working with you

Yours Sincerely

Lee Gryphon
Emelius Northern

Examiner's comments

The fourth requirement asked for a letter setting out the benefits of digital data capture service for Swinburne and three key performance indicators that EN could include in the service level agreement for the new contract. Most candidates were comfortable pointing out the benefits of digital data storage although only the better answers related these to the context of the legal firm in question. Once again not all candidates clearly understand what a KPI is, with some suggesting goals or critical success factors rather than measures that could be applied to service levels. A disappointing number of candidates did not score the mark for laying out the letter properly, either by ignoring it or by setting out their answer as a memorandum.

10 Boom plc (March 2014, amended)

Marking guide

	Knowledge	Skill	Marks
10.1 Directors views and duties	4	10	12
10.2 Commercial and ethical issues	3	9	10
	7	19	22

10.1 Directors' views

Boom's mission states that the company aims "to maximise the return on investment for our shareholders whilst striving to recognise our corporate responsibility to wider society."

Finance director

The finance director believes this is contradictory. In the short term any measures taken by Boom to enhance the health and safety of its employees or to protect the local environment by reducing the amount of natural capital that it uses, such as spending on recycling water or controlling pollution, may increase costs and reduce profits. Reduced profits imply reduced shareholder wealth in terms of dividends foregone or lower capital growth. The finance director's view is consistent with the traditional view that it is the duty of the directors, as agents appointed by shareholders, to maximise shareholder wealth. This might suggest that social factors which sacrifice shareholder wealth should not be taken into account. This is the approach that the finance director is taking when he suggests that money spent 'keeping the environmentalists happy' may make certain projects non-viable.

However the mission statement is not necessarily contradictory – it does not say that Boom has to make sure that society is not disadvantaged in any way by its activities; rather it implies that the company will do its best to take society into account in its decision making and operations.

Non-executive director: corporate responsibility

Corporate responsibility is used to describe the duties which a business has to the wider community. It can be defined as the actions, activities and obligations of business in achieving sustainability. A sustainable business is one which is able to generate continuously increasing stakeholder value by applying sustainable practices throughout all its activities.

The last 100 years has seen a change in society's expectations towards social responsibility and an increased focus on the extent to which a company should exceed its minimum obligations to stakeholders and society. The modification of the Companies Act has shifted the focus for directors from looking solely at shareholders' interests to taking account of other stakeholders as well when fulfilling their statutory duty to promote the success of the company. The aim is to promote an 'inclusive' approach towards the interests of stakeholders and to encourage a long term view to be taken of corporate investment.

This is more the approach that the NED is referring to when he quotes the statement from the conference that 'the directors have a legal duty to run the company for the benefits of its members as a whole.'

Boom's shareholders, as owners of the company, will be primarily interested in the long term profitability of the various mining projects undertaken. However mining is also likely to bring benefits to a wider group of stakeholders than just Boom's shareholders. For example, employees will benefit from pay, job security and employment prospects. There are benefits too for the local governments of the countries in which Boom mines, which need to be seen to satisfy the demands of their electorate. They may argue that they are doing so by attracting foreign investment, thereby creating employment, increasing the wealth of the economy and collecting additional tax revenues. Boom's activities will also financially benefit the suppliers of its materials and equipment, and mining will also benefit those customers who use the gas that Boom produces.

Nevertheless, whilst wider society might indeed benefit from drilling and mining, the local community and environment in which any of Boom's mining activities take place might be adversely affected through pollution or the use of scarce natural capital such as water resources.

If Boom is to be true to its mission statement, it must recognise its responsibility here and this is perhaps where the potential for conflict arises:

Corporate governance and directors' duties

Corporate governance is concerned with the direction and control of the company, and helps determine the structure of an organisation, its objectives and the relationship between the organisation's management, its board of directors and its shareholders.

Responsibilities fall on the Board collectively and there is no legal distinction between the duties of executive and non-executive directors, but they do have differing roles. The executive directors are more involved in the day-to-day running of the business, whilst the NEDs bring an independent view and help facilitate the strategic decision-making process, by providing objective challenge and criticism. Good corporate governance requires the directors to put in place a risk management strategy and the NED refers to this.

Risk management

If Boom is merely paying lip-service to corporate responsibility in its mission statement, then it is much more likely to be subject to risks resulting from the diverse range of issues relevant to external stakeholders. Therefore the possibility of corporate risk failure and potential financial volatility is increased.

Transparent and accountable governance structures should incorporate the highest standards of ethics. Sustainable business practices will help to manage and minimise Boom's exposure to a broad range of risks relating to the environment, and social and workplace issues. Minimising risk ultimately places Boom in a stronger, more sustainable market position than an unengaged competitor who is likely to be exposed to a greater number of external variables.

If Boom undertakes active and responsive engagement with a broad range of stakeholder groups, this will improve its relationships with stakeholders and give it a better understanding of the environment in which it operates. Such procedures will equip Boom to anticipate the inclinations of those who prescribe regulations and sharpen its response to third party pressures.

Conclusion

The link between social engagement and financial performance ultimately suggests that companies should be motivated to implement socially responsible strategies since this will reduce risk and aid long term profitability, maximising the value of shareholder investments.

On this basis, there would appear to be no inherent conflict in Boom's mission statement. Given that the directors' duties are owed to the members as a whole, any actions which foster long term profitability appear to be in the company's best interests and therefore both elements of Boom's mission statement are achievable simultaneously.

If Boom engages sincerely in social, environmental and other sustainability issues, it is, for example, more likely to secure future access to government controlled natural capital resources and therefore more likely to achieve superior profit maximisation for its shareholders.

Examiner's comments

The first requirement asked candidates to discuss the views of the two directors in relation to Boom's mission statement. They were also asked to explain the directors' duties in respect of corporate governance and corporate responsibility. Attempts at this requirement were quite polarised. Many weaker candidates chose to apply the models of Ashridge and Mendelow, but in doing so failed to address the requirement to discuss directors' duties and corporate governance. Most candidates were confident discussing the concept of corporate responsibility, wider stakeholders and sustainability. A surprising number were however unable to distinguish adequately between corporate responsibility (the activities and obligations of a business in achieving sustainability) and corporate governance (the rules governing the structure and objectives of the organisation and the relationship between management, the board and the shareholders). Better candidates discussed the fact that the roles of the FD and the NED might influence their viewpoint and highlighted the latter's responsibility to bring an independent viewpoint to strategy and standards of conduct. Risk management was mentioned in the scenario but only the better candidates discussed the duties of the Board in ensuring an appropriate risk management framework – particularly relevant in the context of fracking and the danger that decisions might be taken to increase profits without having due regard to the risks involved.

10.2 Commercial and ethical issues

Commercial issues

Boom needs to evaluate the costs and benefits of the proposed SA project to assess what level of return the company is likely to make for its shareholders.

However the decision to invest should not be made without considering non-financial aspects or those who might be disadvantaged by the project.

Financial projections can be prepared, incorporating estimates of the production volumes of gas, the price that it will be able to sell it at, the costs of leasing the land, and mining and distributing the gas.

Non-financial or indirect benefits include the number of jobs created in the local economy, the tax revenues paid to the local government, and the environmental benefits from the reduction in the use of coal and other fossil fuels.

Boom also needs to establish the likely costs to society – for example it needs to assess the likelihood of environmental damage from hazardous chemicals and take all steps possible to reduce the risk of contamination. This could increase the operating costs of the project.

Commercially however, as explained by the FD, if the costs of protecting the environment are too great the project may become non-viable which, given the potential benefits to the local community, would not necessarily be in anyone's interests. Therefore Boom would not be expected to incur costs to eliminate all environmental risks, just those that are deemed most likely and most significant, which it would seem reasonable to address.

Ethical issues

Boom needs to consider whether there are any legal or regulatory issues in relation to the project. Given the nature of Boom's business there may be voluntary industry codes of conduct which should be adhered to.

The project appears to have the support of the local government who are willing to grant the lease, and the central government who believe that there will be considerable economic benefits. Provided the government is prepared to grant Boom a lease to mine the land then there would not appear to be a legality issue. However the shale gas is presumably non-replaceable so the government/local region needs to be compensated for Boom's use of the regions limited natural capital – presumably this will be reflected in the price of the lease for the land.

Regulatory issues may also relate to health and safety and the working conditions of employees, who have the right to be safe and to be treated fairly. It is important that Boom acts with integrity to maintain its reputation for the highest standards of health and safety and does not exploit lower standards or the lack of regulation that may exist in the region.

From a sustainability point of view the project is expected to have long term environmental benefits. However Boom and the local government must balance the need to find alternative fuel sources with the need to conserve local water supplies. They need to consult the local population, farmers etc. and take their views into account. Consideration should be given to the alternative sources to using freshwater that exist (eg, salt water or non-drinking water) and the extent to which any waste water can be treated and recycled. This may result in slightly higher costs but will increase the sustainability of the project.

There is an issue of transparency. The environmental groups are claiming that the local population is not fully informed in relation to the impact of the fracking. This claim needs to be investigated and the facts established. Boom must ensure that it has been open and honest in its negotiations with the local government to obtain the lease. It also needs to consider the extent to which the environmentalists have genuine concerns which are backed up by evidence or whether these are merely overreactions or scaremongering claims. Meetings should be held with representatives of the government, the local community and the environmental groups to exchange information and to help address their concerns. One possible issue in relation to environmental damage is the fact that the long-term detrimental effects of fracking, which is a relatively new technique, are not yet known.

In relation to integrity, Boom must ensure that its dealings with the local government and others are honest and above board, that the local community is in no way misled about the development and its long term effects, and that it is not involved in any financial attempts to induce or persuade people to act in its favour.

Conclusion

Boom needs to weigh up the benefits of project SA for its shareholders and the wider stakeholders who benefit from the shale gas production, with the disadvantages to the local environment. Provided Boom has been transparent with the government and the local community and its consultations/negotiations are genuine then the company is probably likely to be deemed to act ethically.

Examiner's comments

The second requirement asked candidates to discuss the commercial and ethical issues for Boom which are involved in the decision to extract shale gas in South America.

A wide number of points could be made in relation to the commercial issues and the better candidates covered a number of these. Only a very few explained that in undertaking an assessment of the viability of the project Boom would need to consider both financial and non-financial costs and benefits, including where relevant the costs to society. A minority of candidates missed this element of the requirement out altogether and concentrated on ethical issues only.

Candidates' answers to the ethics element were quite mixed. Better candidates considered both the negative and positive sides of the problem, identifying that although fracking may bring some environmental problems locally, it will also reduce the need for fossil fuels, Boom has the support of local and central government, and there will be considerable benefits to the area, all of which are consistent with acting sustainably. Some weaker candidates failed to use any ethical language or principles such as transparency and integrity in their answers. Others applied the transparency/effect/fairness framework, but took a simplistic view, asserting that the farmers and local people would be badly affected, that Boom would not want people to find out about this and that as a result the project was probably not ethical. This approach failed to consider the need to assess the facts and evidence before assuming the environmentalists' claims are accurate. It also overlooked the wide range of benefits that fracking is expected to generate for the region. As has been stated before, the ethics issues are not always clear-cut and weaker candidates need to take note that more balanced and questioning answers are required that do not assert conclusions without supporting reasoning and evidence.

An overwhelming majority of candidates failed to present any sort of conclusion to their analysis, which is disappointing. Commercially, if the costs for Boom of protecting the environment are too great the project might become non-viable, which would cause the wider community to miss out on the possible benefits. Thus a balance needs to be found between the interests of the shareholders and the benefits to wider society on the one hand and those that will be affected by damage to the local environment on the other. Provided Boom is transparent and genuine with all parties and addresses the most significant environmental issues then it may well be acting ethically.

11 ElectroInfo Ltd (June 2014)

	Knowledge	Skill	Marks
11.1 Pricing – current and low income			
(a) Calculation of price per chargeable hour	3	2	
(b) Feasibility and benefits of charging different prices	–	8	
			12
11.2 Pricing – IT and Electrical	2	8	9
11.3 Depot heads – set prices locally	3	9	11
	8	27	32

11.1 (a) Total demand

Price £	30	32	34	36
Variable cost £	20	20	20	20
Contribution per hr £	10	12	14	16
Demand	250,000	230,000	200,000	160,000
Total contribution	2,500,000	2,760,000	**2,800,000**	2,560,000

Thus the optimal price if charged uniformly to all customers is **£34** per session generating a total contribution of **£2.8 million**. This implies a price increase of £2 per chargeable hour if uniform pricing is to continue.

Income
Low incomes

Price	30	32	34	36
Variable cost	20	20	20	20
Contribution per hr	10	12	14	16
Demand	85,000	70,000	45,000	20,000
Total contribution	**850,000**	840,000	630,000	320,000

Other customers

Price	30	32	34	36
Variable cost	20	20	20	20
Contribution per hr	10	12	14	16
Demand	165,000	160,000	155,000	140,000
Total contribution	1,650,000	1,920,000	2,170,000	**2,240,000**

With price discrimination based on incomes, the optimal prices per hour would be:

Low income households: £30
Other customers   £36

This would generate a total contribution of:

Low income households:	£0.85m
Other customers	£2.24m
Total	**£3.09m**

(b) **Discussion**

Feasibility

In order to for it to be feasible to gain advantage from price discrimination (ie, charging different prices for a similar product/service in different parts of the market) it is necessary for:

- there to be different levels of price sensitivity in each market (ie, different price elasticities)

- the markets to be segregated, so there is minimal leakage between them

To the extent that market research is reliable, it appears from the data provided that the level of price resistance (ie, price elasticity) for the two income groups is significantly different.

As the home address for IT or electrical services should be known before a price is quoted, it should be possible to estimate the value of the house from various online databases. However, the house value is only a rough representation for income. It is not likely to be feasible that incomes can be directly identified.

Although the market can be separated by charging different prices to different customers, if there is leakage of information between the two groups, then this may cause a loss of goodwill in the 'other customers' group, as they will have paid more per hour for the same work. This may make the operation of price discrimination more difficult, if not unfeasible. In reality, it may be hard for 'other customers' to discern the hourly rate just by knowing an overall price for a job.

Benefits

From the above table, the price discrimination policy based on incomes gives a higher overall contribution than uniform pricing for all customers, as it optimises the price in each of the two separate market segments, rather than merely the market in total.

Using the above data, the price for low income households should be reduced from the current level of £32 per hour to £30 per hour. This is advantageous to EIL, as this low income group is price sensitive (ie, there is high price elasticity) and the 6% price decrease (from £32 to £30) leads to a 21% increase in demand in terms of chargeable hours (from 70,000 to 85,000). This leads to an increased contribution of £10,000 from this group.

This increase in demand might reflect the price spectrum of sole trader competitors which is up to £28 per hour. Pricing at only £2 above this rate, EIL may appeal to many low income households wishing to obtain a good quality service and who are prepared to pay a small amount extra for this, but, for many of this potential customer group, not as much as the current price of £32 per hour.

The sensitivity of demand to price changes for 'other customers' is much lower. Using the above table, the price to 'other customers' should increase from the current level of £32 per hour to £36 per hour. This is advantageous to EIL, as this customer group is less price sensitive than low income households and, although the price increase leads to a fall in demand of 12.5% (from 160,000 to 140,000), the 12.5% price increase (from £32 to £36) more than compensates for this in terms of additional contribution from this group (contribution increases by 16.7% (£1,920,000 to £2,240,000). Overall contribution from using price discrimination increases by 10.4% (from £2.8 million to £3.09 million).

Even if it is not possible to separate the markets, an additional contribution can be gained compared to the current situation by increasing the overall price from £32 to £34 per hour. This will increase total contribution from £2.76 million to £2.8 million.

A key factor in attaining the above benefits is whether the market research is accurate. Concerns may include the following:

- The market research only explored prices up to £36 and the 'other customers' had the optimal price at this level within the range explored. However, had the research gone up to £38 and beyond, then these higher prices may have provided an even higher level of contribution

- Use of questionnaire data where customers' responses may not reflect their actual behaviour

- Past data on reaction to price changes may not reflect future behaviour to a different set of price changes

- The value of a house may not accurately reflect the available income of the householders

- There are likely to be a range of factors other than income which will impact on a customer's price resistance (eg, costs, competitors' prices, wealth, service quality)

Examiner's comments

Most candidates arrived at correct calculations and thereby could make sensible comments regarding the pros and cons of price discrimination based on income. A significant minority, however, incorrectly used revenue, rather than contribution, in their calculations. Some of these candidates said that as variable cost per unit does not change then only price/revenue needs to be used, which is not correct.

Both in this requirement, and the next requirement, a small minority attempted price elasticity of demand calculations, but failed to produce systematic calculations of contribution. Some limited credit was given for such an approach.

A majority considered discrimination based on income, in the way proposed, to be a bad idea for various reasons, especially as house values may be a poor indicator of relative income.

There was a minority who calculated average prices coming out with chargeable rates within pence of each other yet not realising they may have approached it wrongly.

Hardly any candidates made the point that prices beyond £36 could also have been explored by the market research.

11.2

Service type
IT services

Price per hour	£30	£32	£34	£36
Variable cost per hour	£20	£20	£20	£20
Contribution per hour	£10	£12	£14	£16
Demand	125,000	120,000	110,000	100,000
Total contribution	£1,250,000	£1,440,000	£1,540,000	**£1,600,000**

Electricals

Price per hour	£30	£32	£34	£36
Variable cost per hour	£20	£20	£20	£20
Contribution per hour	£10	£12	£14	£16
Demand	125,000	110,000	90,000	60,000
Total contribution	£1,250,000	**£1,320,000**	£1,260,000	£960,000

With price differentiation based on service type, the optimal prices per hour would be:

IT services	£36
Electrical	£32

This would generate a total contribution of:

IT services	£1.60m
Electrical	£1.32m
Total	**£2.92m**

Discussion

Feasibility

There would appear to be few problems of feasibility in charging different prices for the two types of service in terms of operationalising the policy. The two services are carried out by different employees and all that is required is appropriate time keeping records.

In terms of the feasibility in the market place of being able to charge different prices for the two types of service, this will depend on whether such differential pricing is acceptable to customers.

Benefits

This policy is not price discrimination as they are different types of service. The pricing policy that EIL has followed appears to be a cost based pricing policy, in that it would appear (based on the finance director's quote) that the company believes that if costs are the same, then prices should be the same.

An alternative view would be to let markets dictate optimal prices and therefore, if the two types of service are valued differently in the marketplace, they should be priced differently.

If the two services are priced according to their own markets then the above table shows that this policy gives a higher overall contribution than uniform pricing for both types of service, as it optimises the price in each of the two separate markets, rather than merely in total.

Using the above data, the price for IT services should be increased by £4 from the current level of £32 per hour to £36 per hour. The IT services market appears more resilient to higher prices than electrical services. This may be because they are more highly valued by customers or because of the pricing policies and availability of competitors. This higher price is advantageous to EIL as although it leads to a fall in demand for IT services of 16.7% (from 120,000 hours to 100,000 hours), the 12.5% price increase (from £32 to £36) more than compensates for this in terms of additional contribution from this group (contribution increases by 11.1% (£1,440,000 to £1,600,000)).

The table also shows that the current price of £32 per hour is optimal for electrical services. As a result, the contribution from electrical services would be unchanged.

Overall contribution from differential pricing of the two types of service is that contribution increases from £2.76 million to £2.92 million (ie, 5.8%).

As already noted, even if there was homogeneous pricing for both services, an additional contribution can be gained, compared to the current situation, by increasing the price from £32 to £34 per hour. This will increase total contribution from £2.76 million to £2.8 million.

Examiner's comments

Similar points regarding the use of revenue, rather than contribution, as were made in the first requirement above, also apply here.

The majority concluded that considering price variation based on services, rather than incomes, was an improvement and did not suffer from many of the problems associated with the latter.

Many candidates incorrectly referred to the service approach as price discrimination, with only a small minority pointing out that it differs in principle from price discrimination.

11.3 Evaluation

The market analysis above examines only a limited range of the factors that need to be considered in pricing. Namely:

- a narrow range of specified prices
- demand according to incomes
- demand according to type of service
- variable costs

In order to achieve a more robust overall pricing strategy other factors need to be considered.

In so doing, there are two alternatives to the chief executive's suggestion of local pricing:

- The centre sets prices that apply to all depots.
- Separate prices are set for each depot based on local conditions.

Further information is required in this respect to clarify the alternative benchmark against which the local pricing policy is being judged.

In evaluating the chief executive's suggestion two key issues arise:

(1) The way in which prices are set (eg, who, when, how, why)
(2) The factors to be considered in setting prices

(1) **The way prices are set**

The above data analysis is static (ie, at a point in time). Market conditions are likely to change and therefore a method of setting prices according to changing markets over time is required, not just a decision on a revision of existing prices on a one-time basis. Consideration therefore needs to be given to how frequently they are reset and this requires a degree of agility in decision making which would be more appropriate at local depot level than for the company as a whole.

There is therefore some support for the CE's suggestion that local determination of prices by depot managers is a more responsive method of setting prices which can take account of local conditions and indeed, price based on individual transactions, rather than for groups of customers or types of service.

(2) **Factors to be considered in setting prices**

There are a range of factors that need to be considered in setting prices. The key question in this context is whether depot managers are better positioned to consider these factors than the centre.

Leakage – as the depots are 50km apart and the range for each depot is 25km then there is no leakage between markets if differential prices are set between depots (ie, there is no internal competition).

Variable costs – the average variable cost is £20 per hour across the company. However this is an average and may vary both (1) between depots and (2) within depots for different jobs. For example, there may be a variation between depots due to a need to pay higher wages for depots nearer London. Within depots, a job 25km away may be more expensive than a job 1km from the depot. These variations are almost impossible to accommodate centrally, but could be allowed for at local level with local knowledge.

Fixed costs – information is not provided on fixed costs so this is required. However, it seems likely that fixed costs will vary between depots. For example, there may be a variation between property costs, such as rentals, between depots nearer London and those further away from London. Whilst not relevant to short term pricing, the level of fixed costs would be relevant to a long term pricing strategy in order to make a reasonable return on investment.

Price discrimination – local knowledge of housing and individuals could enable a series of prices, based on a series of income levels, rather than just the two suggested by the market survey.

Competition – the industry is quite diverse between smaller sole proprietors and larger IT/electrics companies. The nature and intensity of the competition is therefore likely to vary between depots. Even if the centre is aware of this variation in local competition, it is not easy to set prices centrally for each depot as local conditions may change rapidly.

Employee level price variation – it appears there is uniform remuneration of operational employees. Notwithstanding this, the level of skill and experience is likely to vary between employees which may enable differential prices to be charged for their services based on local knowledge. Thus, for example, higher prices can be charged for more skilled or more popular employees (eg, based on customer requests).

The counter-argument

The above arguments tend to support the CE's view of a local pricing policy based on local knowledge of markets and operating conditions. However the counter view may include a few issues:

- By surrendering price control to depot managers there is a loss of control and more uncertainty at the centre.

- Depot managers may lack the experience of setting appropriate prices.

- Customers may in the long run prefer more certainty over prices and thus prefer uniform and stable prices over variable and varying prices.

Implementation

In order to be able to implement the policy of local pricing at depot level, the degree of autonomy of depot managers needs to increase significantly and this raises a series of questions relating to implementation including decision making authority, accountability, the role and competence of depot managers, and internal reporting mechanisms.

Decision making authority – giving depot managers additional autonomy in setting prices raises the question of whether this should be the only devolution of authority from the centre. For example, it may be difficult to uncouple the pricing decision from other issues surrounding pricing and which arise from a change in price, such as a change in demand. In the above table, the decision to raise the price of IT services by £4 per hour to £36 causes demand to fall from 120,000 hours pa to 100,000 hours pa. The human resource operations of this consequence therefore need to be considered alongside, and possibly in advance of, the pricing decision. To best achieve this, the local manager would also need autonomy over staffing as a consequence of having autonomy over pricing.

Accountability – in devolving decision making there is a corresponding duty of accountability on a depot manager in being responsible for those decisions and their consequences. This is likely to have consequences for internal reporting mechanisms as they report back to the centre.

Training and competence – depot managers would need the appropriate level of training in order to be competent in their wider role and to enable them to make appropriate pricing and related operating decisions.

Conclusion

Greater flexibility is needed in pricing. One conclusion would be to adopt both the policies of price discrimination based on estimated household incomes and differential pricing of IT and electrical services, but at depot level.

Further analysis of existing information from the market survey at depot level is required to be able to do this. It will require analysing responses for each of the two services according to the two income groupings.

Overall, making prices respond more flexibility to market conditions, service types and customer characteristics will present a more complex pricing structure, but there is significant scope to increase profits if this can be implemented at local level by competent managers with local knowledge and the consequences controlled at central level.

Examiner's comments

This part was the weakest part of the question for most candidates. Many referred to goal congruence issues, but often without providing examples of a lack of goal congruence.

A few candidates made the point that the geographical boundaries between depots may be unclear, thereby questioning the quality of any relative performance data.

Many candidates talked about customers going to another depot – they were failing to notice the point that this is a home service where an engineer comes to your house and you will be served by a specific depot. Those who discussed implementation issues arising from the change in structure for decision making scored well, but many ignored this element of the question.

12 Forsi Ltd (September 2014, amended)

	Knowledge	Skill	Marks
12.1 Performance analysis/non-financial information	2	16	16
12.2 Existing structure	2	5	7
12.3 Knowledge management/implementation	3	6	8
12.4 (a) Subsidiary/forensic science division	3	6	
(b) Change management recommendations	2	5	
			14
	12	38	45

12.1 Data Analysis

Appendix of calculations

Tutorial note

A wide range of calculations is provided here for marking purposes. Candidates were not expected to produce all of these for the marks available

	Forsi 20X2	Forsi 20X3	Aussi Forensic science division 20X3
Sales revenue £million	5.4	5.088 (2.3% of Aussi)	220.3
Direct costs £million	4.175	4.165 (2.5% of Aussi)	165.225
Gross profit £million	1.225	0.923 (1.7% of Aussi)	55.075
R&D £million	0.254	0.260 (5.9% of Aussi)	4.4
Marketing £million	0.108	0.090 (1.0% of Aussi)	9.000
Other operating expenses £million	0.268	0.270 (3.1% of Aussi)	8.645
Operating profit £million	0.595	0.303 (1.0% of Aussi)	33.03
Asset value £million	4.02	3.91 (2.1% of Aussi)	183.5
Gross margin	22.7%	18.1%	25.0%

	Forsi 20X2	Forsi 20X3	Aussi Forensic science division 20X3
Operating margin	11.2%	6.0%	15.0%
ROCE	14.8%	7.7%	18.0%
R&D as % of sales	4.7%	5.1%	2.0%
Marketing as % of sales	2.0%	1.8%	4.1%
Other operating expenses as % of sales	5.0%	5.3%	3.9%
Order book as % of revenue	25%	16.8%	29.5%
Order book (months)	3	2	3.5
No of employees	45	45 (2.25% of Aussi)	2,000
Revenue per employee	120,000	113,067	110,150
Per project			
Average value of project	50,000	48,000	89,992
Direct cost per project	38,657	39,292	67,494
GP per project	11,343	8,708	22,498
No of projects	108	106 (4.3% of Aussi)	2,448
No of projects completed on time	90 (83%)	81 (76%)	2,179 (89%)
No of projects completed late	18 (17%)	25 (24%)	269 (11%)
No of projects completed in budget	78 (72%)	69 (65%)	2,252 (92%)

Forsi: Year on year change	%
Sales revenue	-5.8
Direct costs	-0.2
Gross profit	-24.7
R&D	+0.2
Marketing	-16.7
Other operating expenses	+0.7
Operating profit	-49.1

Forsi: Year on year change	%
Net asset value	-2.7%
No of employees	No change
No of projects	-1.9
Order book	-36.7

Analysis of performance

Whilst still profitable, Forsi's performance has deteriorated significantly between 20X2 and 20X3, with a £312,000 drop in sales revenue (5.8%) and a £292,000 drop in operating profit. As a result, operating profit at £303,000 is only just over half the previous year's figure.

Sales

Sales revenue has fallen by just under 6%. The number of projects undertaken in the year was broadly similar (106 compared to 108) but the average project value has fallen from £50,000 to £48,000 which may reflect the price pressure that Forsi has been experiencing and the fact that it has had to agree lower prices to avoid losing clients. Forsi is very small in relation to Aussi's forensic science division – its revenue is only 2.3% of Aussi's. At £89,992 Aussi's revenue per project is almost twice that of Forsi's which could be a result of different pricing strategies or projects of a different size/nature.

In addition by the end of 20X3, the value of Forsi's order book represents two months' worth of sales, compared to three months at the end of 20X2. This suggests that order levels are falling and could either represent a lack of demand or an increased failure to win client tenders. More information is needed in this area (see below).

Forsi spent £18,000 less on marketing in 20X3, a drop of 16.7% compared to the previous year, which could have had a negative effect on revenue, given the increasingly competitive environment. Its marketing expenditure as a % of sales is only 1.8% compared to Aussi's 4.1%. It is possible that awareness of the founders' expertise through word-of-mouth recommendations or existing contacts is diminishing and that more marketing needs to be undertaken to raise awareness of the company's services.

Given the increasing number of specialist providers, Forsi may be losing projects in particular areas of forensic science, so an analysis of revenue by field of expertise would be useful.

Revenue per employee is above that for Aussi (£110,150) although it has fallen from £120,000 to £113,067 which could reflect a lack of productivity due to delays experienced when project requirements are being re-negotiated, or an increase in the amount of scientists' time that is non-chargeable. Alternatively it could reflect the pressure on prices that has been discussed previously or the increased number of fixed price projects. Aussi's figure may be lower if it has more administrative staff – the statistic would be more meaningful if information were available to calculate it based on the number of fee earning employees.

Gross margin

The gross margin has fallen from 22.7% to 18.1%. This is below the 25% achieved by Aussi and less than the 20% target that would be required if Forsi was acquired.

Whilst revenue per project has fallen by 4%, direct costs per project have increased by 1.6%. The deterioration in gross margin could reflect a drop in recovery rates – compared to 20X2, 7 more projects over-ran on time and/or budgeted cost. If clients are increasingly dissatisfied they may be refusing to pay for the over-runs and Forsi may be having to write off time/money spent on the project.

Expenses

With the exception of marketing (discussed above), expenditure on R&D and other operating costs has not changed significantly. As a % of revenue, Forsi spends more on R&D than Aussi, possibly because the latter has greater efficiencies/economies of scale.

ROCE

The halving of operating profit has resulted in a similar drop in ROCE, falling from 14.8% to 7.7%. This is considerably below Aussi's ROCE of 18% and the 15% target that Forsi would need to achieve if it were owned by Forsi.

Lack of management control

The fact that the number of projects over-running on time and/or budget has increased and is considerably worse than that achieved by Aussi suggests that Forsi's founders are not exerting sufficient control over costs and scheduling or that budgets are overly optimistic, perhaps in an attempt to win tenders. In some cases these over-runs may be unavoidable (eg, due to additional client demands) but in this case Forsi needs to ensure it has renegotiated passing these on to the client.

Other non-financial information that would be useful:

- Statistics on the number of tenders won vs the number actually submitted, including an analysis of which fields of forensic science these related to

- Details of the number of new clients won and existing clients lost during the year and the split of new projects/repeat business

- Breakdown of projects by private/public sector

- Amount of hours recharged to clients/hours actually spent on projects

- Breakdown of hours worked by scientists between client work and R&D

- Typical project length to establish average size of project team

Examiner's comments

In the first requirement, candidates were asked to analyse the performance of Forsi, contrasting it with Aussi's where appropriate and to suggest other non-financial information that may be useful.

The data analysis section was generally very well answered. Most candidates made some appropriate initial calculations based on the balance scorecard provided, in order to support sensible comments regarding Forsi's deteriorating performance. The majority of candidates examined revenue, margins and return on capital, and attempted to use the non-financial aspects, such as the increase in delays to project completion and the cost overruns, to explain the financial results. Whilst most candidates set out their calculations in an initial table, a minority mixed calculations within their discussion and this sometimes caused them to lose flow and structure or fail to address certain aspects. Some weaker candidates limited their analysis to the movement in figures across the two-year period.

Narrative explanations of relative performance in comparison to Aussi tended to be variable, depending partly on which calculations had been attempted. For example, those candidates who did not calculate ROCE were less able to discuss the shortfall between Forsi's current ROCE and gross margin and the targets that Aussi would require. The best answers compared and contrasted the performance of Aussi and Forsi, highlighting the vast difference in their size and market, and considering their relative performance in respect of the average size of the projects undertaken and their ability to complete on time and to budget.

The poorer answers made little attempt at identifying cause and effect relationships or key trends, for the most part simply re-stating the calculated numbers in terms of ups and downs. Weaker candidates also produced a generic list of additional information required, which was often financial, failing to address the specifics of the requirement which asked for non-financial information.

12.2 Existing structure:

Forsi undertakes specialised work based on expert knowledge. To some extent its structure has not really evolved from that of a simple entrepreneurial one, with the four original founders exerting total control over the running of the business.

One way of analysing Forsi's structure is with reference to Mintzberg's organisational configurations.

The key component (or building block) within Forsi appears to be the operating core, with scientists working directly on providing the technical forensic science service to clients.

Forsi's structure has developed incrementally and reflects the values and behaviour of the four original founders, who form the strategic apex of the organisation and currently control all client relationships.

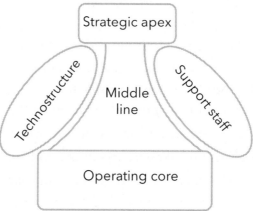

Its existing structure might be seen as Mintzberg's adhocracy or innovative configuration, suitable for a complex dynamic environment.

Key features of Forsi's structure are as follows:

- Research and innovation are key objectives and scientists (operating core) carry out their work independently.

- There is little formalisation (an absence of technostructure) and no layer of middle management (middle line). Staff are likely to be intelligent and self-motivated, with the expertise and knowledge to make the appropriate decisions whilst working in a project.

- Such a structure avoids the trappings of bureaucracy and remains flexible to encourage innovation.

- The number of support staff is limited as these functions (HR, accounting) are largely outsourced.

An alternative model might be Handy's shamrock organisation or flexible firm – with Forsi being seen as a lean organisation comprising a core of essential workers (scientists) providing specialist services to customers and supported by a contractual fringe of outside contractors, whose services are bought in as required.

Whilst the simple, flexible structure promotes innovation and allows Forsi to focus on the activities important for competitive advantage, there are some disadvantages and the informality and lack of control appear to be causing Forsi some difficulties now that it is a bigger organisation:

- The structure is lacking in coordination mechanisms

- Teams and scientists have a tendency to work in isolation rather than sharing knowledge. Such independence may result in a lack of goal congruence with personal interests being put before shared company ones

- Loose control and lack of financial awareness has led to cost overruns and impact on margins

- The founders acting as a go-between between scientists and clients has led to delays and client complaints

Recommendation:

- It may be better to have project managers responsible for liaison with the client

- Senior management could monitor projects and liaise externally to ensure Forsi is keeping abreast of industry developments, changes in competition/market. However this would necessitate an improved management information system to allow monitoring

Examiner's comments

The second requirement asked candidates to discuss the appropriateness of Forsi's existing structure, referring to relevant models. It was well attempted by the vast majority of candidates, who were clearly very well-prepared for this topic. The majority of candidates identified that the informal, largely entrepreneurial structure had initially fostered successful innovation and flexibility in a dynamic environment but was no longer suitable for the growing size of the company and was, at least in part, to blame for Forsi's deteriorating performance discussed in the first requirement. Candidates were asked to refer to relevant models and those who discussed Forsi's structure with reference to Mintzberg's organisational forms and/or Handy's shamrock structure produced answers that had more depth than those who limited their discussion to functional, divisional and matrix structures.

12.3 Why knowledge management is important

The concept of human capital is of critical significance to Forsi as this is concerned with the capabilities, creativity, skills and knowledge of its workforce which enable it to create economic value. Knowledge is a key strategic asset for an organisation such as Forsi which is providing a highly technical scientific service. Forsi may have limited tangible assets other than the technical expertise of its people.

As an organisation grows it needs more formal processes to ensure that the wealth of knowledge within the business is being captured and shared. Eg, knowledge gleaned by scientists on a project for one police force may assist scientists working on a similar project for another force, thereby reducing the learning curve and cutting time or costs.

It is important that the founders recognise that a formal strategy is required and that knowledge does not just flow round the organisation of its own accord.

Forsi's knowledge management (KM) strategy needs to capture the knowledge that is critical to its competitive advantage and then disseminate and use that knowledge in the decision-making process. Eg, KM could help Forsi to identify ways to meet client needs that are better than competitors or to improve processes or develop new and innovative forensic science techniques.

Implementing a knowledge management strategy

Implementing a knowledge management strategy would involve the following steps:

(1) Identifying the knowledge that exists within Forsi

- Human capital eg, specific scientific knowledge held by a particular scientist in a particular field or discipline

- Intellectual property (the result of innovation) eg, patents over any new techniques developed

- Client data eg, lists of client contacts held by founders, details of projects undertaken by client

- Organisational infrastructure (processes and policies) eg, the negotiating skills and relationship management tools used by the founders when dealing with clients

(2) Capture/document the knowledge to create some form of knowledge base. This may include capturing knowledge from outside Forsi (eg, intelligence on competitors, renowned experts in a particular scientific field, the police's in-house labs). Forsi may seek to capture the knowledge available to it by making use of knowledge management systems. Such systems are often particularly helpful in disseminating knowledge among workers (see point 3 below).

(3) Disseminate the knowledge to the appropriate people so it can be harnessed to:

- improve efficiency and performance
- identify opportunities to provide a better service for customers than competitors
- innovate new forensic science techniques

(4) Determine ways in which Forsi's knowledge can be developed and tracked. KM also requires an organisation to identify any knowledge it lacks and to spend time investing in improving the knowledge of its employees (eg, technical training or update courses) or helping them to use it more effectively (organisational learning). Forsi may look to build upon the KM and human capital at its disposal by encouraging its scientists to be creative and to try out new ideas, which challenge existing ways of working. Successful new ideas and ways of working could then be shared with others when undertaking similar projects in the future. This approach is likely to require an acceptance by the founders that some employee directed-schemes may not result in commercially viable solutions. This may help Forsi when tendering for future forensic work as it will have a better understanding of those techniques and procedures which should be avoided.

(5) Ensure that key strategic knowledge is kept secure and confidential within Forsi and does not leak to competitors or is not lost when staff leave eg, ensuring all scientists have confidentiality clauses in their contracts, protecting IP wherever possible

Some knowledge will be explicit eg, particular forensic science procedures or protocols. Other knowledge may be tacit (in the heads of the scientists and/or founders and therefore invisible).

It is more difficult to harness the tacit knowledge and the informal networks and communities or practices that exist within an organisation. However encouraging increased collaboration between scientists would help Forsi to transform tacit knowledge into explicit knowledge.

Forsi needs to try and break down the barriers to sharing eg, scientists may be protective of their knowledge and feel reluctant to give away their value or feel that they are losing their position of influence or professional respect if they share their expertise with everyone.

Encouraging increased collaboration between scientists and creating a culture of openness where knowledge sharing is rewarded, would help Forsi to transform tacit knowledge into explicit knowledge. The project nature of the work undertaken by Forsi's scientists should make it possible to frame work as a 'problem to be solved'. Such an approach may help to encourage Forsi's scientists to draw upon their own expert knowledge and to then share this with others in finding solutions when undertaking forensic work.

In a field such as forensic science negative knowledge is also important. A company with an effective knowledge management process will be able to build a permanent body of awareness of 'negative knowledge' which provides information to improve on – those approaches that didn't work out as hoped or anticipated, or the reasons why a particular tender was lost.

As mentioned above, a KM strategy is likely to place significant reliance on information technology and systems and Forsi may need to invest more money in this area.

Electronic tools such as knowledge management systems, online bulletin boards, blogs, intranets and wikis may all facilitate knowledge sharing.

Examiner's comments

The third requirement asked candidates, on the assumption that the business was not taken over, to explain why knowledge management is important to Forsi and recommend steps to implement a knowledge management strategy. Answers to this requirement, which was the least well done in all the exam, were very polarised and only a small minority of candidates scored the maximum marks. The weakest candidates knew very little about knowledge management or misinterpreted the requirement and wrote about the need for a management information system. Better candidates identified that scientific knowledge was a key strategic asset for Forsi and a source of competitive advantage. They went on to discuss how IP might be protected and the steps Forsi could take to capture and disseminate the knowledge that its scientists and founders possess.

12.4(a) Choice of operating structure

Irrespective of the structure chosen, ownership by Aussi is likely to provide Forsi with additional administrative support through access to its shared service centre and may reduce the need for outsourcing.

Forsi will also have greater access to funding.

Better financial controls and a focus on efficiency and returns may prevent acceptance of unprofitable or unacceptable projects.

Combined organisational knowledge is likely to increase as the businesses differ in geography, culture and operating practices, so sharing experience and best practice may enhance activities for both Aussi and Forsi.

However:

The need for central sign-off of projects by Australia may delay the speed of response so Forsi could lose tenders to competition

Rejection of a project purely on financial grounds may overlook the fact that it leads to repeat business or other more profitable work

Ownership by a larger global company inevitably brings more bureaucracy which could stifle Forsi's innovation and research culture.

Specific issues relating to the two different options for structuring the management of Forsi:

Integration of Forsi within the existing division of Aussi

If Forsi is fully incorporated into Aussi as part of its forensic science operating division, then its strategy and operations will be formalised centrally.

This may help with knowledge sharing etc – Aussi is likely to have procedures in place.

Forsi may be able to increase efficiency by benchmarking its activities against the rest of the division.

Integration may also generate economies of scale. The parts of the business will be geographically separate but there may be economies in areas like procurement, especially if Aussi's shared service centre can offer services in such fields.

However, having too great a technostructure would seem to run counter to the needs of an innovative business and direct supervision is unlikely to be welcomed by scientists, who are used to working independently.

Decision making could become slower and inflexible and barriers between scientists and clients may increase.

Some UK clients may have a negative attitude to Australian ownership, especially those in the public sector. Conversely being part of the acknowledged market leader in Australia/Asia may give Forsi credibility at tenders and help win more business/public sector projects.

Aussi's forensic division may be more conservative in their attitude to risk which might affect the nature of projects undertaken.

Aussi's main activities are in Australia and Asia so it may not make sense to have European activities integrated in the same area when markets, regulations etc may be quite different.

It will be harder for Aussi to assess how Forsi is doing if its activities are subsumed within the existing division – Forsi will only be a very small part of the existing activities.

Separate subsidiary company

Forsi would have more freedom to operate as it has done before, retaining its research-centred culture.

Forsi's founders may continue to negotiate its own projects and have more flexibility re pricing and margins, although it will still be subject to Aussi's project screening procedures so will not be completely autonomous.

Objectives of the subsidiary may become more determined by financial considerations and the need to meet Aussi's targets.

Forsi's culture could change and this may affect the behaviour of the workforce who appear happy with the current loose informal structure.

Australian ownership may be less visible to clients if Forsi continues to operate as a separate subsidiary.

Forsi would be a very small subsidiary compared to Aussi's existing division.

Recommendation:

Forsi should be operated as a subsidiary. Aussi needs to create some overarching management principles to guide activities but not overemphasise rules, regulations and procedures, otherwise research and innovation will be stifled.

ROCE and margin targets may need to be different than for the existing division to take account of the different market place, clients etc.

(b) Change management

The acquisition will involve rapid one-off change to the culture and structure of the organisation and is likely to be viewed by Forsi's employees as transformational. It is likely to involve changes to the way activities are carried out, new management structures and new reward systems.

The change is likely to be greater if Forsi is to be incorporated within the division of Aussi than if it is to continue as a stand-alone subsidiary. The way in which Aussi manages the change will affect the future success of the business.

Integration will require a careful change management programme.

If the founders have agreed to sell then they may encourage and support the change programme, particularly if they are involved in any sort of earn-out. The founders may therefore be able to help break down any forces resisting change.

Intelligent staff such as the scientists employed by Forsi will want to feel like they are being offered the chance to participate in the change process. One danger of consultation however is that should they provide input which is ignored they might become demotivated. Thus some careful negotiation and trade-offs may be required to accommodate the wishes of all parties involved in the change. The acquisition will most likely have the greatest impact upon Forsi's five administrators as some, if not all of their work could probably be undertaken by Aussi's shared service centre. If this is the case then a programme of redundancies will also be required.

Open communication as to the reasons for the change in structure may help Forsi's staff to accept it, although care needs to be taken that such education is not done in a patronising way. Power, coercion or manipulation are unlikely to work with the majority of the scientists and may result in the loss of key staff.

Examiner's comments

The assumption in the fourth requirement was that Forsi's founders did agree to be taken over by Aussi. Candidates needed to discuss whether Forsi should be operated as a subsidiary or as part of Aussi's forensic science division, and to recommend how Aussi should manage the change when the takeover is announced. Again this requirement was well attempted.

Most were comfortable discussing the choice of operating structure, in the light of Aussi's desire to retain Forsi's research-centred culture. Better candidates discussed the impact the choice might have on performance monitoring, given Aussi's project screening process and requirements for target returns, and provided a preliminary recommendation as to the best option. However some weaker candidates seemed to overlook the fact that the two businesses were very dissimilar in size and geographic location. As in previous sittings, candidates were well versed in the technical knowledge for the change management requirement but an inability to apply this knowledge was again evident on the part of the weaker candidates. A key issue here was that the nature of the change, the likely barriers and the appropriate change management practice were dependent on the choice of structure, a fact that the better candidates identified.

13 Water On Tap (September 2014, amended)

	Knowledge	Skill	Marks
13.1 Sustainable enterprise	2	5	7
13.2 Ethics of marketing	3	6	8
13.3 Two proposals	3	9	10
	8	20	25

13.1 Sustainable enterprise

A sustainable enterprise is one that takes account of social and environmental returns as well as financial ones. As a social enterprise, on the face of it Ontap would appear to be such a business.

A key issue is the concept that a sustainable organisation is one that has a long term orientation and does not just focus on short-term results and measures when making decisions. As a social enterprise, Ontap's objectives will be wider than just financial. Its goals will be externally as well as internally focused and will include taking account of customers'/partners' business objectives and meeting the needs of the Indian communities it is serving. Ontap will want to optimise its profits (rather than maximise them), in order to give more money away to fund water projects and raise educational awareness.

To be financially sustainable (ie, to survive in the long term), a business needs an understanding of the changing external environment so that it can respond and adapt to the opportunities and threats presented by it. So for example Nala has developed a product in response to society's changing attitudes to bottled water and the negative impact that sourcing mineral water is having on the world's natural capital.

Sustainability is therefore an issue for any business in relation to risk mitigation, innovation and the development of new skills and capabilities to create and sustain competitive advantage over rivals. One question over Ontap's financial sustainability will be whether refillable bottles prove to be a fad and/or whether other businesses copy the idea, although in a sense this would help Ontap in its desire to persuade individuals to move away from bottled water in order to protect the environment.

In the context of environmental sustainability, an organisation should only use resources at a rate that allows them to be replenished in order to ensure they will continue to be available.

Ontap's whole concept is aiming to protect the environment by persuading individuals to move away from bottled water, thereby reducing the volume of bottles that end up in landfill and reducing the amount of mineral water sourced from around the world. It donates profits to education campaigns and clean water projects and its own bottle is made from recycled aluminium foil.

A socially sustainable organisation is one where decision making is linked to respect for people, communities and the environment. An increased focus on sustainability should support investment in human capital, engaging in innovation and establishing more reliable supply chains even if these do not maximise short-term financial performance. A key issue for Ontap will be ensuring that the supplier(s) of its bottles and the cafes and restaurants it partners with also act in a socially responsible manner.

Conclusion

In social and environmental terms, Ontap would appear to constitute a sustainable enterprise. The steps Nala is proposing to capitalise on the success of the business may help ensure it is also a financially sustainable one.

In the first requirement candidates were asked to discuss the extent to which Ontap is a sustainable enterprise. A significant number of candidates started their discussion with the Brundtland definition of sustainability but did not necessarily explore how this related to the concept of a sustainable enterprise. Many candidates then limited their discussion by concentrating on either the environmental aspects or the financial aspects of Ontap's sustainability and it was extremely rare to see a discussion of all three aspects of sustainability: economic, social and environmental. Clearly, Ontap is striving for environmental sustainability, but the extent to which it is financially sustainable as a model may be more questionable. Disappointingly, despite having been asked to assess the extent of Ontap's sustainability, candidates often failed to reach a conclusion on this matter.

13.2 Ethics of marketing

Bottled water manufacturers

An ethical argument sometimes raised against marketing is that it wastes resources by selling people things that they do not want or using promotional techniques to persuade people that they are dissatisfied without them.

This criticism could perhaps be levied at the bottled water manufacturers, who have spent significant resources on advertising to create brand/lifestyle images in order to persuade consumers to buy water which they could otherwise choose to get free from our taps.

Some would argue that charging money for something that is freely available or certainly cheap to obtain in order to make a profit for shareholders is unethical and does not demonstrate corporate responsibility. However marketing is undertaken by most organisations so is a reality in the commercial world.

One aspect of the marketing mix is 'Product'. The bottled water product itself could also be argued to lead to environmental pollution. The financial costs to both the consumer and the environment are high:

- The cost of the actual product
- Energy required in production
- Pollution created as a result of the production process
- Transportation costs
- Packaging material that has to be discarded (75% of the 18 billion bottles end up in landfill)
- Use of the world's natural capital, which has a limited supply

The way marketing is carried out may also sometimes cause ethical concerns. Information about the content and effects of products needs to be clear otherwise there is an issue of transparency, particularly if the manufacturers, either deliberately or by omission, suggest their product is something that it is not. Hence the example given in the scenario of the UK supermarkets being criticised when it became apparent that some of their own-brand bottled water was simply filtered, purified tap water.

However most businesses will abide by industry and voluntary codes of practice in how they promote their products and would argue therefore that they are behaving responsibly in marketing their products.

The bottled water companies might also argue that consumers have a free choice and, provided they are given clear information, it is up to the buyer to decide whether to buy or to choose not to buy if they think the product is unethical.

Such companies might also argue that there is an ethical good that comes from the marketing of their product in the form of creating employment and jobs. Some of the bottled water companies have also started to try and address ethical criticisms by donating funds to promote clean drinking water in the developing world or selling more ecologically responsible products, using recycled bottles.

Ontap

Marketing will be undertaken by Ontap in relation to:

- sale of water bottles
- promotion of business in order to attract cafes and restaurants as partners
- education relating to environmental impact of buying and drinking bottled water

Ontap's product is not a luxury good – it is aiming to fill a distinct need, saving customers money and protecting the environment at the same time, so it is unlikely to be subject to the same degree of criticism.

In promoting a more ecologically responsible product, aimed at persuading its target audience to voluntarily change behaviour and revert to tap water, Ontap's marketing could be argued to reduce waste and save resources. Also it is aimed at steering people to products that are helpful to them and to society.

However Ontap will face a conflict between spending resources on marketing and generating more profits to donate to good causes. By harnessing social media, the use of logos in cafés and restaurants and on bottles to build its brand image, Ontap may be able to keep its marketing spend to a minimum.

A possible criticism of Ontap might be that, like the bottled water companies, it is also trying to sell consumers a product (in this case a bottle) when they could just ask for free tap water. Also if Ontap's business model proves not to be sustainable, customers will have wasted £8 on a bottle that they may not then be able to refill for free if there are no longer participating cafes.

Overall Ontap's marketing is likely to be seen as more ethical and transparent than some other companies in the bottled water industry. Certainly, since Ontap is a not-for-profit organisation, society is likely to be less cynical about its motives compared to the for-profit bottled water companies.

Examiner's comments

The second requirement asked candidates to compare and contrast the ethics of the marketing activities of Ontap with its competitors in the bottled water industry. This requirement was poorly done by many candidates. Some did apply the transparency, fairness and effect decision-making approach, which tended to at least ensure they were talking in ethical terms and applying a structured thought process. Only the best candidates provided an initial discussion of ethical marketing principles and the arguments for and against marketing in the context of the activities of Ontap and the bottled water companies (providing choice/raising awareness/promoting responsible products vs wasting resources/persuading consumers to buy products they do not need/attempting to portray products as something they are not). Better answers pointed out that, whilst attempting to sell tap water as bottled mineral water lacked transparency, attempts to strengthen brand image through marketing is common place and legal and not necessarily unethical, providing industry advertising standards are adhered to. A small minority did question whether Ontap's own marketing activities were in reality that different, since under the umbrella of corporate social responsibility they were also hoping to make money by marketing a product that in theory people could obtain for free, and that if their business model is not financially sustainable, people will have wasted £8 on a bottle they cannot then use for its intended purpose. Answers to the ethics requirement, which is a consistent feature of the exam, continue to be variable and – as has been said before – candidates wishing to score well are advised to adopt some form of framework for their answer and to produce a balanced argument rather than a one-sided discussion.

13.3 Expansion strategies

Nala's desire to expand – general factors to consider

- Expansion will require finance which may not be available given that a significant proportion of Ontap's profits are donated
- It is likely to be harder for Nala to control a bigger business
- Ontap will need to be sure it can source sufficient supply of water bottles from ethical suppliers
- The business is likely to need to expand by taking on more staff
- There is a limited market – once a consumer has bought a bottle they don't need to replace it
- Will the Ontap concept prove to be a passing fad?
- Product concept is very easy for others to copy
- If you are an existing customer in the restaurant/café/bar you don't need a water bottle. Also Ontap cannot prevent people refilling their own bottles and containers.
- Ontap may face reaction/competition from bottled water companies

Corporate sales scheme

- This will generate significant volumes from persuading one company to buy (less time, cost and effort) although fulfilling the order may be problematic.
- Ontap needs to target businesses which want to be more environmentally responsible. Companies who are keen to improve their image may be prepared to sign up
- A partnership with a large blue chip company will enhance Ontap's reputation and co-branded bottles will raise awareness
- This idea may be popular with staff – Ontap could get existing customers to lobby their employers on Ontap's behalf
- The downside is that Ontap will be relatively small in relation to a large corporate buyer, which may insist on a substantial volume discount. Ontap's image and reputation could be badly affected if the wrong 'partner' is chosen, and Ontap's ability to source sufficient bottles may be a problem
- Perhaps Ontap could offer a corporate customer a trial scheme to start with

Geographical expansion

- It would be easiest achieved by targetting national and regional chains eg, pizza restaurants
- Getting first mover advantage and wider national coverage may create barriers to entry for the competition
- Cafes can also act as sales outlets for the bottles which would increase the potential market

- Ontap should be able to find appropriate partners as the cafes benefit from a page on the Ontap website, increased footfall, free marketing via Ontap's app. They can also attract additional customers rather than replacement ones as they will still also be selling bottled water to other consumers

- Again Ontap will need to be careful about the image/ethics of the cafes and restaurants it chooses to partner with.

- This option is likely to be harder for Nala to control than the corporate option and would result in slower growth, at least initially.

Recommendation:

The options may not both be mutually exclusive – Nala's ability to pursue them will be limited by Ontap's resources in terms of people and finance, and its ability to source bottles.

Both are probably sensible ways of expanding.

Examiner's comments

The third requirement requested candidates to discuss the problems Ontap will face in any expansion of the business and evaluate the two proposed options. Although this was the last requirement in the exam it was generally well attempted. Most candidates pointed out the expansion issues for Nala in relation to control, limited resources and available funding. Better candidates went on to then discuss the two proposals in the light of these and to reach a conclusion on which strategy might be more suitable. A number pointed out correctly that neither were mutually exclusive and that it might be feasible to pursue both options.

14 Drummond & Drew LLP (December 2015)

Marking guide

	Knowledge	Skill	Marks
14.1 Organisational structure	3	8	10
14.2 Expand internationally	3	10	12
14.3 Acquisition v direct investment	2	7	8
	8	25	30

14.1 DD is a professional service provider, based on expert knowledge. There is a need for their formal and informal structures to be appropriate to the communication and control needs of the business. The structure also needs to be appropriate to external client needs as a large amount of time is spent at construction sites.

One way of analysing DD's structure is with reference to Mintzberg's organisational configurations.

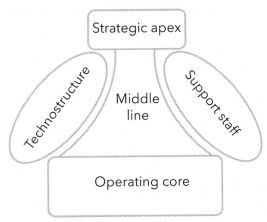

Mintzberg suggests that each component of the organisation has its own dynamic. The precise shape (configuration) of the organisation will be determined by the degree of influence each exerts.

The 12 partners who form the senior management team of the DD partnership are the strategic apex. As the owners of the business, they currently control all strategy and operations by taking all the key decisions.

The key component (or building block) within DD appears to be the operating core, with architects working directly on providing services to clients which are directly fee earning.

The managers comprise the middle line and may seek to increase control over the operating core of architects, even if they do not control the detail of their work.

Other support staff only gain influence when their expertise is vital but this may include IT where it is central to assignments (eg, graphics or management information).

The technostructure consists of the small technical and regulatory team whose reason for existence is the design of procedures and standards. The team seeks an environment that is standardised as it is highly regulated.

DD's existing structure might be seen as Mintzberg's professional bureaucracy configuration, suitable for the standardisation of skills.

Key features of DD's structure are as follows:

- The key building block is the operating core of architects who are fee earning.

- The environment is a complex static which has many elements but is not rapidly changing.

- The internal factors are professional with simple systems arising from working from one geographic location with commissions driving reporting systems.

- Skills are largely standardised professional skills but with some specialisations in complex assignments.

An alternative model might be Handy's shamrock organisation.

Handy defines the shamrock organisation as a "core of essential executives and workers supported by outside contractors and part-time help". This structure permits the buying-in of services as needed, with consequent reductions in overhead costs. It is also known as the flexible firm.

Handy has four elements to the shamrock:

The professional core comprises permanently employed staff who provide the core competencies and distinctive knowledge base of the organisation. For DD this would comprise the partners and architects but also some other employees (IT, administration etc)

The flexible labour force are temporary short-term contract architects who can be deployed when required by peaks in demand (eg, from variations in the number and size of commissions in progress).

The contractual fringe are external providers (specialist architects) who can undertake specialist services on complex commissions but are not required frequently and thus can be engaged more economically on short-term contracts than by being employed permanently.

The use of specialist and non-specialist temporary contracts by DD allows short-term flexibility as the number and size of commissions in operation vary over time, and specialist skills are acquired on an occasional basis as the need arises. In the longer term it permits rapid downsizing in times of recession and can save on the costs of benefits such as pensions, holiday pay and health insurance.

Customers are a fourth cluster, to whom DD may be able to 'sub-contract' some tasks. In the case of DD this is less likely to refer to the clients themselves but rather to other contractors used by clients (eg, construction companies) which may employ staff with skills similar to those of DD staff (eg, chartered surveyors). This may be convenient to DD if the site is geographically remote (eg, in parts of the UK a long distance from London) while construction company staff are on site.

Recommendation

The model of an operating core from the Mintzberg model with a contractual fringe and flexible labour force from the Handy model appears to work well for DD given its current professional bureaucracy configuration around a single head office. The ability of this structure to cope with more complex changes of multiple locations, overseas operations and a wider range of commission types would be questionable.

Examiner's comments

Candidates who used recognised frameworks or models tended to score better than candidates who referred to general types of organisational structure. Those who recognised the direct relevance of Mintzberg's structure and provided supporting contextualised discussion provided the best answers. The best candidates complemented the discussion of Mintzberg with reference to Handy's shamrock organisational structure.

Poorer answers talked vaguely about tall or flat structures or referred, in general terms, to divisionalised, matrix and functional structures. Also, weaker candidates tended to be too generic rather than applying discussion to the particular circumstances of a professional services organisation, as required by the scenario.

14.2 DD already has some revenue from international clients but as this activity expands, the capability of continuing to service clients from the UK for the construction phase of commissions becomes less plausible.

Whilst planning and design could largely be carried out from the UK, the inability to service the construction phase of the Sunrise contract is likely to mean that DD would not be used for design and planning as a single architect firm would normally be used for all phases.

The costs of setting up and maintaining a local presence in the Gulf States needs to be measured against: (1) the cost of servicing clients from the UK and (2) the ability and capacity to generate additional contribution from servicing more clients if there were to be a physical presence in the region.

The expansion being considered by DD can be evaluated using alternative strategic models.

The Ansoff model is a two-by-two matrix of Products (new and existing) and Markets (new and existing).

DD is attempting to enter a new geographical market with its existing professional service of commercial architecture. According to the Ansoff model this is market development. Having a recognised core competence in commercial architecture services, DD has used this in the UK to build its business but, due to competition, it is struggling to expand further. Overseas markets, in particular the Gulf States for DD, offer new opportunities for expansion.

It could be argued that the move into architectural services for domestic housing is a new type of service to be provided in a new market. According to the Ansoff model this is a strategy of diversification. The new service is strongly related to the existing service so it may also be termed related diversification.

Diversification involves developing new products for new markets. It involves the greatest risk of all Ansoff's strategies. In terms of providing the service it can require new skills, new techniques and different ways of operating. In terms of marketing the service it may also require adaptation to a new business-to-consumer model in addition to the existing business-to-business model.

Lynch's expansion method matrix is another two-by-two matrix matching company growth (organic growth and external development) with geographical location (home country and international).

Under this model, all of DD's traditional growth appears to have been carried out organically and services/markets have been developed largely domestically. Over the past five years there has been some international growth, mainly in the Gulf States, which has been serviced from the London office and so has been organic.

Porter's Diamond relates to developing a strategy in a global environment and the need to understand the competitive advantages DD may enjoy as result of physically locating in the Gulf States.

The factors include: firm strategy, structure and rivalry (eg, local cultural factors with respect to the architecture industry, local capital markets, rivalry from local architect firms already established in the Gulf States); factor conditions (eg, local skills available and other human resource factors; local technical knowledge and education; land for building; infrastructure); demand conditions (local demand for building projects in commercial and private building sectors); and related and support industries (eg, a well-developed local construction industry).

The more these factors in Porter's Diamond point towards favourable local conditions for architect firms, the greater the benefits from DD making a local investment and commitment to the region rather than servicing it from the London office.

Ohmae's 'five Cs' framework (The Borderless World) identified a number of reasons which might encourage a firm to act globally. This model identifies factors that may influence DD's decision of whether to establish an office in Dubai.

Ohmae's factors which may influence DD's decision include: the customer (whether the architect service requirements of Gulf States are similar to those of the UK where DD has core competences); the company (a greater volume of sales spreads existing fixed costs, although DD may incur additional fixed costs by local investment); competition (strength and response of local competition); currency volatility (currency of costs to match revenues with local investment); country (access to local resources through setting up a local office, such as HR).

Aside from these models, a key decision is needed as to whether to service client needs from London or to establish an office in Dubai (whether by setting up from scratch or by acquisition).

Key factors include the following:

A new office is likely to involve more fixed costs than servicing from London. This will increase the operating gearing of the Gulf State operations. As a result, if the Dubai office is successful then there may be advantages of lower variable costs of servicing clients (eg, reduced travel time and travel costs for architects). This may depend on whether, under existing arrangements, travel costs can be charged on to the clients without affecting competitiveness.

Under existing arrangements, 10 full time staff were used on Gulf State assignments. The data provided shows that this could increase to 27 in 20X7, then to 39 in 20X8, before falling to 26 in 20X8 and beyond as the Sunrise contract ends. This is quite a significant increase in staff and presumably there are revenues anticipated which, on the face of it, would justify investing in a physical presence in the region.

The presence in the region compared to the scale of staff at the London office would also indicate that it is substantial. If the staff are proportional to fees then this would imply a significant increase in revenue and indicates that the operation would be of a viable scale if forecasts are achieved. If however the venture fails then there may be significant exit costs of terminating the commitment (eg, redundancy, selling the office or terminating the lease).

Operating gearing risks and exit cost risks can be mitigated by keeping the real option and deferring the decision to invest in Dubai until it is known whether or not the Sunrise commission has been won assuming a commitment to future investment is acceptable under the tendering terms of the contract. This will give work for 12 staff in 20X7 along with 10 other staff on commercial work, which is only the equivalent to that already being serviced from London, so looks to be an achievable objective. Any additional staff need then only be taken on as and when new commissions are achieved.

The fall in the number of staff after the completion of the Sunrise contract could be accommodated either by sending London staff to Dubai on a two year secondment or by hiring short term contract staff, or a combination of both.

A further advantage of investing in a physical presence in Dubai would be the ability to hire local architects with local knowledge of regulations, culture and conditions.

Having an office in Dubai to house staff may also release space in the London office which may be useful if there are space constraints there.

A final factor may be foreign exchange risk. It could be viewed that the foreign investment may lead to greater foreign exchange risk but it may also be a form of natural hedging to reduce risk by incurring costs in local currencies to match against revenues earned from those countries.

Examiner's comments

Those candidates who applied a model such as Ansoff, Lynch, Porter's Diamond or Ohmae, often scored higher because their answer had structure and direction. The use of such models also widened the scope of the answers, ensuring key areas were specifically addressed. However, only a minority used such models, with the majority relying on a 'common sense' approach.

While the use of models was not specifically mentioned in the requirement, models are a core part of the syllabus and form part of the 'toolkit' for strategic analysis. Selection of appropriate models, where relevant, should therefore be considered by candidates to structure answers and to solve strategic problems in a variety of situations, and not only where directed to do so by the requirement. Candidates should not feel confined to using only one model in such circumstances.

A minority made use of Porter's Five Forces, and some credit was given for this where the analysis was appropriate.

Answers too often failed to deal with the specific issues that would be faced by DD and instead discussed very general overseas expansion issues/considerations that could apply to any company, in any industry.

The relevance of the key Sunrise development was, rather surprisingly, only referred to by a small minority.

Relatively few candidates made any reference to the data provided in the question. As a general rule, if there are numbers in the question, then there should be numbers in the answer.

14.3 According to the Lynch model, a business can expand organically (internal development) or via external development.

External development can include an acquisition or it can include working with another partner (eg, joint venture or other form of alliance). DD only appears to be considering either an acquisition or internal development.

There are a number of factors that would favour an acquisition of a local architect's practice in Dubai:

- Existing knowledge of the local environment, culture, regulations and markets providing useful initial expertise. It may be that DD has some expertise in these areas from its previous work in Dubai, but local knowledge is likely to be an additional benefit

- An instant skill base in terms of resources and employees is likely to mean faster growth.

- It provides experience of existing supply chain and networks.

- A locally known established brand and reputation with an existing customer base – this may be viewed more favourably by local businesses and government than a foreign-owned brand.

- An acquisition buys out a potential competitor and better enables DD to compete with the other domestic companies.

- There are likely to be synergies as local staff can provide local knowledge but conversely DD can introduce innovations from its UK experience.

- Gets round any barriers to entry in terms of resistance from local architects, construction firms and government.

Direct investment by setting up a new office from scratch offers the following merits:

- It may be difficult to find a suitable partner in terms of size or market positioning in the time scale available, allowing time for negotiation and completion.

- There may be a conflict between strategies and cultures of DD and an acquired local firm which may hinder integration.

- If an acquisition is made in Dubai, the local knowledge acquired may be limited to Dubai and not stretch across all the Gulf States.

- Direct investment will allow DD to be free to pursue its own strategy.

- The price DD is required to pay for a local firm is likely to include a goodwill premium, the cost of which may outweigh the possible benefits noted above. Organic growth by setting up an office from scratch avoids paying for goodwill, therefore DD can acquire a larger tangible asset base for the same cost as an acquisition.

- Direct investment may offer a chance for more gradual expansion and an opportunity to test the market and learn. It also enables a choice of clients rather than inheriting a client list, some of which may be unsuitable for the skills base offered by DD.

- Avoids any hidden or unforeseen losses that do not come out as part of due diligence eg, litigation based on historic work by the acquired firm that has been negligently performed.

- There may be damage to, or dilution of, DD's good local reputation if a local firm is acquired with an inferior reputation or brand name.

The core competencies that have allowed DD to prosper in the UK may not be fully realised in an overseas country. The above arguments regarding the ability of DD to replicate in Dubai what it has achieved in the UK may be summarised within Kay's framework on sources of core competencies:

Architecture

Internal architecture – is the relationship with employees. These are likely to be entirely or largely new employees, where a new relationship needs to be established.

External architecture – this includes relationships with external stakeholders such as suppliers, contractors and clients.

Network architecture – collaboration between businesses and local networks needs to be established from scratch.

Reputation

It is likely that DD will need to establish a new reputation locally. This may prevent it from initially charging a price premium as in the UK.

Innovative ability

Innovation in design is likely to be able to be 'transported' from the UK to the overseas markets but it is an industry where tastes vary across countries and thus is unlikely to give the same competitive advantage.

Conclusion

Much will depend on the price of any acquisition but, given DD already has some experience and reputation in the region and an international reputation, there may be some merit in DD setting up its own office. If further local knowledge is required, an acquisition could take place later. Alternatively, some other form of strategic alliance could take place with a local firm.

Examiner's comments

Most candidates considered both direct investment and acquisition of an existing firm, and most also recognised the significance of existing knowledge and competencies.

Candidates approached this requirement in different ways. Some tried to compare the differences between organic growth and growth by acquisition, whereas others approached it by thinking about the key aspects of expansion and which method best suited DD in that respect.

Only a significant minority gave due emphasis to the importance of timing in the decision. The remainder may not have done so because they had not considered the Sunrise development in the first requirement. Most did nevertheless make the point that organic development will take longer than acquisition, but without much elaboration.

The candidates who scored highest related their answer to the scenario and to DD. Weaker candidates simply listed the advantages and disadvantages of each approach, without attempting to draw emphasis to which issues were more important, or to provide an overall conclusion to provide coherence to the list of points made.

15 Mississippi Muzic Ltd (December 2015)

Marking guide

	Knowledge	Skill	Marks
15.1 Database CRM	3	6	8
15.2 Market research	2	7	8
15.3 Segmentation and pricing	2	7	8
	7	20	24

15.1 To: Jane Flinkstein
From: Business Adviser
Date: XX/XX/XX
Subject: Marketing strategy – Mississippi Muzic Ltd

The use of the database to market to existing customers should be part of a strategy of customer relationship marketing.

This is the marketing process that seeks to attract, maintain and enhance customer relationships by focusing on the whole satisfaction experienced by the customer when dealing with the firm. Building up customer relationships requires a change of focus from the 'transaction-based approach' to a relationship approach.

The concept of a club membership and the holding of a database on members' attributes and purchase habits can facilitate retaining customers over a long period by providing them with good customer service which is appropriate to their particular needs and enables two-way communication. Central to MM's ability to pursue a relationship marketing approach is that its members have consented to MM using their personal data for marketing purposes.

The database can therefore be regarded as a Customer Relationship Management system (CRM). CRM describes the methodologies, software, and usually Internet capabilities that help an enterprise manage customer relationships.

CRM can consist of the following:

- Helping MM to identify and target their best customers, manage marketing campaigns with clear goals and objectives, and generate quality leads.

- Assisting MM to improve sales management by optimising information shared, and streamlining existing processes (for example, taking reservations of table bookings and orders using mobile devices).

- Allowing the formation of relationships with customers, with the aim of improving customer satisfaction and maximising profits; identifying the most profitable customers (eg, large groups) and providing them with the highest level of service.

- Providing employees with the information and processes necessary to know the main customer groups, understand their needs, and effectively build relationships between the company and its membership base.

The information held can be used to market the clubs' activities to individual customers in a targeted manner that will suit their individual circumstances. However, it is unlikely to be cost effective to have individual marketing for each customer's attributes. Some grouping of the data may therefore be appropriate as a form of market segmentation to enable specific marketing on a group basis.

Examples might be:

- People who have not visited for a while. These could be targeted to come back with some inducement (eg, free entry).

- Groups who visit regularly, but who have not used the restaurant (perhaps provide a restaurant voucher).

The existing information could be used to gain better communication through social media (eg, Facebook and Twitter), as a means of achieving competitive advantage. Again some inducement could be offered for initial join-up.

Social media could be particularly effective at creating a community of MM club members. When followers become part of the MM club community, it gains instant access to them. That means MM can find out what challenges they are facing and what they like and don't like about MM's offerings. MM staff can engage in ongoing dialogue that can be more valuable than any kind of paid market research.

Social media also provides MM with the opportunity to remind followers over and over again about what it has to offer, which can shorten the sales cycle dramatically.

Patterns of attendance could be established. If someone visits occasionally, but always on a Saturday when they do visit, then particular events and features on a Saturday could be marketed to that group.

In order to widen the customer base, members visiting regularly could be given incentives to bring a friend to join.

Aside from the specific attributes, more general attributes could be used to analyse and use the database, as part of a strategy of segmentation. One example would by age, whereby as members get older, then individual nights could be themed to their age group (eg, over 30s) or profession (eg, accountant only nights).

Improved data collection, storage and analysis tools may indicate previously unknown opportunities for sales. Such tools may include data-mining software which allows relationships to be discovered between previously unrelated data.

Examiner's comments

Most candidates considered both the database and marketing issues in the context of customer relationship management, a significant minority referring to the latter explicitly.

Many made use of the four 'Ps' of marketing, although only the better ones who did this used the model to focus on particular customer segments.

The majority of candidates did not use a report format for their answer despite being asked to produce a report.

15.2 Market research is the systematic gathering, recording and analysing of information relating to the marketing of goods and services.

Market research can help in identifying the potential size of specific markets and provides information about customer characteristics, needs and wants, attitude to price and quality, and competitors' products. Market research may also help in defining appropriate elements of the marketing mix (product, price, place, promotion).

There are various forms that market research can take.

Desk research

This is the gathering and analysis of existing or secondary data. This is likely to be of background significance in establishing the characteristics of the potential market identified, but is nevertheless important.

In the case of Strategy 2, much of the relevant desk research may already have been collected in relation to the initial establishment of the nightclubs. However, new relevant data might include both general economic intelligence and market intelligence.

General economic intelligence would include data about the general economy as it applies to the target markets. This might include:

- general macroeconomic data on growth, inflation, unemployment etc (as leisure is a luxury good of choice it may suffer disproportionately in a recession)

- spending habits in the UK (family expenditure survey)

- demographic trends (census): this may be of particular importance in the context of the narrow age profile that might normally attend nightclubs.

Market intelligence may include:

- industry information on the nightclub/restaurant industry (eg, prices, new trends, new music tastes, customer volume changes, advertising, trade journals, magazine articles)

- information on the demand for entertainment/leisure activities (national surveys, published local surveys, industry intelligence).

Field research

Field research involves the collection of new, primary information. It is usually more costly than desk research, but it is likely to be more relevant to the circumstances of MM.

A key advantage is that the nightclubs already exist and can thus be used as the basis for some forms of field research, as although most people are young professionals, the database would identify those members attending midweek and their attributes. The database could therefore be a key part of the field research for Strategy 2, as well as helping to develop Strategy 1.

The key answers to establish are:

- what sections of the population attend, or could be induced into attending, nightclubs on Sunday to Thursday

- how much these people would be willing to pay for entrance and for food/drink

- how frequently they would attend

- whether preferences would be concentrated for any particular night in any age group, gender, or income grouping

- whether the clubs are associated with any particular image (which may indicate the type of advertising and target market that might be appropriate)

- whether there is a demand for an alternative use midweek (eg, just as a restaurant)

Trial testing

For Strategy 2, this could involve testing the service provided by the clubs on a sample of the public. This may take the form of random sampling to extrapolate the results into the general population. This could involve free tickets for midweek nights in return for feedback on the experience. Alternatively, quota sampling may be used where the clubs are tested on a sample with predetermined characteristics (eg, age or gender), again with feedback. Some detail of the respondents will be needed if information is required on the differential response of different market segment groupings.

Experimentation

Experimentation may have some similar characteristics to trial testing, but is likely to be more controlled to isolate different factors such as slight changes in the product composition and presentation. For Strategy 2 this might involve changing the format or prices on a certain night during the week to test the appeal to target markets.

Test marketing

Test marketing involves a restricted launch of a new product in a small segment of the total market eg, a geographical region. Ideally, the test should be small, self-contained, representative and adequately promoted. The test may be based upon the results of the above types of market research.

For Strategy 2, this might involve making changes in one of the four London clubs with respect to the types of music, food or prices on particular midweek nights. It may even involve more permanent changes in the environment to develop appeal outside the core market.

Examiner's comments

Most candidates discussed desk and field research and displayed understanding of the differences between the two approaches and the uses to which each could be put. Only a small minority took this further, and considered possibilities for test marketing, trial testing and experimentation.

Stronger candidates were able to suggest specific questions that MM would be seeking to answer, whereas a weaker answer provided only generic desk/field research commentary.

15.3 Segmentation strategy

Segmentation is "the division of the market into homogeneous groups of potential customers who may be treated similarly for market purposes".

Strategy 2

The segmentation strategy for the existing core market is both demographic and socio-economic eg, young professionals.

It may however be appropriate to adopt a different segmentation strategy on mid-week days. The nature of the service offered could then be tailored to the new market.

Examples might include the following:

- **Students** – this is a similar demographic segmentation to the core group, but a different socio-economic segmentation, as they would be a low income group. Students may not have such long working hours and be more willing to socialise, at a lower price, during weekdays.

- **'Middle-aged' people** – a different demographic segmentation might be over 30s/40s/50s nights. More established in their careers, they might be of similar high socio-economic groups to the core market, but have different tastes in music and environment.

- **Retired** – an older age range still would be a further demographic segmentation, and might have more time flexibility, but different social and leisure needs.

- **Unemployed** – significant spare time mid-week. Could also be split demographically.

While the segments may be split on a 'day of the week' basis, there may be a danger of altering the general culture of the nightclub, making it less appealing to the core market. The physical attributes of the nightclubs (eg, décor) may also not lend themselves to different types of entertainment.

As well as splitting on a day of the week basis, segmentation could be by different types of membership. This could vary the membership fee but also facilitate subsequent targeted communication and keep the core group as a separate and distinctive membership.

Pricing

Strategy 2

The core market has a premium pricing strategy, but a nightclub can distinguish its markets on the basis of time – with each night of the week being a separate market. As such, it enables a policy of price discrimination between the different markets by charging different prices on different nights, and would thus be linked to the above segmentation strategy.

Nevertheless, this is only an advantage if there is a different price elasticity of demand in each of the markets. Given the widely different socio-economic groups being targeted, this seems very likely. Thus, while demand may be inelastic for the core market, it may be very elastic for other low income markets such as students and the unemployed. This would suggest a much lower price on these nights.

A key factor in assessing price is the price being changed by the closest competitors, which should be determined in a competitor analysis.

This should include the prices being charged for drinks and in the restaurant as well as the entrance fee. Indeed, one pricing strategy would be to have free entrance (or a minimal cost) on some nights in order to generate revenue from drink and food. This may be possible given the low marginal cost of attracting additional customers.

Examiner's comments

In general, the segmentation element of the question was dealt with much better than the pricing aspects. Poorer efforts at pricing used the four 'Cs' model with little application to the scenario, often simply 'knowledge dumping' by quoting all the pricing strategies that candidates knew. Weaker candidates also did not link their explanation of pricing strategy to their earlier discussion on segmentation.

The best responses covered market segmentation and pricing well, and explained the relationship between these, giving some emphasis to price discrimination between segments and between days of the week.

Some also made the point that it may be difficult for the club to offer a different experience on different days of the week, as it may be too focused in terms of décor and general offering on higher-end customers. Some also referred to problems of leakage between segments, thereby making price discrimination more difficult.

16 Confo plc (December 2014, amended)

	Knowledge	Skill	Marks
16.1 Transfer price	3	7	9
16.2 Performance	2	15	15
16.3 Recovery plan	4	12	15
16.4 Ethics	3	5	7
	12	39	46

16.1 Transfer prices

A transfer price (TP) is the price at which one division in a group sells its products or services to another division in the same group.

The transfer prices will be important for Confo as they have a number of implications:

- They determine the profits of divisions. If the Manufacturing Division charges a high transfer price then most of the total profit from company sales will be attributed to it, with less to the other divisions. This will give a false measure of performance for all divisions.

- As the price to franchisees is the same as the transfer price to the owned shops, this may impact upon the willingness of third parties (favourably or unfavourably) to take up franchises and the volume of goods they purchase whilst a franchisee.

- If high transfer prices are passed on to ultimate customers then sales volumes may fall and overall profits may be distorted.

- Inappropriate transfer prices can lead to internal conflict between divisions. As shops only sell Confo's confectionery, the Retail Division cannot access outside markets to obtain lower cost products from third parties. The Manufacturing Division is therefore a monopoly supplier to owned shops and to franchisees and, from 1 October 20X3, to the Commercial and Export Divisions.

Pre-1 October 20X3 transfer pricing system

The transfer pricing system pre-1 October 20X3 was on a full cost plus 20% basis.

The Manufacturing Division

From the perspective of the Manufacturing Division, the cost-plus formula guaranteed an operating profit margin of 20%. This meant that any cost inefficiencies could be passed on to the Retail Division with an additional mark-up. Perversely, this could mean that the more inefficient the Manufacturing Division was, the more profit it made.

There does not appear to be any rationale for the 20% and this figure appears to be arbitrary. More meaningful is the mark-up overall for the company.

A further concern is that, although fixed costs are not as large as variable costs, they are significant. In attempting to recover fixed costs per unit then an estimate needed to be made at the beginning of the year, not just of total fixed costs to be incurred, but also of the output volume to be achieved in order to determine budgeted fixed cost per unit and hence price. Any error would result in an under- or over-recovery of fixed costs.

A related problem is that costs (fixed and variable) need to be allocated to each type of product to set each transfer price. Given that production is likely to be interdependent between different products, costs are incurred jointly on different products and it can be difficult to identify cost drivers to separate them in order to be able to calculate each product's transfer price.

Conversely, however, there are a number of positive points that could be made for Confo's former transfer pricing system:

- The same prices were being successfully charged commercially to franchisees which may imply it was at (or below) the market rate. However, in this case, franchisees were also paying a fixed fee which needs to be considered alongside the transfer price to determine viability for the franchisees.

- The full cost may be budgeted costs rather than actual so any cost overrun would be incurred by the Manufacturing Division rather than the Retail Division (although the data shows 20% related to actual cost, it could be that the budget equalled actual).

The Retail Division

The Retail Division had no control over the transfer price it paid to the Manufacturing Division and there was no alternative supplier of confectionery it could use. The transfer prices therefore had significant implications for the validity of its status as a profit centre. Being a profit centre would imply that divisional managers had significant control over costs and revenues, but this appears not to have been the case. As a consequence, the divisional loss of £400,000 for the Retail Division had little meaning.

In favour of the transfer prices, it could be that the Confo board had set cost plus 20% as their best estimate of the wholesale market value of the confectionery. The fact that there are no identical confectionery products being sold by rival companies makes this difficult to substantiate.

Post-1 October 20X3 transfer pricing system

The transfer pricing system post-1 October 20X3 is on a full cost basis. This treats the Manufacturing Division as a cost centre and the other divisions (Retail, Commercial and Export) therefore recognise the full profit to be made from the sale by the company.

The Manufacturing Division

The Manufacturing Division is now a cost centre and so its performance cannot be measured on profit, but rather on its ability to control costs (eg, against budget). An example of how well it has performed in this respect is the reduction in fixed costs compared with the previous year (see below).

Given the franchisees are also acquiring the goods at the same full cost, manufacturing has few incentives to promotes sales to franchisees as there is no profit. The only advantage for the Manufacturing Division of more sales to franchisees is that fixed costs are being spread over more units of output thereby increasing its cost efficiency.

The Retail, Commercial and Export Divisions

These divisions are profit centres and have the advantage of acquiring inventories at cost price, whereas rivals would need to pay outside suppliers wholesale market rates including a mark-up for profit.

In terms of incentives, these divisions may be motivated to over-order from Manufacturing Division or under-price to consumers/customers compared to rivals as they can acquire confectionery more cheaply.

Alternative methods of transfer pricing

There may be distortions in incentives given that internal transfer prices and prices to franchisees are unlikely to be at wholesale market rates.

An alternative system of transfer pricing would be to make transfers at market rates.

This could be done by estimating the wholesale market value of each type of sweet by comparison to rivals' products (albeit there are no identical products).

A further alternative would be to let divisional directors negotiate the transfer prices by discussion in a bargaining process. This may cause conflict, but would result in an agreed set of transfer prices, rather than a centrally imposed set. It may also tend towards market prices over time. However, the problem with this is that the strongest negotiator may dominate, possibly providing a sub-optimal outcome overall.

Conclusion

Transfer prices should be set by negotiation where the outcome is influenced strongly by market prices charged to third party customers (or to franchisees) in a competitive market.

Examiner's comments

Answers were variable in quality. A significant minority failed to explain the motivational aspects of transfer pricing, particularly for the manufacturing division. For example, some considered the revised transfer pricing approach as not motivating managers in this division to control costs. Only a few candidates appreciated that any revised performance management/reward approach would incorporate success in cost control for the Manufacturing Division, as opposed to success in generating profits. Even fewer made the point that the downside could be a reduction in product quality in pursuit of lower costs.

Of those who referred to goal congruence, many did not explain this in the context of the question. The same observation applies to discussion of alternative transfer pricing approaches. With reference to transfer prices at opportunity cost, there appeared to be no appreciation of the fact that the manufacturing division only supplies internally and is a monopoly supplier to the shops. Better answers did refer to the use of market prices in this context, but normally did not consider that these may be difficult to determine, given the unique nature of the firm's products. Weaker candidates did not justify the alternative methods of transfer pricing and instead just listed various methods (such as variable cost plus, fixed cost plus, market prices, negotiated prices) without any explanation or discussion. A small minority of candidates discussed methods of pricing in general rather than of transfer pricing.

16.2

	20X3 Owned shops	20X4 Owned shops	20X3 Manufacturing	20X4 Manufacturing
Revenue per shop £	160,000	180,000		
Operating profit per shop £	-2,667	16,500		
Revenue per product £	2	2	1.50	1.25
Operating profit per product £	-0.033	0.183	0.25	0
Total cost per product £			1.25	1.25
Operating profit margin (profit/revenue %)	-1.67%	9.17%	16.67%	0%

Profit from franchisees:

	20X3 £'000	20X4 £'000
Profit on transfers from manufacturing (8,100 × 20/120)	1,350	0
Fees	1,200	2,500
	2,550	2,500
Profit per franchisee shop £'000	28,333	20,833

Manufacturing costs

	20X3	20X4
Fixed costs per unit	50p	50p
Variable costs per unit	75p	75p
Transfer price	£1.50	£1.25

Total profit for Retail and Manufacturing

	20X3 £'000	20X4 £'000
Manufacturing	4,350	0
Retail	(400)	1,320
Fees	1,200	2,500
Total operating profit	5,150	3,820

Overall performance of Retail and Manufacturing

In comparing the data for 20X3 and 20X4 for Retail and Manufacturing Divisions, four significant elements of the recovery plan have occurred. These are:

- the closure of 70 owned shops to scale down the owned network significantly
- opening 30 new franchised shops in replacement of some owned shops
- transfers from Manufacturing Division at full cost in 20X4, rather than full cost plus 20% in 20X3
- more than doubling, in total, of the fixed franchise fee from £1.2 million to £2.5 million

These decisions distort underlying data trends and therefore impact on any comparable assessment of overall performance. This makes like-for-like comparisons difficult for the underlying elements of the business.

> **Tutorial note**
>
> The Commercial and Export Divisions are new lines of business and are analysed separately.

Revenue – owned outlets

Total revenue for owned shops has declined by 40% from £24 million in 20X3 to £14.4 million in 20X4. Similarly, the volume of sales (number of items sold) has declined by 40% from 12 million in 20X3 to 7.2 million in 20X4. The average selling price has remained the same at £2, so this does not appear to be a factor in the change in revenue or volume of sales.

A key causal factor in this decline has been the scaling down of the number of owned shops by 46.7% from 150 in 20X3, to 80 in 20X4.

Thus, rather than reflecting poor performance, the change in revenue has been a deliberate rescaling within the recovery strategy.

Revenue per owned shop has increased from £160,000 in 20X3 to £180,000 in 20X4 (12.5%). This is indicative, in revenue terms at least, that the worst performing shops have been closed and the shops with higher revenue generation have remained open.

Thus, while there has been a downscaling of the number of owned shops in the network, the average sales generation performance per owned shop has improved.

Operating profit – owned outlets

Total operating profit for owned shops has improved from an operating loss of £400,000 in 20X3 to an operating profit of £1.32 million in 20X4.

At first sight, this appears to indicate improved performance, particularly as it has been generated by a scaled down network of owned shops.

Further analysis indicates, however, that a key causal factor in this improvement has been the reduced transfer price from the manufacturing division. Adjusting the data to show the operating profit/loss if the previous transfer pricing policy in 20X3, of full cost plus 20%, had been maintained for 20X4 reveals the following:

	£'000
External sales	14,400
Internal & franchisee transfers (9,000 × 1.2)	(10,800)
Variable costs	(1,080)
Fixed costs	(3,000)
Operating (Loss)	(480)

Tutorial note

A comparable analysis could be carried out by scaling down the 20X3 data.

Thus, rather than operating profit of the owned shops improving, had the transfer pricing policy remained at full cost plus 20%, then the operating losses would have increased from £400,000 to £480,000.

This has occurred, despite the improvement in revenue generation per shop, because the smaller network has meant that fixed costs of owned shops have decreased by only 25% (from £4 million to £3 million) while volumes of sales have decreased by 40% (see above) thereby increasing fixed costs per unit.

Franchised shops

The recovery strategy has been to favour franchised shops rather than owned shops. In this respect there has been some operational success in opening a further 30 franchised shops in replacement of owned shops.

Overall, the profit from franchising has decreased by 2% from £2.55 million to £2.5 million. This is in the context of an increase in the number franchised shops of 33.3% from 90 to 120.

As a consequence, the operating profit to Confo per franchised shop has fallen by 26.5% from £28,333 in 20X3, to £20,833 in 20X4. This may be indicative of poorer performance, but it could also reflect a short term policy to expand the network by offering improved conditions for the franchisee contract.

It may also reflect the fact that the newer franchisees may take some time to become established. More information would be needed on the relative performance of new and existing franchisees.

Manufacturing

The key factor affecting the 'profit' generated by the manufacturing division has been the change in transfer pricing policy from a profit centre (cost plus 20%) to a cost centre. This is a corporate level decision and is not indicative of the underlying performance of the Manufacturing Division itself.

Basing performance on its ability to control costs, it has performed well. The overall output has reduced by 5.7% from 17.4 million units to 16.4 million units. This is a reflection of reduced sales but additional information would be needed to confirm that sales were not constrained by reduced production capacity.

Variable cost per unit has remained at 75p so any reduced scale economies have not been a factor.

More significantly, the fixed cost per unit has remained constant despite the fall in sales and production output. This reflects a good performance in reducing fixed costs.

Examiner's comments

Generally, this requirement was fairly well answered, with most candidates providing up-front calculations in a reasonably well structured table. Analysis often endeavoured to explain changes and results for the two years in terms of cause and effect. Weaker candidates were poor in this regard, merely reiterating the percentage changes. Weaker candidates also provided occasional calculations within their narrative, rather than in an initial structured table.

Calculations most commonly focused on gross and net profit margins and commented on changes year on year. Only the better candidates calculated specific ratios such as revenue per shop, operating profit per shop and cost per shop. There was some good discussion of the differences in results between the franchised outlets and owned outlets.

Better responses recognised problems in comparisons between the two years, particularly due to the change in the transfer pricing system and organisational structure changes. A very small minority adjusted the data to take out this distortion, normally by adjusting the 20X3 data by removing the 20% mark-up on internal transfers, thus arriving at more sensible comments regarding the relative performance of the manufacturing and retail divisions. Weaker candidates omitted to comment on problems in making comparisons, or to suggest additional information that would assist analysis, despite these being required in the question.

16.3 (a) To: The Confo plc board
From: A Student
Date: 10 December 20X4
Subject: Strategy review

Both divisions are in the start-up phase of their life cycle so it is difficult to make judgements about the success of the performance or strategy at this stage. Nevertheless, there are some early indicators.

Using the Ansoff matrix these are both examples of market development whereby existing products are being sold in new markets.

Export Division

In the case of the Export Division the new markets in the Ansoff matrix are new geographical markets.

In terms of the Lynch Expansion Method it would be regarded as growth through internal development abroad (ie, exporting).

These sales are likely to all be incremental with minimal leakage between home and export markets. While this is positive in terms of generating more revenue, the strategy has a number of problems in relation to costs and risks:

(1) The costs incurred in penetrating new markets may be significant compared to the revenues earned

(2) The downstream supply chain is lengthened significantly, thereby increasing costs of getting goods to customers

(3) There may be different tastes in different countries such that products developed for the UK market tastes may be unsuitable (eg, some sweets may be unsuitable in hot climates)

(4) Additional risks apply (eg, international physical distribution and foreign exchange rate risk on settlement)

The Export Division has made a small profit of £200,000 for the year. Whilst this is unlikely to be sufficient in the long run to justify the investment, this is the start-up phase to penetrate markets.

The profit is small but, based on the above argument, it is all incremental, with little or no damage to the existing business. Indeed, as an international brand it may enhance the existing business in the UK in terms of reputation.

Commercial Division

In the case of the Commercial Division, the new markets in the Ansoff matrix are new distribution channels.

In terms of the Lynch Expansion Method it would be regarded as growth through internal domestic development.

The key strategic issue in this case is that there may be competition between Confo's existing markets and the new commercial market. If consumers become aware that the supermarkets are selling the same products as Confo's owned shops and franchisees, but at a lower price, then this strategy may reduce contribution and destroy value for Confo overall.

The Commercial Division has made a small profit of £300,000 for the year. Unlike the Export Division, we cannot be certain that this is entirely incremental. Indeed, the lost contribution on existing sales (if consumers perceive it is the same product but own-labelled) may be greater than £300,000.

(b) **Evaluation of success of the recovery plan**

In pure financial terms Confo has generated less profit in the year following the introduction of the recovery plan (£4.32 million) than in the year before the plan (£5.15 million). This is a reduction in operating profit of 16.1%.

However as the marking director pointed out, it would be unwise to judge performance on one year's data. This is particularly the case as it is a transitional period and only the first year of the three year recovery plan.

Positive signs included the following:

(1) The willingness of 30 franchisees to take up new franchises
(2) Profit in first year for Export Division
(3) Profit in first year for Commercial Division

Negative signs include the following:

(1) Overall reduction in volume of sales
(2) Significant fall in operating profit per franchisee shop

Given that several simultaneous changes have been made by Confo, it is difficult to determine precisely which changes have impacted performance most in the short term. Given that the planning horizon is three years, it is appropriate to review progress after one year, but unreasonable to draw firm conclusions as to whether the changes will be successful when the three year planning horizon is reached.

The main weakness in this requirement was inadequate evaluation of the overall recovery plan, which was unsatisfactory in nature and in the level of detail in the answers of most candidates.

The majority of candidates incorporated analytical frameworks, and most who used models made use of Ansoff's matrix. A smaller number also referred to Lynch.

Only a small minority recognised potential cannibalisation of the Retail Division's sales by the Commercial Division, combined with consumer awareness that the products are identical apart from packaging. More saw the revised packaging as a protection against this.

In terms of the overall recovery plan for the company, of those who considered this, most concluded it to be favourable, on balance, as time is needed for it to come to fruition. Better candidates included calculations to support this conclusion. A few explicitly referred to the three-year time horizon.

16.4 Ethical issues

Ethics pertains to whether a particular behaviour is deemed acceptable in the context under consideration. In short, it is 'doing the right thing'.

In making any ethical evaluation it is first necessary to establish the facts. In this case, it would seem that the facts are reasonably clear in terms of what has happened, although the lack of documentary evidence to support the facts may limit the actions that can be taken.

The issue of legality and compliance with the Bribery Act needs to be considered and legal advice taken by Confo. If a crime has been committed there may be a duty to disclose in the public interest.

Both the offering, and the receiving, of an inappropriate inducement may be considered illegal and/or unethical.

In making a decision as to how to proceed, it is helpful to apply the Institute of Business Ethics three tests:

- Transparency
- Effect
- Fairness

Transparency – would CCC mind people (existing customers, suppliers, employees) knowing that these transactions have taken place. In the first instance, there appears to be a degree of internal transparency as Kirsty reported the initial Christmas gift to the commercial director. It is not known whether John reported the gift within Lenton but, given his subsequent behaviour, this seems unlikely. At this stage Kirsty may be deemed to have taken actions which are not inappropriate give the scale, context and disclosure.

Subsequent gifts made by Kirsty were not disclosed and hence the ethical test of openness does not appear to have been met. Since March 20X4 Kirsty has made gifts of company property without notification, consultation or authority, which appears both fraudulent and unethical. The question of how she obtained the goods needs to be asked and who knew about this (as opposed to the purpose for which they were being used), if anyone.

Her refusal to make undisclosed gifts beyond £100 is appropriate, but does not compensate for her earlier actions.

Effect – whom does the decision to make the ever larger transfers of sweets affect or hurt? The initial Christmas gift may be appropriate based on its scale (small amount of £10), context (seasonal gift and industry norm) and expected frequency (annual at Christmas) in that it would be unlikely to be of sufficient size to affect John's commercial decisions about the Confo contract. However, subsequent larger gifts may have had the effect of John choosing to make purchases from Confo, rather than a rival company which might be offering preferential commercial terms to Lenton, but with no personal inducement for John. The effect in this case would be that Lenton shareholders are suffering due to John receiving inappropriate personal inducements. Conversely, Confo may be the best commercial provider and the ceasing of gifts may have made John choose an inferior provider, to the detriment of Lenton shareholders.

In this context, sweets with a relatively small financial value (even at £100) could trigger decisions on a commercial contract worth many thousands of pounds.

Fairness – would the transfers be considered fair by those affected? Confo may be obtaining an unfair commercial advantage over rivals through paying inappropriate (and possibly illegal) inducements. Similarly, John has gained a significant and unfair benefit compared to more honest colleagues who would not have engaged in such actions. Whilst the benefit is in kind, rather than cash, this is not the key issue if it amounts to an inducement. Moreover, it is possible that the confectionery could be sold by John to convert to cash.

Honesty and integrity

Further issues are those of honesty and integrity. The inducements may fail the honesty test as they are not earned, authorised or disclosed by, or on behalf of, the giver or the recipient.

Actions

An initial action for Kirsty would be now to act honestly and make transparent what has occurred to the commercial director by full disclosure of all the facts, with any supporting evidence to which she has access. The matter is likely to be of sufficient seriousness that she may offer her resignation in anticipation of possible legal action against her for misappropriating goods belonging to the company to a third party without authority.

Kirsty should cooperate in all investigations made by the company or the police.

The fact she received no direct financial benefit may mitigate, but not remove, her culpability. Indirectly, in making more sales, she may have benefited in the long run by achieving promotion or more job security.

Confo may have benefited initially from Kirsty's action and may suffer reputational damage by external disclosure, but nevertheless there is a public interest disclosure requirement if, on the basis of legal advice, a crime has been committed. The Confo board should therefore inform the Lenton board of what has occurred in order that it can make its own investigations. If the Lenton board does not make disclosure to the police then the Confo board should consider doing so, notwithstanding that documentary evidence is limited.

Examiner's comments

This requirement was well answered, on the whole, with most candidates making use of ethical principles and language to assist their balanced discussion, and recognising the potential adverse effects to be much greater than a few boxes of chocolates as it could have impacted on the cessation of the supply contract between the two companies. Legal aspects were also often referred to, including bribery, though a worrying minority dismissed the idea of there being any legal ramifications out of hand. Some considered the culpability to be only with John Drake, rather than also relating to Kirsty at Confo.

Only a minority recognised the need for a clear formulation of a company policy on the issue of gifts to business contacts. Poorer candidates failed to deal with required actions and instead just analysed the scenario in general terms using transparency, fairness and effect.

17 Radar Traditional Radios Ltd (December 2014, amended)

	Knowledge	Skill	Marks
17.1 Porter's 5 Forces	3	8	10
17.2 Segmentation	4	9	12
17.3 Abandon	2	8	9
	9	25	31

17.1 Porter's Five Forces

Substitutes

A substitute product is a product or service produced by another industry which satisfies the same customer needs as the industry under consideration.

Where there are readily available substitutes accessible to consumers at reasonable cost, then this acts as additional competition and competes away industry profitability.

In the radio manufacturing industry, close substitutes exist in a range of other devices which can receive digital audio transmissions to replicate the function of radios. These include digital televisions, internet devices and smart phones.

The growth in the use of internet and smartphones for listening to the radio in the five years up to 20X7 (see table) indicates that they are relatively close substitutes.

Moreover, while some of the other devices are more expensive than buying a radio, they also perform other functions, so consumers are, for example, already likely to have a television and there is no incremental cost to listening to the radio. In addition, switching costs are minimal if other devices are already owned.

While the other products noted above are close substitutes, they are not perfect substitutes. For example:

- The other devices do not receive analogue broadcasts
- The sound quality (eg, from many smart phones) may not be as good as a radio
- A radio is portable unlike some other devices (eg, a television)

Nevertheless, these substitutes affect the profitability of the radio manufacturing industry through the following:

- Putting a ceiling on prices eg, it is unlikely very high prices could be charged, even for high quality radios

- Affecting volumes of demand as the market is split not only between rivals in the industry, but with manufacturers of substitute products

- Forcing expensive investments and technology improvements to keep pace with technology changes outside the industry

Defining the industry as radio manufacturing is quite narrow. Many of the larger consumer electronics manufacturers are also likely to make the substitute products noted above and hence are internally diversified. The companies most exposed to the threat of substitutes in the industry are those (like RTR) who only make radios.

Conclusion

Overall the threat from substitutes is significant and could, in the longer run, be industry destroying.

Competitive rivalry amongst existing firms

The intensity of competition amongst existing rival firms in the industry will tend to compete away the collective profitability of participants in the industry.

Competition in radio manufacture is global, even if some companies in the industry are focused, like RTR, on one national market. There are major international companies which, although not based in the UK, can distribute efficiently to the UK.

The level of competitive rivalry in radio manufacturing will depend on the following factors.

Digital radios

- Rate of market growth – the market for digital radios is changing:

    - It may be rising as fewer people buy analogue radios, which will reduce competitiveness and make the industry more profitable; or

    - It may be falling as the overall market for listening to radio is fairly constant (in listening hours) and the availability of substitutes means that the remaining demand for radios is falling, leaving the incumbent manufacturers chasing a smaller market.

- Ease of switching for buyers – buyers of digital radios can easily switch to rival products when a radio is replaced thus competition is intense in relation to every product cycle.

- Degree of uncertainty over the actions of rival firms – new digital technology could emerge on a regular basis meaning that profits could fall away for many firms in the industry. This requires high R&D budgets which reduce industry profitability.

Analogue radios

- Level of fixed costs – if there is a smaller market for analogue radios in future and as volumes fall across the industry then fixed costs per unit increase and industry profitability therefore falls

- Importance of capacity utilisation/economies of scale – a shrinking market means fewer economies of scale and more spare capacity thereby reducing industry profit

- Exit barriers – these may be high (non-current assets with a low break-up value; redundancy payments, costs of withdrawal) due to the specialised nature of the equipment which means competition remains in the industry much longer than would otherwise be the case (zombie companies)

Conclusion

Overall, the threat from competitive rivalry amongst existing firms is significant and could cause less efficient companies to exit the industry.

Examiner's comments

This requirement was generally very well answered. Most recognised the relevance of substitutes and competitive rivalry to industry competitiveness and concluded that both forces are relatively strong, hence tending towards an increasingly unattractive competitive environment. Fewer candidates emphasised the fact that analogue radio faces less of a threat from substitutes than digital.

The competitive rivalry section was less well done than substitutes, with candidates often failing to recognise that the market for radios was changing. Candidates tended to conclude that competitive rivalry was high, but often without really justifying why.

Weaker efforts tended to confuse substitutes with competitive rivalry and spent a lot of time discussing how digital radios are substitutes for analogue.

17.2 Market segmentation

Market segmentation is the division of the market into homogeneous groups of potential customers who may be treated similarly for marketing purposes.

Focus players like RTR may only be able to use market segmentation in a limited way as one segment might be their sole consumer group. Broader market players may use market segmentation to market in different ways to different groups.

RTR has a premium pricing strategy. Necessarily, there are fewer people that can afford expensive radios than can afford cheaper radios, which limits the size of the market, but also changes the characteristics of the consumer group (see pricing section below).

Market segmentation is therefore a tool of marketing strategy that can help RTR management to focus on relevant customer groups, and to use a marketing mix to arrive at a desirable marketing proposition. This enables RTR to customise its marketing mix to make it appropriate to likely customers.

The market can be segmented in a number of general different ways. For example:

- Age
- Income
- Gender

More specific segmentation might refer to the number of hours listening to the radio, or technology spending of consumers (eg, identified by purchasing technology magazines or other technology products purchased).

Different types of market segmentation can be combined in order to refine the sub group which is most likely to appeal as potential consumers of RTR radios. Thus, for instance, a particular type of radio programme might appeal to higher income groups with an age group of around 55, perhaps with more females in the audience. These can be targeted for radio advertising during these programmes.

There are a number of problems in doing this type of market segmentation:

- The groupings are crude (eg, 55% female buyers for RTR is only just above half and there is therefore little benefit above mass marketing to the population generally).

- Obtaining the information to target these groups may be difficult. It may be necessary to use databases which tend to be typical of the market segments identified, rather than use the characteristics (age, income and gender) directly.

The marketing mix

Following market segmentation, targeting involves selecting the most appropriate market segments.

Target marketing tailors a marketing mix for one or more segments identified by market segmentation.

Promotion

Advertising is the most obvious form of promotion, and it should be appropriate to the targeted market segment.

Radio manufacturing is related to the media industry, so advertising through this means seems one of the most obvious channels to use. This may include transmissions through other rival devices such as TV, mobiles and the internet including social media.

The internet may take target marketing down to very small groups who have shown an interest in radios and radio broadcasting through their choice of websites.

In terms of broader radio audiences, data may be available by audience characteristics for particular programmes and placing adverts adjacent to these programmes would stand the best opportunity of reaching the RTR target customer base and gain best value for its advertising spending.

Other media might include journals and magazines used by older, high income age groups, ideally with some radio listening theme.

Price

RTR has a premium pricing strategy. Necessarily, there are fewer people that can afford expensive radios than can afford cheaper radios, which limits the size of the market, but it also changes the characteristics of the consumer group willing to pay more for radios, compared with the mass market of radio purchasing consumers.

Even within the high income group who buy RTR's radios, more customers could be created by lowering the price, but this has some disadvantages:

- Lowers the profit per unit

- Demand is likely to be inelastic in this market niche thus sales volumes may not increase significantly even if prices are substantially lower

- It sends the wrong marketing signal where this is a luxury good and the quality cannot be readily observed, thus price is a signal of quality

A key factor in assessing price is the prices being charged by the closest competitors, which should be identified in market research of competitors. In this case, however, as a signal of quality, a virtue is being made of setting prices above competitors.

Product

A product is not just the physical item with features, but the perception of the item to the customer and the package of benefits that it provides.

The technology features used by RTR are good quality, but the styling of the goods is important and is distinctive, being part of the brand image.

The brand name is key in representing these qualities and making the RTR radios distinct from other brands.

In the case of RTR, the company name is the brand name.

Thus, for example, the 'retro' old fashioned style may particularly appeal to the older age market segment who can remember when all radios were styled in that way.

Place

Given RTR currently only sells through retail outlets in the UK, this limits the geographical market. The distribution network should be reviewed to make sure that the shops where RTR radios are being sold are consistent in image with the high income, middle age market segmentation strategy.

However, there may also be scope for widening the perception of the attainable geographic market by marketing to similar high income, middle aged groups overseas. Further market research could reveal whether the same segmentation groups apply in other countries as they do in the UK.

In terms of distribution, a radio is small and portable so the costs of transporting them may be low and this would enhance the opportunity to open up international markets through online sales without damaging the relationship with UK retailers, as there is likely to be little leakage between markets.

Examiner's comments

This requirement was well answered on the whole. Most began with definitions of segmentation and applied this to the question.

A minority wasted time discussing in detail market research approaches to segmentation, but then often proceeded to ignore the data which had been provided in the question.

The best answers related each different type of segmentation to the marketing mix. Weaker efforts only discussed the latter in generic terms.

There was little discussion by most candidates of the problems of applying market segmentation.

Virtually no candidate attempted to discuss the marketing mix in the broader context of an overall marketing strategy for the firm.

17.3 Factors to consider

RTR currently makes both digital and analogue radios. Analogue still makes up most of the sales of RTR by volume at 60%, although by value it is less than this at 53% (see below) as digital radios are more expensive.

In sales value terms at retail prices:

	20X7 £'000	
Analogue radios (60,000 × £150)	9,000	53%
Digital radios (40,000 × £200)	8,000	47%

While analogue radios are the more important product in terms of sales volumes, they are declining as they near the end of their product life cycle, due to both technology and regulation. In terms of a BCG matrix analysis of its product portfolio, RTR's analogue radios are the company's key 'cash cows' as they still generate significant cash flows which can be used to fund increased marketing and/or investment in R&D for the 'problem child' digital products. Cash flows are likely to decline soon however, as analogue radios head towards 'dog' status. In contrast, digital radios are in the growth phase of their product life cycle, but at a slow rate of only 1,000 radios per year on average.

The immediate abandonment of the major product seems implausible, and this is not being suggested. Rather, the suggestion is that RTR should no longer invest in analogue R&D and marketing and thus gradually let sales decline (perhaps over two to three years) to the point where they will then be abandoned.

If the process of decline in analogue is rapid, this is very risky as the major product may be in its decline stage of the product life cycle but is still generating most of the major cash flows for RTR. Indeed, any R&D and marketing costs may be self-financing in terms of additional sales.

Despite the above, it seems clear that the UK government intends to abandon analogue broadcasting eventually, thereby ending sales of analogue radios in the UK. Whilst there may be overseas markets to sell analogue radios to (eg, developing nations) it seems clear this market will disappear over time in favour of digital radios.

In essence therefore, the key decision for RTR is not **whether** to abandon producing analogue radios, but **when**.

In making this decision the key factors are as follows.

In favour of abandoning analogue sooner and investing in digital radios

- Analogue is to cease being broadcast. In anticipation of this, consumers will cease to buy analogue radios some time before the switch-off date

- Industry support appears to be in favour of digital, so working with broadcasters in digital research may be more fruitful than analogue research

- Less than half of households own digital radios, but in total 90% of people have access to digital reception, so there is a big potential first time buyer market

- As technology develops rapidly, consumers will wish to replace their radios more frequently with the new features

- Distribution outlets for analogue radios may shrink as retail chains stop selling them

- New features like Bluetooth are needed to keep pace with changes in technology in order to compete and R&D is needed for this

Against abandoning analogue sooner and continuing to invest in it for longer

- Digital reception is only available to 90% of the UK population. This not only restricts the market but makes it less likely in the short term that government will switch off analogue

- Uncertainty arises from the intensity of future competition in digital communications (within the industry and with substitutes)

- Analogue is still a larger market than digital by current sales volumes and current listeners

- Digital may fail to take hold in the global market and therefore fail commercially as a technology

- Analogue may continue for many years, perhaps due to the greater sound quality.

- If other companies exit the analogue market, but RTR remain in it, then it may be less competitive for RTR

Conclusion

There are significant uncertainties about the nature and timing of the relative popularity of digital and analogue. It may be appropriate to keep the real option and continue with both technologies until it is clearer about the pace of change in market preferences and the timing and certainty of the analogue switch off.

Examiner's comments

The responses to this question were mixed. The best answers were well balanced and often explicitly introduced either the product life cycle or the BCG matrix, or both. Many were implicitly aware of the relevance of these frameworks, so some credit was given.

Only a few referred to the uncertainty of the analogue switch-off date. The weakest answers concluded that the firm should quit analogue production as soon as possible, with little consideration of the adverse cash flow impact this would have. Weaker answers also failed to make any reference to the data provided.

The higher scoring answers recognised that if other companies exited the analogue market, then RTR could benefit from this as the industry supply would be reduced to offset, to some degree, falling industry demand for analogue devices.

Additionally they tended to spend a lot of time discussing partially relevant issues such as redundancies, with little focus on the timing, product portfolio and cash flow issues.

Very few referred to the real option characteristics of the choices faced by the firm.

18 The Norgate Bank plc (December 2014)

	Knowledge	Skill	Marks
18.1 KPIs	2	11	12
18.2 Benchmarking	4	8	11
	6	19	23

18.1 KPIs

KPIs are metrics in relation to a target that will deliver the organisation's objectives in the area to which they relate.

KPIs should therefore be related to the relevant critical success factor. In the case of the call centres this means dealing with customer enquiries to satisfy customer expectations, build relationships and achieve this as efficiently as possible in terms of time and cost.

The actual KPIs achieved are given in the Exhibit but there is no target measure against which to judge these metrics in order to determine whether performance has been at an appropriate level. The idea of benchmarks to determine an appropriate target is examined below.

Dealing with the nature of the KPIs used by Ron:

Average time taken to answer a customer call

This is measure of efficiency, but also it is a measure of capacity to take calls. If the KPI achieved is not at an appropriate level of efficiency (eg, customers are ringing off before the call is answered) then this may damage relationships with customers and cause dissatisfaction leaving customer enquiries unsatisfied.

There is therefore a trade-off between efficiency, capacity and cost. If sufficient resources are dedicated to call centres then all calls could be answered immediately, but this may not meet the objective of cost efficiency as too many staff may be idle waiting when call volumes are low.

Being efficient would be trying to meet customer expectations, including unexpected peaks and troughs in call volumes, without undue idle time and therefore excessive cost.

Overall this seems to be a reasonable measure in that long waiting times are likely to be viewed unfavourably by customers. What is not clear is how to determine the target for the optimal time that customers should wait to balance service delivery with cost.

Average length of a customer call

This KPI is, to a degree, ambiguous. If the average call is long then it could be sign of quality in meeting customer needs by giving due time to resolve all the issues raised and make the customer feel in receipt of a good service.

Conversely, it could be a sign of inefficiency in being unable to deal with customer enquiries quickly and efficiently and so wastes customer time as well as NB staff time and costs.

A further alternative may be that the length of the call is dependent on the subject matter. Thus business customer calls may deal with more complex issues than calls from private individuals and may therefore take longer on average.

Overall, therefore, this seems a difficult measure to determine, not just the level of the KPI, but the direction relative to target. In this respect many of the relevant factors may be captured in the final KPI which is:

Scores from customer satisfaction surveys

Scores from customer satisfaction surveys are a good measure of whether objectives are being achieved in relation to building customer relationships and offering appropriate service.

On their own however crude measures of how satisfied customers are with a call does not of itself indicate why they are satisfied. Further qualitative detail is needed to better understand customer satisfaction (eg, whether it is the length of the call, ability to resolve issue quickly, friendliness). It also leaves open the question of satisfaction relative to cost.

Conclusion

The KPIs selected emphasise effective service delivery by omitting measures of the efficiency with which that service is delivered.

Additional measures of efficiency (eg, meeting peaks and troughs with the right scheduling of staff hours to meet demand at key times in the day, and for key days of the week) and capacity (idle hours to total hours ie, utilisation) would be useful.

Also there are no financial KPIs which is key to call centre financial efficiency. Cost per call could be one such measure. In this case, the costs of the Vietnam centre per call may be much lower than the London centre, even if operational efficiency is lower in Vietnam.

Examiner's comments

The quality of responses was mixed for this requirement. The best answers provided critical evaluation of each of the three KPIs after an introduction defining KPIs, their role and their relationship to critical success factors or goals. Alternatives were suggested during the course of the evaluations and, often, afterwards. Weaker candidates failed to link the KPIs with CSFs.

Relatively few candidates explicitly or implicitly discussed the trade-offs between efficiency, capacity and costs. Likewise, only a significant minority considered the issue of different types of customers and/or locations.

Additionally, a few referred to direct sample monitoring of calls as well as using the 'mystery shopper' approach to direct quality evaluation.

In order to consider critical success factors, some attempted to use the Balanced Scorecard framework, but in many instances suggested goals and measures which were largely unrelated to the performance of the call centres.

Some candidates redefined the entire requirement in terms of the Balanced Scorecard, which tended to lead to poor marks.

18.2 Benchmarking

Benchmarking is: "The establishment, through data gathering, of targets and comparators, through whose use relative levels of performance (and particularly areas of underperformance) can be identified. By the adoption of identified best practices it is hoped that performance will improve."

Benchmarking compares the use of assets and activities across the firm, or across the industry, and indicates where they might be used better or where they are already a source of superior performance. Once a business has identified its CSFs and core competences, it must identify performance standards which need to be achieved to outperform rivals and achieve sustainable competitive advantage. These standards are sometimes called key performance indicators (KPIs).

Benchmarks can therefore provide a means of determining target KPIs which, if achieved, will match the best standards in the industry. Such benchmarks not only set targets for existing KPIs, but may suggest different types of KPI to measure new CSFs.

In so doing, by comparing performance with other entities, NB can learn how to reduce costs and improve customer service quality. Additionally, benchmarking may help NB better understand whether it is achieving competitive advantage and superior performance in the call centre operations area of its activities.

Different types of benchmarks may provide different types of guidance:

Historic or internal benchmarking – internal benchmarking would be at the level of comparing individual units (for businesses and individuals) at each call centre (London and Vietnam) with each other to determine those that are under- or over-performing when considering the different demands and circumstances. At the moment however this is the first year of operation of Vietnam and learning may still be taking place. Conversely London may still be adjusting to losing the French customer calls. Nevertheless, internal benchmarking attempts to raise performance to the standard of the best internal unit and demonstrates to other units that this level of performance is achievable.

Historical comparison looks at performance over time to ascertain trends/significant changes, but the danger is that performance against competitors is ignored and long-standing internal inefficiencies are not highlighted. For the first year of operation this is not possible in Vietnam.

In the Exhibit, it would appear that data could be used (for example) to compare the number of hours of calls handled per annum for each member of staff. In the UK call centre for individuals this is 800 hours pa $((1{,}200{,}000 \times 4/60)/100)$ but in the other three functions (UK individuals, Vietnam business and Vietnam individuals) it is 1,000 hours pa. This would at least raise some questions. The differences in satisfaction also vary between centre and between types of customer, but there is no obvious pattern.

Competitive benchmarking – compares performance with other firms in the same industry or sector. This may assist NB in ascertaining ways to improve performance – eg, comparing the performance with other banks' call centres. An alternative is to widen the definition of the industry from banks to financial services and include the experience of Ron's deputy who has worked in the related industry of insurance. The differences may be accounted for in the differences in the types of calls received by banks and insurance companies but questions may be asked to improve performance even though the comparisons are not identical.

This may involve the use of league tables, but more detailed information may be difficult to achieve as competitors may be reluctant to share data with rivals. Partnerships or industry groupings or a benchmarking centre may help overcome this lack of information.

Activity (best in class) benchmarking – compare with best practice in whatever industry can be found eg, could compare with a hotel telephone booking system, or ticket booking or emergency telephone system, whichever is 'best in class' for the function dealing with telephone calls efficiently. This has the advantage that a firm may share operations in common with non-competitor external organisations, which might be 'best in the class' for a particular function, more readily than with a rival firm in the same industry.

Generic benchmarking – this is benchmarking against a conceptually similar process eg, compare an online system of banking compared to telephone calls which can achieve the same outcome (eg, simple transactions online or by telephone). It is unlikely that this will result in comparison of detailed measures but it could identify conceptual areas for improvement.

Disadvantages

There are disadvantages to benchmarking. A full programme can overload managers with demands for information, restrict their attention to the factors that are to be benchmarked and affect their motivation by seeming to reduce their role to copying others. It can also undermine competitive advantage by revealing trade secrets. Strategically, it can divert attention away from innovation and the future by focusing it on the efficiency of current operations.

Since benchmarking is about processes rather than results, measures would have to be linked to outcomes at some stage.

Examiner's comments

Most candidates discussed three or four types of benchmarking and many also provided an introduction to the purpose of benchmarking in the performance management process of identifying critical success factors and related KPIs.

A significant minority described the approaches with little or no evaluation of advantages and problems in their application in this particular scenario. Many did mention, in general terms, the difficulties involved in obtaining competitor/comparator data. Additionally, there was a tendency to evaluate internal benchmarking only, tending to ignore the other types of benchmarking, beyond an initial description.

Good answers also related their discussion to their previous consideration of KPIs. However, a minority of weaker candidates displayed a lack of awareness of the benchmarking process and simply carried on evaluating KPIs.

19   Rocket Co (March 2015, amended)

Marking guide

	Knowledge	Skill	Marks
19.1 Performance	2	18	18
19.2 Consideration of factors	3	9	10
19.3 Change management	4	7	10
19.4 Ethics	3	6	8
	12	40	46

Appendix: Further analysis

> **Tutorial note**
>
> A wide range of possible calculations have been given here for marking purposes and to illustrate the scope for additional numerical analysis.

Analysis of income

	20X4	20X3
Fee income F'000 (given)	7,091	6,653
Mix of fee income:		
Accounting: tax	47:53	45:55
Absolute fee income:		
Accounting F'000	3,333 (increase 11.3%)	2,994
Tax F'000	3,758 (increase 2.7%)	3,659
Average fee charged		
Accounting	F335 (increase 11.7%)	F300
Tax	F415 (increase 15.3%)	F360
Premium charged for tax (tax rate/accountancy rate)	23.9%	20%
Hours billed		
Accounting	9,949	9,980
Tax	9,055	10,164
	Total 19,004	Total 20,144
Change in total hours:	(5.7%)	
Accounting	(0.3%)	
Tax	(10.9%)	

Market information

	20X4	20X3
Fee income F'000 (given)	7,091	6,653
Market share (given)	12%	14%
Hence market size F'000	59,092 (increase 24.3%)	47,521

Profitability

	20X4	20X3
Fee income F'000 (given)	7,091	6,653
Net profit margin	20.8%	23.1%
Net profit F'000	1,475 (decrease 4.0%)	1,537
Total costs F'000	5,616 (increase 9.8%)	5,116
Fee income per partner F'000 (given)	1,773	1,663
No. of partners	4	4
Average profit per partner	368.75 (4% decrease)	384.25

Variances on non-financial indicators

	20X4	20X3	Variance
Market share	12%	14%	2% decrease
% Satisfied clients	75%	85%	10% decrease
Total staff turnover	23.5%	17.6%	5.9% increase
Error rates	10%	8%	2% increase
Utilisation rate	70.5%	66.5%	4% increase

Rocket uses a balanced scorecard approach to performance measurement which combines financial and non-financial information. Some of the non-financial factors in the scorecard can be used to help explain the financial performance of and the prospects for the business and give much greater insight into key operational issues within the business.

Income and market share

Fee income is up by 6.6% compared to an increase of 9.2% the previous year which suggests that growth is slowing and may explain Rocket's desire to consider new products.

However referring to the market share information (customer perspective), it is clear that Rocket has underperformed the market, losing 2% of its share at a time when the market for services (measured by revenue) has increased by 24.3%. It would be helpful to have the market share information analysed between tax and accounting to consider both lines of service separately and assess whether one is out-performing the other. The sales mix has altered with the more lucrative tax work representing only 53% of income (F3.758 million), compared to 55% in 20X3 (F3.659 million), so it may be that Rocket is falling behind in this market. Since tax services command a premium rate compared to accounting, the change in sales mix will have an adverse effect on income.

The cause of the growth in fee income needs to be analysed between price and volume:

Rocket increased the fees charged for both services – accounting by 11.7% and tax by 15.3%. As a result the hours billed have fallen by 5.6% in total, from 20,144 to 19,004. This is consistent with a drop in market share. One possible reason for the increase in price would be to cover the pay rise that Rocket has had to offer staff to keep its salaries more in line with competitors.

It can be seen from the analysis that the tax services seem to have been more sensitive to the change in price, with chargeable tax hours reducing by 10.9% and thus only a 2.7% increase in overall tax revenue (compared to 11.3% for accounting). It would be useful to know to what extent the level of WIP (work done not yet billed) is comparable across the years and to try to ascertain whether the loss of chargeable hours is a timing issue or symptomatic of a loss of clients. It would also be useful to obtain competitor charge-out rates for the sports and leisure sector to see whether Rocket's fees are reasonable, although as discussed above the fact that Rocket has lost market share may be in part due to over-pricing.

Another reason for the drop in hours billed may be to do with loss of clients due to client dissatisfaction. The 20X4 customer survey has revealed that only 75% of clients are satisfied, compared to 85% in 20X3 – a 10% adverse variance. The cause of the dissatisfaction needs to be investigated. It may be linked to an increase in error rates from 8% to 10% of jobs (internal business) or to staffing issues – see below. Certainly if clients are being asked to pay higher fees they are likely to expect standards and quality of service to be at least maintained, so a 25% increase in the error rate is unlikely to be acceptable. It would be useful to know the reasons for the dissatisfaction and to ascertain whether one service has been affected more than the other.

Rocket has not been paying staff the appropriate market premium and this has probably led to demotivation and dissatisfaction, as evidenced by the increase in staff turnover (17.6% to 23.5% – innovation and learning). This represents one more fee-earner (5.9% × 17 fee earners) leaving and needing to be replaced. The pay rise offered may have come too late for some staff and more may choose to leave given the increasing employment opportunities in the marketplace. Continuity of staff is important as clients may resent revealing personal financial details to a variety of different people each year. Recruiting replacement staff costs the business money and there is then a learning curve period, during which perhaps errors may be made. In addition the business does not appear to be investing much in training, with qualified staff only receiving two days per year. In a specialist sector this may not be sufficient to keep abreast of developments and may be an additional cause of the error rates.

Profitability

Despite the 6.6% increase in fee income, Rocket's net profit for 20X4 of F1.475 million is 4% lower than in 20X3.

The net profit margin has fallen from 23.1% to 20.8% as a result of the total cost increase (9.8%) exceeding that of the revenue increase. A number of factors have caused Rocket's costs to increase in 20X4:

- Rent review

- Increased PII premiums

- Pay rise for staff (it would be useful to know how much this was and at what point in the year it was made as it does not yet appear to have stemmed the staff turnover)

One factor which will be adversely affecting profitability is the poor staff utilisation rate. Although this has improved from 66.5% to 70.5% it still means that staff are spending a considerable amount of time engaged in activities that are not billed to clients. This may be due to having to incur write-offs of time eg, on fixed fee jobs or because staff are spending time on business development, or too much time on administrative issues. Assuming staff work 7 hours a day, 5 days a week for 48 weeks, there are 1,680 hours available per fee earner. Assuming utilisation rates were between 85% and 90%, Rocket would only need 13 staff to achieve the 20X4 billed hours. In the change management memo the partners identify the need for qualified staff to consider delegating more tasks to concentrate on higher value activities which would increase profitability.

Summary

In conclusion, although the revenue has grown and margins are still reasonable, the financial results do not show the full picture. Rocket appears to have some fundamental weaknesses in its core business that need to be addressed, if it is to continue to grow into the future. The success of the MDP proposal will be dependent on existing clients' willingness to buy additional legal services from Rocket, which they will not do if they are dissatisfied with the existing services and perceive staff to be inadequately trained.

Examiner's comments

Candidates were asked to analyse and evaluate the performance of Rocket between 20X3 and 20X4, using the balanced scorecard.

The data analysis requirement was reasonably attempted but certainly not as well answered as in recent sittings. The fact that a balanced scorecard of performance indicators was provided in the Exhibit seemed to discourage a surprising number of candidates from undertaking any further numerical analysis. Better candidates provided some additional up-front calculations in a reasonably well structured table to help explain some of the changes in the scorecard (fee income per service stream, billable hours, market size, profit per partner). Weaker candidates were very poor in this regard, merely reiterating the KPIs that had been given or at most providing occasional calculations of changes in figures, within their narrative.

Most candidates structured their narrative explanation using the four headings from the scorecard and made good links between the different sections, successfully drawing conclusions from the non-financial information to explain the reasons behind the financial performance.

Only the stronger candidates suggested additional information that would assist their analysis and concluded that Rocket would need to address some of its internal issues relating to client and staff dissatisfaction before becoming an MDP.

19.2 Factors affecting ability to create a multi-disciplinary practice (MDP)

Human resource capabilities

Rocket's existing partners and staff are all experienced in accountancy and taxation, not law, so it does not currently have the human capital needed to implement this strategy. It would appear that it intends to use its existing support staff by establishing its own shared service centre but will need to employ new 'fee-earners'.

It is critical to the venture's success that the legal staff have appropriate specialist expertise, otherwise there will be no incentive for existing clients to switch their legal services to Rocket. The MDP will take longer to set up if Rocket recruits piecemeal rather than acquires an existing team. However the advantage of the former is that Rocket may be more likely to integrate individuals into its own culture and may experience less resistance from staff.

From a cost point of view, Rocket may have to offer higher pay/rewards to induce staff to move, particularly if it has a reputation for poor pay and high staff turnover. The upside of recruiting an existing team however is that they may bring some clients with them.

Increasingly law firms are employing para-legal/non-lawyers to do routine work such as document processing, so Rocket will need to consider how many staff are required and what the appropriate mix is. This will depend on the expected demand for its legal services.

Legal and regulatory issues

These forces may relate to/be affected by government policies and be politically driven. They are largely outside Rocket's control.

Changes in the regulations affecting the legal services market appear to be an attempt by government to increase competition in the market. However this could change.

The new MDP will need a licence to operate and will be monitored by the new regulatory authority. It is not clear how easy it will be for Rocket to acquire the licence, the time and cost involved, what terms and conditions will apply eg, in relation to the mix of partners, governance requirements etc. and what the costs of compliance are likely to be. Rocket is presumably used to being accountable to the relevant accountancy and tax regulators so it has some experience in this area.

It will also need to consider the prospect of further regulations affecting MDPs/law/accountancy firms and also in relation to the sports sector where there are likely to be rules and regulations of different sports governing bodies, disciplinary matters etc.

Competitors and market structure

The reduction of barriers to entry is likely to increase competition and give rise to a number of alternative professional services providers.

Other accountancy firms may also decide to create MDPs.

Alternatively legal firms could develop their own accountancy and tax businesses so Rocket may lose referrals that it is currently getting from these firms.

Possible consolidation in the market place is likely to increase the size of the various players and if they are able to reduce costs, this may result in lower prices for services which will affect margins.

Rocket's advantage is that it specialises in sports and leisure, so it may face less competition in this niche than if it were targeting the whole market.

Candidates were required to analyse various factors that might influence Rocket's ability to create an MDP.

The second requirement was very well answered on the whole. The majority of candidates identified that Rocket does not currently have any legal expertise and that recruiting the necessary staff and obtaining the licence would be critical success factors for the creation of an MDP. Better candidates discussed the two different approaches to resourcing suggested in the question, in light of Rocket's current staffing issues. They also highlighted the uncertainty surrounding the MDP licence and rules given that the regulatory framework is new and designed to increase competition. Weaker candidates typically found it more difficult to discuss competition and market structure, although candidates who used their knowledge of rivalry and barriers to entry from the Porter's 5 forces model had more to say.

19.3 Change management

The change to an MDP is a major transformational change for Rocket, which is being made in response to changes in the external environment. As the internal memo points out, it may have a significant effect on the staffing and management structure of the firm.

The Gemini 4Rs framework to change involves reframing, restructuring, revitalising and renewal. To an extent, in advance of the memo, Rocket's partners have already addressed the first three of these:

- Reframing – Rocket has asked fundamental questions about what the organisation is about, decided to become an MDP and created a vision of what it will stand for: a mid-market professional services practice offering one-stop legal, tax and accounting advice for its existing wealthy sporting clients.

- Restructuring – the alignment of the physical organisation with the plan. Again the partners have addressed this by identifying the need to recruit resources, creating a shared service centre and setting up appropriate account teams.

- Revitalising – this is the process of securing a good fit with the environment and explains the motivation for the change – here the partners of Rocket have quickly decided to adopt a new business model in response to the deregulation of the legal services market and are one of the early adopters in the hope of gaining competitive advantage.

This leaves the critical element – renewal – which is ensuring that people in the organisation support the change process and have the necessary skills to contribute to it.

Here the partners appear to have left the major change of culture and structure to be announced to staff in a memo. This is a coercive change approach, with little attempt at participation. As a result they have possibly underestimated the forces of resistance to change and do not appear to have attempted to harness support in favour of the new structure.

The problem with this is that change affects individuals in different ways and that the way change is introduced can influence the degree of resistance to it. Staff are likely to have lots of questions about the MDP and there will be a great deal of uncertainty surrounding the impact that the new legal staff will have on the firm's culture, structure and systems. The fact that the partners state they will 'be examining the potential for cost savings and efficiencies across the firm' is likely to cause staff to worry about earnings and job security.

Existing staff may see the change as a threat for a variety of reasons: administrative staff in particular are being told to increase efficiency and informed that there will be target staffing ratios. Qualified staff may fear that in delegating work to juniors they lose their power base or may become redundant. Junior staff may feel ill-prepared to take on the additional work that is expected of them and worry about their lack of appropriate skills and training.

Such an approach can lead to low staff morale, which may already be a problem given that Rocket is not paying the market premium for specialist staff and has experienced an increase in staff turnover.

Instead of presenting staff with a fait accompli, Rocket would have been better undertaking some consultation process in advance of the announcement, allowing discussion about individual needs and creating opportunities for staff to contribute to the changes. This would have given staff time to get used to the idea and reduced the resentment and feelings of helplessness.

Thus whilst Rocket is taking a proactive approach to changes in its environment, its chosen method of communicating the change falls short of best practice. In the aftermath of the email, Rocket would be well advised to hold meetings to address any concerns and offer staff the chance to become involved in the implementation phase of the change process.

Examiner's comments

Candidates were asked to discuss, in light of the partners' email, the extent to which Rocket's approach meets best practice in change management, referring to an appropriate change model such as Gemini 4Rs.

The main difference in the answers to this requirement related to whether candidates were familiar with the specific model suggested for use. Candidates are normally well versed in the technical knowledge for the change management requirement but the Gemini 4Rs model proved to be an exception. A significant number of candidates, clearly unable to recall the Gemini model, made comments along the lines of "whilst Gemini 4Rs is useful, so is Lewin Schein's iceberg model" and then went on to use that as an alternative.

Candidates are advised that if the examiner recommends an approach, there is usually a good reason for doing so. Whilst credit was awarded to candidates who used an alternative model, the use of the recommended Gemini model would have created scope to make a wider variety of points. Faced with changes in the external environment, Rocket appears to have **reframed** what the practice should stand for, is **restructuring** (recruiting lawyers and creating a central admin team) and attempting to **revitalise** by being an early adopter of the MDP model. However this is a major transformational change and staff are already unhappy, yet Rocket appears to have adopted a coercive change approach with little consultation. Thus the critical element of **renewal**, ensuring people in the organisation support the change, is lacking. Better answers were produced by the very few candidates who understood the model and recognised this.

As usual, weaker candidates failed to apply their knowledge to the question, simply discussing the type of change and the likely barriers rather than evaluating Rocket's decision to announce the change via email.

19.4 **Ethical issues**

This situation gives rise to a number of different potential ethical issues:

- Facilitation by the manager of unethical behaviour or even possibly illegal actions by the client

- Conflict between Alina's obligations as an ICAEW professional accountant and her obligations to Rocket, her employer

- Possible issues with the tone at the top within Rocket

Every employee has a duty of loyalty to their employer and in this case Alina owes a duty to Rocket Co. As a result Alina must not just turn blind eye to suspected wrongful behaviour because saying something might put her in an uncomfortable position with colleagues or because of self-interest in relation to her job or career. Thus if there is evidence of wrongdoing then keeping quiet should not be an option. Instead she needs to consider morally and ethically what the right thing to do is in relation to her suspicions.

A longstanding personal relationship with a client may have given rise to a familiarity threat to the manager's fundamental principles of objectivity. However it is important that Alina does not automatically assume that the manager has done something wrong. She needs to try and ascertain the facts. An effective relationship with superiors needs to be open, honest and trusting – the culture of Rocket should be such that Alina feels able to go to the managers and partners she works for and discuss opinions/ask questions/even challenge. It is not clear to what extent Alina has already done this with the manager concerned in relation to the statement of wealth and what evidence she has that the client's personal wealth has been misstated. If Alina has felt unable to raise her concerns then there may be a cultural issue to be addressed here by Rocket (the manner in which the change management was handled may suggest that this is the case).

Alina also needs to consider whether there is any statutory duty here and what legislation applies. Professional accountants need to be mindful of their responsibilities to their clients and employers to keep any information they learn confidential. Certainly Alina needs to avoid spreading news of the potentially dishonest activity by discussing it with colleagues or others who do not have responsibility over the matter. However there may be anti-fraud and/or anti-money laundering legislation that might govern reporting requirements. Whistle-blower protection provisions are common in most of Europe so she also needs to consider what legislation exists in the country to protect whistle-blowers, particularly for example in relation to the disclosure of confidential information about the client concerned.

In determining the appropriate action, Alina should consider whether there is any guidance in her employment contract, staff handbook, Rocket's code of conduct, or any internal guidance on whistleblowing. She also needs to consider her professional responsibility as a qualified accountant and the IESBA code of ethics (which is likely to apply to her manager and Rocket's partners to the extent that they are qualified accountants). Alina may be able to contact the firm's HR representative for assistance and/or seek legal advice.

Discussing her concerns with superiors in Rocket may be key as a means of preventing/detecting possible fraud. It would also highlight the inadequacies in Rocket's systems and culture which have allowed this to happen. Were Alina not to take any action, this would be allowed to perpetuate.

Examiner's comments

Candidates were requested to discuss the ethical issues associated with Alina's concerns and advise her on appropriate actions to take.

This requirement was well answered, presumably because the ethical issues (the suspected provision of misleading information to the bank and the need for internal/external disclosure) were reasonably easy for most candidates to identify. The vast majority of candidates recognised that there is likely to be a legal issue here – possibly fraud or money laundering. Most candidates made good use of ICAEW ethical principles and ethical language to assist their discussion and were able to identify the potential actions open to Alina. Some weaker candidates did apply the transparency, fairness and effect decision-making approach, although this is often more relevant in relation to a business dilemma and was much less useful here.

20 The Scottish Woodlands Commission (March 2015, amended)

Marking guide

	Knowledge	Skill	Marks
20.1 Strategic fit	3	7	9
20.2 Financial benefits	2	8	10
20.3 Risks	2	6	7
20.4 Governance issues	3	7	8
	10	28	34

20.1 Strategic fit

To: SWC's Trustees
From: Business adviser
Date: XX/XX/XX
Re: Woodsaway LLP

Strategic fit

SWC's mission is to "manage, protect and expand the public woodlands in Scotland and to increase their value to society and the environment". In order to achieve this, it is authorised to undertake woodland management, nature conservation and provide facilities for public recreation.

The Woodsaway venture is likely to increase the number of people who are able to enjoy Campbell Forest and assist SWC in fulfilling one of its subsidiary objectives, of providing the general public with widespread access to the natural woodlands environment, and to promote woodlands as a location for sports and leisure activities.

It would not appear to directly assist with woodland management or nature conservation. Indeed construction of the log cabins may have a negative impact on the habitat for local wildlife, the maintenance of which is the other of SWC's subsidiary objectives.

However if the LLP generates additional income for SWC (see financial benefits below), then it may indirectly allow it to better achieve its primary and secondary objectives by providing more financial resources. Also woodland activities undertaken by Woodsaway's customers may have educational benefits by raising awareness and, if paid for, could also generate funds for conservation.

For the venture to be a success the two members of the LLP need to have complementary and aligned objectives.

CabinCo's mission is 'to be one of the UK's leading providers of luxury short breaks in natural surroundings'. It has created a strong brand and is seeking competitive advantage from having access to Campbell forest to develop a holiday village, and first option on the development of future villages on SWC woodlands in Scotland. As a private commercial company, CabinCo's aims are likely to involve growth and profits. Its primary objectives are more likely to be financial rather than non-financial, with a probable focus on cost control and margins. However the sustainable tourism market it is targeting may be more in line with SWC's environmental aims. Also the benefit to SWC is that CabinCo brings commercial experience to the venture, which may help increase profits and hence SWC's share.

There may be possible conflicts of interest about the strategy and activities of Woodsaway, between CabinCo as a private entity and SWC as a public body, since they have very different stakeholders and different planning horizons. CabinCo as a company accountable to its shareholders is likely to have a shorter term focus than the 20 year planning horizon that woodland management entails. A balance will need to be struck between financial return and delivering a service to customers and the general public.

Also conflicts may arise between the interests of the LLP and the separate interests of the two participating members. For instance CabinCo's desire to increase the profitability of the Woodsaway venture may conflict with SWC's mission to protect the woodlands and increase their value to society.

This is further discussed under the governance heading below.

Examiner's comments

In the first section of the report, candidates had to assess the strategic fit of the proposed venture. It was well answered. Most candidates were comfortable discussing the extent to which the venture is aligned with SWC's mission and secondary aims, recognising that construction of the log cabins might be inconsistent with the achievement of some of these aims (eg, protection of the woodland and nature conservation) but might facilitate others (increasing access and education). The better candidates also highlighted the very different nature of the two organisations involved in the LLP and questioned the conflict that may arise as a result. Most, but surprisingly not all candidates, scored an easy format mark for setting out their answer in the report format required. Some candidates created a time management issue for themselves by using all three headings from the suitability, feasibility, acceptability model when in fact 'suitability' is sufficient to assess strategic fit.

20.2 Financial benefits

The public/private partnership reduces the need for investment from SWC which would have to come from central government and SWC's limited commercial funds.

CabinCo (and possibly Woodsaway) will be able to raise funds privately from banks etc as it is not under the same restrictions regarding borrowing as SWC. The access to finance could provide opportunities for SWC, which would be unlikely to be able to find the £2 million building costs. In the future it would also allow extension of the concept to other sites.

The venture provides SWC as landlord with a guaranteed income stream in the form of the lease rentals of £30,000pa. Depending on the occupancy levels, SWC, as a member of the LLP, will also receive a 50% share of the profits. Provided Woodsaway does not make a loss of more than £60,000 then SWC will avoid any financial loss.

Looking at the figures in the exhibit, the financial returns to SWC are highly sensitive to occupancy, which is likely to be lower in the early years:

Occupancy rate	40%	65%	90%
	£'000	£'000	£'000
Rental	30	30	30
Share of Woodsaway (loss)/profit	(153)	118	372
Net return to SWC	(123)	148	402
Annual return on £2m land value invested	-6.15%	7.4%	20.1%
Occupancy rate	40%	65%	90%
	£'000	£'000	£'000
Cabin revenue	1,752	2,847	3,942
Contribution	1,226	1,993	2,759
Fixed costs incl rent	(1,532)	(1,757)	(2,015)
Loss/Profit	(306)	236	744

The cabins are projected to generate a gross profit of £84 per night (eg, £1,226,000/(365 × 40)). There are 36,500 available cabin nights (365 × 100 cabins). If operating costs were £1,532,000 including rent then for the Woodsaway venture to breakeven it needs to sell £1,532,000/84 = 18,238 cabin nights which equates to 50% occupancy.

Were operating costs to be £1,757,000 including rent then it would need 20,917 cabin nights or 57% occupancy. In reality it appears that some operating costs are stepped (14.7% increase in operating costs for 25% increase in occupancy), so breakeven occupancy is somewhere between 50% and 57%.

It would be useful to know what occupancy CabinCo currently achieves in its other holiday villages, which is said to be 'high', but if Woodsaway achieves anything over 65%, it would appear to be providing SWC with a decent return.

It is not clear who has supplied the figures and how these compare to other CabinCo ventures. More detail on the breakdown of operating costs would be useful and the assumption of 365 days availability may be over-optimistic.

As discussed above, money from Woodsaway can be used to fulfil SWC's other objectives and is a useful source of income given its reliance on government funds.

Examiner's comments

Answers to this section on financial benefits were varied and there were a considerable number of poor answers, resulting in this section having the lowest overall mark. Once again a surprising number of candidates made no reference to the numbers provided in the question, despite the fact that this was the obvious place to do so. Weaker candidates simply discussed the fact that SWC is limited in its ability to raise finance and that the venture may help with this, without considering the financial returns.

The key to evaluating the financial benefits was to identify the two separate roles of SWC in relation to the Woodsaway venture:

- As landlord in receipt of annual rental
- As a member of the LLP, sharing in 50% of the profits or losses

Better candidates recognised this and used the various projections to calculate SWC's profit share for the different occupancy levels. The best candidates used the financial projections provided to give some indication of the likely return on SWC's £2 million land investment and examined the sensitivity of the venture (eg, by calculating a breakeven occupancy).

20.3 Risks

A key issue for SWC is risk and who will take responsibility for managing those risks.

Compared to SWC operating a holiday village on its own, the risk of the Woodsaway venture is reduced because it is structured as an LLP and risk is shared with CabinCo, an experienced partner in the holiday sector. The public/private partnership integrates the complementary resources of the two parties. However as discussed above, a conflict of interest may arise between the interests of the LLP and the separate interests of the two participating members.

The Woodsaway venture brings its own additional risks:

Economic risk – financial events that would affect the management of the holiday village and/or the forest. This might include the volatility of revenue streams and profit share due to the state of the economy. Also any impact that operating the holiday site may have on revenues from the sale of timber. The construction of the cabins may require tree felling which could generate revenue initially but may then reduce the areas available for replanting, adversely impacting SWC's future revenue.

Reputational risk – the possible negative impact of the LLP and the holiday site on the image of SWC in the minds of other organisations it deals with, the general public and the government. If Woodsaway is very profitable it may not be appropriate for SWC to be seen to be associated with this, conversely the same may be true with a financially unsuccessful venture. There may also be reputational issues if Woodsaway is seen to pay high salaries/bonuses or alternatively if it treats staff poorly or causes environmental damage (see below).

Environmental risk – the creation of a holiday site exposes the woodland estate to possible additional threats in relation to damage and disease. There is a possible risk of urbanisation of forest through construction of cabins, which might destroy natural habitats, and there may be ongoing issues relating to damage due to footfall, more vehicles, creation of waste etc.

Hazard risk – similar to the environmental risk above, there is an increased risk of fire damage from the use of the forest as a holiday site.

Social risk – the holiday site may open the woodland up to more people but if CabinCo's customers are largely in England and Wales, these may not necessarily be from the community which SWC serves. Also the luxury cabins may only be affordable by a small minority and could be seen to be elitist.

SWC will need to ensure that appropriate risk management processes are put in place to address the additional risks that arise as a result of the Woodsaway venture. It needs to insist on controls in relation to woodland management, protection of habitat and leisure.

Examiner's comments

The majority of candidates were clearly well prepared to discuss the risks associated with the proposed venture and scored very highly on this section of the report. Most candidates identified a range of risks and discussed their potential impact. Better candidates also discussed their likelihood and suggested how they might be mitigated/managed if SWC is to go ahead with the proposal, pointing out that the risks are reduced by the creation of the LLP to operate the venture.

20.4 Governance issues

Applicability of corporate governance

Corporate governance generally refers to the system by which companies are directed and controlled. The aim of corporate governance is to facilitate effective, prudent management in order to deliver long term success. It is underpinned by the principles of accountability, transparency, probity (honesty) and focus on long term sustainable success.

Whilst the second SWC trustee is correct that the UK *Corporate Governance Code* applies to listed companies only, good governance is essential not just for companies but to any organisation, irrespective of whether it is private or public, if that organisation is to be well led and high performing.

It could be argued that good governance is even more important in the context of a public sector body, like SWC, which needs to ensure that public funds are wisely spent and that resources such as Scotland's woodlands are properly safeguarded and are used economically, efficiently, and effectively. This is the view expressed by the first trustee.

More generally therefore, governance relates to the framework of accountability to users, stakeholders and the wider community, within which organisations take decisions, and lead and control their functions, to achieve their objectives. As such it would apply to both SWC and Woodsaway. Without effective governance, the proposed public/private partnership is unlikely to be successful.

Nolan principles

Governance in the public sector has much in common with corporate governance for companies. As a publicly funded body, SWC's management board needs to act in accordance with the Nolan principles, which include the principles of integrity, accountability, openness (transparency) and honesty (probity). These are very similar to the core corporate governance principles. In addition, holders of public office are expected to comply with the additional principles of selflessness, objectivity and leadership.

Of particular relevance in the context of the Woodsaway venture are:

Selflessness: holders of public office should take decisions solely in terms of the public interest. They should not do so in order to gain financial or other materials benefits for themselves, their family, or other friends. Thus SWC needs to balance its different responsibilities and ensure that its involvement in Woodsaway does not give rise to the risk of appearing to act in a manner contrary to public interest.

Objectivity: in carrying out public business, including making public appointments, awarding contracts, or recommending individuals for rewards and benefits, holders of public office should make choices on merit. The trustees need to be seen to have considered alternative partners as well as CabinCo, which has been selected because it is the best option

Public sector organisations operate in complex legislative, political and local contexts, in which they have to make difficult decisions. Well-governed organisations balance their different responsibilities and use information to decide where to allocate effort and resources to meet competing demands.

Governance of Woodsaway

The principles of governance will apply to Woodsaway, as an LLP. A key part of good governance is risk management and this will be particularly important to SWC given the additional risks that arise as a result of the Woodsaway venture (discussed above).

CabinCo and SWC will each be entitled to appoint three representatives on Woodsaway's senior management committee so neither party would appear able to dictate decisions.

SWC needs to insist on controls to ensure Woodsaway LLP does not undermine SWC's objectives in relation to woodland management and the protection of habitat and nature. It will also need to agree on the methods for resolving any disputes and the exit arrangements should either party want to terminate the venture.

Conclusion

Overall the project appears likely to generate financial returns and would appear to help SWC further some of its aims. It seems to have the support of government, which has granted preliminary approval for the formation of the LLP. More work should be done on the financial projections and SWC could engage in stakeholder consultations to assess the public perception of the proposals. The LLP will need to be set up carefully to ensure that the risks and governance issues identified are properly addressed.

Examiner's comments

Answers to the governance section were very variable in quality. There were really two issues here: addressing the trustees' comments in relation to governance and considering the governance of the proposed LLP. A significant minority failed to appreciate the distinction between the UK *Corporate Governance Code* that applies only to listed companies and corporate governance, which is the system by which companies are directed and controlled. The better candidates recognised that the principles of good governance (accountability, transparency etc) are very similar to those enshrined in the Nolan principles and are best practice for the prudent and effective management of any organisation. Thus governance may be more, rather than less, relevant for a public sector organisation such as SWC with a wider group of stakeholders to account to and a need to act in the public interest.

Having discussed this in the light of the trustees' comments, better candidates also went on to consider governance in relation to the LLP as a critical factor in the likely success of the venture, and discussed the proposals for the structure of Woodsaway's senior management committee.

Recognising that the overall purpose of the report was to evaluate the proposed venture, most candidates provided reasoned advice at the end as to whether SWC should go ahead with the Woodsaway venture. This was pleasing to see.

21 WeDive Ltd (March 2015, amended)

Marking guide

	Knowledge	Skill	Marks
21.1 Strategic options	3	12	14
21.2 Decision tree	2	5	6
	5	17	20

21.1 Evaluation of options

Option 1: expand the range of products for the UK market

Option 1 in terms of the Ansoff matrix constitutes product development.

Advantages

- It may be less risky than targeting overseas markets as there are no language/cultural barriers.

- WeDive's brand name is already known to the UK market and seen as high-quality, so it can easily capitalise on it.

- Casual lifestyle clothing is related to the existing product range so there is some strategic fit and it may appeal to existing recreational dive customers.

- These products can probably sell through the existing distribution channels which facilitates implementation of the strategy.

- The new products may also appeal to other market segments, so this strategy could involve an element of market development too.

- The marketing of the product via social media may fit with the appeal of lifestyle clothing to a younger market.

Disadvantages

- From a generic strategy point of view, WeDive's existing product is very differentiated and it protects itself from competition by operating in a market niche. There are high levels of competition in the lifestyle clothing market already and the products are more homogeneous.

- Margins on casual clothing may be lower than on existing drysuit products and will be affected by the level of competition and the fact that there are low-cost producers outside the UK.

- There is likely to be a short product life cycle as typically these lifestyle brands come and go as far as fashion is concerned.

- 65% of sales are to professional divers and these products may be less attractive to them than the recreational divers.

- WeDive will need to source a supplier(s) as it has no experience in manufacturing.

- There is little scope for using WeDive's existing expertise.

- The new strategy will require marketing expenditure and social media may be insufficient to attract a wide customer base.

- This strategy is still UK-focused and may offer limited scope for growth.

Option 2: focus on core product but expand market overseas

Option 2 in terms of the Ansoff matrix constitutes market development.

Advantages

- Exporting drysuits builds on existing competences and is consistent with WeDive's differentiation strategy.

- WeDive already have a tried and tested product that has been well received by the market.

- It may be possible to achieve better expansion by targeting contracts with professional divers rather than recreational ones, using existing links with police, armed forces etc.

- Overseas markets may be more price sensitive/have different price elasticities which could increase their profitability.

- It may be sensible to try out one or two markets initially that are more close to the UK in terms of the size, fit and climate requirements.

Disadvantages

- WeDive's brand name may not be recognised in export markets although once established, this strategy will help to create a global brand.

- The nature of the product may not work in some countries – eg, different fabric may be required for tropical rather than cold water diving.

- The product may require amendments to the fit to suit different population sizes and characteristics.

- Risk arises due to the lack of familiarity with overseas markets although this will be reduced if WeDive find the right distribution partner.

- WeDive is likely to face competition from existing players in these markets.

- A factor to consider is where the suits will be made and whether WeDive has the production capacity to cater for the increased volumes.

Preliminary conclusions

- The existing product has a three year warranty and may not involve frequent repeat purchases so it seems sensible to consider opportunities to expand revenue.

- Either option will help reduce dependence on the existing UK market and on professional dive contracts in particular.

- Market research of either strategy offers the opportunity to reduce the risk of expansion.

- WeDive needs to consider financial projections before making a decision.

- Option 2 is probably more likely to be successful in the longer term as it makes use of existing expertise and builds on WeDive's differentiation strategy. The company could consider selling online initially as a means of export then find distributors if it becomes clear that there is demand.

Examiner's comments

The requirement to evaluate the two alternative strategies was straightforward and well done by most candidates. A significant number of candidates identified that WeDive is currently a differentiator, focused on a niche market. Many started their discussion by positioning the proposed strategies within the Ansoff matrix as product development and market development respectively. Most candidates produced sensible answers setting out the advantages and disadvantages of the two strategies and showed good knowledge of the specific issues relating to overseas expansion. Some used the 'suitability, feasibility, acceptability' approach to good effect to generate a range of points. The better candidates went on to reach a conclusion as to which of the strategies might be more appropriate for WeDive, recognising the need to obtain more detailed financial projections before making a final decision.

21.2 Decision tree

Initial decision	Prob	Demand		£'000
LAUNCH NOW	0.1	Low		-100
	0.9	High		300
MARKET RESEARCH -£15,000	0.1	Low	Abandon	0
	0.9	High	Launch	300

Launch now without MR: $(0.9 \times 300k) + (0.1 \times (-100k)) = 260k$

With MR: $(0.9 \times 300k) + (0.1 \times 0) = 270k$ less 15k research cost = 255k

Hence financially it is better not to undertake MR but this is based on EV which is a long term average and not necessarily applicable to a one-off decision. It also ignores risk:

Without MR, actual outcomes are +300 or –100, spread of 400k in potential return

With MR, actual outcomes become +300 or zero. Therefore depending on WeDive's attitude to risk it may be worth paying £15k for the ability to minimise downside risk despite the lower expected outcome.

Examiner's comments

This was the first time that a decision tree had been examined and answers were very variable. For candidates who knew how to prepare the tree, and then do the simple expected value calculations, this requirement was a source of easy marks. Many lacked the required technical knowledge however which resulted in some non-attempts. Sensible candidates who used the numbers in the scenario to produce an expected value calculation and then went on to make some relevant comments were still able to score a pass however.

22 Reyel plc (June 2015)

Marking guide

		Knowledge	Skill	Marks
22.1 (a)	Quarterly data analysis	1	11	
(b)	Comparative data analysis	1	8	18
22.2	Capacity management and pricing	4	7	10
22.3	Estimated loss	1	7	7
22.4	Ethics	3	4	7
		10	37	42

22.1(a) Quarterly data analysis: The Clarre

	Quarter to 30 June 20X4	Quarter to 30 September 20X4	The Clarre Quarter to 31 December 20X4	Quarter to 31 March 20X5	Year ending 31 March 20X5	The Zoy Year ending 31 March 20X5
Capacity (nights)	21,600	21,600	21,600	21,600	86,400	108,000
Number of nights actually occupied	15,552	17,280	16,848	15,120	64,800	62,640
Operating profit % (based on guestroom revenue)	18.3%	28.1%	28.1%	16.6%	23.3%	*21.7%
% of annual revenue	22.8%	27.5%	27.5%	22.1%	100%	–
% of annual nights	24.0%	26.7%	26.0%	23.3%	100%	–
% of annual operating profit	17.9%	33.1%	33.2%	15.8%	100%	–

* 18.2% If based on total revenue

Revenue

The Clarre was a new start-up on 1 April 20X4, which is the beginning of the current financial year. As such, it is likely to take some time to establish a customer base and grow, particularly as this is a new type of hotel for the Reyel group. The first year of operations is therefore probably atypical and there is likely to be growth in future years. Similarly, there is likely to be growth between quarters as the hotel becomes established during the year. Some of the underlying quarterly variation may therefore be due to early growth, rather than just seasonal variation.

Revenue in each of the two quarters ending 30 September 20X4 and 31 December 20X4 (Q2 and Q3) was greater than in each of the other two quarters (Q1 and Q4). In terms of revenue generated 55% of annual revenue occurred in Q2 and Q3, being equally split between these two quarters.

In terms of volumes (ie, number of guest nights) the seasonal variation is less pronounced with only 52.7% of guest nights occurring in Q2 and Q3 (being 26.7% and 26% respectively). This variation however understates the variability in seasonal demand as the lowest occupancy rates in Q1 and Q4 were incurred despite the lowest average prices of £68 per night, compared with averages of £74 and £76 per night respectively for Q2 and Q3. Had the same prices been charged throughout the year then a much more pronounced seasonal variation is likely to have occurred.

In summary, the highest demand occurred in Q2 and Q3 despite these quarters having the higher average prices. Whilst Q1 may have been disadvantaged as the start-up quarter, the same cannot be said for Q4 which had longer to establish a customer base than Q2 and Q3.

Additional information, which would be an indicator of the Q1 start-up effect, can be found by comparing revenue for Q1 with the quarter ended 30 June 20X5, which is near completion.

Additional useful information would be:

- seasonal variation of any other extended stay hotels in the London area to use as a benchmark to strip out industry average seasonality in the geographical area (though this information may be difficult to obtain)

- variations in prices and occupancy within each quarter.

Operating profit

The quarterly operating profit margins for Q2 and Q3 (28.1% for each) show that they are much more profitable than Q1 and Q4 which had margins of only 18.3% and 16.6% respectively.

A similar picture can be seen from analysing the percentage of total operating profit for the year earned in each quarter. Almost two thirds (66.3%) of total operating profit for the year was earned in Q2 and Q3, being 33.1% and 33.2% respectively. This trend is far more pronounced than that for revenue, discussed above, which amounted to only 55% in Q2 and Q3.

There are number of causal factors which are likely to have given rise to this:

- The average price per night is higher in Q2 and Q3 so the margins are higher.

- There will be a large element of fixed operating costs in running a hotel. These will have an operating gearing effect, such that variations in revenue are magnified in operating profit as the fixed costs must still be covered when revenue falls. This means the lower demand in Q1 and Q4 gives rise to a disproportionate decrease in operating profit.

- The average length of a stay is greater in Q2 and Q3 (at 15 and 18 nights respectively, against 14 and 13 nights in Q1 and Q4), so the costs of room change-overs are reduced.

(b) **Comparison of The Clarre and The Zoy**

Difficulties in making valid comparisons should be recognised. These include:

- a different business model, although both are in the same industry
- the Clarre is a start-up whereas The Zoy is well established

Despite this, the two hotels are operating in the mid-market hotel sector, are of similar size and are in similar locations. Reasonable comparisons are therefore possible.

A key distinction is that The Zoy has two sources of revenue: room revenues and other revenues (from the restaurant and bar). The operating costs provided are not divided between these two revenue streams and this would be useful additional information in identifying the source of the performance. The interdependence of revenues and costs between these two revenue streams would however need to be recognised, even if this cost analysis information were to be available.

Guestroom revenues

Guestroom revenues generated by The Zoy are 34.9% higher than those of The Clarre. In analysing the underlying causes of why the revenue is greater there are three key factors:

- Capacity (number of room nights available)
- Occupancy
- Price

It can be seen from the above table that the number of nights occupancy (ie, volume) is similar for the two hotels, with The Clarre and The Zoy being 64,800 and 62,640 respectively for the year ended 31 March 20X5. These figures are determined as a function of capacity and occupancy.

Despite the volume of room nights being similar, this is achieved in a different way with The Zoy having a much higher capacity (108,000 room nights compared to 86,400), but a lower occupancy (58% compared to 75%).

Given the similar volumes sold (ie, the number of room nights) the fact that The Zoy has revenue that is 34.9% higher than The Clarre is caused by an average price of £100 for The Zoy per night, compared with £71.70 per night for The Clarre (ie, 39.5% higher).

Data could meaningfully be calculated based on revenue per guest if comparing two traditional hotels or two extended stay hotels. However, given that the relative business models create very different average stays, such a comparison would be almost meaningless in comparing The Clarre with The Zoy as it would not compare like with like.

Other revenue

'Other revenue' for The Zoy is £1.2 million, which is 16.1% of the total revenue of £7.464 million for The Zoy. This is therefore reasonably substantial and makes the total revenue for The Zoy 60.7% higher than that of The Clarre. (However, the operating costs of the restaurant and bar are not separately provided so it is difficult to draw conclusions about the profitability of The Zoy restaurant.)

Operating costs

Additional information is needed analysing operating costs into the component accounts.

Overall, however, The Zoy has operating costs which are 71.5% higher than those of The Clarre. The underlying causes of this are likely to be:

- costs of the restaurant and bar

- greater levels of service (eg, daily cleaning)

- more frequent change-overs (as average stay is 3 days rather than 15 days for The Zoy)

Note however that the volume of room nights actually used is similar for both hotels.

Further information indicating the breakdown of fixed and variable costs may be useful to determine how costs relate to volumes and how operating costs are likely to change in future.

Operating profit

As already noted, The Zoy has revenue 60.7% higher than The Clarre, but operating costs 71.5% higher. Despite this, in absolute terms, The Zoy has made more profit than The Clarre in the year ended 31 March 20X5, as revenue is greater than operating costs. Indeed, the operating profit of The Zoy is 25.3% higher than The Clarre.

Conclusion

The Zoy has outperformed The Clarre but this is not unexpected given this is the latter's first year of trading. Greater sales in future, as The Clarre generates a more established customer base, seem likely to close the gap and perhaps permit the performance of The Clarre to exceed that of The Zoy.

Examiner's comments

(a) Candidates' answers were generally reasonably good on this requirement. For most candidates, there was an improvement over previous sittings on the presentation of the data analysis by using an initial table of calculations, followed by a qualitative analysis of the results.

The majority recognised the seasonality evident in the data. Many also identified the need for a breakdown of costs into fixed and variable after recognising that there had been a more than proportional increase in operating profit relative to the increases in revenue.

The better scoring scripts analysed occupancy rates per quarter and the overall impact of occupancy on profitability. The discussion part of the question was done quite well with candidates linking seasonality, location and hotel type back to the scenario.

However, only a small number identified that the data presented was from a start-up business and could be subject to major variations in the future.

Weaker candidates merely copied data from the question, often without calculating any new ratios. Where new ratios were calculated, weaker candidates tended to provide only very general ratios such as operating profit margins, without considering any indicators of performance specific to the scenario. In their narrative, weaker candidates tended to merely describe what had happened, rather than providing an analysis determining causal factors and explaining how and why a movement in the data had occurred.

(b) Calculations were mostly limited to percentage changes and basic margins. In terms of analysis, only the strong candidates highlighted the difficulties in making comparisons due to the differences in the business models of the two hotels and the fact that the Clarre was a start-up. While trying to make similar comparisons, candidates wanted to 'strip out' the restaurant but, in doing so, often deducted the revenue while not recognising some of the operating costs would be attributable to the restaurant. Conclusions were not always offered.

22.2 Capacity management and pricing

Capacity planning

Capacity planning is the process of determining the capacity needed by an organisation to satisfy changing demands for its products or services.

Effective capacity in the hotel industry is the maximum number of guests that a hotel is capable of accommodating in a given period, due to constraints such as physical resources (guestroom capacity), human resources, quality threshold issues (guestrooms in good repair and cleaned) and delays (room turnaround).

A difference between the capacity of a hotel and the demand from its guests results either in under-utilised resources (eg, available guestrooms unoccupied) or unsatisfied demand (guests turned away when the hotel is full). The goal of capacity planning is to manage this difference.

Capacity can be increased through introducing new techniques, processes or assets, or varying the number of employee hours. In an effort to address issues relating to capacity management a growing number of organisations have started to embrace the concept of workforce flexibility, particularly in relation to flexible working arrangements. This is discussed in greater detail below.

Capacity management in the hotel industry can be short-term or long-term. Within each of these time frames, capacity management can also be viewed from the supply side or the demand side.

Long-term capacity management

Supply side

In the context of a hotel, the number of guestrooms sets an upper limit on physical capacity in the medium to long term. Whilst it may be possible, from the company perspective, to build new extended stay hotels, from the perspective of the manager of The Clarre, an extension of physical capacity is difficult as there are limitations of building in a city such as London. Possibilities in the longer term to raise physical capacity might be to: change common areas into more guestrooms; build additional floors; reconfigure the guestrooms to make them smaller, but more plentiful; use an overflow venue.

It would be a mistake however to consider capacity solely in terms of either (1) physical capacity or (2) only increasing capacity.

Capacity could have a number of aspects. For example, the need may be to reduce capacity in order to reduce costs, rather than increase capacity. The average utilisation of The Clarre is 75%. Maintaining the ability to service 100% occupancy, if long-term demand remains at 75% occupancy, would be an inefficient use of resources and would involve the provision of expensive and unutilised capacity.

Demand side

Demand management might involve increasing demand in order to utilise surplus capacity. This might include, in terms of long-term demand management: improving facilities to attract more people to stay at the hotel (eg, business centre, bar); improve guestroom quality; recruit more staff; reduce standard prices.

Short-term capacity management

Supply side

Flexibility in short-term capacity is needed as hotel bookings may vary unpredictably, so the need to match variations in demand with variations in capacity reduces underutilised resources or lost sales.

Labour is a key aspect of planning short-term capacity. As mentioned above a growing number of organisations, particularly those in the leisure and retail sectors, have taken to employing workers on flexible contracts. Embracing these developments may help to address Kevin Kloster's (manager of The Clarre) concerns in relation to short-term capacity management. The Clarre could look to hire a proportion of its workforce on flexible contracts, where staff might be required to work overtime or shifts at short notice to meet changes in demand from bookings. This should enable resources to be acquired quickly to match demand changes in the short term. Offering working arrangements such as these may appeal to those individuals with flexible lifestyle commitments, for example, University students.

Short-term closure of a section of rooms, or a floor, may reduce short-term capacity (eg, from the data provided, demand is seasonal for The Clarre). This would save costs such as heating a floor.

Demand side

The use of IT (including data analytics tools) and marketing models to predict variations in demand will help give management more time to manage capacity.

Demand management capacity planning may be used to reduce peak demand by switching it to the off-peak periods, such as by offering relatively lower off-peak prices. This is a form of price discrimination which is discussed below. The utilisation of the advertising budget may also be applied disproportionately to attract demand in the low season.

Pricing

Flexible prices, taking the form of price discrimination, can include charging customers different amounts to reflect their individual price elasticities. To be able to do this, there needs to be separation of markets.

Examples of effective separation of markets can include businesses which make a large number of bookings compared to individuals who may only make a single booking. The individual cannot access the business price as he/she does not normally require as many hotel stays as a business.

The objective of the pricing strategy needs to be clear. Setting prices to maximise utilisation is not necessarily a good idea if revenues can be maximised by a higher price with less than 100% utilisation.

Even revenue maximisation may not be appropriate as it may not equate to profit maximisation.

The data in the exhibit shows that demand varies between quarters, but will also vary within quarters (eg, if a major event is on in London, higher prices can be charged and yet there may still be full utilisation). These demand peaks can generate higher prices in order to reduce demand (in terms of guest nights) to the capacity level of the hotel.

Conclusion

Where there is a strict physical limit on the number of guestrooms (at least in the short term) then pricing can be one of the most effective means of capacity planning. If capacity management is aligning capacity and demand then, where capacity is upwardly inflexible, pricing is the primary means in the short-term of adjusting effective demand to match available capacity.

Examiner's comments

Most candidates only considered the short-term when discussing capacity management. However a range of interesting suggestions were provided. Good quality candidates tried to link capacity management and pricing policy. Few candidates distinguished supply-side and demand-side aspects of capacity management.

The treatment of pricing was variable in quality. A high proportion of candidates used the 4Cs approach to structure their answers. Many candidates recognised that varying prices could be charged due to the seasonality of the business, but many failed to recognise key issues such as price discrimination or price elasticity.

Some candidates conflated the issues of capacity management and pricing within a single narrative, which usually limited the clarity and scope of their answers.

22.3 Estimate of lost revenue

The impact of opening The Clarre on the revenues of The Zoy is the difference between the following two figures:

(1) The revenues actually generated by The Zoy

(2) The revenues that would have been generated by The Zoy had The Clarre not been opened (the counter factual).

Whilst figure (1) is known, figure (2) needs to be estimated.

The starting point is that if The Clarre had not been opened it may have been the case that The Zoy's revenues may have changed over the past year anyway, due to other factors. These other factors need to be evaluated in order to make an assessment of the figure in (2) above.

Macro and industry factors

In estimating the change in The Zoy's revenue from last year, industry trends and macroeconomic trends need to be considered, particularly in the context of the London market. Thus, if London hotels generally suffered a fall in revenues compared to last year, then this factor could be stripped out of last year's The Zoy revenue in estimating (2) above.

Internal changes

Any changes that Zoy management has made this year compared to last year need to be considered. Price changes may have had an effect on demand, as may other factors including staffing, refurbishment (or lack of it), customer service policy and advertising. These factors need to be stripped out in estimating (2) above.

Data analysis

An analysis of data might reveal more information.

For instance, if there has been a sharp fall in the number of long stays at The Zoy (of over 8 days) then this seems more likely to have been caused by the opening of The Clarre than if there had been a fall in the number of short stays, which are not the same market sector as The Clarre.

If there is a Reyel loyalty card, or company credit card, then specific evidence could be gathered on individual customers who stayed at The Zoy last year but transferred over to The Clarre this year.

Examiner's comments

The answers to this requirement were the weakest in the exam, and formed the highest rate of non-attempts. Many candidates failed to grasp the key issue of what would have happened to the revenue of The Zoy if The Clarre had not opened. Weaker candidates, implicitly or explicitly, assumed it would have remained at the level of the previous year.

Many candidates did not give due consideration to external factors, in addition to the internal ones, relevant to the possible impact on The Zoy arising from opening The Clarre. Few focused on what had happened specifically to the longer stay customers of the Zoy.

22.4 Ethical issues

Ethics pertains to whether a particular behaviour is deemed acceptable in the context under consideration. In short it is 'doing the right thing'.

In making any ethical evaluation it is first necessary to establish the facts. In this case, the claims made against Kevin need to be established to assess their validity. This may include establishing the use of vouchers by The Clarre customers and tracing these back to the prices they have paid for staying at The Clarre.

The issue of legality applies; where an inducement has been given then this may come under the Bribery Act. It may also be fraud. Legal advice should be taken.

The offering of vouchers may not, of itself, be unethical and may be common practice in the industry. However, two other factors to consider are:

- the value of the vouchers and whether they are sufficiently significant to amount to a material inducement; and

- the fact that vouchers are not being offered for booking a guestroom on normal commercial terms but, rather, for individual business guests agreeing that their employers should pay in excess of the standard price set for other guests, with no clear commercial cause or benefit to the employer. There is a clear and possibly substantial benefit to the employee as an individual.

In making a decision as to how to act, it may be helpful to apply the Institute of Business Ethics three tests:

- Transparency
- Effect
- Fairness

Transparency – would the Reyel board mind people (existing customers, suppliers, employees) knowing what has happened? In particular, the issue of transparency will apply to the employers who have paid inflated amounts. This is likely to have consequences in refunding money to employers.

Effect - whom does the decision to provide inducements affect/hurt? Clearly this includes the employers who have paid more than the market rate. Other rival hotels, who were offering lower prices to employers but without additional inducements, may also have suffered.

Fairness - would the inducement be considered fair by those affected? The issue for Reyel's board is that the company may have benefited from the action of the manager, even though the board did not itself instigate the particular actions nor was even aware of them at the time.

Honesty - A final issue is one of honesty. The inducements fail the honesty test on the basis of Rexel making an improper gain. There is now the onus to make other parties (eg, employers) aware and return the excess amounts received.

Response

Where there is appropriate evidence an initial action would be to inform the employers and return any excess amounts charged. The manager's continued employment should be reviewed. The operation of the discount voucher scheme company-wide should also be reviewed.

If there is suspicion there has been a crime then disclosure to the police, based on legal advice, may be appropriate.

Examiner's comments

On the whole, this requirement was reasonably well answered. Most candidates considered the legality issue, although many then immediately dismissed it as not relevant in this case.

Many candidates adopted the transparency, effect, fairness framework. Only better students went on to identify other ethical issues outside this framework. Actions to be taken by management were often ignored. Frustratingly, this included some students who produced excellent commentary on the ethical issues, but then failed to identify any subsequent actions.

---

23 Home of Leather plc (June 2015)

Marking guide

	Knowledge	Skill	Marks
23.1 Breakeven/volume of sales	3	6	9
23.2 Three strategies	2	10	10
23.3 Mendelow's matrix	3	4	7
23.4 Change management	3	6	8
	11	26	34

23.1 (a) Breakeven and sales volume

To: Home of Leather plc Board
From: A Business Advisor
Date: 10 June 20X5
Subject: Proposed reorganisation strategies

Breakeven price

Strategy 1

B/E contribution $= £14.4m/120,000 = £120$
B/E price $= £200 + £120 = £320$

Strategy 2

B/E contribution $= £10.8m/120,000 = £90$
B/E price $= £160 + £90 = £250$

Strategy 3

B/E contribution $= £1.8m/120,000 = £15$
B/E price $= £280 + £15 = £295$

(b) **Sales volume to achieve a profit of £7.2m**

Strategy 1

$(£14.4m + £7.2m)/(360 - 200) = 135,000$ units

Strategy 2

$(£10.8m + £7.2m)/(324 - 160) = 109,756$ units

Strategy 3

$(£1.8m + £7.2m)/(324 - 280) = 204,545$ units

Examiner's comments

The performance on this requirement was generally good, although it did tend to polarise between the many candidates who managed to arrive at the correct calculations, thereby scoring full marks, and the minority who scored nominal marks. Weaker candidates often provided breakeven sales volumes, rather than the volumes necessary to achieve an annual profit of £7.2 million. Others determined breakeven volumes, instead of breakeven prices.

Many candidates failed to achieve the mark available for presenting their answer to this question in report format.

23.2 Evaluation of proposals

	Strategy 1 £'000	Strategy 2 £'000	Strategy 3 £'000
Sales	43,200	38,880	38,880
Variable cost	(24,000)	(19,200)	(33,600)
Annual fixed costs	(14,400)	(10,800)	(1,800)
Profit	**4,800**	**8,880**	**3,480**

Strategy 1

While this strategy involves some downsizing, it is the least transformational change and therefore has fewer transition costs. Nevertheless, there would be a loss of 60% of the employees who have skills which may be difficult to replicate with a new workforce.

In terms of ongoing production, the product quality is maintained and therefore the risk of alienating existing customers in the hope of attracting new customers through a lower price-quality mix is avoided.

In terms of the data offered Strategy 1 is not as profitable as Strategy 2 (see above), but more profitable than Strategy 3.

There is however less risk with Strategy 1 than the other two strategies in a number of respects:

- There is currency matching between the currency of 70% of sales and the currency in which costs are incurred. There is therefore less risk from currency fluctuations.

- As the proposal is based on existing production there is more certainty surrounding estimates

- There is no change in market positioning

This strategy however has greater risk than the other two in having more fixed costs and therefore higher operating gearing. As an example, if the Grint contract is lost then the high fixed costs still need to be incurred and a large loss will be made.

Also, in respect of the Grint contract, the breakeven price of £320 is only £40 less than the price indicated by the Grint board as a maximum, making profits only marginal on this contract.

Strategy 2

Based on the data provided, this is the most profitable contract, with an estimated annual profit of £8.88 million.

There are, however, a number of operating and financial factors which increase risk and mitigate against the higher return.

In the first instance, this strategy is likely to be the greatest transformational change and therefore have the highest initial costs from change. It is unclear whether these initial costs have been annualised into the fixed costs in the table or whether they have been treated separately.

The supply chain is lengthened significantly which may cause operational uncertainty in meeting customer delivery needs.

The breakeven price at £250 is £70 lower than the breakeven price for Strategy 1 at £320. However, the quality of the output is better with Strategy 1, making any given price easier to achieve. Nevertheless, if the quality differential in relation to price is correct, then Strategy 2 remains more competitive than Strategy 1 in price-quality terms.

That said, the market positioning in Strategy 2 is different from the existing market positioning and there is a risk that it may take time to adjust to a new customer base which prefers a lower price-quality mix.

Looking at the breakeven data in (the first requirement) above there appears to be a greater margin of safety for Strategy 2 than the other two strategies. This indicates lower risk in terms of variation of price and demand.

Strategy 3

On the basis of the data presented, Strategy 3 looks to be the least favourable option as it has the lowest expected profit and the least favourable margins of safety in terms of price and volumes demanded.

The issues of price-quality mix and currency risk are the same as for Strategy 2.

The key area where outsourcing in Strategy 3 has an advantage however is that it has the lowest fixed costs and therefore the lowest operating gearing. If the Grint contract were to be lost then high fixed costs would not need to continue to be incurred. There is more financial agility with Strategy 3, even though the expected return is lower. There is therefore downside protection. Exit costs are also likely to be lower as there is only a supply contract to exit and a warehouse to sell, rather than an entire factory.

Conclusion

For the renewal of the Grint contract, it would seem that Strategy 2 and Strategy 3 offer the potential to make a more competitive bid on price than Strategy 1. However much will depend on how significant quality is to Grint in the tender process.

Examiner's comments

Generally, there was a good performance by most candidates. Not all made use of financial data in their commentary. Others made good use of the data, for example determining profits and margins of safety, but then provided limited narrative (eg, on supply chain issues). Some candidates drifted into a discussion of change management, despite being explicitly told they were not to do so. Those who used the suitability/acceptability/feasibility framework often wrote too much, yet missed key points, and were not normally helped by structuring their answers in this way. Most candidates provided a reasoned conclusion as to which strategy appeared best.

23.3 Mendelow

Strategy 1

Current employees

Power – low
Interest – high negative

The current employees have high negative interest as they are under immediate threat of losing their jobs. The power of current employees to stop or moderate any relocation decision is limited. If the entire UK workforce is united against the move then significant costs to HoL can arise from disruption.

Given however that not all jobs are under threat, there may be limited cooperation in industrial action from the 40% of employees who are willing to relocate 150 kilometres away. This may be particularly the case if HoL pays generous removal expenses to relocate employees.

Even amongst the employees losing their jobs some may be happy with redundancy as they intend to retire or move jobs anyway.

Despite the above, it is likely that most employees have a strong negative interest in the relocation, particularly as the company is a key part of the town and perhaps families and friends are located there, who may suffer from a decline in the local economy following the closure of the factory. This may also make it harder for redundant employees to find new employment locally and therefore reinforce their negative interest.

One final qualification is employees may have a strong negative interest compared to the status quo of the factory in Puddington. If however there is an acceptance of the board's decision of the commercial need to make a change then, in relative terms, compared with the other two strategies, employees could favour Strategy 1 as there are fewer redundancies.

Grint

Power – high
Interest – moderate

Given that 35% of HoL's sales are from Grint, it has considerable power over HoL and is likely to be in a position to influence the decision to relocate production. The cost savings from transferring production are likely to be a factor in the next tender, but also the level of quality of the products that HoL can provide is dependent on which of the three strategies is selected.

Grint may however be only moderately interested in the relocation as furniture manufacture is a competitive industry, with a range of alternative suppliers being available if HoL fails to deliver the required quality at the required price. Nevertheless, HoL is presumably currently Grint's preferred supplier for good reasons, so there may be a moderate wish to continue the relationship, despite the concerns over price expressed in their communication.

Examiner's comments

This requirement was very well answered by the majority of candidates and was, on average, the best answered requirement in the exam. Relatively comprehensive rationales were usually provided to support the positioning of current employees and Grint on Mendelow's matrix.

23.4 Change management

The change management process needs to be appropriate to the nature of the change.

In this case, the change is fundamental and transformational for either Strategy 1 or Strategy 2.

The transformational and reactive nature of the change classifies it as 'Forced Change' in the sense that the company will be unable to continue to compete if it does not reduce costs by making major changes.

Whilst there are commonalities between the two strategies which may require similar change management procedures, there are also differences which suggest a different change management approach for each strategy.

In terms of managing the impact of change, then there are very different effects for employees staying with the company and those being made redundant.

While there is a major effect on those being made redundant, in the longer term they will not be employees so, while the leaving process needs to be managed, there may be limited long-term effects on motivation if the change is well-managed. For Strategy 2 the change impacts on nearly all employees.

However, in the shorter term, following announcement the employees may not know which of the two groups they will fall into, and thus all employees may be demotivated by the uncertainty in this period. This may have adverse effects on quality of work and reputation.

There is also a danger of focusing only on change with respect to employees. Other stakeholders should also be considered in change management including:

(1) Continuing customers – who need to be reassured that they will continue to be supplied quality goods and that the delivery will continue to be reliable, particularly with Strategy 2 where the supply chain is geographically extended.

(2) Suppliers – to manage the continuing relationship with Strategy 1 and the issues that may arise from the change in geographical location. With Strategy 2 there is a need to ensure reliability of supply in the closing months when UK suppliers will be aware that contracts are to be terminated.

However, change does not only involve people but also:

(1) changes in management structure due to the change in the nature of the business (eg, automation with Strategy 1) and the location of the business (with Strategy 2).

(2) change in culture. There is likely to be a change in culture particularly in Strategy 2 where employees will have a different national culture as well as management having the opportunity to work with employees to set up a new corporate culture.

Much more than Strategy 2, Strategy 1 has the change management issue of managing employees who are continuing in employment with HoL, but who may need to adapt to new practices in an automated environment and deal with a new culture.

In this context, for continuing employees, Lewin and Schein's Iceberg model has three stages in managing change:

- Unfreeze
- Move
- Refreeze

Unfreezing involves a trigger, a challenge of existing behaviour, involvement of outsiders, alterations to power structures.

Moving means making the changes, and communicating and encouraging adoption of the new situation.

Refreezing means consolidation and reinforcement of the new situation.

While these phases may be appropriate to employees moving or changing roles within the company, the changes to the factory are absolute (ie, closure) and thus there is no concept of refreezing a new situation for employees who are leaving.

The model's application is therefore limited in the context of this factory closure, as some employees are lost to the company rather than having to accept a new structure or culture.

The **coercive change** approach is where change is forced without participation. This requires the ability to push through the change without cooperation but it may be appropriate in these circumstances as there is no requirement to maintain the goodwill of most of the factory workforce post changes, as they will no longer be working for HoL.

The **Gemini 4Rs** model of reframing, restructuring, revitalising and renewal is, like the Lewin model, largely based on the needs, not just of getting rid of the old structure, but also of reformulating the new structure. In the case of factory closure and for Strategy 2, the latter part of the model is largely redundant as there is little scope for renewal for employees who are leaving.

There are likely to be barriers to change, particularly from employees, which need to be managed as part of the change management process.

(1) **Cultural barriers**

Strategy 1 is more difficult to manage as it involves maintaining elements of the existing culture/structure/workforce despite closing the factory. In contrast, Strategy 2 is more about managing closure and a new start up than managing a continuing process.

Strategy 1 puts forward fundamental changes that will affect the culture of the organisation. Power structures within the company may be threatened by the redistribution of decision-making authority or resources, or the changing of lines of communication.

For example, this will affect management and thus management may be reluctant to implement changes which will be contrary to their own interests.

(2) **Stakeholder groups**

Group inertia may block change where the changes are inconsistent with the norms of teams and departments, or where they threaten their interests.

Examples might include the following:

- Strikes and other forms of resistance to change implementation by staff who are to be made redundant

- UK raw material suppliers taking legal action for contract termination if the business is now to be switched to overseas suppliers under Strategy 2

- Shareholders selling shares as a result of the changes.

(3) **Individuals**

There are also barriers which affect individuals and result in them seeing the change as a threat to earnings and job security.

Conclusion

The transfer overseas in Strategy 2 is operationally more difficult as it involves setting up in a new country and almost starting the manufacturing process again. However, managing employees who are to move from the old factory to the new factory in Strategy 1 also presents challenges and a greater opportunity for resistance to change from those involved in that change. Each will require elements of common change management and differences in change management.

Examiner's comments

Answers were variable in quality. Weaker candidates' answers were unstructured and often did not refer to models at all, but merely discussed common sense issues such as uncertainty, redundancy and a lack of buy-in by the employees.

For those candidates that did use change management models, such as Lewin's iceberg model, answers were mixed. Where models were used, the weaker candidates did not apply the model to the scenario, while stronger candidates tended to analyse each strategy separately and conclude how best to manage change in each case.

24 Zuccini plc (June 2015, amended)

Marking guide

	Knowledge	Skill	Marks
24.1 Typhoon	3	10	12
24.2 Hurricane	3	10	12
	6	20	24

24.1 The product life cycle

The product life cycle (PLC) describes the phases of development that a product goes through. The key stages of the life cycle are as follows:

- **Introduction** – a new product or service is made available for purchase and organisations attempt to develop buyer interest.

- **Growth** – a period of rapid expansion of demand or activity as the product finds a market and the product demonstrates its potential.

- **Maturity** – a relatively stable period of time where there is little change in sales volumes year to year but competition between firms intensifies as growth slows down.

- **Decline** – a falling off in sales levels as the product becomes less competitive in the face of competition from newer products.

The PLC can be viewed in conjunction with the BCG Matrix in determining the impact on the company's cash flow from a portfolio of products at various stages in their life cycles. The BCG Matrix portfolio analysis is useful because it provides a framework to consider and forecast potential market growth and to evaluate the competitive dimension through an evaluation of market share. (As Zuccini is a niche player then, in one sense, all of its products have a small market share in relation to the largest companies in motorbike industry. Zuccini's relative market share therefore needs to be considered in comparison to the other niche players.)

The Typhoon4 appears to be in its decline phase with sales falling, and may be viewed as a 'Dog' product (or perhaps a Dodo) within the BCG Matrix with low market share, low or negative growth, and modest or negative cash flow.

The StormRaider appears to be in the growth phase with replacement not due until 20X9. It may therefore be viewed as a 'Star' within the BCG Matrix.

The Hurricane is in its R&D phase. It will not enter its introduction phase until either 20X6 or 20X8 (see below). It may therefore be viewed as an infant in the BCG Matrix with negative cash flow.

Overall, the benefit of the BCG Matrix is to view Zuccini's portfolio of products as impacting cash flows and liquidity in different ways at different points in their life cycles. Thus, for example, established or growth products are financing the development of new products.

When to end Typhoon4 production

In deciding on the timing of change for the Typhoon4 it is necessary to consider it in the context of the wider company product portfolio.

Whilst Typhoon4 sales are declining, the product is not necessarily unprofitable. As it is made in a separate factory in Italy, most of the costs associated with the Typhoon4 should be readily identifiable in order to make an assessment of product profitability.

In order to determine how long the production of the Typhoon4 should be allowed to continue in its decline phase, the following factors should be considered:

- How much inventory of the Typhoon4 exists (ie, how many months' sales). If inventory is significant, then production will need to cease some time prior to sales ceasing.

- Evaluate the exit barriers to determine the optimum time to cease production (eg, at the end of a lease agreement on machinery specific to the manufacture of the Typhoon4 or at the end of the useful life of machinery for making the Typhoon4).

- Potential response of competitors to any change.

- Need for new updates (eg, a change in regulations on emissions with which the Typhoon4 does not comply, but with which the Typhoon4A and Typhoon5 do comply).

- Availability of cash to replace or modify. Even though its sales are declining, the Typhoon4 may still be cash generative. In contrast, the introduction of the Typhoon4A or the Typhoon5 would be likely initially to consume cash at a time it may be needed on R&D projects, eg, for the Hurricane (see below).

Whether to produce the Typhoon4A or the Typhoon5

At this stage, there is insufficient information to make a firm decision as to whether the Typhoon4 should be replaced or modified. There are however a number of indicative factors which can be considered.

In terms of the product life cycle (PLC) replacing the Typhoon4 with the Typhoon4A will provide an extra two years of product life, effectively pushing it back into the maturity phase, and extending its life before the replacement of the Typhoon4A is needed with the Typhoon5 in 20X7.

Replacing the Typhoon4 with the Typhoon5 on the other hand will, in PLC terms, in effect commence a new introduction phase with a much longer extended life cycle.

One of the problems of replacing the Typhoon4 with the Typhoon4A is that it is a two-stage process, as the Typhoon4A will then need to be replaced with the Typhoon5 two years later.

This raises two key questions:

- Will the transition costs of converting from the Typhoon4 to the Typhoon5 in one step be significantly different from the transition costs of converting from the Typhoon4 to the Typhoon4A, and then later from the Typhoon4A to the Typhoon5, as a two-step process?

- If the Typhoon5 starts production two years later, will its life cycle finish two years later, or at the same time for both options, irrespective of its introduction date?

The cash needed to replace a product is much greater than the amount needed to modify one, therefore the introduction of the Typhoon5 is likely initially to consume much more cash than the modification to the Typhoon4A. This may be at a time it is needed on R&D projects, eg, for the Hurricane (see below).

Turning to marketing aspects, in trying to compete in a difficult external market it is important that Zuccini's product reputation is maintained and improved. This would indicate that the best product should be launched as soon as possible, which would be the Typhoon5. Prolonging the introduction of the Typhoon5 with the Typhoon4A may damage reputation and make future sales of all Zuccini's products more difficult.

Conclusion

Subject to more detailed information becoming available, based on the current information the Typhoon5 should be introduced as soon as possible. This will save a double change of product type and ensure that the best product is available to customers as soon as possible. The life cycles are driven by market conditions and so could well be coterminous for the Typhoon5 under either option. It may be that sales of the Typhoon4 continue to be made from inventory but, in this case, a short period of overlapping life cycles, where the old product price is discounted, is likely to be more acceptable than forcing customers into buying Typhoon4A technology which is not the best that Zuccini can offer.

Candidates appeared to be comfortable in the application of the product life cycle and the BCG matrix, identifying that the Typhoon 4 was in decline and could be classified as a dog product. The higher scoring answers also identified capital investment and the resulting liquidity position as key factors in making the decision. Disappointingly, most answers did not discuss the wider product portfolio context that in order to manage a product range, it is a sensible strategy to have a range of products all at different stages of the life cycle. Many candidates did not make sufficient distinction between types 4A and 5.

24.2 Factors

The launch of the Hurricane would introduce an extra model to the product portfolio, making it three in all. It would sit at the bottom end of the Zuccini quality range whether introduced in June 20X6 as a basic product, or in June 20X8 as a mid-market product.

Strategic factors

The StormRaider is an upmarket motorbike and the Typhoon4 is a mid to upmarket motorbike. The introduction of the Hurricane as a basic motorbike extends the product portfolio down the quality spectrum, which may cause brand confusion and damage reputation for the two other products in the portfolio.

There will be a significant delay of three years (until 20X8) before the mid-market version of the Hurricane can be launched. There is significant uncertainty here as competitors are likely to launch new models during this period so the degree of competition by 20X8 is difficult to estimate, causing additional uncertainty.

R&D plays a key role in product strategy and a number of strategic models are relevant in this context.

Porter's generic strategies: product innovation could be a source of differentiation. Process innovation may enable differentiation for the £9,000 motorbike or cost leadership for the £6,000 motorbike.

Porter's value chain: R&D is included within the support activities of technology development. It can be harnessed in the service of lower costs or improved differentiation for the £6,000 motorbike.

Ansoff matrix: R&D supports all four strategic quadrants. Strategies of market penetration and product development are relevant to Zuccini in this context.

Industry and product life cycles: the obsolescence of existing products can be accelerated by R&D by other companies and so R&D is required to provide Zuccini with replacements to compete.

Operational factors

There appear to have been uncertainties relating to technical factors in the R&D process. In this sense R&D is key to determining the nature of the product and the way it is positioned in the market. However, the very nature of R&D means that it has uncertainty of operational outcomes. The mid-market product appears to present more difficulties and therefore more delay and more uncertainty. This would favour the earlier launch of the basic product in order to reduce uncertainty.

The R&D process may have unintended externalities. In other words, R&D may discover processes and products which may be of use, not just on the Hurricane, but also on the other two models, even though this was not the original purpose of the R&D.

Financial factors

Given that the company may have liquidity issues over the next few years then this may be a key factor in deciding between the 20X6 launch and the 20X8 launch.

Comparing the two choices, the 20X8 launch is cash negative in the next few years. R&D tends to be expensive and over the next three years the mid-market motorbike R&D project will be consuming cash in its R&D efforts whilst delaying the product launch and therefore the future cash inflows. Even after the 20X8 launch, the Hurricane would be in the introductory phase of its PLC and it may take a while before it will be any more than cash neutral.

In contrast the basic model will complete the R&D outflows in 20X6 and launch thereafter with the ability to generate cash as it comes out of its introductory phase.

More information is needed to decide which alternative will ultimately generate the greater NPV over its life cycle but if short-term liquidity is an issue this points towards the basic model.

In pure undiscounted cash terms (ie, zero discount rate) the cash flows from one unit of each product (in the absence of information on volumes) would be generated as follows:

20X6 launch: £6,000 × 7 years = £42,000
20X8 launch: £9,000 × 6 years = £54,000

Whilst the 20X8 mid-market product generates more revenue, there are several financial factors which mitigate against this, in favour of the 20X6 launch of the basic product:

- The 20X6 launch generates cash flows earlier and so will have a higher present value on average per £1 generated

- Additional R&D costs will be incurred for the 20X8 mid-market product

- It seems likely that for the 20X8 launch there will be greater operational costs in producing a mid-market product rather than a basic product

Conclusion

More information is needed on costs and volumes. However, based on the information available there seem too much delay and too much uncertainty to favour the 20X8 mid-market product. Moreover, in financial terms the 20X6 basic product generates more cash earlier. This may support the development of other products.

Rather than damage reputation it may be considered that the 20X6 basic product could be launched under a different brand name.

Examiner's comments

This part was attempted reasonably well, with better candidates structuring their discussion using the headings provided in the question of strategic, operational and financial factors. In this part of the answer, most candidates did think about the overall strategy of where to position the product in the market and how a delayed launch would be perceived. The majority also identified the generic strategy issue in launching the low cost model, given the firm's differentiated niche focus. Conclusions were not always offered and, if they were, they were usually not fully explained or justified.

25 Kentish Fruit Farms (September 2015)

	Knowledge	Skill	Marks
25.1 PESTEL factors	3	6	9
25.2 Evaluation of two strategies	2	18	18
25.3 Ethical issues	3	6	8
25.4 Control procedures	3	6	8
	11	36	43

Tutorial note

Only 3 forces need to be analysed but these need to be justified as Key. There was plenty of obvious information in the scenario to discuss Social/Technological/Ecological/Legal. There was less in the scenario to support Political/Economic.

25.1 **The key forces are:**

Social – consumers' attitudes to organic food are changing because of concerns about health and the environment. Organic food is seen to be more socially responsible – it helps address issues around global warming and the environment and reduces concerns about the consumption of harmful pesticide and fertiliser residues. These factors will work to increase industry demand. The accountability of farmers as a result of organic certification is also likely to increase consumer confidence in what they are buying. A focus on the procurement of local goods will benefit organic farmers in their region, as will public sentiment against genetically-modified crops.

Technological – the industry relies on the use of technology to avoid using harmful fertilisers and pesticides. As a result it has developed sophisticated weather management systems and atmospherically controlled growing and storage tunnels. These factors will help increase yields and also reduce the seasonality impact and perishability problems by extending the life of the product through storage, thus benefiting cashflow. Further technical advances may help the industry reduce costs and hence prices, making the products accessible to more consumers.

Ecological (Environmental) – a key factor in the growth of the organic farming industry has been a drive for more environmentally friendly products. Organic farming is seen to be more ecologically sound – the farming methods reduce harmful waste from the manufacture and use of agrochemicals and, since it is often also more local, there is less carbon footprint associated with its distribution. However the need for environmentally friendly farming methods may mean the industry struggles to compete on price with traditional farming methods. The latter may be more pest-resistant due to the use of fertilisers or may be able to achieve greater yields through artificial growth methods. A further environmental issue is the weather which can have a significant impact on crop quality and yields and which the industry attempts to manage through technology (discussed above).

Legal (regulatory) – there is significant regulation in the food industry generally and particularly for organic produce. As well as complying with the Food Standards Agency (FSA) and regulations regarding production, packaging and labelling, organic farmers also need to comply with regulations specifying organic farming methods. In addition they need to be approved for and obtain certification, then comply with its terms. There are severe sanctions for breaching regulations, and as a result compliance is critical and costs are likely to be high. Any changes in standards in the future will have an impact on the industry – also different countries have different standards which can be an issue for exports.

Political (there is much less in the scenario to go on for this)

Political factors refer to the attitude and approaches of the government and other parties to the organic farming movement. Any change in government may affect future regulations. The Green Party for example supports changes in the farming industry to make food production more sustainable and protect the environment and its resources; they are also in favour of local food production. Government initiatives to promote sustainability and healthy eating are likely to increase demand for organic products and hence benefit the industry. Inevitably these are links between political factors and legal factors such as consumer protection regulations and the certification of organic farmers.

Economic (there is much less information to go on in the scenario for this)

Historically organic produce has been seen as a luxury product and is therefore less in demand when disposable incomes fall. However the move towards organic as a lifestyle choice reduces this risk for the industry, which appears to be in a growth phase. As demand increases there may be pressure to intensify farming operations which may not be consistent with organic methods. Many smaller organic farmers may find it challenging to deal with the size and bargaining power of large retail buyers, which could dictate prices and hence margins. From a financial point of view organic farmers, like traditional ones, are at risk due to seasonality of cashflows and unpredictability of weather.

Examiner's comments

This requirement was very well answered and was, on average, the best answered requirement in the exam. Most candidates used relevant information from the scenario to justify the importance of their selected PESTEL factor and explain its likely impact on the industry. A common mistake among weaker candidates was to treat PESTEL as if it were a company rather than industry model and/or to discuss relatively unimportant factors. A minority of candidates wasted time by completing a full PESTEL analysis when only three factors were required.

25.2 Data Analysis

Table 1:	20X3	20X4
Hectares of KFF orchards yielding fruit	40	55
Tonnes of apples harvested	480	720
Yield (tonnes produced/hectare)	12.0	13.1
Tonnes of apples sold as fresh fruit	288	468
Tonnes of own apples used for juice	192	252
Crop mix: fruit:juice	60:40	65:35
Tonnes of own apples used for juice production	192	252
Tonnes of apples bought in	–	48
Total tonnes of apples used for juice production	192	300
1 litre bottles of juice produced and sold	96,000	150,000
Bottles produced per tonne	500	500
Revenue: fresh fruit £'000	576	889
Tonnes of apples sold as fresh fruit	288	468
Fresh fruit: Revenue per tonne	2,000	1,900

Revenue: juice £'000	336	525
Total tonnes of apples used for juice production	192	300
Juice: revenue per tonne £'000	1,750	1,750
Juice: revenue per 1 litre bottle £	3.50	3.50
Sales revenue mix: fruit:juice	63:37	63:37
Cost of sales £'000	540	812
Tonnes of apples sold as fruit/juice	480	768
Cost per tonne used £	1,125	1,057
Gross profit £'000	372	602
Gross profit per tonne £	775	784

Table 2:	20X3	20X4
Gross profit margin	41%	43%
Operating margin	12%	10%
Operating costs as % of sales	28%	32%
Interest cover	2.13	1.97

Table 3: analysis of yield from new trees

Incremental land	15 hectares
Incremental apple crop	240 tonnes
Yield (tonnes produced per hectare)	16 tonnes/hectare
15 hectares at standard yield of 12 tonnes	180 tonnes
Increased yield due to efficiency of new planting	60 tonnes

Table 4: analysis of changes in revenue 20X3-20X4

	£
Revenue generated from additional trees: Strategy 1	
Incremental fruit crop: (468 – 288) × £1,900	342,000
Incremental juice crop: (252 –192) × £1,750	105,000
	447,000
Revenue generated from fruit bought in: Strategy 2	
48 × £1,750	84,000
	531,000
Revenue lost due to reduction in market price of fresh fruit:	
288 × £(2,000 – 1,900)	(28,800)
Total incremental revenue (**Note:** £1,414 – £912k = £502k)	**502,200**

Commentary:

KFF's profitability is limited by its capacity to meet all the demand for its products. To generate additional capacity, KFF have implemented two new strategies that impact on 20X4 results:

(1) The purchase of land and intense planting of new trees to increase apple production and also improve yields per hectare. The first crop from this was produced in 20X4.

(2) The decision from 20X4 to purchase apples from local farmers to increase juice production. This will increase sales volumes of juice but is likely to reduce the margin if it is more expensive to buy in apples than to home grow them.

It is not clear whether these strategies will have had a 12 month impact or only affected results for part of the year, and more information would be useful to assess the timing of the change.

The overall performance of the business in relation to the objectives set is as follows:

	Objective	Actual 20X4	Comment
Annual revenue growth	15%	55%	Achieved
Gross margin	45%	43%	Not achieved

On the face of it therefore the new strategies have achieved the required revenue growth, although since this is the first year of impact, the growth achieved may not be sustainable. The gross margin target has not been met, although gross margin has increased from 41% to 43% so it is moving in the right direction.

However further analysis is required, of each strategy, of performance overall and of performance in relation to the objectives.

Strategy 1: new trees:

The purpose of acquiring the land is twofold:

- To increase supply of apples
- To improve profitability by increasing the yield per hectare

The supply of apples has increased as the new orchard has come on stream, providing an additional 15 acres which in terms of land base increases the capacity of the farm by 37.5%. Ordinarily at KFF's 20X3 yield the new land would have produced 12 tonnes per hectare or 180 tonnes of apples in total. The new farming method was expected to increase yields by 30%. In 20X4 the new trees actually generated an additional crop of 240 tonnes, 60 tonnes above standard output, which is an increase in yield of 33.33% and resulted in a yield of 16 tonnes per hectare.

As a result the purchase of the land and the switch to more intensive planting appears to have been successful in increasing capacity. Table 4 shows that the fruit grown on the new trees increased revenue by £447,000 in 20X4, although as we have no detail on costs we do not know how profitable this was.

A greater proportion of the crop was sold as fresh fruit (65% compared to the previous year's 60%) which perhaps suggests better quality output, but the revenue per tonne fell which, as KFF is a price-taker, is likely to be due to market factors.

Strategy 2: purchase of other fruit:

During the year KFF acquired 48 tonnes of fruit from neighbouring farms, which it turned into juice and from which it generated £84,000 extra revenue. The additional volume of bottles did not have any impact on the price per bottle, which remained constant at £3.50 and therefore suggests strong demand. Again more information on the costs of buying in and processing the fruit would be useful. Also there is now some doubt about whether all fruit bought in met the required organic standards, and this may give rise to concerns over this strategy in the future.

Success of strategies:

No breakdown is given of the costs of either strategy. In total, they have allowed KFF to increase revenue by £531,000 in 20X4 (58% of 20X3 revenue). The actual revenue increase of 55% (or £502,000) is lower because the market price for fresh fruit has fallen from £2,000 to £1,900 per tonne in 20X4.

Overall the revenue mix of fresh fruit and juice has not changed.

The increase in revenue of 55% exceeds the objective of 15%. However this type of growth would be expected in the first year of the capacity increase. The objective is for annual revenue growth of 15% but it is not clear whether that is expected to be each year or on an average basis. In 20X5 KFF will only be able to generate more revenue by purchasing additional apples for juice or adopting more new farming methods to increase yields.

Profitability

The gross profit margin has increased overall. Purchasing fruit is likely to have reduced margin on the bottles of juice which incorporate it. The increased yield per hectare will have an upward effect on margin, although this may depend on how expensive the new farming method is. The fact that the cost of sales per tonne has fallen from £1,125 to £1,057 implies that the net effect has been positive.

In order to assess the profitability of the decisions, it would be useful to know:

- the cost per hectare of farming the new trees on the new land compared to the existing trees on the existing land

- the cost per tonne that KFF has had to pay to buy in the fruit

Although the gross margin has increased, the operating margin has fallen from 12% to 10% which is due to increased operating costs. Thus £502,000 of additional revenue has generated £230,000 of additional gross profit but only £33,000 of extra operating profit. More information is needed about the increase in operating costs.

Cash flow

Interest cover has fallen from 2.13 times to 1.97 times because of the 40% increase in interest costs. The customer mix may have changed and the additional sales may have come from retailers who have dictated longer credit terms. Thus the business' cash position has deteriorated and interest charges have increased. More information on cash flows, and on KFF's capital structure, would be useful.

Further details:

To better explain performance, the business needs to analyse costs between the old and the new trees and also separately analyse the profitability of the two product lines, juice and fresh fruit. Management accounts for 20X4 showing monthly statement of profit or loss and cash flow would help better assess the seasonality of the business and also the impact of the new strategies.

Examiner's comments

The data analysis requirement was well attempted by the majority of candidates. Most were well practised at providing a table of up-front calculations and a list of additional information, although this was not always tailored to the scenario. The key to a good answer was to identify appropriate financial and operational calculations which would help determine the impact of each strategy separately: both the planting of the additional trees and the purchase of apples from other farmers. The better candidates did this, providing calculations to assess the impact of the additional land capacity and the change in yield, and structuring their evaluation under two separate headings. Weaker candidates were poor in this regard, merely providing calculations of changes in financial figures, within their narrative, and evaluating the performance of the company overall, rather than the impact of each strategy against the objectives that had been set. The best candidates recognised that there was sufficient information to assess the revenue impact of the strategies but not their overall profitability.

25.3 Ethical issues

Ethics pertains to whether a particular behaviour is deemed acceptable in the context under consideration. In short, it is 'doing the right thing'.

In making any ethical evaluation it is first necessary to establish the facts. In this case, it would seem that the facts are reasonably clear in terms of a batch of KFF juice being identified as containing non-organic pesticides and the fruit having been traced to a supplier. What is uncertain is how KFF should react to this.

Given the extensive regulations affecting the organic food industry, the issue of legality needs to be considered and legal advice taken by KFF as to its responsibility. Although the fruit concerned may have come from another farm, the juice is sold under the KFF brand and KFF are likely to be held responsible for the breach by the FSA, which may apply sanctions. KFF may face losing their organic certification, which may require that everything they sell should be 100% organic.

Joe Fielding appears to be prepared to behave ethically in relation to the undistributed product, which would be relabelled and sold as non-organic, presumably at a lower price. It is the action suggested in relation to the bottles that have already been distributed which raises ethical issues.

In making a decision as to how to proceed, it is helpful to apply the Institute of Business Ethics three tests:

- Transparency
- Effect
- Fairness

Transparency – a public recall of the juice already distributed would be transparent and in the public interest. It would be consistent with the reputation KFF has built as an ethical farm. Keeping quiet about the bottles that have already been distributed and only addressing the remaining inventory is less transparent and KFF should consider whether it would mind people (existing customers, regulators, employees) knowing that it has taken this action. Lack of full disclosure may in fact not be an option as it may be imposed by the regulator as a matter of public interest.

Effect – a full recall may embarrass KFF and the retailer but would prevent harm to the end-consumers. The effect of a partial action would be to keep information from the retailer, and consumers who have already bought the juice would suffer due to KFF acting in its own and not the public interest. As a minimum this would be because consumers pay higher prices for organic juice which is in fact non-organic. More serious, although perhaps less likely, is the fact that their health may be affected by the consumption of pesticide residues.

Fairness – it is likely that competitors, the retailer and consumers would not take kindly to the fact that KFF has knowingly deceived them and mis-represented its product.

Actions

KFF should be guided by legal advice and its discussions with FSA, and should cooperate in all investigations made by the FSA. The matter may be of sufficient seriousness for FSA to apply sanctions. The best action would be for KFF to act honestly and with integrity, making a full disclosure of all the facts. Even if the FSA does not require disclosure, KFF should consider doing so, to avoid further damage to its reputation. KFF should then have discussions with the supplier concerned to establish how the use of non-organic pesticides has arisen and why it was not detected. It may have recourse against the supplier depending on the contractual terms.

Having made the suggestion that the company should be dishonest, the board should consider discussing with Joe Fielding the importance of ethical behaviour, and should review the company's overall culture to ensure that all staff are in line with the importance of maintaining ethics and also the organic status of the company's produce.

Examiner's comments

This requirement was well answered. The ethical issues relating to the possible production and sale of non-organic juice were reasonably easy for most candidates to identify. The vast majority of candidates also recognised that there was a legal/regulatory issue here given the FSA and the need for organic certification. Some candidates restricted their marks by not providing clear actions. Better answers distinguished between the actions that might be appropriate in respect of the contaminated juice that has already been distributed and the action that the company should take regarding the remaining bottles.

25.4 Control procedures and information systems

Given the nature of KFF's business, quality is a critical success factor. Quality assurance and quality control are critical to standardise the quality of fruit and juice products and also ensure that they are safe to consume.

Even if KFF was not an organic farm, the requirement to produce safe foods in a hygienic way is part of the law and there are serious penalties for contravening hygiene and food safety legislation.

In creating a new relationship with suppliers, KFF should establish a service level agreement, agreeing not just on the financial terms of supply but also on key targets/standards that need to be met and the consequence of not doing. Any expectations that KFF has in relation to ethics and sustainability and the need for suppliers to conform to KFF's policies in these areas would need to be set out.

Suppliers should be selected based on their experience and the quality of their products. Clearly verifying a supplier's organic certification and credentials would be a critical step in early due diligence, before contracts are agreed. KFF should carry out an annual inspection visit where the supplier is required to confirm that organic standards have been met. If suppliers are local then occasional drop-in visits may be feasible.

Once a supplier has been contracted then a key control procedure is to measure and monitor supplier performance. Joe is correct that early detection of problems is desirable but costs (both financial and reputational) are generally lower if KFF is able to prevent defective output rather than simply detecting it.

KFF should go through each stage of processing, from purchase of apples and other ingredients/packaging products to the bottling of the final juice, to identify where factors exist that could influence either product quality or safety and then devise procedures that control those factors.

Quality assurance focuses on procedures and standards that will ensure product problems are eliminated or minimised during the production process. In KFF's case this might include inspecting or sample testing fruit that is bought in, before using it in production, in the hope that any poor quality fruit is identified and rejected or that any traces of pesticides would be identified.

Fruit that is to be stored before use might need testing on arrival at KFF and then inspecting again after storage but before use. Any bottles, caps or other items involved in the juice production should also be inspected and tested, since these may cause quality issues.

Quality control is associated with checking a product after it has been produced and this might involve sample testing bottles of juice from every batch of production. Even if there are no pesticide issues, this may be a good idea to ensure consistency of the product over time in relation to flavour, appearance etc.

Given the importance of local reputation, the need for certification and the high level of regulation in the industry, KFF would be advised to apply quality control procedures to all its own fruit and juice production, as well as to suppliers' fruit, if it is not already doing so.

If it is unable to expand its own capacity, then for long-term sustainability of the farm, KFF needs to establish partnerships with local farmers which are transparent and add strategic value. An information system can be used to enhance this, not just from the point of view of supplier control and monitoring but also for measuring KFF's own performance, by capturing a range of data.

An information system can track performance overtime, and may be useful in identifying trends or detecting early warning signs of future problems. It also provides KFF with evidence for its own organic certification and in relation to supplier performance when discussing or renewing contracts with suppliers.

Appropriate operational measures (KPIs) to monitor supplier performance might include:

Quality assurance

Rejection rate of apples per tonne purchased – this could be compared against KFF's own achievement and also across suppliers and harvests

The reasons for reject could then also be broken down as this will help identify and address the cause of the problem eg:

- Level of pesticide/fertiliser detected on apple crop
- % of apples contaminated eg, by insects
- % of apples that were mouldy/physically damaged

These would need to be considered in relation to any agreed tolerances that have been established with the supplier but also in relation to organic standard requirements.

Quality control

- Rejection rate of bottles per batch of juice
- Level of wastage during production process
- % of bottles not meeting specifications (weight, volume, appearance, labelling etc)

Other measures useful for supplier monitoring might include the following:

- Tonnes delivered vs tonnes promised
- Number of disruptions to production caused due to late delivery/apple shortages
- Price per tonne

Examiner's comments

This was one of the worst attempted requirements in the exam but answers were quite polarised. The main difference in the standard of answers to this requirement related to whether candidates were familiar with the concept of quality assurance and control procedures. Weaker answers simply listed brief checks that KFF could undertake in relation to suppliers. Stronger candidates identified procedures and processes that could be used to prevent and detect quality issues and monitor performance. A significant number of candidates ignored the requirement to suggest some specific KPIs.

26 Premier Paper Products plc (September 2015, amended)

	Knowledge	Skill	Marks
26.1 Business development and CSFs	3	8	10
26.2 Risk register	3	6	9
26.3 Memorandum	3	10	11
	9	24	30

26.1 CSFs for PPP

PPP's growth

Ansoff

The Ansoff model is a two-by-two matrix of Products (new and existing) and Markets (new and existing).

PPP started out as a manufacturer of banknotes (existing product) for its country's central bank (existing market). The growth of its business has then come from both geographical expansion and the development of new products.

Market development – existing products and new markets.

The expansion of the banknote production into over 100 countries across Europe and Asia is market development on a geographical basis, as is the sale of security paper to the state-owned printing works which use it to produce their own banknotes. In terms of CSFs, PPP's design skills and innovative security features are likely to have helped it build market share.

Product development – new products and existing markets.

PPP realised that its existing customer base of central banks would benefit from other products. As a result, 60 years ago, it capitalised on one of its CSFs – its existing customer relationships and contracts – by expanding its product range and moving into the related area of banknote sorting and counting machines and inspection equipment.

Further product development or Diversification – new product, new market

Growth continued with the establishment of a new product range: passports and identity cards. PPP continued to leverage its expertise in designing and printing security paper and its reputation for maintaining security and confidentiality by extending this to government identity schemes. 15 years ago PPP won its first contract to print passports and driving licences for its own government and now produces documents for 65 countries.

Although closely related to central bank clients, governments might be said to be a different market and hence this strategy might be deemed diversification.

Lynch Expansion method matrix

The Lynch model is another two-by-two matrix of method of company growth (organic growth and external development) and geographical location (home (domestic) and international). Under this model, the primary focus for PPP's growth has been through organic growth and international development. Both banknote and identity card production started with the domestic market, but because the size of this is limited, to achieve economies of scale PPP had to expand internationally, targeting a variety of global central bank and government clients.

PPP's CSFs have allowed it to grow organically rather than through acquisition. It has achieved this by continuing innovation through in-house research and development and also by leveraging its client base.

Critical success factors are the product features that are particularly valued by customers and/or the activities that an organisation must excel at to outperform the competition.

In the case of PPP, a summary of the key critical success factors discussed above that have facilitated its development are as follows:

- Innovation - expertise in evolving innovative and sophisticated security features for paper, notes and identity documents

- Reputation - for the design of high quality, elegant banknotes and for maintaining security/confidentiality

- Relationships and partnerships/contracts with central banks and governments

- Operational excellence in relation to quality, accuracy, reliability

Examiner's comments

Candidates were asked to assess the ways that PPP has expanded. A number of models could be used here and many were comfortable using Ansoff, though Lynch and Porter's generic strategies were also relevant. The better answers combined their discussion of the various expansion strategies (product development, market development etc) with an explanation of the CSFs that had facilitated each move. Candidates who merely positioned each strategy on the Ansoff matrix and then separately produced a bulleted list of CSFs tended to score less well.

26.2 Risk register

A variety of key business risks facing PPP's banknote division are set out below:

Nature of business risk	Impact and likelihood	Risk management
Strategic: technological change renders the need for banknotes obsolete	Technological developments in the form of credit cards, contactless payment systems and cryptocurrencies are clearly having a big impact on the industry and are changing the nature of the product and market as the demand for cash reduces. Changes in technology may reduce the volume of business but for the present time it seems unlikely that it will remove the need for banknotes entirely. Also the technology is likely to be adopted at different rates in different markets. This is supported by the fact that at present only a small number of online retailers have started to explore accepting cryptocurrency payments from customers.	Reduce risk in short term by developing different technologies eg, polymer notes so PPP will retain central bank customers even if they switch from paper. May have to accept this as a risk in longer term, especially if cryptocurrencies become a mainstream form of payment for goods and services purchased online. PPP as a whole has reduced risk by diversifying product range eg, identity cards and passports
Strategic: failure to produce technologically advanced and competitive banknote products	Industry standards and security features are continually evolving. Failure to innovate would likely result in lost market share and lower margins.	Reduce risk through: continued investment in R&D, design, and human capital by employing skilled designers. Consider JV with universities/scientists

Nature of business risk	Impact and likelihood	Risk management
Strategic: failure to win or renew key contracts	Contracts are often long-term so timing of renewal may be predictable. The loss of contracts is likely as this is a competitive environment and contracts are awarded by central banks which can be affected by political factors outside PPP's control. Failure to win contracts may result in PPP operating below optimal capacity, restricting growth and profitability	Reduce risk by maintaining close, trusted relationships with customers. Monitor sales pipeline and undertake production planning to ensure critical mass. Monitor activities of competitors where possible. Maintain brand and reputation for design and operational excellence. Implement/maintain a CRM system and focus on key contracts as they come due for renewal.
Operational: poor quality product or standards of service damage the company's reputation	Highly technical contracts with very detailed specifications mean this is a key risk. The very public nature of the product and the high profile central bank customer mean that if a problem does occur reputational damage is quite likely, with a serious impact including possible loss of contracts. Poor quality banknotes or errors would require re-working or perhaps contract penalty payments.	Reduce risk through quality assurance/total quality management and operational excellence programmes.
Operational: product security. A breakdown in security procedures resulting in theft of products from a site or loss of notes in transit	Likelihood: PPP's past history suggests this is reasonably unlikely Impact: PPP may be contractually liable	Reduce risk by: Security screening for all staff. Physical controls regarding site access, material stores etc would reduce the risk on site. Use of stringent controls for personnel and carriers involved in distribution. Transfer risk through Insurance.

Nature of business risk	Impact and likelihood	Risk management
Hazard: loss of a key manufacturing site or inventory at a site eg, through fire	Depending on the details of the contract, this may result in litigation. The impact would be severe, the likelihood is unknown.	Reduce likelihood by having preventative measures such as advanced smoke detection and sprinkler systems, plus 24 hour monitoring. Transfer through insurance. Contingency plan for other sites to operate as back-up.
Compliance: failure to comply with legal or regulatory requirements	Value and nature of product means there is some likelihood here and reputational impact would be high	Avoid/reduce by: Implementing code of conduct and ethics Screening and security clearance for all employees Disciplinary procedures Training in rules and procedures

Tutorial note

Other relevant key risks were awarded credit. Only **three** were required.

Examiner's comments

The majority of candidates produced a well-structured table, identifying three risks facing PPP's banknote division, although weaker candidates did not always concentrate on the key ones. Some candidates limited their marks by not addressing all elements of the requirement comprehensively eg, focussing on the impact of the risk and its management, without considering its nature and likelihood. The strongest answers identified a range of key risks and used the TARA model to identify appropriate risk management strategies. A number of candidates wasted time and marks discussing risks facing PPP as a whole rather than the banknote division.

26.3 Memorandum

To:	PPP Board
From:	A Manager, Banknote division
Date:	September 20X5
Re:	Polymer bank notes

Factors to consider in deciding whether to invest in the technology to produce polymer banknotes include the following:

Competition

Uniquel is currently the only competitor producing polymer notes, but if these are deemed by central banks to be the way forward, then other printing companies are likely to follow suit. This will have an impact on the following:

(1) The demand for PPP's paper product

(2) The number of contracts that PPP can retain on renewal

Likely buyers and their preferences

Potential customers for polymer notes include the following:

- Central banks who already outsource production to PPP

- Central banks who outsource production to PPP's competitors (private companies or other in-house printers)

- Central banks who currently print in-house

Since a major issue for the industry is security it appears likely that more central banks will move to polymer or alternatively demand increasingly expensive security features for paper notes. A way of ensuring optimal production is to approach other in-house state printing works that do not have PPP's economies of scale and may increasingly find it too costly to keep up with security developments for a small volume of notes.

Environmental considerations

Greater awareness among governments, businesses and consumers around issues related to natural capital and sustainability, are likely to lead to increased demand for more environmentally friendly products, and may influence the move away from paper to polymer.

Timing of any adoption of new technology

PPP could wait and see to what extent central banks move to polymer as their contracts come up for renewal and make a decision once it has more information. However this will allow Uniquel and any other competitors which enter the market to steal market share. Since banknote contracts are long-term (10 years on average) and this may increase, given the seven year lifetime of the new notes, it could be locked out of the market for a long time. PPP must also consider the impact on its reputation for innovation of being seen not to adopt new technology.

Resources and competences

New machinery is required which may necessitate more factory space. In addition it will take time to develop the necessary human capital, ie, a workforce with the required skills and expertise to develop, design and print polymer banknotes, especially as PPP is only currently involved in producing security paper products. It will also take time to source suppliers of polymer. Any errors or issues of quality in the early stages of the process may affect its reputation and position in the paper banknote market.

Costs

A contract for paper notes requires production of notes every three years, compared to every seven for polymer. Thus PPP will need to tender for and win new contracts every year or persuade existing customers to switch to ensure efficient utilisation of production facilities.

Other issues to consider if a decision is taken to introduce polymer are as follows:

- Whether to run the two technologies side by side or cease paper production and switch to polymer

- Whether eventually demand for banknotes will cease altogether as payments move to electronic systems (contactless payments and cryptocurrencies) in the longer term

Product portfolio

Paper notes appear to be a cash cow product for PPP currently. The question is to what extent demand will decline and to what extent PPP, as a major industry player, might influence this decline by making the move to polymer. The immediate abandonment of

PPP's major product seems implausible, however over the next few years sales may decline to the point where paper notes might then be abandoned.

The adoption of polymer notes is at an early stage in the lifecycle. PPP could aim to stay in the paper notes market all the time it is making sufficient returns and as one of the biggest players it has economies of scale which will probably allow it to outlast smaller competitors. However whether in the long term there will be a dual market for both paper and polymer, or whether eventually paper notes will disappear over time in favour of polymer, needs to be considered.

The future of the banknote

The lifecycle of the banknote industry appears uncertain. Changing consumer preferences appear to have reduced demand for traditional cash payment. Thus the banknote division faces a long-term threat posed by phone, card and other digital currency and payment mechanisms. Scenario planning may help to identify future risks and possible strategic responses. However although demand for cash is reduced, it appears likely that it will not disappear altogether and that there may be more demand for cash in some parts of the world than others, because different countries are at different stages in the lifecycle of cash and electronic payment mechanisms.

Conclusion

On balance it appears that there is a sound strategic argument for the introduction of the new technology. However forecasts need to be prepared and a detailed cost benefit analysis/investment appraisal undertaken to assess the incremental effect of introducing polymer.

Examiner's comments

Most, but surprisingly not all candidates, scored an easy format mark for setting out their answer in the memo format required. Candidates who used sub-headings to structure their answer tended to produce a wider range of points than those who merely listed a range of unconnected factors. Better candidates provided a balanced argument regarding the benefits and problems associated with investing in the polymer technology, linking their answers to the risks identified in respect of the second requirement. Most candidates provided an initial recommendation as to whether the investment was advisable and the best candidates identified the steps that should be taken to reach a decision.

27 Taxi Tracker (September 2015)

Marking guide

	Knowledge	Skill	Marks
27.1 Cost and value drivers	3	6	8
27.2 Benefits of dynamic demand-based pricing	3	6	8
27.3 Calculations and evaluation	1	11	11
	7	23	27

27.1 Cost and value drivers

An organisation's value chain is the sequence of activities by which value is added to its service. This influences the margin a customer is prepared to pay over the costs the organisation incurs in delivering the service.

Within the value chain there can be both cost and value drivers. Whilst cost drivers influence the cost of a given activity, value drivers help an organisation to differentiate itself from competitors. TT's success has been built around its smartphone app which facilitates ease of booking, cashless payment, and improved customer service compared to both Citicabs and existing PHVs. As a result it appears to be following a differentiation strategy.

> **Tutorial note**
>
> Only **three** were required.

In the case of TT, the key drivers include:

Technology as a value driver of customer service – TT makes widespread use of existing technology (GPS, phone, electronic payments) to add value by making it easier for customers to book a car, track it and pay for it. Using the phone as a meter makes prices more transparent for customers and the payment system is also more secure as drivers do not handle money.

- Technology as a cost driver – the use of the smartphone app reduces the costs to TT of matching drivers and customers since this largely happens without any need for intervention by TT. It means that TT can provide a very high level of customer service at a low cost to itself, connecting customers with the nearest available driver at the touch of a button.

- Procurement (cost driver) – TT's HR model is one of independent contractors rather than employees. While this reduces cost the dynamic demand-based pricing model would also ensure that there is flexibility of supply, as drivers are incentivised to make themselves available when more cars are needed.

- After sales (value driver) – asking customers to rate journeys and drivers creates a perception that TT cares about the customer experience. The fact that drivers have to score at least 4 out of 5 to be able to continue is likely to give the customer confidence in the quality of the service.

- Customer service (value driver) – fast booking and reduced waiting times for cars, the ability to track cars and the ease of payment all create an enhanced customer service experience.

- Firm infrastructure (cost driver) – TT operates a low-cost, flexible model. It has little in the way of infrastructure costs (no requirement for investment in non-current assets such as cars) or employment costs of drivers.

Examiner's comments

This requirement was well done by most candidates, who as usual demonstrated good knowledge of Porter's value chain analysis. The better candidates linked their discussion to TT's generic strategy, identified whether each key driver selected was a cost or value driver, linked it with the relevant aspect of the value chain, and explained how it gave TT a competitive advantage.

27.2 Benefits of dynamic demand-based pricing

Dynamic demand-based pricing is an attempt by TT to find a price at which supply and demand are equal and hence could be argued to be a market-driven approach. TT increases the price in periods of peak demand, when the supply of available PHVs is lower than the number of customers. This has the effect of attracting more drivers because the journeys are more lucrative, hence increasing supply, whilst potentially reducing demand temporarily as the more price-sensitive customers decide to make alternative arrangements for their journey or wait until prices fall again. The extent to which this happens will depend on the price elasticity of demand.

Essentially this strategy is similar to one of price discrimination, used for example by railways or cinemas, where prices vary according to the time of day, or dynamic pricing used by airlines, where prices vary according to the actual level of demand compared to what is deemed a normal level.

The model allows TT to extract the maximum possible revenue by charging higher prices to people who are willing to pay more. Whilst some may argue this is unfair to customers, TT is transparent about their approach to pricing and customers have alternative forms of transport and other PHVs/Citicabs available so are making a free choice.

It could be argued that customers benefit as this approach to pricing is not just about exploiting demand but also about incentivising drivers to work at peak times in order to increase supply, thereby offering the customer a better service. Also drivers benefit as they earn more money and are therefore compensated for having to work at times that are perhaps less sociable eg, public holidays.

To some extent it is a matter of perception as to which price (the high or low fare) is seen as the norm and therefore whether TT are seen to exploit customers by increasing the price in busy periods, or considered to be offering a discount at quieter times.

Unlike Citicabs, whose prices are fixed by the regulator, TT is free to set its own prices. It would be interesting to see how the maximum prices charged by TT compare to those of Citicabs.

Examiner's comments

The discussion of the benefits of demand-based pricing was well done by the majority of candidates, with many identifying both demand and supply side factors. The requirement to consider whether this was unfair to customers was less well done and some weak candidates ignored it altogether. Better answers identified that the use of price discrimination is common in many industries. They pointed out that TT's demand-based pricing model will serve to balance supply and demand, facilitate its promise to make cars available in five minutes, and be transparent so customers can choose rivals such as Citicabs if they are cheaper.

27.3 **Calculations and evaluation**

(a) Evaluation of fare reduction strategy:

Current fares received	**£**
130,000 × 4 × £10	5,200,000
Split:	
Drivers 80%	4,160,000
TT 20%	1,040,000

Fares reduced by 25%, demand unaffected	**£**
130,000 × 4 × £7.50	3,900,000
Split as now:	
Drivers 80%	3,120,000
TT 20%	780,000

TT would lose £260,000 (£780,000 compared to £1,040,000) and drivers would be £1,040,000 worse off (£3,120,000 compared to £4,160,000).

Fares reduced by 25%, demand increases 15%

	£
130,000 × 1.15 × 4 × £7.50	4,485,000
Split to maintain drivers' income:	
Drivers	4,160,000
TT	325,000

TT is £715,000 worse off (£325,000 compared to £1,040,000 previously).

Drivers are unaffected.

(b) For neither TT nor the drivers to be worse off, and there to be no change in the 20% commission structure, revenue would need to be maintained at £5,200,000 still.

Where n is the number of journeys: n × 4 × £7.5 = £5,200,000

Hence n = 173,333 (£5,200,000/£30)

This requires an increase in demand of 33.3% for the month.

(c) Evaluation of fare reduction strategy

	TT £'000	Drivers £'000
Current strategy	1,040	4,160
25% reduction, no change in demand, 20% commission	780	3,120
25% reduction, 15% increase in demand, maintain driver income	325	4,160
25% reduction, 20% commission, 33.3% increase in demand	1,040	4,160

If fares are reduced by 25%, with no corresponding increase in demand, the total fares received are £3,900,000 and under the 20% commission, both TT and the drivers are worse off: TT would lose £260,000 and drivers £1,040,000.

This is likely to cause drivers to move away from TT and contract with other PHV operators in an attempt to maintain their income levels. A lack of availability of drivers may then affect TT's customer service levels or cause higher demand-based prices.

If fares are reduced and demand increases by 15%, the new fares received are £4,485,000.

If TT guarantees that drivers will receive the same income, then TT suffers all the impact of the fare reduction and would be £715,000 worse off than in a normal four week period.

However if the increase in demand is permanent as customers stay loyal to TT, then in future months TT's income will increase. Also TT would be able to advertise this to drivers as a reduction in its commission to 7% (£325k/£4,485k) and may actually attract more drivers as a result. This seems a sensible strategy.

For neither TT nor the drivers to be affected by the fare reduction, an increase in demand of 33.3% for the month is required, which seems an ambitious target and may depend on the elasticity of demand as well as the reactions of competitors.

Other factors to consider:

Although the fare reduction may be attractive, in peak periods when the demand-based pricing model kicks in, the reduction may not be obvious to customers and hence may not have the desired effect.

TT's price reduction may lead to a price war in the PHV market, which will end up permanently reducing every operator's prices and hence margins.

The level of demand will be stimulated if demand for TT's product is price-sensitive, but the customer's decision to use TT may be more about ease of use, service, age of customer – in which case the price reduction may not stimulate demand.

Ultimately TT may be prepared to suffer a short-term reduction in income in the hope of strengthening its loyal customer base and ensuring it retains its drivers before the entry of a new rival.

Examiner's comments

This was the worst attempted requirement in the exam. Candidates seemed to score very well or very poorly. Common mistakes in the calculations included not considering the impact for a 4 week period, confusing the percentage commission with the percentage price reduction and ignoring the constraint of maintaining the driver's income in the second calculation. Many weaker candidates ignored either the calculation element or the discussion element of the requirement completely, limiting the marks available. Better candidates used their calculations as a starting point to discuss whether the strategy was sensible, identifying that the numbers are based on certain limiting assumptions and that wider issues may be relevant.

28 Outil plc (March 2016)

Marking guide

	Knowledge	Skill	Marks
28.1 Performance analysis	3	16	17
28.2 Discussion of proposals	2	9	10
28.3 Stakeholder analysis	3	6	8
28.4 Evaluation of test marketing and opening stores	3	6	8
	11	37	43

28.1 Report on performance

To:	Outil Board
From:	Business Advisor
Date:	XX/XX/XX
Re:	Future strategic direction

Calculations are shown in the appendix:

	Outil total 20X5	UK total 20X5	Outil total 20X4
Gross margin	34.0%	34.7%	35.9%
Contribution as % revenue	6.9%	6.5%	9.0%
Operating margin	6.1%	5.8%	8.2%
ROCE	22.4%	21.7%	30.9%

% change in

	20X4 to 20X5 Outil total	20X4 to 20X5 UK total
Revenue	+24.9%	+5.7%
Gross profit	+18.1%	+2.1%
Traceable costs	+26.0%	+10.7%
Divisional contribution	-5.1%	-23.7%
Apportioned central costs	+14.3%	-2.9%
Operating profit	-7.0%	-25.7%
Net assets	+28.4%	+5.4%

Divisional performance year to 31 December 20X5

	Homestyle	Fixing	Targi
Gross margin	29.3%	42.0%	30.1%
Divisional contribution as % revenue	5.7%	7.6%	8.7%
Operation profit margin	5.0%	6.9%	8.0%
ROCE	18.0%	27.3%	25.2%
Share of total sales	49%	36%	15%
Divisional contribution mix	41%	40%	19%
Share of net assets	49%	33%	18%
Revenue per store (£m)	10.46	4.95	7.26
Profit per store (£'000)	520	342	583
Ave store size (sq m)	10,000	3,500	5,600
Revenue per sq m	£1,046	£1,414	£1,296
Profit per sq m	£51.98	£97.65	£104.04
Employees/store	58	18	30
Sq metres covered per employee	172	194	187
Revenue per employee (£'000)	181	272	243

Commentary on overall company performance

Despite a 24.9% increase in sales revenue, Outil's total operating profit has fallen 7% and ROCE has dropped from 30.9% to 22.4%. Both gross and operating profit margins have fallen by approximately 2 percentage points.

However it is hard to properly compare the performance of the business between 20X4 and 20X5 due to substantial changes during the year, notably the acquisition of the Targi stores and the expansion of the Fixings division.

Targi needs to be excluded from the 20X5 results so that a more relevant comparison can be made of the combined results of the Homestyle and Fixings divisions. Once this is done it becomes apparent that whilst revenue has increased 5.7%, operating profit has fallen by 25.7%.

The Homestyle director says that the division's revenue is relatively unchanged year-on-year so the increase in revenue is likely to have arisen as a result of the 50 new Fixings stores. The scenario suggests the deterioration in profit is due to the Homestyle division's sales mix, increased delivery costs and promotional pricing strategies.

Segmental information for 20X4 would enable more analysis of the causes of performance.

Commentary on divisions

Comparing the divisional performance:

Almost half the company revenue comes from the Homestyle division but this only accounts for 41% of the divisional contribution. Whilst the Homestyle stores have a similar gross profit margin (29.3%) to the new Targi stores (30.1%), their operating margin is much lower (5% compared to 8%) and the ROCE considerably less (18% compared to 25.2%).

ICAEW 2019

This is borne out by the fact that despite each Homestyle store being almost twice the size of the Targi ones (10,000 sqm vs 5,600), with about 45% more revenue per store (£10.46 million compared to £7.26 million), the average profit per store is lower at £520k compared to £583k.

This may reflect the differences in the markets (UK v Eastern Europe), customer base (consumers v tradespeople) and operating models (the Targi division carries a limited product range which it sells in large volumes at low prices).

There may also be exchange differences arising in the Targi results.

The UK based Fixings division, which sells to a mix of tradespeople and consumers, has the highest gross margin (42%) and the highest ROCE at 27.3%. It accounts for 36% of group sales and 40% of the contribution.

The Fixings stores are the smallest (3,500 sq metres and £4.95 million revenue per store) but it is the most efficient revenue generator at £1,414 per sq metre, which is consistent with the information in the scenario about the majority of the store space being used to display products.

There may be differences in rental costs between the stores eg, smaller stores may be in town and therefore more expensive per sq metre than larger, out of town stores.

Given the different store sizes it is not particularly useful to compare performance measures on a per store basis, instead comparisons have been made per square metre. These show that the Homestyle division lags quite a long way behind both the Fixings and Targi divisions in terms of revenue per sq metre, profit per sq metre and revenue per employee. Since it accounts for almost half the net assets of the group, Homestyle's weak performance will have had a significant impact on the overall results.

Further information

Additional information that would be useful includes the following:

- Rental costs of the stores operated by each division

- Information regarding the age and current value of assets used by each division, including any operating leases, since this will influence ROCE

- In addition to profit-based performance measures, investors may also use measures such as EPS, PE ratio. Information regarding the investors in Outil and their target ratios would be useful.

- Wider non-financial performance measures for the divisions would also assist in comparing performance and assessing underlying causes of profitability.

Conclusion

The Homestyle division does appear to be underperforming relative to the other divisions currently. This division is the only one that relies exclusively on consumers and the performance may be a result of internal inefficiencies or a permanent decline in the DIY market. In deciding what to do with the division it is not just historic performance but also future prospects that are relevant. Therefore details of budgets/plans for the Homestyle division for 20X6 onwards would be useful.

Examiner's comments

This requirement was well answered. The majority of candidates included an initial table (or an appendix) of data calculations, covering both the company and divisional performance. The weaker candidates failed to provide sufficient quantitative analysis, often restricting their answers to a discussion with a few percentage changes thrown in. Many answers did not use a report format for their answer despite being asked to do so.

The quality of the calculations varied; stronger candidates identified that, for a like-with-like comparison with 20X4, Targi's results needed to be excluded from the overall company results for 20X5. For comparability, they also provided divisional calculations on a per square metre or per employee basis. Weaker answers considered overall movements (including Targi's 20X5 results) and/or provided calculations which ignored the differing sizes of the three divisions.

In terms of the qualitative analysis, weaker candidates who had performed more limited calculations had less to discuss and ended up repeating information already provided in the question, with little or no added value.

The stronger candidates commented on the fact that the revenue improvements in 20X5 arose as a result of the acquisition of Targi and the 50 new Fixings stores, and used the differences in the store models and the target markets to explain the varied divisional performance.

28.2 Homestyle division strategies

The managing director and the Fixings director both support focusing on the trade business and believe the group would be better off without the Homestyle division, favouring closure and sale respectively. The logic for this is to improve overall company performance, either by reducing costs or increasing return on assets by deploying resources to activities with a bigger return on capital.

On a basic level the Homestyle division is making £151 million positive contribution to group results and without it absolute profit would decrease significantly. The loss of the Homestyle division, which is contributing 49% of net assets and sales, and 41% of divisional contribution, would make Outil a much smaller company, albeit a more profitable one in terms of margins and ROCE. The fact that the company is smaller in terms of revenue, profits and net assets might affect its ability to raise finance.

The exact impact would also depend on the extent to which UK divisional sales are interdependent – if the Homestyle division is closed or sold, would customers buy from Fixings instead or would the Homestyle division customers who currently also buy from the Fixings division transfer their business elsewhere?

Other financial factors to consider are the extent to which central costs would be saved by closing or selling the division. The exit costs referred to by the managing director in terms of lease penalties and redundancies also need to be ascertained.

Sale of division vs Closure

Closure of the Homestyle division would necessitate change management, discussed in 43.3 below. However it would allow Outil to retain those Homestyle stores that are located in prime sites and creates an obvious opportunity to expand the Targi brand into the UK and to continue to open more Fixings stores. To some extent this will depend on how easy store sites are to come by and to what extent the existing Homestyle stores are located in areas where the company wants to operate.

If the change management issues and disruption arising as a result of restructuring are significant then a sale may be better and would obviously generate cash. However a key factor in the decision to sell would be whether there are any buyers and the price that they are willing to pay. This will depend on expectations of future prospects for the home improvement market. One possibility is that the managers of the division might be interested in a purchase, since according to the Homestyle division director the market is due to improve.

Retention of the division

The Homestyle director believes that the division has performed well in difficult circumstances and managed to survive when a near competitor has had to close. Whilst it is relatively not as profitable as the other divisions, it is at a different stage in the lifecycle and may be seen as a cash cow, making £151 million positive contribution.

A key consideration is whether the decline in the demand for DIY products from Homestyle consumers is a temporary or permanent situation. If the latter, then Outil may feel it is best to sell or close the division before the market declines even further. If the decline is temporary then a decision to close or sell the division may be premature.

Conclusion

Ultimately Outil needs to consider what is best for its shareholders. Outil's objective is to maximise the wealth of its shareholders, although as a listed company there may be a conflict between different groups of shareholders as to which direction the business should take.

One possible way to resolve the conflict is to consider demerging the Homestyle division so that shareholders can decide for themselves whether they wish to retain shares in it. A demerger is the opposite of a merger – the splitting up of a business into separate operating companies. Existing shareholders exchange shares in Outil plc for shares in the individual companies, but no cash is raised.

Examiner's comments

This requirement was reasonably well attempted. Most candidates used the comments from the directors to structure their answers regarding the future of the Homestyle division.

Weaker candidates tended to consider only two of the three options however and often failed to discuss the Homestyle director's proposal that the division should be kept going until the market improves. They also ignored the requirement to refer to their calculations in respect of the first requirement.

Stronger candidates used their analysis from the first requirement (as requested) to identify that the Homestyle division makes up a significant element of the group and that the group's performance might be significantly affected by any closure or sale. Many discussed the division's position in the industry lifecycle and considered the related issues of divisional interdependence and central costs.

Only a minority of candidates identified that Outil's board needs to consider what is best for its shareholders.

28.3 Impact on two stakeholders of closure and strategies to reduce barriers to change

The nature of the change being proposed for the Homestyle division, which involves downsizing and redundancy, is transformational and likely to be met with resistance for a variety of stakeholder groups, (for example):

- Employees
- Customers
- Investors
- Suppliers

Mendelow's matrix could be used to assess the power and interest of the various stakeholders and to identify key stakeholders who are likely to cause problems by resisting the change. For example the Homestyle employees are likely to have high levels of interest and may have some power to disrupt the change, depending on the degree of unionisation.

Barriers to change	Impact	Strategies to reduce barriers
Employees		
Group inertia may block change where the changes are inconsistent with the norms of the teams/stores or where they threaten their interests	There may be strikes and other forms of resistance from the staff who are to be made redundant or transferred. Staff who are to remain may be demotivated by the loss of colleagues or the need to relocate/transfer stores.	Lewin Schein's iceberg model could be used here to assist with appropriate change management strategies. Unfreeze existing behaviour: • Identify those stores to close and those to re-brand. Unions and staff must be consulted and the case for change made clear. • Make redundancy announcements. If staff are to be made redundant they may be motivated by reasonable redundancy terms, the provision of references and outplacement assistance, contingent on their cooperation
Cultural barriers: Internally the new proposal put forward will result in fundamental changes to the structure and culture of Outil. Power structures may be threatened by the re-distribution of resources and decision-making authority.	This will particularly affect the director of the Homestyle division and the store managers who may be reluctant to implement decisions that they perceive to be against their own interests.	
There are also barriers which affect individuals and result in them seeing the change as a threat to earnings and job security.	This will not only affect employees of the stores that are closed but also those employees who are required to work in a re-branded store for a different division which may have different working practices	Move to the new structure: • Implement redundancies and provide appropriate exit support • Get retained staff on side and ready for the change. • Participation in the process may improve motivation Refreeze: Once the changes have been made, remaining staff will need support to adapt to the new business model.

Barriers to change	Impact	Strategies to reduce barriers
Customers		
Customers may block change where the changes are inconsistent with the norm or where they threaten their interests	Homestyle customers who also buy from the Fixings division may choose to transfer their business to competitors	Change management will need to focus on communication of which stores will close and which will be re-branded. Key trade customers will need to be reassured that as far as the Fixings division is concerned it is business as usual. Homestyle division customers will need to be encouraged to source supplies where possible from the Fixings division. Outil will need to manage its reputation through the media by explaining how and why the decision has been taken.
Investors		
Investors may block change where the changes are inconsistent with the norm or where they threaten their interests.	Shareholders may consider selling shares as a result of the changes.	Change management will need to focus on the following: <ul><li>Identifying those stores which are to close and those which are to be re-branded</li><li>Announcing the change to market and other stakeholders</li><li>Managing investor relations</li></ul> Communication will be an essential part of the process: Shareholders will be interested in the impact on share price, profitability and dividends. Outil will need to provide reassurance regarding the state of their investment and how the strategy will benefit them. Outil will need to manage its reputation through the financial press and analysts by explaining how and why the decision has been taken.

Barriers to change	Impact	Strategies to reduce barriers
Suppliers		
Suppliers may block change where the changes are inconsistent with the norm or where they threaten their interests.	Suppliers may take legal action for breach of contract in the event of termination.	Legal advice should be sought regarding contractual obligations with suppliers. Change management will need to focus on the following: • Communicating the change to suppliers • Managing supplier relations Communication will be an essential part of the process

Tutorial note

In the answer above Lewin Schein's model is used to assess appropriate change management strategies, you could have also used Gemini's 4 Rs model.

Examiner's comments

This requirement was one of the best answered in the exam. The vast majority of candidates had no problem identifying two stakeholder groups that would be affected by the closure of the Homestyle division and were clearly well-versed in technical knowledge for the change management discussion. Marginal candidates tended to demonstrate one of the following weaknesses: ignoring the requirement to refer to change models, discussing the model(s) in generic terms without application to the scenario, or focusing their discussion on one stakeholder group only (usually the employees).

28.4 Expansion of Fixings division: Merits of test marketing/opening trial stores

Test marketing involves a trial run of a product or concept before proceeding to a full launch.

Test marketing the plan to expand internationally would involve a trial of all aspects of the marketing mix in a limited area. It is designed to reduce risk and gather information about the likely success prior to a full roll-out.

The marketing strategy for the Fixings division may need to be modified for international business differences in language, culture and customs. There may also need to be obvious product modifications, such as voltage changes for power tools etc. This could be minimised by using overseas suppliers rather than shipping from the UK.

Determining the appropriate pricing strategy for the international market may need to take into account increased costs – for example, shipping and export services. Fixings will need to assess competitor pricing. If the expansion is to be in Germany, Euro currency fluctuations will also need to be considered.

The test market selected should normally be small, self-contained and representative of the wider market.

Problems:

- Even the largest test market is not totally representative of the national market.

- Although the main objective of test marketing is to reduce the amount of investment put at risk, it may still involve significant costs. If a major part of the investment has already been made the reduction in risk may be minimal, for example if the Fixings division has to develop an international website or create a large central depot to service a small number of test stores.

- Test marketing may give competitors advance warning of Outil's intentions.

Conclusion:

If test marketing enables large parts of the investment costs relating to an international expansion strategy to be deferred until a reliable estimate of national sales can be made, then it is desirable.

Trial stores

Opening trial stores in Germany offers two important benefits. First, it provides Fixings division with an opportunity to test demand for its products under typical market conditions in order to obtain a measure of its sales performance. As well as enabling top management to make an accurate prediction of its potential national turnover, it may familiarise international customers with the Fixings brand.

Second, it provides an opportunity for management to identify and correct any weaknesses in the strategy or marketing plan before making the commitment to a national sales launch.

Questions to be considered are as follows:

- Where to open the stores?
- How long a test?
- What are the success criteria?

The strategy requires a specific German website to be launched which will need to be tested by a local language and culture expert.

The stores will need a wide range of inventory and if there are only a handful of them, there may not be sufficient volumes for minimum order quantities to get best prices.

If the decision to open stores is taken, this can be done organically (which is how the Homestyle division has previously grown) by opening company-owned stores, or venturing overseas via licensing deals and joint-venture partnerships.

An alternative to opening trial stores would be to test the international demand for Fixings division products via an e-commerce site in the first instance. This would allow it to see which products sell. Goods could then be dispatched from UK or direct from German/European suppliers. (Outil already operate in Eastern Europe through Targi so may already have supply and distribution networks in place.)

Conclusion:

Expanding delivery via a website is likely to be a better way of testing the waters of the German market initially. If this is successful then trial stores could be opened.

Examiner's comments

This was the lowest scoring requirement, but was still reasonably well answered. In general, candidates coped well with identifying the benefits of test-marketing prior to international expansion, although only the better candidates identified this as a risk management strategy. Stronger candidates then went on to consider the merits of the specific proposal to open up four trial stores in Germany. Weaker candidates tended to mix up both elements of the requirement in one discussion, often focusing on one part to the detriment of the other.

29 Dreamy Potato Products Ltd (March 2016, amended)

	Knowledge	Skill	Marks
29.1 Elements of Porter's five forces	3	6	9
29.2 Evaluation of contract (proposal 1)	2	10	10
29.3 Assessment of proposal 2	2	5	7
29.4 Discussion of ethical issues	3	5	7
	10	26	33

29.1 Porter's five forces model is used to analyse the competitive environment within an industry. An analysis of the key forces can help DPP understand the factors which will affect its profitability.

Barriers to entry:

Unless incumbents have strong and durable barriers to entry, profitable markets attract new entrants, which erodes profitability.

Barriers to entry in DPP's industry seem relatively high. They include the following:

- Economies of scale from large volume processing – evident from the fact that the ready meal manufacturers have decided to outsource and that Estima controls 30% of the market

- Investment required for capital intensive processing and specialised logistics (fresh food products)

- Existing players have three year contracts with the large ready-food manufacturers

- Heavily regulated industry with high compliance costs

- Existing firms may have access to suppliers of ingredients, possibly on favourable terms

Barriers are reduced by the following:

- Limited product differentiation and low switching costs

- Smaller entrants could avoid the need for expertise in the distribution of fresh products by outsourcing distribution

It appears that DPP is more likely to face competition from existing firms than new entrants. Local potato farmers may be too small to enter the market.

Power of suppliers:

A key issue is the availability and quality of potatoes. The price is driven by market factors so one individual supplier is unlikely to be able to drive up the price. Limited product differentiation and low switching costs also reduce supplier power. Suppliers are likely to have more power when potato harvests are poor and supplies are limited.

DPP's workforce are also a supplier but the work is probably relatively unskilled and there is likely to be a plentiful supply of workers so individually they will have low power.

DPP has exclusive contracts with four local farms which will help guarantee supply. To the extent that the farms rely on DPP for income, DPP may be in a stronger bargaining position than the suppliers. It has a weekly-paid workforce on the minimum wage and there is no indication of labour supply issues.

Power of customers

The power of customers is driven by the number of buyers in the market and the cost to the buyer of switching from one supplier to another. It is likely to be high.

If there are a few powerful ready-meal manufacturers, they will be able to dictate terms. Here the power of the buyers' buyers is also relevant. Since ready-meal manufacturers supply to large retailers their margins are likely to be low and this will influence the amount they are prepared to pay for processed potatoes. Contracts are also renewed regularly and there is little to differentiate the product.

DPP is dependent on a small number of key customers and its customers are themselves very dependent on the large retailers who have high power, as evidenced by the example of Giant and Potters Pies. This is also reflected in the fact that DPP's contracts are renegotiated every three years and contract terms tend to change frequently.

Examiner's comments

Candidates were well-prepared to discuss three of Porter's five forces and this was the highest scoring element in the exam. The best candidates discussed the model as it applies to the potato processing industry, summarised the strength of each force in the industry and then recognised the impact this would have on DPP. Weaker candidates tended to confuse the industry and company discussion.

29.2 Evaluation of fast food contract

Appendix of possible calculations

Potato prices: EV calculation

Year 1 price = £125

Year 2 price: $(0.40 \times £125) + (0.60 \times £160) = £146$

Year 3 price: $0.40 \times [(0.45 \times £115) + (0.55 \times £135)] + 0.60 \times [(0.65 \times £150) + (0.35 \times £170)] = £144.60$

Annual profits from contract

		Year 1 £	Year 2 £	Year 3 £	Total £
Revenue	9,000 × £210	1,890,000	1,890,000	1,890,000	5,670,000
Potatoes	9,000 × £125/£146/£144.60	1,125,000	1,314,000	1,301,400	3,740,400
Labour and other VC	9,000 × £65	585,000	585,000	585,000	1,755,000
Contribution	9,000 × £20/(/£1)/(£0.40)	180,000	(9,000)	3,600	174,600
Other operation cost		25,000	25,000	25,000	75,000
Profit		155,000	-34,000	-21,400	99,600

Tutorial note

A range of different approaches could be used to determine profitability

Alternative calculation of contract profitability:

Costs	Working	£
Labour and other VC	9,000 × £65 = £585,000 pa × 3	1,755,000
Operating costs	25,000 pa × 3	75,000
		1,830,000
Potatoes	Year 1: 9,000 × £125	1,125,000
	Year 2: 9,000 × £146	1,314,000
	Year 3: 9,000 × £144.60	1,301,400
Total costs		5,570,400
Total revenue	27,000 × £210	5,670,000
Expected profit		99,600

Sensitivity to price of potatoes:

The annual revenue of £1,890,000 less labour and increased operating costs of £610,000 generates £1,280,000 per annum to cover the costs of purchasing 9,000 tonnes potatoes.

This amounts to £142.20 per tonne.

Anything paid above this price will be loss-making for DPP.

The EV is a long-term average and in fact the purchase price of potatoes will vary from £115 to £170 per tonne.

The profitability at different purchase prices can be considered:

Price	115 £	125 £	135 £	150 £	160 £	170 £
Net revenue	1,280,000	1,280,000	1,280,000	1,280,000	1,280,000	1,280,000
Costs of Potatoes	1,035,000	1,125,000	1,215,000	1,350,000	1,440,000	1,530,000
Profit/loss	245,000	155,000	65,000	-70,000	-160,000	-250,000

Evaluation

At the proposed fixed price of £210 per tonne for the three year contract, DPP will make an additional £99,600 of operating profit overall, so on the face of it the contract is financially viable. However this is an operating margin of only 1.8% (99,600/5,670,000), which is less than the current margin (352k/10.8m = 3.3%). Also the profit is not spread evenly.

The key issue affecting profitability is the price that DPP is going to have to pay for potatoes.

On the basis of the agreed price of £125 for Year 1 of the contract, there will be a profit in Year 1 of £155,000. However based on the expected value calculations, the contract will make losses of £34,000 and £21,400 in the subsequent two years.

Potato prices are dependent on crops planted and harvested and market supply. It is not clear how accurate or reliable the price forecasts are. The average price used in the contract profitability calculation will not actually apply. There is a 40% chance that the actual price in Year 2 is £125 and DPP will make a further £155,000 profit. However it is more likely (p=0.6) that the price will be £160, and the actual loss will be £160k.

The maximum that DPP can afford to pay for potatoes is £142.20 per tonne (see sensitivity working). Thus in Year 3 the contract will be profitable if purchase prices are £115 or £135 and loss making at £150 or £170.

Other factors to consider:

(a) Are all the additional costs of the machine and premises space reflected in the £25,000 incremental fixed costs?

(b) If DPP turns the contract down, will it go to a competitor?

(c) If the fast food chain does not renew the contract after three years will DPP be able to use the machine and the additional warehouse space it has rented?

(d) Is there scope to add a clause to the contract for variation in prices depending on the market conditions?

(e) Can DPP pass the risk on to their suppliers by agreeing three year supply prices now?

Conclusion: further research should be undertaken before a final decision to go ahead is taken.

Examiner's comments

Answers to this requirement, which produced the lowest scores in the exam, were polarised. The weakest answers either concentrated on a numerical analysis of the proposed fast-food contract but provided no discussion, or simply produced a qualitative discussion with no supporting calculations.

The better candidates produced more balanced answers and showed good knowledge of expected values and conditional probabilities, scoring full marks on the calculations. Weaker candidates were unsure how to calculate an expected price in Year 3, often averaging the numbers rather than applying the conditional probabilities. They also made errors on the fixed overheads, including the absorbed overheads as well as the incremental element.

29.3 Sustainability involves using natural resources in a way that does not lead to their decline. The Bruntland definition is: "meeting the needs of the present without compromising the ability of future generations to meet their own needs." In a wider context sustainability does not just address environmental issues but also economic and social sustainability, so would encompass long-term financial stability, working conditions and fair treatment of suppliers, among other things.

It is not really clear whether the motivation for DPP's proposed use of waste products is primarily commercial (reduced costs and increased revenues) or based on wanting to adopt a more sustainable approach to business. Certainly the conversion of potato peelings to power will reduce DPP's consumption of energy resources. The sale of starch residue is likely to generate additional revenue at relatively low cost. Whether it will be a net benefit to the environment will depend on how the residue is currently disposed of. Irrespective of environmental sustainability, the diversification of earnings streams and the ability to generate additional revenue will make DPP's business more financially sustainable.

Benefits of proposed strategy:

- In the long-run the use of waste as an energy source will reduce costs

- Sale of potato peelings for cattle food will generate additional revenue

- Accreditation for its sustainable approach may enhance DPP's reputation

- It may attract new environmentally conscious customers

- Large retailers who place emphasis on CSR may insist on suppliers adopting sustainable practices and this may help DPP win contracts.

Costs of implementing a sustainability strategy:

- Additional fixed costs associated with installing the digester

Overall the strategy would appear to be commercially viable and may help increase DPP's environmental and financial sustainability.

Other possible sustainability contributions could come from:

- Increasing the proportion of more modern, fuel efficient vehicles through a regular replacement programme
- Use of cleaner high grade diesel fuel even if this is more expensive
- Improved vehicle utilisation to reduce the number of empty load journeys which waste fuel
- Better refrigeration/chilling processes to reduce emissions
- Ensuring that health and safety is maintained at the highest standards
- Promoting diversity and equal opportunity and providing fair pay and benefits for all workers
- Working in partnership with suppliers, making sure suppliers are treated fairly and that contract terms are transparent and fair to both parties

Examiner's comments

Most candidates were well prepared for a sustainability discussion, although a surprising number still seem to believe this is limited to environmental aspects. Whilst this did gain credit, weaker students who adopted this approach restricted the marks available to them. Better answers identified the financial and environmental benefits of the proposals for waste management and considered a range of alternative proposals to improve sustainability in all three areas (economic, environmental and social).

29.4 Ethical issues

Ethics pertains to whether a particular behaviour is deemed acceptable in the context under consideration. In short, it is 'doing the right thing'.

In making any ethical evaluation it is first necessary to establish the facts. In this case, it would seem that the facts are reasonably clear: Potters is asking DPP to drop its price on one contract (Giant) but is prepared in return to pay more on another contract (Quality). A key question here is whether there is an ethical issue at all or whether this could be deemed to be a normal part of price negotiations in the ordinary course of business.

Andrew's proposal implies a lack of personal ethics on his part, both in relation to his willingness to mislead Quality and also given the implied threat in respect of DPP's contract with Potters. This may be symptomatic of a wider cultural issue within Potters. Alternatively it may be that Andrew is simply passing on the pressure that Potters has come under from Giant and reflects Andrew's desperation to retain a prestigious contract.

The issue of legality needs to be considered and legal advice taken. Andrew has not promised any direct financial incentive but has offered the inducement of a guaranteed contract renewal which might be considered a bribe.

In making a decision as to how to proceed, it is helpful to apply the Institute of Business Ethics three tests:

- Transparency
- Effect
- Fairness

Transparency – would DPP mind people (other customers, suppliers, employees) knowing that it has agreed to this transaction? In the first instance, there appears to be a degree of transparency between DPP and Potters but the same cannot be said in relation to Potters' retail customers. In particular Potters intends to deliberately mislead Quality regarding the price increase.

Effect – whom does the decision affect or hurt? To an extent the impact on Giant is positive since they win by renewing their contract with Potters at a lower price. However this is at Quality's expense. If the contract volumes are the same, DPP will be no worse off financially. However DPP might be accused of colluding with Potters to procure a contract and this may be deemed unfair to other ready-meal manufacturers who are also tendering.

Fairness – would the action be considered fair by those affected? It is likely that competitors and Quality would not take kindly to the fact that DPP has acted with Potters to knowingly deceive them and misrepresent its product as having improved in quality.

Honesty

A final issue is one of honesty. The inducements may fail the honesty test as they are not earned, authorised or disclosed by, or on behalf of, the giver or the recipient.

Actions

DPP should be guided by any legal advice.

Whilst DPP may benefit initially by agreeing to Andrew's request, it would suffer reputational damage if the transaction came to light. Having succumbed once to the implicit threats from Potters, DPP may in future come under more pressure from Potters, in return for its silence. The best action would be for DPP to act honestly and therefore not agree to Andrew's request, which is asking the company to turn a blind eye to dishonesty. DPP might also consider whether it needs to raise the issue of Andrew's behaviour with Potters' directors.

Examiner's comments

The ethics requirement was very well attempted. The vast majority of candidates now acknowledge the need for a balanced discussion which addresses any legal as well as ethical issues and uses appropriate ethical language. Weaker candidates are still tending to limit their analysis to a discussion of transparency, effect and fairness. Better candidates went beyond this to consider Andrew's thinly disguised intimidation threat and to question whether DPP would be demonstrating integrity and honesty by colluding with Andrew's proposed deception. It was encouraging to see that most candidates went on to propose some appropriate next steps to resolve the issue, which was expected for maximum marks.

30 The Zed Museum (March 2016)

Marking guide

		Knowledge	Skill	Marks
30.1	Analysis of stakeholders	3	6	9
30.2	Licensing strategy	2	7	8
30.3	Performance measurement	2	6	7
		7	19	24

30.1 Stakeholders

As a NFP organisation, Zed is likely to have multiple stakeholders with a range of different interests and potentially conflicting goals. A challenge is to integrate the interests of the museum's internal stakeholders (trustees, volunteers, staff) and external stakeholders (donors, visitors, community, government donors) to allow the museum to achieve financial sustainability, make efficient use of its resources, and fulfil its educational role and public interest remit.

Stakeholders can be analysed using Mendelow's power and influence matrix:

Trustees

Trustees have significant power and influence over the day-to-day running of Zed. They may be interested in status/reputation/external recognition. They will also be concerned about the possibility of being found liable for losses if the museum is insolvent. Some trustees may have a network of contacts to assist Zed with funding/expertise or access to new collections/donations.

Trustees are key stakeholders and it is important that they are kept on board as they may attempt to block changes to the status quo, such as the proposed licensing strategy.

Donors

Donors may be interested in the proper use of their funds/artefacts. They may seek recognition or confidentiality. Overall their interest in the museum is probably medium-high. Their power may depend on the size/value of any donation and the donor's ability to raise the profile of the museum or their connections in the art world.

Given the current financial crisis, retention of existing donors or attraction of new ones is critical to the survival of the museum.

Staff

Paid staff will be interested in job satisfaction, pay and security, although volunteers may be doing the job for the love of art and the learning and experience it brings. Power and influence are based on the museum's need for their resources and the availability of labour, but it could be argued that staff are likely to have little power as individuals. However it would be easy for volunteers to withdraw their labour in disgust, since they have nothing to lose as they are not reliant on the museum for income. This could cause the museum problems, depending on the extent to which it relies on volunteer labour rather than paid staff. As a result the level of power is difficult to identify fully.

As the staff are likely to be stakeholders with high interest but possibly medium power, the key here is communication so they feel informed and involved in the museum's future.

Examiner's comments

Most candidates considered the interest and influence of the three stakeholder groups identified. Better candidates used their knowledge of Mendelow to draw this together and analyse the relative importance of each group and the impact of their relationship with the museum in light of the current scenario.

30.2 Desirability of licensing

Advantages

- The museum is in financial crisis and licence fees would offer it a quick, new source of revenue which could ensure survival.

- The assets cannot be sold and there is insufficient room to display them all so this ensures they are generating value for Zed.

- Licensing increases awareness and knowledge of the museum and raises its profile/reputation.

- Expansion risk is shared with the licensee.

- This strategy allows more people to share in/enjoy the donated items

- It increases the opportunities for learning and education due to wider reach and is consistent with Zed's constitution to "encourage visitors to explore collections for inspiration, learning and enjoyment".

Disadvantages

- Licensees may have their own agendas and the museum may suffer as a result of their self-interest.

- Zed may lose control of its collections which goes against its constitution to safeguard the long-term public interest in the collections.

- There may be conditions regarding the use of the building and the collections - restrictive legacies may prohibit them leaving the museum or specify they are for the benefit of Italian citizens only.

- The licensed museum's staff may not have suitable experience/expertise.

- Zed may be accused of allowing commercial objectives to override its constitution and licensing may not be deemed ethical for a NFP organisation.

- Licensing may create financial ties with foreign governments/nationals that restrict the museum's independence.

Specific issues relating to the Japanese museum:

- There may be disparity between the cultural priorities of Italian Zed and the Japanese billionaire.

- The sizeable donation may compromise Zed's independence.

- Will there be a demand for imported Italian culture on the Japanese island?

- There will be significant costs and logistics of transporting collections and ensuring their safety/security/conditions.

- There may be significant language and cultural differences.

Conclusion

It is not unusual for museums and art galleries to share objects and exhibitions and to put collections on loan. Some other international museums have embarked on licence strategies to strengthen their global brand.

Zed's founding principles require it to "recognise the interests of people who made, owned, collected or donated items in the collections" and to "consult and involve the local community, users and supporters" and it should engage with these people before making a final decision.

Clearly some action is required since the museum is in imminent danger of insolvency. In addition to licensing, other strategies may be available to raise revenue eg, increase admission fees, charge for special exhibitions, and sell merchandise online.

Examiner's comments

The approach required here was a consideration of the benefits for Zed of a licensing strategy in general, together with the specifics of the Japanese proposal. Many candidates mixed up the two elements under one discussion of advantages and disadvantages. Whilst this approach usually scored acceptable marks, those who first considered whether licensing was a sensible option for the museum before considering some of the issues associated with the particular Japanese option tended to make a more diverse range of points. The better candidates recognised that, given the museum's financial crisis, imminent action was required.

30.3 Approach to performance measurement

Currently Zed is looking at performance from a very narrow angle: the number of people through its doors. One of its founding principles is to "review performance to innovate and improve". To fulfil this Zed needs a wider system of performance measurement and, given its NFP status, this needs to take into account both financial and non-financial aspects. An effective system of performance measurement will demonstrate to external stakeholders that the museum's founding principles and objectives are being met and show Zed's stewardship of its assets: its collections, intellectual capital, and brand.

Given the broad range of stakeholders, a balanced scorecard approach may be relevant. This highlights four perspectives: financial, customer, internal business processes, and innovation and learning. The trustees should identify critical success factors – the areas that are vital for the museum to be a long-term sustainable organisation – and these should guide the choice of KPIs and the setting of targets within each area.

Financial

It is difficult to assign monetary value to art/culture and many of the traditional financial measures of performance (eg, ROCE, profit margin) will not apply here. However given the financial crisis that Zed finds itself in, the financial perspective is vitally important. To remain viable the museum may have to manage its costs more closely. It could consider the 3Es commonly used in the public sector: Economy, Efficiency and Effectiveness. These will help assess whether the museum's resources have been put to good use to add value to society.

Appropriate financial KPIs might include the following:

- Admission fees received
- Grant income received
- Average value of financial donations
- Average value of exhibits donated
- Sales of merchandise
- % of budget spent on marketing
- Licence fees received
- Ratio of income to operating costs
- Revenue generated from café
- Cost of restorations undertaken
- Cost of fund-raising activities

Customer

This is the only area currently being monitored. However Zed needs to know what its users feel about the museum and its exhibitions. They may be seeking education and/or entertainment.

Appropriate KPIs might include the following:

- Monthly attendance figures
- % of return visitors
- Number of first-time visitors
- Average score in visitor satisfaction ratings
- Mix of visitors – local: tourists
- % of time museum open to visitors

Internal business processes

This considers how Zed goes about delivering its services and the impact this has on its effectiveness.

Appropriate KPIs might include the following:

- % of total collection on display
- Number of new pieces acquired in the year
- % of income spent on admin rather than collections and activities
- Ratio of paid staff: volunteers
- Ratio of staff: visitors
- Number of damaged artefacts

Learning and development:

The museum should be a place of personal growth for both its staff and its visitors and it also wants to play a role in encouraging learning on the part of the visitors to the museum.

Appropriate KPIs might include the following:

- No. of articles published by museum staff in journals
- No. of institutions to which museum has lent items
- % of budget spent on staff training
- Staff turnover/absenteeism
- No. of new collections/exhibitions acquired
- No. of visits by schools/colleges

Examiner's comments

Answers to the performance measurement requirement were sometimes disappointing. Poorer efforts tended to ignore the request to recommend a suitable approach to performance measurement and simply provided a list of KPIs. Stronger candidates discussed the need to extend the current and very narrow approach to measuring performance (visitor numbers). A number of options were acceptable here in the context of a NFP experiencing financial difficulties and included balanced scorecard, the 3 Es or consideration of a range of financial and non-financial measures. The weakest candidates still appear to be confused about the difference between CSFs/goals and KPIs which are measures of the extent to which these goals have been achieved.

31 The Healthy Vegetarian plc (June 2016)

	Knowledge	Skill	Marks
31.1(a) Data analysis	2	9	10
(b) KPIs	3	6	8
31.2 Budgeting	2	5	7
31.3 Procurement	3	9	11
31.4 Ethics	3	6	8
	13	35	44

31.1(a)

	Leeds £	Hull £	Average for all shops £	Average for 50 worst performing shops £	Average for 50 best performing shops £
Per sq m					
Revenue	3,269	4,063	6,000	4,875	4,833
Op Profit	131	138	375	250	375
NCA/Sq m	4,231	3,750	3,875	3,688	3,750
Per employee					
Revenue	38,636	46,429	68,571	55,714	58,000
Op Profit	1,545	1,571	4,286	2,857	4,500
Rev/NCA	0.77	1.08	1.55	1.32	1.29
Op profit margin %	4.0%	3.4%	6.3%	5.1%	7.8%
% of average for all shops					
Revenue	88.5%	67.7%	100.0%	81.3%	120.8%
Op profit	56.7%	36.7%	100.0%	66.7%	150.0%
Operating costs	408,000	314,000	450,000	370,000	535,000

Leeds shop

General issues

Based on the information available, the Leeds shop is larger in terms of floor space than the Hull shop and any of the three 'averages' given as benchmarks. This implies it could have greater potential to make more sales, so it may have an unfair advantage over smaller shops to generate revenue and profit.

Perhaps, more significantly, the cost of the property in Leeds is greater than the Hull shop and any of the three 'averages' given as benchmarks. This is true in absolute terms, but also in terms of non-current assets cost per square metre. The reason for this may be that the Leeds shop is better positioned in a prime location. This may enable it to generate more revenue. Comparisons of revenue per shop in absolute terms therefore gives unfair advantage to higher cost, bigger shops such as Leeds. Operating profit in absolute terms may also be greater for higher cost shops like Leeds, but in this case it needs to cover the additional depreciation costs.

Where the Leeds shop performs badly by comparison to all the other shops is in the ROCE KPI. Any additional profit it earns needs to be proportionate to the additional capital invested, and in this it seems to be failing.

Revenue

In terms of the total revenue generated, the Leeds shop outperforms the worst performing shops benchmark and generates 88.5% of the revenue of the average shop. Whilst not a good performance this would not place it in the very bottom of the rankings which would warrant being placed in closure review procedures.

However, when revenue is adjusted for scale using floor space, then the revenue per square metre at £3,269 is far lower than the Hull shop or the three benchmarks.

Also, revenue per employee at £38,636 is lower than the Hull shop and the three benchmarks. This may be a further reflection of scale or as a result of the inefficient use of labour resources.

Operating profit

In terms of the total operating profit earned, the Leeds shop outperforms the Hull shop, but is below the worst performing shops benchmark, despite the greater size of the Leeds shop. It generates only 56.7% of the operating profit of the average shop.

The operating margin is low at only 4%. This is little more than half the margin of the best performing shops benchmark, although it is above the margin for the Hull shop. In general it shows that despite generating significant revenue, operating costs are high.

Indeed, the operating costs of the Leeds shop are £38,000 higher than the worst performing shops benchmark despite generating only an extra £35,000 in revenue.

Operating profit per employee is the lowest of the shops in the table although similar to the Hull shop. Again this could reflect inefficient use of labour resources.

ROCE

As already noted, the ROCE of the Leeds shop is by far the lowest at 3.1%. This reflects poor utilisation of resources and a low level of return.

The ROCE uses the historic cost, but this was some years ago and the fair value may far exceed this which would make the ROCE far worse in fair value terms.

Closure decision

A distinction needs to be made between the performance of the manager and the potential performance of the shop. The causal factors therefore need to be identified to ascertain whether the poor performance is due to controllable factors (eg, poor staff management) or non-controllable factors (eg, difficult market conditions). A recovery plan can then be put in place and acted upon.

If the factors causing poor performance are non-controllable then alternative and more efficient use of the resources tied up in the Leeds shop could be gained by closing it and reinvesting the cash in alternative locations. As noted, the cash generated may far exceed the price originally paid.

Hull shop

General issues

The Hull shop is of similar size and value to the average and worst performing benchmarks, so reasonably valid comparisons can be made.

However the Hull shop was the most recently opened of the shops and therefore could still be regarded as in the start-up phase, with greater potential for future growth than other shops.

Revenue

The low level of total revenue generated appears to be the main problem. It is the lowest of the shops disclosed in the table with only 67.7% of the revenue of the average shop (ie, about a third lower) and 83.3% of the revenue of the worst performing benchmark.

In terms of revenue per square metre, the Hull shop is about the same proportion lower than the average as in absolute terms, given they are of similar size.

By the same argument, the revenue per employee for the Hull shop, compared to the average shop and the worst performing benchmark, is similarly lower as they all have the same number of staff.

Operating profit

In terms of the total operating profit earned, the Hull shop is by far the worst. This seems likely to be due to low revenue and high operating gearing, with staff and depreciation being key fixed costs.

The operating margin is the lowest at only 3.4%. This is little more than half the margin of the average shop at 6.3%. In general, it shows that low revenue and high operating gearing are having a detrimental effect on margins.

Operating profit per employee and per square metre of floor space are both higher than the Leeds shop but below that of the worst performing benchmark. Again this could reflect poor revenue generation and/or inefficient use of labour resources.

ROCE

While the ROCE of the Hull shop at 3.7% is not as low as the Leeds shop it is far below the worst performing benchmark at 6.8%, reflecting low profitability.

Closure decision

Unless there is strong evidence that the Hull shop can quickly emerge from the start-up phase and make significant improvement, consideration should be given to closure. If the Hull shop were to be sold then more efficient use of resources could be gained by reinvesting the cash in alternative locations, even if the new shop were only to earn the worst performing benchmark rate of return. There may however be closure costs and, as the shop was acquired recently, the sale price might not exceed the price paid.

(b) Closure review procedures may possibly have benefits of motivating staff at the lower end of the performance range but may also generate issues in terms of stress and uncertainty which may reduce staff morale.

Closure review procedures are unlikely to have either positive or negative motivational effects for strong performing units as it is not probable they will be affected.

Some form of criteria to decide on the viability of shops seems necessary in order to promote the efficient use of capital of the business as a whole. In this respect there are two factors:

(1) How the criteria are applied
(2) Which criteria are applied

How the criteria are applied

The current criteria are applied only annually. This is a long period, over which performance can deteriorate a great deal. More regular monitoring (eg, quarterly or even monthly) seems appropriate.

Conversely however once a shop is placed in closure review procedures it can be closed within three months which gives little time for it to be turned around and improved.

There also seems insufficient distinction between poor performance of the shop and the poor performance of the shop manager. Changing the shop manager may seem to be an appropriate initial response to poor performance rather than closure of the shop. Replacement of the manager only appears to occur in response to budget deficits rather than closure review procedure measures.

The measures appear to be applied in terms of relative performance compared to other shops, rather than absolute performance against a predetermined target. If all shops are performing well in absolute terms, then one shop still has to be at the bottom of the rankings and at risk of being closed. Conversely, if a large number of shops are performing badly, it is only the very worst that will be captured by closure review procedures using relative measures. Other shops, performing badly but not quite as badly, will then escape scrutiny but may warrant closure.

Moreover, relative performance measures create uncertainty in that shop managers do not know the level of performance that will place them in closure review procedures, as they do not know, in advance, how other shops are performing. Absolute criteria for closure review procedures (eg, a 5% ROCE) would at least make clear, from the beginning of the year, what is an acceptable level of performance.

Which criteria are applied

Revenue

Absolute revenue fails to allow for scale, and can therefore hide the underlying level of efficiency. A large expensive shop (such as Leeds) will easily achieve this revenue criterion, whereas a small shop may be well managed but may struggle to generate significant revenue.

Operating profit

Similarly, the absolute level of operating profit rewards scale. It also hides such factors as food wastage and theft of products amongst much larger costs.

ROCE

The ROCE as used in the closure review procedures bases the capital on the price paid for non-current assets. For older purchases, the fair value of the property may have increased a lot over historic cost. Conversely, for fixtures and equipment, they may be largely depreciated and in need of urgent replacement.

Alternative measures

Operating profit margin – this addresses the scale issue by relating operating profit to revenue generated.

Gross profit margin – this would be the difference between revenue and the cost of sales (ie, the cost of the food/drink acquired). As selling prices are uniform and the price paid for products is constant this measure would reveal inefficiencies in usage (eg, wastage and theft).

ROCE based on fair values – would give a more accurate picture of opportunity cost and the realisable value on closure. It would make comparisons between shops more valid as they would be measured on the same basis.

Non-financial measures – may include: customer satisfaction ratings; number of items sold per square metre; and number of customer complaints. A balanced scorecard could be used to identify some key non-financial measures.

Examiner's comments

Part (a) of the first requirement was generally very well answered by most candidates calculating relevant data and presenting their figures in a structured table. Weaker candidates did not produce an initial table of calculations, but weaved occasional random calculations into their narrative. Other weaker candidates mainly used the figures already provided in the question, with few additional new calculations.

Most candidates produced a good commentary on the data with a reasoned opinion on whether Leeds and Hull should be closed or not. The vast majority also highlighted additional information required, with most tending to do this separately, rather than integrating it into their discussion. The vast majority also provided a conclusion, although there was a lot of sitting on the fence.

In respect of part (b) of the first requirement, the overall the critique of the KPIs was poorly done. Relatively few candidates identified the issue of scale or concept of absolute versus relative KPIs. Even fewer candidates highlighted the issue of using a ranking system for the KPIs as opposed to measurement against a target.

Candidates performed better in suggesting other KPIs with most predictably using the Balance Scorecard. However, many failed to justify the additional KPIs in the context of the given scenario. Most candidates identified the need for non-financial KPIs and a good proportion highlighted the issue of asset values and ROCE.

31.2 Budgeting

A budget is a plan expressed in financial terms.

THV appears to be currently using budgeting for three purposes:

(1) Planning – promotes forward thinking so resources can be put in place in time (eg, a cash shortfall can be financed by a planned overdraft). Potential problems are identified early, therefore giving managers time enough to consider the best way to overcome that problem.

(2) Motivating performance – having a defined target can motivate shop managers in their performance. Shop managers may be motivated by a target to achieve, but this is reinforced by the policy of penalties such as dismissal if targets are not achieved.

(3) Providing a basis for a system of control. Budgets provide a yardstick for measuring performance by comparing actual against planned performance and investigating budget variances.

Possible improvements

At the moment there may be a conflict between the ways in which THV is using budgeting.

Participation in setting targets by shop managers may lead to more commitment to achieving those targets but may also lead to a degree of biasing the budget downwards to improve budget variances. If managers fear they are going to be judged, and possibly dismissed, if they do not achieve their budget target they are likely to build in slack to make the budget more achievable. Budgets that contain slack are less useful for planning purposes as they contain bias.

An improvement would be to have less of a budget-constrained style of management and instead treat variances as an opportunity to make improvements rather than dismiss managers. With reduced consequences may come more cooperation and more accurate budgeting.

The fact that budgets below the previous year's level are not acceptable may fail to take into account changing market conditions (eg, a new competitor in a local region). If last year's performance is now unachievable, the budget may need to be revised. Only realistic budgets can form the basis for planning and control, and therefore they should be adaptable. A zero-based budget would start from first principles rather than adjust last year's figure.

Budgets enable senior managers to 'manage by exception', and thereby focus on areas where things are not going to plan (ie, the exceptions). This is done by comparing the actual performance to the budget to identify the variance. However, not all variances are under the control of shop managers. The principles of controllability and accountability apply. Shop managers can only be held responsible for budget variances arising from causes over which they have control.

The use of budgets could be extended by THV for other purposes. At the moment, there seems limited use of budgets for authorisation. Shop managers appear to have complete discretion of the number of staff hired at their shop. If they were forced to budget, then they would need to plan staff usage in advance which would make it subject to senior management scrutiny before the event. Similarly, variations from the staffing budgets would need to be justified before being authorised.

If the policy of permitting shop managers to make external purchases of food from local suppliers were to take place (see below) then this could be implemented, authorised and controlled by a budgetary mechanism at individual shop level.

The use of budgets could also be extended beyond shop level. Budgets could be applied to each of the 40 product lines to assess the profitability of each product line and trends in demand compared to expectations. Poorly performing product lines could be dropped where highlighted by adverse budget variances. Similarly, new product lines could be introduced and monitored by budgets.

Examiner's comments

There was discussion about the nature of the current budgeting system and the problems with it, but there tended to be limited detail and justification for how better use could be made of budgeting by THV. Weaker candidates struggled on this requirement providing only brief answers that lacked any real cohesion. The better responses gave due consideration to controllability by store managers in the context of performance measurement/management.

31.3 Procurement processes

Purchasing of food products from local suppliers

Currently there is a limited degree of autonomy given to shop managers. The selling prices are fixed by head office; the prices paid to suppliers and recharged to shops are fixed by head office; the location of the shop and capital expenditure are determined by head office.

The only real factors that shop managers can control therefore are:

- the amounts of food ordered each day from within the narrow range of 40 products lines purchased by head office
- staffing levels

Key advantages to permitting some purchases from local suppliers are:

- use of local knowledge to accommodate local tastes
- managers are more motivated if they have more autonomy.
- learning by head office from successful new products sold on a trial basis which can be rolled out across all 200 shops.

Disadvantages are:

- costs – head office can take advantage of economies of scale to lower the cost of purchase. Individual shops are likely to pay more.

- some central purchases would be displaced and therefore there may be the loss of quantity discounts.

- less control – risk of fraud if shop managers sell their own goods through shops and understate revenue.

- loss of homogeneity – if customers obtain different goods at different shops there may be some loss of brand identity.

Use of information technology systems for procurement

The use of automatic reordering at the level of individual shops would reduce the amount of autonomy for shop managers. In this sense, it is the opposite of the above proposal for purchasing from local suppliers. It is also probably initially incompatible with the above proposal as introducing purchases from local suppliers would make historical data patterns unreliable predictors of future sales.

Aside from the behavioural issues, there are risks of future sales patterns not following historical patterns. Local conditions, such as a new competitor, could be accommodated by a shop manager but may not be fully reflected by historic data recognition patterns over a prolonged period.

If errors are made by IT systems ordering so wastage occurs, it may not always be clear who is responsible. It would be difficult to hold shop managers responsible for wastage if they had not ordered the goods, yet wastage figures impact on profit.

Advantages would include the following:

- Releasing shop manager time to focus on customer service and staff management rather than order quantities

- Orders could be placed on a consistent basis if the shop manager was ill or on holiday

- Data management would be easier if IT systems were used rather than orders from 200 separate managers

- IT systems could be integrated with suppliers' IT systems for more efficient ordering. This could make systems more efficient as there are only four suppliers. Improved transfer of information may make the logistics and distribution systems of suppliers more efficient.

Examiner's comments

This was generally well answered with most candidates scoring well. The merits and problems of procurement and IT were well considered by most, recognising the tensions inherent in centralisation versus de-centralisation in decision making. Fewer recognised the problems associated with conflicts in brand identity due to local sourcing and/or the possibility of fraud by store managers.

31.4 Ethical issues

Ethics pertains to whether a particular behaviour is deemed acceptable in the context under consideration. In short, it is 'doing the right thing'.

In making any ethical evaluation it is first necessary to establish the facts. In this case, the claims made by Andrew need to be established to assess their validity before taking any action. This may include establishing the sugar content of a sample of products. It might also include determining the validity of Diana's counter-claim that: "…the sugar content in grams is marked on all our products…."

The issue of legality may apply if the labelling is incorrect, misleading or contrary to regulations. Legal advice should be taken.

Assuming that Diana's claim that products are labelled is correct, this leaves open the question for the board of whether the marketing theme of healthy vegetarian food is inconsistent with the facts, notwithstanding that they are labelled individually.

In making a decision as to how to act, it may be helpful to Andrew and the board to apply the Institute of Business Ethics three tests:

- Transparency
- Effect
- Fairness

Transparency – would the THV board mind people (existing customers, suppliers, employees) knowing about the sugar content in a more open way? In particular, the issue of transparency will apply to the customers who may have believed the heathy eating marketing but, if told more overtly and transparently about high sugar content, would have acted differently. The key issue is whether the prominence and clarity of the labelling amounts to adequate transparency that would lead one to believe that the customers were making an informed choice on the sugar content of their purchases.

Effect – whom does the high sugar content, without clear disclosure, affect/hurt? Clearly this could include the health of customers who would have acted differently on the basis of full information. Other rivals selling genuinely healthy food may also have suffered financially.

Fairness – would the level of disclosure of sugar content be considered fair by those affected? The issue for THV's board is the boundary between the individual customer's responsibility to read labelling about sugar and the company's responsibilities: to make labelling sufficiently clear for it to be observed, and readily understood, in the context of making a food purchase of this nature; to be fair, open and accurate in the information it provides to customers via its marketing efforts.

Honesty – A final issue is one of honesty. Is there an intention to mislead in holding out products to be healthy in marketing communications and then making the minimum possible disclosure in the expectation that customers will not understand the reality of the sugar content?

Actions

Andrew's actions should be consistent with his obligations and duties as a non-executive director. His initial action should be to inform the board. Three issues are to be highlighted: (1) whether the labelling is transparent, clear and in compliance with regulations such that there is evidence that customers are making an informed choice on the sugar content of their purchases; (2) whether the marketing message is misleading; and (3) if the labelling is within regulations, whether it is also in line with custom and practice in the industry.

Andrew needs to give the board reasonable time to respond to the issues that he has raised. If there is no adequate, timely response, and he believes the actions are illegal, then he may have a duty as a non-executive director to report to the relevant regulatory body, having taken legal advice.

He should consider resigning if this becomes necessary.

A large majority of candidates adopted the transparency, effect, and fairness structure. However, the application of this structure varied, with weaker candidates not completely sure of the correct interpretation of the principles in the context of the scenario. Many candidates failed to go beyond this TEF framework to discuss any other ethical principles. Overall the use of ethical language and principles was not as comprehensive as in previous sittings. Many candidates failed to address the legality issue or to identify suitable actions for Andrew given his role as a non-executive director. Although most candidates (but not all) identified potential actions for Andrew, there was generally a poor understanding of Andrew's role as a non-executive director in relation to this issue.

32 Elver Bloom Recruiting plc (June 2016)

Marking guide

	Knowledge	Skill	Marks
32.1 Elements of PESTEL	3	7	10
32.2 Fee reduction	4	14	16
32.3 Amy's proposal	2	8	9
	9	29	35

32.1 Key issues – notes

Economic

- Economic growth – more employees required

- More prosperity – higher salaries on which fees are based

- Labour market conditions – as the market nears full employment, it is more difficult for employers to find the right people without specialist outsourced help

- Economic cycle makes labour market and therefore recruitment particularly volatile

- Specialist companies with dependency on one sector (eg, finance or IT) generate risk of dependency on the fortunes of that sector

Technological

- E-recruitment through social media and internet makes quick access to more potential recruits cheaper and easier

- International recruits can be accessed with social media and internet without physical presence in other countries

- Groups can be easily targeted (eg, financial services or IT potential recruits) using relevant websites and industry electronic journals

- Makes market place more competitive when cheap access makes low barriers to entry for new recruitment companies

- Makes pricing more transparent

- Clients can more easily recruit themselves through Linkedin etc so less need for agency services

Legal

- Employment law advice is a source of income

- Employment legislation may constrain the recruitment process to avoid discrimination and promote equality. This may impose additional costs.

- Data protection may prevent e-recruitment details being accessed

- International recruitment may be constrained by immigration laws

Conclusion and synthesis

Profitability in the recruitment agency industry is dependent on cycles in the labour market which in turn are a function of the economic cycle. Agencies dependent on one sector (eg, finance or IT) will be dependent on the fortunes of that industry, which may or may not follow macro-economic conditions. Revenue generated in the recruitment agency appears to have benefited overall from the general economic recovery, thereby enhancing industry profitability.

The increased use of social media and e-recruitment seems to be lowering costs in the industry so may appear to add to profitability. However, this is not unambiguously the case if it simultaneously reduces barriers to entry and thereby increases industry competition and forces down prices.

Legal issues may similarly have an ambiguous effect on industry profitability in constraining actions of recruiters and requiring additional processes, but also offering an opportunity for advisory work.

Overall the three factors appear to have recently enhanced industry profitability but there is sufficient ambiguity of effect that not all industry participants may benefit from this.

Examiner's comments

Answers tended to use the three headings provided however the economic analysis was generally poor with few answers clearly stating the link between economic activity, the labour market and the recruitment industry. Better answers used examples for technology from social media, for employment law, and data protection. Poorer efforts tended to be somewhat generic.

32.2 To: EBR board
From: An Adviser
Date: 7 June 20X6
Subject: Report – fee level review

Year to 31 March	20X6	20X5	Change %
Fee per appointment	£16,000	£17,000	-5.9%
Rebate/revenue %	12.0%	10.1%	
Operating profit % fees	41.6%	44.2%	
Operating profit % total	46.4%	48.9%	
VC/Revenue %	20.0%	18.0%	
FC/Revenue %	26.4%	27.7%	
VC per appointment £	£3,200	£3,060	4.6%
FC per appointment £	£4,230	£4,714	-10.3%
TC per appointment £	£7,430	£7,774	-4.4%
Recruitment operating profit per appointment	£6,649	£7,511	-11.5%

% changes

Revenue	4.9%
Operating profit recruitment	-1.4%
Other services	8.9%
Operating profit total	-0.4%

Impact of price reduction

In comparing 20X6 with 20X5, the working assumption adopted is that, in the absence of the fee change, the 20X6 financial statements would replicate those of 20X5. In other words it has been assumed that any changes in 20X6 are due entirely to the 10% fee reduction.

There has been:

- growth in revenue of 4.9%, but operating profits on fees and overall have fallen by 1.4% and 0.4% respectively. The increase in revenue as a consequence of fee reduction implies that demand is elastic. Nevertheless, the increased revenue has been outweighed by the increased costs caused by the higher level of activity, leading to a fall in operating profit.

- more appointments have been made, up 11.4%, increasing from 700 to 780. According to the working assumption, this has been generated by lower prices. This gives the opportunity for future growth and cross selling of other services (which have also increased).

- there is a danger of price being a signal for quality and the perception of positioning downmarket when trying to attract upmarket clients and recruits.

- fee per appointment has only fallen by 5.9% not 10%. This may mean a better mix of higher quality appointments or that the 10% reduction policy has not been fully implemented.

- rebates increased in absolute terms and also as a % of revenue, so there may be poorer quality appointments (although variable cost per appointment has gone up which could imply increased quality, or increased inefficiency).

- operating profit has changed only marginally in absolute and % terms. However operating profit per appointment has fallen significantly by 11.5%. This has been driven by the 10% fee reduction but also the increase of 4.6% in variable cost per appointment already noted.

- 'other services' has increased contribution – this may indicate more cross-selling.

Retain or reverse price reduction

The short term impact in 20X6 from the price reduction would indicate that the effect has been unfavourable as the operating profit has fallen. However, before deciding on the best future action, the working assumption that there were no other relevant factors affecting profit may be challenged.

Also, it may be inappropriate to judge the pricing strategy based on one year alone. The increase in the number of appointments may have a longer term beneficial effect in improving reputation and increasing cross-selling of other services.

However the longer term effects may also be detrimental to the company and the damage to the company's reputation for quality may increase over time adding to the short term adverse effect on operating profit.

Examiner's comments

Calculations were variable, with some students producing few or no calculations, whilst others made a reasonable attempt. There was generally a poor appreciation of the relationship of price/volume/variable costs, with only a minority considering the growth in other services or price elasticity and sensitivity. The discussion of the case to retain or reverse the price reduction was generally thin. Sometimes it was just added as an assertion as part of the conclusion.

32.3 Key issues

Amy's proposal is to move EBR further upmarket, not just from the current market positioning (following the 10% price reduction), but further upmarket than the traditional market position prior to the recent price reduction. This could be viewed as part of a differentiation strategy.

This would mean that EBR, under Amy's suggestion, would be charging higher prices than ever, despite the fact that it has been having difficulty in winning tenders since the end of the recession at lower prices.

Price can be taken as a signal of quality, particularly where objective evidence of underlying quality may be difficult to attain. Amy's other suggestion is therefore consistent with reinforcing the quality signal, by going beyond the industry norm in offering rebates. This gives a self-imposed penalty for poor appointments, and therefore incentives to make good quality appointments. If this is perceived by customers and potential customers, it is a consistent signal of quality with the price increase.

In terms of risk shifting, it transfers much of the risk of bad appointments from the client onto EBR. The increase in price may therefore be regarded as a risk premium being paid by clients.

From EBR's perspective there is a significant downside risk. The costs of the rebates may significantly outweigh the benefits of increased prices, particularly if the change fails to attract new customers. There is therefore a need for more information to quantify the risk to EBR. In this respect:

- Historical information about how long appointed employees have stayed with clients is needed in order to model the effects of rebates in the future.

- Market research is also needed to evaluate the likely client response to the rebate offer and to increased prices, so historical trends can be better extrapolated.

A further risk arises from competitor response. While such a policy is not common in the industry, and therefore differentiates EBR from its competitors, this is only the current position. Markets are dynamic and, if the policy is initially successful, then competitors may copy it, thereby reducing the benefits to EBR and possibly forcing down industry profits.

A final issue is that the swings in pricing policy within a short period of time, and in opposite directions, are likely to cause market confusion as to EBR's market positioning. In this respect, the previous reduction in prices may harm this proposed strategy, particularly as it is based upon the perception of quality being influenced by price, which requires stability of pricing policy.

Recommendation

The increase of prices suggested by Amy is significant and has a risk of losing existing customers and causing wide swings in pricing following the recent 10% reduction.

One proposal would be to offer all customers a choice of prices: (1) the higher price with a higher rebate; or (2) the existing (or original) pricing with existing rebates. This would enable customer preferences to determine the price-risk package, rather than the EBR board to guess what all customers may want.

Many candidates used the Suitable/Acceptable/Feasible structure but were not normally helped by this framework as they consequently tended to overlook the strategic re-positioning and quality changes. Better approaches were to discuss the price/quality relationship and the change to a differentiation strategy, followed by discussion of the price/profit/risk trade-off. A minority made direct reference to Porter's generic strategies framework, often identifying the proposal as one of focused differentiation.

33 TechScan Ltd (June 2016)

Marking guide

	Knowledge	Skill	Marks
33.1 Impact on R&D	2	4	6
33.2 Expected net present value	3	14	15
	5	18	21

33.1 Impact on R&D

Research should be intended to improve products or processes in order to gain competitive advantage. R&D should support the organisation's strategy, be properly planned and be closely coordinated with marketing.

There may be an impact on the R&D department arising from behavioural issues. This could arise from abandoning the current development project in favour of using licensed Ursa technology. If the best R&D staff are to be retained for developing the next generation of technology over the next five years, then motivation and staff retention will need to be prioritised. Loss of key core competences from losing key staff could be a key issue that damages the R&D capability of TechScan for many years.

R&D can have long term horizons and if Option 2 is selected, then it would seem that the next critical time is in about six years (ie, the new technology is licensed from next year and will last for five more years).

It is important that the R&D strategy should be carefully controlled; new products and technologies can be a major source of competitive advantage but can cost a great deal and have a degree of uncertainty. A screening process is necessary to ensure that resources are concentrated on projects with a high probability of success.

In this respect, R&D can be important but only if it is successful. Otherwise it is a wasted cost. If Option 2 is selected, the previous R&D project would not have produced outcomes as the board would have decided to license alternative technology from another company. Whilst it may have been successful if the final R&D phase had been financed, this would not have the opportunity to occur if there is an immediate decision in favour of Option 2. Any money spent on earlier phases is therefore wasted. A review or debriefing of what went wrong with the previous R&D project may now be appropriate in order to learn lessons about the future of the R&D department.

In the context of the board accepting Option 2, the future of R&D can be seen as part of the next product life cycle. In preparing for the obsolescence of Ursa technology, successful new technology needs to be in place for the next product life cycle in approximately six years' time. If there is early success in the new R&D, then the current product life cycle for Ursa technology may be shortened, but it is likely that contractual commitments have been made to Ursa to make licence payments over five years so these would need to be treated as a sunk cost.

Examiner's comments

This was reasonably well answered, although most concentrated either on R&D and possible closure of the department together with redundancies, or alternatively on the move to licensing. Only a minority addressed both the issue of impact on the R&D department and on the future R&D strategy. Only a minority made explicit reference to core competences in R&D and related problems, although many alluded to this indirectly.

33.2 (a) **Option 1**

Initial investment	R&D cost outcome	Price outcome	NPV	Probability	Expected value
(£45m)	Fail* (£100m)	High +£160m	£15m	(0.4)(0.7) = 0.28	£4.2m
(£45m)	Succeed (£20m)	Low +£110m	£45m	(0.6)(0.3) = 0.18	£8.1m
(£45m)	Fail* (£100m)	Low +£110m	(£35m)	(0.4)(0.3) = 0.12	(£4.2m)
(£45m)	Succeed (£20m)	High +£160m	£95m	(0.6)(0.7) = 0.42	£39.9m
Total				**1.0(proof)**	**£48.0m**

* If the R&D project fails, TechScan will move to Ursa Inc licensing, as future benefits exceed future costs even in a low price scenario (even though there is a loss overall, the initial £45 million is a sunk cost at this stage).

Option 2

Initial investment	R&D cost outcome	Price outcome	NPV	Probability	Expected value
0	(£100m)	High +£160m	£60m	0.7	£42.0m
0	(£100m)	Low +£110m	£10m	0.3	£3.0m
Total				**1.0**	**£45.0m**

Tutorial note

A decision tree diagram can also be used to do this calculation.

Alternative approach:

Revenue in each case = (0.7 × 160 + (0.3 ×110) = 145

Costs:

Option 1: –45 + (0.6 × –20) + (0.4 × –100) = 97

Option 2: 100

Profit:

Option 1: 145 – 97 = **48**

Option 2: 145 – 100 = **45**

(b) The issues of investment in R&D or licensing deals with the concepts of risk, expected values and probabilities.

The TechScan board has to deal with decision making under uncertainty. In these circumstances there are two levels of uncertainty:

- Uncertainty of R&D success – which leads to uncertainty of costs for the R&D option but not the licensing option

- Uncertainty of market conditions – which leads to uncertainty of revenues, which is the same for both types of technology

The two types of uncertainty are independent of each other, but occur simultaneously.

The table above shows that Option 1 has a higher expected NPV than Option 2. As a result, in terms of expected values alone, Option 1 is preferable ie, undertake the final phase of the R&D project and invest £45 million.

However there are some weaknesses in using these expected values as the sole decision making criterion:

- The probabilities used when calculating expected values are likely to be estimates, particularly as R&D activity tends to have unknown uncertainties. The probabilities provided may therefore be unreliable or inaccurate.

- Expected values are long-term averages most suitable for decisions involving a high number of similar outcomes. They are less suitable for use in situations involving one-off decisions such as whether to buy the licence or engage in further R&D, where the expected value itself will never occur. They may therefore be useful as a guide to decision making rather than as a strict rule for one-off decisions.

- Expected values do not consider the attitudes to risk of the people involved in the decision making process. They assume risk neutrality which may not be appropriate for the owners of TechScan.

Looking at the data above more specifically, although Option 1 has the higher expected value (by £3 million) it has a greater risk in terms of dispersion of outcomes. There is a 12% chance of making a significant loss of £4.2 million, where the R&D project fails and there are low prices. For Option 2 there is no loss expected to be incurred in any circumstance.

Similarly, under Option 2 there is a 70% probability of achieving profits of £42m, which is greater than any envisaged outcome under Option 1.

Other factors

If TechScan uses Ursa technology under licence its R&D function may diminish and lose capability to engage in future R&D projects (see above)

Also, If TechScan uses Ursa technology under licence then it becomes dependent on another company which is a rival and on the terms of the licence agreement. Thus, for instance, the opportunity to export may unexpectedly arise over the next five years but TechScan would not be able to exploit this under licensing, as it only has UK rights, whereas it could export with its own R&D where it owns the intellectual property.

There is a risk that the licensing payments may vary. It is possible they are fixed in US$ terms but exchange rate fluctuation may alter their value in sterling.

It may be more difficult to legally enforce UK exclusivity under the licensing agreement than would be the case under a patent for a product that has been developed internally.

It is possible there are internal behavioural issues which could create untoward optimism for the internal R&D under Option 1. This may mean that the probability of success of the R&D project may have been exaggerated. A degree of professional scepticism should therefore be applied to these probabilities until there is supporting objective evidence.

If the R&D project is successful it may be possible to gain revenue from licensing it out to rival companies in other countries.

Conclusion

If there is reasonable confidence that the probabilities provided are reliable estimates which have been objectively determined, then there is a strong case for Option 1 and thereby retaining the core competence of R&D and control over the intellectual property rights to the technology. It also has the higher expected value.

If the R&D project fails, the licence can still be accessed from Ursa Inc at the same cost, but £45 million in initial R&D will have been wasted. The wider financial strength of the company to withstand such a financial loss needs to be ascertained.

Examiner's comments

Most candidates calculated the expected NPV for Option 2 correctly. Common errors for Option 1 included selecting a zero NPV if the R&D project failed, rather than reverting to licensing. The most common incorrect answers for the ENPV of Option 1 were £80 million and £30 million. A small minority ignored expected values altogether in their calculations. Other errors included multiplying the NPV figures by 5 years.

In their narrative, some made use of real options terminology and concepts to enhance their analysis. Very few considered the limitations of expected values or questioned the validity of the probabilities provided. Whilst most candidates mentioned risk, far fewer spelt out the nature of the risks in using the numbers in the scenario and the limitations of expected values in this context. Consideration of other relevant factors tended to focus on keeping the option open for future R&D developments via Option 1 and thereby preserving the firm's core competences, although it was often not expressed in these terms.

34 Guayaporto Ltd (September 2016)

Marking guide

	Knowledge	Skill	Marks
34.1 Scenario planning	2	5	7
34.2 Data analysis	2	18	18
34.3 Data sharing	2	5	7
34.4 Proposals	4	10	12
	10	38	44

34.1 Scenario planning

Scenario planning is useful in providing a long-term view of strategy, where a few key factors may influence success. In the face of a changing industry environment, organisations can choose to do nothing, continue to make short-term forecasts or use scenario planning to consider potentially substantial shifts in the industry and its environment.

Technology has already radically changed the market for discs and this appears to be affecting GPT's results. The company is now operating below capacity.

A key question for GPT is where the disc industry will be in 5-10 years' time.

Using scenario planning GPT would attempt to consider possible future situations (favourable or unfavourable) that may occur – 'what if?' – and how these might impact on its business – 'what is the effect of?'. Consideration of these changes will help GPT determine how it can achieve a sustainable business model for the future.

The success of GPT's business depends ultimately on the demand for discs from the entertainment and education sectors. Possible scenarios to consider could be as follows:

- A reduced but ongoing demand from certain markets for discs (either geographically or based on end use)

- Complete cessation of demand for all discs as they are replaced by alternative technologies

In assessing the impact of these different scenarios GPT needs to consider the whole supply chain of which it is a part. This will include asking what will film and music producers do faced with this future, and what might competitors do?

This type of scenario planning would give general rather than precise answers because of the uncertainties involved, but might allow GPT to anticipate changes, develop contingency plans and perhaps respond earlier than some of its competitors.

Options might include the following:

- Becoming more of a niche business, servicing markets where demand remains eg, gaming

- Offering a range of complementary services eg, digital printing

- Abandoning discs and moving into a new business area/sector

- Selling the business whilst there is still some value in it

Examiner's comments

Answers to this requirement were generally disappointing.

Only a minority of candidates demonstrated a clear understanding of the nature of scenario planning. Weaker candidates failed to address the key issue of the fundamental uncertainty regarding the long-term direction of the industry. Many answers confused scenario planning with a company's normal strategic planning process and produced a PESTEL analysis. Others discussed how GPT could undertake sensitivity analysis/simulation to help evaluate the risk of the two strategies being proposed.

34.2 Data analysis

Tutorial note

The requirement asked candidates to quantify the financial impact of each of the factors that have caused the decline in performance. This analysis could have been undertaken in a variety of ways. A possible approach is shown below.

Calculation are shown in the appendix:

Analysis of the differences in profit	francs
Refer to figures in (W) for 20X4 results adjusted for impact of volume change:	
Impact of reduction in sales volume on gross profit:	(451,205)
(1,563,330 actual 20X4 – 1,112,125 revised)	
Increased selling price	210,000
(2,205,000 – 1,995,000)	
Increased cost of master-disc (525,000 – 284,375)	
This may be sub analysed:	
Due to exchange rate movement:	(240,625)
1,050,000/1,000 × (500 – 325) = 183,750	
Due to smaller order size	
((1,050,000/1,200) – (1,050,000/1,000)) × 325 = 56,875	
Increase in other production costs	(31,500)
(630,000 – 598,500)	
Reduction in overheads	146,400
(835,000 – 981,400)	
Net movement in profit	(366,930)
(Check: 215,000 – 581,930)	

Other more standard performance evaluation calculations:

	20X5	20X4
Gross profit margin	47.62%	55.75%
Operating profit margin	9.75%	20.75%
Selling price per disc	f2.10	$1.90
Other production costs/disc	f0.60	$0.57
Cost/Master-disc in francs	f500	f325

% change in

	%
Sales	–21.4
Master-disc (cost of sales)	+31.3
Other production costs	–25.1
Gross profit	–32.8
Admin and distribution overheads	–14.9
Operating profit	–63.1
Volume of discs sold	–28.9
Other size	–16.7
Number of orders	–14.6
Exchange rate	–53.8
Selling price per disc	+10.5
Other production costs per disc	+5.3
Local cost of Master-disc	+53.8

Working	20X5 (based on 1,050,000 disks) francs	20X4 (adjusted, based on 1,050,000 discs) francs	Working
Sales	2,205,000	1,995,000	(1,050,000 × $1.90)
Cost of sales:			
Master-Discs	525,000	284,375	(1,050,000/1,200 × $325)
Other production costs	630,000	598,500	1,050,000 × 0.57
	1,155,000	882,875	
Gross profit	1,050,000	1,112,125	
Overheads	835,000	981,400	
Operating profit	215,000	130,725	

Commentary

During the year profit has fallen by f366,930 (63%). Gross profit margin has fallen from 55.75% to 47.62% and operating margin has fallen from 20.75% to 9.75%. The decline in profit is a result of a variety of different factors which are analysed below:

Sales

In total sales have fallen by 21.4%.

The biggest impact has been the decline in sales volume, leading to a loss in profit of f451,205. Sales volumes have fallen 28.9% by 426,000 discs which reflects the decline in industry demand and is largely due to external market factors. The number of orders placed has declined by 14.6% and customers appear to be ordering fewer discs, since the average order size has fallen by 16.7% from 1,200 discs per order to 1,000. Demand may also have been affected by customers being unhappy with delays or errors caused by manual packaging.

GPT Ltd has addressed some of the sales shortfall by increasing the price per disc from f1.90 to f2.10, leading to an overall increase in profit of f210,000. This may have been an attempt to pass on to the customer some of the increase in the cost of the master-disc or the other production costs (see below). However it is not clear whether, as a result of this price increase, customers have gone to competitors or have reduced their order volumes. Thus some of the decline in sales volume may be a result of the increase in price.

Cost of sales

A key component of cost of sales is the master-disc. The increase here has caused a profit shortfall of f240,625.

Two factors are at play:

The smaller order sizes being placed by customers has led to the need to buy more master-discs (had the order size remained at 1,200 then only 875 master-discs would have been required in 20X5 (1,050,000/1,200). This has cost an additional f56,875.

The exchange rate has depreciated significantly during the year (by 53.8%) and as a result despite the fact that the supplier has kept Asian dollar prices constant, the imported master-discs have cost an additional f183,750.

In addition other production costs have increased from f0.57 to f0.60 per disc causing an overall drop in profit of f31,500. Some of this has been recouped via the increase in selling price. This could reflect increased costs for polycarbonate, printing materials or labour rates/productivity – more information is needed to confirm this.

Overheads

These appear to have been well controlled with the effect that costs have reduced (and hence profit increased) by f146,400.

However, the machines are not working at anywhere near capacity. GPT is capable of processing 45,000 discs per week which on a 50 week year is 2,250,000 discs. Thus in 20X5 it had spare capacity of 1,200,000 discs, and is operating at 46.7% of capacity. As a result GPT will not be benefitting from economies of scale. The company needs to address this if it is to improve profitability.

Further information

Additional information that would be useful includes the following:

- A breakdown of sales and gross profit by customer and type of disc to ascertain whether some products/jobs are more profitable than others

- Competitor prices to compare with GPT

- A breakdown of overheads to assess whether there are any discretionary elements that could be cut further

- The extent to which GPT has hedged the exchange rate movements

- A forecast of market demand and exchange rates for 20X6/20X7

Conclusion

The company is in a declining market which has resulted in demand falling significantly. In addition a depreciating currency has caused the cost of importing master-discs to increase. GPT is now operating below 50% capacity and unless the company can find alternative sources of demand, its results are likely to deteriorate further.

Examiner's comments

Candidates scored reasonably well here although very few candidates fully addressed the requirement. The majority of candidates included an initial table (or an appendix) of data calculations. Most candidates were comfortable undertaking a straightforward analysis of the financial and operating data provided and discussing the causes of the decline in performance. However an extremely small minority properly answered the requirement by quantifying the financial impact of each cause separately. As a result very few candidates scored full marks on this requirement.

34.3 Data sharing

GPT Ltd is party to confidential data files which it receives from its customers and then shares in the course of its supply chain with the Asian manufacturer of the master-disc. This information may be valuable and sensitive and GPT has a contractual obligation to protect the data from unauthorised modification, disclosure or destruction.

However, once it is shared by GPT, direct control of the data files is lost. This leads to an increased risk of their confidentiality, integrity or availability being compromised.

The data files from the customer also qualify for intellectual property rights so there is some element of legal obligation for GPT to consider.

The risk of data loss or misuse occurs at various stages in GPT's process:

- The information is transferred from the customer to GPT
- GPT shares the information with the disc supplier
- The master-disc containing the information is returned to GPT
- The master is replicated and many copies of the information are made

GPT needs to ensure appropriate security measures are in place to protect the data at each stage and to prevent theft of IP, since confidential data files are only valuable if stored in an accessible form and then disclosed to others.

From customer to GPT

Make sure communication of confidential information is by secure means.

Asian supplier

Use of a single master-disc supplier reduces the risk as information is only shared with one party. GPT needs to assess the information risk in relation to the contract with the Asian supplier. It should assess the probability and impact of a potential breach and undertake assurance around controls at the supplier.

GPT should ensure there are controls in its outsourcing agreement that place specific confidentiality obligations on the recipient of the confidential data before it is disclosed. With respect to particularly valuable data files, express prior agreement to such obligations could be gained (eg, by the return of a signed confidentiality letter).

Finally it is important that the master-disc is returned via secure means and that appropriate contracts are in place with the secure courier.

At GPT

Employees

Employees automatically have duties to their employer to not knowingly misuse or wrongfully disclose confidential information. These obligations are also often expressly confirmed in their employment contracts.

GPT should only disclose confidential information to employees or third parties where reasonably necessary, and it should ensure that recipients of confidential information know that it should be treated as such, imposing express confidentiality obligations wherever possible.

Processes

GPT should ensure master-discs are kept secure whilst in use and are destroyed or returned to the customer, as agreed, after replication has finished.

It should also ensure there is no breach of intellectual property rights such as copyright eg, using information from the customer to print for other customers (see below).

GPT needs to ensure that the replicated discs do not fall into the wrong hands (eg, theft by staff). It also needs to ensure that wasted or spoilt discs produced are disposed of securely, especially those where the disc is playable but has been rejected for errors in printing or packaging.

Examiner's comments

This was generally well answered with most candidates scoring well. The problems of sharing confidential data with the Asian supplier and the IT risks involved were well considered. Most candidates made some sensible suggestions as to how these issues might be addressed. Better answers recognised GPT's legal and contractual obligations in respect of confidentiality and clients' intellectual property, and extended their discussion to encompass these issues at all stages in the supply chain. A number of candidates referred to the 3Rs of supply chain management (responsiveness, reliability and relationships) in their answer.

34.4 Packaging strategy (production director)

Advantages:

- Automation may reduce packaging costs and increase margins.

- Improved efficiency may lead to faster processing of customer orders and increased customer satisfaction.

- A new machine may reduce error rates and wastage.

- This would increase GPT's processing capacity and may reduce bottlenecks.

- The new machine is likely to be able to cope with higher volume runs.

Disadvantages:

- GPT are not operating at full capacity (see above) – it appears the number and volume of orders rather than the manual packaging process is the factor that is restricting production.

- If demand for discs is declining there may be no point in increasing capacity.

- Investment may require significant capital expenditure and GPT may not be able to access sufficient funds in future.

- Automation may convert variable costs (labour) into fixed cost (machine) and hence increase operating gearing.

- Manual packaging may have given scope to fulfil bespoke customer demands; this service will now be lost.

- Automation will result in redundancies which will incur costs.

- The change of strategy may be negatively received by the remaining workforce (change management issues).

- Redundancies will affect jobs and livelihoods – historically GPT have wanted to support the community and this goes against their previous stance on corporate responsibility.

- Adverse publicity regarding redundancies and job cuts is likely to damage GPT's reputation in the local community.

- Automation will require training and could lead to some downtime during installation and commissioning.

Alternative revenue streams (sales director)

Advantages:

- Since the market is declining, GPT needs alternative revenue streams if it is to survive.

- According to Ansoff, this can be achieved by considering new markets and/or new products.

- There may be other markets where the industry lifecycle is at a different point and has not yet reached the decline stage.

- New revenue streams will give rise to a more balanced product portfolio and diversify risk.

- The education market may represent one of the areas where demand for discs is declining more slowly.

- The Alegre proposal specifically would generate incremental contribution and utilise some spare capacity.

- GPT could explore the possibility of producing own-brand versions by licensing IP from educational businesses.

Disadvantages:

- The IP for the Alegre revision guides does not belong to GPT but to Alegre.

- In theory the Alegre master-disc should have already been destroyed according to the contract which would prevent GPT producing the guides.

- If Alegre were to find out they might stop using GPT and sue for breach of contract/use of IP.

- This specific strategy is not ethical and could also be illegal.

- It may damage GPT's brand and reputation in the marketplace.

- GPT may lack the necessary competencies/experience, particularly for a diversification strategy that involves new products and new markets.

Conclusion

Whilst the purchase of the new machine might improve efficiency and reduce costs it does not address GPT's main issue which is that of lack of demand. The sales director is correct that GPT needs to consider alternative revenue streams. Whilst it does appear that GPT needs to do this to survive, the specific suggestion does not appear to be ethical and should be rejected. Further research needs to be done to establish where demand for discs is likely to remain and GPT should then target these markets.

Examiner's comments

Answers to this requirement were mixed. Often candidates produced a good evaluation of one proposal at the expense of the other. Many candidates identified that GPT were already operating significantly below capacity and that the production director's suggestion, as well as creating reputational and change management issues, would not help to address this. However it was surprising how many candidates failed to spot the ethical and possible legal issues associated with the specific proposal to re-use Alegre's master-disc. Only the better candidates extended their discussion to consider the sales director's suggestion of other possible revenue streams.

35 MHD (September 2016, amended)

Marking guide

	Knowledge	Skill	Marks
35.1 Governance procedures	3	6	8
35.2 Sustainability	2	4	6
35.3 Monitoring performance	3	7	9
35.4 Ethical issues	3	6	8
	11	23	31

35.1 Governance

As a charity, MHD can be considered a not-for-profit organisation (NFP). The Nolan principles set out seven standards for public sector governance which the trustees need to take into account: (selflessness, integrity, objectivity, accountability, openness, honesty and leadership). Some of these are discussed further below.

Governance is a term used to describe the trustees' role in directing the charity in the long term, including its objectives or purposes, implementing policies and activities to achieve objectives and complying with legal requirements.

The following are the main issues that MHD need to be concerned about in respect of governance:

Stakeholders and public interest

When MHD sets objectives it must balance the interests and concerns of a wide range of stakeholders, which may conflict. This may result in a range of objectives, rather than a single over-riding one. Given that MHD is accountable to a wide range of stakeholders, the trustees need to consider to what extent they are legally obliged to involve stakeholders in the objective-setting process.

The trustees' role is one of leadership. They must act in the interests of the charity's beneficiaries, but this may not always coincide with the priorities of the board and the management team or the wishes of any corporate sponsors.

Financial solvency

Whilst MHD may not have a pure profit-making objective, it will need to ensure that it has sufficient funds to cover its costs. In addition to its stated aims of providing services and support for a range of people experiencing mental health issues, MHD's trustees will need to try and derive maximum benefit from a limited amount of resources whilst remaining solvent.

Accountability and openness

This is fundamental to the corporate governance of the charity with regard to the proper stewardship of public and donated funds.

The trustees of MHD should be as open and honest as possible about the decisions and actions that they take. They should give reasons for their decisions and restrict information only when the wider public interest clearly demands.

MHD's Board must be prepared to submit to an appropriate level of scrutiny. This will lessen any risk of being accused of acting improperly. Vishal's comment about not upsetting the trustees suggests that there may not be a culture where the trustees can be challenged.

Actions/interests of the board

Board members must take decisions in line with the objectives of the charity and in the interests of its beneficiaries. They should not do so to gain financial or other material benefits for themselves, their family or their friends. Nor should they place themselves under any financial or other obligation to outside individuals or organisations that might influence them in the performance of their duties.

Those trustees whose companies have donated funds should not be allowed to dominate or unduly influence the decision-making.

The board should ensure that they have complied with the principles set out above regarding openness, honesty and selflessness.

Composition of Board

Whilst some stability may be helpful it appears that the current trustees have all been in situ for a while and are very comfortable working with each other. Vishal's point about the meetings being easy to manage and decisions being made quickly may not necessarily be a good thing. The familiarity among the trustees may have led to a lack of pro-activity and the close relationships may make people reluctant to challenge mismanagement for fear of upsetting friends/peers. Also failure to appoint new trustees means that MHD does not have an effective succession plan. The introduction of some new trustees with a wider range of commercial experience may, as Jennifer suggests, bring fresh thinking from different sectors to assist the charity and achieve sustainability going forward.

Risk management

Charities can face a wide variety of risks which could negatively affect their beneficiaries if not dealt with properly. A risk is any event that could prevent MHD from achieving its aims or carrying out its strategies. Risks for MHD include:

- possible damage to the charity's reputation
- receiving less funding or fewer public donations
- changes in government policy affecting income or activities

The trustees have ultimate responsibility for managing risk but in practice this is often delegated to the management team.

John Adams is incorrect when he says that the management team needs to avoid risk at all costs. Risk management requires the trustees/management to identify any potential risks and put processes in place to assess and manage those risks. Risk avoidance is one such strategy but risks can also be transferred (eg, by insurance), reduced (eg, by widening the sources of funds) or accepted.

Conclusion

The resignation of the previous CFO may suggest that there have been some governance issues or problems between the management and trustees in the past. MHD is in a difficult situation financially and is facing possible ethical issues so implementing more robust governance procedures may help address this.

Examiner's comments

On the whole the governance requirement was well done. There were plenty of points to build on in the scenario regarding the composition of the board of trustees, risk management and MHD's financial problems. Poorer efforts tended to overlook the nature of MHD as a charitable organisation or simply reiterated the views expressed at the meeting without further analysis of the implications for MHD's achievement of objectives.

35.2 Sustainability

A sustainable enterprise is one that takes account of social and environmental returns as well as financial ones. A sustainable organisation is one that has a long-term orientation and does not just focus on short-term results and measures when making decisions.

Financial sustainability:

To survive in the long term MHD needs to be financially sustainable and financial solvency is therefore a key issue in relation to risk mitigation.

Given the low reserves, MHD will only be sustainable if it has the ability to retain existing grants/sponsors and attract new funding. The better its reputation, the more successful its activities, and the more relevant it is to a wide range of people, the greater its chances of success. The development of some income-generating services that still meet its core mission might help contribute to the development of a diverse and sustainable funding base.

Social and environmental sustainability:

As a non-profit making enterprise, MHD's objectives will be wider than just financial and its goals will be externally as well as internally focused. This will include taking account of wider stakeholders' objectives and meeting the needs of the mental health sufferers it is serving.

A socially sustainable organisation is one where decision making is linked to respect for people, communities and the environment. The nature of MHD's activities would suggest it is socially sustainable and the research it undertakes is a forward-looking activity. However MHD has a responsibility to continue to provide services to those who are depending on it. This responsibility can only be fulfilled if it is financially sustainable.

In the context of environmental sustainability, an organisation should only use resources at a rate that allows them to be replenished in order to ensure they will continue to be available. There is little information about the extent to which MHD is environmentally sustainable.

Conclusion

With low reserves and concerns about the management of the organisation it is questionable whether MHD is currently a financially sustainable organisation. This is a problem given the needs of the beneficiaries it serves and the fact that, should the charity become insolvent, a lot of people would be left without services and many people would lose their jobs.

Jennifer is right that MHD needs to address its financial situation as soon as possible.

Examiner's comments

Candidates seemed well prepared for a requirement on this topic. The vast majority of candidates had no problem defining sustainability in a general sense. Better candidates were able to apply this to the scenario, discussing what sustainability means for MHD and identifying that unless the charity addresses its financial issues it will not be able to sustain the provision of mental health services in the future.

35.3 Monitoring performance

The board needs to implement an effective system of performance measurement as this will demonstrate to external stakeholders that MHD's mandates and objectives are being met. It may, as Jennifer says, help MHD raise more funds. However the system for measuring must not be so complicated that implementing it is prohibitively expensive.

Key performance indicators need to be established, targets set, and actual performance measured and monitored for each of those indicators, possibly in relation to other charities engaged in similar activities.

However:

(1) There is no profit motive objective so many of the traditional financial performance indicators cannot be applied.

(2) Since MHD is a large mental health charity, it may be difficult to find other, similar organisations that can be used as benchmarks for assessing MHD's performance.

Value for money is a measure often applied in the public sector. This could be used to assess whether MHD is providing an economic, efficient and effective service.

Economy – an input measure. Are the resources the cheapest possible for the quality of service desired? Eg, cost of staff in residential settings

Efficiency – Is the maximum output being achieved from the resources used? Eg, £ of funds raised per £ spent on marketing

Effectiveness – an output measure, looking at whether MHD's objectives are being met. Eg, number of new research projects undertaken

Balanced scorecard

A significant number of MHD's objectives are likely to be of a non-financial nature and as a result the balanced scorecard approach to performance measurement is likely to be particularly relevant.

The BSC approach looks at four perspectives in order to provide operational control so that the organisation's mission and objectives can be met. These perspectives are financial, customer, internal processes, and learning and growth. They are balanced in the sense that managers are required to think in terms of all four perspectives to prevent improvements being made in one area at the expense of another. MHD can identify critical success factors in each of these areas, set targets for achievement and implement KPIs to measure this. These could also take into account any government performance targets.

Financial perspective

Here the financial perspective will be in terms of economy and efficiency: allowing the available resources to be put to best use to add value to beneficiaries, providing value for money for the fund providers.

Appropriate KPIs include the following:

- Average donations
- Growth in funds raised year-on-year
- Costs of providing individual services
- Cost control of care centres (residential and day)
- Level of marketing spend

Customer perspective

A not-for-profit organisation such as MHD needs to know what its users and beneficiaries feel about its services. MHD aims to provide a range of services and fund research.

Appropriate KPIs include the following:

- Service user satisfaction statistics
- Increase in number of service users and/or areas covered by MHD
- Number of research projects funded
- Hours of mental health services provided
- Waiting list of users requiring services
- Ranking in government or local authority performance tables
- Performance in inspections carried out by regulators

Internal business process perspective

This perspective asks what processes MHD must excel at to achieve its financial and customer objectives. It aims to improve internal processes and decision making.

MHD must assess how it goes about delivering its services and what impact this has on its effectiveness.

Appropriate KPIs include the following:

- Number of service users catered for
- Percentage of revenue spent on administration
- Percentage of revenue that is spent on the publicised cause
- Number of marketing/fund-raising events held
- Number of services offered eg, counselling, workshops
- Ratio of paid staff/volunteers

Learning and growth perspective

This considers MHD's capacity to maintain and grow its position through the acquisition of new skills and the development of new services.

MHD will benefit from learning from the past (both successes and failures), to enable processes to improve over time leading to improved user satisfaction.

Jennifer is keen to attract new funding and develop services, so this is a key perspective for MHD.

Appropriate KPIs include the following:

- Number of new services implemented by MHD
- Amount of training undertaken by staff
- New funding sources identified

The introduction of a new performance measurement system may create fear and uncertainty among staff since it raises their visibility and accountability. It will be important to implement an appropriate programme of consultation, communication and training.

Examiner's comments

Although performance measurement and KPIs are a mainstream topic it is surprising how often requirements such as this one are poorly done. There were two elements to this requirement: explaining an approach to performance measurement and suggesting some specific KPIs. A reasonable proportion of candidates overlooked the former, limiting the marks available.

Most candidates identified the need for non-financial KPIs and many predictably used the Balance Scorecard. However candidates often failed to explain what each area would be measuring in the context of MHD. Weaker candidates produced a bullet list of quite generic KPIs – the better answers identified critical success factors under each balanced scorecard heading and linked their KPIs to these.

35.4 Ethical issues

A key risk for MHD as a result of the newspaper article is that the charity may suffer long-term loss of credibility with fund-providers and volunteers who trust MHD to use their money or time effectively in support of its cause.

The first step in assessing the implications would be to assess the extent to which the newspaper article is based on fact and the criticisms levied at MHD are valid.

High salary packages

Assuming the charity has indeed given substantial pay increases, the issue here is potentially one of integrity and self-interest and links to the governance discussion raised earlier.

It is not unethical for charities to pay their staff or to give them pay-rises. Employees of MHD, as any other organisation, are entitled to be paid a fair wage for the work that they do.

In order to attract an appropriately qualified and competent chief executive MHD needs to offer a sufficient salary that is commensurate with the complexities of the job. This may have to be at a certain level to attract relevant candidates from the private sector (or to prevent staff leaving to join the private sector).

However it may be unethical for senior staff to be given large pay-rises if this is at the expense of providing more services or reimbursing expenses to volunteers. This is particularly true if they have not earned the pay rises or are deciding on the salaries themselves. The pay rises also come at a time when the charity appears to be struggling financially.

It is important that the chief executive and management team's salaries are set independently and that they are appraised on the extent to which the charity's performance and financial position has improved.

MHD needs to ensure that:

- it is transparent about amounts paid to senior staff

- all senior staff salaries are approved by the board of trustees

- salary scales are benchmarked against other sectors

- information is provided to all stakeholders about the charity's financial position and performance

Fundraising

All charities rely on donations to provide services and the more funds MHD is able to raise, the more services it can offer.

Key ethical issues are:

(1) the cost of marketing and fund-raising activities
(2) the amount of donations spent on the end-cause.

A specific issue here is that FFY are being paid commission according to how much money they raise. This type of pricing agreement is common in the private sector and it could be argued that here it is a good thing, since it is likely to raise more money for MHD.

However this type of approach may be unethical for reasons such as these:

- The charitable element may come second to personal gain so the interests of fund-providers and service users may suffer

- FFY staff may lack involvement and interest in MHD's purpose

- FFY may use excessive pressure on potential donors to maximise their own payment

In addition, as a result of behaviour or pressure from FFY, potential donors may become disillusioned and lose faith in the charitable cause, ceasing to support MHD in future and withdrawing their permission for MHD to use their personal data to contact them. Since it is in need of additional funding to ensure sustainability, this could present a major problem.

MHD should require any professional fund-raiser to comply with the highest legal and ethical standards eg, accurately describing the charity's work and the intended uses of the funds, not being overly aggressive or applying undue pressure to potential donors, being honest about whether the fund-raiser will benefit personally from any funds raised, and to what extent.

MHD should also be fully transparent by reporting on the percentage of income spent on raising funds and administration. It will need to ensure that donations are used to support the published purposes of the charity and are in line with the purpose for which they are solicited.

Examiner's comments

Overall the use of ethical language and principles was not as comprehensive as in previous sittings with weaker candidates simply discussing the issues raised by the newspaper in terms of their likely impact on the charity's reputation and ability to raise funds in future. A number of candidates adopted the transparency, effect, and fairness structure but only the better answers went beyond this TEF framework to discuss any other ethical principles, such as the self-interest of the management team in taking large pay-rises. A surprisingly small number demonstrated professional scepticism with regard to the factual accuracy of the claims made by the newspaper. Some marginal candidates limited their discussion to that of management pay and failed to consider the issue of the aggressive fund-raising altogether.

36 Thistle Engineering Services Ltd (September 2016)

Marking guide

	Knowledge	Skill	Marks
36.1 Risks and mitigating factors	1	7	8
36.2 Forecasts	2	10	10
36.3 Structure of venture	2	6	7
	5	23	25

Business Plan for UK Bank

Subject: Proposed Maltese Base
Prepared by: Thistle Engineering Services Ltd
Date: September 20X6

36.1 Risks and mitigants

The bank is likely to want to understand the key risks facing Thistle which will affect the profitability of the proposed venture and the ability of the business as a whole to service debt. Where possible Thistle should provide details of mitigating factors which will reassure the bank that the risks can be monitored and managed.

The risks and potential mitigants that should be covered in this section include the following:

- **Management team**

  A key risk is the fact that the management team at Thistle is small and only experienced in UK operations. International expansion is likely to take up a significant amount of their time and attention which may result in a lack of focus on existing activities. The business is heavily dependent on Joshua's knowledge, experience and contacts, though even without the expansion this may be a problem.

Mitigants: given Joshua's age, a succession plan is required to reassure the bank. Tom has good sector experience and has worked in the business for many years. Joshua and Tom could divide up the roles (UK/International) between them and develop a management team underneath them to take responsibility for the day-to-day operations.

- **Uncertainty of demand**

A lack of demand beyond Romiou's current scheme would make the venture unsustainable. There is also a risk that even Romiou's proposed exploratory drilling does not prove to be as successful as expected.

Mitigants: the bank will want to see details of industry research and results of any exploratory drilling. The fact that Romiou has suggested a contract indicates the existence of gas may now be confirmed rather than speculative.

- **Competition**

Thistle is likely to face competition from much bigger global engineering and construction companies and may not win tenders for other contracts relating to gas extraction in the Mediterranean. It is not clear if Thistle has experience of the production and installation of under-sea pipelines, or of international tenders.

Mitigants: initial contract with Romiou provides a good base from which to expand the business. Also a number of Thistle's existing customers are multi-national businesses so there may be scope to get contracts from them. Using the Romiou contract, Thistle will be able to establish first mover advantage in the Mediterranean area.

The patented pipe-wrapping system is a differentiator although this is more relevant to repairs and maintenance and may not apply to the construction of new pipelines.

Thistle is certified as compliant with global oil and gas regulatory standards and is an industry leader in environmental aspects which should act as a barrier to entry for others.

- **Supply chain**

It is not clear whether the intention is to manufacture steelwork overseas or to continue to manufacture in the UK and ship abroad. If manufacture is to take place in the UK then the plan needs to consider capacity and ability/costs to ship overseas. Currently all suppliers are based in the UK. The expansion to production overseas is likely to require the development of new supply chain relationships.

Mitigants: some existing suppliers may be able to provide additional capacity for overseas expansion, particularly if they already supply internationally.

- **Labour force**

The project will require new staff and the availability of competent qualified engineers for installation will be a critical success factor.

Mitigants: staff may need to be seconded or transferred from the UK to support those recruited locally. The use of local engineers may reduce any language and cultural barriers.

- **Exchange rate issues**

All business is currently conducted in the UK from both a sales and supply chain point of view. International expansion will bring exchange rate risk which Anya may not have experience of.

Mitigants:

- Hedging strategies can be adopted to manage the exchange rate risk.

- Agreeing prices in the local currency may be a better strategy if costs are to be incurred locally.

- Alternatively if manufacturing is to be done in the UK, using UK suppliers, then pricing in £ may be more appropriate.

- **Health and safety risks**

  A key issue for the industry is poor H&S performance which could result in fatalities or environmental damage. Health and safety/environmental standards in the Mediterranean may be different from those in the UK.

  Mitigants: Thistle is certified as compliant with global oil and gas regulatory standards and is an industry leader in environmental aspects.

- **Financial risks**

  The new venture entails additional borrowing and will increase the financial gearing of the company.

  Mitigants: The UK business has a good track record and comfortable interest cover (8.5 times) which reduces the risk of Thistle not being able to service the debt.

Further information required:

- Evidence of any market research undertaken by Thistle
- Results of any exploratory drilling
- Details of contracts with Romiou or other potential customers
- Details of existing loan finance and repayment terms
- Further information on key staff members
- Details on existing and potential new suppliers

Examiner's comments

This was reasonably well answered. Most candidates identified a good range of risks associated with the new venture. However weaker candidates failed to set out factors that might demonstrate to the bank how these risks could be mitigated.

36.2 Forecasts

> **Tutorial note**
>
> The requirement asked candidates to consider the sensitivity of forecasts. This could have been done in a number of ways. Some possible calculations are shown below but candidates who attempted other sensible versions of a 'what-if' calculation were given credit.

The bank will want to understand Thistle's ability to afford the debt. This may in part depend on whether the new venture is likely to provide sufficient funds to service any debt, although the loan is to the company rather than the project so if the project fails but the company is sound, the bank will probably still get paid. Thistle will want to consider whether the numbers are accurate and have been based on credible assumptions and how sensitive the forecasts are to changes in key variables and to the timing of sales.

As well as providing a commentary on the expected level of profits, forecasts should give an indication of the best and worst case scenario.

Analysis of forecasts:

Appendix:

	Year 1 £'000	Year 2 £'000	Year 3 £'000	Total £'000
Sales	633	1,266	1,582	3,481
Sales growth		100%	25%	
Gross profit	190	443	634	1,267
Gross margin	30.0%	35.0%	40.1%	36.4%
Fixed costs	310	335	365	1010
Operating (loss)/profit	(120)	108	269	257
Operating margin	(19.0)%	8.5%	17.0%	7.4%
Annualised ROCE [(257 × 1/3)/425)]				20.2%
Sensitivity:				
Breakeven sales (£'000)	1,033	957	910	2,775
Margin of safety	(63.2)%	24.4%	42.5%	20.3%
GP margin required to breakeven (FC/Sales)	49.0%	26.5%	23.1%	29.0%
% change in fixed costs to achieve breakeven in Y1	(38.7)%			

Commentary:

Sales

Year 1 sales are based on the contract with Romiou.

Sales are expected to double in Year 2 as presumably new contracts are won and growth is expected to slow in Year 3. Average annual sales are £1,160k over the period which means the overseas venture would represent 17.6% of UK sales.

Gross profit

Gross margin has been assumed at 30% which is similar to the UK margin (30.6%). This is forecast to grow in Year 2 and 3 due to economies of scale. The average GP margin required to breakeven over the life of the project is 29%.

Fixed costs

Fixed costs are expected to increase over the period reflecting the steps in activity level.

At the assumed margin, the breakeven sales for the three year period are £2,775k – giving a margin of safety of 20%

Return on Capital employed

Over three years the expansion project is expected to make an annualised return on investment of 20.2% compared to a return on existing activities of 22.5%. At a cost of £425k, the investment is likely to have paid back after 4 years.

Further information that may be required:

- Sight of the contract or letter of intent from Romiou

- List of assumptions made by Anya when creating the forecast, including assumptions re exchange rates

- A more detailed breakdown of fixed costs

- Market research and other evidence confirming the likelihood of other potential customers

Weaker candidates either produced a narrative analysis of the forecasts with few supporting numbers or alternatively focussed on calculations without appropriate discussion. Only a minority of candidates considered the sensitivity of the forecasts, despite a specific requirement to do so. This could have been done in a variety of ways and candidates who attempted some form of 'what if' analysis scored well. Whilst candidates have become well practised at data analysis in the context of performance appraisal, in BST they are expected to be able to undertake data analysis in a variety of forms. Candidates seem less comfortable with requirements that involve the analysis of management accounting type data. They need to develop the ability to analyse and challenge budgetary assumptions and to sensitise forecasts.

36.3 Structure of venture

The bank will want to ensure that the business is structured in such a way as to minimise the risks involved and to allow the performance of the new business to be monitored effectively by management. It may also want reassurance that the new venture will not adversely affect UK operations.

Various options exist for the new business.

(1) Run as a one-off project within Thistle
(2) Set up an overseas division of Thistle
(3) Set up a separate company (subsidiary)

If long-term demand is expected, a further consideration which will influence structure is whether to set up a manufacturing operation overseas or manufacture all steel/pipework in the UK and distribute from there.

Since it appears that the expansion is to consist of more than just the initial project, setting up a division or subsidiary is probably a better option.

A division may have less autonomy than a subsidiary but may be more appropriate if the manufacturing is to remain in the UK. In which case issues of transfer pricing and the recharging of central costs will need to be considered.

If manufacturing is to be undertaken locally then the new business may be better as a subsidiary, fully accountable for its own results and with the freedom to make its own decisions and create its own culture. Management and employees may also be more motivated under this structure as there may be less scope for the dysfunctional decisions that sometimes occur in assessing divisional performance.

Whatever structure is chosen the business will need additional administrative support in relation to:

- financial controls
- hedging of overseas transactions

The choice may depend on the size of operations initially. To start with it may be sensible to operate the new venture as a division then expand to a subsidiary if more contracts are forthcoming. By evolving the venture in this way, Thistle retains flexibility and reduces risk.

Other considerations that might influence the choice of structure may include local tax, local regulations, the ability to raise funds in future.

Further information that may be required:

- Exact nature of the proposed base (eg, will it involve construction as well as the provision of services)
- CVs of the existing management team and other key members of staff who may be involved in the venture
- Details of likely staffing requirements in Malta

Examiner's comments

This requirement was generally well answered. Most candidates suggested some form of divisionalised structure for the new venture and discussed the need for local knowledge and input in deciding the degree to which decisions should be decentralised. Better candidates discussed the impact that the choice of structure could have on risk. In their narrative, some made use of real options terminology and concepts to enhance their analysis, recognising that the expansion may be phased over time and that initial choices could be made to provide more flexibility as the market develops.

37 Pinter Shipping Panels Ltd (December 2016)

Marking guide

	Knowledge	Skill	Marks
37.1 Data analysis	3	17	18
37.2 Sourcing steel	4	11	13
37.3 Procurement	3	8	9
	10	36	40

37.1

	20X5			20X6					
	Tinner	FMC	Total	Tinner	FMC	Total	Tinner % change	FMC % change	Total % change
Steel cost per tonne	300	300	300	150	150	150	(50.0)	(50.0)	(50.0)
Tonnes (000s)	30	20	50	26	22	48	(13.3)	10.0	(4.0)
Panels (000s)	120	80	200	104	88	192	(13.3)	10.0	(4.0)
Price per panel	200	205		180	190		(10.0)	(7.3)	
Steel cost per panel	75	75		37.5	37.5		(50.0)	(50.0)	
Other VC per panel (£s)	60	65		65	70		8.3	7.7	

| | 20X5 | | | | 20X6 | | | | |
| | Tinner | FMC | Total | Tinner | FMC | Total | Tinner % change | FMC % change | Total % change |
	£'000	£'000	£'000	£'000	£'000	£'000			
Revenue	24,000	16,400	40,400	18,720	16,720	35,440	(22.0)	2.0	(12.3)
Cost of steel	9,000	6,000	15,000	3,900	3,300	7,200	(56.7)	(45.0)	(52.0)
Other VC	7,200	5,200	12,400	6,760	6,160	12,920	(6.1)	18.5	4.2
Contribution	7,800	5,200	13,000	8,060	7,260	15,320	3.3	39.6	17.8
Fixed costs			9,000			9,000			–
Operating profit			4,000			6,320			58.0

Revenue analysis

Total revenue has decreased by 12.3% in 20X6, compared with 20X5. The causes for the decreased revenue can be analysed in terms of price and quantity changes. Alternatively, they can be analysed in terms of the revenues generated by each customer.

The overall volume of panels sold fell from 200,000 to 192,000 between 20X5 and 20X6, which is a fall of 4%. This overall fall hides a significant difference between the sales volumes to each of the two customers. Sales volumes to Tinner fell by a significant 13.3%, while sales volumes to FMC increased by 10%.

The cause of the fall in sales volumes to Tinner is likely to be a reduction in the production requirements of Tinner as there is a single supplier agreement, so there is no competition from elsewhere. Tinner running down inventory is an alternative explanation but perhaps less plausible given the extent of the change and the regular usage and scale of annual sales.

The cause of the increase in sales volumes to FMC is more uncertain as there is a multi-supplier agreement. This means it could be because of an increase in the production requirements of FMC. Alternatively it could be that PSP's pricing has become more competitive than its other suppliers this year and so FMC is purchasing a higher proportion of its requirements for steel panels from PSP in 20X6 compared with 20X5.

Another factor causing the overall fall in revenue in 20X6 is the reduction in selling prices. Sales prices to Tinner and FMC have been reduced by 10% and 7.3% respectively. A primary cause of the fall in selling price appears to be the significant fall in the cost of steel in 20X6 (see below). Since prices have fallen across the steel panel industry it is likely that rival companies have also reduced prices, even if the full extent of the steel price reduction has not been passed on to customers. The price to FMC might also have reflected changes in the £/euro exchange rates, although there may be have been currency hedging to offset this.

Cost analysis

Steel

Steel prices paid by PSP have fallen by 50% between 20X5 and 20X6 from £300 per tonne to £150 per tonne. This is a significant percentage fall, but it is made more significant by the fact that in 20X5 steel costs of £15 million made up 41.2% of the total cost of £36.4 million.

The amount of steel used in 20X6 was also slightly lower at 48,000 tonnes compared with 50,000 tonnes in 20X5. Overall, this meant a fall in steel costs of £7.8 million which is far greater than the increase in operating profit in 20X6 compared with 20X5 of £2.32 million (see below on sensitivity of profit to steel prices).

The fall in the price of steel was therefore a key driver of the increase in profitability, although slightly moderated by the fall in selling price that seems likely to have arisen largely from the fall in steel price.

One note of caution about steel prices is that they reflect the price under an annual contract with Coastal at 1 January 20X6, rather than the average spot price during the year. As such, they may represent the benefits of the contract terms and price movements in steel prior to the commencement of 20X6 rather than favourable price movements during the year.

Other variable costs

Other variable costs per panel increased for both Tinner and FMC by 8.3% and 7.7% respectively. Both increased by the same absolute amount of £5 per panel. These are fairly significant but any increase was more than offset by the fall in steel prices.

FMC has higher other variable costs per panel than Tinner. This could be because of transport costs to Italy.

Fixed costs

Fixed costs remained constant and hence were not a contributory factor in changing absolute profit although they create high operating gearing so make profit more sensitive to changes in sales levels.

Fixed costs have not been allocated between the two customers but have been treated as a lump sum cost for the company as a whole. Analysis of the two customers can therefore only be performed at contribution level, rather than an operating profit level.

Profit and contribution analysis

The contribution from Tinner has only increased by 3.3%, despite the 50% fall in steel prices. A key factor in this respect has been the significant fall in revenue of 22% arising from a decrease in both sales volume and selling price.

In contrast, the contribution of FMC has increased very significantly by 39.6%, driven by a combination of the fall in steel prices and the increase in revenue of 2% which is turn was driven by a volume increase of 10% that outweighed the selling price decrease of 7.3%.

The operating profit showed more sensitivity to change and increased by 58% due to the high level of fixed costs and operating gearing already noted.

Sensitivity analysis

Cost of steel per tonne	=	£7.2m/48,000 tonnes
	=	£150 per tonne
Operating profit	=	£6.32m
Increase to breakeven is	=	£6.32m/48,000
	=	£131.67 per tonne
Breakeven price per tonne	=	£150 + £131.67
	=	**£281.67**

Implications

The superficial implication is that if steel prices rose by 87.8% from their present level of £150 then PSP would break even.

This may appear to suggest that if steel prices in 20X7 were to return to the 20X5 level of £300 per tonne then PSP would make a loss. This may appear to represent a significant risk.

However this type of sensitivity analysis is univariate in assuming all other factors will remain unchanged if steel prices increase. This seems unlikely as there appears to be a strong interdependency between the prices of panels and the price of steel (as evidenced by the fall in selling prices in 20X6 and the email from the Tinner procurement director). As a consequence, it seems likely that if steel prices did increase significantly then PSP would be able to raise its selling price – assuming it is not tied into an annual contract.

This is not to suggest that an increase in steel prices is not a significant risk to profitability for PSP, not least because of an annual contract but also because the steel price increase may not be able to be fully passed on to customers in the same way the decreases in steel prices have not been fully passed on.

Conclusion

The difference between the cost at which steel is purchased and the extent to which this influences the price at which panels can be sold is a key driver of profits. The nature of supply contracts (fixed annual or contract by contract) is important in determining the level of profit, but also the variability of profit.

Other key issues include obtaining security of supply for steel as the main raw material. In this respect, there are trade-offs between profitability and risk.

Overall, the level of profit for 20X6 seems unsustainable as PSP has been favourably affected by steel price movements and contract terms that are unlikely to be systematically repeated in future.

Examiner's comments

The data analysis was generally well answered, with most candidates calculating relevant data and presenting their figures in a structured table with appropriate columns. Weaker candidates did not produce an initial table of calculations, but weaved occasional random calculations into their narrative which tended to produce limited answers with only partial data. Other weaker candidates mainly based their discussion on the figures already provided in the question, with few additional new calculations.

Many candidates tended not to perform a sufficient number of calculations. Many calculated steel cost per panel, but fewer calculated revenue per panel. However, a number of candidates failed to analyse the data more deeply, such as splitting revenue streams between the two customers.

Most candidates produced a good commentary on the data with a reasoned discussion of the issues revealed by their data analysis. Most identified the key drivers as requested, although not all specifically mentioned 'key drivers'.

Weaker candidates failed to structure their discussion sensibly (eg, revenue/costs/profits/ conclusion). Similarly, they failed to address the two customers separately – including some of those who had done so in their calculations.

Only a minority directly addressed the issue of the sustainability of business performance. Those who did tended to reflect only on continuing steel price falls, rather than the alternative possibility of prices rising in the future.

The majority provided a conclusion, although this was often very brief, taking the form of a mere unsupported assertion which failed to make reference to their prior argument.

37.2 The key factors are:

(1) Price
(2) Terms of contract (annual, quarterly, spot)
(3) Reliability, timing and frequency of deliveries.
(4) Other risks (eg, foreign currency, security of supply)

Quality could also be an issue but as a commodity product this is assumed to be largely standardised.

The issue of multi- or single-supplier arrangement needs to be considered (see separate section below).

Price

It would seem that both prospective suppliers are charging higher prices than were offered by Coastal in 20X6 (£150 per tonne). However, the prices proposed by the prospective suppliers may be higher because global steel prices are expected to be higher at 1 January 20X7 than they were at 1 January 20X6, rather than Coastal being a lower cost supplier.

Lipp is offering two prices: a lower price of £180 per tonne for the exclusivity of a single-supplier agreement and a higher price of £190 per tonne for a multi-supplier agreement. This may be due to economies of scale in production, economies of scope in making deliveries or part of the negotiating stance to provide a financial incentive for PSP to award Lipp the exclusive contract. Given Lipp's difficult financial circumstances it may be possible to negotiate lower prices than those currently being offered.

Kerr is offering a price of £185 per tonne on 1 January 20X7. This is the mid-point between the two prices offered by Lipp and does not appear to depend on whether it is a single- or multi-supplier agreement.

Terms of contract

Aside from the level of price, a key difference is that Lipp is offering a fixed price for the year while Kerr's prices will vary according to the price of steel on a contract by contract spot price basis.

Also, Lipp's price is fixed in £ sterling, while the Kerr contract is denominated in US$. Kerr's price may therefore vary if the £/$ exchange rate moves, even if the $ price of steel is stable.

Any movements in the steel price or the £/$ exchange rates could be favourable or adverse for PSP on the Kerr contract, but represent additional risk. These risks could be hedged but this may not be a perfect hedge and there would an additional cost to hedging.

Hedging could be achieved by matching the nature of the contracts to suppliers and customers. The contract with the customer Tinner is currently on an annual basis and therefore matching this with the Lipp contract, which is also on an annual basis, would mean that there is risk protection from steel price movements.

The contract with FMC is determined on a quarterly basis which is not a good match for either the Lipp or Kerr supplies, which are on an annual and spot basis respectively. Thus, if global steel prices fall and PSP is locked into an annual contract with Lipp, FMC may still demand price reductions.

Deliveries

Kerr is a US supplier so the geographical distance in the supply chain is significant.

- The lead times and uncertainty of delivery time are greater if the geographical distances are greater, such as from the US. This is made worse if Tinner is demanding supplies at more regular intervals of varying amounts.

- Cross border supply chains may produce regulatory, cultural, exchange rate and tax problems.

Risks

Lipp in particular could cease production at short notice (as Coastal did), given the competitive nature of the steel market. This gives uncertainty over security of supply for PSP, which may mitigate towards a multi-supplier arrangement.

Multi- or single-supplier arrangement

If PSP has multiple suppliers there are a number of benefits:

- PSP can drive down prices charged to it by encouraging competition between suppliers who know that it has a choice of alternative suppliers.

- There is greater flexibility in that if steel prices rise and Kerr raises its price, then PSP can purchase more from Lipp. This is particularly the case as the minimum is only 40% of total supplies so one supplier could be favoured with 60% of purchases. Conversely if steel prices fall then PSP can purchase more from Kerr which will lower prices in accordance with steel prices using the pre-agreed pricing formula.

- There is greater security of supply in case one supplier ceases to trade. Given that Lipp has difficult financial circumstances, this is particularly relevant.

However, if PSP has multiple suppliers there may be a number of problems:

- Each supplier has a smaller income from PSP than from a single source supplier agreement and so may lack commitment to the contract.

- The cost of steel is £10 per tonne higher under a multi-supplier agreement with Lipp compared to a single supplier arrangement. Using 20X6 purchases, with 40% bought from Lipp, this would cost an additional £192,000 (40% × 48,000 × £10).

- Multiple supplier communications could become more difficult and more expensive for PSP.

- Reduced scale economies and economies of scope may increase suppliers' costs and may make them more reluctant to offer reduced prices in negotiation.

- Both of the potential suppliers will be new and therefore this may create some initial uncertainty and front-end costs in establishing new relationships and communications systems.

Advice

A multi-supplier arrangement appears to offer the best option in terms of flexibility (in allocating the final 20% of supplies to either supplier) and security of supply. The two different contracts (annual and spot) are together a reasonable match for the current customer contracts.

Given that they are both new suppliers the reduction in risk and increase in flexibility appear to outweigh the relatively small short-term cost advantages from a single supplier arrangement.

Examiner's comments

This requirement was well answered by the majority of candidates. Most identified many of the key factors relevant to deciding between the two suppliers. However, the quality of answers provided tended to vary in terms of how comprehensively each factor was addressed, which allowed some candidates to score higher marks.

Some candidates concentrated on pricing and contracts but largely ignored supply chain issues. Others did the reverse. It was surprising that many candidates did not mention price as being a factor in choosing between suppliers, despite different prices being provided in the scenario. Few performed meaningful calculations for comparison.

Also surprising was the fact that a number of candidates did not address the single- versus multi-supplier issue. Others restricted their treatment to a brief mention within their conclusion. Those who did cover single- versus multi-supplier issues tended to pick up on some key points, but often missed out on some relatively straightforward marks.

Most concluded that a multi-supplier arrangement was the best way forward, usually justifying this conclusion on the basis of risk management.

37.3 To: Ms Kelly Jones, Procurement Director of Tinner plc
     From: Assistant to CEO
     Date: 6 December 20X6
     Subject: Pricing policy

Dear Ms Jones

Thank you for your recent email regarding our pricing policy and delivery scheduling.

Pricing

PSP constantly strives to price its products competitively for our customers and to provide the highest level of service. We do so in competitive markets measuring ourselves against rival companies.

As I am sure you are aware, the contract agreed between our two companies for sales in 20X6 was an annual fixed price contract. This has the advantage for both companies of giving certainty of pricing over the year and reducing the risk of significant changes in the price of panels.

A consequence for PSP of an annual fixed price agreement is that if our costs, such as the cost of steel, increase within the year we would need to bear this cost and would be unable to pass it on to Tinner in higher prices within the year. We accepted this risk as the downside from our agreed annual contract.

As it happened, in 20X6 steel prices fell and we benefited from this as the upside of our agreed contract. We believe it was clearly understood by both companies that this should happen and there was no agreement to pass on steel price reductions within the year of our annual contract.

While the price of our panels sold to Tinner was not reduced in response to steel price changes within 20X6, it was reduced by 10% from 20X5, when the price was £200 per panel to £180 in 2016.

We would not expect the prices of panels to fall by the same percentage as steel prices, as PSP has other costs which have in fact risen in 20X6 compared to 20X5. Any price based on cost would need to reflect all costs, not just steel, which is only one component of cost.

The removal of annual pricing would create uncertainty for both companies and therefore requires more discussion. If we are to move to weekly contracts for 20X7 then the formula needs to be agreed to reflect not just steel costs but other factors. We sell to our other customer in a competitive market with rival companies and these market factors need to be considered alongside other factors.

Delivery schedule

We note your comments on the requirement for weekly deliveries and penalties. As a valued customer we will do our best to accommodate your needs but 1 January 20X7 is only a few weeks away so there would need to be discussion of the logistics while we revise our operations. I am sure that you understand that this cannot be achieved instantly. In addition I am sure you will appreciate that more frequent deliveries will increase the level of delivery charges significantly.

As our production facilities are located so close to each other, we believe we can provide the best possible service in this respect.

Conclusion

Tinner is a valued customer of PSP and we wish to continue to build our relationship and provide the best possible service at competitive prices. I suggest a meeting takes place to discuss further the issues you have raised.

With kind regards

38 Zeter Domestic Chemicals plc (December 2016)

Marking guide

	Knowledge	Skill	Marks
38.1 First-year post acquisition review	3	10	11
38.2 Second-year post acquisition review	3	10	11
38.3 Ethics	3	6	8
	9	26	30

38.1 In-sourcing all distribution services

The first decision was for ZDC to in-source all distribution services by bringing them in-house using its subsidiary, Trann. This is a form of vertical integration. The rationale given by David (the CEO) was that ZDC should not use the other two external distribution companies as there would be additional costs incurred.

While the other distribution companies will charge a profit margin in addition to costs, a similar margin would be required by Trann if ZDC requires a return on its investment. Using Trann may not therefore be a lower cost to the group. (See issues below.)

A key issue is that the change-over is sudden for Trann and may create logistical problems in adjusting from supplying many customers to supplying just one customer. There is therefore a serious question of whether Trann can immediately replicate the core competences of the other two distribution companies in terms of skills and assets (eg, size and type of lorries) even though the deliveries are all for ZDC which is an existing customer.

Despite these transitional issues, in the long run the greater scale of operations may permit more efficiency and better utilisation for Trann, and provide a more coherent distribution function for ZDC with better interconnectivity of information systems for transport requirements.

Terminate the contracts with all other Trann customers

In deciding to source all distribution services internally, there is an opportunity cost from cancelling the other customers of Trann in order to create the required capacity. The opportunity cost comprises the lost revenue and lost contribution from these other customers.

In order to evaluate this decision the opportunity cost needs to be compared with any reduction in costs of using Trann rather than the other two distributors previously used. (This is in addition to any lost return on the funds invested to acquire Trann.)

An additional consideration in evaluating this decision is whether Trann could have invested to create new capacity and, as a result, been able to keep its existing customers as well as providing all of ZDC's distribution requirements.

Price reduction of 10%

In the year ended 30 September 20X5, Trann seems to have been operated as an autonomous subsidiary within the ZDC group. This would mean that its financial performance could be assessed largely independently from ZDC, notwithstanding that ZDC is a major customer, as transactions are negotiated on an arm's length basis, as they were prior to the acquisition, including pricing.

Similarly, in 20X5 the transport managers of ZDC appear to have been free to use, or not to use, Trann as they had previously. As a result, in the year ended 30 September 20X5, evaluating Trann as a profit centre, or even as an investment centre, would have been broadly appropriate.

The decision to impose a transfer price at 10% below the arm's length price previously set by negotiation significantly altered the autonomy of Trann management. This reduction in autonomy was reinforced by the decision to force ZDC transport managers to acquire all distribution services from Trann and to terminate Trann's contracts with all other customers.

As a result, the financial results of Trann would, after 1 October 20X5, no longer reflect the performance of Trann as the degree of financial interdependency between ZDC and Trann would thereafter be increased. By imposing the reduced transfer price, the recorded profit of Trann would no longer act as a reasonable measure of performance or means of control.

Conclusion

The decision to make Trann the exclusive supplier of distribution services and to impose transfer prices is likely to set up dysfunctional behaviour for managers in both Trann and ZDC as it simultaneously distorts market prices, provides dysfunctional incentives, damages control mechanisms and distorts performance measures.

The decision to terminate Trann's contracts with all of its other customers may be a necessary consequence of the in-sourcing decision, and thereby impose further costs. However further consideration could have been given to increasing capacity to enable existing customers to be retained despite the exclusive in-sourcing policy.

Examiner's comments

This requirement on the first-year acquisition review produced reasonably good answers by most candidates.

The vast majority displayed an understanding of transfer pricing. A significant minority identified vertical integration but fewer candidates displayed an understanding of divisional autonomy. The answers provided for in-sourcing the distribution and contract termination for other customers were of a reasonably good standard, although some weaker candidates failed to address at least one of these issues. Marks were lost by some candidates due to the fact they attempted to cover both issues simultaneously.

Regarding the relationship with Trann, most candidates displayed an understanding of the tensions between synergy and responsiveness in corporate structures. The better candidates related the discussion of in-sourcing of all distribution back to the original decision to acquire Trann. Most considered the synergistic benefits from integration. Many considered capacity issues.

The 10% transfer price reduction was often supported by those advocating the benefits of vertical integration. However, many appropriately considered the 10% to be arbitrary. Better answers suggested that Trann was now effectively a pseudo cost centre and so conventional profitability measures for Trann were no longer valid in assessing its performance. Weaker candidates struggled to get to the crux of the transfer pricing issues and instead offered some generic commentary on transfer pricing.

A number of candidates diverted into change management and, as a result, drifted away from the requirement.

Many failed to offer a conclusion at all and often, when it was provided, it did little more than summarise what had already been stated.

38.2

	20X5	20X6
Deliveries:		
For ZDC	4,250	8,000
Other	3,300	-
Average journey km	1,100	1,050
Total km	8,305,000	8,400,000
Revenue	£16,610,000	£15,120,000
Price per km	£2.00	£1.80
Variable cost per km	£1.40	£1.40
Variable cost	£11,627,000	£11,760,000
Fixed cost	£4,000,000	£4,000,000
Operating profit	£983,000	(£640,000)

NB uses data from both exhibits

Return on investment:

20X5 £983,000/£7m = 14%
20X6 £(640,000)/£7m = (9.1%)

Residual income:

20X5 £983,000 – (£7m × 10%) = £283,000
20X6 £(640,000) – (£7m × 10%) = (£1,340,000)

Finance director

The argument of the finance director (Lisa) relates to what she perceives to be the poor performance of Trann.

In respect of the year ended 30 September 20X5 she argued "the performance of Trann was poor in the first year after acquisition".

The above table shows that Trann made an operating profit of £983,000 in the year ended 30 September 20X5, giving a return on investment of 14%. While not as high as ZDC at 18%, it is above the cost of capital threshold and therefore reasonable (without adjusting for risk). Moreover the 14% is calculated on a fair value asset basis for Trann. It needs to be ascertained that the 18% for ZDC is on a comparable basis, as if historic cost has been used for the ROI of ZDC this would artificially inflate this figure.

In the year ended 30 September 20X5, residual income for Trann is positive at £283,000, hence performance is value enhancing for the ZDC group. It may be that improvements to performance can be made but, as it stands, based on the year ended 30 September 20X5 figures, the acquisition is having a favourable impact on the group value taking account of a capital charge for the funds invested.

In respect of the year ended 30 September 20X6, Lisa argued that performance "has continued to decline in the second year."

The recorded financial information shows a decline in operating profit in the year ended 30 September 20X6 such that an operating loss of £640,000 was incurred. This clearly creates a negative ROI and residual income.

However, as already noted, the profit of Trann in the year ended 30 September 20X6 no longer provides a reasonable measure of the performance of Trann in terms of its contribution to the ZDC group, specifically because of the artificial pricing imposed by the ZDC board.

The market price of the services at £2 per kilometre was in force in the year ended 30 September 20X5 and immediately prior to the acquisition when Trann was autonomous. The 10% reduction is a cost saving to ZDC and this is reflected in the ZDC accounts as a benefit, but in Trann's accounts as a revenue reduction, leaving the group unaffected.

If the market price is reinstated to £2 to show the value to the group of the services provided by Trann by adding back the 20p per kilometre, this would amount to additional revenue and profit for the year ended 30 September 20X6 of £1.68 million (£0.20 × 8.4 million km).

The revised profit figure would therefore be £1.04 million (£1.68m – £640,000). In turn, this gives the following ROI and residual income figures for Trann for 20X6:

Return on investment:

20X6   £1.04m/£7m   =   14.9%

Residual income:

20X6   £1.04m – (£7m × 10%) =   £340,000

Using these revised figures and therefore making comparisons on a consistent basis: operating profit, ROI and residual income have all increased in the year ended 30 September 20X6, compared with the year ended 30 September 20X5.

The finance director's assertion that performance has continued to decline therefore lacks substance. As the ROI continues to be above the cost of capital and the residual income continues to be positive, Trann is adding value to the ZDC group, even if it is reducing the overall ROI as it is below the 18% achieved by ZDC itself.

Marketing director

Professional scepticism should be exercised over the data provided by the marketing director as he is reporting on his own area of responsibility and was key to the decision to make the acquisition. Intimidation may also have come from the CEO (see below) which may reinforce the motivation of the marketing director to present favourable data. However the argument below assumes the data to be valid in the absence of evidence to the contrary.

The key argument of the marketing director is not to refute the data presented by the finance director, but to argue that the KPIs presented show an improvement (in the year ended 30 September 20X6 compared with the year ended 30 September 20X5) in the efficiency and effectiveness (in terms of pleasing customers) of the distribution function now that it has been brought in-house entirely.

In comparing the data of the years ended 30 September 20X5 and 20X6 it is important to note that direct comparisons about efficiency may not be valid for two reasons:

- A high proportion of the deliveries made are: different journeys; to different customers; in different locations. In particular, in the year ended 30 September 20X5 only 56% of the delivery journeys were to ZDC customers, whilst in the year ended 30 September 20X6 it was 100%.

- There were more deliveries and more kilometres covered in the year ended 30 September 20X6, so comparison of absolute amounts is unlikely to be valid.

Percentage of on-time deliveries – this has increased from 91% to 96%. As noted, this could be due to different customers, but is nevertheless very high in absolute terms and can be taken to represent good performance.

Number of customer complaints related to deliveries – this has fallen significantly in the year ended 30 September 20X6 from 184 to 163. This represents complaints of 2.4% and 2.0% of total deliveries in the years ended 30 September 20X5 and 20X6 respectively. This is a low percentage but more information is needed in terms of the seriousness of the complaints. A more valid like-for-like comparison would be the number of complaints from ZDC customers who had deliveries from Trann in both the years ended 30 September 20X5 and 20X6.

Percentage of full loads operated – the increase in the percentage of full loads from 44% to 56% is an improvement in utilisation and efficiency. However, rather than resulting from effective management, the concentration of deliveries to ZDC customers is likely to produce larger single loads and higher utilisation may be an inevitable consequence of this decision to have a sole distributor.

Number of delivery journeys made – the number of journeys made is indicative of an increase in scale arising from the decision by the ZDC board to have all its distribution carried out by Trann. Thus, while the increased scale and concentration may lead to greater efficiencies, they are not of themselves evidence of greater efficiency or effectiveness by Trann management.

Average distance per delivery journey – the average distance per journey is a function of the location of customers, given the revised customer base, rather than any measure of efficiency. The short journeys may however be a challenge to improving efficiency as the turnarounds at customer premises are more frequent.

Conclusion

The arguments of the finance director are based on the data she provided. When the data is adjusted there is evidence to suggest that the financial performance of Trann is reasonable and does not unambiguously support the director's proposition that the acquisition was a mistake.

The data presented by the marketing director is less certain and it is difficult to make comparisons of efficiency between the years ended 30 September 20X5 and 20X6 given the extensive change in the nature of the distributions made in the two years. More data is needed but there is limited evidence to confirm or refute the arguments of the marketing director based on the KPIs he has provided.

Examiner's comments

Most candidates correctly calculated ROI, but a large majority failed to perform correctly the simple calculation of residual income. Many candidates did not even attempt the residual income calculation.

The weakest answers simply agreed with the finance director's comments based on the ROI data, but then also went on to agree with the marketing director as well (who had the opposite view), often referring to the KPIs in varying degrees of detail. Reference was often made to the Balanced Scorecard in this context. Only a minority attempted to evaluate the conflict of views or reconcile the positions of the two directors.

Only the best candidates performed additional calculations to revise the second year ROI by adding back the 10% transfer price reduction, in order to make like-for-like comparisons, thereby concluding that the finance director was essentially wrong in her evaluation of financial performance. This once again highlights a weakness in many candidates when they need to critically evaluate information provided. Too many just took the numbers provided at face value.

Some candidates mistakenly said it was not surprising that, for example, the number of customer complaints had reduced given that Trann now only had one customer in ZDC.

Overall most candidates scored reasonably, but only the best candidates scored very high marks for this requirement.

38.3 Ethics pertain to whether a particular behaviour is deemed acceptable in the context under consideration. In short, it is 'doing the right thing'.

In making any ethical evaluation it is first necessary to establish the facts. In this case, a conversation about a rumour is not good evidence that what was claimed actually took place. Moreover, it is not good evidence to present to third parties in the sense that David or Kevin could deny the conversation occurred. Nevertheless, it would be appropriate as a starting point to establish the basic facts of whether David has a niece working as a senior manager for Trann and whether she has been promoted twice.

The issue of legality needs to be considered in terms of directors' duties under the Companies Act and consideration should be given to whether legal advice should be obtained.

Aside from any legal issues, there are a number of ethical issues that arise.

The first ethical threat is a potential conflict of interest between David's duty to act in the interests of the shareholders and any personal self-interest to act in favour of his niece. If self-interest were to have overridden the company's interests this would be a serious ethical breach with potential serious consequences. The issue here is David's motivation for the supporting the decision to acquire Trann and his expectations of the benefits of the acquisition for shareholders at the time the decision was made, rather than whether the outcome of the acquisition turned out to be favourable or not.

A second ethical threat is one of intimidation. David could not have voted through the acquisition on his own and may have 'pressured' or intimidated Kevin to vote with him at that time. This may have affected Kevin's motivation and willingness to make an independent decision about the acquisition for the benefit of ZDC shareholders. A second occurrence of intimidation is now taking place by David attempting to suppress Kevin's concerns and thus avoid the possibility of disclosure.

In making a decision as to how to proceed, some guidance is given by applying the Institute of Business Ethics three tests:

- Transparency
- Effect
- Fairness

Transparency – whether his niece's employment should be disclosed (ie, made transparent) by David is a key issue in this case. David needs to bear in mind how people (shareholders, directors, existing customers, suppliers, employees) would react if they found out subsequently that David may have been influenced by the interests of his niece, rather than solely by those of the ZDC shareholders. As a minimum, David should have disclosed the relationship to the other directors at the time. The idea that he "did not want to influence the board, favourably or unfavourably, in the acquisition decision" lacks credibility.

Effect – whom does the decision to disclose or not disclose affect or hurt? Clearly if the acquisition was not in the best interests of the ZDC shareholders then share value may fall as a result of the decision. It is also possible that subsequent decisions favouring Trann may have been motivated by David's personal family interests such as the decision to bring all distribution in-house with Trann. This would also have adversely affected the other two distributors which lost ZDC as a customer. In contrast to ZDC shareholders, the Trann shareholder group could have been favourably affected by the acquisition as they willingly accepted its terms, which may not have been offered in the absence of David's conduct.

Fairness – would David's non-disclosure be considered fair by those affected? Shareholders expecting directors to act on their behalf probably would not consider it fair to suffer a loss to favour David's niece. Also, in terms of the other stakeholders, knowingly not disclosing the personal interest may be seen as unfair and a breach of business trust. For example, the other two distributors losing ZDC as a customer for non-commercial reasons may regard the decision as unfair.

Honesty and integrity

Further ethical issues are those of honesty and integrity, which involve not just non-disclosure of personal interest but also hiding the consequences of, and motivation for, the acquisition of Trann.

Actions

Transparency remains important in seeking to make clear, if only in retrospect, David's personal interests and the risk that it may have influenced his commercial decision-making.

Kevin should approach David to encourage him to make full disclosure, initially to the board. If he refuses then Kevin should disclose the circumstances initially to the chairman and then the board should be informed. This should include the potential intimidation threats by David against Kevin.

The board should decide on any appropriate further disclosure (eg, to shareholders in the annual report).

However, establishing the fact of the relationship with David's niece is not direct evidence that this influenced his decision. Further independent examination of the evidence would be needed surrounding David's support of, and rationale for, the acquisition.

The niece's two promotions could also be examined to ascertain whether they were on merit and whether David had any influence. However, this would only be indirect evidence that David's decision on the acquisition was influenced.

If the facts can be established, David should consider resigning and, if not, the board should consider whether there are grounds to remove him. If there has been a legal breach there would be an impelling case for David's removal.

Examiner's comments

Generally good answers were provided by most candidates.

Ethical language and principles tended to be used by a majority. Many used the transparency, effect, fairness structure, but weaker candidates limited themselves to this framework without using the scenario to identify further ethical issues.

The majority of candidates were able to identify self-interest and intimidation threats as two key ethical issues relating to the scenario. Only better candidates noted that ethical issues arose at two different dates: the time of the acquisition and the current date of the scenario.

Many explicitly considered corporate governance, but a much smaller percentage highlighted anything specific relating to directors' legal duties.

Weaker candidates tended to provide answers that showed little cohesion but made some valid, though random, points.

An area for improvement is the actions recommended as they were, at times, too simplistic or extreme (eg, to resign as a first response) or failed to show a clear understanding of the situation. Some candidates only dealt with actions for either David or Kevin, but not both, as required by the question. Better candidates provided recommended actions for both David and Kevin that were realistic and linked well with the ethical issues previously discussed.

39 Hartley's Traditional Footwear Ltd (December 2016)

Marking guide

	Knowledge	Skill	Marks
39.1 Branding strategy	2	6	8
39.2 Pricing boots	3	4	7
39.3 One-off payment	1	7	7
39.4 Quality control	2	6	8
	8	23	30

39.1 (a) **HTF v Ayres brands**

Brands add value to products by making them recognisable and endowing them with associations attractive to the target segment. This ability of a brand to create future value is sometimes referred to as brand equity.

As a retailer, the HTF brand is a company name, associated with good quality products. This can be contrasted with the Ayres brand, which is the name of a product, but not of the company producing it.

A further difference is that the HTF brand is owned by HTF and therefore long term, while the Ayres brand is, in effect, rented by HTF as part of the contract with ABC, and therefore temporary. In this respect, HTF is unusual in not owning a brand from which it is benefiting.

Another difference between the brands is the difference in the underlying products (HTF shoes and Ayres boots). The brand image may further distinguish the products in terms of the celebrity, young person, fashion image of Ayres, compared with the more traditional quality, over 40s image of the HTF traditional shoes. This may cause brand confusion (see below).

(b) **Benefits and problems of the association with Ayres**

HTF is reaping some benefits from its diversification into a product with different characteristics from its core products. Favourable effects of the Ayres brand on the HTF brand include that, after the first year, there is a distinct upmarket image to Ayres with an even higher average price than HTF shoes. This may reinforce the upmarket image of HTF and establish both products as differentiated niche items.

A further favourable effect comes from cross branding with Ayres in increasing the brand recognition of HTF by exposing it to potential new consumer sectors, albeit that they may not be one of the original target segments for HTF.

There are a number of problems that arise for the HTF brand arising from association with the Ayres brand and brand conflict:

- At first, during 20X5, Ayres boots were being sold at £60 and were low price by comparison to HTF. While making an additional positive financial contribution it seems, based on available knowledge at the time, an unusual decision in selling two very different products, with different market positioning and different target consumers. Damage to the HTF brand seems to have potentially been greatest at this time.

- In 20X6 the price of the two products is much more closely aligned, even though the products remain different. There may however be further brand confusion as, not only are the consumer groups likely to be different between the two products, they are also likely to be different between the customer buying Ayres boots at £60 a pair in 20X5 and at £200 a pair in 20X6.

- Even at £200 per pair of Ayres boots, the brands are so different there may be brand confusion by customers as to what the HTF brand stands for in terms of values, quality and image. This may damage the value of the HTF brand.

- The association with Ayres may not end at the end of the contract but it may be much reduced and may not in the longer term be directly associated with HTF, as other retailers will in future be selling the Ayres brand. As such, the significant financial benefits may be temporary but the damage to the HTF brand may be permanent.

- The HTF infrastructure (shop fittings, staff training and characteristics) have been long established to service the HTF brand image rather than the Ayres image. The appropriateness of this internal infrastructure may have been compromised in actuality, or perception, due to selling Ayres boots. For example, staff may not be able to offer as good a service selling Ayres boots to a young person as they are selling traditional shoes to an older person.

- In 20X6, Ayres boots were the dominant sales item by sales volume. The HTF brand was therefore not so much shared with the Ayres brand as potentially dominated by it. This may change the culture of the shops and relationships with long-term HTF customers, some of whom, as a consequence, may purchase shoes elsewhere in future.

Examiner's comments

This requirement was well answered by most candidates. The majority correctly analysed positioning for the two brands into quality and market segment, as well as making comparisons between them. Benefits and problems of Ayres' association with HTF were also well considered by most, referring to diversification benefits and potential brand damage in particular. Poorer efforts failed explicitly to consider quality and/or segmentation when discussing positioning.

39.2 A traditional downward sloping demand curve would suggest that a lower volume of Ayres boots would be sold at a higher price.

In this case, much higher volumes have been sold in 20X6, at a much higher price, for a product which is physically the same as it was in 20X5.

Although the physical product is the same, the perceived value to consumers of the product was greater in 20X6 as it was then a fashion item with an upmarket celebrity image. As such, the demand curve has shifted to the right so significantly that, not just more can be sold at the same price, but more at a higher price.

The price for HTF is also enhanced by the supply side constraint from ABC of 10,000 pairs per month. This means that price can be increased to the point where demand is reduced to 10,000 per month whereas, if supply was potentially larger, then market forces of supply and demand could have set a potentially lower market clearing price.

In terms of product positioning, there is a relationship between price and quality. It could be argued that the price-quality relationship has shifted against consumers by the price increase from £60 to £200 (see diagram below). However, it is perceived quality that matters and the improvement in image from celebrity use could be argued to increase significantly the perceived quality.

In this case, in the diagram below, the price-quality trade-off for Ayres boots could be said to move from **B** in 20X5, to **A** in 20X6.

A further view could be to look at the change in terms of brand positioning. In the diagram below, it could be argued that in 20X5 Ayres was towards the top right area of the 'Economy brands' box. By increasing price substantially, but not altering the physical quality of the product, it could be that it moved upwards vertically to the 'Cowboy brands' sector.

If however quality is interpreted as perceived quality, then a more feasible and sustainable positioning is to move up into the 'Premium brands' sector.

Examiner's comments

Demand and supply relationships were generally very poorly understood. Many candidates displayed a limited understanding of how demand and supply would interact to cause both the price and volume demanded to increase. Relatively few correctly identified the difference between a shift of the demand curve as opposed to a movement along the curve. Many confused a shift of the demand curve with elasticity along the curve. Better candidates noted the restricted supply of boots from ABC may also have resulted in a higher price.

Various pricing models were presented. The better answers focused on price and perceived quality relationships, relating this to willingness to pay. However, the concept of perceived value, while often cited, was often not expanded upon enough.

For many candidates, appropriate pricing models became a 'knowledge dump' with many providing discussion on as many pricing models and approaches as possible, rather than selecting those which were relevant to the scenario.

Few candidates mentioned anything to do with the brand positioning matrix.

39.3 The potential contribution to be made by extending the ABC contract is:

120,000 × (£200 – £40) = £19.2m

The alternative contribution from the unbranded Russian boots is:

120,000 × (£60 – £40) = £2.4m

The incremental contribution is £16.8 million.

These basic calculations raise a number of concerns about paying this amount of money to ABC as the one-off payment for extending the exclusive supply contract.

- If the contract with ABC lapses at 31 December 20X6, would the alternative action by HTF be to take on the other, Russian contract? Although it generates a positive contribution, would HTF want to sell a downmarket boot with potentially much greater brand confusion and movement downmarket than has been the case in relation to the Ayres boot?

- Another alternative could be to still sell Ayres boots in 20X7 despite other retailers selling them and even though sales volumes and prices are likely to be lower in 20X7 than in 20X6. The contribution for doing so would need to be determined when sales prices and quantities can be established. The cost is also likely to increase from £40 under such an arrangement. However the one-off payment would need to reflect that some contribution from the sales of Ayres boots could be made for HTF even if the exclusive contract with ABC is not extended.

- There is a suggestion that, as a fashion item, Ayres boots will have a life cycle and it may be starting to move into the downward phase of that cycle in 20X7. The above calculations assume that demand will remain at the 20X6 level, which may be optimistic.

- Even if demand remains at the 20X6 level for 20X7, the above calculations would not indicate the amount of the one-off payment to ABC for a one-year extension, as this would mean all additional contribution would be captured by ABC in the one-off payment, rather than being shared between the two companies.

- The above amounts reflect only gross margins. Any incremental fixed costs or other costs would also need to be considered in determining the final one-off payment in terms of marginal benefit.

- Aside from the amounts of financial benefit, the longer term strategic impact of extending the ABC contract need to be considered. There may have been some brand confusion over the two-year contract period. An extension of the contract may mean that damage to the HTF brand may become more embedded and permanent. The end of the contract is therefore a time to form a clear long-term strategy for the HTF business as a whole, including the image and the product lines it wishes to sell.

Examiner's comments

The qualitative aspects of this requirement were answered reasonably, but the quantitative aspects were very poor.

For many candidates, structure was again an issue, as many did not use the structure provided in the question ie, quantitative and qualitative factors.

Quantitative: this was poorly done. Only a minority made any attempt at any numerical calculations, and the vast majority of those who did simply failed to grasp the calculations needed. Candidates rarely referred to contribution, mainly using the term profit. Some determined the contribution of £19.2 million from ABC's boots, but then failed to consider the incremental contribution relative to the alternative Russian contract.

Qualitative: this was better but still many failed to acknowledge the alternative Russian contract. The most common points identified related to fashion trends and maintaining exclusivity.

39.4 Given the nature of HTF's business, quality is a critical success factor. Quality assurance and quality control are critical to selling upmarket products.

HTF should establish a service level agreement with the Russian supplier, agreeing not just on the financial terms of supply but also on key targets/standards that need to be met and the consequences of not doing so. Any expectations that HTF has in relation to ethics and sustainability and the need for suppliers to conform to HTF's policies in these areas would also need to be set out.

Suppliers should be selected based on their reputation and the quality of their products. Clearly this would be a critical step in early due diligence, before contracts are agreed. HTF should carry out an annual inspection visit where the Russian supplier is required to confirm that quality standards have been met.

Once the Russian supplier has been contracted then a key control procedure is to measure and monitor supplier performance. Early detection of any problems is desirable but costs (both financial and reputational) are generally lower if HTF is able to prevent defective product rather than simply detecting it.

HTF should go through each stage of production processing to identify where factors exist that could influence either product quality or safety and then devise procedures that control those factors.

Quality assurance focuses on procedures and standards that will ensure product problems are eliminated or minimised during the production process. Quality control is focused on detecting defects in the output produced. In HTF's case this might include inspecting or sample testing boots that it has bought.

An information system can be used to enhance quality control, not just from the point of view of supplier control and monitoring but also for measuring HTF's own performance, by capturing a range of data (eg, returned items and complaints from customers).

An information system can track performance over time, and may be useful in identifying trends or detecting early warning signs of future problems.

Measures might include the following:

- Customer complaints and returns per 100 pairs sold – this could be compared with HTF's own footwear and also Ayres boots.

- The reasons for returns could then be broken down as this will help identify and address the cause of the problem.

- These would need to be considered in relation to any agreed tolerances that have been established with the Russian supplier.

- % of boots not meeting quality criteria on initial goods receivable inspection (eg, faults in manufacture or inferior materials used).

- % of boots not meeting specifications (size, volume, appearance, labelling).

- % of on-time deliveries.

Examiner's comments

Overall candidates did not perform particularly well on this requirement.

The majority of candidates displayed some knowledge of quality control but very few mentioned quality assurance. Where they did so, only a minority correctly distinguished between quality control and quality assurance.

Only a minority provided good examples of quality measures, and those who did tended to focus on customer-related measures such as customer feedback and product returns. Better candidates provided good examples of KPIs or other measures.

40 Ignite plc (March 2017)

	Knowledge	Skill	Marks
40.1 External factors	3	7	9
40.2 Product portfolio	3	22	22
40.3 Sales and profit margin/growth strategies	6	8	13
	12	37	44

40.1 External factors influencing demand for Ignite's cigarette lighters

To: Ignite Board
From: Business Advisor
Date: X/X/XX
Re: Product portfolio

The demand for Ignite's cigarette lighters is derived from the demand for cigarettes.

When Ignite was launched in the late 1940s, smoking was seen as fashionable and elegant. Over time demand has declined for a variety of reasons, with sales of Ignite's lighters falling from a peak of just over 1.2 million lighters in the 1960s to less than 400k by 2015.

The various external factors that have caused this decline can be analysed using PESTEL and Porters Five Forces. Key factors are as follows:

Increased health consciousness (social factors)

An awareness of the addictive nature of cigarettes and health concerns has led to people cutting back on or stopping smoking. It also puts people off taking up smoking in the first instance.

Research (1960s) and health warnings (1971) have led to a decline in sales of cigarettes and hence lighters.

Taxation (political and economic factors)

From the 1990s onwards, governments have adopted a strategy of continuing to raise the price of cigarettes through taxes with a view to reducing smoking but also raising revenue to pay for the health costs associated with it. The increased cost is likely to have put consumers off buying cigarettes (a 10% price increase results in 5% reduction in demand) and also led to a drop in demand for lighters. This is particularly true during recessionary periods when there is increased pressure on disposable income.

Regulation (legal factors)

To address health concerns governments have introduced successive pieces of legislation which have had a negative impact on the image of smokers and the demand for smoking and hence lighters:

- Advertising and sponsorship restrictions (2002)
- Ban on smoking in enclosed public places (2007)

In addition to the advertising ban's indirect impact, it will have had a direct impact on Ignite's ability to advertise its own product/ brand. However the ban on smoking in public places may have helped make Ignite's windproof lighters more popular among those who continue to smoke.

Alternative products (technological factors, substitutes and competition)

Technological developments have facilitated the development of alternative products to the Ignite lighter:

- The introduction of cheap disposable lighters (1961), which were widely in use by the 1980s, can be seen to have had a significant negative impact on demand for Ignite's lighters, which almost halved between 1960 and 1980.

- e-cigarettes, first introduced in 2004, have seen almost a 300% increase in the period 2012-2016. Where consumers are switching to these for all their smoking there will be a negative effect on demand for lighters.

Summary:

The external factors considered have all had a negative impact on the UK demand for Ignite's luxury cigarette lighters, partly due to a reduction in the number of people smoking and partly due to the fact that many of those who continue to smoke are using e-cigarettes which do not require a lighter. Thus the decline exhibited on the graph is likely to continue and Ignite will need to look to international markets and/or other products to achieve sales growth.

Examiner's comments

This was well answered by the majority. Most understood that demand for lighters was derived from demand for smoking cigarettes and went on to identify several external key factors that had driven changes in demand. Many used PESTEL and/or Five Forces to structure their answers, thereby generating a better answer and ensuring a full range of points was covered. A surprising number failed to set their answers out in the form of a report.

40.2 **Analysis of existing product portfolio**

(a) **Appropriate calculations**

Appendix:

Analysis of historic and forecast financial information 2015-2017

Sales mix	2015	2016	2017
Luxury cigarette lighters	59.62%	54.00%	48.42%
Multi-purpose lighters	15.96%	19.00%	21.05%
Lighter fuel	15.02%	15.00%	15.79%
Lifestyle accessories	9.39%	12.00%	14.74%

Gross profit mix	2015	2016	2017
Luxury cigarette lighters	66.45%	59.92%	52.63%
Multi-purpose lighters	10.46%	12.62%	14.44%
Lighter fuel	7.78%	7.49%	7.67%
Lifestyle accessories	15.31%	19.97%	25.26%

£million	Luxury cigarette lighters	Multi-purpose lighters	Lighter fuel	Lifestyle accessories	Total
Gross profit margin					
2015	41%	24%	19%	60%	36.8%
2016	40%	24%	18%	60%	36.1%
2017	38%	24%	17%	60%	35.0%
Sales growth					
2015–2016	(15.0)%	11.8%	(6.3)%	20.0%	(6.1)%
2016–2017	(14.8)%	5.3%	–	16.7%	(5.0)%

Appendix: BCG analysis of existing portfolio

Product	Ignite market share	Market leader's share	Ignite's share relative to market leader	Estimated market growth rate	Analysis	Position
Luxury cigarette lighters	26%	38%	0.68	(5)%	Large share, low growth	Cash cow
Multi-purpose lighters	18%	22%	0.82	14%	Large share, high growth	Star
Lighter gas/fuel	11%	45%	0.24	2%	Small share, low growth	Dog
Lifestyle accessories	Negligible	n/a	Negligible	12%	Small share, high growth	Question mark

A market growth rate of less than 10% is typically considered to be low, although this does depend on the type of market.

Positioning Ignite's products in a BCG matrix shows:

Relative market share

	High	Low
High % rate of market growth	Star Multiple purpose lighters	Question mark Lifestyle accessories
Low	Cash cow Luxury cigarette lighters	Dog Lighter fuel

ICAEW 2019

Ignite's products may actually be in a different position in different markets, for example luxury lighters may be a dog product in the UK but a star or cash cow in Asia. More information on the individual markets would facilitate a more detailed analysis.

(b) **Implications for future corporate strategy:**

Sales growth

The business has experienced a 6.1% drop in revenue between 2015 and 2016, and a further 5% fall is estimated for 2016-17. Clearly this means the Board will fail to hit the 15% growth target that it has announced to the market.

Cigarette lighters account for the majority of Ignite's sales, although for the first time in 2017 they are estimated to make up less than 50% of the overall total. This product is currently a cash cow, having reached maturity. However demand has declined as a result of the reduction in the popularity of smoking and the introduction of e-cigarettes, and it is expected to continue declining by approximately 15% per annum.

Due presumably to the popularity of outdoor activities, sales of multi-purpose lighters are increasing. However the sales growth of 11.8% is below that of the market (14%) which implies that Ignite has lost some market share and may need to increase its investment in marketing. The growth rate is expected to slow to 5.3% in the 2017 forecast.

Demand for lighter fuel is presumably derived from sales of both types of lighters, so although it has fallen by 6.3%, it would presumably have been worse without the increased sales of multi-purpose lighters.

The demand for Ignite's lifestyle accessories shows a healthy growth rate, and is the only one in excess of the Board's target. However some products eg, fragrance, have been less successful than others. More information is needed to assess the sales and profitability of the individual items within this range.

Profitability

The total gross profit has fallen by 8.0% in 2016 and is estimated to fall a further 7.8% in 2017. The overall gross margin has fallen from 36.8% in 2015 to an estimated 35% in 2017, again falling short of the Board's 38% target. This reflects declining margins on both cigarette lighters and lighter fuel.

Margins on cigarette lighters are relatively high but are expected to continue falling as the market becomes increasingly mature. This is worrying since in 2016 cigarette lighters contributed 59.92% of the overall gross profit.

Overall the lifestyle accessories are the most profitable, with a consistent gross margin of 60%. Sales growth in this market means these products have contributed 19.97% of the 2016 gross profit and are expected to generate 25.26% of Ignite's profit in 2017, despite representing only 14.74% of sales. As demand for its traditional product declines, Ignite is becoming more dependent on the success of this product range.

Margins on multi-purpose lighters remain steady at 24% but are significantly below the Board's target of 38%, which may be over-optimistic.

The overall results for each product are an amalgamation of sales in different markets at different prices, and will have been translated into £. More information is needed on sales volumes, sales prices, costs and exchange rates. Information about the running costs of the business is also required to be able to evaluate Ignite's operating profit.

Risk

Currently the product portfolio is unbalanced. Ignite's business is over-reliant on cigarette lighters which make up almost 50% sales and over 50% of gross profit. This product is a cash cow but is likely to be nearing the end of its lifecycle: the market for the company's most important product is in decline and this is an industry trend which is likely to continue in the future. However there may come a point below which demand does not fall (a core of regular smokers). Identifying markets where Ignite lighters are still in demand, because a significant of the population smoke, will extend the life of the product. When these markets cease, there may remain a small income stream from sales of lighters to non-smoking collectors and to core smokers. Ignite needs to monitor the performance of its cigarette lighter range and pull out before/at the point that cashflows become negative.

Since a significant proportion of lighter fuel sales is likely to derive from sales of cigarette lighters, this interdependence increases the overall risk for the business.

To an extent Ignite have mitigated some of this risk by using the same technology for multi-purpose lighters, sales of which are increasing. This product is well-established now and although it needs promotional support, it is classified as a star and should present good prospects for the future as the market is growing.

The expansion in 2010 into lifestyle accessories has reduced the risk of the portfolio. These are expected to make up 14.74% of sales and 25.26% of gross profit in 2017. Ignite has a very small share of a growing market however and this is likely to be extremely competitive. Hence this product is classified as a problem child. Ignite has already been faced with counterfeit products which risk damaging the brand image. There is also a risk that the product sales are interdependent and that these purchases are being made because of the brand's historic image. If so, sales would be lower if Ignite withdrew its cigarette lighter product.

The products are very heavily dependent on a narrow market (males, aged 18-34) which again increases risk.

Ignite has reduced risk by targeting international sales – products are now sold in 160 countries. This helps reduce reliance on a single geographical region and also offers the opportunity to capitalise on markets where demand is at a different point in the lifecycle.

Conclusion

The Board is right to be concerned about Ignite's future profitability. Ignite appears to have under-invested in the development of new product lines. Until 2010 its entire portfolio was based on lighter-related products. Developing a wider range of products is vital if the business is to have a sustainable future. The existing portfolio is also focused on a relatively small core market of 18-34 year old males. Widening the market of customers will also help increase sales – this should be possible for the multi-purpose lighter and accessories.

Examiner's comments

The data analysis was generally well answered although some candidates clearly mis-managed their time on this requirement as a whole.

Most candidates calculated relevant data for 2015-2017 and presented their figures in a structured table with appropriate columns. The vast majority of candidates also made a good attempt at analysing the product portfolio using the BCG matrix, although on the whole their conclusions regarding each product could have been better presented, for example using a table or diagram.

Weaker candidates did not produce an initial table of calculations, but weaved occasional random calculations into their narrative which tended to produce limited answers with only partial data. Another common error was not to calculate relative market share or for weaker candidates to assume that a relative market share of anything less than 1 counted as 'small' in the BCG analysis.

Many candidates produced a good commentary on the data with a reasoned discussion of the issues revealed by their data and product portfolio analysis, specifically identifying that Ignite's main product is in the decline phase of its product lifecycle. Weaker candidates, as usual, reiterated the figures they had calculated, without adding value.

The requirement had been constructed in two parts, asking for calculations first and then narrative using a given set of headings. A significant number of candidates provided an evaluation of the 2015-2017 figures using their own headings and then repeated something very similar, using the specific headings given in the question. This meant that they mismanaged their time considerably.

Few candidates identified further information that might be useful and only a minority provided a brief summary of whether the Board was right to be concerned about the balance of the existing portfolio and its implications for future success.

40.3 (a) **Calculation:**

£m	Target 2017	Forecast – existing products 2017	Performance required of new products (balance) 2017
Sales	230 (200 × 1.15)	190	40
Gross profit	87.4 (230 × .38)	66.5	20.9
GP margin	38%	35%	52.25%

(b) **Growth strategies**

Trackr:

Using the Ansoff matrix, this would be classified as market penetration or product development, depending on whether it is seen as a new product or a revamp of an existing one. Whilst there may be some demand for this product, it is still focused on the declining market of cigarette smokers. The reputed 'health benefits' are likely to be small and Ignite may be accused of being unethical and damage its reputation if it makes too much of this angle for its marketing. This product is likely to have a short life-cycle. It may also be costly to produce because of the technology involved and there is no evidence that Ignite has expertise in this area. It may be better to launch this product as a joint venture with one of the businesses that specialise in fitness apps.

Outdoor range:

These products are more likely to be within Ignite's range of expertise. If these are targeted at the existing customers then this strategy would be considered one of product development.

However barbecues may also attract a new and wider market. This strategy is likely to be the least risky option and could probably be implemented fastest. However the current 'outdoor' multi-purpose lighters only achieve a margin of 24% so this range may not be sufficiently high margin for the Board.

Female market:

To the extent that Ignite already sells multi-purpose lighters to women, the sale of candle lighters might be seen as one of market penetration. Were Ignite to sell its existing sunglasses, pens and fragrance to the female market, this strategy could be seen as market development (a new target market for existing products). However if these products are to be radically different then the strategy could be seen as one of diversification (new products and new market).

The evidence to date suggests that Ignite's products have had limited appeal to the female market.

Although historically the brand image was one of elegance and glamour the existing brand appears to have developed more of a 'rugged outdoor' image, and comes with the negative connotations of smoking. It is sensible to attempt to widen the market beyond 18-34 year old males but it may be necessary to do this under a different brand. Alternatively Ignite may need to identify a range of celebrities to help promote the product and change its image.

Board's targets:

If the Board's sales growth target is to be achieved, new product sales would need to be £40 million (see (a)) – the same level as those forecast for the multi-purpose lighters in 2017. This may be ambitious if the products have not yet been launched. The margin of 52.25% from new product sales also looks to be unachievable, unless Ignite is successful in introducing higher margin accessories for the female market.

Conclusion

In order to generate a financially sustainable business, Ignite should focus on changing the brand image from a lighter brand to a lifestyle and outdoor brand, and widening the appeal to reduce reliance on a young male market. In addition to considering new product streams, the Board should identify other geographical markets for market development of the existing products. The targets set by the Board for 2017 look over-ambitious.

Examiner's comments

Whilst candidates were generally comfortable with the discursive element of the requirement, answers to the calculation element regarding sales and gross profit margin were polarised, with many candidates scoring full marks but also a disappointing number scoring zero. Candidates are expected to have a degree of numerical agility and the calculation of target sales and profit figures is a basic skill that should have offered easy marks.

The requirement to analyse the three proposals for new products was well answered by the majority. Most used the Ansoff matrix to position each strategy. Better candidates went on to discuss whether the strategy was likely to be successful in delivering the additional sales and profit required by the board.

Many candidates who had mismanaged their time attempting the second requirement gave a truncated answer to this part of the question.

41 Eclo Ltd (March 2017)

	Knowledge	Skill	Marks
41.1 Organisational structure	2	5	7
41.2 Control procedures	2	8	9
41.3 Strategic and financial considerations	3	10	12
41.4 Ethical issues	2	7	8
	9	30	36

41.1 Structure

Eclo currently appears to have a simple structure. It is a small business which is relatively young and the organisation is very flat: Eve the entrepreneur sits at the top with a wide span of control and the rest of the employees are encouraged to participate in decisions. As the organisation grows, this structure may become less flexible if all decisions have to go through Eve.

According to Mintzberg's theory of organisational forms, Eclo seems to fit with the adhocracy/innovative configuration. Eve the entrepreneur sits at the strategic apex with the operating core as the key building block, likely to be coordinated by mutual adjustment.

There is little formalisation (absence of technostructure) and no layer of middle management (middle line). This means the organisation is flexible and quick to adapt/innovate but it may limit the scope for expansion.

An alternative model is that of the flexible firm or, according to Handy, the shamrock organisation – a core of essential workers supported by a contractual fringe of external providers (the strategic partnerships with suppliers and the agent in India). This sees Eclo as an organic organisation which can respond to changing circumstances and evolve incrementally. For example if the new printing app is introduced, Eclo will subcontract some of the printing tasks to its customers (as the fourth part of the shamrock).

Modern businesses are developing along the lines of the boundary-less/borderless structure.

There is some evidence of this at Eclo:

- Collaborative approach with suppliers
- Outsource non-value added activities
- Outsource some operations to specialists
- Offshore some elements of process to different countries

Overall Eclo appears to have a reasonably flexible structure. The relatively informal, fluid approach reflects the values and behaviour of Eve at the top of the organisation (social entrepreneur). Should Eclo take on a new investor, this may change the structure as they may want a different approach. As the business grows it may need some more formal mechanism for control over finances, and more people responsible for customer relationships.

The requirement on structure produced good answers from most candidates, with many referring to models such as Handy's shamrock and Mintzberg. Some candidates also identified the elements of Eclo's structure that reflect the newer types of flexible organisation. The weakest answers tended to discuss Eclo's flat, entrepreneurial structure but not go beyond this.

41.2 Control procedures

The ethos of Eclo is that of a social enterprise. Its own ethos is one of sustainability and it targets organisations that have created brands based on sustainability. In a wider context sustainability does not just address environmental issues but also economic and social sustainability, so would encompass long-term financial stability, working conditions and fair treatment of suppliers, among other things.

Ensuring that all elements of the supply chain reflect Eclo's brand ethos is critical as there is a big reputational risk if they do not. Eclo can achieve this by working in partnership with suppliers, making sure suppliers are treated fairly and that contract terms are transparent and fair to both parties. For long-term sustainability Eclo needs to pay suppliers enough so their businesses are economically sustainable (although suppliers may have other customers/economic relationships and therefore may not be entirely reliant on Eclo).

To ensure suppliers are compliant with Eclo's sustainability approach:

- Eclo should undertake appropriate due diligence on suppliers – quality assurance and quality control are critical to ensure sustainability compliance so Eclo should seek assurances that suppliers are also firms with an ethically sound CSR policy.

- There may be reputational and other penalties if Eclo advertises products as organic/sustainable when they are not. Also a key marketing message is that every Eclo product can be traced back to its origins. Eclo must ensure that suppliers are able to produce this information for its simple eco-labelling system and that it is verifiable.

- In developing its relationship with suppliers, Eclo should instigate a service level agreement, agreeing not just on the financial terms of supply but also on key targets/standards that need to be met and the consequences of not doing so. Any expectations that Eclo has in relation to ethics and sustainability and the need for suppliers to conform to Eclo's policies in these areas would need to be set out. Aside from product quality, other aspects that Eclo should consider are processes to ensure that health and safety is maintained at the highest standards and that suppliers promote diversity and equal opportunity, providing fair pay and benefits for all workers.

- Suppliers should be selected based on their experience and the quality of their products. Clearly verifying a supplier's certification and credentials would be a critical step in early due diligence, before contracts are agreed. Eclo should arrange for an annual inspection visit where the supplier is required to confirm that all Eclo's standards have been met. This could be undertaken by a third party agent.

- Once a supplier has been contracted then a key control procedure is to measure and monitor supplier performance for prevention and early detection of problems.

Monitoring the quality of output:

This is critical as there have been an increasing number of client complaints about product quality and errors in printing. Eclo has also experienced delays between client order and delivery.

- Eclo should go through each stage of the production process, to identify where factors exist that could influence product quality and then devise procedures that control those factors. Quality assurance focuses on procedures and standards that will ensure product problems are eliminated or minimised during the production process. In Eclo's case this might include inspecting or sample testing fabrics and dyes before using them in production, so that any traces of toxic materials would be identified.

- Quality control is associated with checking a product after it has been produced and this might involve sample testing garments from every supplier. Even if there are no toxic/ non-organic issues, checking is still a good idea to ensure consistency of the quality of the product over time.

- An information system can be used to track performance over time, and may be useful in identifying trends or detecting early warning signs of future problems. It also provides Eclo with evidence for its own eco-friendly certification and in relation to supplier performance when discussing or renewing contracts with suppliers. Eclo could monitor areas such as quality of service (eg, the percentage of deliveries received on time) and the level of customer complaints/returns.

Examiner's comments

After a couple of recent sittings where the topics of sustainability and control procedures were not always well done, it was nice to see that the vast majority of candidates were well-prepared for this requirement. The candidates whose answers covered both quality assurance (linked to sustainability) and quality control (linked to output) tended to score higher marks.

41.3 **Bringing some/all operations back to the UK**

There are two issues:

(a) whether to use UK suppliers instead of Indian suppliers; and

(b) whether to bring printing in-house

Strategic considerations:

(a) In relation to Indian vs UK suppliers

Key considerations in supply chain management are responsiveness, reliability and relationships. As far as relationships are concerned, Eclo currently has partnerships with three Indian garment suppliers and an Indian printing company. This may be consistent with the ethos of a sustainable enterprise and a circular economy – providing jobs and returning income to the economies where the raw materials are sourced. Eve should consider to what extent this has been part of Eclo's marketing strategy as there may be reputational damage if contracts with Indian suppliers are terminated.

However there have been issues with the Indian suppliers in relation to quality (reliability) and lead times (responsiveness) which are affecting customer service. The issue of delays may be reduced if suppliers are in the UK rather than India as the speed of supply should increase. However raw materials may need to be imported into the UK, in which case the delay may simply be transferred to an earlier point in the supply chain.

Political and cultural risks relating to overseas operations will be reduced if the supply chain is brought back to the UK. However relationships would need to be established with a range of new UK suppliers and Eclo's bargaining power may be limited if it is small relative to potential suppliers. The issue of quality control will remain, although the lack of language barriers and the proximity of supplier locations may make it easier to undertake test visits and ensure adherence to standards if UK suppliers are used.

(b) In relation to a decision to bring printing activities in-house:

Eclo has limited direct experience of printing and an outsourced company will have greater expertise. An outsourcing model also allows Eve to focus on what she is best at (design) and makes best use of her skills.

An outsourcing model for printing allows greater flexibility (expansion/contraction) and shares risk. For a small business like Eclo it increases the scaleability of the business model – which is particularly important if there is rapid growth. Eclo's structure (see above) is one of a flexible business/network and bringing activities in-house will move away from this.

However the downside of continuing to outsource printing is the possible issue of lack of control over standards and quality. There is an option to establish a printing facility in a nearby factory unit. If the printing errors in India have been ongoing and are indicative of poor supplier performance then this may be a sensible opportunity. Eclo will be able to control quality and ensure processes are sustainable.

Since Eclo's strategy is based on customisation of the garment, to the extent that this takes place at the printing stage it may be sensible to bring it in-house as a core added value activity, rather than use a supplier which also works for competitors.

The facility to allow clients to create their own designs via an app may help Eclo increase sales (although it is possible that this could still be done using an external printing supplier).

Financial considerations:

(a) In relation to Indian vs UK suppliers

More information is needed about the relative costs of UK/Indian suppliers. The garments may be more expensive to manufacture in the UK. However the increased cost of manufacture may be offset by reductions in transport and distribution costs and the profit margins paid to the third party agent and suppliers.

The decision to use UK-based suppliers only would remove exchange rate risk for Eclo and transfer it to each UK supplier which is importing the materials (although this may be reflected in the cost of the garment to Eclo).

(b) In relation to a decision to bring printing activities in-house:

The current arrangement keeps printing costs variable and reduces operating gearing. An in-house printing facility will convert variable costs to fixed costs and potentially raise the breakeven point.

Currently financial risk is reduced by not committing to the expense of a printing facility. However Investment in a printing facility requires relatively small investment (£100,000) and if a suitable equity investor can be found, this may be a good first step.

Eve needs to consider whether an investor can be found who would support the ethos of the business.

Conclusion

Eclo is a small company. A sensible transition approach may be to evaluate the Indian suppliers, then to identify a suitable UK-based garment supplier and use them in conjunction with the better performing Indian suppliers. A cost benefit analysis should be done of the in-house printing facility. If a suitable equity investor can be found, a UK-based garment supplier may facilitate the strategy of allowing customers to create and print their own designs, as it will increase the speed to market.

Overall most candidates scored reasonably, but only the best candidates scored very high marks for this requirement. The question asked for the strategic and financial considerations relating to two different issues – (a) bringing the supply chain back to the UK and (b) bringing printing in-house. Typically weaker candidates let themselves down by not considering all four elements or by producing imbalanced answers. Few candidates scored full marks on this requirement. This was often due to discussing supply chain management using a common sense approach which, whilst scoring reasonably well, did not demonstrate some key areas of technical knowledge such as the relative risk of international vs domestic operations and the impact on financial and operating gearing.

41.4 Ethical issues

Ethics pertains to whether a particular behaviour is deemed acceptable in the context under consideration. In short, it is 'doing the right thing'.

There are two ethical issues to consider here:

(a)   The contamination of the river by wastewater from the supplier
(b)   The marketing manager's suggestion regarding the way this should be dealt with

In making any ethical evaluation it is first necessary to establish the facts concerning the original incident.

It appears reasonably certain that one of Eclo's Indian suppliers, AMG, has discharged damaging wastewater into the river, which may be illegal. The uncertainty surrounds whether Eclo has any responsibility for this – the supplier appears to be saying that it does not.

A key question here is whether there is an ethical obligation on Eclo to be aware of all activities at the supplier or just those involving its own production processes and products.

Even though Eclo may not have had any involvement, its reputation may be damaged by association with AMG when the incident comes to light. However AMG appears to be intending to deal with the problem in an open and transparent way and to make good its fault. Assuming the contamination is an accident, it is not necessarily indicative of deliberately unethical behaviour on the part of the supplier.

There are two elements to the marketing manager's proposal.

Depending on the terms of the supplier contract, Eclo may be within its rights to cancel all orders with AMG, although this may be seen as unfair/unethical if it results in job losses for local workers without any notice.

The proposal to release confidential information to the market, which AMG has supplied in good faith, implies a lack of personal ethics on the marketing manager's part, since this is a breach of confidentiality. Also the issue of legality needs to be considered and legal advice taken. Eclo does not know for certain that the high-fashion retailer is responsible and could face legal action if it states this publicly.

In making a decision as to how to proceed, the Institute of Business Ethics three tests:

- Transparency
- Effect
- Fairness

could also be applied.

Transparency – AMG's intention to make an announcement suggests it is dealing with the incident in a transparent manner. If this is the case, there may be no need for Eclo to pre-empt AMG's statement.

Effect – an earlier announcement by Eclo and any termination of the supply contract would have a detrimental effect on AMG's business and its employees. This is not in keeping with the concept of sustainability.

Fairness – the marketing manager's suggestion to allocate blame away from Eclo may be unfair to the high-fashion retailer, particularly given that Eclo may not yet have all the facts and AMG has provided this information in confidence.

Actions

Eclo should be guided by any legal advice.

The most reasonable action would appear to be to draft a statement that can be released at the same time as or soon after AMG publicises its apology.

Rather than terminating the supply contract, which would compound the supplier's problems, if Eclo has a long-standing relationship with AMG then it might take steps to help the company identify the problems in its processes and implement control procedures to prevent this happening again.

The marketing manager's suggestion to make an advance statement is unethical and this should not happen. Eve should discuss the inappropriateness of this suggestion with the manager, and consider whether there is a good fit between the manager's values and those of Eclo as a social enterprise.

Examiner's comments

This requirement was very well attempted by most candidates. The majority of candidates were able to identify that there were really two key ethical issues in the scenario – the first being the contamination of the river by the supplier and the second relating to the proposed announcement by the marketing manager.

Many candidates recognised that ethically the supplier is proposing to do the right thing by making an open and honest apology and offering compensation. The less clear issue is whether there is a public interest argument for Eclo making an announcement before the supplier has a chance to do so, and what the marketing manager's motives are for suggesting that Eclo breaches confidentiality by naming and shaming the other business involved.

Ethical language and principles tended to be used by a majority. Many used the transparency, effect, fairness structure, but weaker candidates limited themselves to this framework without using the scenario to identify further ethical issues, such as confidentiality. Weaker candidates tended to provide answers that showed little cohesion but made some valid, though random, points.

It is encouraging that more candidates seem to have developed the ability to provide recommended actions that are realistic and linked well with the ethical issues previously discussed.

42 Gighay Ltd (March 2017, amended)

	Knowledge	Skill	Marks
42.1 Outsourcing and KPIs	3	9	11
42.2 Data analytics and competitive advantage, and big data strategy	2	8	9
	5	17	20

42.1 Benefits and problems for Oxna of outsourcing IT

Benefits:

- Outsourcing services to Gighay provides Oxna with greater flexibility which is especially important if Oxna is growing rapidly and its IT requirements are changing.

- This is likely to result in reduced service and support costs as Gighay is likely to have better purchasing power and will benefit from economies of scale. It also allows Oxna to budget more predictably.

- Oxna will benefit from better quality of service, fewer IT failures and less downtime. This is important given the recent server crashes.

- Oxna does not have a core competence in IT. It will get access to accredited technical expertise and a wide range of skills without having to train its own staff. There is also a reduced risk of an in-house IT specialist leaving the company and taking their knowledge with them.

- Gighay provides round-the-clock access to a 24-hour support desk that can resolve problems for staff remotely and rapidly, whatever the time of day or their location. This is critical given that Oxna's remote employees need to connect 24 hours a day. It should also help reduce the need for costly emergency support.

- Oxna has experienced a recent cyber-security issue. Gighay will have access to the latest applications and hardware and will be better placed to ensure security of systems and data and prevent such attacks in future. An outsourcing agreement helps to transfer the risk and responsibility for dealing with problems to Gighay.

- Oxna gains access to consultancy advice on other IT issues

Problems:

- Oxna will have to trust Gighay with potentially confidential information about its business.

- If IT services are outsourced it will be very difficult to bring them back in-house at a later date.

- Oxna may become very dependent on Gighay and find it difficult to switch IT supplier in the event that Gighay increases its prices in future or Oxna becomes unhappy with the service.

- Outsourcing does not necessarily prevent a cyber-security attack occurring although it may reduce the financial consequences.

- Gighay's particular expertise is in data capture and data analytics which are not services that Oxna requires.

- Oxna will need to draw up a service agreement to carefully monitor the quality of the service provided.

Managing the contract: KPIs

A balance of measures will be important to cover all aspects of the support service. It could include some of the following:

- Cost per help request
- Number of help requests dealt with in the period (to give an indication of workload)
- Speed of response to initial query – how long does it take for Gighay to answer the phone or respond to emails?
- First contact resolution rate
- How often do Gighay provide a solution or outcome to a request for support at the first instance or on the same day the issue was raised?
- Average time taken to resolve issue (how soon are technicians put to work and problems resolved?)
- Number of unplanned IT security or downtime incidents
- Average amount of server downtime per week/month
- Number of cyber-security incidents detected and prevented
- Average score in customer satisfaction feedback surveys (voluntary short questionnaires could be sent to Oxna staff after each support case is closed).

Examiner's comments

This requirement was very well answered by most candidates, who were clearly well versed in the arguments for and against outsourcing. It was pleasing to see that most tailored their discussion and their KPIs to the scenario in the question. Weaker candidates tended to ignore the cyber-security issue, and make generic points. Some continue to confuse KPIs with goals or targets.

42.2 Big Data

Big Data encompasses information from multiple internal and external sources. It might include information from Feltar's systems, transactions with its customers, social media, mobile devices etc.

Companies can analyse this data and use it to adapt their products to better meet customers' needs and find new sources of revenue.

Big Data is often defined by considering the Vs: volume, velocity, variety, value:

Volume – refers to the scale or amount of data which is now available for organisations to access, store and use. Widespread use of the internet, smart phones and social media has increased the volumes of data available to businesses. This data can be used to give insights to customers' requirements by identifying trends and buying patterns. Currently Feltar are only collecting a very limited amount of data from customers.

Velocity – refers to the speed at which 'real time' data is gathered and used by modern organisations. At the moment Feltar simply records the final sale at the end of a customer transaction. Many online retailers compile records of each click and interaction a customer makes while visiting a website and use this to recommend additional purchases to a customer when they visit the company's website.

Variety – big data comes from a variety of sources and in different forms, structured and unstructured. For example Feltar could gather unstructured content from social media eg,

Twitter, YouTube, and use it in conjunction with more structured database information which Feltar's customers have consented to provide via the website.

Value – refers to the uncertainty that surrounds the accuracy of a lot of the data. The reliability of the data will influence the value of the predictions/outcomes of the data analysis.

Using data for competitive advantage

Marketing and sales:

Feltar could build brand loyalty by establishing a customer loyalty scheme – this would allow it to collect data and analyse and profile customers and their needs/buying habits. To comply with data protection regulations, Feltar would need to obtain consent from its customers if it intended to use the data collected to direct promotional material at its customers.

Data analytics software could be used to analyse the type of coffee individual customers buy, the frequency of purchases and the amounts typically spent.

In addition to collecting database information, Feltar could use Twitter/social media data to get better insights into what customers plan to buy, rather than just reacting to historical purchases.

Recording customers' preferences and obtaining their consent to use their personal data will help Feltar tailor its marketing eg, by delivering targeted advertising and discounts directly to customers' mobile devices. It could also help increase sales volumes by promoting related/similar products to those purchased before they check-out on the website or recommending items purchased by customers with similar tastes.

Inventory and pricing:

Collecting data about customers will not only help tailor the shopping experience to each individual but will also help Feltar to predict inventory requirements and potentially negotiate favourable rates with suppliers of the most popular coffee lines.

Trends identified in online sales in real time could be used to help improve inventory and pricing decisions. If a particular line of coffee is not selling very well, then an automatic price offer could be triggered.

Alternatively Feltar could send discounts to consenting customers whose buying behaviour shows that they have not returned to the site for a while.

Competitors' prices can be monitored and analysed so that Feltar can respond quickly with its own deals.

Customer service:

Many retailers offer customers the opportunity to leave feedback on the experience of shopping with the company. Some customers also give public feedback via social media.

If Feltar were to capture and analyse such feedback it could deal proactively with potential issues and respond quickly to customer complaints.

Practical implications

IT strategy

Feltar currently operates a basic website and captures limited data. This suggests that it has made limited investment in IT. The management team may need to take a more strategic attitude towards the use of technology.

Cost

A big data strategy is likely to need significant up-front investment in IT systems, which will require funding. Capturing and processing more data about customers will also have an ongoing cost.

Regulation

To comply with data protection regulations regarding the use of customer data, Feltar would need to put in place a mechanism for obtaining customer consent to store and use such data. Failure to process data in accordance with any customer consent given and holding personal data for longer than needed may result in significant fines.

Skills

As Feltar is a small business it may not have people with the skills to identify the appropriate data to capture, nor to extract meaningful insight from the data that is captured and processed. An alternative to employing its own experts is to outsource this to Gighay, since it has expertise in this area.

Time

Establishing the necessary databases and acquiring suitable analytical software is likely to take a significant amount of time.

Impact on customers

Consideration will need to be given to any potential disruption that the implementation of a big data strategy may cause, particularly if enhanced data capture requires changes to the website.

Data protection and security

Collecting and holding personal data about customers has legal and security implications. Feltar's management team will need to ensure that appropriate controls are put in place to prevent customer information falling into the wrong hands and to ensure compliance with the *Data Protection Act (2018)*. Again Gighay may be able to assist with this.

Examiner's comments

Most candidates were able to make some general points about how retail businesses can capture and use customer data. Better candidates picked up on the three areas highlighted in the scenario – marketing, inventory and pricing – and illustrated specifically how this might be done in the context of a coffee business. It was noticeable that those candidates who had studied the new topics in the learning materials were able to talk about big data and data analytics, rather than just the analysis of data traditionally captured in a company's customer database. Surprisingly few pointed out that Gighay, with particular expertise in data capture and data analytics, would be well placed to help Feltar overcome any practical difficulties. Candidates who discussed the 4Vs of big data and applied it to the relatively small coffee business tended to score highly.

43 Holidays Direct plc (June 2017)

Marking guide

	Knowledge	Skill	Marks
43.1 (a) Data analysis	2	11	
(b) Risks	2	7	19
43.2 Website	2	6	8
43.3 Structure	2	8	9
43.4 Ethics	3	5	8
	11	37	44

43.1 (a)

	20X6	20X7	% change
European (£'000s)	348,000	360,000	3.4%
Worldwide (£'000s)	148,000	184,000	24.3%
Total (£'000s)	496,000	544,000	9.7%
Bookings by consumers			
European (000s)	290	300	3.4%
Worldwide (000s)	74	92	24.3%
Total (000s)	364	392	7.7%
Average time of booking before departure (days)	87	76	(12.6)%
Hotel rooms booked (000s)	473	470	(0.6)%
Flight seats booked (000s)	1,092	1,176	7.7%
Hotel rooms vacant (000s)	14.2	4.7	(66.9)%
Flight seats empty (000s)	32.8	11.8	(64.0)%
Number of people per hotel room	2.31	2.5	
Value of discounts given to consumers (£'000s)	14,880	5,440	(63.4)%
Cost of additional bookings by HD (£'000s)	4,960	27,200	448.4%
Website visits (000s)	6,916	8,624	24.7%
Revenue per booking:			
European (£s)	1,200	1,200	–
Worldwide (£s)	2,000	2,000	–
Total (£s)	1,363	1,388	1.8%
Revenue per person (ie, flight seat) (£s)	454	463	2.0%
Discounts as a % of revenue	3%	1%	
Additional HD bookings as a % of revenue	1%	5%	
% vacant hotel rooms	3%	1%	
% empty seats	3%	1%	
Website visits per booking	19	22	15.8%

Financial performance

Overall revenue has increased by 9.7% in 20X7 compared with 20X6. In total, both the number of flight seats booked and the number of bookings have increased by 7.7%. However, these overall figures hide different trends in the European and Worldwide Divisions.

The European Division has experienced revenue growth of only 3.4% in the year. There has been an equivalent change in the number of bookings of 3.4% between 20X7 and 20X6. An initial conclusion might therefore be that the increase in revenue for the European Division has been the result of an increase in volumes rather than prices.

The Worldwide Division has experienced significant revenue growth of 24.3% in the year. Again, there has been an equivalent change in the number of bookings of 24.3% between 20X7 and 20X6. An initial conclusion might again be that the increase in revenue for the Worldwide Division has been the result of an increase in volumes rather than prices.

The initial conclusions of revenue changes resulting from volume changes rather than price can be challenged based on changes in underlying trends in consumer behaviour. Specifically, the number of hotel rooms booked has fallen by 0.6% despite the increase in the number of flight seats booked of 7.7%. This is due to the number of people per hotel room increasing from an average of 2.31 to an average of 2.5.

Operating performance

The increase in the number of people per hotel room may be part of a trend for more people squeezing into a hotel room to save on the price of the holiday. An alternative explanation is that the hotel rooms being sold are larger (eg, family rooms).

Overall, it seems likely that the revenue generated from operations relating to flights has increased more than that from accommodation operations, as there are more individuals flying. Also, the greater growth in the Worldwide Division may suggest that a larger part of the price of these holidays comprises the flight, compared with shorter haul European holidays.

Some trends can also be explained by the fact that a greater proportion of revenues in the mix are being generated by the operations of the Worldwide Division compared with the European Division. For example, there has been an overall increase of 1.8% in revenue per booking, despite the revenue per booking being stable for each individual division.

Additional information

- The information provided relates mainly to revenues and sales. Information on costs would be needed to determine margins and profit for each line of business and to make a more complete analysis of performance.

- A breakdown of discounts and additional flights between destinations would help to assess where the forecasting errors are occurring (eg, in one division in particular).

- Information on competitor performance from industry intelligence would help to assess HD's relative performance compared with competitors in a changing market.

- Monthly data would help to assess short-term patterns and trends in demand within the year, rather than just between years.

- Granular data on each hotel (eg, bookings, margins, occupancy) would help to determine differing trends in demand for individual hotels within destinations to assess performance at the level of individual hotels.

(b) **Operating risks**

Demand from consumers appears to be volatile.

Two issues arise from variations in demand:

- The extent to which demand is predictable (eg, through forecasts and market research)

- The extent to which demand is controllable (eg, through discounts, advertising, new or improved hotels and better destinations)

For HD predicting demand involves:

- predicting industry demand for the UK tour operators sector (eg, macroeconomic growth; competition from self-packaging; competition from consumer trend to holiday within the UK)

- predicting market share (pricing, marketing and quality of flights/hotels/service)

The key operating risks of **underestimating** demand:

- Lost goodwill and lost repeat bookings from customers who cannot book through lack of availability

- The feasibility of late additional bookings of flights and hotels by HD is limited, and are likely to be residual bookings that other tour operators do not want (eg, less favourable destinations/hotels)

- Late bookings by HD on top of block bookings require a double coincidence of availability of flights and hotels for the same location

- If an airline or a hotel cancel a booking (eg, mechanical failure of an aircraft or flood at a hotel) then there is no operational flexibility to cope with the excess demand

- If a destination suffers an incident (eg, terrorist attack or natural disaster) there is limited operational flexibility to offer alternative accommodation or flights

The key operating risk of **overestimating** demand:

- Late discounts may need to be offered which may damage goodwill of customers who have paid full price.

- Discounts may become expected, therefore incentivising consumers to delay bookings until they are available. This could make discounts the norm for an increasing proportion of consumers, thereby reducing profit and increasing uncertainty in forecasting demand.

The issues of under- and overestimating demand relate to each destination rather than overall. However, there is a little more flexibility for flights as each airport can serve multiple destinations for hotels.

As a result, there may be overestimated demand at one location and underestimated demand at another with limited operational ability (eg, due to flights) or consumer desire to transfer between the two locations.

Turning to specific data analysis in respect of the above:

Flight seat utilisation

The total of seats which were unoccupied in 20X7 was 11,800. This was a significant decrease of 64.1% from 32,800 unused seats in 20X6.

One of the factors causing the higher utilisation rate may have been that demand increased in 20X7 compared with 20X6 and this increase was not expected. It may have been that, following low demand in 20X6, HD expected demand to remain at a lower level for 20X7 rather than attempting to predict demand afresh.

This data may suggest that variations in demand have not been well predicted by HD and predictions for next year may have been too much influenced by demand in the current year.

Even when demand is high in 20X7 there are still 1% of flight seats vacant. This may suggest operating inefficiency, poor prediction of demand for some locations or random events at some locations (natural disasters).

In 20X6, when demand was lower, 3% of flight seats were vacant. The causal factor here however is not that demand was low per se, but that demand was not predicted to be low and so it was unexpected, resulting in overcapacity.

Vacant hotel rooms

The total of vacant hotel rooms in 20X7 was 4,700. This was again a significant decrease of 66.9% from 14,200 vacant rooms in 20X6.

The factors causing the higher utilisation rate in 20X7 are likely to have been the same as for flights.

Even when demand is high in 20X7 there are still 1% of hotel rooms vacant. In 20X6, when demand was lower, 3% of hotel rooms were vacant.

Whilst these data may suggest that there was operational inefficiency in misestimating demand, it does suggest, at least, that the hotel block bookings and flight block bookings were aligned at each destination.

Other operating risks

Other operating risks which may cause a difference between block contracts and demand:

- Random events (natural disasters and terrorist attacks)

- Flights – disruption of schedules (grounding of aircraft for technical problems, strikes, weather events)

Financial risks

Financial risks of overestimating demand

A key financial risk of overestimating demand relates to the cost of unsold flight seats and hotel rooms which still need to be paid for by HD even though there is no revenue from bookings.

Another of the key financial risks in overestimating demand is that discounts need to be offered in order to sell holidays (ie, flight seats and hotel rooms).

In this respect, the above data represent the residual effect in being unable to sell holidays to some destinations even after discounts.

Again, these effects are particular to each location. It is likely some destinations are overbooked and some underbooked.

The discounts have decreased by 63.4% from £14.88 million to £5.44 million. This is further evidence that the increase in demand in 20X7 compared with 20X6 was not fully anticipated. However, the overall increase in demand may not have been present across all destinations, as some discounts were still required in 20X7, which amounted to 1% of total revenue, despite this being lower than the 3% of total revenue in 20X6.

Financial risks of underestimating demand

The key financial risk of underestimating demand relates to lost revenues from unsatisfied demand and this will impact on profit.

One of the financial risks in underestimating demand is that additional late bookings of flights and hotel rooms may need to be made by HD. These are likely to be at higher cost than block bookings and are subject to availability of the flight and hotel at the same destination.

It may be that this results in lower profit or that the increased cost can be passed on to consumers in higher prices. Notwithstanding this, better operational efficiency in forecasting would have enabled better planning of flights, hotel rooms and prices.

Other financial risks

Other financial risks which may arise from a difference between block contracts and demand:

- Foreign exchange – if the £ falls (eg, between the time of the block contract booking and the time of consumer bookings), then oil prices (and therefore fuel costs) in $ will rise in sterling terms. Also, the cost of Worldwide accommodation will rise in sterling terms if the £ falls in relation to a range of currencies. These changes in sterling costs may need to be passed on by HD in price increases to consumers, which will impact demand and profit.

- Counterparty credit risk from failure of hotel chains and airlines holding deposits may cause a short-term reduction in supply and financial loss.

Examiner's comments

Part (a) of the first requirement was generally well answered. Most candidates provided a well-structured table for data analysis, focusing on changes between the two years, financial data and non-financial data.

The qualitative discussion was also good in many cases, providing reasons for the data trends and suggesting causal relationships. However, the non-financial data was generally less well analysed than the financial data.

Many candidates initially considered the firm's demand forecasting ability to be good, as evidenced by the decline in the value of discounts given to customers, but then often changed their minds when they came to consider the increase in the cost of additional bookings.

The weaker minority did not produce a data table and instead tended to weave some numbers into their narrative. They tended to lose marks by failing to present the data systematically, thereby failing to identify data patterns which would have revealed important issues facing the firm.

Of the better candidates, a few made the point, in the additional information section, that a complete evaluation of the firm's overall performance cannot be made as information provided was mainly restricted to revenues, with no overall cost or profit data given.

Many produced rather lengthy lists of additional insignificant information requirements, which were often very generic in nature and not directly relevant to the question.

In respect of part (b) most candidates performed well on this requirement. The majority devoted most of the discussion to the central issue of over/under estimation of demand. However, most candidates made insufficient use of the basic data provided in the question to illustrate their arguments.

Some candidates did not separate out the risks into operating and financial, thereby providing an unstructured, and frequently generalised, risk answer.

43.2 Website visits

Monitoring of the number of website visits in each period may be a lead indicator of the level of interest in the holidays and therefore the number of eventual bookings.

This may help predict future demand and therefore improve on the operational inefficiencies noted above.

The total number of visits in 20X7 increased by 24.7% compared with 20X6. This meant there were over 22 visits per booking in 20X7, compared with 19 per booking in 20X6.

This could have been an early indication of increased demand in 20X7 compared with 20X6 but it would have been necessary to monitor the visits each day/week/month rather than annually. An alternative explanation is that more visits occurring is consistent with more people accessing the internet from more types of devices.

Better data relating to visits would be obtained if the particular pages visited could be identified on the website, so changes in consumer tastes for each destination or type of holiday could be better monitored to estimate future demand in each segment of the business. This data indicating future demand could be used to support a segmentation strategy.

Bookings

Monitoring the numbers of, and trends in, actual bookings is key data in predicting eventual demand.

The fact that there has been a trend for later bookings in 20X7 (76 days before departure) compared with 20X6 (87 days) may be indicative of a change in customers' behaviour relating to the later timing of making a booking. In this case, extrapolating trends by comparing bookings this year with the number of bookings at the equivalent time last year, may be less valid, or at least may need to be adjusted.

The bookings system provides key information for Harriet and Penny in adjusting the block bookings of hotels and flights for each destination and for each week of the year. This may impact not just on block bookings but on the timing and extent of discounts and additional bookings.

Further details on demographics and social attributes of consumers, provided consumer consent is given for HD to process this data, may help tailor marketing of particular locations (eg, for retired people who may be flexible with travel arrangements) and timings (eg, families who are not flexible on timing and may be sensitive to price changes).

Data Analytics

HD can use data analytics software to organise and analyse the website data collected to discover trends and patterns that might not otherwise be apparent.

The website data collected can also be combined using data analytics software with other internally (eg, previous bookings) and externally (eg, from social media) available data about customers to build up a more detailed profile.

This can help HD gain a deeper understanding of customer requirements. This information can then help predict future demand, for example by using models to forecast sales trends and the likely impact on costs.

Examiner's comments

This was reasonably well answered by most candidates. Most recognised the relevance of the website information for overall demand prediction. Fewer discussed issues around segmentation and/or seasonality and how this information can be used to estimate future variations in demand in different geographical areas or segments of the business.

A minority discussed, in some detail, the technicalities of 'Big Data' - displaying knowledge in this area - but then some became distracted by this theme, missing the key issues of demand/segmentation prediction.

The validity of the data for prediction of demand was raised by a minority.

43.3 The current organisational structure seems to be a divisionalised structure which is the legacy of a previous acquisition.

In essence, the two operating divisions are based upon different geographical markets according to the location of the consumers' holidays.

It also has elements of a matrix structure as it includes Penny and Harriet reporting to both divisional heads, as flights and accommodation bookings cut across both geographical divisions. This may cause conflicts of interest, confused reporting lines and clouded areas of performance measurement.

The first key issue is whether the booking and marketing aspects of the business need to be split between Europe and Worldwide Divisions. Both use the same booking system and there appears to be little difference in the nature of the holidays to justify separation. The main difference is just distance of travel.

Joining marketing and booking into one division may generate economies of scale in sharing marketing and advertising. If the divisions are being monitored for performance separately it may also avoid competition between divisions.

The accommodation function is currently split across two divisions, despite the hotel chains having global presence across both geographical regions. This may be preventing composite contracts for the company as a whole, or at least some flexibility between bookings within and beyond Europe.

The booking of flights does appear to be in line with the current system of Europe and Worldwide with two airlines serving Europe and one elsewhere. However, this may be a consequence of having two divisions, rather than being coincident with them. If the divisions were to be merged, then there may be the facility to have all airlines serve both European and global markets with consequent economies of scale.

Revised structure

A revised structure could be for three main separate operating divisions (sales, hotel bookings and flight bookings) reporting into a single head of operations who would have overall control. Other support divisions (eg, HR, administration etc) may also be needed but could be monitored separately from operating divisions.

A key issue for business efficiency and risk is integrating sales, flights and accommodation for each location. This requires shared information and shared decision making which could take place between functions under the umbrella of a single divisional head.

The consequence of the need for coordination is interdependency so performance measurement is difficult under the old two divisions. However, it can be measured with one operating division and one operating head who can take overall responsibility for all aspects of operating performance.

Examiner's comments

Most candidates identified the current structure as divisional. Some also considered it to be partly matrix as well, or they considered it to be, in part, functional. A significant minority referred to Mintzberg and/or Handy, but often inappropriately. Most candidates were able to identify some advantages and disadvantages of the current structure.

Most candidates also provided reasonable suggestions for an alternative structure, after outlining the drawbacks of the existing structure. Many suggested a functional structure. Fewer provided a strong justification for their suggested structure in the specific context of the firm's operations.

43.4 There are two potential ethical issues:

(1) Penny disclosing information to customers about car hire charges.

(2) HD using its position of access to information, and trying to persuade consumers to pay more than necessary for car hire, in order for HD to take a commission.

In making any ethical evaluation it is first necessary to establish the facts. In this case, the claims made by Penny need to be established to assess their validity before taking any action. This may include establishing not just what Penny has disclosed but the extent of her actions (which she may have understated). In particular, it needs to be established whether over-charging of customers for car rental is actually taking place. It also needs to be established that Penny has not taken any money as she asserted.

A key issue is that she has disclosed general market information **to** customers, not **about** customers.

The issue of legality may apply if the charging information or personal details have been accessed in order to provide information to selected customers. Legal advice is needed to ascertain whether this is contrary to criminal law in the UK or other countries where HD operates, or breaches regulations or contractual agreements signed by HD.

For HD, illegality may relate to mis-selling if pressure was applied to customers, but again legal advice is required.

Irrespective of legality, in making an ethical decision as to how to act, it may be helpful to Penny and to HD apply the Institute of Business Ethics three tests:

- Transparency
- Effect
- Fairness

Penny

Transparency – would Penny mind people (divisional heads, the HD board, existing customers, suppliers, other employees) knowing about what she has done? In particular, the issue of providing transparency in disclosing car hire rates to customers could be viewed as the opposite side of a breach of confidentiality of HD's pricing.

Effect – whom does Penny's disclosure affect or hurt? Clearly this could include the benefits of reduced car hire fees to some customers who acted differently on the basis of full information. On the other hand, her employer could lose legitimate commission income. Car hire companies in Spain dealing with HD would lose income but Penny's friend could gain.

Fairness – would it be considered fair by those affected? The issues are whether mere disclosure of information is unfair and whether the circumstances under which it was made (by an employee) are fair. Also, disclosure was only made to holiday-makers going to Spain. Other holiday-makers may feel it is unfair that they did not gain the same information. In addition, the disclosure was not just general information that car hire through HD was expensive but a specific recommendation to use a firm related to Penny.

HD

Transparency – would HD mind people (existing customers, suppliers, employees) knowing what it was doing? In particular, the issue of deliberately pushing customers towards high car hire rates to make commissions for HD could be viewed as inappropriate exploitation of their position and therefore mis-selling. Conversely, it could be argued that earning commission for recommendations of firms with which it has contractual relationships is a legitimate business activity given that the consumers were free to look elsewhere if they chose to do so.

Effect – whom does the disclosure affect or hurt? Clearly this could include the harm to customers, who would have acted differently on the basis of full information, of being persuaded to pay higher car hire fees.

Fairness – would it be considered fair by those affected? The issue could be whether HD's superior information position was exploited or that information was readily available (eg, on websites) to customers to enable them to make an informed choice, but they were willing to pay an additional amount for ease and reassurance.

Actions

Penny's actions should be consistent with her obligations and duties as a senior HD employee.

Although Penny made no direct personal gain (if her claims are true), it may have facilitated a relationship with her Spanish friend to her benefit and may therefore still have involved self-interest.

Harriet's initial action should be to inform the HD board. It seems unlikely there is illegality but unauthorised direct contact with HD customers for a purpose contrary to the interests of HD whilst an employee of HD may be a breach of Penny's duties as an employee.

Harriet may also question the board on whether the arrangement amounts to mis-selling.

Examiner's comments

The answers to this requirement were variable in quality. Most candidates did not apply professional scepticism to establish the facts. For example, many candidates uncritically accepted that the firm is over-charging customers for car rental, and that Penny has not taken any money as she asserted. Discussion also often tended to focus on Penny to the exclusion of HD although, with some candidates, it was the other way around.

Many candidates used the Transparency, Effect, Fairness (TEF) structure and language, although surprisingly not everyone. However, many candidates limited their discussion to these three TEF principles rather than going on also to explore other ethical principles and issues raised by the scenario. They thereby produced a restricted and narrow answer which was constrained by the TEF framework rather than enhanced by it.

Some candidates provided a reasonable discussion of the ethical issues/principles but then provided a weak discussion of the actions. Most candidates set out suggested actions for Harriet as required, but others then went on to stray beyond what was asked in the requirement by also setting out actions for HD and Penny.

44 Jason Smyth Textiles Ltd (June 2017, amended)

Marking guide

	Knowledge	Skill	Marks
44.1 (a) Value chain diagram	4	8	
(b) Value chain – low cost strategy	2	7	19
44.2 (a) New business model	2	7	
(b) Change management	2	5	14
	10	27	33

44.1 (a)

	IL	O	OL	M/S	S
FI	Profit-orientated culture. Tight financial and operating control.				
TD	IT ordering systems, inventory control, payables management		Delivery IT systems	IT systems and data capture to facilitate relationship marketing	IT receivables/payables management systems IT based marketing support
HRD	Some training for skilled staff	Some training for skilled staff Limited training for unskilled staff	Delivery IT systems training	Discipline relating to customer issues	
Procurement	Bulk buying, managing supplier relationships, payables management	Low cost factory historically used			Financing and administration of payables systems
Primary activity	Optimal delivery systems, JIT, sourcing low cost synthetic materials	Low cost factory, low cost unskilled labour Labour intensive Colouring and design	Direct delivery to customers in bulk	Relationship marketing	Make good defaults Receivables administration and management Credit facilities

Tutorial note

In the Business Strategy and Technology exam if you are required to present your answer in a diagrammatical form then it is perfectly acceptable to present your work in a tabular or columnar format as shown above.

(b) The value chain can be used to examine where value can be created using the resources of the business to generate strategic options.

The primary activities are those that create value and are directly concerned with providing the output of soft furnishings. The support activities do not create value of themselves but enable the primary activities to take place with maximum efficiency and effectiveness.

Value drivers for JST include the colouring and design activities that have enabled JST to distinguish its products from those of competitors and create competitive advantage.

Overall, JST is pursuing a cost leadership strategy in accordance with Porter's generic activities and should thus focus upon low cost resources to produce a low-cost product. This requires identification of cost drivers within the value chain.

Examples are the low labour and materials costs on the supply side and efficient operating activities throughout the value chain up to the truncated delivery chain to customers, which provides only a basic service.

However, to maintain the position of cost leadership it is not just internal costs that need to be controlled, but costs throughout the supply chain. This includes costs from suppliers of raw materials and other inputs.

In particular, costs relating to support activities that do not support appropriately the primary activities in adding value for customers, or that create excess costs in so doing, should be reduced or removed.

Examples of low cost features, built in throughout JST's value chain, include:

- low cost production machines (acquired from a liquidator)

- low cost labour at the minimum wage for unskilled staff

- low cost raw materials (polyester) which are imported from developing countries

- low distribution costs through own lorry fleet and improved efficiency using IT

- costs of inbound logistics shifted to suppliers so inward transport and inventory holding costs are minimised (JIT)

- only a small number of suppliers, so payables management and procurement systems costs are reduced.

The abilities to add value by reducing costs to a minimum need to be linked and applied consistently for all costs in the value chain to be able to sell at a low price and therefore be competitive in the market for basic soft furnishings.

Whilst this model has been successful historically, two key costs are increasing: wages, due to the increase in the minimum wage; and raw materials, due to the decrease in the value of the £. These changing cost drivers in the value chain make it more difficult for JST to add value and remain competitive on a sustainable basis.

Examiner's comments

Part (a) of the first requirement was well answered by most candidates. Most correctly identified the primary and secondary activities of the value chain and provided descriptions of the relevant activities. The descriptions were sometimes within the value chain diagram boxes and sometimes cross-referenced to a more detailed narrative outside the value chain diagram. Either approach was acceptable.

Some candidates answered parts (a) and (b) jointly, normally resulting in an unstructured approach to answering these requirements.

Weaker candidates did not know the basics of the activities within the value chain or the structure of the diagram. Examples would be: mixing rows and columns inappropriately; treating support activities as primary and vice versa; or just simply omitting some activities completely.

In respect of part (b) of the first requirement, a significant minority failed to identify the cost leadership strategy pursued by the firm as central to their answer. Only a small minority referred to cost/value drivers. However, most candidates were able to use examples from the scenario to illustrate the nature of the low-cost strategy.

Linkages between primary and support activities were only explicitly considered and evaluated by the best candidates. Many candidates tended to provide a rather generic/descriptive discussion of each activity in isolation.

Better candidates were able to link the strategy to the value chain activities and discuss the relevance of value drivers and cost drivers.

44.2 (a) The new strategy consists of two elements:

- Abandoning the current model of low cost production and its associated markets

- Entering a new position in a related market with revised production techniques and improved procurement quality

Benefits

- The current market is one of cost leadership according to Porter's generic strategies. It appears to be an unsustainable strategy due to low margins and increasing costs. The new strategy offers higher prices with the potential for increased margins. The new strategy would be a move to be a differentiator in Porter's generic strategies by creating tangible and intangible product features that consumers are willing to pay for and therefore to create margin.

- The new strategy is to launch a new product in the existing market (Ansoff's product development), so there is likely to be some overlap of market knowledge and networking contacts. However, it could be argued that the new strategy is in a different sector of the same market.

- The JST brand name for soft furnishings is still relevant to the industry under the new business model.

- If competition in the new sector of the market is more about quality, design and service, and less about cost and price, then there is an opportunity to compete on more favourable terms with imported goods by taking advantage of proximity to customers.

- Whilst rival companies in developing nations may benefit from lower wage costs and lower production costs compared with JST they may suffer from the fall in the value of the £. Rivals' products will have become more expensive in £ terms and the revenue generated for these rival in £s is less attractive when converted back into their own currencies.

- Whilst the new natural products are largely a departure from existing production and markets, the continued use of polyester (albeit of better quality) may give JST a continued foothold in existing markets and production techniques as a transition to the new business model.

- The new strategy requires the purchase of advanced robotic machinery which is to be operated through the use of an intelligent control system. As highlighted by the JST board, the introduction of the new machinery should enable JST to achieve significant efficiencies in the manufacturing process. This is a considerable benefit as its existing manufacturing machinery is nearing the end of its useful life, and has resulted in an increasing number of defects in batches of production. As such the introduction of the new machinery and intelligent control system should help support JST as it transitions from its current business model to its new strategy.

Problems

- The new strategy may involve new skills (eg, in processing natural fabrics) which may not be primarily within the existing core competences of JST, notwithstanding some overlap.

- The move upmarket may mean that new relationships need to be established with an entire range of new customers. The existing customer relationships may be largely lost as the new quality products may be outside the price range for their customers' range of products.

- Whilst the JST brand name may continue to have some relevance, it may send the wrong signal in suggesting a low-cost product when the firm is trying to promote the opposite, upmarket image.

- One of the reasons that a low-cost operation has been sustainable is that the factory and machinery were acquired at low cost from the liquidator. Now that this initial machinery is failing, the proposed purchase costs of the new automated robotic machinery and intelligent control system will need to be considered. The advanced nature of the new machinery proposed for use in manufacturing is likely to require significant capital expenditure. This has a number of risks:

  - The increased costs of the new machinery and intelligent control system will increase overall costs and this may mean that the new business model may not be competitive even at higher prices.

  - The increase in machinery costs are fixed costs which raise operating gearing further and increases operating risk.

  - Any new investment would be a sunk cost and may not be recoverable if JST's new strategy becomes unviable.

  - The associated costs of maintaining the intelligent control system infrastructure also need to be factored into the proposed new strategy. Again, due to the technologically advanced nature of this type of system these costs will most likely be significant.

Conclusion

The new strategy is extremely risky and a better response to the demise of existing markets may be to exit the industry. Much will depend on market research and the ability to establish a new range of customers in sufficient quantity to make the new business model viable.

(b) The type of change will strongly influence the way in which change is managed. Change in this case seems transformational (a major significant change) and is planned to take place on 1 January 20X8 as a rapid one-off change on the introduction of the new robotics machinery and intelligent control system. This will affect all employees significantly, but unskilled employees are most at risk.

The changes also affect other stakeholders such as suppliers and customers, although customers are well protected in competitive markets where they can purchase elsewhere.

The way in which the changes are introduced will be very important in them being implemented successfully. There will be cultural and individual barriers to change. Resistance and barriers to change need to be acknowledged and may be lessened by involving the employees in planning and implementation. There are two main groups of employees which will need to be managed differently and present different barriers to change:

- Those skilled employees who are required to retrain and have changed roles
- Those unskilled employees who may be required to leave the company

Barriers to change

Change management to reduce barriers to change involves managing people's expectations and attitudes since many changes may be resisted by employees. The key staff affected here will be the skilled employees to be retrained to use the new automated machinery and those unskilled employees whom JST wishes to retain. The change is unlikely to be successful unless key employees can be persuaded of the need for change and the benefits of change to them.

The current business model is generating losses for JST and these are expected to worsen, so convincing employees of the need for change is facilitated as the current business model is unsustainable. However, this does not mean employees will approve of the specific new business model being proposed.

Various barriers to change are possible.

(1) **Cultural barriers**

Power structures within JST may be threatened. This will, in particular, affect management and others in authority who may be protective of their current roles and decision-making authority and be reluctant to implement changes which will be against their own interests.

Structural inertia: the existing systems of planning and decision making may act as a barrier to change to a new approach.

Group inertia may block change where the changes are inconsistent with the norms of team working and departments, or where they threaten their interests. JST's unskilled workers may therefore bond together to resist change (eg, strike action) as they are most affected, particularly as they may not obtain other jobs as local unemployment is high.

(2) **Personnel barriers**

There are also barriers which affect individuals and result in them seeing the change as a threat. Here habit and fear of the unknown may mean some individual JST managers are unwilling or reluctant to take on additional responsibility involved in new roles.

Approach to change

A mixture of the adaptive and coercive approach is likely to be appropriate. Adaptive change alone may be too slow, and JST's management may need to emphasise that it is vital that changes are made soon if the company is to survive.

Jason may need to actively demonstrate a willingness to delegate and adopt a more hands-off approach to management of the change. Otherwise managers may perceive that their involvement is simply a token and that the substance of decision making is outside their control. JST managers will need educating that the existing manufacturing systems are insufficient to allow successful improvements to meet competitive conditions. Jason will need to provide managers with training and support to increase their ability to make decisions within the new business model.

Models

Lewin/Schein's 3-step iceberg model of change would prescribe the following approach:

- Unfreezing standard operating procedures (identifying the restraining forces and overcoming them);

- Move to new patterns of behaviour (eg, carrying out the change to higher quality production); and

- Refreezing to ensure lasting effects (eg, reinforcing working with the new automated machinery and intelligent control system and natural fabrics).

While these phases may be appropriate to employees retaining roles within JST, they will not apply to those who are to be made redundant, as they will not have to accept a new structure or culture.

The **Gemini 4Rs** framework could also be used here:

Reframe – create the will and desire to change (the current JST business model is unsustainable due to rising costs of labour and imported materials).

Restructure – redesign the structure and culture to facilitate the new approach of higher quality materials and outputs. This may involve setting up new teams and processes as part of a learning culture.

Revitalise – creating a culture of teamwork between the new incoming employees and the existing employees who are being retained.

Renewal – ensure the change is supported on an ongoing basis and that individuals involved have the necessary skills eg, training in the new manufacturing systems.

The **coercive change approach** is where change is forced without participation. This requires the ability to push through the change without cooperation.

Examiner's comments

Part (a) of the second requirement was well answered by the majority of candidates. Most recognised the proposal as a change in generic strategy, moving towards differentiation and away from cost leadership. Most candidates also recommended that the new business model should not be adopted, even though the current strategy is not sustainable.

Those who clearly structured their answer by separately identifying benefits and problems tended to score well. Weaker candidates did not separate out the benefits and problems and therefore tended to produce generic and unstructured answers. Weaker candidates also tended to produce rather thin answers. For example, for key benefits their discussion got little beyond obtaining higher prices.

Part (b) of the second requirement was well answered by most candidates. A majority incorporated a relevant model for change management, mostly Lewin, and a variety of barriers to change. However, weaker answers tended to provide very generic discussion of models and barriers to change.

45 Portland Prawns Ltd (June 2017)

Marking guide

	Knowledge	Skill	Marks
45.1 FFF Contract	2	15	15
45.2 Rental	1	7	8
	3	22	23

45.1 (a)　The FFF contract is rejected.

Price £	10.00	10.50	11.00
VC £	4.50	4.50	4.50
Selling cost £	1.00	1.00	1.00
Contribution pu £	4.50	5.00	5.50
Sales volume kg	400,000	350,000	300,000
Total contribution £	1,800,000	1,750,000	1,650,000
FC £	1,200,000	1,200,000	1,200,000
Profit £	600,000	550,000	450,000

Thus **£600,000** remains the highest attainable profit which is achieved at a price of £10 per kilo if the contract is rejected.

(b)　The FFF contract is accepted and demand is **150,000 kilos**.

	Existing customers per (a)	FFF	Total
Price £	10.50	8.00	
VC £	4.50	4.50	
Selling cost £	1.00	-	
Contribution pu £	5.00	3.50	
Sales volume kg	350,000	150,000	500,000 (capacity)
Total contribution £	1,750,000	525,000	
FC £	1,200,000	420,000	
Profit £	550,000	105,000	**£655,000**

Alternative presentation of calculations

Total contribution from FFF = £[8 – 4.5) × 150,000] – £420,000 = £105,000

Maximum contribution from existing customers:

Capacity = 400,000 kg/0.8 = 500,000 kg

Maximum available supply for existing customers = (500,000 – 150,000)kg = 350,000 kg

Highest price to sell 350,000 kg = £10.50

Profit from existing customers = £550,000 (see schedule above)

Total profit = **£655,000** (£105,000 + 550,000)

(c)　The FFF contract is accepted and demand is **200,000 kilos**.

	Existing customers per (a)	FFF	Total
Price £	11.00	8.00	
VC £	4.50	4.50	
Selling cost £	1.00	-	
Contribution pu £	5.50	3.50	
Sales volume kg	300,000	200,000	500,000 (capacity)
Total contribution £	1,650,000	700,000	
FC £	1,200,000	420,000	
Profit £	450,000	280,000	**£730,000**

Alternative presentation of calculations

Total contribution from FFF = £[8 – 4.5) × 200,000] – £420,000 = £280,000

Maximum contribution from existing customers:

Maximum available supply for existing customers = (500,000 - 200,000)kg = 300,000 kg

Highest price to sell 300,000 kg = £11

Profit from existing customers = £450,000 (see schedule above)

Total profit = **£730,000** (£280,000 + 450,000)

Discussion

If the FFF contract is rejected, the market research indicates that the optimal price for PP is the current price of £10 per kilo (see schedule above).

In the short term, the FFF contract would generate additional profit irrespective of whether demand is as low as 150,000 kg or as high as 200,000 kg.

If FFF demand is low (150,000 kg) however the additional profit is small at only £55,000 and this can be achieved only by reducing the volumes sold to existing customers by 50,000 kg (ie, to 350,000 kg) due to the annual operating capacity constraint of 500,000 kg. The reduced target level of sales to existing customers does however enable the price to these customers to be increased to £10.50 in order to maximise operating profit.

If FFF demand is high (200,000 kg) the additional profit is £130,000. This is achieved by reducing the volumes sold to existing customers by 100,000 kg (ie, to 300,000 kg) due to the annual operating capacity constraint of 500,000 kg. The reduced target level of sales to existing customers does however enable the price to these customers to be increased to £11.00 in order to maximise operating profit.

Clearly if demand is between these limits then the additional profit would be between £55,000 and £130,000.

These results however depend on a number of assumptions:

- Penalties are avoided.

- The quality of processing can be maintained with additional output and with the new freezing process.

- A supply of quality additional prawns can be obtained to satisfy both FFF and existing customers.

- If demand is seasonal (and fresh prawns cannot be effectively stored) then processing may already be at full capacity at certain times of the year and thus the opportunity cost of lost sales from existing customers may be greater than indicated.

- Demand from FFF is known at the beginning of the year, so the price to other customers can be set accordingly at that time to accommodate residual capacity (ie, at the beginning of the year it might not be known whether demand from FFF is 150,000 kg or as high as 200,000 kg, so PP does not, at that time, know whether to set a price to other customers of £10.50 or £11).

If the FFF contract is terminated after one year or after two years, there is a longer-term issue that the existing customers, who have been discouraged by price increases, do not return.

The contract with FFF may improve PP's reputation and lead to further sales in future or alternatively to a hardening of selling prices.

With the new FFF contract, production would be at capacity, so there is a risk that any stoppage of processing (strike, breakdown etc) will result in lost sales and profit. Penalty clauses may apply if there is such a failure.

Each current customer is small and thus there is little individual customer power. FFF however is a significant customer and may be able to dictate future terms.

There is no certainty of contract renewal in future thus lost customers may be a permanent opportunity cost. Similarly, the marketing survey may be incorrect and existing customers may be more resistant to price increases than the survey indicates.

There are significant additional fixed costs associated with the new contract and this increases operating gearing.

Examiner's comments

This requirement was not well answered by most candidates, but a number of the better candidates scored full marks. The marks therefore tended to polarise.

The calculations were not complex but they required an understanding and application of the basic business issues of demand and pricing where there is a capacity constraint.

Many candidates initially used a structured approach and obtained £600k if the contract is rejected. However, some jumped to this answer without demonstrating it as optimal by exploring the alternative price/volume relationships provided in the question (ie, they ignored the market research data provided). Some candidates incorrectly calculated the theoretical 'maximum profit' as if 500 kg were sold. Other added the sales volumes (400k + 350k + 300k) and multiplied by the price, completely missing the point of the price/demand market research information.

Other calculation errors were: failing to alter the variable distribution costs for selling lower volumes; deducting the £65,000 rental cost which only applies to the final requirement (as explicitly stated in the requirement).

Even some of those candidates who arrived at the correct calculations did not then provide much comment or qualitative analysis.

Weaker candidates failed to grasp the fundamentals of how to deal optimally with the capacity constraint while accepting the new contract.

Where candidates made incorrect calculations, credit was given for their discussion under the 'own answer' principle. There were also marks for discussion of non-data issues relating to the terms of the contract, although candidates' answers were often too narrow and did not address these issues.

45.2 The FFF contract is accepted and demand is **150,000 kilos with rented factory**

	Existing customers per (a)	FFF	Total
Price £	10.00	8.00	
VC £	4.50	4.50	
Selling cost £	1.00	–	
Contribution pu £	4.50	3.50	
Sales volume kg	400,000	150,000	550,000
Total contribution £	1,800,000	525,000	
FC £	1,200,000	420,000	
Profit £	600,000	105,000	**705,000**
Factory rental cost £			(65,000)
Revised total £			**640,000**

The FFF contract is accepted and demand is **200,000 kilos with rented factory**

	Existing customers per (a)	FFF	Total
Price £	10.00	8.00	
VC £	4.50	4.50	
Selling cost £	1.00	–	
Contribution pu £	4.50	3.50	
Sales volume kg	400,000	200,000	600,000
Total contribution £	1,800,000	700,000	
FC £	1,200,000	420,000	
Profit £	600,000	280,000	**880,000**
Factory rental cost £			(65,000)
Revised total £			**815,000**

With the rental contract, the total capacity of both factories would be 650,000 kilos (500,000 + 150,000).

This would be sufficient to satisfy both the optimal demand from current customers (400,000 kg) and the highest demand from FFF (200,000 kg). It would also leave 50,000 kg spare capacity to accommodate any sales growth.

At the maximum demand from FFF, this would generate a total contribution of £880,000 (£600,000 + £280,000), an increase of **£150,000** compared with not having the extra capacity (£880,000 – £730,000).

At the lower demand from FFF, this would generate a total contribution of £705,000 (£600,000 + £105,000), an increase of **£50,000** compared with not having the extra capacity (£705,000 – £655,000).

As a result, if demand from FFF is at the lower end of the range in the year ending 30 June 20X8 then the additional contribution generated by having the new factory (£50,000) would not be sufficient to cover the additional rental cost in that year of £65,000.

In contrast, if demand from FFF is at the higher end of the range in the year ending 30 June 20X8 then the additional contribution generated by having the new factory (£150,000) would be more than sufficient to cover the additional rental cost in that year of £65,000.

An assessment would need to be made of how probable it is that demand from FFF would be towards the higher end of the contractual range.

More significantly, there are major risks arising from the fact that this is a three-year rental agreement and there is no guarantee that the FFF contract will be renewed for either 20X8 or 20X9. This would leave PP with unnecessary spare capacity serving its existing customers and an obligation to pay rentals of £65,000 pa for possibly two more years.

It may however be possible to sub-let the factory to a third party if the FFF contract does not run for more than one year, although this may not be for £65,000 pa or for the full period.

There is some upside potential if the FFF operations lead to obtaining similar customers requiring frozen prawns and thereby utilise the spare capacity.

Overall the advice is that the risks of signing the rental contract are too great at 1 July 20X7 as this would add to the existing risks from the FFF contract. Deferring the decision to keep the real option of waiting to see how the FFF succeeds may be the best decision. It can then be determined whether spare capacity is needed, either at the new factory currently being offered, or at an alternative location.

Marks on this requirement again tended to polarise with some better candidates scoring full marks while many candidates failed to grasp some fairly basic principles on contribution and decision making in a situation of constrained capacity.

As with the first requirement, the calculations were basic, but they required an understanding and application of the fundamental business issues of the costs and benefits of obtaining additional capacity by entering into a rental agreement for an additional factory.

These basic calculations were then 'pegs' on which to hang a brief discussion of the quantitative benefits, alongside the more general qualitative business issues relating to uncertainty of demand over the period of the rental contract.

46 Blakes Blinds Ltd (September 2017)

Marking guide

	Knowledge	Skill	Marks
46.1 Factors creating competitive advantage/ sustainability	2	5	7
46.2 Analysis of financial performance/areas of concern	1	22	20
46.3 Advantages/disadvantages of acquisition/transfer pricing	4	8	11
46.4 Ethical issues	3	5	7
	10	40	45

46.1 Competitive advantage

In accordance with Porter's generic strategies, BB operates a differentiation strategy manufacturing and installing high quality blinds and shutters. This means that clients are prepared to pay a premium to the extent that they perceive BB's product is different or has added value. BB's strategy is focused on the niche market of corporate clients in the UK.

The following are value drivers which give BB a competitive advantage in terms of its differentiation strategy:

- Unlike most blind and shutter companies, which buy in ready-made products, BB undertakes all its manufacturing in-house. This allows it to control the quality which is important to the underlying strategy.

- It also provides a one-stop service from site visit through to servicing. BB is able to tailor products to individual requirements and take into account delivery dates, installation times, and specific budgets.

- The offer of a service contract also helps tie customers into BB and generate future repeat business.

- Through Research and Development BB has developed its innovative 'Auto-close' system which appears to be highly valued by corporate clients. This competitive advantage is protected in a sense as a result of the brand being trademarked.

Sustainability:

Porter's five forces looks at how easy it is to sustain profitability within an industry given the nature of the competitive forces. There are a number of businesses in the blinds and shutters market making it a competitive market and it appears that barriers to entry are relatively low. Switching costs for clients are also likely to be low so retention of clients and customer loyalty is key to sustaining market share, since there is little to stop other businesses operating a similar strategy to BB. The 'Auto-close' system offers a distinct competitive advantage, however it depends heavily on technology, which is constantly evolving and it appears that other competitors have already brought out similar products.

As a result it is likely that BB has first mover advantage here only rather than a long-term sustainable advantage. This is especially true if competitor's products can be retro-fitted to BBs blinds.

Examiner's comments

This was very well answered by the vast majority of candidates who were very comfortable discussing competitive advantage. However surprisingly few chose to use a specific model to structure their answers and ensure a full range of points were covered.

In terms of Porter's generic strategies, many answers either referred to differentiation or focus, but not focused differentiation which is the strategy being adopted by BB. Some better candidates used Porter's value chain to analyse sources of competitive advantage linked to the chosen generic strategy.

Very few used Porter's five forces to analyse the sustainability of competitive advantage, although this was implicit in many of the better answers. Some candidates missed this element of the requirement out altogether. A significant minority focused on the broader Bruntland definition of sustainability which was not really relevant here, although since most did consider economic sustainability as part of this discussion, they were awarded some marks.

46.2 Data analysis

Evaluation of performance 20X5–20X6

The Board is right to be concerned. Despite an increase in revenue of £5.9 million (56.3%) between 20X5 and 20X6 ,operating profit has fallen by £7,000 from £417,000 to £410,000. There are two reasons for this reduction in profitability:

- The gross profit margin has fallen from 43.2% to 40.5%; and
- The fixed costs have increased by 51% between 20X5 and 20X6.

As a result the operating margin is only 2.5% for 20X6, compared to 4% the previous year.

To further explain the reasons for the decline it is important to analyse the individual revenue streams. The fall in gross margin has been driven by the reduction in the profitability of the core business – blinds and shutters. Here the margin has fallen from 36% in 20X5 to 29.7% in 20X6. Over 60% of BB's components are sourced from China. One reason for the loss of profits is the increase in cost of sales caused by exchange rate movements. Between 20X5 and 20X6 it appears that CNY has appreciated from £0.105 to £0.115. This resulted in purchases costing an extra £265,000 in 20X6 (CNY26,456 × (0.115 – 0.105)). More information is needed about the extent to which BB undertakes hedging of its foreign exchange risk and whether this was down purely to exchange rate movements or included foreign currency losses.

The sales growth is largely attributable to the development of the new 'Auto-close' system which launched at the beginning of 20X5. This accounted for 5% of sales in 20X5 but had grown to 17% in 20X6.

Without the development of the auto-close system the decline in gross profit in 20X6 would have been greater. The fact that this is trademarked, sought after technology explains why this product is relatively more profitable, with a GP margin of 49.2% in 20X6 (45.0% 20X5). This is to be expected as early adopters of the technology will be prepared to pay a premium, however as competitors bring out similar automated systems price competition is likely to increase and profitability will fall as BB loses market share. Thus the long term margins may not remain at this level. Also BB is likely to have spent large sums on research and development to generate the system, which effectively need to be recovered. Thus if costing were to be done on a life-cycle basis, taking into account all the costs of design and development, the product would appear less profitable.

The service business accounts for a relatively consistent proportion of sales, 20% in 20X6 (22% 20X5) and is BB's most lucrative area, generating a margin of 67% in both years. It would be useful to know what % of clients take up service contracts be whether there is scope to develop this area further. Again to properly assess the profitability, the warranty costs associated with the free-of-charge repairs should be taken into account. These seem to have increased given that they represented 8% of cost of sales in 20X6, compared to 5% in 20X5, which may indicate some quality problems.

A key issue for BB is that the product lines are interdependent, since service demand is a derived demand from the sales of the underlying product. Also the existence of the service contracts then provides BB with the opportunity to undertake upgrades or install replacement products.

To the extent that the auto-close system can be retro-fitted to any blinds/shutters there is an element of sales that is independent. However it is again likely that the many clients using this system have already purchased BB blinds and shutters and that some clients are attracted to buy BB blinds and shutters because of the system. An analysis of auto-close sales by existing and new customers would be helpful.

In conclusion, it is really the overall price for any contract that matters, rather than the price for each of the three elements. Therefore in evaluating performance it is not really possible to evaluate the performance of each element separately in any meaningful way. More information is also required about the sales volumes for each revenue stream.

Ability to achieve 20X7 budget

Sales

The 20X7 budget is ambitious. It assumes another year of very high revenue growth (46.8%), presumably on the back of further sales of the Auto-close systems. This may not be achievable if competitors have brought out similar products. Indeed the growth achieved in the first six months of 20X7 is only 26% (assuming no seasonality). More information is required to understand the seasonality of BB's sales including a breakdown of budgeted revenue by revenue stream. However on the face of it the 20X7 sales budget may be over-ambitious unless there are significant contracts planned for the second half of the year.

Gross profit

The budget assumes a margin of 41%. This may be due to an assumption that the auto-close systems, which are highly profitable (20X6 margin 49.2%) will represent a greater mix of sales in 20X7. However the actual overall margin in the first six months is only 40% so again this does not seem to have happened. Since over 60% of components are bought from China, the margin on shutters and blinds is also affected by the exchange rate movement. The cost of sales note suggests that the CNY has continued to strengthen during the first six months of 20X7 (average rate for purchases of CNY = £0.12) and this will have further reduced the margins on blinds and shutters.

If the first six months of the year are replicated, then compared to the budget, by the end of 20X7 there will be a 14.2% sales shortfall and a 16.3% shortfall in gross profit.

Again the detail of the budget by revenue stream is required.

Fixed costs

Fixed costs have grown by 18% in the first six months of 20X7, assuming no seasonality, whereas the budgeted increase for the year is only 11.3%. This, coupled with the GP margin has resulted in a margin of safety of 10.9% compared to a budget of 29.7%.

In 20X6, warranty costs rose from 5% of cost of sales (COS) to 8% and this trend may explain some of the higher actual costs in 20X7. In 20X6 there was a cutback of R&D expenditure in relation to sales. BB may have had to increase this if competitors have started to bring out new products. Indeed, if it has not done so, this would give further cause for concern in relation to its ability to achieve the sales growth.

The fixed costs figure may also have been affected by timing issues and may not represent the true costs for a six-month period if accounting adjustments such as accruals have not been made in the six-month management accounts.

A detailed breakdown of fixed costs by cost category is required.

Conclusion

Ultimately in the first six months of 20X7, BB has achieved more operating profit than it did in the whole of 20X6 (£451,000 compared to £4,210,000), however it has only actually achieved 15.4% of its budgeted operating profit. Admittedly, we are only comparing six months of actual figures to the budgets for the full year, but nonetheless unless significant contracts are planned for the second half of 20X7 it would appear that the 20X7 budget is unrealistic and over-ambitious.

Appendix of additional calculations

	Blinds and shutters	Auto-close	Service contracts
20X5			
GP margin	36%	45%	67%
Sales mix	73%	5%	22%
GP mix	61%	5%	34%
20X6			
GP margin	30%	49%	67%
Sales mix	63%	17%	20%
GP mix	46%	21%	33%

	20X5	**20X6**	**20X7**
Exchange rate for purchases CNY =	£0.105	£0.115	£0.12

Components cost	Increase 20X5–X6
CNY	35%
£	48%

	20X5	**20X6**
Fixed costs as % of total cost	40.9%	39.0%

	Actual 6 months to 30 June 20X7 £'000	Estimated Scaled to 12 months £'000	Budget Year ended 31 December 20X7 £'000	Variances Estimated 12 months vs budget £'000
Revenue	10,370	20,740	24,165	(3,425)
Cost of sales	6,225	12,450	14,260	1,810
Gross profit	4,145	8,290	9,905	(1,615)
Fixed costs	3,694	7,388	6,970	(418)
Operating profit	451	902	2,935	(2033)

	% changes		
	20X6 vs 20X5	20X7 budget vs 20X6 actual	20X7 12mth estimated vs 20X6 actual
Revenue	56%	47%	26%
Cost of sales	64%	46%	27%
Gross profit	47%	49%	24%
Fixed costs	51%	11%	18%
Operating profit	-2%	616%	120%

	Actual 6 months to 30 June 20X7	Budget Year ended 31 December 20X7
GP margin	40.0%	41.0%
OP margin	4.3%	12.1%
Margin of safety	10.9%	29.7%
Sales growth compared to 20X6	26%	46.8%
Increase in overheads compared to 20X6	18.0%	11.3%

Examiner's comments

The data analysis requirement was generally well answered, although comparing performance was better done than evaluating whether the budget would be achieved. Several performance indicators were already provided in the scenario. Many candidates identified and calculated additional relevant data (such as exchange rate movements and analysis by product) and presented their figures in a structured table with appropriate columns. Weaker candidates often reproduced all the data already given in the question, which simply wasted time without scoring marks. Some weaker candidates only considered percentage changes in data or did not produce an initial table of calculations, but weaved occasional random calculations into their narrative which tended to produce limited answers with only partial data.

Many candidates produced a good commentary on the actual data with a reasoned discussion of the performance of the various product streams. Weaker candidates, as usual, reiterated the figures they had calculated, without adding value. Evaluation of the company's ability to achieve the budget was less insightful, although most concluded that the budget is optimistic and, given current performance, unlikely to be achieved. Only a very small minority referenced the Board's concerns or discussed the issue of interdependencies between product lines. Most candidates identified further information that might be useful although in some cases this was very generic.

46.3 Acquisition of supplier

The acquisition of RX, BB's major Chinese supplier is a strategy of vertical integration, with BB moving backwards in the supply chain.

Advantages of Vertical integration

- This removes the margin that is currently being paid to RX and means BB are only covering the cost of producing the components, so may improve profitability or allow BB to reduce prices.

- This may give BB greater control over quality, which is important given the bespoke nature of its products. BB already has a close relationship with RX but the increased warranty costs may suggest there have been some problems recently.

- BB may be able to take advantage of the fact that they will control the supply chain to ensure more reliable delivery dates and shorter lead times which would enhance customer service. However there will always be some lead time given the location in China.

- If components are a source of competitive advantage then this allows BB to prevent competitors using the same ones and enhances their differentiation strategy.

- The acquisition of RX may provide BB with a foothold in the Chinese market and could use this to develop sales of the main products in Asia which would represent market development.

Disadvantages

- This does not remove currency risk which appears to have been a significant contributor to the decline in profit.

- In addition to the exchange risk on transactions, acquisition of the Chinese supplier will create exchange risk on asset values as well.

- BB's operating gearing will be increased significantly by the acquisition which will convert variable costs into fixed operating costs. The high fixed costs may raise the breakeven point and means that profits will be more volatile relative to changes in sales. Any additional borrowing generates additional financial gearing which raises financial risks.

- This strategy may not improve performance – it depends on how RX supplier is performing and what % of its sales are external.

- Exit costs are likely to be significant if the venture fails, as there is likely to be a large financial commitment.

- Flexibility of operations is reduced eg, the ability to shop around if other suppliers bring out better or more technologically developed components.

- Further operational risk arises from the management of the Chinese business which may be outside the core competences of the current BB management team that has UK experience only.

- It will involve some costs of integration (although BB may continue to run it as two separate businesses).

Transfer pricing

The transfer price is the price at which RX (the component division) will sells its components to BB's manufacturing division.

The following factors should be considered:

- Whether the divisions are to be treated as cost or profit centres. If they are to be profit centres then the transfer price will determine the profits of divisions. If the component division charges a high transfer price, then most of the total profit from company sales will be attributed to it, with less to the manufacturing division. This will give a false measure of performance for both divisions.

- If high transfer prices are then treated as costs by the manufacturing division and passed on to BB's ultimate customers, sales volumes may fall and overall profits may be distorted.

- Inappropriate transfer prices can lead to dysfunctional decisions or internal conflict between divisions. If either division believes it can get a better deal from an outside market it may take it. For example, if the manufacturing division could obtain supplies of equal quality at lower cost from third parties eg, alternative Chinese suppliers, then it may, if permitted, choose to purchase outside the company. This could leave the component division with reduced sales. Conversely, if transfer prices are too low, then management of the component division might prefer to sell its supply through alternative channels at a higher price and leave the manufacturing division without components.

- There are various methods of setting transfer prices:

  Basing the transfer price on standard cost rather than using RX's actual costs should incentivise the component division to control costs. An issue to consider is whether to base the price on variable costs or to include an element of fixed costs, which brings with it the need for apportionment. If the component division is to be a profit centre then some form of cost plus price may be appropriate.

  The capacity of the component division should also be considered – if it will lose out on external sales by transferring components to BB's manufacturing division then this opportunity cost should be reflected in the transfer price.

Preliminary conclusion

A lot will depend on the price of the acquisition – BB already have a close relationship and a strong partnership with RX so acquisition may not help. It reduces flexibility and does not remove the exchange rate risk. If the only motive is in relation to the supply chain then it may not be sensible. However the Asian market is large and profitable so if there is an opportunity to sell BB's products through RX then the acquisition may be worth considering.

If the acquisition goes ahead, transfer prices could be set by negotiation and need to recognise the opportunity for either division to buy from or sell into external markets on an arm's length basis.

Examiner's comments

This requirement was reasonably well answered, on the whole, although a sizeable number of candidates talked in terms of acquisition generally rather than explicitly mentioning BB's backwards vertical integration of its main supplier. Most were well rehearsed in the advantages and disadvantages of this form of strategy, and the international considerations, although only a minority considered increase in operating gearing among the disadvantages.

The requirement on the implications for transfer pricing was generally poorly done. Few candidates discussed the concept of cost and profit centres and the need to identify how the division would be assessed. Suggestions for different approaches to setting the transfer price were on the whole very wooden, although better candidates did justice to behavioural considerations and taxation issues.

46.4 **Ethics**

Ethics pertains to whether a particular behaviour is deemed acceptable in the context under consideration. In short, it is "doing the right thing".

The issue here seems to be one of possible fraud and is potentially a legal issue as well as a moral one. In making any ethical evaluation it is first necessary to establish the facts. In this case, it would seem that the facts are reasonably clear. BB's Financial Controller (FC) has been told by the Managing Director (MD) to apply for a grant from Lemchester City Council, stating that BB fulfils all the application criteria.

The council's criteria for the grant are that the company provides local employment and has an entirely local supply chain. BB would appear to fulfil the criteria in relation to providing local employment and if it is awarded the grant, may be able to use this to increase capacity and benefit the local area. However more information is needed to ascertain the Council's definition of local supply chain and also to understand whether the Council's criteria are open to interpretation, since whilst BB manufactures its products in the UK, it sources over 60% of its components from China.

What is not clear is the extent to which the MD is deliberately trying to mislead the council by telling the Financial Controller to make a materially inaccurate/false statement or whether the MD has misinterpreted the criteria and equated local manufacturing with local supply chain.

If the MD is trying to get the grant under false pretences then this conduct is dishonest, lacks transparency and implies a lack of personal ethics. The application may even be considered fraudulent and potentially illegal.

As the Financial Controller is a qualified ICAEW Accountant, they are bound by the ethical code for professional accountants. Going along with such behaviour would conflict with the fundamental principle of integrity and objectivity and if the Financial Controller signs the application they may also be guilty of a criminal act.

The MD may also be using their position to pressurise the Financial Controller who is likely to be concerned about the implications of going against the MD's wishes and perceive some form of intimidation threat.

Actions

Before making the application, the Financial Controller needs to consider the grant documentation and obtain more information in relation to the Council's criteria for awarding the grant, in particular their definition of local supply chain.

If the Financial Controller believes the Managing Director intends to act dishonestly then the FC should tell the MD that the application should not be submitted as it stands and that they are unable to sign it. If however BB provides full information to the council about its manufacturing activities, including its supply chain, then it may reasonably leave it up to the Council to decide whether to award the grant.

If the MD continues to insist that the application is submitted then the FC will be left in a difficult situation since if they go against the MD they may find their position untenable or end up facing dismissal. The FC may need to consider BB's whistleblowing policies, seek legal advice, and contact the ICAEW ethics helpline about their position.

Examiner's comments

The ethics requirement was very well attempted by most candidates. The majority of candidates were able to identify the key ethical issues in the scenario - the MD's desire to be less than transparent in applying for the grant and the threats presented to the Financial Controller's fundamental principles. Ethical language and principles tended to be used by a majority and many referred to the ICAEW Code of Ethics. However weaker candidates limited themselves to the transparency, effect, fairness structure which restricted their ability to score marks. Many candidates pointed out that the application for the grant may be fraudulent as well as dishonest. Better candidates identified that this may depend on the council's definition of "entirely local supply chain", discussed how the possible acquisition of RX may impact on this and suggested that BB have an open conversation with the council about whether it could apply.

It is encouraging that more candidates seem to have developed the ability to provide recommended actions that are realistic and linked well with the ethical issues previously discussed.

47 Air Services UK Ltd (September 2017, amended)

	Knowledge	Skill	Marks
47.1 Consistency of three-year goals	2	9	10
47.2 Functional strategies (HR and RD)	2	9	10
47.3 Cyber-security risks/risk management	3	7	9
	7	25	29

47.1 Vision and goals

Joan's vision is for ASU to be "the global leader in innovative airspace management."

To achieve this she has set the following goals:

- Achieve business growth by diversification
- Reduce the risks of accidents linked to airspace management
- Reduce emissions related to airspace management
- Increase the efficiency of ASU's internal operations

Consistency of Goals and Vision

Business growth through diversification is likely to raise awareness of ASU's brand and increase its customer base, thereby helping it to become a global leader.

Three of the four goals are focused on safety, cost efficiency and environmental management. If ASU succeeds in these areas it is more likely to achieve its goal of growth as it will be a supplier of choice. ASU currently has an excellent track record but any accidents or incidents linked to poor air traffic management would be very damaging for ASU's reputation and brand image and hinder the achievement of Joan's vision.

Currently ASU is in a monopoly position in the UK so growth can only come internationally. If ASU can demonstrate a good track record in safety, cost efficiency and environment it will be in a position to win international contracts. This will lead to increased market share and facilitate its vision to be global market leader. So there is some consistency between the vision and the goals.

However innovation is also key to the vision and to ASU's competitive advantage and yet no specific goals have been set in this area (although some innovation may be implicit in the other goals). So given the vision of "innovative airspace management" Joan should consider setting an additional goal in this area.

Consistency of Goals and Stakeholder objectives

ASU's key stakeholders include private shareholders, the government (as shareholder), CAA (representing public interest), airlines, airports, passengers and staff. Since there are multiple stakeholders, some of their objectives may conflict.

- Reducing the risks of accidents associated with airspace management

  This goal is likely to appeal to CAA, government, airlines, airports and passengers. A first class safety record is also likely to help ASU win contracts - for example this is one of the criteria for the European airspace tender and is likely to be relevant to the drone contract.

- Reduce emissions related to airspace management

  Again this is likely to appeal to CAA, government, airlines and airports. It will also help reduce negative interest from environmental groups. Whilst some private shareholder's may not want to pursue sustainability at the expense of profits, environmental impact is one of the criteria for the European airspace tender and therefore reducing emissions may enhance future profits

- Increase the efficiency of ASU's internal operations

  This is most likely to appeal to shareholders (private and government) as the efficiency of operations will directly affect ASU's profitability. However more efficient air traffic control is also in the interests of the users of ASU's services - the airport and airlines and the CAA as regulator. It may also make life easier for staff although some may perceive this goal as threatening their jobs.

- Achieve business growth by diversification

  Again this goal is likely to be more of interest to private shareholders as growth should provide an opportunity for added value in terms of shareholder wealth. Indirectly it may also appeal to staff since growth will facilitate job security and career development prospects. However it may be less appealing to the UK government who may prefer ASU to concentrate on activities closer to home.

Conclusion:

Whilst some of ASU's stakeholders may be more or less interested in certain goals, three of the four goals are likely to be consistent with the objectives of most of the stakeholders. The one concern is over the government's attitude to diversification and as a key stakeholder Joan would be advised to consult with them as soon as possible to ascertain whether this goal has their support.

In general terms the goals do not seem to be in conflict with each other and could therefore be said to be aligned. Indeed if ASU succeeds in reducing accident risk, reducing emissions and increasing efficiency, then growth is likely to follow and in a sense the goals could be seen as forming a hierarchy which will help Joan achieve ASU's vision.

Examiner's comments

This requirement was very well answered by the majority of candidates, who considered Joan's vision for ASU to become "the global leader in innovative airspace management" in relation to both the four stated goals and the likely objectives of key stakeholders.

Many good answers identified that ASU has multiple stakeholders whose objectives are likely to conflict. However weaker candidates tended to focus on only one element of the requirement or restricted their consideration of stakeholders to ASU's owners. The best candidates reflected critically on the goals and identified that, given Joan's vision, an explicit goal was missing in relation to 'innovation'.

47.2 Functional strategies

A successful company is often one that is outward looking, and has accepted the reality of constant change. As well as delivering business as usual to the highest standards, ASU needs to look to the future towards new markets, innovative processes, and improved efficiency.

Functional strategies that are critical to ASU's vision include:

- Human resources
- Research and development

These areas are both interlinked with technology:

Human resources

Human resources considers ASU's requirements in terms of people as they represent its human capital. Human resources is also concerned with how ASU's requirements may be met:

- As part of succession planning ASU needs to recruit and retain the best talent – innovative organisations tend to attract and retain higher quality staff, who want the opportunity to contribute to the development of a forward-looking organisation. Today many organisations operate their own talent management programmes which are aimed at identifying and retaining individuals considered to be important to the future success of the organisation. ASU could look to introduce its own similar scheme.

- Staff retention does not seem to be the issue – ASU has staff with long employment records but a significant number will retire in the next few years and as part of succession planning ASU needs to start hiring appropriate numbers of staff with the right skills.

- Different skillsets may be required for international markets which may increase staff diversity. ASU operates in a dynamic environment and needs staff to be flexible and adaptable to change. It is likely that the drone contract would need to be operated from the Middle East. Consideration needs to be given to whether to employ local staff or second staff from the UK. Language skills may also be required.

- ASU is likely to need people with scientific and engineering backgrounds, as well as wider business skills such as finance, administration. In order to expand the business it may also need staff with sales skills.

- Continued success depends on getting the best from its employees. ASU needs to foster a culture of innovation (see below). Cross-disciplinary teams may allow employees to be more involved in the development of new processes, to move around and generate fresh ideas. Training and development will also be key.

- ASU has already invested significantly in technology: this is evident given the development of the drone management system which incorporates cutting edge intelligent system design. ASU's investment in technology allows staff and business partners to make better use of information and ensures its IT systems can be connected with others across a wide range of organisations and countries. This should help facilitate international expansion.

- ASU needs to ensure it has an appropriate knowledge management system. This needs to capture all the knowledge that is valuable and deliver it to the people in such a way that it can be acted on quickly, to the competitive advantage of the business. This is particularly true in relation to the knowledge held by the staff who are due to retire.

Research and development

Research and development is aimed at the innovation/improvement of both products and processes. This is a key source of competitive advantage and ASU needs to ensure that it continues to invest in this area, particularly given Joan's vision.

ASU can help foster a culture of innovation by:

- creating a culture that promotes and rewards creativity and inventiveness and supports individual and team abilities;

- implementing a management style and structure designed for innovation: praising new ideas, encouraging staff to explore possibilities;

- being aware of and making use of common information/resources available to the airline industry and monitoring the development and processes used by other air traffic control organisations; and

- using multiple sources of innovation – R&D, employees, customers, partners, outsourcing and joint ventures, working with the government and other public sector initiatives.

A key area of research will be finding new technological developments. ASU has already developed expertise in the management of unmanned aircraft systems and drones which make use of intelligent system design. This development has created the opportunity for the new contract in the Middle East.

Continued investment in technology is therefore key, particularly given how fast technology changes. However technology is also a key area of risk that needs to be managed (see below). As it is partly privately funded, ASU may be better placed than the government owned bodies it is competing against to attract finance for ongoing investment in research and development.

Examiner's comments

Answers to this requirement were polarised. There were some excellent attempts but some candidates omitted answering the second requirement entirely. This is surprising given the fact that functional strategies are covered in detail in the learning materials and candidates should at least have been able to include points from a common sense point of view, based on their own experiences and using the information in the scenario. Human resource strategy was generally answered well but for RD many candidates only gave consideration to process innovations rather than product innovations. The better candidates discussed how these strategies could be implemented to help ASU achieve the goals and vision discussed in respect of the first requirement.

47.3 Cyber security

Tutorial note

This answer includes a wide range of points for marking/learning purposes and is longer than candidates were expected to produce in the time available.

Cyber risk is any risk of financial loss, disruption or damage to the reputation of an organisation from some sort of failure of its IT systems. Cyber security refers to the prevention of systems failure and the protection of networks and data from unauthorised modification, disclosure or destruction.

ASU's business is extensively reliant on computer systems. ASU's cyber security needs to be directed towards protecting its IT systems from risks which will threaten its ability to ensure the safe and uninterrupted operation of the airspace system.

The risks to ASU's IT systems and data predominantly feature some degree of human involvement:

- Human threats: hackers may be able to get into ASU's internal network, either to steal data (personnel or financial) or to damage the IT system. Political terrorism is a major risk in the era of cyber-terrorism and there have been a number of real-life examples of coordinated attacks on the computer systems of different airlines/airports. For ASU in extreme situations this could involve hackers taking control of aircrafts or drones.

- Denial of Service (DoS) attack: an attempt by attackers to prevent legitimate users of a service from using that service. Such an attack could be intended to cause communication difficulties eg, between the plane and the air traffic controller or to prevent systems responsible for scheduling aircraft and flight plans from operating properly.

- Viruses and other corruptions: could spread through the network to all of ASU's computers eg, malware in staff email accounts or embedded Trojans which may prevent radar systems or communication channels from operating effectively .

- Deliberate sabotage: for example, malicious damage by employees or other users with access to the system could disrupt ASU's operations

- Accidents: on a more minor level, staff are a physical threat to IT installations, and there is a risk of accidents including spilling a cup of coffee over a desk, or tripping and falling, thereby doing some damage to an item of IT equipment.

ASU has developed its IT infrastructure to allow widespread use by a variety of parties which delivers more efficiency and competitive advantage but in doing so increases the risk that it is vulnerable to attack – particularly through the weakest links in the systems chain. Its use of cloud-based systems, for example in relation to drones, may also increase cyber security risks.

Risk management

Effective risk management is integral to ASU's competitive advantage and is fundamental to survival in the longer term. Global airspace is extremely crowded and a systems failure could in the worst case scenario result in a plane crash and fatalities. If a system is not operating properly ASU may need to ground all planes as a precaution since it cannot run the risk of this happening. Whilst this minimises the risk of an accident, it causes disruption for airports, airlines and passengers, potentially leading to financial loss for ASU. A key issue for ASU is that any technical failure has a significant and immediate impact and is likely to be high profile, as evidenced by the recent incident leading to flight cancellations and delays and a £7 million fine. Reputation is a key aspect and ASU may need to undertake PR to manage the negative publicity associated with the recent flight delay incident that has arisen.

ASU needs to ensure that there is a clear responsibility and accountability for cyber security and that it has individuals with the specialist skills and expertise to help the organisation protect itself against cyber-attacks. It also needs to take into account the fact that facilities and systems are accessed by third parties. ASU's board need to regularly consider their risk tolerance and risk appetite in relation to cyber security and reflect this in risk management strategies.

ASU needs to spend time identifying the various potential causes of a system breach, take steps to reduce the likelihood of this occurring and plan different strategies so that it is ready to react in the event that a breach occurs. Risks may be transferred, avoided, reduced or accepted. ASU must take steps to minimise the risk of systems failure, protect the integrity of its systems, safeguard information and ensure the continuity of its operations.

However accepting that there is still the possibility of a breach, ASU should consider putting appropriate insurances in place to mitigate the effects of any cyber-attacks that do occur. It also needs a business continuity plan in place to reduce the need to shut down the systems or at least minimise the time that this has to be down for (see below).

The international security standard, ISO17799 recommends various measures for combating IT risks and ensuring security, which ASU could consider:

- Personnel security: this covers issues such as recruitment of trustworthy employees, and also reporting of security-related incidents. Training is particularly important, with the aim that users are aware of information security threats and concerns and are equipped to comply with the organisation's security policy.

- Physical and environmental security: measures should be taken to prevent unauthorised access, damage and interference to ASU's premises, assets, information and information facilities and prevention of theft.

- Systems access control: this includes protection of information, information systems, networked services, detection of unauthorised activities and security when using the systems. ASU needs to ensure that all the different users of its systems have appropriate controls in place.

- Systems development and maintenance: this includes security measures and steps to protect data in operational and application systems and also ensuring that IT projects and support are conducted securely.

Business continuity plan (BCP)

- A BCP is concerned with crisis management and disaster recovery. It must specify the actions ASU will take to recover and restore operations interrupted by the occurrence of a massive risk event eg, a major breach of security resulting in a major systems failure or air disaster.

- ASU already has such a plan but it should be reviewed in the light of the recent incident to assess how successful it is and whether additional steps can be taken.

- All members of ASU staff should be aware of the importance of business continuity planning, training should be given and the plan tested regularly.

- Factors that should be considered by a BCP include:
    - Restoration of data and other IT systems
    - Securing interim premises
    - Securing interim management and staff
    - Management of the PR issues – this is a key issue for ASU

- Methods of recovery might include:
    - Carrying out activities manually until IT services are resumed (eg, via the call centre)
    - Moving staff at an affected building to another location
    - Agreeing with another business to use each other's premises in the event of a disaster
    - Arranging to use IT services and accommodation provided by a specialist third-party standby site.

Examiner's comments

Overall most candidates were well prepared for the discussion of cyber risk and scored highly. Relevant cyber risks were generally well identified although the suggestions for managing the significant risks were weaker. Some candidates introduced the TARA framework but did not then make use of it to aid discussion of risk management strategies.

Given the critically important nature of air traffic management it was surprising that only a minority of candidates made reference to the need for a business continuity plan. More candidates referred to a back-up plan, but often only in relation to IT systems back-up.

48 Purechoc Ltd (September 2017)

	Knowledge	Skill	Marks
48.1 Control section of report	3	5	8
48.2 Risks section of report	2	6	7
48.3 Strategic fit section of report	2	6	7
48.4 Preliminary advice section of report	1	3	4
	8	20	26

To: Purechoc Board
From: Business Advisor
Date: XX/XX/XX
Re: Future strategy

Two possible options are being considered:

- Sale of shares to Koreto Inc
- Franchising

48.1 Control

Sale of shares

If all the directors sell their shares to Koreto then they will lose control in the form of ownership. Purechoc becomes dependent on Koreto which is a much bigger business. Although Koreto have promised that Purechoc can be run semi-autonomously, they own the business and may interfere in its running, as evidenced by their desire to appoint a new CEO.

The Bernard family will have reduced influence on the board of directors and this may lead to their wishes being overridden when it comes to important operating decisions. It may be very difficult to work with new American owners who are used to a much bigger business.

Despite the loss of ownership, Purechoc may have more influence over day-to-day running of the shops than under a franchise arrangement.

Franchise

Purechoc will maintain some general contractual control over franchisees but will lose some operational control.

If franchising is to be taken up by many small operators, then Purechoc is not dominated by its business partner(s). However it may be more difficult to influence or change the strategic direction of the business in the future if franchisees have a degree of autonomy in the running of their shop, as they may each have different objectives.

In a niche market, brand image is critical, so Purechoc will need to monitor quality control and consistency of products. Franchisees must be chosen carefully and contracts need to be drawn up to ensure Purechoc's reputation is protected.

Purechoc will need to provide training in chocolate production. Franchisees may also expect central support with procurement and marketing. Purechoc may need to take on additional manpower to provide training and support and manage the franchisees.

Examiner's comments

This was very well answered, although as usual some candidates lost easy marks by not presenting their answer in report format. Most candidates recognised that there was a difference between control in the context of ownership and control in relation to day-to-day operations. A small minority assumed that not all shareholders would be selling their shares. Although this may be a possibility, none referred to the need to seek agreement from the American company given that they are, initially at least, interested in 100% ownership. As usual, most candidates were good at discussing franchising although some weaker ones appeared to think that this option would involve relinquishing complete control of operations to the franchisees – better candidates pointed out that control could be maintained by choosing franchisees carefully and implementing a carefully worded franchise agreement.

48.2 Risks

Sale of shares

The sale of shares to Koreto means the directors no longer own the company and therefore lose their voting rights as shareholders. This transfers the risk of ownership from the Bernard family and may help reduce the risk to the business that is presented by Marine's ill-health and the current lack of cashflow.

However there is a risk that resources input by Koreto may not compensate for the loss of control by the Bernard family. Whilst Marine is keen to retire, the other members of the family are not and Koreto may decide to replace the current team.

Koreto may not fulfil their initial promises in respect of brand retention, autonomy of operations or finance. Requirements for dividends/management fees or exit route by Koreto may limit future availability of funds for Purechoc's expansion.

Koreto has no experience of the UK and there may not be able to transfer its core competences to operate successfully in a different market. Also Koreto's ownership may bring adverse publicity or damage Purechoc's brand (see below).

Franchise

Purechoc faces reduced financial risk by having franchisees' own capital for expansion.

Compared to organic growth, there are fewer risks from franchisee losses as the cost of failure is shared with the franchisee. This reduces the maximum potential loss from the failure of a shop but also provides an increased incentive for the franchisee to succeed.

However:

Franchisees will gain access to Purechoc's intellectual property (in the form of the recipes) and successful franchisees may break away to set up in competition.

Poor quality franchisees may harm Purechoc's brand name which risks damaging the existing business and shops. There is a need to monitor the franchisees and the existing management may be overburdened as the number of franchises grows.

There is a risk that franchisees may not want to take up the opportunity – there needs to be some incentive to purchase a franchise and Purechoc may be relatively unknown outside its immediate geographical market, especially given its lack of marketing.

Again this was a high scoring requirement. Most candidates were able to make sensible points about how each of the strategic options increased downside risks for Purechoc. However only the better candidates identified that the strategies may also help the business reduce or share some risks. The strongest answers also considered upside risk from the point of view of the existing owners, recognising that, in the case of Koreto, the risks of ownership would be removed from the family entirely.

48.3 Strategic fit

Sale of shares

Koreto offers opportunities for expansion in two respects:

- Access to increased financial capital and other resources
- Possible access to Koreto's market in the USA

Purechoc is a small-scale business, operating an ethical procurement policy. It has a premium pricing policy based on its differentiation strategy. Koreto is more likely to adopt a low cost, high volume business model. It is not clear what Koreto's procurement policy is – some of the other dominant confectionery producers have already attracted adverse publicity for their sourcing of cocoa and their treatment of suppliers. Thus Purechoc's business may not fit with the existing strategy and brand image of a large confectionery manufacturer like Koreto.

However this may not be a problem if Purechoc is to be retained as a separate brand. Koreto will be able to provide access to more resources, established distribution channels and a marketing budget to raise awareness of the brand. It also provides strong potential for overseas expansion.

Franchise

Franchisees are likely to be individuals so unlike Koreto will not be able to provide financial or operational support for any large scale expansion. Under a franchise, Purechoc grants the franchisee the right to use its brand, its know-how and its products. There is also likely to be a requirement for Purechoc to provide some degree of central control and support. In return, the franchisee will provide a lump sum upfront and contribute a share of earnings.

In the context of the chocolate shops, a franchise is likely to be on a geographical basis in order to segregate the markets for the individual franchisees. The expansion of the business through individual shops may be more in keeping with the niche market and the brand ethos. Since each franchise will be unique to its area, this may help to maintain its image as a family company.

Purechoc can screen applicants carefully to identify like-minded franchisees and use the franchise agreement to ensure that franchisees adhere to the appropriate quality.

Examiner's comments

Generally the requirement to discuss strategic fit was well attempted, with many referring to the need to protect Purechoc's niche strategy and values, the latter often considered with regard to the firm's ethical procurement policy.

The best responses compared Purechoc and Koreto in terms of their respective generic strategies, assumed (reasonably) to be high volume cost leadership in the case of Koreto. The possible implications of this for Koreto's future business conduct were also well explored. Some candidates chose to adopt a suitability, feasibility, acceptability approach to this requirement which often proved disappointing and also caused them to run out of time.

48.4 Preliminary Advice

Before deciding on which option to pursue, the objectives of the different shareholders and their eventual plans for exit need to be considered.

Both options address the issue of limited resources and share the risk of expansion but also require the family to accept reduced control and share the future profits of the business.

If significant new capital is provided by Koreto, then growth could be rapid in terms of the number of outlets. Purechoc's business will be able to benefit from access to Koreto's expertise in the confectionery market and Koreto may be able to provide support for procurement, marketing, training etc, which is the inverse of the franchise situation.

Franchising offers a slower growth route, with Purechoc providing the expertise, but retaining control of the direction of the business. More consideration needs to be given to the terms of a franchise agreement and whether there would be any interested franchisees.

If Marine wants an exit in the short term then the Koreto offer may be attractive, depending on the price Koreto are prepared to pay. If she needs to raise cash then it may be better to sell now than a few years down the line when there is increased competition and a more mature market. As he is less reliant on the income, Thomas's decision may be more influenced by quality of life than money. However if he were to decide to sell too then Koreto would have sufficient shares for a majority holding, although it is not clear whether partial ownership would be acceptable to Koreto – they will need to be consulted on this. Jonathan and Anne seem more likely to want to retain control of their own destiny. They may not take kindly to reporting to a new Chief Executive appointed by Koreto. If this option is not attractive then an alternative may be for them to offer to buy out Marine and then to implement the franchising model.

Examiner's comments

The requirement to give preliminary advice was well answered by most, although omitted by a considerable number. Weaker efforts tended to concentrate on either sale or franchise, with little or no consideration of alternatives as a means of comparison. A significant minority suggested that, if the franchise option is chosen, the other shareholders can offer to buy out the founder.

49 Fullerton Office Furniture Ltd (December 2017)

Marking guide

	Knowledge	Skill	Marks
49.1 Data analysis	1	24	22
49.2 Premises choice	4	7	10
49.3 New technology	2	5	7
49.4 Ethics	3	5	8
	10	41	47

49.1

	FOF - business 20X7	FOF - business 20X6	FOF schools 20X7	FOF schools 20X6	% change Business	% change Schools
Number of items sold	79,200	72,000	16,000	19,200	10.0%	-16.7%
Price per item (net of discounts)	£98	£100	£50	£50	-2.0%	0.0%
VC per item	£44	£40	£15	£16	10.0%	-6.3%
Distribution costs outward per item	£8	£8	£1	£1	0.0%	0.0%
Commission per item	£2.45					
Contribution per item	£43.55	£52	£34	£33	-16.3%	3.0%
	£	**£**	**£**	**£**		
Returns inwards	2,000	2,000	10,000	1,000	0.0%	900.0%
Sales	7,761,600	7,200,000	800,000	960,000	7.8%	-16.7%
Fixed production costs	3,000,000	2,800,000	240,000	240,000	7.1%	0.0%
Variable production costs	3,484,800	2,880,000	240,000	307,200	21.0%	-21.9%
Sales staff commissions	194,040	-	-	-		
Returns inward	2,000	2,000	10,000	1,000	0.0%	900%
Administration	250,000	250,000	100,000	100,000	0.0%	0.0%
Distribution						
– fixed	6,000	6,000	6,000	6,000	0.0%	0.0%
– variable	633,600	576,000	16,000	19,200	10.0%	-16.7%
Operating profit	**191,160**	**686,000**	**188,000**	**286,600**	**-72.1%**	**-34.4%**

	FOF - business 20X7	FOF - business 20X6	FOF schools 20X7	FOF schools 20X6	% change Business	% change Schools
Number of schools			125	150		-16.7%
Number of customers	300	320			-6.3%	
Number of items sold	79,200	72,000	16,000	19,200	10.0%	-16.7%
Number of new customers	12	18			-33.3%	
Sales to new customers	£480,000	£756,000			-36.5%	

	FOF – business 20X7	FOF – business 20X6	FOF schools 20X7	FOF schools 20X6	% change Business	% change Schools
Operating margin	2.5%	9.5%	23.5%	29.9%		
Sales per school			£6,400	£6,400		0.0%
Sales per customer	£25,872	£22,500			15.0%	
Sales per new customer	£40,000	£42,000			-4.8%	
Sales per existing customer	£25,283	£21,338			18.5%	
Commissions	2.5%					
Discounts	2.0%					
Sales (net of commissions)	£7,567,560	£7,200,000				

Analysis

The causes for the change in operating profit need be analysed between the two segments as different causal factors apply in each case.

Business Segment

Revenue

In 20X7, there have been price and quantity changes impacting on revenue. The working assumption is that "Sales revenue and sales volumes in the Business Segment would have been the same in 20X7 as in 20X6 if the new policy of offering sales discounts to customers and commissions to sales staff had not been introduced". The changes in revenue can therefore be isolated to these two factors.

The average selling price has been reduced from £100 to £98. This means that an average discount has been given of 2% compared to last year, which is a significant proportion of the maximum permitted discount of 5%.

Average revenue per item, net of commissions (average £2.45 per item) and discounts, has therefore decreased from £100 to £95.55 (£100 – £2 – £2.45), a decrease of 4.45%.

On the positive side, sales volume has increased by 10% which, given the working assumption, is because of the new discounting and sales commission policy. The causal factors are that lower prices on a selective basis make the furniture more competitive, enabling more to be sold. The commissions mean the sales staff are better incentivised to make more sales.

The sales in 20X6 can therefore be reconciled with the sales (net of commissions) in 20X7 as follows:

£7,200,000 × 1.1 × 0.9555 = £7,567,560

This is a net revenue gain of £367,560, which is 5.1% growth. This demonstrates that demand is price elastic.

The wider industry picture should also be considered in assessing the revenue growth. FOF is one of the larger companies in the industry, so it has some economies of scale and protection against smaller new entrants. However, while industry sales are estimated to grow at about 3% in 20X7, the working assumption is more modest at zero growth. Using the industry as a benchmark to judge performance, rather than FOF 20X6 figures, the changes are less encouraging.

Costs and contribution

While revenues have increased, there has also been an increase in costs.

Total variable costs have clearly needed to rise as volumes produced have increased by 10%. The assumption is that they would move in a linear fashion in relation to volume. This includes variable production costs and distribution costs outward.

In addition to volume related changes, there have also been changes in variable production costs per unit from £40 to £44 (10%). The increases in these costs could be due to the volume changes (eg, additional overtime costs to make the additional units or capacity problems reducing efficiency) or they could be due to factors independent of volume changes, such as changes in sales mix or production inefficiencies.

Assuming they are due to independent factors, then the change in contribution due to discounting and commissions (ie, using 20X6 unit costs) is:

20X7:	79,200 × (£95.55 – £40 – £8) – £3,765,960
20X6:	72,000 × (£100 – £40 – £8) – £3,744,000

There has therefore been a marginal improvement in contribution of £21,960 (0.6%) based on these assumptions.

However, this is a best-case scenario. As already noted, some of the increase in variable production cost per unit may have been due to increased production volumes.

In addition, fixed production costs have increased by £200,000 (7.1%). This may have been due to these costs being a stepped function, where a significant increase in volume has caused increases in fixed costs. Specific reasons would need to be investigated.

Overall, a commission based on sales, rather than on contribution, may not provide the best incentives, as sales staff may give discounts too readily to secure a sale and focus on products with the highest price, rather than the highest contribution.

There has been a reduction in the number of new customers. This is important for future growth but it may be that sales staff are more incentivised to sell to existing customers for current sales rather than attempt to establish long-term relationships for future sales, where they may not benefit personally from commissions, as they would in the short term.

Similarly, the total number of customers has fallen, which may be because sales staff are focusing on the larger customers. The fact that sales per customer have increased by 15% may provide some support for this proposition.

Overall, the Business Segment operating profit has decreased significantly (by 72.1%) from £686,000 to £191,160. This can be reconciled as follows:

	£
20X6 operating profit	**686,000**
Increased contribution from discounts and commissions	21,960
Change in fixed production costs	(200,000)
Change in variable cost per unit (£4 × 79,200)	(316,800)
20X7 operating profit	**191,160**

Conclusion – key drivers

Overall, there has been a significant decline in the operating profit of the Business Segment despite expanding industry sales. The key drivers affecting operating profit have, however, been related not to revenues and sales, but rather to the increase in variable production cost per unit and the increase in total fixed production costs.

Schools Segment

Revenue

The schools segment operates in a well-defined, finite, local geographical market. The size of the market has reduced given the reductions in the local authority's budget.

Market share in this sector is a key issue, where one competitor, EE, is dominating the market. However, while EE is larger in this market, it is smaller than FOF overall, as it has no business customers outside this market.

A summary of changes in market participants in terms of the number of schools supplied is provided below:

	20X7	20X6	% change
FOF	125	150	(16.7%)
EE	263	254	3.5%
Other	87	71	22.5%
Total	475	475	

Both the number of school orders and the volume of sales of the Schools Segment have decreased by 16.7%. The volume of sales per school is therefore constant.

The selling price is constant at £50 per item so this is not a key driver of change in operating profit. However, in an environment of reduced local authority expenditure, maintaining selling price at the 20X6 level is evidence of good performance.

The key driver of the change in total revenue therefore appears to be the number of schools to which sales are made, which in turn depends on the number of tenders won.

The reduction in tenders of 16.7% in one year is significant and causal factors need to be identified.

The most obvious causal factor is the reduction in FOF's furniture quality based on the number of faults and returns inwards. This has damaged FOF's reputation in this market (it may also have affected Business Segment sales as the two segments use the same brand name).

A further factor could be increased competition in the sector. It appears that, of the 25 school customers lost from 20X6, 9 have gone to EE and 16 to other smaller manufacturers.

In this respect the rumour that EE has been providing inducements to Jayne to win new tenders from FOF is not strongly supported by the data as EE has only won 9 of the 25 schools lost by FOF (see below).

The personal issue between Jayne and Trevor (see ethical issue below) seems unlikely to be a major factor as this did not take place until towards the end of 20X7.

Costs and contribution

Variable production costs have fallen by £1 per unit sold from £16 in 20X6 to £15 in 20X7 (6.3%). Based on the information provided this, in part at least, seems due to the reduction in the costs and quality of wood as a raw material. Whilst generating a total £16,000 cost saving, it also seems likely to have caused adverse financial effects, being:

- increased cost of returns inward
- reduced sales volumes

There is also likely to be a longer term reputation effect.

While it may be inappropriate to attribute the whole of the volume change to the decision to source low-cost, low-quality wood, it is credible that this is a key driver of the fall in sales volume.

Overall, the Schools Segment operating profit has decreased significantly (by 34.4%) from £286,600 to £188,000. This can be reconciled as:

	£
20X6 operating profit	**286,600**
Sales volumes (lost contribution)	
3,200 (£ 50 – £16 – £1)	(105,600)
Variable cost saved per unit	
16,000 × £1	16,000
Returns inwards	(9,000)
20X7 operating profit	**188,000**

This analysis demonstrates that the cost saving from lower costs of wood is largely offset by the increased cost of returns inwards, leaving a net saving of only £7,000 (£16,000 – £9,000).

Also, even if the lower quality wood is only one driver in causing sales volumes to fall then £7,000 is only a small proportion of the lost contribution from the reduction in sales volumes of £105,600. Given there is also likely to be non-financial reputational long-term damage, the reduced cost of wood from the new source appears likely to have adversely affected short-term performance and will impact long-term performance.

Conclusion – key drivers

The key driver of the change in operating profit in the Schools Segment is the decrease in sales volume.

Examiner's comments

This requirement was reasonably well answered on the whole. Most candidates provided a well-structured table with columns for data analysis, focusing on changes between years and by segment.

However, in many cases the analysis focused exclusively on headline percentage changes between periods, plus operating profit margin and per item/per customer/per school ratios. Far less common was any deeper analysis such as the effects of volume, discounts, commissions or costs. Similarly, many candidates did not identify the key drivers of change in profits in either segment.

The weakest candidates did not produce a data table and instead tended to weave some numbers into their narrative. They tended to lose marks by failing to present the data systematically, thereby failing to identify data patterns which would have revealed important issues facing the firm.

The discussion was generally reasonable in most cases, providing reasons for the data trends and suggesting causal relationships. Weaker candidates merely asserted whether the numbers had increased or decreased, which is not sufficient.

Most candidates used sensible sub-headings for the discussion, separately analysing each segment, but weaker candidates merged their analysis of the two segments.

49.2 The key factors relating to the choice of premises include:

- Cost
- Lease term
- Location (for logistics of inward and outward distribution)
- Size
- Transition and relocation

Cost

It is clear that, based on the figures presented, the direct rental cost is significantly greater for the existing factory under the proposed new leasing agreement (£360,000) than for the prospective Liverpool factory (£260,000). While both rentals are greater than the current rental, this is of no direct relevance to the decision for the selection of future premises.

In absolute terms, the difference is substantial at £100,000 which is 26% of the operating profit of £379,160 for 20X7. The issue is therefore important in financial terms. It is however possible that these costs are negotiating positions and will change during the process of making a final agreement.

The above costs only relate to direct costs. FOF currently spends £12,000 a year on inward distribution costs of wood from Liverpool to Birmingham. If the factory moves to Liverpool then this cost is likely to be minimal. This would give a cost saving of around £12,000.

However, there are likely to be additional costs associated with outward distribution for both the Business Segment and the Schools Segment. In particular, all the Schools Segment sales are local to the current factory in Birmingham, hence the distribution cost of only £1 per item. This is likely to increase significantly if FOF is to be based in Liverpool.

The Business Segment case is less clear, as its customers are throughout the UK. Whilst Birmingham is central to the UK this does not mean it is central to the dispersion of FOF's business customers. An assessment of the logistics would need to be made to determine the difference in distribution costs.

Other non-financial distribution factors are considered below.

Lease term

The leaseholder for the Birmingham premises is requiring a 10-year commitment while the Liverpool leaseholder requires only 5 years. The 10-year commitment has greater risks if the scale, nature or existence of the FOF business were to change. Possible methods to mitigate risks could include: break clauses; the ability to sub-let; and the nature of rent reviews.

Overall, the five-year lease would appear to be a lower risk choice, particularly as the sales volumes have changed in 20X7, and may change further in future.

Location for distribution logistics

Aside from the costs of distribution, there is an impact on the logistics of the upstream and downstream supply chain.

While the Liverpool location is important for the import of wood, this occurs only once per month and, if suitable levels of inventories are held, the location near the port does not appear to be a major advantage.

Much more frequent and significant is outward distribution, where there are many more orders. Lead times to customers and the ability to service customers efficiently are therefore key factors. This needs to be assessed for Business Segment customers, but the Schools Segment very clearly has a major advantage from its current Birmingham location, compared with Liverpool, in terms of logistics and speed of delivery.

Aside from the physical delivery of goods, the building of relationships with schools and the local authority and the negotiation of contracts are facilitated by the Birmingham office premises location.

Size

The Liverpool factory is larger than the Birmingham factory. This may facilitate the new design and production systems (see below). Even if this does not take place, there could be other uses of the additional space, such as increasing production capacity or furniture storage for customers.

Transition and relocation

A key factor is the transition to the new factory. Much of this will be temporary disruption from moving equipment and other facilities. This will have a financial cost and may disrupt production activities for a short period.

The main issue however is relocating employees. Many employees may not want to relocate to Liverpool and there may be the loss of some key staff as a result of the move. Legal advice will need to be taken in respect of employment law regarding the level of required financial compensation for those employees not willing to relocate.

Even those employees who do move may be unhappy at doing so and there could be a demotivating effect. Relocation costs would need to be paid to these employees.

Consultation with employees will be needed and an assessment made of their resistance to any relocation. The ability to employ new staff with the right skills in Liverpool will need to be assessed.

Conclusion

The new premises may of themselves have a lower direct cost than the current premises and better meet the needs of FOF, but the change in location is likely to disrupt the logistics of distribution and cause some problems in the longer term.

In the shorter term, in the transitional period the disruption and demotivation of staff are likely to be major factors. Further information is needed but the possibility of an alternative facility may persuade the Birmingham leaseholder to reduce the rent from the level being requested in negotiations.

Examiner's comments

Generally, this requirement was answered well, with better answers identifying and discussing the key differences between the two locations. Weaker candidates generally spent too much time on the change management and staff movement issues and failed to give a good all-round assessment of the key factors such as supply chain management, cost, lease term and size. Better answers used the numerical data in the question.

Some candidates' answers were structured around a Suitability, Acceptability and Feasibility framework (SAF) and these tended not to score well, as the key issues were not normally illuminated by applying the framework

---

49.3 The new system is likely to provide a number of distinct benefits:

- improved production efficiency, which will lower variable production costs per unit

- improving management information for marketing decisions in identifying customer needs

- improved customer service in designing space requirements for new furniture.

The above advantages come at a price. This includes a financial cost of £180,000 per annum. There may also be an opportunity cost in terms of alternative use of the space in the Liverpool premises (eg, it could alternatively be used for additional production capacity or furniture storage for customers). Such a cost would need to be assessed but the allocation of a proportion of the rental cost would not be valid to help decision making as it would be arbitrary.

Production efficiency

The annual production cost savings at current production levels would be:

$79,200 \times £1.50 = £118,800$

The net additional annual cost is therefore £180,000 - £118,800 = £61,200

An alternative perspective is that sales volumes may grow and the savings will be greater with a reduced variable cost.

The contribution in future would, if other costs remain constant, be:

£95.55 - £42.50 - £8 = £45.05

Annual sales will therefore need to increase by the following in order to recover the annual fixed costs for the digital system:

£180,000/£45.05 = 3,996 units

This is a 5% increase in sales volume compared with 20X7 sales.

Marketing information

Useful marketing information can be gathered by the new website software when customers use it to help select the appropriate office layout and plan furniture installations. It gives information to FOF that they may be thinking about making a purchase and the pages of the website being used may give information about the type of furniture they are interested in. This may enable email and other advertising communications to be directed at the customer (provided data protection regulations are complied with) or a visit from sales staff for larger orders.

This targeted relationship marketing may increase sales by improved information specific to the customer. It may also provide better general understanding of how and when FOF customers make purchases.

Data analytics could also be applied to the data captured to enable better understanding of customers and markets plus improved production planning.

Customer service

A better customer service improves the overall perceived quality by customers of the purchase from FOF and may increase sales without the need for sales staff to travel to client premises. Better suiting the client needs would help competitive advantage particularly over the smaller competitors. For example, with one third of industry competitors having revenue below £1 million it is unlikely that they will have sufficient scale economies to afford an annual cost of £180,000 for the digital system.

Examiner's comments

The answers to this requirement were the weakest in the exam. The numerical analysis was very poor for most candidates - the vast majority did not calculate the correct breakeven quantity, and only a minority managed even to arrive at the correct additional cost of the new technology. Some credit was given for understanding the impact of the decision on variable cost and displaying an awareness of breakeven. The discussion was a little better and many candidates did recognise the value of the data analytics to the business.

49.4 In making any ethical evaluation, it is first necessary to establish the facts. In this case, an overheard conversation is not good evidence. The claims about Jayne having been receiving free tickets for major sports events from the chief executive of EE may not have occurred. Moreover, even if it had taken place, the extent is unclear.

Even if tickets had been provided by the CEO, to a greater or lesser extent, this is not strong evidence that Jayne has necessarily been favouring EE in awarding tender contracts for furniture for schools. While EE has increased the number of schools it supplies by nine in 20X7 compared with 20X6, the increase is far greater for other smaller suppliers at 16.

It would be appropriate, as a starting point, to establish the basic facts of whether Jayne has been accepting tickets from the CEO of EE. If she has accepted tickets, it is important to establish whether they were free (a gift) or she paid market value in an arm's length transaction. In the latter case, the issue of personal benefit is much reduced as it is an exchange, rather than a transfer of value.

As the context of the case is in the public sector, consideration should be given to the Nolan Principles on Standards in Public Life. Relevant principles, for Jayne, in the current context include:

- **Selflessness**: holders of public office should take decisions solely in terms of the public interest. They should not do so to gain financial or other material benefits for themselves, their family or their friends.

- **Integrity**: holders of public office should not place themselves under any financial or other obligation to outside individuals or organisations that might influence them in the performance of their duties.

- **Honesty**: holders of public office have a duty to declare any private interests relating to their public duties and to take steps to resolve any conflicts arising in a way that protects the public interest.

The issue of legality needs to be considered in terms of whether an inducement has been given under the Bribery Act. If the claimed facts are established, then consideration should be given to whether legal advice should be obtained.

Aside from any legal issues, there are a number of ethical issues that arise.

The first ethical issue is a potential conflict of interest for Jayne. This is between Jayne's duty to act in the public interest in the disbursement of public funds in obtaining 'best value' and her self interest in obtaining free tickets. If she awards a contract to EE when she knows they are not the best value provider, then there is a strong case that self-interest has overridden the public interest and this could be a serious ethical breach with potential legal consequences.

A second potential ethical threat is one of intimidation. Potentially this could be perceived to be in either direction. Trevor confronted Jayne about this issue over lunch. If Jayne is innocent of the claimed facts she could perceive this as being intimidated by Trevor, even if it was not intended to be so. On the other hand, if the facts about free tickets are true, then Jayne's counter-claim to report Trevor to her superior for attempting to intimidate her could itself be a form of intimidation towards Trevor to deflect any criticism.

In making a decision as to how to proceed, some guidance is given by applying the Institute of Business Ethics three tests:

- Transparency
- Effect
- Fairness

Transparency – whether the EE CEO's gift/transaction (if any) should be made transparent by being disclosed at least within the LEA is a key issue in this case. Jayne needs to bear in mind how people (the public of Birmingham, EE shareholders, directors, competitors, schools and employees) would react if they found out subsequently that she may have been influenced by self-interest, rather than solely by the public interest. As a minimum, Jayne should have disclosed the nature of any transactions/gifts that took place. The local authority should have in place a code of conduct for employees receiving gifts or undertaking transactions with suppliers. Jayne should have disclosed whether or not she complies with such a code.

Effect – whom does the decision to disclose or not disclose affect or hurt? Clearly if the gift/transaction was not in the public interest, local taxpayers and businesses would not have received full value on an arm's length basis. Schools will also not have received value for their budgets. Competitors in the industry, such as FOF, may also have suffered from unfair competition.

Fairness – would Jayne's acceptance, then non-disclosure, be considered fair by those affected? The public and schools expect the local authority to act properly on their behalf and would not consider it fair to suffer a loss in order to favour Jayne's personal interests. Also, in terms of the other stakeholders, knowingly not disclosing the personal interest may be seen as unfair and a breach of business trust. FOF would almost certainly not regard the loss of business to further Jayne's personal interests to be fair.

Honesty and integrity

Further ethical issues are those of honesty and integrity, which involve, not just non-disclosure of personal interest, but also hiding the fact of, and consequences of, any gift/transaction for tickets.

Actions

Transparency remains important in seeking to make clear, if only in retrospect, the basis on which any gifts/transactions between Jayne and the EE CEO took place. It is also necessary to establish evidence that it may have influenced her decision-making in awarding contracts.

Unless a formal communication shortly arrives from Jayne's superior, Trevor should attempt to contact Jayne in writing, setting out his concerns and requesting a meeting to discuss the issues.

If Trevor knows the staff that he overheard, it may be possible to speak to them to obtain any more details.

Clarification of the basis on which FOF's recent tenders have not been successful should be obtained.

If there is no response to his enquiries, then Trevor should contact senior staff in the LEA to discuss the issues and obtain clarification and evidence. If there is no response, then Trevor should contact legal representatives of the LEA.

Examiner's comments

The answers to this requirement were variable in quality. Most candidates did not apply professional scepticism. For example, many candidates did not question either the validity of the claim about the tickets or Jayne's assertion that Trevor's behaviour was intimidating, when he appeared to be merely attempting to establish the facts.

Discussion also often tended to focus on Trevor to the exclusion of Jayne although, with some candidates, it was the other way around.

Many candidates used the Transparency, Effect, Fairness (TEF) structure and language. However, many candidates limited their discussion to these three TEF principles, rather than going on also to explore other ethical principles and issues raised by the scenario, including a conflict of interest and issues of honesty and integrity. They thereby produced a restricted and narrow answer which was constrained by the TEF framework, rather than enhanced by it.

Most candidates made some reference to legal issues, including bribery. Only a small minority referred to the public sector context and the Nolan principles.

Some candidates provided a reasonable discussion of the ethical issues/principles but then provided a weak discussion of the actions. Most candidates set out some suggested actions for Trevor as required, but others then went on to stray beyond what was asked in the requirement by also setting out actions for Jayne.

50 Berlina Kitchen Appliances (December 2017)

Marking guide

	Knowledge	Skill	Marks
50.1 Benchmarking	2	8	9
50.2 Performance management	3	9	11
50.3 (a) Implementation of change			
(b) Barriers to change	3	9	11
	8	26	31

50.1 Benchmarking uses comparisons with best practice to encourage improvement and change to achieve sustainable competitive advantage.

There are various types of benchmarking which BKA can use:

Internal: Internal benchmarking could involve a comparison between the four BKA production lines. The four production lines use similar processes of mass production so reasonable comparisons could be made for at least some processes. In terms of inputs, this might include taking a reasonably standardised task and comparing: cost; time taken; quality (eg, measured by faults or complaints). It may also provide overall comparisons of cost and operating efficiency between production lines, after adjusting for variations in the type of product. In so doing, internal benchmarking may raise questions of why differences occur, rather than direct answers as to what to do about any differences.

Internal benchmarking may also apply in terms of outputs such as selling prices, customer satisfaction and growth.

The strength of internal benchmarking is that it attempts to raise the standard of the weakest performing production line to that of the highest performing production line by showing what can be achieved within the same company.

A weakness of internal benchmarking is that it is inward looking and ignores the relative performance of competitors over whom we are attempting to gain a sustainable competitive advantage.

More aspirational internal benchmarking could be against Stigel's factory in Germany. If ultimately sales are to be made on global markets, then the German factory standards may better indicate what can be achieved and what needs to be achieved. These benchmarks may not be attainable in the short term for BKA, given current plant and equipment and working methods, but such benchmarks could illustrate the gap that needs to be closed for goals of international competitiveness to be achieved.

Competitive (or External): External benchmarking compares the performance of BKA to other companies operating in the same industry. In the current context, this might be similar companies such as Muskov, or more generally, companies manufacturing kitchen appliances operating in Eastern Europe. However, such companies may have similar problems to BKA and may not represent best practice. Under the new strategy in the change management plan, competitive benchmarking may involve global comparisons if this is the market in which the company intends to operate. For this exercise, any competitive benchmarking carried out by Stigel in respect of its own rivals may also be appropriate as an aspirational benchmark for BKA.

External benchmarking attempts to identify any competitive advantage or disadvantage compared to rivals. A weakness is that the quality of information is much lower than internal benchmarking as only information in the public domain is usually available, unless there is shared information within a benchmarking group.

Activity (or Best in Class): This involves comparing each of the activities or processes to similar activities in whatever industry they can be found. This could be different for each function: eg, production; marketing, procurement.

Comparators for production processes could be other industries where mass production is a key factor. This could perhaps be for motor vehicle manufacture where competitive pressures for production efficiency, yet high quality and reliability, may have given rise to innovative and efficient processes. Similarly, marketing activity could be benchmarked against specialist marketing companies or advertising agencies which are hired by many companies for their expertise.

Generic: This involves benchmarking against conceptually similar processes. This might involve examining processes in environments where the quality of manufacture is fundamental eg, medical equipment. Alternatively, procurement activities could be benchmarked against leaders across industries such as Amazon or Toyota. Customer satisfaction could be benchmarked against relationship marketing activities by leading hotel chains.

Examiner's comments

Marks tended to polarise on this requirement. The major problem for a significant number of candidates was a lack of basic knowledge in being unable to identify the four types of benchmark.

Those candidates who were able to identify the four types of benchmark normally scored well, although in some cases discussion often displayed confusion between competitive and best-in-class benchmarks. With regard to internal benchmarking, only a minority considered the additional possibility of benchmarking against Stigel's factory in Germany.

With competitive benchmarking, many referred to comparisons with Muskov, but hardly any recognised that the latter may well have similar problems to BKA. Most candidates did recognise the difficulties in accessing competitor information.

Weaker candidates displayed a lack of understanding of benchmarks, often confusing these with KPIs.

50.2 General comments

CSFs are those factors which are essential to the success of an organisation. Outperforming competitors in these areas is essential to gain competitive advantage.

KPIs are performance standards to measure and control the achievement of the areas critical to success (ie, CSFs). They include target measures of what needs to be achieved in each area in specific quantitative terms. Actual performance is then compared with these targets. However, KPIs do not of themselves indicate how these targets can be achieved.

Overall assessment of KPIs

The KPIs need to be well defined and quantifiable. All of the three KPIs suggested appear to meet this criterion and although there may be some issues of data collection, these do not appear to be insurmountable.

They must be well communicated. All of the three KPIs suggested appear to be capable of being clearly communicated to the relevant staff.

They must be relevant to the line of business. It would appear that these KPIs are being applied to BKA as a whole. Given the apparent intended autonomy of each production line as a profit centre, it is important to measure the performance of each division separately by using separate KPIs for each production line. In this way, a good performance by one production line does not hide the poor performance of another.

Customer satisfaction

KPIs

The measure of the number of customers being 'satisfied' might not be enough to outperform the competition and may be too low a hurdle. Perhaps the KPI would be better as a relative measure compared to a key competitor (see benchmarking above) or industry norms.

A further problem is that the measure of itself is not enough to indicate the reasons for customer satisfaction or dissatisfaction. More targeted measures about whether the customer is satisfied with specific aspects (eg, delivery, design, reliability, features) might elicit measures that can more easily be acted upon.

The responses to questionnaires by customers may exhibit bias, as not all customers have responded. For example, dissatisfied may have a greater motivation to respond to the questionnaire.

As noted above, separate measures of customer satisfaction for each type of product (ie, production line) would also focus management attention where required.

Alternative KPIs may include (for each division):

- Proportion of satisfied customers compared with the market leader.
- Customer retention rates.
- Number of customer complaints received.

Targets

The level of current achievement of customer satisfaction is low at 72%, being less than three in four customers. This might be due to a lack of customer choice under central government control in the past. It seems unlikely that BKA will retain over a quarter of its customers (who are less than satisfied) under the new regime in Ruritania where there is more choice by customers.

The targets for 20X8 and 20X9 require substantial improvement, but still tolerate 10% of unsatisfied customers in 20X8 and 5% in 20X9 which may still be considered high. It may however be that some customers responding to questionnaires in 20X8 receive their goods and service in 20X7.

It should be noted that the type of customer in 20X8 and 20X9 will be partly different from the customers in 20X7 as there will be a proportion living in overseas countries. These customers may be more used to purchasing electrical appliances from global suppliers and therefore have higher expectations to judge satisfaction. The figures for 20X7, 20X8 and 20X9 may therefore be non-comparable as the population of the respondents will differ. Segmentation of the responses into Ruritanian and other customers may give more intertemporal consistency in the data.

Production quality

KPIs

Production quality is important but has a number of aspects. The KPI of 'number of faults reported in the first year after sales' measures only one aspect of quality – reliability. Other aspects could include the capability of (say) a washing machine to clean clothes well at a range of temperatures when it is working as it should. More subtly, it could include quality of design. At best, therefore, this KPI is only a partial measure of the achievement of the CSF.

Alternative KPIs may include (for each division):

- The number of faults compared to the market leader; one month, one year and three years after sale.

- Cost of faults repaired under guarantee, stratified in cost ranges.

- Rankings in consumer press reports on product performance.

Targets

The target of the number of faults reported in the first year after sales is a lagged measure. Even if immediate improvements in quality are made on the first day of the change management plan (eg, by importing into Ruritania washing machine motors from Germany) then faults could still be reported in 20X8 in respect of sales made in 20X7 under the 'old regime'.

Currently the proportion of faults is high and, whilst improvements are targeted, they remain high in 20X9. Targets set relative to competitors are required (see benchmarking) in order to ascertain whether these levels are likely to give competitive advantage, even for a low-cost product.

Penetrate export markets

KPIs

This KPI is not sufficiently specific in specifying whether the measure is sales volume or sales value. If sale prices are higher outside Ruritania then this measure may be distorted, or at least not what was intended.

Also, measuring the proportion of sales outside Ruritania may not be the best measure of success if Ruritanian sales are falling as long-term government contracts are not being renewed. An absolute measure to target overseas sales might better capture the plan to expand outside Ruritania.

The nature of the markets is also not specified in the KPI. It could include neighbouring countries which are similar to Ruritania and are still developing closed or semi-closed economies which are not competing in global markets. This is different to selling in countries exposed to global competition in global markets.

Alternative KPIs may include (for each division):

- Sales revenue in each of the following geographical areas: Western Europe; Ruritania; Rest of Europe; America; Rest of the World.

- Growth in sales revenue in each of the following geographical areas: Western Europe; Ruritania; Rest of Europe; America; Rest of the World.

Targets

By 20X9, there is a target to have 30% of sales outside Ruritania. This is a stretching target within two years in the context of a five-year plan, particularly as there is a low lase to start from, with very few existing customers outside Ruritania.

The KPI may provide inappropriate incentives to BKA marketing staff in attempting to achieve the target by focusing on 'easier' sales in less developed countries, rather than in open economies subject to global competition, such as in Germany.

Examiner's comments

This requirement provided a clear direction to address each agreed CSF and provide KPIs based on the information in the scenario and the tabulated data provided. However, many candidates ignored this guidance and, instead, tried (inappropriately) to shoehorn the structured information given in the scenario into a Balanced Scorecard framework. Models can help to structure an answer when the information provided is diverse and unstructured, but this was not the case in this requirement. There were clearly defined and structured performance issues, based on the specific needs of the company, which should have been used directly to address the issues as required.

Most candidates appraised at least some of the suggested KPIs but very few provided a critique of the targets set or suggested that KPIs should be set at divisional level rather than company-wide level. The great majority of candidates only set out alternatives at the firm level, usually without consideration of targets or the timeframe within which they are being applied.

50.3(a) **Rapid implementation or piecemeal change**

Rapid change is appropriate when the organisation is in crisis. This appears to be the case with BKA given the under-investment in the past and the lack of competitiveness. This is particularly the case as it is losing customers as long-term contracts are not being renewed. However, while rapid change may be desirable, it may not be feasible given:

- The potential barriers to change (see below)
- The need to retrain and develop new skills in updating production processes
- The need to establish new global markets for the products
- The need to implement new investment
- The scale of change needed – which is transformational change in this case

As a consequence, a flexible plan may be appropriate. This covers not just controllable events but the need to change the culture of existing managers and employees and the need to create new markets.

The five-year plan and the required KPIs in the first two years set some challenging targets (see above). A two-year plan would mean that revised targets to achieve ultimate goals become extremely challenging and may not be perceived as attainable.

They may therefore cause employees and management to dismiss the change management as unreasonable.

Also, the plan involves achieving internal and external goals. Whilst internal factors may be pushed through, wisely or unwisely, external factors are less controllable. To change customer perceptions of the BKA products may take time given the company's history. Attempting to change customer perceptions in international markets at the same time as being in the process of improving production quality and customer satisfaction may be unreasonable.

If the plan is to rebrand BKA products as Stigel at the end of the planning period, then two years may be overoptimistic and there may be real risks of damaging the core Stigel brand by a premature launch.

50.3 (b) Barriers to change

Cultural barriers

Structural inertia is the cumulative effect of all the systems and procedures that the organisation has installed over the years to ensure consistency and quality. These act as barriers to change.

The BKA change management plan proposes fundamental changes that will affect the culture of the organisation. In order to mitigate the damaging aspects of this, Lewin argues that the old culture of cost centres and lack of divisional responsibility will need to be unfrozen; the changes should be made; and then a refreezing of the new culture of profit centres and more divisional autonomy should take place.

Power structures may be threatened by the redistribution of decision-making authority or resources, or the changing of lines of communication.

This will in particular affect lower levels of management and thus they may be reluctant to implement changes which will be against their own interests.

Personnel barriers

There are also barriers which affect individuals and result in them seeing the change plan as a threat. This may affect employees who perceive that the goal of increasing the number of units of output produced per employee to result in downsizing. It may also apply where there are likely to be substantial changes in work practices and redundancies of old skills in favour of new skills. These fears may be countered by transparency as to who may be affected or reassurance that retraining will take place and that the number of units of output produced per employee can be increased by raising output without making any redundancies.

Habit – habitual ways of work are hard to change, and the new and unknown is often uncomfortable. This may be part of the old centralised top-down culture of BKA.

Security – is almost inevitably threatened. Both job security and the security of familiarity are threatened with Stigel as the new foreign owners. This may vary according to whether particular production lines are most seen as under threat of closure.

Effect on earnings – continuing cost reductions and changes in work practices may affect the earnings of individuals. Increasing pay contingent on the change programme and improved performance may mitigate this by 'buying off' some of the resistance to change.

Fear of the unknown reduces people's willingness and interest in learning new skills; they may lack the confidence to take on a new challenge where work practices change. New foreign ownership and unfamiliar processes and practices may increase this fear.

Selective information processing results in employees ignoring management arguments for change. An effective communication strategy with consultation by the BKA senior management is therefore needed to help mitigate this.

One model that can be used to mitigate barriers to change is the Gemini 4Rs model comprising:

- Reframing – establish a new emphasis and vision on quality and creating the willingness to change

- Restructuring – create new divisions and profit centres with increased automated production methods, and align the new culture to these

- Revitalising – adapt to the new international competitive environment appropriate for selling in global markets

- Renewal – gain staff commitment for the new structure and processes through a new reward structure and individual learning.

Examiner's comments

In respect of the first part of the requirement many candidates were critical of rapid change with reference to behavioural factors and barriers to change, as a result many answered aspects of the second part of the requirement when attempting the first. Only a minority saw the issues in a broader strategic context, with the need for rapid change driven by the changing competitive and technological environment.

Most candidates showed awareness of personnel barriers to change, fewer also being aware of cultural barriers. A minority confused organisational culture with international cultural differences between Germany and Ruritania. Most discussed mitigation measures and the majority referred to Lewin's framework (but also Gemini).

Weaker candidates made no use of any framework, just referring generally to motivational issues.

Some weaker candidates also merged their answers to the first and second parts of the requirement. This normally resulted in unstructured and often confused responses.

51 Cancer Concern Ltd (December 2017)

Marking guide

	Knowledge	Skill	Marks
51.1 Report			
(a) Stakeholder impact			
(b) Funds allocation	5	11	14
51.2 Mission statement	3	5	8
	8	16	22

51.1(a) Patients and future patients

To reduce expenditure on research projects, stricter filtering criteria could be applied to potential projects to raise the probability that funded projects will succeed.

To reduce expenditure on hospices consideration could be given, for example, to closure of underutilised hospices (if any) and transferring patients to other hospices. Replacement of paid staff with volunteers and reductions in the scope of service provided to patients could be considered. However, all these proposals are likely to have an effect on the effectiveness of the service provided to patients and therefore reduce achievement of the aims of the charitable trust.

Universities, hospitals and researchers

Universities, hospitals and researchers may be affected by a reduction in funding allocated by CC to research projects. Aside from the self-interest of these stakeholders, reductions in funding may reduce the effectiveness of the research outcomes although, by its nature, research is uncertain, so the impact of funding withdrawal is also uncertain. Withdrawal of funding from some existing projects may mean that historical allocations of funds may not have the opportunity to yield successful research outcomes.

Professional staff and volunteers at hospices

Reductions in professional staff at hospices to save money may lead to demotivation and reduced effectiveness of the services provided to patients. While volunteers are not paid, they may be unwilling to work more hours to compensate for the loss of professional staff, or may be less effective if they do so.

Consultations with all staff to discuss the issues arising from reduced income may be a means of gaining acceptance of changes and participation in developing solutions.

Donors to CC

Reduction of funding to either of the two activities may indirectly affect donors' perception of CC and therefore their willingness to continue to make donations to CC in future. For example, the closure of a hospice which had helped a relative may cause future donations to cease and thereby limit the benefit of any cost reduction by also reducing income. In addition, legacies to CC may be cancelled if the historic activities of the charity are rebalanced.

51.1(b) In deciding, at the margin, whether to make donations to research projects or hospices there is a trade-off between the interests of current cancer patients and potential future cancer patients. There is also a trade-off between the near certainty of the activity of looking after patients in hospices and the uncertainty of a research project which may yield widespread, long-term benefits or may fail completely.

In deciding how to allocate the reduced level of income between activities, CC trustees must ensure that they are complying with legal and other regulatory requirements and are within the terms of the trust deed.

This may require a choice, not just between the two main activities but between any other obligations within those activities (eg, restricted funds may become repayable if a hospice is closed; or there may be duties in the trust deed to fund certain activities).

There may also be obligations in the trust deed with respect to the level of reserves which must be maintained (which are currently 'limited'). It may be that funds need to be allocated to increase reserves rather than for either of the two activities to maintain financial stability.

Funds not set aside for the above purposes need to be allocated by trustees and, while this requires judgement, it is important that there are criteria to guide that judgement.

In particular, it is important that best use is made of the available funds in order to promote the aims of the charity. Continuing an equal split may be arithmetically appealing but may not satisfy appropriate criteria for judging where the greatest benefit from fund allocations can be achieved.

Key stakeholders are the patients suffering from cancer and patients who will suffer from cancer in the future. While their interests may be the primary purpose of the charity in determining the allocation of funds, it is also important to consider the interests of other stakeholders who are important in enabling the care of patients and on whom the purposes of the charity are dependent. There is significant subjectivity in making these judgements, but priorities need to be established based on agreed principles.

Such principles make include:

- The 3Es – economy, effectiveness and efficiency
- Cost-benefit trade-offs
- The value based on qualitative and quantitative outcomes
- Reputational impact

Examiner's comments

Answers to the first part of this requirement were normally quite good.

Relevant stakeholder groups were generally well identified, although weaker efforts tended to ignore the cancer research charitable activity for some reason.

Addressing the issue of conflicts tended to be restricted to problems associated with lower allocations of funds, rather than conflicts between stakeholders. Only the better candidates considered the longer-term consequences of current reductions in funding. A number of candidates reverted to Mendelow's matrix which meant they identified stakeholders but then often failed adequately to cover impact.

In respect of the second part of the requirement most candidates restricted their discussion to the prioritisation criteria and cost-benefit analysis and tended to ignore legal/regulatory/trust deed considerations.

Nevertheless, a significant minority addressed most areas very well, additionally identifying tensions between the need to secure financial stability for the charity and perceptions of outsiders, donors in particular.

51.2 Mission statement

We exist to promote the discovery of new treatments for cancer and care for those suffering from terminal cancer.

We aim to achieve this by:

- supporting innovative and effective research projects, by established researchers, relating to diagnoses, treatments and prevention of cancers; and
- delivering expert care for people suffering from terminal cancer and emotional support for their families.

We will enable these aims by raising funds in a cost-effective and ethical manner and by making distribution decisions based on our values and the best use of funds in effectively promoting our aims and providing the greatest probable benefit to the greatest number of people suffering from cancer, now and in the future.

We will pursue these aims within the constraints of the law, other regulations, the terms of the CC trust deed, the public interest and financial constraints.

We do not seek to make a profit or surplus, but we will aim to secure the financial stability and sustainability of the CC charitable trust by maintaining appropriate reserves to meet its current and future obligations.

Justification

The revised mission statement sets out more clearly the purposes and scope of CC's activities. It clarifies why the organisation exists and sets out the activities it will undertake to achieve these purposes.

The mission statement also provides broad guidance to help judgement to be exercised to discern how funds will be allocated between the two key activities.

It also sets out the financial, legal and regulatory constraints on CC's activities and the standards and values by which decisions will be guided.

It contains the four aspects on the Ashridge model for mission statements:

- Purpose
- Strategy
- Policies and standards of behaviour
- Values

Examiner's comments

Candidates' performance varied in quality for the justification of the revisions to the mission statement, with many referring to generic criteria for mission statements such as Ashridge. However, fewer mentioned the need for financial stability and sustainability for the charity.

The presentation of mission statements produced variation in quality and length. Generally, the mission statements provided were of the correct tone. However, there was a tendency for weaker candidates to be too brief, despite the instruction in the question for a longer mission statement to include key purposes and values, and recognition of the impact of financial constraints. In particular, many candidates failed to recognise funding limitations explicitly within their mission statement.

52 Just Houses Ltd (March 2018)

Marking guide

	Knowledge	Skill	Marks
52.1 Barriers to entry and impact of technology	2	6	8
52.2 Data analysis	2	19	19
52.3 Proposed strategic alliance	2	9	10
52.4 Ethics	3	6	8
	9	40	45

52.1 Barriers to Entry and Impact of technology

Barriers to entry are one of Porter's five forces that determine the degree of competitive rivalry in an industry. High barriers to entry make it more difficult for new entrants to join the market so it becomes more competitive.

The combined impact of the barriers to entry for new entrants to the estate agent industry appears to be relatively low to moderate. Barriers consist of:

Capital investment

Traditional estate agents operate from high street branches which may require capital investment, however this is not true for those that choose to rent. The new online agency model removes the need for premises and reduces overheads, thereby lowering entry barriers.

Economies of scale

In the traditional model there are limited opportunities for economies of scale which reduce entry barriers. The industry is fragmented with many small local estate agents. National chains may have some cost economies due to their greater purchasing power eg, in relation to printing and advertising. Technology has given the online property portal operators some opportunity for economies of scale since they possess large databases that they can leverage. However it also provides an opportunity for smaller estate agents to advertise on a wider scale, making it easier for them to start up.

Product differentiation and switching

The product offering (sale of the house) is relatively homogeneous with most estate agents operating a similar pricing model so differentiation is via the level of customer service or additional services offered (eg, mortgage advice, legal assistance etc).

There are some switching costs – the vendor normally signs a contract with the estate agent for exclusive rights to sell the property during a set period. Costs for selling through another agent or withdrawing from the contract make switching more restricted.

Qualifications and membership of professional bodies

Typically it is not compulsory for estate agents to undergo lengthy training to obtain formal qualifications, nor is it mandatory to be a member of a professional body which reduces the formal barriers to entry.

Advantages to incumbents

There may be some advantages to incumbents as a result of:

(1)   Brand names of the national chains

(2)   Knowledge and expertise on industry standards and regulations

(3)   Access to suppliers on favourable terms eg, online portals such as Pozla/Nextstep, advertising in newspapers

Impact of technology on barriers to entry:

As noted in the scenario, technology has created a change in the behaviour of buyers and sellers. The social/technological trend for shopping online has seen the growth of several large online property portals which has caused a major shift in buyer behaviour - looking for properties online rather than through visits to high street agents. This has considerably reduced the capital barriers to entry since agencies can operate without a physical presence. It has also potentially made it easier for small agencies to broaden their operating remit and marketing reach.

Technology has had limited impact on requirements for qualification and membership, although it may have made training more accessible online. The IT skills required to operate in the industry may have created a new skill barrier. Conversely the ability to create large databases, provide data to buyers online and offer virtual tours means that agencies require less staff which reduces a key cost.

A relatively small percentage of sellers currently choose to sell through an online agent or use the internet to sell the property themselves. However as this behaviour increases, the market for traditional estate agents is likely to shrink further.

Summary

There appear to be relatively few barriers to entry to the traditional estate agency market. There is a limited market in the form of the number of people wanting to sell houses and the market is mature. Technology has changed the market model and further reduced the barriers to entry. As a result the market share and performance of traditional estate agents is threatened by new online entrants. This means that there is increased competition both online and through traditional channels, as larger national agents may defend their market positioning by aggressive marketing and/or pricing.

Examiner's comments

This requirement was well answered by most candidates. Many candidates discussed barriers from a common sense point of view, using information in the scenario. Those candidates who used knowledge from the learning materials to structure their answer tended to come up with a wider range of points and a better analysis. Only a very few referred to Porter's Five Forces explicitly, although these were implicit in most responses. Only the better candidates specified the relative overall strength of the entry barriers.

Most provided a separate discussion of the impact of information technology on barriers to entry, although weaker candidates tended to discuss the impact of technology in general rather than in relation to barriers specifically. Better candidates discussed the fact that technology might both strengthen and weaken the barriers to entry, justifying their perspective.

52.2 **Evaluate comparative financial and operating performance of Branch A and B**

Appendix of calculations

> **Tutorial note**
>
> A wide range of analysis could be undertaken – the table demonstrates the range of calculations. Candidates are not expected to have produced all of them.

	Average JH Branch £'000	Branch A (note 1) £'000	Branch B (note 2) £'000
Financial KPIs			
By branch:			
Sales commission earned	514	368	422
Fees from other services	171	170	140
Total revenue (Commission + fees)	685	538	562
Branch costs	414	326	408
Contribution – pre central costs	271	212	154
Operating profit	171	112	54
Operating profit margin	25%	20.8%	9.6%
Contribution margin	39.6%	39.4%	27.4%
Fees from other services as a % of revenue	25%	31.6%	25%

By properties sold:

Value of completed property sales	34,286	24,500	28,100
Number of properties sold	94	70	84
Average value of each property sold	£364,745	£350,000	£334,524
Average commission per sale	£5,468	£5,257	£5,024
Total revenue per sale	£7,287	£7,686	£6,690
Branch costs per sale	£4,404	£4,657	£4,857
Contribution per sale	£2,883	£3,029	£1,833
Average commission per employee	£85,667	£73,600	£60,286
Other fees per employee	£28,500	£34,000	£20,000
Average initial asking price of properties sold (sales value/% price achieved)	£392,199	£372,340	£375,870

Operating KPIs

Number of viewings	1,131	675	1,176
Number of employees	6	5	7
Properties sold per employee	15.7	14	12
Viewings per employee	189	135	168
Average viewings per sale	12	9.6	14
Average time taken to sell property	15 weeks	12 weeks	18 weeks
Sales price as % original asking price	93%	94%	89%
Number of enquiries from vendors	171	225	153
Conversion of enquiries into sales clients (properties sold/enquiries)	55%	31%	55%

Commentary

JH performance in relation to industry

JH charges a commission of 1.5% on the final sales value of the property compared to the industry average of 1.8%. This may be due to market positioning or JH's location in the North West which may be a less buoyant market than, say, London and the South.

Overall JH takes 5 weeks longer than the industry average to sell each property (15 weeks compared to 10) and requires more viewings to achieve a sale (12 compared to 10) – this may be due to regional market differences but may also reflect JH's lack of online advertising. The fact that JH typically achieves 93% of the initial asking price suggests that the accuracy of initial valuations and the strength of sales negotiations are consistent with the industry.

Branch performance and other possible closure criteria

Initial closure criteria

The two branches have been identified for possible closure as a result of their low levels of commission and operating margin. Both Branch A and B are preforming notably worse than the JH average:

	Average JH branch	Branch A	Branch B
Sales commission earned £'000	514	368	422
Operating profit margin	25%	20.8%	9.6%

Unless the branches are operating in areas of a similar size, with similar housing markets, comparing an absolute figure such as total sales commission may not be valid.

Alternative closure criteria

An alternative closure criterion might be to compare commission per employee, which would allow for different staffing levels, albeit still does not reflect any differences in local housing markets.

Similarly operating profit margin is calculated after taking account of central costs. These appear to have been divided equally across the branches £0.7m/7 = £100k per branch.

A more relevant measure for comparing branch performance in advance of closure, or at least for evaluating the performance of the branch manager, might be to consider contribution margin, which focuses on controllable costs.

	Average JH branch	Branch A	Branch B
Commission per employee	£85,667	£73,600	£60,286
Contribution margin	39.6%	39.4%	27.4%

Although both branches are still generating less commission per employee than the average, it can be seen that Branch A's contribution margin is almost equal to that of the average JH branch, whereas Branch B's contribution margin is relatively poor at 27.4%.

A more detailed analysis of performance is required to ascertain whether the two branches are indeed underperforming:

Branch A

This branch is located in a town with a local population of 180,000. The town has a university and is home to the regional headquarters of a major bank, which suggest that it is a reasonably promising location. If a significant proportion of housing is student accommodation, this may have affected average prices in the area.

This branch appears to be being well-run. It is selling houses faster than the JH average (12 weeks), with fewer viewings required than both the JH and industry average (9.6 compared to 12 and 10 respectively) and achieving a higher percentage of the asking price (94%). The branch has 5 employees (1 fewer than the average) who are selling 14 houses each compared to the JH average of 15.7. Another area of success for the branch appears to be the fees from other services per employee which at £34,000 are significantly higher than the JH average £28,500 which suggests staff are doing well at augmenting the service offering.

The main area of underperformance appears to be in converting enquiries into clients, where branch A only has a 31% success rate compared to the JH average of 55%. This needs further investigation as the quality of the branch's service suggests they would be able to attract potential vendors. It may be due to the fact that branch A faces more competition due to the nature of the town, or is less good at promoting its success.

Branch B

Branch B is located in a large seaside town and seaside resort with a population of 140,000. A significant number of the town's population are retired and the town's economy has suffered due to the rising popularity of foreign holidays.

Specific problems for the town, coupled with the general economic uncertainty, are likely to have adversely affected the local housing market, reducing house prices. This may explain the branch's poor results.

The average value of a house sold by Branch B is £335k (compared to JH's average of £365k) and it has only been able to achieve 89% of the average asking price. It takes longer than average and Branch A to sell properties (18 weeks) and requires more viewings per sale (14 compared to an average of 12). In addition the fact that a large number of people in the town have retired may reduce the number of housing transactions that are likely to take place. This could explain why Branch B only received 153 sales enquiries in the year compared to the branch average of 171.

The branch's conversion rate of enquiries to sales is the same as the JH average. This suggests that potential customers are choosing Branch B because they believe the branch will be able to offer a good service but that there is a lack of potential customers in the first place. The branch has one more employee than the average but they are selling fewer properties, so costs could be potentially saved and results improved by reducing headcount. However employees are undertaking more viewings per person (168) than Branch A (135) and a cut in numbers may reduce the service it is able to offer.

More information is required to be able to draw final conclusions:

- 20X7 Budget to identify how branches and JH overall were expected to perform

- Information on the size of each branch and its market, including details about the properties in each area since the property types and values may depend on where the branch is located

- A breakdown of the fees for other services, including details of services offered and price

- Details of the central costs to help ascertain whether these can be allocated more accurately

- Results for prior years to identify trends in performance

- Forecasts for JH as a whole and for individual branches, together with industry/regional market forecasts for house sales and prices to assess future potential

- Regional industry information to benchmark JH's performance against similar sized estate agents in the North West

- Details of competitors for each branch

Conclusion

The two branches have both produced lower revenue and operating margin figures than average. However these are not necessarily indicative of poor performance nor are they necessarily grounds for closure.

The other performance measures considered suggest that Branch A is offering a good service to its customers by selling houses relatively quickly and achieving a good percentage of the asking price. However it needs to improve the rate of conversion of enquiries into clients.

More information is required to ascertain whether Branch B is being poorly managed/offering a lower quality service or whether its results are due to the fact that it seems to be operating in a more challenging marketplace.

Both branches are still contributing to the wealth of the Haldar family and it would be naïve to close them without further investigation and further information (see above). However depending on the forecasts, Branch B in the struggling seaside resort may be a better candidate for closure than Branch A in the thriving town, as the latter might be more easily supported to improve performance.

Examiner's comments

Answers to this requirement were somewhat polarised and the average score, whilst reasonable, was lower than some previous data analysis requirements. This is likely to be due to the fact that the candidates could not usefully perform standard ratio calculations or look at percentage changes, and instead needed to give some thought to selecting the most useful calculations and analysis in the context of branch closures.

Most candidates provided a well-structured table with columns of data analysis showing figures for both Branches A and B, and the better candidates also included industry benchmarks or figures for the average JH branch.

The weakest candidates did not produce a data table and instead wove some numbers into their narrative. They tended to lose marks by failing to present the data systematically, thereby failing to identify data patterns.

The discussion was generally reasonable, and many candidates used sensible sub-headings. Better candidates produced a reasoned discussion of the performance of the two branches relative to the JH and industry averages, typically using the operating data to explain the financial performance, and addressing the usefulness of the commission revenue and operating margin criteria directly. Weaker candidates, as usual, reiterated the figures they had calculated, without adding value, or tended to provide either financial analysis or operating analysis and not both.

A minority considered the impact of the equal but arbitrary split of central costs and the implications for relative performance evaluation of the branches.

Most candidates identified the need for additional information to inform any decision regarding branch closures, although weaker candidates tended to produce a generic list which did not attract many marks. Few referenced the lack of information about competitors in the scenario.

A surprising number did not give an initial assessment of whether either branch should be closed, and very few discussed other possible closure criteria despite the specific requirement to do so.

52.3 Strategic alliance with OurCasa

A strategic alliance is an agreement between two companies to act together with mutual interest.

Advantages

- Most buyers look for property online – this alliance will allow JH properties to be listed and seen by more people, widening the potential customer base.

- Although JH advertises on its website it will only attract potential purchasers who have already heard of JH; the alliance with OurCasa is likely to attract buyers from outside the immediate local area, increasing JH's geographic market without requiring capital investment in premises.

- Availability 24/7 – this strategy allows people to book viewings/give decisions on offers electronically. It may help persuade vendors to choose JH to sell their property who are currently going to competitors (given its enquiry conversion rate is lower than average).

- This starts to address the risks of a declining industry for the traditional model.

- It provides JH with access to a business that has resources and expertise in technology so reduces the risk to JH of implementing a digital strategy and removes the need for in-house expertise.

Disadvantages

- Vendors who pay for JH's traditional 1.5% model may feel they are paying over the odds/being exploited if they are paying the average commission fee of £5,468 compared to the premium package from OurCasa of £1,250.

- Potential customers who learn of OurCasa at their initial enquiry with JH may go direct to OurCasa because it is cheaper, as a result the strategic alliance may cannibalise JH's existing business.

- OurCasa is relatively new and may not have the same reputation as the large online property portals and so may not have access to as wide a pool of buyers as NextStep/Pozla.

- JH will be making a lower profit per sale and will be required to provide staff to support the premium service – it may not have the capacity to do this or this may detract from its own service that customers are paying substantial extra money for.

- The two businesses will each have their own interests at heart and this could result in disputes/disagreements about key issues.

Conclusion

The advantage for JH is that the alliance provides wider access to potential buyers and improves the service it is able to offer its customers. As Rebecca says it also helps JH respond to the technological changes in the industry without requiring significant capital investment. Not partaking in the alliance may have a significant opportunity cost since a competitor could take up OurCasa's offer and make profit at JH's expense.

However JH needs to consider whether it would be better paying to advertise its properties on the existing well-known online portals and developing its own website further to provide email alerts/a 24 hour online service rather than risk cannibalising its existing market by getting involved with a business that is relatively unknown.

On the face of it the alliance may not last long as it is hard to see that JH has much to offer OurCasa which OurCasa could not get itself by employing people on a contract basis to accompany viewings.

Examiner's comments

This requirement was reasonably well answered and most candidates were comfortable discussing the advantages and disadvantages of the proposed strategic alliance. A surprising number did not specifically recognise risk sharing as an advantage and some weaker candidates produced an imbalanced response, emphasising the advantages without considering possible disadvantages such as cannibalisation of the existing JH business. Most candidates arrived at a conclusion with regards to the overall viability of the alliance.

52.4 Ethical issues

In making any ethical evaluation, it is first necessary to establish the facts. In this case, an overheard conversation may not be good evidence. Also we do not know whether Sarah has actually chosen to do what her brother requests, or even seriously considered whether to do so.

The issue of legality needs to be considered in terms of whether the additional commission represents an inducement under the Bribery Act. There may also be implications in relation to money laundering regulations. Once the facts are established, consideration should be given to whether legal advice should be obtained.

Aside from any legal issues, there are a number of ethical issues that arise.

A key issue is one of honesty and integrity. JH is regulated by the Estate Agents Act which requires estate agents to act in the best interests of their clients, and to treat both buyers and sellers honestly and fairly. Whilst Sarah might argue that the seller is only interested in getting the highest price and that she is therefore acting in the client's interests, revealing the buyer's bid to Jim breaches confidentiality and is neither honest nor fair. It will particularly affect Vera who will thereby be deprived of her rightful opportunity to purchase the property. Sarah is likely to be in breach of any code of conduct issued by her professional body.

Sarah is facing a conflict of interest. This is between her duty to act in the client's interest in obtaining 'best value', her duty to treat buyers fairly, and her self-interest in earning extra commission and promoting the interests of her brother.

Sarah should aim to act as transparently as possible and should also bear in mind how people would react if they found out subsequently that she may have been influenced by self-interest. If it came to light, JH's reputation is likely to suffer.

Actions

The fact that Jim has asked Sarah to release confidential information implies a lack of personal ethics on his part. As a minimum, Sarah should have disclosed the fact that she is related to the potential purchaser and probably therefore withdrawn from handling this particular sale.

As financial controller, I am subject to ICAEW ethical guidelines. Having overheard the conversation, the most reasonable action would appear to be for me to try and establish the facts and whether Sarah has acted on the request.

I/JH may need to take legal advice and be guided by it, particularly in relation to money laundering and bribery legislation.

Once I have all the information, I may need to consult any policies/codes of conduct that JH has and consider appropriate steps to report the matter. If Sarah has revealed the information to Jim, there may grounds to remove or at least discipline her.

Moving forwards, JH should establish a policy for staff, requiring them to declare any personal interest or connections they have and ensuring that affected transactions are handled by other members of staff.

Examiner's comments

The ethics requirement was very well attempted by most candidates. Most candidates were able to identify the key ethical issues in the scenario and it is encouraging that more candidates are now applying professional scepticism, in this case in relation to the reliability of an overheard conversation as evidence of unethical behaviour.

Those candidates who relied on the Transparency, Effect, Fairness (TEF) structure and language typically produced a much more restricted answer than candidates who explored the other ethical principles and issues raised by the scenario, which included conflict of interest and confidentiality. Most candidates made some reference to legal issues, including bribery and/or money laundering.

Some candidates provided a reasonable discussion of the ethical issues/principles but then provided a weak discussion of the actions. Some weaker candidates limited their potential marks by focusing their discussion on the implications and actions for Sarah only.

53 Bagaj Lux Ltd (March 2018)

	Knowledge	Skill	Marks
53.1 Value chain and competitive strategy	3	8	10
53.2 Cyber security risks and management	2	7	8
53.3 Financial and non-financial factors	2	11	12
	7	26	30

53.1 Key elements of Value Chain

The value chain is the organisation of resources through a sequence of activities that enables BL to add value, in this case to the luggage product that it produces. BL is pursuing a differentiation strategy in accordance with Porter's generic activities – its luggage is perceived to be of high quality and sells at a premium price, allowing it to earn an average gross margin of 48%. So BL needs to focus on resources and processes which support its differentiation strategy.

Primary activities (inbound logistics, operations, outbound logistics, sales and marketing, and service) are those that create value and are directly concerned with providing the output: luggage. Support activities (Firm infrastructure, Procurement, HR, Technology) do not create value directly themselves but enable the primary activities to take place and result in a high quality product and high quality customer service.

The crucial activities that allow BL to sustain its competitive advantage as a differentiator are known as value drivers. Value drivers are evident at each stage in BL's value chain:

Inbound logistics/Procurement:

Inbound logistics is supported by procurement, sourcing the very best quality leather from Belgium, which is hand dyed and contributes to the premium product. There is likely to be a relationship of trust with the single supplier. Other materials come from Turkey – these need to be of appropriate quality to maintain BL's brand image.

Operations/HR:

BL has a very labour-intensive production process. Highly skilled craftspeople undertake most of the production by hand, differentiating the luggage from mass-produced items and adding to the image of luxury. As this is a key value driver, the HR function needs to support operations to ensure that employees with appropriate skills are hired and receive suitable training.

Outbound logistics/Technology

Distribution is outsourced to an international logistics company, Pello, which undertakes some value-added services associated with the initial delivery of the product: pre-wrapping of the luggage and care-label tagging. This relationship and the services Pello provides help BL differentiate its product from competitors and technology is used to integrate the two systems and coordinate operations and distribution. The fact that BL regularly inspects Pello's operations ensures that the service it provides is consistent with BL's brand image.

Marketing and Sales

This is a key value adding activity. BL spends a considerable amount on advertising. In particular its use of product placement strategies and celebrity promotion help to create an image of the luggage as a "must-have" product that customers are prepared to wait for. The adoption of BL's products by celebrity internet bloggers help add to its perceived value.

Service

After purchase, BL offers a lifetime guarantee as evidence of its quality product and its after-care service allows customers to send their bags back to the factory for any repairs. The offer of this sort of service guarantee is likely to give the customer confidence in BL's products although as customers may want to stay on-trend with the latest colour and design they may in fact replace items regularly rather than keep using them for life.

Firm infrastructure – The firm culture/ethos of "hand-made in England" helps to sustain BL's brand image particularly with overseas customers.

Linkages

BL's competitive advantage is sustained by the linkages in its value chain and its wider value system of suppliers and distributors.

For example the fact that BL secures the highest quality leather (procurement/inbound logistics) and its product is made by hand by highly skilled craftsmen (HR/operations) is likely to ensure high quality production. This reduces the need for and hence the cost of the lifetime guarantee/repairs service.

Also the use of technology to integrate and coordinate activities (evidenced by BL's online ordering and payment system, interface with Pello and real-time reporting of deliveries) allows for smooth functioning of the distribution process and a higher quality service.

Some activities that add value to BL's product extend beyond BL itself. For example the Belgian supplier's success in producing high quality hand-dyed and printed leather is critical to the overall quality of the product. BL regularly inspects its distributor Pello to ensure that it complies with the most stringent quality and security standards.

Examiner's comments

This requirement was well answered by the vast majority of candidates, who appeared well prepared for a question on value chain and competitive strategy. The majority recognised the firm's strategic focus to be differentiation, and were able to identify and discuss primary and support activities, although in order to score full knowledge marks candidates also needed to use cost/value driver terminology.

Weaker candidates tended to either ignore support activities or simply described all BL's primary and support activities without explicitly linking them to its generic strategy or each other. Better candidates focused on those activities that were key to the strategy and the linkages in the value chain that gave rise to BL's competitive advantage.

53.2 Key cyber security risks and risk management

Cyber risk is any risk of financial loss, disruption or damage to the reputation of an organisation from some sort of failure of its IT systems.

In addition to the general risks faced by all businesses, BL faces some specific cyber risks because its business with customers is done online. Any technical failure would have a significant and immediate impact because problems with the e-commerce site are immediately visible to customers/prospective customers. It is likely to lead to loss of customer confidence and damage BL's brand and reputation.

BL must take steps to minimise the risk of systems failure, protect the integrity of its systems, safeguard information and ensure the continuity of its operations. BL should ensure it has a business continuity plan in place so that the business can continue to operate in the event of a crisis. Risks may be transferred, avoided, reduced or accepted.

Specific cyber risks and recommendations for risk management:

- Denial of service attack

  An attack by hackers could result in BL's website being inaccessible or too slow, or the payment system could go down. Alternatively BL may have to withdraw the website if there is a virus/malware attack on its systems or if hackers access the website and deface it, for example.

  This is likely to result in frustrated customers. Sales could be lost if customers decide to switch to a competitor although the fact that the luggage is sought after and customers are prepared to wait for items to be produced may simply mean the transaction is delayed rather than lost.

  Risk can be reduced by ensuring appropriate systems development and maintenance takes place and by having back-up servers. Systems need to be upgraded regularly to ensure they are capable of providing the necessary capacity, particularly given the growth expected. BL's website should be regularly updated and tested to ensure it is fully functioning.

  BL could also reduce the risk by ensuring that customers are directed to alternatives such as phone ordering in the event of system delays or failures. BL could transfer the risk by outsourcing the provision of the website to a specialist provider.

- The company's online ordering and payment system could potentially be abused. Any identity theft/card fraud arising would severely damage BL's reputation.

  BL should ensure it reduces this risk by having access controls, data encryption, appropriate payment verification software, firewalls and secure communication.

- Hackers may be able to gain access to sensitive data, either for malicious reasons or to gain competitive knowledge. Loss of critical data relating to customers personal data held in databases eg, through viruses or deliberate sabotage would damage BL's reputation with existing and potential customers. Customers will expect BL to have appropriate security systems in place. If it does not, any cyber security issues or concerns about vulnerability will damage customer confidence and threaten the success of the business.

  Any failure to comply with data protection legislation could also result in BL facing penalties/litigation.

  The risk can be reduced by ensuring appropriate security features are in place to control access and content. BL must ensure its ordering and inventory system and any customer databases that it operates are kept up-to date, and backed up regularly with hard copies kept off-site. It must have systems in place to monitor compliance with data protection regulations and ensure all data held is secure (eg, via encryption).

- Risk is increased due to BL's shared system access with Pello. Whilst sharing information brings competitive advantage the inter-connectedness reduces the control that BL has over its digital security and increases the risk that it is vulnerable to attack – particularly through the weakest links in the systems chain. If Pello's system is hacked or fails this could result in delayed deliveries, customer complaints and lost customers which would severely damage BL's brand image.

BL needs to ensure that there is clear responsibility and accountability for cyber security, particularly in relation to the integrated system. In addition to inspecting the quality of Pello's operations BL should satisfy itself regarding Pello's cyber security.

General risk management procedures:

BL needs to ensure that it has individuals with the specialist skills and expertise to help the organisation protect itself against cyber-attacks. The board need to regularly consider the organisation's risk tolerance and risk appetite in relation to cyber security and reflect this in risk management strategies.

Where risks cannot be reduced or eliminated it may be possible to transfer them via:

- Insurance (however this may be costly and it may be problematic to quantify the extent of business loss from a security incident)
- Contracting out the management of e-commerce to a third party who can host the system. The loss may still occur and impact on the business, but the service level agreement can stipulate penalties

Examiner's comments

This requirement, on cyber security, was the highest scoring in the exam, which seems fitting at the first sitting of CBE, and in view of the addition of 'Technology' to the exam's title! Most candidates identified a range of key cyber security risks and risk management procedures and it was encouraging that in the main these were applied well to the scenario. Only the better candidates explicitly discussed the increased risk arising from the shared system with Pello and few gave due consideration to the need for a business continuity plan.

53.3 Taraf contract

Non-financial factors

Taraf is a luxury airline and so its image of high quality is consistent with that of BL.

However wealthy customers may not be happy that the cabin crew have luggage with the BL label if they view themselves as superior in status.

There is a waiting list for the existing product as customers have bags made to order and are prepared to wait for up to three months. Making the product available "en masse" to Taraf's cabin crew may detract from the high-end brand image and reduce the attraction of the label as a limited edition item.

There is a risk associated with using lower quality leather but printing it with the same logo which means the bags are clearly identifiable as BL items, presenting an image to the marketplace that the bags are the same as BL's existing products. If there are any problems with the quality or life of the bags this may have a knock-on impact on the existing brand.

BL is planning to introduce two new suppliers which increases the risk as these relationships are not tested. BL will need to carry out due diligence on the suppliers and ensure quality control is in place to ensure the leather, etc whilst being cheaper, is still of appropriately high quality. Depending on the location of the suppliers it may also give rise to additional exchange risk

Financial factors

See appendix for costing and pricing calculations.

In fixing a price for the contract BL needs to bear in mind the following:

The variable costs for the new bags are cheaper than the current range (£310 per bag compared to £416/£520). Presumably this is largely due to savings in the leather costs because the bags are of lower quality. If incremental fixed costs are considered then the production cost per bag and hence the breakeven contract price would be £490 per item.

BL normally makes a 48% gross margin which would result in a selling price of £942 per bag. However this margin is on sales of one-off items to consumers and Taraf is likely to require a volume discount.

Currently the factory can produce 600 items per week and, given the waiting list, can be assumed to be at full capacity. The Taraf contract represents 7.5 weeks' worth of production in total (4,500/600). If the bags cannot be made alongside the existing luggage (eg, by running an extra shift), then there may be an opportunity cost associated with accepting the contract because it will replace existing production. However it is possible that sales may not be lost if customers are simply prepared to wait another month for their order. More information is required about when/how the bags are to be delivered.

BL need to consider the impact of any predicted exchange rate movements on the cost. Also no information has been provided on the distribution and delivery costs associated with the contract.

Recommendation

BL needs to consider the other parties that may be asked to tender and the likely price that Taraf is prepared to pay. It does not appear likely that the contract will offer any scope for renewal since at the end of two years the cabin crew will all have flight bags, so there is no benefit in reducing the price now in anticipation of further revenue later, particularly if accepting the contract merely replaces sales to existing customers who are not prepared to wait.

The contract is sizeable and would probably generate an attractive amount of additional contribution provided it does not result in lost sales to existing/potential customers. One option to minimise the impact on BL's brand would be to consider making the bags as a Taraf own-label product.

Appendix of calculations:

Taraf contract:

	£ per bag
Leather (0.6 × 95) + (0.4 × 105)	99
Buckles	26
Labour and VC	185
Total VC per bag	310
Bags required	4,500
Total VC for contract	£1,395,000
Incremental FC = 2 years × £405,000	£810,000
Total contract costs	£2,205,000
Production cost per bag = selling price to breakeven	£490
Selling price to achieve 48% margin (£490/0.52)	£942.31

Existing luggage:

Selling price	Production cost (assuming 48% GPM)	Variable cost per item = 2/3 total production cost	FC per item = 1/3 total production cost
£1,200	£624	£416	£208
£1,500	£780	£520	£260

Examiner's comments

This was the worst scoring requirement in the exam. Candidates consistently appear to find requirements that ask for supporting calculations to be more challenging. Often this is because they fail to produce a balanced answer that covers both financial and non-financial considerations. There was a roughly 50/50 split between those who did justice to the numerical calculations and those who did not or even ignored the numbers all together. Many candidates failed to deal correctly with fixed overheads (only the incremental element was relevant). Hardly any arrived at the correct 48% margin price, or even attempted it, although many more made an attempt at calculating the breakeven price.

Non-financial considerations were reasonably well addressed, although the issue of capacity constraints was ignored by a surprising number. Better candidates included a reasoned recommendation as to whether to pursue the contract, despite this not being explicitly requested, which was a pleasing approach.

54 Jacmel Products plc (March 2018)

	Knowledge	Skill	Marks
54.1 Report			
Matrix structure			
Challenges in implementing change	4	9	12
54.2 Market research factors			
Marketing mix	5	9	13
	9	18	25

54.1 **To:** Jacmel Board
From: Business Advisor
Date: XX/X/XX
Re: Expansion into developing markets

Proposed change in organisational structure

Benefits and problems of proposed matrix structure

Matrix structures are common in organisations that span different products and countries, and will allow Jacmel to adopt a multi-disciplinary approach. Instead of the current divisionalisation by product, the new matrix structure will be a cross between a territory-based and product-based structure. The current markets in USA and Europe have probably been quite similar and as a result product-based divisionalisation was sufficient. Given the planned expansion into East Africa, a matrix by product and geography should facilitate information flow and reduce response time to customers. However it may present challenges because each employee reports to multiple managers.

Advantages:

- The matrix structure is likely to be more flexible and may allow Jacmel to respond faster to the different needs of a new market and new customers in a developing economy

- Allows Jacmel to exploit economies of scale but still react to the different needs of the existing markets (USA and Europe) and the new market in East Africa

- Should improve communication within the organisation and enable staff to benefit from a wider range of specialist skills and knowledge, so the manager of East Africa can get expert product support from the pens or razors specialist.

- Supports collaboration which can foster creativity and may help Jacmel develop new products or new processes eg, in relation to marketing

- Prevents people operating in silos and requires them to consider views of others in the organisation, so can reduce divisional rivalry

Disadvantages:

- May create challenges as employees have to report to a product and territory manager. Lines of authority can be blurred and this can create stress/demotivation and impact on productivity.

- Managers are interdependent so will need to spend time coordinating efforts/work. It may be hard for Jacmel to coordinate teams working in different geographies and time zones (USA, Europe, Africa) and this may exacerbate any disputes.

- The move from divisional to matrix will create overlaps in the structure which may result in costly duplication and as there are more people to gain consensus from, Jacmel's decision making may be slower.

- Jacmel's existing managers may find it hard to accept the new structure and feel their authority is being threatened, leading to conflict/resistance (see below). Also some managers may lack the skills to work with staff more flexibly across the organisation.

Challenges implementing new structure

Cultural barriers

Structure plays a large role in shaping organisational culture. Here the chief executive, Tom, is proposing planned structural change to facilitate the company's growth. These changes will affect the reporting and management structure of Jacmel, which has been in place for a considerable time. Structural inertia is the cumulative effect of all the systems and procedures that the organisation has installed over the years to ensure consistency and quality. These act as barriers to change.

In order to change this, Lewin argues that the old culture of product divisional responsibility will need to be unfrozen; the changes made; and then a refreezing of the new culture of a matrix organisation by geography and product should take place.

The power structures of the existing general managers may be threatened by the redistribution of decision-making authority or resources, or the changing of lines of communication. Management may be reluctant to implement changes which will be against their own interests – managers within the pens and razors divisions who have previously been autonomous may perceive they have been downgraded if they need to report to or seek input from someone else eg, a territory manager.

Personnel barriers

There are also barriers which affect individuals and result in them seeing the proposal to change the organisational structure as a threat.

Habitual ways of work are hard to change, and the new and unknown is often uncomfortable or frightening. Managers may feel insecure about their position and need reassurance that their jobs or earnings are not under threat. Some managers or employees may be concerned that the new structure will require them to relocate to East Africa and fear of the unknown may reduce their willingness to take on a new challenge. They may be concerned about the impact if they turn down the offer of a move. Selective information processing can result in managers focusing on their personal concerns and ignoring the business argument for change.

Action:

An effective communication strategy with consultation by the Jacmel senior management is therefore needed. Tom needs to communicate and explain the strategic reasons for change and involve managers in the proposals, to get them on board.

Fears may be countered by transparency as to which managers may be affected and how.

Once the new structure is in place, support should be provided and visible rewards given to those who embrace the change.

Tutorial note

Candidates were not specifically asked to refer to change models. References to Lewin have been made above but credit was awarded for other appropriate models eg, Gemini.

Examiner's comments

This requirement was well answered overall, although answers were quite polarised. As usual a significant minority did not produce a report format, thus losing an easy mark.

The nature of a matrix structure, even if understood, was poorly explained by many, and a significant number of candidates talked about decentralisation instead of focusing on the differences between the existing divisional structure and the new matrix, and the advantages and disadvantages arising from this. Those who did justice to the requirement tended to cover duplication of effort and two-way reporting among the disadvantages of the proposed structure.

As usual candidates were well prepared to discuss barriers to change and change models, but weaker candidates discussed these in relation to employees in general, rather than focusing on the barriers to change for managers specifically. Many candidates made suggestions for dealing with the challenges, although in a surprising number of cases this was limited to increased communication of the proposed change.

54.2 Marketing strategy for new markets

An appropriate marketing strategy involves segmentation, targeting and positioning:

Segmentation – requires identification of the bases for segmenting the market and the characteristics of different market segments.

Targeting – is about evaluating the attractiveness of each segment and selecting those to target.

Positioning – requires a detailed marketing mix to be developed for each selected segment.

Jacmel need to undertake market research to understand the market and consumer requirements in East Africa. Research can take the form of analysing existing secondary data (desk research) or gathering new primary information direct from consumers through interviews, surveys etc (field research).

Since the characteristics of the emerging markets are expected to be very different Tom, the chief executive, is correct that Jacmel cannot use US/European data to draw conclusions. The markets are at different stage in the lifecycle (whilst the current market is mature, the emerging markets are at the stage of introduction/growth) and buyers will have different characteristics.

Factors to consider when deciding on appropriate research include:

- Markets are rapidly growing so buying patterns will be less stable

- Product life cycles may be shorter or certain stages truncated

- The retail system is likely to be less organised and fragmented into smaller but more widespread units

- The online market will be less developed due to lack of technological infrastructure

- Buyers across East Africa are likely to be less homogeneous – multiple languages, religions, ethnicities and wider income differentials will mean more options for segmentation

- It is likely to be more of a rural market than an urban one

Jacmel therefore needs to customise the market research and consider using different methods:

- Depending on which emerging market segments Jacmel wants to target within East Africa, there may be some customer data available in the form of desk research. The advantage is that this is cheaper but Jacmel is unlikely to be able to rely on this alone.

- Field research is likely to be more valuable than desk research. Phone and internet surveys may be less useful as not everyone will possess these – so face to face interviews/on-street surveys/product testing may be more relevant.

- Jacmel needs to make use of local interviewers with the right language and cultural skills. It also needs to take into account cultural differences in evaluating responses – consumers may feel the need to be polite and therefore be less honest in their replies.

- Test marketing the products by distributing samples of items packaged in different quantities or at different prices may help determine what consumers are likely to purchase (see below).

Marketing mix

The marketing mix consists of the 4Ps: Product, Price, Place and Promotion.

Product – Developed markets are more focused on brand, service and value added i.e an augmented product. The new emerging market segments are likely to be more price conscious and lower income consumers may demand a more basic product. As a result Jacmel's existing pens and razors may need modification for new markets eg, the consumer may be prepared to settle for something that lasts a bit less time if it is cheaper, so Jacmel could consider a razor that only does five shaves or may need to package the product in smaller units rather than multipacks to keep costs down.

Price – As discussed above this may be the key issue and price may be closely linked to the design and packaging of the product. Packaging the pens and razors in smaller quantities would allow for more affordable prices. Jacmel may consider using price penetration to establish brand name and market presence.

Place – channels to market may be more fragmented. There may be many smaller outlets such as kiosks rather than large retailers. As a result distribution will be more dependent on local knowledge and relationships. Jacmel may decide to incentivise the sales of pens and razors to boost demand (see below). Jacmel may need to establish a permanent local presence in the different countries within East Africa.

Promotion – this is required to create awareness and educate retailers/consumers about Jacmel's products. Jacmel needs to encourage customers to try the pens and razors, then establish demand and build brand preference. It needs retailers to present the products in an attractive location and to promote their use. Promotion to retailers could involve trade fairs. Jacmel could offer free samples, introductory offers and coupons.

Conclusion

Given the maturity of the US and European market, it seems sensible to target emerging markets such as East Africa. Since this market has quite different characteristics, careful and appropriate market research will enable Jacmel to develop a marketing mix for its pens and razors that gives the expansion strategy the best chance of success.

Examiner's comments

There were some excellent attempts at this requirement and many much poorer ones. Although there was no overall evidence of time pressure, some weaker candidates who mismanaged their time on earlier requirements produced a truncated attempt at this one. The differentiating feature in the quality of responses was the ability to tailor what might at first sight appear to be a very knowledge-based requirement to the specific scenario of a developing market. Many answers were so generic that it was not possible to tell what was to be marketed or to whom.

In relation to market research, the best answers discussed the specific purposes of the research, the relative merits of field and desk research and the need to tailor research to the local, developing market. Weaker candidates restricted their discussion to field and desk research, which they described in very generic terms, although most recognised field research to be more appropriate under the circumstances.

The four Ps of the product marketing mix were typically well addressed, with most candidates applying the model well to the scenario even when they had failed to do so in relation to marketing research. A minority of weaker responses produced generic answers that were not appropriate to the developing market and often only considered one or two of the four Ps.

55 Ten Ten Burgers Inc (June 2018)

	Knowledge	Skill	Marks
55.1 Lima app	3	6	8
55.2 Data analysis	4	25	27
55.3 Franchise v owned	3	7	9
	10	38	44

55.1 Increase revenues

The capacity for the Lima app to increase revenue relates to its ability to increase sales volumes and to optimise prices.

The use of the app in advertising and marketing has the capability to communicate marketing messages effectively to a target group known to have some interest in the TTB product. This group is either a previous customer (evidenced by sales made and credits earned using the app) or somebody with sufficient interest in the TTB product to take the trouble to download the app.

As a targeted marketing tool, it can be used to send messages to all users, for example a new type of burger, new offers, new services or new feature at restaurants.

Alternatively, market segmentation can be used where the marketing message to increase sales is targeted at a sub group of app users which has particular characteristics (eg, young people, high socio-economic groups, regular customers).

In addition to a mere communication device, the app can be used to make a substantive difference to customers and to customer experience which may improve sales.

For example, the fact that customers do not need to wait for the meal to be cooked, but can still have a freshly cooked meal on arrival, may enhance customer service and boost sales volumes. Similarly, if a seat can be booked shortly before the meal it may help customer experience, or at least the availability will be known.

Aside from increasing sales volumes, revenue can be increased by price discrimination by enabling flexible prices using knowledge of particular customers' behaviours using algorithms. This may enable TTB to recognise individuals' price elasticity based on their prior behaviour.

The flexibility of price is achieved through the use of targeted discounts/credits which may also be an incentive for regular customers to buy more if greater discounts are given to customers who, on a cumulative basis, make more purchases from TTB.

The data in Exhibit 1 supports the proposition that the app is generating revenue by affecting volumes in particular, although caution needs to be exercised in that sales via the app may in part be displacing sales through traditional channels. In addition, the app allocates credits which effectively reduces the prices charged.

Operating efficiency

In terms of operating efficiency, the app provides demand management information on a macro basis (for all customers or customer groupings) and on a micro basis (for individual customers).

The usefulness of the macro data is however limited as only 22.1% (ie, (£2,584k – £176.8k)/ £10,880k) of all sales for the year were made through using the app. This had risen by the half year, but non-app sales data are not provided on a quarterly basis, so the precise figure is not known.

More specifically, operating efficiency in terms of meal preparation can be improved as app users provide prior information, not just of their intention to eat at the restaurant as in a normal booking, but also the precise nature of their order. If the lead time is long, this can enable better scheduling of food orders and staffing. If the lead time is short, the cooking schedule can be better planned.

Utilisation of tables is likely to be improved as tables are saved only when an order and payment are received. This reduces 'no-shows' by customers and encourages timely arrival. This may improve utilisation of capacity at busy times.

Efficiency relating to table utilisation is also improved, as customers using the app are not occupying the table while ordering and waiting for the food to be cooked.

The incentives to provide feedback through the Lima app (using credits) may help by acting on customer suggestions to improve service and efficiency.

Examiner's comments

This was the highest scoring requirement in the exam. Most candidates clearly structured their answers to show the two distinct parts in terms of increasing revenues and improving operating efficiency. Better candidates provided a balanced answer between the two parts, recognised market segmentation and/or price discrimination as key marketing issues and showed insight into how the app can be used to generate revenue and improve capacity utilisation.

Weaker candidates however failed to address each element separately and tried to blend their answer in to one combined solution, which did not clearly address the two elements.

55.2

PER OUTLET	Owned 20X7	Owned 20X8	Franchised 20X8	Average 20X8
Revenue per outlet	1,000,000	1,080,000	1,100,000	1,088,000
Operating profit per outlet	90,000	160,000	165,000	162,000
Fixed fee per outlet			30,000	
Variable fee per outlet			110,000	
Franchise profit per outlet			25,000	
Initial capital cost	400,000	400,000	400,000	
Outlets	4	6	4	
Variable fee as % of revenue			10%	
Costs to TTB per franchise			50,000	

In £s	Owned 20X7	Owned 20X8	Franchised 20X8	Total 20X8
Revenue	4,000,000	6,480,000	4,400,000	10,880,000
Operating costs	3,640,000	5,520,000	3,740,000	9,260,000
Operating profit	360,000	960,000	660,000	1,620,000

In £s	Owned 20X7	Owned 20X8	Franchised 20X8	Total 20X8
Fixed franchise fees to TTB		120,000	(120,000)	
Variable (10%) TTB share of revenues		440,000	(440,000)	
Less TTB's franchise costs		(200,000)		
TTBUK profit from franchisees		360,000		
Profit retained by franchisees			100,000	
TTB total profit	360,000	1,320,000		
Op profit margin % (owned)	9.0%	14.8%		
Op profit margin % (franchise, gross)			15.00%	
Op profit % margin (franchise, net)			2.27%	
Op profit margin % (total) (1,320)/(6,480 + 120+ 440)				18.75%
Capital employed	1,600,000	2,400,000	1,600,000	
ROCE owned	22.5%	40.0%		
ROCE % (franchise, gross)			41.25%	
ROCE % (franchise, net)			6.25%	
ROCE % total (owned and franchised) 20X8				
- Equity basis (960 + 360)/ (400 × 6)				55.0%
- Entity basis (960 + 660)/ (400 × 10)				40.5%

Compare and evaluate the performance of owned restaurants with franchised restaurants in the year ended 31 March 20X8

There were four owned restaurants opened on 1 April 20X6 which generated an average revenue of £1 million per restaurant and an operating profit of £90,000 per restaurant for the year ended 31 March 20X7. There are no comparable figures for franchised restaurants for this period.

The year ended 31 March 20X7 was the first year TTB operated in the UK hence it not only achieved a profit but also began to establish presence in the UK and to develop recognition of the TTB brand name. This seems likely to be to the subsequent benefit of both owned and franchised restaurants.

There were two further owned restaurants and four franchised restaurants opened on 1 April 20X7.

Comparisons of the overall revenue and operating profit are invalid as there are six owned restaurants and only four franchised. Comparisons are therefore made below on a per restaurant basis.

In the year ended 31 March 20X8 the franchise restaurants, in operational terms, performed marginally better than the owned restaurants with a 1.9% higher revenue per restaurant. Whilst this seems a small amount extra it is not comparing like with like as four of the six owned restaurants were more established, being in their second year of operation, and so may have been expected to do better than the newer franchised restaurants.

Similarly, in the year ended 31 March 20X8, the franchise restaurants were more profitable than the owned restaurants with a 3.1% higher operating profit (before franchisee charges) at £165,000 per restaurant.

A possible explanation for the better performance of franchised restaurants is that franchisees have higher motivation than employed managers of owned outlets, as they have high personal investment of their own capital. Also, arguably, they may have better knowledge of potential customer requirements in their respective local areas.

An alternative possible explanation is that the franchised restaurants are larger, or in better locations, than the owned restaurants. However, as the initial cost of all the restaurants is £400,000, this does not seem to be plausible as a significant factor.

A further possibility is that, given the small number of restaurants, there may be an outlier distorting the average for either grouping. For example, there may be, for whatever reason, a very poorly performing owned restaurant or a very well performing franchised restaurant. Once any outlier is stripped out of the data then it may be that the comparison of the averages of the remaining restaurants presents a different picture. Data for each individual restaurant is really needed to identify a clear cause and effect relationship between franchising and performance.

An alternative explanation of the differences relating to the higher operating profit of franchisees could arise from charging arrangements for central costs. This could arise from the fact that the operating profit of £165,000 per franchised restaurant is before franchisee charges. In contrast, the costs of services provided to owned restaurants (eg, the Lima app and management costs) seem likely to have already been charged to owned restaurants in arriving at the £160,000 operating profit figure, unless these are retained centrally.

Once franchisee charges are made, then profit per franchisee restaurant is only £25,000 compared with £160,000 per owned outlet. On this basis, the owned restaurants have performed better but more information is needed on the method of recharging central costs to owned restaurants.

Evaluate and explain the financial and operating performance of TTB UK in the year ended 31 March 20X8 compared with the year ended 31 March 20X7.

Revenue

Overall revenue has increased by 170% in 20X8 compared with 20X7 (from £4 million to £10.8 million) however the number of restaurants has increased by 150% (from 4 to 10).

Much of the increase in revenue is therefore due to expansion, rather than improved performance.

It should be noted that all the restaurants were opened on the first day of each financial year so they were able to make a full contribution in each year. The timing of the openings within the year is therefore not an issue.

In order to assess performance, the revenue per outlet (for all 10 outlets) could be reviewed. This has increased from £1 million in 20X7 to £1.088 million in 20X8, which is an increase of 8.8%. One of the drivers of this improved performance is the fact that franchised restaurants have performed better than owned restaurants and they only opened for the 20X8 financial year. This factor has already been discussed above.

In order to strip out the effect of the 'franchise factor' the performance per owned restaurant in 20X7 can be compared to the performance per owned restaurant in 20X8. This shows that revenue per owned restaurant has increased from £1 million in 20X7 to £1.08 million in 20X8, which is an increase of 8%. One factor could be that the initial four restaurants are becoming established over time with a greater base of regular customers. More information is needed on individual restaurants to establish whether the evidence supports this notion of the initial four restaurants performing better than the new two restaurants.

A further factor affecting revenue is price. In 20X8 gross prices increased in steps from £10 in the first quarter to £10.50 in the final quarter. If demand is inelastic then this may have increased revenues, particularly for non-app users not obtaining credits.

The Lima app and the credits/discounts may affect revenue but this is considered separately in a later section.

Overall operating performance

Overall operating profit has increased by 350% in 20X8 compared with 20X7 (from £360,000 to £1.62 million). This is much more substantial than the 150% increase in number of restaurants or 172% increase in restaurant revenue (from £4 million to £10.88 million).

One key factor to explain this increase is likely to be that there is a high element of fixed costs relating to the properties which need to be incurred irrespective of the numbers of customers. This operating gearing effect means that, as sales increase, operating profit will increase disproportionately compared with revenue.

The operating profit per outlet has increased from £90,000 in 20X7 to £162,000 in 20X8, which is an increase of 80%. This shows a significant increase in performance per outlet in 20X8.

Again, in order to strip out the effect of the 'franchise factor' the performance per owned restaurant in 20X7 can be compared to the performance per owned restaurant in 20X8. This shows that operating profit per owned outlet has increased from £90,000 in 20X7 to £160,000 in 20X8, which is a significant increase of 77.8%.

A further factor affecting operating profit is price. In 20X8, gross prices increased in steps from £10 in the first quarter to £10.50 in the final quarter, thereby improving margins on sale, particularly for non-app users not obtaining credits.

Overall therefore, the performance has increased significantly in 20X8 compared to 20X7. However, for a start-up business in a new country it would be surprising if there was not strong initial growth. A key question is whether growth is sufficient and how it compares with planned growth.

Financial performance for TTB UK

The above analysis examines operating performance of the restaurants as operating units irrespective of whether they are owned or franchised.

An alternative analysis would be to look at the financial performance from the perspective of TTB UK in terms of the returns to TTB, rather than considering the success of the franchisees' restaurants (ie, the financial performance of the TTB UK investment, rather than the operating performance of the restaurants).

In this respect, TTB UK has two income streams:

(1) Operating profit from owned restaurants
(2) Franchise fees received, net of the cost to TTB of running franchises.

In 20X8, the six owned restaurants made a total operating profit of £960,000 (ie, £160,000 per restaurant).

The four franchised restaurants made a total return to TTB in the form of gross fees of £560,000. This is reduced to £360,000, net of the £200,000 franchise costs. Of the total gross fees, £120,000 are fixed, which covers a majority of the costs incurred by TTB on franchising. The remaining fees are variable and so can vary with the success of the franchisees.

Superficially it would seem that the owned restaurants have performed better in total than franchised restaurants. However, a key issue is that owned restaurants require an initial investment of £400,000, whereas there is no initial investment by TTB for franchised restaurants. ROCE or ROI measures from the perspective of TTB's financial investment are therefore very different. This is demonstrated in comparing the ROCE measures for the entity perspective (ie, both owners and franchisees capital investment) with the equity perspective (owners capital investment only – ie, TTB)

– Equity basis (960 + 360)/(400 × 6)   55.0%
– Entity basis (960 + 660)/(400 × 10)   40.5%

The future prospects of owned and franchised are considered in more detail in a later section below.

Evaluate the effect of the Lima app on revenue, so far as the information permits.

Impact of Lima app on revenue

Without Lima app

	Owned 20X7	Owned 20X8	Franchised 20X8	Total 20X8	% change owned
Revenue per outlet	1,000,000	1,080,000	1,100,000	1,088,000	8.0%
Revenue without Lima (×0.95)	1,000,000	1,026,000	1,045,000	1,033,600	2.6%
Incremental revenue	0	54,000	55,000	54,400	
Gross sales on App per restaurant				258,400	
Displacing existing sales				204,000	

Of the 8% total increase in revenue per owned restaurant in 20X8, compared with 20X7, 5.4% can be explained by the Lima app. The remaining 2.6% growth therefore is caused by other factors (see earlier answer).

Gross sales through the app are £258,400 per restaurant, so £204,000 of app sales are displacing existing sales that would have been made anyway without the app.

This is however a narrow interpretation of the data, as there is significant variation in app usage within the year ended 31 March, so whole year averages are less relevant, particularly in the first year of usage.

Moreover, there are strategic pricing benefits that may not be fully captured in the first year of usage, including the app enabling flexible pricing.

A critical factor is that there is no data for costs. The existing operating margin could be applied to the incremental sales from the app but such a simple extrapolation seems inappropriate given the first year set up costs needed to establish the app. More cost information is therefore needed.

A long-term view would consider the scale benefits of rolling out the app to US operations, which could cover initial set-up costs many times if it is successful.

Quarterly intra-year data analysis on Lima app

A minority of customers use the app, but the proportion is growing.

As already noted the proportion of total food sales made through the Lima app is only 22.1% in 20X8. However, it may be that other sales were influenced by information from the app (eg, advertising) but the customer actually made the purchase without the app.

It is clear that usage of the app has increased substantially over the year. Comparing Q1 with Q4, visits to the app have increased by 185.7% and gross sales (ie, before discounts) have increased by 200%.

It would be wrong however to conclude automatically from these increases that the app is a success. It could be that sales are not increasing because of the app, but customers previously buying TTB meals normally are now using the app (ie, app sales have merely displaced normal sales – see table). It could be that there is therefore a substitution of app sales for other sales but no net increase. The fact that sales are higher in 20X8 than 20X7 is consistent with the notion of the app increasing overall sales but there may also be other, additional or alternative, reasons for the improved performance as noted above.

As a working assumption, if total sales are constant each quarter, then the percentages of gross app sales to total sales each quarter are:

Q1 10% (ie, £272,000/(£10.88m × 3/12))
Q2 25%
Q3 30%
Q4 30%

Under this assumption, it shows that app sales are growing within the year but are still a minority of total sales.

Moreover, a concern is that the growth has flattened out between Q3 and Q4 so the capacity for further growth may be limited, if for example most people intending to use the app have already downloaded it.

A substantial factor regarding the influence of the app is the value of credits/discounts given as a means of achieving flexible prices. The discounts have grown substantially as the use of the app has increased. However, the value of discounts has grown by 380% between Q1 and Q4 which is more than the growth in the use of the app itself, which was only 185.7% over the same period.

One explanation of this 'excess' growth is that the percentage discount has increased over the year as gross prices have also increased. The discount as a percentage of gross sales from the above table has increased from 5% in Q1 to 8% in Q4.

Given the increased discounts are being awarded against higher gross prices, it can be seen from the above table that the net price to app users has only risen from £9.50 to £9.66 between Q1 and Q4. However, in the same period, the gross price to non-app users increased more substantially from £10 to £10.50.

The benefit of flexible and targeting prices could be significant for app users but, as the majority of customers are non-app users, sales may suffer if they believe they are being overcharged (price elastic) and do not want to download the app.

Examiner's comments

This was the lowest scoring requirement in the exam. Good candidates clearly presented their answer according to the three separate requirements: owned v franchised; 20X7 v 20X8; and impact of Lima app on revenue. Some weaker candidates however again tried to merge these elements into a combined answer. More generally, it has been a common weakness over many sittings of weaker candidates failing to structure their answers in line with separate requirements.

Very few candidates specifically identified the essential difference between the operating performance of each franchised shop and its performance in terms of the fees it generates for TTB UK. However, this was sometimes implicit in the discussion of 20X8 v 20X7 performance of TTB UK.

Many candidates lost marks for poor numerical analysis, with the weakest answers failing to provide calculations per outlet for revenue or operating profit. This often led to further weaknesses where inappropriate or incomplete conclusions were arrived at in terms of relative performance between owned and franchised outlets. Also, reasons for improved performance of TTB UK sometimes ignored the fact that the number of restaurants had grown between 20X7 and 20X8.

When comparing franchised and owned outlets, the timing of start-up was discussed by only a minority, but a significant number considered the impact of outlier performance given the small number of restaurants. The majority made the point that the marginally better performance of the franchised outlets may be explained, partially at least, by higher motivation among owners to generate more profit due to relatively high investment of own capital and also due to better local knowledge of customers.

Few candidates showed calculations for ROCE or, more generally, any return on investment measure.

Tables were used in nearly all cases by candidates to both calculate and visually present their calculations, but some weaker candidates just weaved random calculations into their commentary on a piecemeal basis. This is not recommended.

Some candidates produced a combined answer for the first two elements of the requirement (ie, owned v franchised; and 20X8 v 20X7). Combining requirements, or sub requirements, in a single narrative answer is not a good strategy as it asks the marker to decide which points are related to which requirement. A better approach is for the candidate to exercise judgement as to the relevance of points and to address each requirement separately.

With regard to the Lima app, most provided data on downloads and sales made but only a significant minority provided quarterly growth analysis. Many did, nevertheless, recognise the drop off in growth in the final quarter. The possibility of displaced existing sales rather than incremental growth was only recognised by a few of the best candidates.

55.3 Evaluate the factors to be considered by TTB UK in deciding whether to expand further within the UK by opening new franchised restaurants or owned restaurants.

Business franchising is the granting of a licence by one person (the franchisor) to another (the franchisee), which entitles the franchisee to own and operate their own business under the brand, systems and proven business model of the franchisor.

The agreement means that the franchisee obtains all the elements of the successful franchised business. This includes everything from branding, products, supplies and designs to marketing and advertising support. Thus, part of the attractiveness to franchisees is that they are buying into an established business model.

One attractive aspect of franchising for TTB UK is that the financial risk is limited. The restaurant style is a tried and tested venture that has succeeded in the US. However, there are risks about 'exporting' this to a new country, the UK, where there is less brand recognition and different tastes and cultures. The initial investment in a new restaurant of £400,000 will contain a significant element of sunk costs and hence, if the UK venture fails, the exit costs will be high.

To some extent there is assurance over the risk of lack of acceptability in the UK as TTB has now been operating there for two years with reasonable profitability and success.

Aside from risk factors, a key advantage of franchising for TTB is that if its financial capital is constrained, then more outlets can be opened in the UK more quickly as the capital of the franchisees is being used to provide initial financing of restaurants. The personal equity of franchisees also provides strong incentives and motivation for them to succeed, which is consistent with the better relative performance of franchised outlets compared with owned outlets in 20X8.

More rapid growth through franchising can mean that TTB gains from economies of scale. On the supply side, this means that TTB may find it cheaper to purchase food ingredients and fixtures. On the demand side, there is likely to be greater brand recognition and consumer confidence as the number of restaurants grows into a nationally recognised chain.

There are however risks in franchising in that there is less control and oversight by TTB than for an owned restaurant. For example, poor franchisees may damage the brand. Also, dishonest franchisees may attempt to under-record revenues in order to reduce the 10% variable franchise fee.

Risk mitigation is possible by ensuring the franchising contract has clauses that monitor and constrain the behaviour of the franchisee. For example, TTB could use rule violations to terminate contracts and recover the franchise. This monitoring maintains some control over the activities of franchisees, although this is less than with owned restaurants.

It has been noted above that, in 20X8, the six owned restaurants made a total operating profit of £960,000 (ie, £160,000 per restaurant). The four franchised restaurants made a total net return to TTB (ie, franchise fees net of costs to TTB) of £360,000 (ie, £90,000 per restaurant).

Superficially it would seem that, on average, owned restaurants have performed better than franchised restaurants as an investment for TTB. However, they require an initial investment of capital of £400,000, whereas there is no initial investment for franchised restaurants. This means that operating risk is much higher for owned restaurants than franchised restaurants from the perspective of TTB UK.

However if a capital charge of 10% (the required return) is made, then the residual income would be:

Owned	£160,000 − (£400,000 × 10%)	=	£120,000
Franchised		=	£90,000

Thus, with the capital charge at 10%, the owned restaurants still perform better than franchised restaurants.

The breakeven capital charge would be 17.5%:

Owned	£160,000 − (£400,000 × 17.5%)	=	£90,000
Franchised		=	£90,000

Overall 17.5% would appear to be a good return, even for a risk adjusted rate, and it exceeds the required rate of 10%. However, much would depend on the availability of financial capital in the TTB group.

Conclusion

There are different merits for TTB of ownership and franchising.

The ownership model provides a good return, in excess of the required return of 10% and gives greater control of operations.

The franchising option permits a return without investment and the ability to expand the UK operations much more quickly with less financial risk. Franchisees may also be more motivated than employed managers.

Overall the 'franchising only' model looks to be favoured as economies of scale can be achieved quickly, enhancing international reputation while generating a significant return on capital at low financial risk.

Most candidates showed a structured approach to assessing both the franchise and owned options for growth. Many gave due consideration to key issues of profit, return on capital, risk and control issues. Gearing was only considered by a small minority and speed of expansion was considered by only a significant minority. Weaker candidates often displayed misunderstanding in believing that the up-front capital for franchises was being paid by TTB UK.

Weaker answers appeared to focus on the franchise option only and did not mention the owned option, thereby limiting their overall marks due to providing an unbalanced answer which failed to address key issues of ownership.

56 Maya plc (June 2018)

Marking guide

	Knowledge	Skill	Marks
56.1 Risks and risk mitigation	3	9	11
56.2 Supply chain management	2	10	11
56.3 Independent operation/strategic alliance	3	9	11
	8	28	33

56.1 Risks

Business Plan Extracts – Development of Vardex

Risk	Mitigation
Product quality and effectiveness. The new chemical, Vardex, is unproven in commercial use. It may be insufficiently effective in actual commercial use thereby damaging reputation and incurring sunk costs.	• Pre-testing on a commercial scale outside of a laboratory. • Robust manufacturing and quality control processes.
Lack of diversification of the product base for agrochemicals in general and South American operations in particular. This gives dependency risk.	• Add resources to R&D to build on existing research to develop more agrochemical products to complement Vardex. • Consider acquisition of an existing agrochemical company, ideally in Brazil, where it would buy out a rival and create critical mass locally. • Consider manufacturing 'out of patent', generic agrochemical products to gain critical mass.

Risk	Mitigation
A key risk is the fact that the existing management team has no experience of South America, although it does have other international experience. There is therefore a risk of inability to compete with local rivals. Language and cultural barriers. A risk of costly marketing errors.	• Consider hiring local management with industry experience (eg, from a rival company). • Using existing management with relevant language knowledge for South America (Portuguese in particular or Spanish). • Provide appropriate training.
The existing management team also has no experience of agrochemicals as they do not fit into any of the existing business models. It therefore lacks core competences in agrochemical production, marketing and distribution. There is therefore a risk of inability to compete with more established rivals. Also a risk of costly production errors.	• Consider hiring local management with industry experience (eg, from a rival company). • Hire management from agrochemical companies globally. • Second a member of the R&D team with Vardex product knowledge to South America. • Provide appropriate training.
Health and safety risk with chemicals may damage reputation, ligation, breach of local laws. Risk of environmental damage.	• Safety culture. • Safety procedures. • Investigation procedures.
Lack of local reputation in South America. Resistance to sales by local farmers makes growth difficult to get a market foothold.	• Advertising. • Sell via wholesalers. • Marketing to promote brand awareness.
Supply chain risk. This is a new product, with a new supply chain, in a new location.	• Prior research of local suppliers. • Investigate inward distribution channels into Brazil from international suppliers. • There may be scarcity of supply of HaDx.
A competitor may develop a more effective product than Vardex	• Continue with R&D to develop the features of Vardex. • Engage in further R&D to develop a portfolio of agrochemical products.
There may be problems hiring a labour force with relevant and adequate skills to work in the desired location.	• Staff may need to be seconded or transferred from the UK or elsewhere to support those recruited locally. • Appropriate training could be provided to develop the necessary skills. • The use of local chemical engineers may reduce any language and cultural barriers.
Failure in South America may have significant exit costs	• Short-term contracts. • Plan possible exit arrangements in advance.

Risk	Mitigation
Loss of intellectual property if Vardex is copied by a rival company	<ul><li>Intellectual capital management eg, international patents.</li><li>Appropriate security around product specification.</li><li>Use of patents and other legal protection.</li></ul>

Examiner's comments

Very few candidates included a "business plan" heading or phrased the sections as part of a business plan and therefore lost a presentation mark. Most candidates identified relevant risks and provided mitigation specific to each risk. Some candidates only provided risks and did not include any mitigation. Other weaker candidates provided a collection of risks followed by a collection of mitigation factors, without linking each risk to each mitigating factor.

Some candidates listed trivial risks but missed some key risks and this received limited credit.

56.2 Supply chain management

Maya has an extended global supply chain which will be expanded further by setting up a factory in a foreign country. In this context the 'Rs model' of SCM identifies three main themes:

Responsiveness – the ability to supply customers quickly. This includes for example Just-In-Time (JIT) systems to keep raw materials acquisition, production and distribution as flexible as possible.

Reliability – the ability to supply customers reliably.

Relationships – the use of single sourcing and long-term contracts so as better to integrate the buyer and supplier.

In the context of the scenario there are two key issues:

(1) Which supplier to select in a single supplier agreement.

(2) Whether to have a single supplier, or use both suppliers, under a dual supplier agreement.

Some of the advantages from a single sourcing with Gomez may include:

- Communication, integration and synchronisation are easier for Maya's South American operations as they are local.

- Lead times for urgent orders are shorter than Veng, as distances for delivery are shorter.

- As the shelf life is only six weeks, deliveries from Gomez can be held in inventories longer as there is less time in transit.

- The purchase cost is lower.

Some of the advantages from a single sourcing with Veng may include:

- There is an established relationship between Veng and Maya so communication, integration and synchronisation with Veng are easier for Maya's UK operations.

- Experience has established Veng to be reliable, so although lead times to South America are longer than Gomez, they may be more reliable.

- Product quality is more reliable than for Gomez. While Gomez's product quality is an issue only "very occasionally" this can be important in agrochemicals where contamination of human food and the environment could be serious risks even if it is happening only very occasionally.

- Veng may be more dependent on Maya as a major customer if it also supplies its industrial chemicals division. It may therefore be more responsive to Maya's needs than Gomez, if a large amount of its income is being earned from Maya overall.

If Maya has multiple suppliers (ie, both Veng and Gomez) there are a number of benefits:

- Maya can drive down prices charged to it by encouraging competition between suppliers who know that Maya has a choice of alternative suppliers.

- Switching sources of supply is possible by dropping a supplier altogether if it is delivering a poor quality product or service.

- If there is a problem with obtaining sufficient HaDx from one supplier then it can be satisfied by the other.

However, if Maya has multiple suppliers there may be a number of problems:

- Each supplier has a smaller income from Maya than a single source supplier and so may lack commitment.

- Multiple communications become more difficult and more expensive for Maya (eg, more difficult to integrate multiple IT systems).

- Reduced scale economies.

- Cross-border supply chains may produce regulatory, language, cultural, exchange rate and tax problems.

Advice

The current supplier, Veng, has proved reliable and therefore reduces risk and gives assurance over quality. Maya may thus be best having Veng as sole supplier but, in negotiations on price and service, the possibility of using Gomez is useful.

A key factor would be the issue of cost. If HaDx is a significant cost in producing Vardex, then this may mitigate in favour of Gomez as the cheaper supplier.

Examiner's comments

Many better candidates used the Rs model to frame the discussion. However, rigid use of the Rs model sometimes resulted in ignoring some key points, such as the relative costs of supply from Veng and Gomez.

Better candidates structured their answer by analysing Veng, then Gomez, and then considering a potential dual support arrangement. Weaker candidates did not follow this structure, with some just talking generally about a single supplier arrangement (with no reference to Veng and Gomez).

Single versus dual supplier arrangements were also given due consideration by the majority. However weaker candidates did not address the issue of a dual supplier arrangement at all. The weakest answers also ignored altogether the logistical problems associated with using Veng as the main supplier.

56.3 Strategy

Independent operation or strategic alliance with AMB

Both strategies offer the opportunity to enter new geographical markets, with a new product market. This is diversification according to the Ansoff matrix. Whilst offering new opportunities it combines the significant risks of both a new geographical area and a new product.

In addition, setting up a new division may add significant new financial risk through the need to finance the increased investment.

If the project succeeds, then as an independent operation, all of the benefits will come to Maya through its new agrochemical division. However, if the project fails then it will suffer all the losses. With a lack of local knowledge then there may be an increased probability of failure.

In contrast, the strategic alliance with AMB has a number of benefits which would not be experienced by an independent operation.

Some costs and risks are shared with AMB. As the capital outlay is shared, a strategic alliance is attractive to Maya if it is risk-averse. Also, in this case, expensive new technologies are being established. AMB may not bring much new financial capital, but the utilisation of the AMB land reduces Maya's initial outlay. There are also shared operating costs (eg, unskilled labour). These common costs and economies of scale are likely to be a major financial benefit to Maya and reduce operating risk.

There is also reduced risk from the alliance in a reduction in exit costs if the venture fails, as the set-up costs are lower.

There may be reputational enhancement as, locally at least, AMB is likely to be a more recognisable brand, as Maya has not previously operated in this area. AMB may therefore bring increased initial credibility and there may be an opportunity to cross brand to enhance Maya's local reputation.

There are likely to be synergies. Maya's expertise can be supplemented by AMB's marketing and distribution facility. For example, there may be economies of scope in distribution of both partners' products throughout South America. However, this would not seem to apply to any sales outside of South America.

AMB may also provide local knowledge of South American law, culture, customers and language. This may also extend to local knowledge and experience of supply chains.

A strategic alliance arrangement may also have a number of problems and risks which would not be experienced by an independent operation.

There may be conflicts of interest between Maya and AMB. This may be in terms of prioritization of the short-term use of resources (eg, use of pooled labour for competing urgent deliveries). They may also have different longer-term objectives for the arrangement – for example, if one is looking for short-term profits, while the other wants to invest in longer-term growth.

Disagreements may arise over the initial agreement of, and subsequent measurement of, profit shares. There may also be disagreement over amounts invested, the management of the alliance, and the marketing strategy. In particular, there needs to be a degree of business trust between the parties requiring openness and access to information, and acknowledgement that the relationship should be mutually beneficial.

One example of profit measurement problems and business trust is that the internal R&D charge may be a means to reduce AMB's profit share, as an excessive charge may transmit profits back to Maya in the UK, which might have legitimately belonged to the alliance arrangement.

There may be a finite life of four years if AMB decides to terminate the arrangement after the minimum period. This may leave open the ownership and other rights over the factory which was built by Maya on AMB land. In contrast, an independent operation would have an open-ended life to be determined solely by the interests of Maya. One risk mitigation strategy would be for Maya to obtain an option to purchase the land in four years' time with legal rights of continued access and usage.

Examiner's comments

Most candidates correctly assessed both the strategic alliance and independence options and made a reasoned recommendation based on their analysis, with most choosing the strategic alliance as the better option. Many candidates did not, however, recognise the risk sharing benefits of a strategic alliance.

A significant minority did not give sufficient consideration to the possibility of independent operation.

Some candidates used the Suitability, Acceptability and Feasibility structure. However this was, as in some previous sittings, not helpful in guiding candidates towards the specific issues in the scenario, instead leading them towards wider issues which were only generally relevant.

57 Muple plc (June 2018)

Marking guide

	Knowledge	Skill	Marks
57.1 Sensorex: efficiency and profitability	4	13	16
57.2 Ethics	3	5	7
	7	18	23

57.1 Sensorex

Accurate predictions of customer occupancy (footfall × dwell time) give reasonable forecasts of demand for staff time to deal with customers who require advice on purchases and to carry out transactions.

The availability of data to predict staffing needs is one side of the problem. Obtaining the right number of staff to meet those needs on a timely basis can help provide a solution to that problem.

There are essentially two issues, each of which can be costly to Muple in different ways.

Overstaffing – there are too many staff on duty than required for the number of customers in the store and in individual departments. In this case there will be underutilised staff and excess staff costs where staff are being paid with no benefit to customers or increase in sales.

Understaffing – there are too few staff to deal, in a timely manner, with the number of customers in the store. Customers may not wait for staff to become available to help them and may leave the Muple stores without making a purchase. They may purchase elsewhere on the same day but also may not return in future to Muple stores due to the bad service and poor customer experience. There will therefore be a lost contribution from lost sales and damage to Muple's reputation.

Predictability of staffing requirements and workforce flexibility in terms of staffing procurement are therefore two key issues where using data analytics to forecast staffing needs can be an instrument in matching staffing supply with customer demand.

The 4Vs model gives an indication of the qualities that big data may have, enabling it to be useful to Muple:

Volume – large volumes of data may help Muple to gain a detailed understanding of customer movements and their consequent staffing requirements.

Velocity – refers to the speed at which 'real time' data flows into Muple and the speed at which the data is processed by Muple's systems to produce a meaningful output and to enable real time staffing decisions.

Variety – is concerned with the diverse range of forms that big data can take. Capturing, processing and storing unstructured data presents challenges but adds to the richness of the data and potentially its usefulness.

Veracity (value) – is concerned with the truthfulness of the data collected ie, it must not present a bias or contain inconsistencies. In Muple's case this means that customer movements can be captured and faithfully represented.

Patterned predictability of peak demand during the day (eg, around 13.00 on Saturdays and 12.30 on Sundays from pilot evidence) and for days of the week (eg, Saturday and Sunday from pilot evidence) will allow an appropriate number of staff to be scheduled to work at these peak times.

However, the Sensorex system enables customer flows also to be monitored within the store (ie, between departments) not just for the store as a whole. Thus, for example, if the software and computers department has a different peak time to the entertainment equipment department, then staff can be moved across to satisfy customer demand where it is most needed. This requires flexibility in terms of working arrangements in respect of staff allocations between departments but also flexibility of staff product knowledge. This could be gained by staff rotation between departments as a normal part of training.

While recording historic patterns of customer demand is useful for booking staff time for each department in advance (as above) there will inevitably be real-time and unexpected variations in customer demand from historic trends. This requires a real-time response from staff which might amount to more than just moving staff between departments (eg, if all departments are busy at the same time).

The staff app can add workforce flexibility in terms of labour availability by calling in staff at short notice who are not on duty. The advantage of the app, over a telephone call to staff, is that staff can indicate in advance their willingness to work when not on duty (perhaps with a pay premium for a short-term response).

The pilot data on its own provides only a relative comparison over a given week. This week may be atypical for most weeks over the year or between stores. Trends may emerge if data is collected over a year or over a number of years. For example:

- There may be a seasonal impact: summer and winter

- There may be cultural times of year for high or low spending: Christmas, other festivals, school holidays.

- There may be local events that effect only one region – local festivals, sporting events. This emphasises the need to predict customer demand for each store separately rather than for all stores.

Dealing with the specific data in the pilot:

Footfall – is a sales opportunity and demonstrates the potential demand, not just for sales on the day but to build reputation with customers through staff service. The quantitative variation in footfall (the highest is 7.6 times greater than the lowest) shows the degree of variation in staffing requirements needed to satisfy selling opportunities.

Dwell time – may be indicative of the level of interest of each customer and the seriousness of their intention to make a purchase. It may also be affected by the level of interest shown by staff to retain customers in the store. It may therefore be a consequence of additional staff time, not just a cause.

Conversion rate – this distinguishes between the number of customers who are serious in making purchases and those who do not intend to purchase or have not seen what they want. Increases in staffing may raise this percentage in retaining customers in store and persuading them to make a purchase. Increased staffing can improve this percentage but any benefit needs to be weighed against the greater staffing cost at the margin.

The above factors may be linked. For example, an increase in dwell time may be causally linked with the conversion rate in that if customers stay in the store longer they are more likely to make a purchase.

Examiner's comments

This was fairly well answered by the majority. Many used the 4Vs framework. While some found it helpful, for others, rigid adherence to this framework manifested itself. Many of those who used the 4Vs rigidly missed some of the key points that were relevant in the scenario, but did not fit the model.

The best answers gave intelligent consideration to the significance of footfall, dwell time and conversion rate data in assisting improved operations.

Most candidates mentioned data analytics and also explored the staff availability and staff forecasting and scheduling improvements. Many also explored the impact of real time data and how it can assist in scheduling.

Many failed to draw upon the pilot data provided in the question. Better answers included the pilot data and discussed the real time aspects of customer demand v staff availability/supply.

57.2 Ethics

There are two potential ethical issues for Tony:

(1) Conflict of interest between his new employer and existing employer during contract negotiations, and over the next six months of his continued employment with Muple. Tony also has a personal conflict between his own self-interest and that of his current employer. He stands to make a personal gain in his new job, which incentivises this conflict of interest.

(2) Transparency – Muple is unaware of the conflict of interest and Tony's intention to leave Muple and join Pergola. The issue of providing transparency in disclosing his new job offer to the Muple board could be viewed as the opposite side of the confidentiality requested by Harriett.

There are two potential ethical issues for Harriett:

(1) Intimidation – there may be an issue of her intimidation of Tony as a potential new employee with the implied threat that, if the contract with Muple is not won, Tony may not have a future role with Pergola, despite the job offer, as he is to work on the Pergola contract.

(2) Dishonesty/lack of integrity – intending to keep secret from Muple that Tony could be acting in the interests of Pergola in the negotiations between the companies despite being employed by Muple at the time.

In making any ethical evaluation, it is first necessary to establish the facts. In this case, the intentions of Harriett may not be entirely dishonest, but may be seen as such by an informed and reasonable third party. She has not asked Tony directly to favour Pergola in contract negotiations, but she has incentivised him to do so.

The issue of legality may apply depending on the terms of Tony's employment contract with Muple and his legal duties as a director of Muple. The actions or non-disclosure may be a breach of this contract and a breach of the duty for a director to act in good faith and in the best interests of the company. Acting in the interests of Pergola in negotiations while employed by, and acting as a director of, Muple may constitute a criminal offence such as fraud.

Actions

Tony's actions should be consistent with his obligations and duties as a director of Muple and his employment contract.

Tony can make personal gain from helping Pergola by benefiting in his new role, but this should not influence his ethical actions.

Tony's initial action should be to inform the Muple board of the fact that he intends to join Pergola and the content of the conversation with Harriett.

Tony may also want to rethink his acceptance of the job with Pergola as it appears to be willing to act unethically. If so, he should inform the Muple and Pergola boards.

Tony may wish to persuade the Muple board to consider obtaining sensor technology from an alternative, and more honest, supplier.

Acting in the interests of Pergola in negotiations while employed by, and acting as a director of, Muple may be criminal offence and legal advice should be taken by Tony.

Examiner's comments

Most candidates were able to identify the key ethical issues in the scenario and it is encouraging that more candidates are now applying professional scepticism in questioning the facts.

Those candidates who rigidly relied on the Transparency, Effect, Fairness (TEF) structure and language typically produced a much more restricted answer than candidates who explored the other ethical principles and issues relevant to the scenario. These included: conflict of interest, transparency, intimidation and honesty/integrity. Candidates who used appropriate ethical language tended to score more highly.

Candidates are encouraged to consider a wide range of ethical issues that may be relevant in ethical scenarios and not restrict themselves merely to those included in the TEF model.

Most candidates made some reference to legal issues.

Candidates tended to focus on Tony but less so on Harriet, some ignoring the issues for Harriet altogether. Actions for Tony were sometimes very generic or brief.

58 Innotoy Ltd (September 2018)

	Knowledge	Skill	Marks
58.1 Data analysis	3	16	17
58.2 Management information systems	3	6	8
58.3 Merits of strategies	3	8	10
58.4 Ethics	2	7	8
	11	37	43

58.1 Analysis of Digiwhirl performance

Appendix of calculations

> **Tutorial note**
>
> A wide range of analysis could be undertaken – the appendix demonstrates the range of calculations. Candidates are not expected to have produced all of them.

Digiwhirl sales and profitability analysis

	Sales revenue £'000	Gross profit (55% markup) £'000	% change	Sales volume £'000	Selling price £
20X6	10,500	3,726	–	700	15
20X7	15,000	5,323	42.9%	1,000	15
20X8	12,000	4,258	-20%	800	15

Digiwhirl quarterly sales mix

	Q1 £'000	Q2 £'000	Q3 £'000	Q4 £'000	Total sales £'000
20X6	750	1,950	3,300	4,500	10,500
%	7	19	31	43	
20X7	2,750	5,550	3,700	3,000	15,000
%	18	37	25	20	
20X8	1,200	2,400	3,600	4,800*	12,000
%	10	20	30	40	

Product sales mix 20X7

	Toy 1	Toy 2	Toy 3	Digiwhirl	Innotoy
Mix per Exhibit 1	10%	7%	13%	70%	100%
Revenue (£'000)	2,143	1,500	2,786	15,000	21,429
Gross profit (£'000)	760	532	989	5,323	7,604

Market share/market growth

	20X6	20X7	20X8
Total market volume ('000)	700	1,450	1,600
Market growth	–	107%	10.3%
Digiwhirl sales ('000)	700	1,000	800
Digiwhirl market share (volume)	100%	69%	50%
Competitors' volume (balancing figure)	Nil	450	800
Competitors' revenue × £12 (£'000)	0	5,400	9,600
Digiwhirl revenue (£'000)	10,500	15,000	12,000
Total market revenue (£'000)	10,500	20,400	21,600
Digiwhirl market share (revenue)	100%	73.5%	55.6%

Expected market volume in 20X9 = 1,600,000 × 40% = 640,000

Profit potentially lost as a result of unfulfilled customer demand for Digiwhirl

> **Tutorial note**
>
> Assumes that sales are lost to other competitors

	20X6	20X7	20X8
Unfulfilled orders ('000)	100	250	0
Digiwhirl revenue potentially lost × £15 (£'000)	1,500	3,750	
Gross profit lost (£'000)	532	1,331	
% of GP for year	14.3%	25%	

IT director's data

	20X6	20X7	20X8 to date
Number of hits on Innotoy website ('000)	3,200	5,000	2,000
% change		+56%	-60%
Number of #Digiwhirl references	1,400	3,000	1,000
% change		+114%	-67%
Number of results from internet search for hand-held spinner	6,507	17,430	23,512
% change		+168%	+35%

Commentary

The sales revenue and profitability of Digiwhirl increased by 42.9% between 20X6 and 20X7 but then fell by 20% in 20X8. It is unclear what share of the market it will have in 20X9 but at best, if it retains its 50% share of volume and sees no fall in price, then sales revenue and profitability will fall by 60%. In reality if the market is maturing and Digiwhirl remains more highly priced than competitors, the decline is likely to be greater.

The finance director has asked for an evaluation of whether the performance of Digiwhirl is down to short product life cycles in the toy industry or poor management decisions.

Supply and demand

Perhaps a key management error was to choose to restrict supply in both 20X6 and 20X7 rather than to capitalise on demand that was high, but almost inevitably was going to be short-term. This led to sales shortfalls and appears to have cost Digiwhirl £532,000 profit in 20X6 and at least £1,331,000 profit in 20X7. The profit from unfulfilled orders in the year is however only lost if these customers do not buy in the following year. It could be that customer purchases from 20X6 were deferred to 20X7 rather than lost altogether. However given the advent of competitor products in 20X7, these sales are more likely to have been lost.

Without the advent of copies, Innotoy's strategy of restricting supply might have managed to create a sought-after image, sustain high prices and lengthen the life cycle. Looking at the quarterly analysis it is clear that sales are seasonal and that in 20X6 and 20X8 the bulk of sales took place in Q4 (43% 20X6, 40% 20X8). However, this is not the case in 20X7 – it would appear that Q2, 20X7 marked a peak in demand for Digiwhirl (37% of that year's sales). This was a result of the sudden social media coverage which took Innotoy by surprise – in 20X7 there was a 56% increase in website hits and a 114% increase in references to #Digiwhirl compared to 20X6. Had Innotoy identified the surge in demand in Q2 and been able to make more products available at this point, it may have been able to maintain its market dominance for longer.

Innotoy's failure to capture external information and monitor the market resulted in a failure to accurately predict demand. This was exacerbated by the fact that it is forced to place orders with suppliers annually in advance, so by the time it did respond to the increased demand by placing 25% more orders in 20X8, it was too late. Innotoy would be well advised to reconsider its supplier relationship because it does not give sufficient flexibility in the dynamic toy industry.

Pricing and competition

Copies may have had a substitution effect in 20X7 (in that customers may have bought competitors' products instead of Digiwhirl when it was not available). This may have been exacerbated by the difference in price between Digiwhirl and competitors (£15 vs £12) and Innotoy's choice not to reduce selling prices. The issue here is that once competitors bring out cheaper products, the market is flooded and there is little incentive for customers to buy Digiwhirls at the higher price of £15.

Innotoy's pricing strategy is the same for all products and appears to be based on an arbitrary 55% mark-up on cost. In a competitive market such as the toy industry, it would be better to consider external factors when setting prices and vary these at different stages of the product's life cycle depending on the level of competition and demand. The average rating of Digiwhirl falls from 5/5 in 20X6 to 3.5 in 20X7 – further information is required to assess whether this is down to product features and quality or reflects the fact that customers start to see that other products offer better value-for money

The fact that the number of sellers on one of the major online retail sites increases from 20 to 150 between 20X7 and 20X8 suggests significant competitive rivalry. Although the market for hand-held spinners continued to grow in 20X8 (35% increase in website searches and a 10.3% increase in sales volumes), Digiwhirl's market share fell in volume terms from 69% in 20X7 to an estimated 50% in 20X8. The promotional strategy of emphasizing that Digiwhirl was the original product appears not to have worked as well as was probably wished. The IT director's statistics also reflect this with significantly reduced website hits and refs for #Digiwhirl in 20X8 (respectively 60% and 67% lower than in 20X7).

The trend of decline in the market appears to indicate that demand for Digiwhirl would be sustained for little more than one more year, and that there is little need to purchase any more stock since the company already has spare inventory of 450,000 units.

Protection of IP

Innotoy's initial decision to protect only its product brand names means that any differentiation it enjoys over competitors is short-lived, since its designs can be copied by competitors provided the design differences are sufficient to avoid litigation. More information is needed as to the costs of patenting designs to assess whether the long-term benefits arising from a protected competitive advantage outweigh the costs and time involved.

Product life cycle

Most individual products in the toy industry have a finite product life cycle, although the life cycle of the industry itself is longer. There are some examples of popular toys with long life cycles eg, Lego, however toys such as the Digiwhirl, which become a sudden hit, are likely to have a short life cycle. For these products brand image, advertising and product development may be able to sustain the life cycle for a while but not indefinitely.

In the case of handheld spinners, the market experienced rapid growth between 20X6 and 20X7, more than doubling, was close to maturity in 20X8 (growth of 10.3%) and a significant decline in the overall market is expected by 20X9 (60%).

An indication of the scale of decline in the overall market is that the entire market in 20X9 is predicted to be smaller at 640,000 spinners than the sales of Digiwhirl alone or the products of the combined competitors in 20X8 (800,000 spinners each). This implies Digiwhirl sales would have declined substantially by 20X9 even without the entrance of competitors.

There is a possibility that had Digiwhirl captured the full market in 20X7 then this may have extended the life cycle for a little more time.

Innotoy's product portfolio/research and development

The BCG matrix considers the concept of a balanced product portfolio – Innotoy should have a range of products at different stages of their life cycle which can contribute cash flows to varying degrees at different points in their development, growth, maturity and decline. If we consider Innotoy's sales analysis however this does not appear to be the case, since Digiwhirl accounted for 70% of sales in 20X7. The fact that the business is so dependent on the success of Digiwhirl increases risk. One year after launch the three other toys between them only account for 30% of sales and none of them exceed 13%.

It would appear that after launching Digiwhirl, Innotoy had no other designs in the pipeline to replace Digiwhirl when maturity approached. This might be because Innotoy lacked the core competences to develop other new products (a shortfall of the R&D department which the sales director hints at) and/or it may be they were just lucky with the success of Digiwhirl.

Conclusion

It appears that the performance of Digiwhirl is partly a result of short product life cycles in the toy industry but has been exacerbated by a series of questionable management decisions (lack of patent protection for design, restriction of supply, inflexible supplier, maintaining a constant selling price).

The quality of these decisions may reflect on the managers that took them or the quality of information that was available at the time. The IT director's suggestion that the company's information system is too internally focused may have contributed to this and improvements in data capture and analysis therefore merit consideration, as do strategies to reduce reliance on Digiwhirl.

Examiner's comments

The data analysis requirement was generally well answered. The average score, whilst reasonable, was lower than some previous data analysis requirements. This is likely to be due to the fact that candidates could not just rely on standard ratio calculations or look at percentage changes and needed to give some thought to selecting the most useful calculations to perform in the context of the FD's request.

Most candidates produced a structured table of calculations but some weaker candidates just included random calculations in their commentary on a piecemeal basis, which is not recommended. Only a minority presented an analysis of the quarterly data provided.

The discussion was generally reasonable, although some candidates would have benefitted from the use of sub-headings to structure their answer. Better candidates identified key management decisions (such as patenting the brand only, restricting supply, buying annually and maintaining high prices in the face of increased competition) and produced a reasoned discussion of the extent to which these had contributed to the current situation, often using the online data in Exhibit 2 as additional evidence to back up their comments.

Weaker candidates, as usual, reiterated the figures they had calculated, without adding value. A minority of very weak candidates devoted most of their response to a chronological description of events since the introduction of the Digiwhirl with little, if any, consideration of the relative quality of management decisions. Although many referred to the fact that Digiwhirl accounted for 70% of sales, only a minority recognised the implications of this in the context of product life cycles and Digiwhirl's position in the BCG matrix.

58.2 Management information: data capture and analysis

Innotoy's IT director is suggesting that Innotoy can use information systems as part of a strategy to gain and then sustain competitive advantage. Innotoy's board need information for:

- estimating industry trends and future demand
- competitor analysis
- forecasting sales growth and market share
- new product development plans

Innotoy's strategic management information system therefore needs to provide both quantitative and qualitative information, and as the IT director has recognised, it also needs to incorporate information from internal and external sources. Big data is a term used to describes the large volume of data – both structured and unstructured – that encompasses a variety of internal and external sources. It might include information from Innotoy's systems, transactions with its customers, social media, mobile devices etc. The IT director's reference to the photos, videos and conversations happening online relates to data that is unstructured and real time, which can be analysed for insights that lead to better decisions and may have prevented some of the management errors noted earlier.

Data analytics is the process of collecting, organising and analysing large sets of such data to discover patterns. Innotoy could use big data analytics to help translate market signals into demand signals. One of the benefits of big data is the velocity with which it can be collected and analysed which would allow Innotoy to react in real time eg, had Innotoy been monitoring its website hits and #Digiwhirl references it may have identified and responded faster to the change in demand that occurred in Q2 20X7.

Pricing decisions

Trends identified in sales (volumes, prices and demand) in real time could be used to help improve inventory and pricing decisions. For example, if Innotoy were able to capture real-time sales information it could integrate this with inventory data and information about competitors' prices to flex the prices it charges for its toys. Had Innotoy monitored customers' average ratings for its product it may have realised that Digiwhirl was losing ground compared to competitors in terms of value for money and adjusted its price accordingly.

Marketing and supply chain

Digiwhirl benefitted from being featured on social media but this was perhaps more by luck than judgement. Innotoy could more actively use social media to influence customers and their purchasing behaviour as a means of achieving competitive advantage, eg, using blogs, vlogs, Twitter feeds etc as a form of promotional activity. However it could also capture information that is useful to managers. Social media analytics allows an organisation not only to measure quantitative metrics such as the number of times its Facebook account has been 'liked' but also to capture qualitative data. For example key words posted by customers about Innotoy's products can be used to perform 'sentiment analysis' which would allow Innotoy to respond to any positive and negative trends.

A big challenge for Innotoy is the seasonality of the industry with large volumes of sales taking place in Quarter 4. Innotoy needs to try and define well in advance what types of toy will be in demand so they can inform suppliers about production requirements early enough to have sufficient toys available to meet customer demand at the right time for sale. Had Innotoy identified the amount of online traffic generated, it might have been able increase the supply of Digiwhirl to capitalise on this.

Development of new products

Innotoy operates in a highly competitive industry where product innovation and being first to market are both highly desired. As a result, continual product development is critical to success. A key issue for Innotoy is being able to develop toys that are going to be different from the competition and be successful. To do this it needs to be able to predict and then respond to likely trends in the toy market and what customers want. Management information that captures the factors shaping the toy industry and the competitive strategy and position of competitors (nature of products, market share) will assist with modelling and forecasting. Integrating data obtained from the marketing department about competitors, customer transactions and shopping habits with data from the R&D team about the feasibility of new products could help Innotoy develop new and existing products to meet customer needs and reduce the time to market.

Customer service

Many companies already offer customers the opportunity to leave feedback on their experience with the company and its products or services. Customers also give unsolicited public feedback via social media. If Innotoy were to capture and analyse such feedback it could deal proactively with potential product issues and respond quickly to customer complaints. There can however be issues with the veracity of such data, which may be biased.

Conclusion

If the IT director wants to implement a big data strategy, Innotoy need to identify what data it would be useful to collect, how to capture it and how to process and analyse it. A big data strategy is likely to need significant up-front investment in IT systems, which will require funding. Capturing and processing more data will also have an ongoing cost. As Innotoy is a small business, an alternative to employing its own experts is to outsource this to a company with expertise in this area.

Examiner's comments

This was well answered, on the whole. The best answers correctly considered how Innotoy could improve its data capture and analysis, with many making reference to Big Data, often coupled with consideration of the four Vs (veracity, volume etc), and how big data analytics might help with Innotoy's issues.

Weaker efforts tended just to provide descriptive discussion of the data provided by the IT director whereas the better scripts considered the implications for competitive advantage. The potential outsourcing of data analytics was only considered by a minority.

58.3 Growth strategies

Currently Innotoy's product portfolio is unbalanced and the business is over-reliant on Digiwhirl. Under the BCG matrix, this product is a cash cow (high market share, low market growth) but it is likely to be nearing the end of its life cycle. Using the Ansoff matrix, growth strategies can involve:

- market penetration
- product development
- market development
- diversification

Marketing director

The marketing director's suggestion of marketing Digiwhirl as a desk toy for stressed executives and as a therapeutic aid to concentration for children with attention deficit disorders is one of market development – finding new markets for an existing product. This strategy may help address the seasonality issues that Innotoy has faced with 40% sales in the children's toy market taking place in Q4 in 20X8. It builds on Innotoy's existing core competences but would require the product to be marketed differently for the different audiences. Market research should be undertaken to assess the extent of the two possible markets. The Board could also identify whether there are any other geographical markets for market development of the existing Digiwhirl product.

Sales director

As the sales director recognises, Innotoy was initially able to justify a premium price for Digiwhirl due to its first mover advantage. The declining sales of Digiwhirl suggest that customers no longer believe it is worth paying extra for. So if Digiwhirl chooses to maintain its pricing strategy to protect its brand then market penetration (selling more existing product to existing markets) is likely to be difficult given the extent of competition from cheaper copycats.

The sales director's suggestion to bring out a wider range of Digiwhirl models with added features such as LED lights, Bluetooth speakers, or personalisation could be seen as an attempt to create a new USP and achieve market penetration via differentiation. Alternatively it could be seen as a product development strategy (new products, existing market). By adding additional features it is the intention to get brand-loyal customers to buy more than one version of the product, although this strategy alone is unlikely to bring long-term competitive advantage as all these ideas will be easily copied.

The BCG model talks about the need for a balanced product portfolio. In an industry such as the toy industry where products have relatively short life cycles, success depends on having a mix of yesterday's product, today's product, tomorrow's product and the product of the future. That way cash inflows from today's successful products can be used to fund the development and promotion of new products for the future. This is particularly important if, as experience suggests, only 1 in 4 of Innotoy's products has really been successful. The sales director has identified that as the market for hand-held spinners matures, it is critical for the R&D team to start looking for Innotoy's next new successful product. This is a strategy of product development or diversification depending on the target market. Both market development and product development are ways of spreading the risk Innotoy currently faces. The final step, diversification, involves risk in the sense that the product and market are both new but it does reduce risk in the sense that it would reduce Innotoy's dependence on Digiwhirl.

Conclusion

Innotoy appears to have failed to successfully develop any further new products since its initial launch. This may be due to a lack of investment or a lack of ability on the part of the R&D department. Widening both the market of customers for Digiwhirl and the product range will help Innotoy to increase sales. In order to generate a financially sustainable business, Innotoy urgently needs to have a wider range of products and a more balanced product portfolio to reduce reliance on Digiwhirl. Innotoy needs to have products at each stage of their life cycle.

Examiner's comments

This was well answered by the vast majority of candidates who seemed very comfortable identifying and discussing the strategies proposed by the two directors in the context of Ansoff's product/market matrix.

Some candidates used the Suitability, Acceptability and Feasibility structure to evaluate the strategies. However, as in some previous sittings, this was not always helpful in guiding candidates to address the specific issues in the scenario.

Some weaker candidates limited their discussion of the sales director's proposals to the ideas on developing alternative versions of Digiwhirl, failing to pick up on the other comments relating to pricing and Innotoy's need to develop a wider product portfolio as a matter of urgency.

The best responses were nevertheless pessimistic about Innotoy's current prospects, given the short life cycle of Digiwhirl and related products and the lack of new products in the pipeline.

58.4 Ethical issues

The R&D director is suggesting that Innotoy launch a copy of the inventor's toy that is sufficiently different for the company to not be sued. A key question here is legality in relation to the intellectual property for the new toy. There are two issues:

(1) Whether the IP for the new product belongs to the inventor
(2) Whether Innotoy would be acting legally if it did as the R&D director suggested

The company's lawyer has suggested that Innotoy may be able to copy the product without breaking the law and can minimise its risk of being sued by modifying the design. It is possible that this advice is faulty and a second opinion should be sought. Even if the suggested actions by Innotoy are not illegal they are probably not ethical. The inventor has approached the company and shared confidential information about her design in good faith. Thus there is an issue here of honesty and integrity – the suggestions of the R&D director and the lawyer cast doubt on their personal ethics. This is particularly the case in respect of their claim that Innotoy can act with impunity as the inventor can probably not afford to sue, which would be a form of exploitation.

Innotoy needs to be open and transparent in its actions and comply with its own ethical code/any applicable industry codes. In an industry where IP is critical to competitive advantage, using a product idea that belongs to someone else appears to amount to theft and is unlikely to be considered ethical. It cannot be justified simply on the grounds that competitors have behaved in a similar way in respect of Innotoy's designs. Innotoy's requirement and expectation to make profits needs to be constrained by its obligations to behave responsibly. Innotoy has been on the receiving end of copycat products and suffered as a result. It risks reputational damage if it came to light that it had used someone else's IP for a new toy.

A clear loser here is the inventor who was expecting to share in 50% of the profits if Innotoy adopted her design. Even if Innotoy did not intend to go ahead with the product itself, if the IP belongs to the inventor then she could have approached other toy firms with the concept. In the context of business ethics, Innotoy's behaviour is unfair, if it knowingly uses someone else's IP without paying for it. The R&D director's suggestion amounts to exploitation and relies on the fact that Innotoy, as a larger company with access to greater financial resources, will be able to intimidate the investor and prevent her from suing.

Actions

It appears that the R&D director has already sought legal advice. Legally and commercially Innotoy may be within its rights to use the product concept if the IP has not been protected. However if it wants to be seen to act ethically, then Innotoy should reject the R&D director's proposal. Taking up the inventor's proposals to share the designs in exchange for a share of the profits seems reasonable. Innotoy would be better trying to negotiate a different profit share instead of stealing the inventor's idea.

The R&D director may be motivated by the failure of their department to come up with new product ideas. Innotoy needs to consider whether the suggestions of the R&D director are those of an honest employee and whether there is a good fit between the director's values and those of the organisation. Such behaviour may cause them to reconsider his employment, especially as it is likely that it is an attempt to cover up R&D's failure to produce successful new designs. Innotoy may also want to consider appointing a different lawyer.

Examiner's comments

The ethics requirement was well attempted by most candidates who were able to identify the key ethical issue relating to theft of intellectual property (IP). Those candidates who relied only on the Transparency, Effect, Fairness (TEF) structure typically produced a much more restricted answer than candidates who explored the other ethical principles and issues raised by the scenario, which included honesty, integrity and confidentiality. Most candidates made some reference to legal issues relating to IP. The better answers applied professional scepticism in relation to the lawyer's statement that Innotoy could copy the inventor's product without being sued and to the R&D director's personal motives, given that his department is lacking in new ideas. They also discussed the fact that Innotoy's actions would constitute exploitation of the inventor who has approached Innotoy in good faith.

As usual some weaker candidates provided a reasonable discussion of the ethical issues/principles but then provided a weak discussion of the actions. Virtually all concluded that Innotoy should not go ahead with the proposed action as advocated by the R&D director, instead negotiating with the inventor to arrive at a deal that satisfied everyone. A minority suggested that Innotoy should in fact take action against the R&D director, and possibly the lawyer, given their apparent lack of personal and professional ethics.

59 Balad Ltd (September 2018)

	Knowledge	Skill	Marks
59.1 Conflict of objectives	3	6	9
59.2 Break-even	2	9	10
59.3 Joint venture	3	14	16
	8	29	35

59.1 Conflict of objectives

Balad and the Government will have different objectives, which will themselves be linked to their different stakeholders. As a profit making company, key stakeholders for Balad will be its shareholders (the Balad family). Their main aim may be to generate as much profit as possible. As the public sector body responsible for the running of Ambrosia, key stakeholders for the Government will be residents, businesses, the wider community and any partners in other public services such as health, infrastructure. The Government as a not for profit (NFP) organisation has a wider range of stakeholders and is likely to have to balance the use of limited resources to ensure it provides the best possible services and maximises benefits for the country.

For the College to be a success, the two members of the JV need to have complementary and aligned objectives and in certain cases their aims and objectives may coincide. If the college is successful, this will generate profits for Balad but will also facilitate the achievement of the Government's strategic priorities for education to:

- increase the number of Ambrosian-born residents, aged 17–18, who undertake state-funded further education; and

- develop technological expertise to provide Ambrosia with future resident IT specialists and reduce the need for expatriate resources.

However, there is also scope for conflict of interest about the strategy and activities of the College between Balad as a private entity and the Ambrosian Government as a public body, and the two parties may have different planning horizons. A balance will need to be struck between financial return annually and delivering a public educational service in the longer term.

Also conflicts may arise between the interests of the JV and the separate interests of the two participating members. Balad's aims for the College are likely to involve growth and profits. Its primary objectives are more likely to be financial rather than non-financial, with a probable focus on cost control and margins. Balad's desire to increase profitability may conflict with the Government's obligations to society. This may give rise to conflict for example over admissions policies and who decides on the balance between expats and residents. The Government may be less keen on selection criteria like those applied within Balad School if this reduces the number of resident children who qualify for attendance. The Government will need to insist on controls to ensure that decisions/actions by the JV do not undermine its objectives in relation to national education.

However, Balad brings commercial experience to the venture, which may help increase profits from the college. If the JV generates additional income for the Government then it may indirectly allow the Government to better achieve its other objectives by providing more financial resources. As a public body, the Government needs to act in the public interest and is likely to have to uphold certain principles including integrity, accountability, transparency and honesty. These are very similar to the core corporate governance principles of a company and so the values of Balad and the Government should be aligned in this respect.

Conclusion

Although Balad and the Government have different stakeholders, they both have a vested interest in the success of the College and their objectives are sufficiently aligned for the joint venture to succeed. Since each party is entitled to appoint two representatives to the JV's senior management team, neither would appear able to dictate decisions. However, there is some scope for conflict and they will need to agree on the methods for resolving any disputes.

Examiner's comments

This requirement was reasonably well answered. Most candidates identified the different objectives of Balad (profit maximiser) and the Government (public sector) and many gave due consideration to the broader stakeholder view of the latter, covering the benefits to Ambrosia's economy etc.

Most answers identified conflicts between Balad and the Government, but fewer recognised the degree to which common objectives might exist. However, the better candidates did discuss the degree to which the perspectives of the Government and Balad align, which would be necessary for a successful joint venture.

59.2 Break-even attendance and financial implications

Fee per pupil = $8,000

Contribution per pupil = $8,000 × 0.85 = $6,800

Fixed costs = $794k + Rental $225k + Management fee $375k = $1,394k

Break-even attendance = $1,394,000/$6,800 = 205 pupils p.a.

The IBAC programme and technology diploma is a two year course. In year 1 the College will only have one year-group, starting their two year programme. In year 2 and subsequent years there will be two year-groups. The 205 pupils would represent the total number of pupils in attendance required to break-even over a year, so once the College is up and running this would equate to two intakes/year-groups. For example if, as expected, the College attracted 120 pupils in the first year and 144 in the second (20% increase), then it would be loss making in year 1 (120 pupils in attendance) and profitable in year 2 (264 pupils in attendance compared to 205 break-even, a margin of safety of 22%). The calculation therefore suggests that the College will be a financial success.

The fact that the College will break-even if it has an attendance of 205 pupils does not necessarily mean that this is the point at which the individual JV parties will break-even on their investment, since each has different income and costs arising from the JV. However it is clear that the College will start to generate a profit share for both Balad and the Government from year 2 onwards.

It would be useful to have some further information to substantiate the forecasts of the likely attendance of the College – the numbers of children currently attending Balad's 17–18 programmes and the FAE programme that the Government is proposing to close would give some more idea of the level of demand.

The break-even calculation depends on the assumptions that have been made about the average fee, contribution and fixed costs. In reality these may vary over the five-year period. Some sensitivity analysis would be useful to identify the assumptions that are most critical. As with most colleges the model is one of high operating gearing.

The attendance of the College may depend on its exam success. Thus the financial success of the venture will partly depend on the College's ability to retain the academic standards and quality that Balad's reputation relies on. It would also be important to understand if there are any other schools/colleges operating in competition. Expats may prefer to send their children to an IBAC-only school rather than one offering a mix and the fees charged by competitors may influence demand.

Examiner's comments

Answers to this requirement were very polarised. Candidates consistently appear to find requirements that ask for both calculations and narrative more challenging, often because their answers lack balance. There was a roughly 50/50 split between those who did justice to the numerical calculations and those who did not or even ignored the numbers completely.

Many candidates displayed an understanding of the break-even formula and were able to correctly calculate contribution per student. However, many failed to correctly identify the relevant fixed costs, which included the rental and management fee as well as the fixed overheads. Some weaker candidates confused the costs of the joint venture with the costs incurred by the individual parties to the venture. A surprising number ignored the requirement to discuss the assumptions behind the calculation.

Many provided only the briefest of comments on the implications of their calculation for the financial success of the college. Even where candidates had calculated the breakeven attendance correctly, it was disappointing that hardly any picked up on the fact that the college course lasts for two years, resulting in two intakes of students after the first year. As a result the breakeven point for the College will be reached much sooner than the vast majority realised.

59.3 Benefits and risks

Government

Benefits

- The venture is consistent with the Government's strategic priorities for education and the economy.

- It provides access to the resources and expertise of Balad that the state schools may lack to train students in international qualifications and technology.

- If successful this will provide home-grown IT skills and reduce the country's need for expats.

- There is a guaranteed return on the College building in the form of the $225k annual rental from the JV. Also the Government retains ownership of the building in the event that the JV is not a success.

- Balad's experience may help improve exam results and hence the quality of education received.

- The Government and Balad are sharing the cost of the initial investment. The contribution from Balad reduces the financial risk for the Government compared to funding the College set up alone.

- The Government's 50% profit share can be used to fund other public sector projects and hence benefit wider stakeholders.

Risks/downsides

Risk identification will be particularly important for the Government. Risks include the following:

- The Government will need to finance the $250k up-front investment for refurbishment which may take funds from other projects.

- The Government may attract adverse publicity as a result of closing the state school for 17-18 year olds and may be criticised for becoming involved with a commercial organisation and prioritising profit over education.

- Although profits are shared 50/50, the Government receives less in fixed annual payments from the JV than Balad does (£225k compared to £375k).

- The College costs the Government an extra $1,500 per pupil if they switch from an existing FAE programme and $8,000 if they were previously not in education aged 17-18. Some residents whose parents previously paid for education may now take up their offer of state funding (the data suggests that approximately 20% of Ambrosian parents currently pay privately between the age of 11-16) and if the College is successful in attracting some of the 40% of students who are not currently in 17-18 education, this will significantly increase costs for the Government.

- There may be conflicts of interest with Balad - the fact that Balad has 50% control and profit share may mean public interest arguments are not always the priority and the Government may have to compromise on certain objectives.

- It may take a while for the venture to become profitable and it is unclear what evidence there is for demand for the new technology qualification (what research has been done?).

- If the JV is loss making then the Government has to take a 50% share of losses, although it will still own the building that the College is using.

- The new College may reduce demand for FAE at other state schools, which could appear a second rate option in comparison.

Balad

Benefits

- The JV frees up space for Balad School to use for education of 11-16 year olds. Since there is a waiting list this should increase Balad school's profits from these courses.

- It widens the audience for 17-18 year old courses which are currently undersubscribed and extends the market beyond the expat community.

- Balad is guaranteed an income stream in the form of the $375k management fee.

- Balad are likely to be able to staff the College by transferring existing staff from the IBAC programme which may increase their utilisation rate and will be faster.

- There may be corporate social responsibility (CSR) benefits of being associated with an innovative state education programme. The additional publicity may increase Balad's reputation and attract other pupils to Balad School.

- If the venture is successful Balad could extend this model to other countries.

Risks/downsides

- Balad will need to finance the $250k up-front investment in equipment and resources.

- Balad loses $400k net income from closing existing 17–18 programme, although the guaranteed $375k management fee means most of this is recovered and Balad will break even provided the College makes at least $50k profit.

- Balad is responsible for the day-to-day control of the College. Balad has no apparent experience of technology and the existing tutors may lack the necessary skills so Balad may initially have difficulties managing the College operations. Management time on the College may distract managers from running Balad School's operations effectively.

- Balad will not be free to set prices/decide on strategy as it will need to take the Government views into account. The Government may be reluctant to accept fee increases in future if it is funding some of the pupils.

- A JV with the Government may damage Balad's reputation, particularly if the College has to accept resident children using lower selection criteria than Balad would normally apply. This may have a knock-on impact on the success of the Balad School.

- If the College is too successful it will provide home-grown IT skills and reduce Ambrosia's need for expats, potentially reducing the market for Balad school.

- If the College is not successful and the venture ends, Balad may find it hard to re-open its own courses for 17–18 year olds.

Conclusion

Overall the College looks likely to be a financial success and is probably beneficial for both parties. Balad will generate a financial return from the JV and have the capacity to earn more profit from Balad School. It will also strengthen its ties with the Ambrosian Government. Partnering with Balad will reduce the costs and risks for the Government of setting up the College and help the Government achieve some of its strategic priorities for education.

More work could be done in the form of market research to assess the demand for the new College and the Government could engage in stakeholder consultation. The JV will need to be set up carefully to ensure that the risks identified for each party are properly addressed and that exit arrangements are clear should either party want to terminate the venture.

Examiner's comments

Answers to this requirement about the benefits and risks of the proposed joint venture were variable in quality. Most candidates considered sharing of risks, profits/losses and resources as potential benefits to both parties, but fewer explicitly considered control issues as potential risks. Some weaker candidates produced an imbalanced response, over-emphasising the benefits without considering possible risks or over-focussing on one party to the joint venture at the expense of the other. Another common mistake was the failure to use any of the numerical data provided in the scenario to quantify the financial benefits and risk, thereby restricting the marks scored by only covering strategic issues. Only the better candidates arrived at a conclusion with regards to the overall viability of the joint venture.

60 Vision Bank (September 2018)

	Knowledge	Skill	Marks
60.1 External factors	2	9	10
60.2 Change management	3	10	12
	5	19	22

Report

To: Vision Bank
From: A N Consultant
Date: September 20X8
Re: Open Banking

60.1 Three key external factors driving change in the banking industry

> **Tutorial note**
>
> Examples of some of the key factors driving change are given below. Candidates were only required to identify three key factors which could have been taken from either or both models. Some credit was given for other relevant points.

Key PESTEL forces

Technology

Technology is a key force for change in the banking industry, with digitisation changing the nature of banking. There has been a move from branch to online banking and a move from paper to mobile payments methods. These changes will reduce people and processing costs for the banks facilitating greater profitability but meaning that banks that are slow to adapt may lose business. New technology has also changed the nature of the competition in the form of digital challengers, which have an opportunity for competitive advantage as they are able to use cloud-based solutions and open-banking platforms to meet customer requirements in a more innovative way than traditional banks, without needing huge infrastructure. However new technology also increases the risk to banks of cybercrime and presents data security issues which can damage a bank's reputation and may result in costly fines and penalties. Data security concerns may also mean customers are slow to adopt new methods (see below).

Social

Like many other sectors, the banking sector is changing as consumers increasingly prefer to manage their bank accounts online. Customers are demanding increasing service levels and shorter reaction times and banks that want to remain profitable will need to find a cost effective way to deliver this. This is harder for the traditional banks due to their complex infrastructures and legacy systems. Also due to the banking crisis there has been an erosion of trust in the traditional banks which may pave the way for digital challengers. Some of the change may have been driven by the younger generations who place less reliance on relationship banking and face-to-face contact. However, there may be a limit to these trends as only 5–10% customers classed themselves as early adopters and 53% said they would not share information/change their banking habits so the uptake of new apps and other banking providers may be slower than anticipated.

 ICAEW 2019

Legal

Regulatory change is forcing banks to provide platforms for data sharing with authorised third parties and banks will have to alter their systems to comply with this. The open banking regulations may represent an opportunity for banks to provide a wider range of services. However it is also a threat as it reduces the barriers to entry and gives scope for increased competition in the form of digital challengers. The blog refers to the fact that, as a result of legislation threatening their monopoly, traditional banks may lose up to 31% of their profits. However the need for a banking licence and the requirement to comply with data protection regulation regarding data sharing may put some new entrants off.

Key Porter's 5 forces

Barriers to entry

Barriers to entry in the banking sector have been significantly reduced by the European open banking legislation. This removes the banks' monopoly by providing other businesses with access to the data necessary to provide banking services to customers. It also allows digital challengers to focus on a narrow product or segment, reducing the capital required. However, the fact that new entrants still need to apply for a licence and the fact that new challengers may not have the existing financial and legal competences of traditional banks may put some entrants off.

Substitutes

The removal of some of the barriers changes the nature of competition in the industry and gives rise to new players in the market (online retailers, technology giants) which are not traditional banks. Effectively their technology platforms allow them to become substitutes for the banks. These new challengers may be more agile and may have access to resources/infrastructure /information systems of their own to harness. These alternative providers may develop new-style banking products or ways of managing finances eg, via apps that the traditional banks may struggle to offer.

Power of customers

The changing demands of customers are forcing traditional banks to change as more customers want a digital approach that offers faster, more personalised financial services. The open banking regulations increase the power of customers to use a range of providers for their banking services and reduce the switching costs they face. Technology also facilitates transparency of data regarding the products and services offered by different banks and their prices. This increases customer bargaining power and makes it easier for customers to shop around.

Examiner's comments

This requirement was extremely well answered by most candidates, who typically made use of the PESTEL framework to identify the key factors disrupting the banking industry. Others chose to apply Porter's five forces which was also relevant. Most candidates made good use of the information in the scenario. Better candidates were able to link the two models, explaining for example how the new open banking legislation (PESTEL) was reducing the barriers to entry (Porter) or how technology (PESTEL) was giving rise to substitutes in the form of digital challengers (Porter).

Some weaker candidates provided more than three key factors, wasting their time and often not doing justice to their first three points. As usual a significant minority did not produce a report format, thus losing an easy mark.

60.2 Change management

VB's launch of its banking app and the closure of its paper processing centre will result in a large number of redundancies and the move to digital only banking will impact the day-to-day behaviour of customers.

Employees

The type of change will strongly influence the way in which change is managed. Change in this case seems transformational (a major significant change) since it involves closing a central part of the bank's operations (the paper processing centre) and is planned to take place within a short timescale. The introduction of new systems for the digital platform and the creation of the digital help centre will affect all employees significantly, but those employees at the processing centre are most at risk.

Change management involves managing employees' expectations and attitudes. Resistance and barriers to change will need to be acknowledged and may be lessened by involving the employees in the planning and implementation process. The bank needs to try and reduce any potential damage to its reputation as a result of adverse publicity eg, over redundancies.

Barriers to change

Given that the paper processing site would close, the barriers are likely to be substantial and would occur immediately following the announcement.

There are two main groups of employees which will need to be managed differently and present different barriers to change:

- Those employees required to retrain and change roles
- Those employees who are required to leave the company

Likely barriers to change include:

(1) **Cultural barriers**

   Power structures within VB may be threatened. This will in particular affect management and others in authority who may be protective of their current roles and decision making authority and be reluctant to implement changes which will be against their own interests.

   Structural inertia: VB's embedded systems and procedures are currently set up for paper processing and may need to be changed significantly for a digital strategy.

   Group inertia: if large numbers of employees are affected they may block change where it threatens their interests. Employees at risk of redundancy may therefore bond together to resist change (eg, strike action). The strength of their reaction may depend on their ability to get other jobs in the area.

(2) **Personnel barriers**

   There are also barriers which affect individuals and result in them seeing change as a threat. Here habit and fear of the unknown may mean some of the employees identified for transfer may be unwilling or reluctant to take on the new roles which require them to learn and embrace the new technology in order to be able to help customers.

   #### Approach to change

   Change management essentially relates to the preparation for change, announcing the change, managing the closure and the creation of the new digital help centre and the steps afterwards for operationalising and embedding the change.

The way in which the changes are introduced will be very important in them being implemented successfully. A mixture of the adaptive and coercive approach is likely to be appropriate. The change is unlikely to be successful unless key employees can be persuaded of the need for change and the benefits of change to them. The fact that the change is driven by an external change in regulations may help convince employees that the current business model is unsustainable. VB's management may need to emphasise that it is vital that changes are made soon if the bank is to adapt to a dynamic environment and survive. However, this does not mean employees will approve of the new strategy and business model being proposed.

Issues may include:

(1)   Motivating the staff in the period from announcement to closure

(2)   Facilitating the handover

(3)   Reassuring staff in other parts of VB that their long term security and conditions will not be affected

(4)   Managing any short term sympathy reaction in other parts of the bank (eg, a strike by VB employees in the same union)

(5)   Redundancy and change management costs incurred

Models of change

The **Gemini 4Rs** framework could be used here:

Reframe – VB must start by creating the will and desire to change. VB should announce its plans to employees as soon as possible, explaining the fact that the bank's current business model is unsustainable given changing technology and regulations. Allowing some time for discussions and negotiations with staff may help reduce resistance eg, consulting with employees to ascertain those that may wish to be made redundant and those that are prepared to retrain/transfer.

Restructure – This requires steps to be taken to implement the closure of the paper processing centre and to redesign the structure and culture of VB to facilitate the new digital only approach. This will involve a transition period as paper services are phased out, staff are made redundant and the app is introduced. Before the final closure and change takes place VB will need to set up the new help centre, hire technical staff and create new employee teams and processes as part of a digital learning culture. New contracts may need to be put in place as roles change and staff who are to be transferred will need training.

Revitalise – Given that VB is likely to require additional technological skills, management will need to create a culture of teamwork between any new incoming employees and the existing employees who are being retrained. Communicating the benefits of change for employees and demonstrating the benefits for customers overall of the digital strategy may have a positive impact on employees. VB can also emphasise the new employment opportunities available.

Renewal – once the paper processing centre has closed and the switch to a digital only strategy has occurred, VB must ensure the change is supported on an ongoing basis and that individuals involved have the necessary skills eg, continued training in the new online processes and systems. VB should also ensure reward systems reinforce those that embrace the new model.

Note: As an alternative, Lewin/Schein's 3-step iceberg model of change could also have been used:

- Unfreezing standard operating procedures (announce the new strategy, identify those employees who are to be made redundant, consult with those that are to be transferred/retrained);

- Move to new patterns of behaviour (eg, carry out the change by closing the paper processing centre, creating the digital help centre, training or recruiting employees and launching the app); and

- Refreezing to ensure lasting effects (eg, reinforcing new teams and patterns of working, supporting employees with ongoing training, rewarding conformity with the new system).

While the move and refreeze phases may be appropriate to employees retaining roles within VB they will not apply to those who are to be made redundant, as they will not have to accept a new structure or culture.

Customers

Customers are a key stakeholder when it comes to the change as they are being asked to change their methods of operation:

(1) as a result of the new regulations which require VB to share data and therefore require the customers to give permission for their information to be shared; and

(2) as a result of VB's decision to switch to digital banking and remove all paper processes.

VB may face resistance to change from customers who prefer the status quo.

Unfavourable aspects for VB include:

(1) The level of customer service may be perceived as being reduced if customers are pressured into accepting e-statements

(2) If the bank is unwilling to provide paper copies of statements and correspondence then it may lose existing customers who are unwilling to embrace the technology

(3) There is a risk that the take-up rate by customers is low and the initial set-up costs of the digital help centre will already have been incurred. The blog suggests that 53% of customers don't want to share info or change banking habits and that only 5–10% are likely to be early adopters.

Although customers have little power individually they may be able to form a collective and increase their bargaining power.

Like employees, individual barriers to change are likely to arise due to the fear of the unknown and a preference for existing systems and processes. Customers' preferences for digital over paper may vary depending on their age or ability to use technology. Selective information processing may result in customers focussing on the negative aspects of change and ignoring the overall benefits from a customer service point of view. Some of this can be addressed by education and communication. The digital help centre will help to educate customers in the new processes.

It may help to sell to some customers if VB concentrates on consequences for the environment of the use of natural wood resources in the paper required to produce bank statements each year. However the fact that employees are being made redundant may detract from VB's corporate social responsibility argument.

Customers are likely to need reassurance about the security aspects of going digital and may fear increased cyber security risk. There is an ethical issue of releasing private and confidential information to a third party. The question arises of VB seeking authorisation for disclosure of customer details and also what controls it will have over the data and how it is used.

Examiner's comments

As usual candidates were well prepared to discuss barriers to change and change models and there were some excellent attempts at this requirement. It was pleasing to see more candidates applying their knowledge to the specific scenario rather than quoting generic points from the learning materials.

The differentiating feature in the quality of responses was the ability to produce a well-balanced answer considering both barriers and approaches to change management for both employees and customers. Weaker candidates tended to focus on employees only or concentrate on Lewin's iceberg model. Only a minority explicitly recognised the transformational nature of the proposed change.

REVIEW FORM – BUSINESS STRATEGY AND TECHNOLOGY: Question Bank

Your ratings, comments and suggestions would be appreciated on the following areas of this Question Bank

	Very useful	Useful	Not useful
Number of questions in each section	☐	☐	☐
Standard of answers	☐	☐	☐
Amount of guidance on exam technique	☐	☐	☐
Quality of marking guides	☐	☐	☐

	Excellent	Good	Adequate	Poor
Overall opinion of this Question Bank	☐	☐	☐	☐

Please return completed form to:
The Learning Team
Learning and Professional Department
ICAEW
Metropolitan House
321 Avebury Boulevard
Milton Keynes
MK9 2FZ
E learning@icaew.com

For space to add further comments please see overleaf.

REVIEW FORM (continued)

TELL US WHAT YOU THINK

Please note any further comments and suggestions/errors below.